QUIC[KEN] 2002

USING QUICKEN IN A BUSINESS

QUICKEN 2002

USING QUICKEN IN A BUSINESS

Stephen L. Nelson, C.P.A.

REDMOND
TECHNOLOGY
PRESS

Quicken 2002:
Using Quicken in a Business

Published by
Redmond Technology Press
8581 154th Avenue NE
Redmond, WA 98052
www.redtechpress.com

Library of Congress Catalog Card No: Applied for

ISBN 1-931150-52-4

Printed and bound in the United States of America.

9 8 7 6 5 4 3 2 1

Distributed by
Independent Publishers Group
814 N. Franklin St.
Chicago, IL 60610
www.ipgbook.com

Acknowledgments

A lot of people at Redmond Technology Press worked hard to see that this book provides you with maximum value. They spent weeks and, in some cases, months of their time thinking about you and how to make one part of your life—using Quicken 2002 for a business—easier.

Many thanks to editor Paula Thurman, desktop publisher Minh-Tam S. Le, technical editor Mike Jang, and indexer Joann Woy.

Contents at a Glance

Contents

INTRODUCTION

Quicken 2002: Using Quicken in a Business is not like other Quicken books you have seen. First, those other books (including the one I've written, *Quicken 2002 for Dummies*) are essentially organized by product feature or menu command, while this book is *task-oriented.* Second, those other books assume you're using Quicken as a personal financial management tool, while this book assumes you're one of the 5 million Quicken users who is using Quicken as a business accounting tool.

NOTE *This book works both for Quicken 2002 Deluxe users and Quicken 2002 Home & Business users. Quicken 2002 Home & Business, which is a superset of Quicken 2002 Deluxe, provides special tools for tracking accounts payable (refer to Chapter 16) and for invoicing customers and tracking accounts receivable (refer to Chapter 17).*

How to Use This Book

If you haven't yet installed Quicken, start with Appendix A to find out how to install the software and set up your first account.

If you're totally new to Quicken, you'll want to start with Part I, "Core Quicken Skills," which covers the mechanics. You need this information before you can truly unleash the power of this simple yet sophisticated product. Once you're familiar with the basic operations, you're ready to begin using it for your business financial management.

When you're ready to read about how to use Quicken as a business accounting tool, turn to Part II, "Quicken in a Small Business." It describes how Quicken can help you with a variety of business financial record-keeping and management tasks: credit cards, cash loans, mortgages, taxes, budgeting, payroll, accounts payable, invoicing, accounts receivable, fixed assets record keeping, and measuring cash flow and profits.

Because it would be a shame to ignore all the powerful tools that Quicken provides for personal financial management, I also included a short collection of personal finance chapters in Part III, "Investments and Insurance." You'll find information and advice about using Quicken to track investments in mutual funds, stocks, bonds, and real estate. And you'll find information here on using Quicken both to help you select possible new insurance policies and terms and to track your existing policies.

By the way, scattered throughout the book—but mostly in the chapters in Parts II and III—are tangential sidebars. These sidebars discuss financial and business management concepts and techniques related to the material covered in the chapter. You'll find tips and tricks on achieving financial independence, becoming a smarter manager, simplifying your financial affairs, being a good business owner, and more. You can skip this material if you're interested only in the mechanics of using Quicken. But if you have time even to skim one or two of these sections, you'll find them well worth your while.

At the end of this book, I've provided two appendixes. Appendix A describes how to install the Quicken 2002 program. Appendix B briefly describes how to use Quicken's features for Canadian users.

Versions of Windows, Versions of Quicken, and This Book

Through the first 15 chapters of this book, Quicken windows and dialog boxes show Quicken 2002 Deluxe. From Chapter 16 on, Quicken windows and dialog boxes show Quicken 2002 Home & Business. While this seems potentially confusing, Quicken Deluxe users shouldn't have any trouble. As compared to Quicken Deluxe, Quicken 2002 Home & Business just includes an extra menu, the Business menu, that supplies commands for tracking accounts payable and accounts receivable and for invoicing customers. If you're using Quicken Deluxe, just ignore the references to the Business menu commands. (I do describe alternative accounting techniques for people who don't have Quicken Home & Business, by the way, so you'll clearly see which discussions apply only to Quicken Home & Business.)

NOTE *For the most part, the unique features of Quicken Home & Business are covered in Chapters 16 and 17.*

If you're using Quicken Basic, which comes free on some personal computers, frankly, you'll find this book a bit more confusing. A larger number of the features you'll read about here aren't available in your version of the program. What you'll need to do is remember your program is a subset of the program described here and then simply skip discussions of features you know your program doesn't contain.

All of the windows and dialog boxes that appear in this book were captured on a personal computer running Windows 2000 Professional. That means that your windows and dialog boxes may look a bit different. But the differences are, almost everywhere, only cosmetic. And where true mechanical differences exist, I tried to provide instructions for every common Windows operating system.

Conventions Used in This Book

The early chapters of this book give explicit directions for making menu selections and filling out dialog boxes with both the mouse and the keyboard. In later chapters, I simply tell you to select, click, or enter, and I leave it to you to choose the method that works best for you.

To indicate how you choose a menu command, this book uses the symbol ➤. For example, to instruct you to select the Open command from the File menu, the text says, "choose File ➤ Open."

To identify screen elements, the first letter of each word in the description is capitalized. This convention may look a bit strange at first, but it makes it easier to understand some instruction as "click the Assign Category To Group button."

To highlight important aspects of Quicken operations, you'll see Notes, Tips, and Warnings. Notes give you a little more information about a topic. Tips tell you a technique for getting something done more efficiently. Warnings alert you to problems you may encounter in carrying out a function discussed in the text.

That's everything you should need to get started. Good luck with Quicken. Good luck with your business.

Stephen L. Nelson,

steve@stephenlnelson.com

Seattle, Washington, November 26, 2001

Part 1

CORE QUICKEN SKILLS

In This Part

Chapter 1

GETTING STARTED

In This Chapter

- Starting Quicken
- A quick geography lesson in Quicken
- Finding help when you need it
- How to be a good bookkeeper with Quicken

You'll find it helpful to learn a few things about Microsoft Windows and the Quicken product before you start using Quicken for your business. In this chapter, you'll learn the basics: how to start Quicken, how to find your way around the Quicken windows and dialog boxes, and how to get help as you use Quicken. If you've already worked with Quicken or if you're comfortable using another Windows application, you can skim this chapter.

Before You Begin

In this chapter, I assume you've already done the following two things:

- You have installed the Quicken software.
- You have set up at least one bank account.

If you haven't done either of these things, refer to Appendix A. It tells you how to install Quicken and how to set up your first account.

NOTE *If you're just starting to use Quicken in a business setting—say you're the new bookkeeper—these two things may have already been done. This chapter is the right place for you to begin.*

Starting Quicken

Once you (or someone else) has installed Quicken, starting Quicken is easy. When you turn on your personal computer, Windows starts and then displays the Desktop, as shown in Figure 1.1. To start Quicken, double-click the Quicken shortcut.

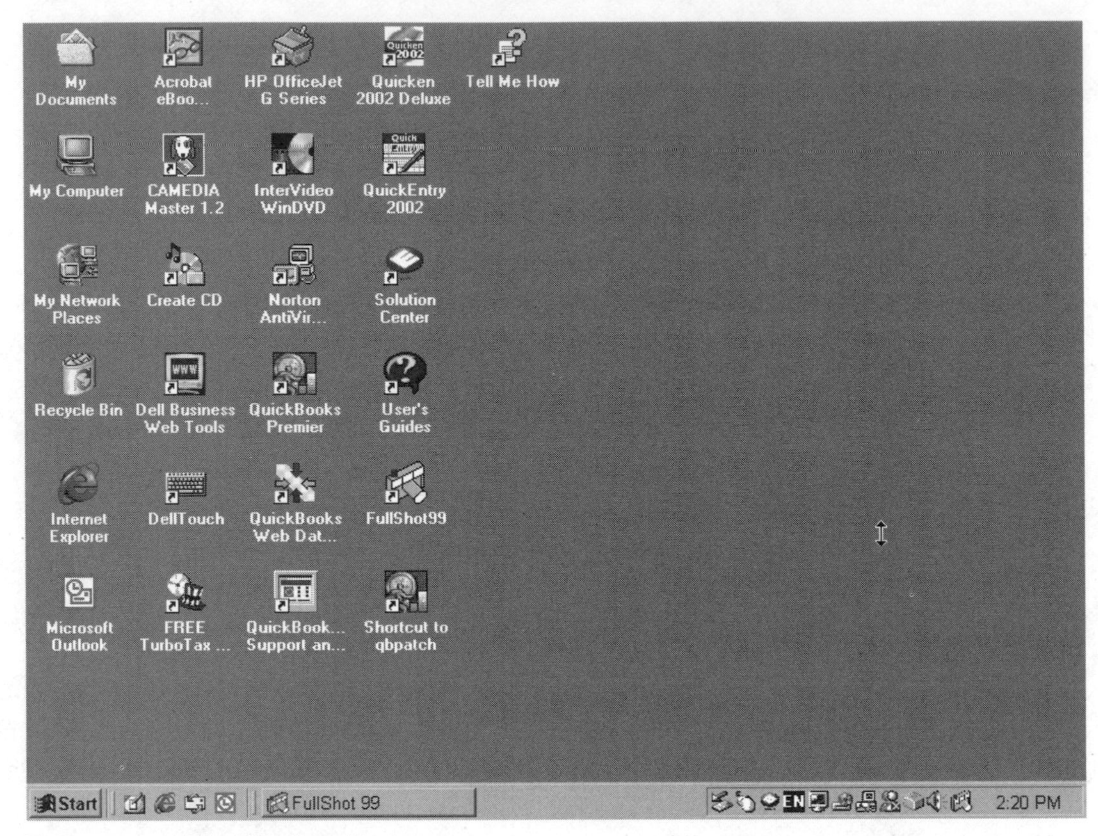

Figure 1.1: The Windows Desktop.

NOTE *Your Desktop probably looks a little different from the one shown in Figure 1.1 because you may use a different operating system and because you most likely have different software installed on your computer. Figure 1.1 shows the Windows 2000 desktop.*

When you first open Quicken, you'll see the Quicken My Finances window, as shown in Figure 1.2. From this page, you can access almost every area of Quicken and immediately accomplish most common tasks. For example, you can click one of the Create New Account buttons to start the Quicken wizard that walks you through the steps for setting up a new account. (A Quicken wizard displays a series of dialog boxes which prompt you to provide the information necessary to complete some task—such as setting up an account.)

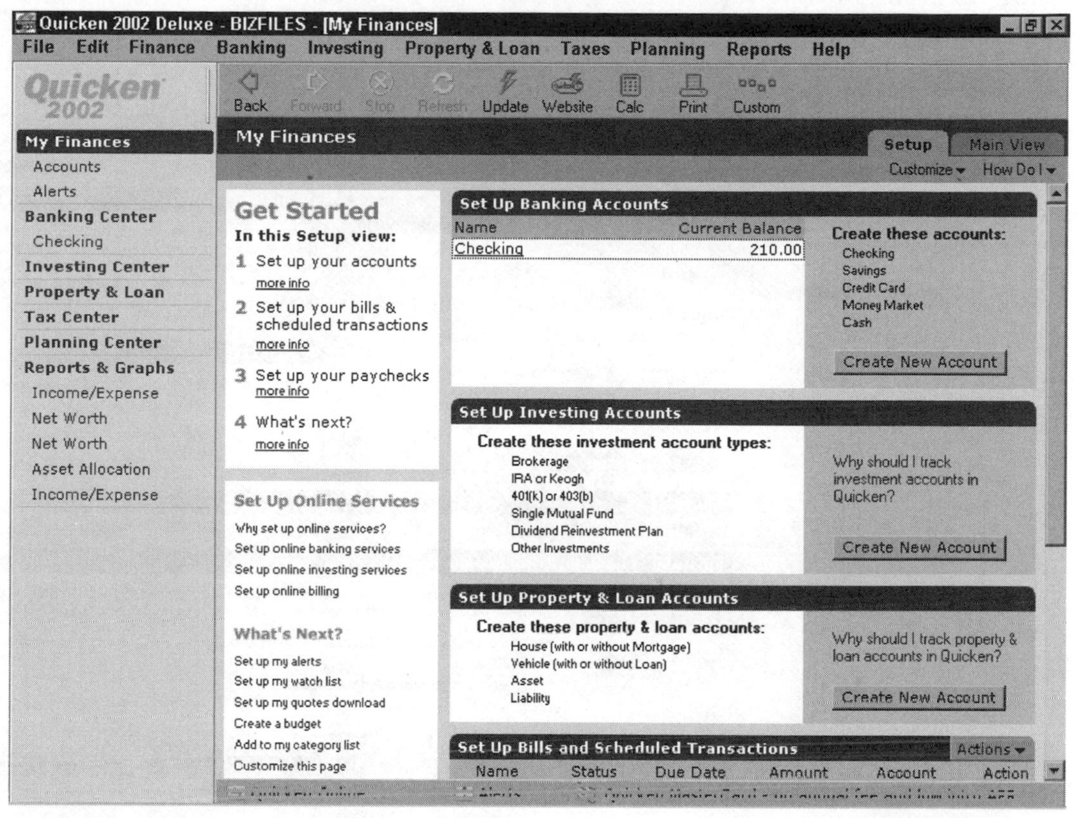

Figure 1.2: The Setup tab of the My Finances window.

NOTE *Your screen will look different from the one in Figure 1.2 depending on the number and type of accounts you've set up.*

The My Finances window provides two tabs. The Setup tab, as shown in Figure 1.2, provides buttons you can click to set up accounts for tracking bank accounts, investing accounts, and property and loan accounts, as well as hyperlinks you can click to get more information on some topic (such as why you might want to set up online services) and how to set up regularly scheduled transactions.

The Main View tab, as shown in Figure 1.3, lists the accounts you or someone else has set up, an alerts list of reminder messages, and, if you scroll down the Main View tab, an abbreviated net worth graph and hyperlinks to help information.

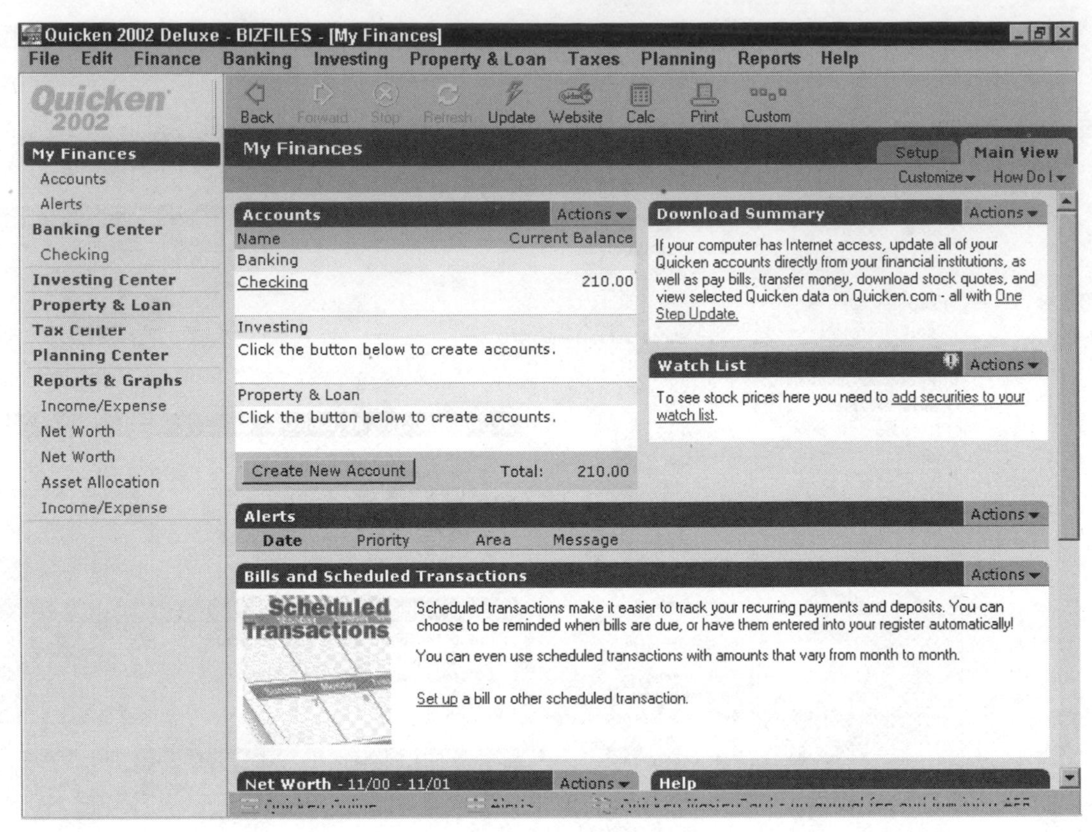

Figure 1.3: The Main View tab of the My Finances window.

TIP *To return to the My Finances window, click the My Finances QuickTab on the left side of your screen.*

Now, let's get to the heart of the matter—the Quicken application window. The Quicken application window provides a menu bar, QuickTabs, the toolbar, and a document window. Figure 1.4 identifies these items.

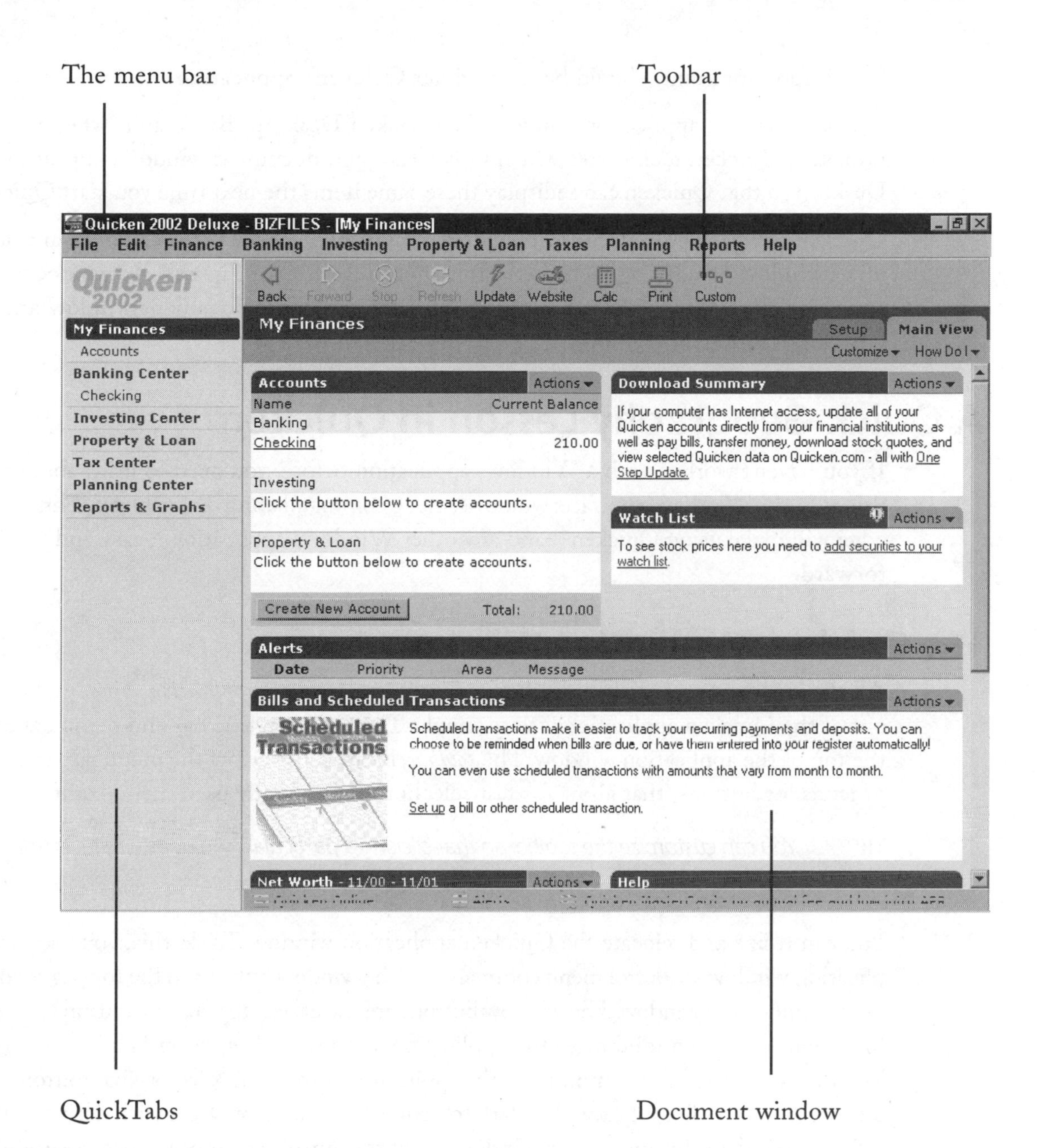

Figure 1.4: The Quicken window with labeled items.

Two important points should be made about Quicken's application window:

Quicken calls its application window the Quicken Desktop. By default, when you exit Quicken, Quicken memorizes which QuickTabs and document windows appear on the Desktop so that Quicken can redisplay these same items the next time you start Quicken.

Quicken lists each open document window in the QuickTabs list. You can open any document window by clicking its name in the QuickTabs list. In Figure 1.4, two documents appear in the list with the other QuickTabs: the Accounts document window and the Checking document window.

A Quick Geography Lesson in Quicken

If you haven't worked with a Windows application before, you need to learn about three things in the Windows interface: windows, menu commands, and dialog boxes. This knowledge will make using Quicken—and any other Windows application—easy and straightforward.

The Quicken Application Window

All the information Quicken displays for you appears in an *application window*. The layout of the Quicken application is very simple: The Quicken title bar and menu bar are at the top of the application window. The *toolbar*, located just below the menu bar, is a series of icons, or buttons, that allow for fast selection of frequently used menu commands.

TIP *You can customize the toolbar so that clicking a particular icon does whatever you want it to do. For details, see Chapter 6.*

You can resize and relocate the Quicken application window. To do this, you use the application window's Control menu commands or the window buttons in the top-right corner of the application window. The window buttons are the easiest to use. The button that looks like a bar or hyphen minimizes the application window so it appears as a button on the Windows Taskbar. (To "unminimize" the application, simply click its Taskbar button.) The button that looks like a box with a dark top edge or a couple of boxes with dark top edges either maximizes the application window to fill the entire screen or restores a window to its previous, unminimized size. The button with the × closes the application window (which is the same thing as closing the application). To move a window, drag its title bar.

TIP *If you want more information about resizing and relocating windows and how to use the Control menu commands, refer to a good book on Windows, such as Pat Coleman's* Windows XP From A to Z *(Redmond Technology Press, 2001).*

Working with Menus and Commands

To tell Quicken what you want it to do, you issue *commands*. For example, if you want Quicken to print what appears in a document window, you choose the File ➢ Print command (open the File menu and select Print). A *menu* is simply a list of commands.

Much of this book talks about how you use commands to accomplish specific personal finance, business management, and investment tasks with Quicken. To use the commands, you'll need to know how to choose commands in Quicken.

In the Windows operating environment, there are usually at least three ways to choose most commands. Let's look at these methods now. In subsequent chapters, I'll assume you've already selected the method you want to use, so I won't describe mouse-clicking or keystroke mechanics.

NOTE *Although Quicken's windows and dialog boxes look slightly different in Windows 95/98, Windows 2000, Windows Me, and Windows XP, the Quicken program works the same way in each of these operating system environments.*

Using the Mouse to Select and Deselect Commands

To choose a command with a mouse, point to the menu you want to display and click the mouse's left button. (This action is called "clicking the object.")

Once you click the menu, Quicken displays it. Next, you simply click the command you want to use. For example, choosing the File ➢ Print List command in the Account List document window requires two clicks:

1. Click the File menu name.
2. Click the Print List command.

Quicken then displays the Print dialog box, as shown in Figure 1.5.

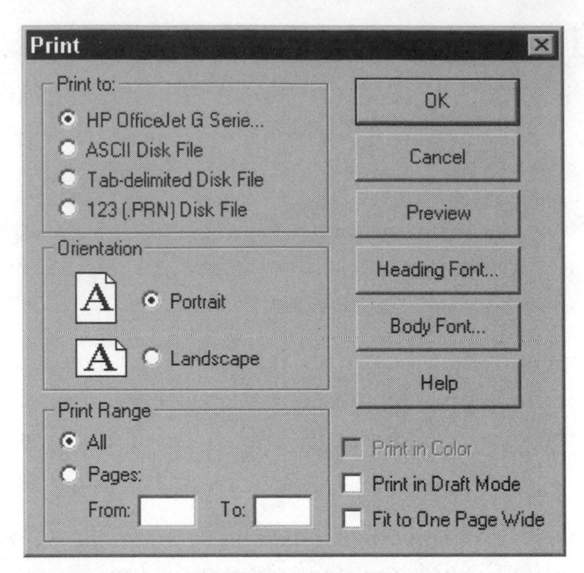

Figure 1.5: The Print dialog box.

To deselect a command you've selected with the mouse, you can press the Esc key on your keyboard or click an empty area of the screen. If choosing a command causes Quicken to display a dialog box, you can remove the dialog box by clicking the dialog box's Close button (the × symbol, located in the upper-right corner of the dialog box). I'll talk more about the Close button and the other Windows command buttons later in the chapter.

Using the Keyboard to Select and Deselect Commands

You can select any command using the keyboard. To do this, you do three things: activate the menu bar, display a menu, and then choose a command. To illustrate this, let's suppose you want to choose the File ➤ Print List command. (Go ahead and follow along with the discussion here; you can't hurt anything or damage your data.)

1. Press the Alt key and the underlined letter in the menu you want to display. For example, to activate the File menu, press Alt and then F. This activates the selected menu. To show you've selected the menu, Quicken drops down the menu, or activates it, as shown in Figure 1.6.

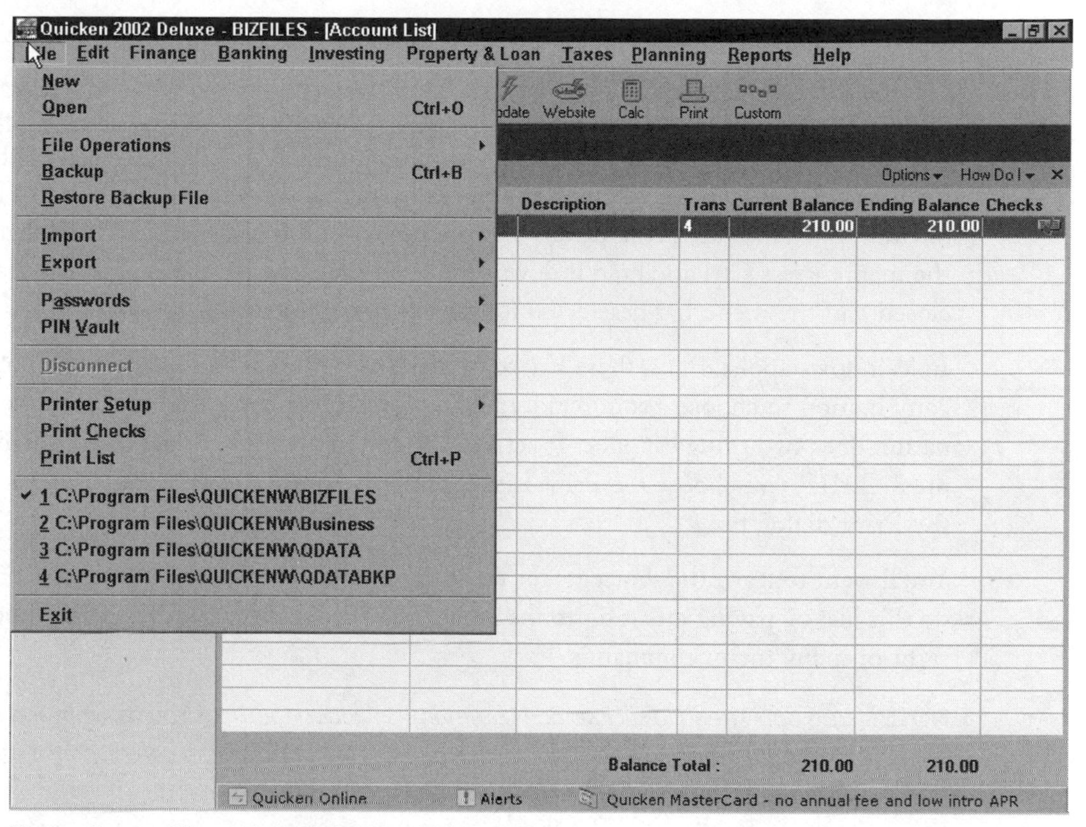

Figure 1.6: The activated Quicken File menu.

NOTE *In some versions of Windows, underlined letters on menus don't appear until you press the Alt key.*

2. Select the command you want. You can use the arrow keys to highlight the command and then press Enter, or you can press the underlined letter of the command name. To select the Print List command once the File menu is displayed, you can press P.

Some menu items contain additional commands. If a command name is followed by a triangle, that command displays a menu of additional commands. For example, the File Operations command is followed by a triangle. This tells you that choosing the File Operations command actually displays another menu of commands.

Not every command makes sense in every situation. Quicken disables commands that you shouldn't or can't choose. To identify these disabled commands, Quicken displays their names in gray letters.

Using Shortcuts to Choose Commands

Take another look at Figure 1.6, which shows the Quicken File menu. To the right of some of the commands, the File menu shows key combinations. For example, to the right of the File ➤ Open command, you see the key combination Ctrl+O. To the right of the File ➤ Print List command, you see the key combination Ctrl+P. When you see such a key combination listed in a menu, this means that you can select this command in a way that bypasses the menu: Press Ctrl and hold it down, and then press the letter key. The menus must be closed and the menu bar deselected for these key combinations to work.

In Windows applications, these key combinations represent *shortcuts*; you can press a key combination to choose a command. In effect, pressing a command's shortcut key combination does two things at once: It activates the menu, and it chooses a command. If you press Ctrl+P, you choose the Print List command from the File menu. Quicken displays the Print dialog box.

You'll want to learn the shortcuts for those commands you choose over and over. You can do this just by paying attention to the menus you display. Key combinations appear to the right of many menu commands.

NOTE *You don't need to stick to one command-selection method. You can mix and match the keyboard, shortcut, and mouse methods. For example, you can display a menu using the mouse, and then use the keyboard to select a command.*

Navigating within Quicken's Document Windows

Quicken uses the document window area beneath the menu bar to display a variety of information. The main areas (Banking, Investing, Property & Loan, Taxes, Planning, and Reports) contain numerous hyperlinks you can click to perform common financial tasks within the area. For example, click the Banking Center QuickTab and click an account's hyperlink, and Quicken displays that account's register, as shown in Figure 1.7 (which shows a checking account register). Quicken's areas display many other kinds of information as well.

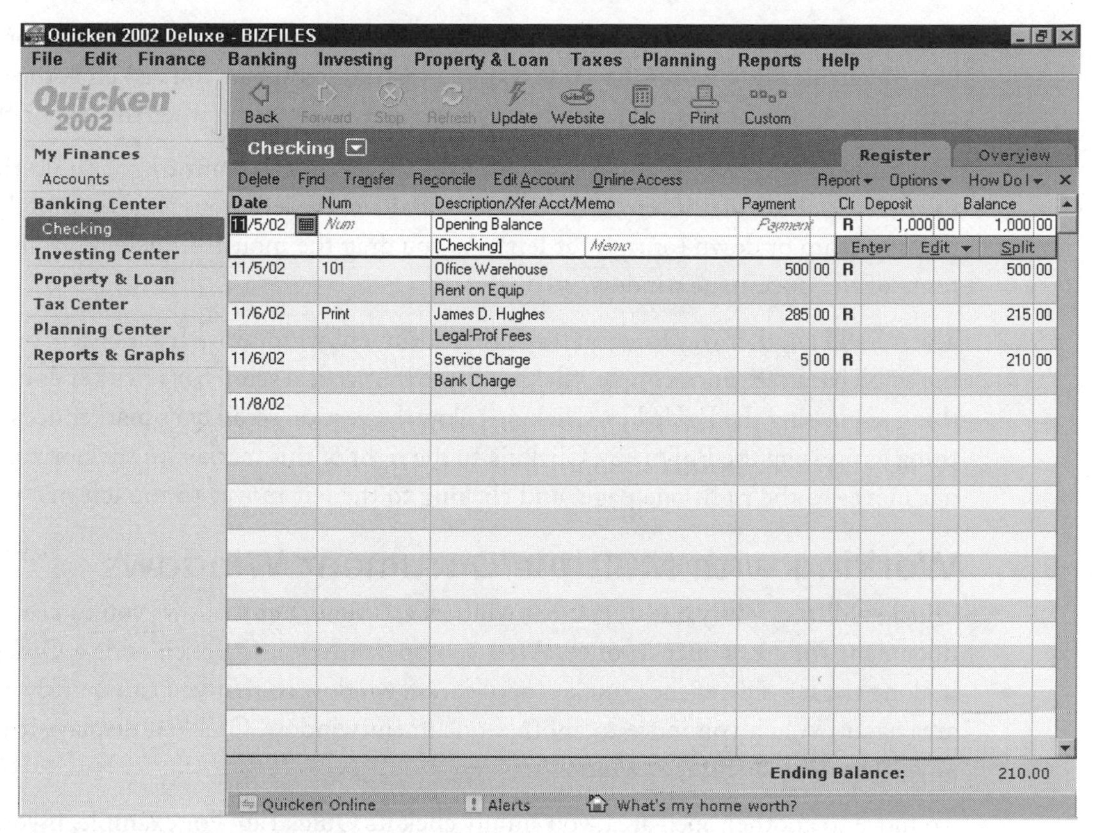

Figure 1.7: The Quicken checking account register.

NOTE *Quicken's document windows don't look like regular document windows (such as a word-processor program might use.) They are, however, document windows.*

Moving Around in a Document Window

If a document window isn't big enough to display everything that's supposed to fit in it, Windows puts a *scroll bar* along the right and bottom edges of the window. Look at the window in Figure 1.7; you'll see a vertical scroll bar along the window's right edge.

One way you can move up and down in a document window that has a vertical scroll bar is by pressing the PgDn and PgUp keys. You can also use your mouse to move up, down, left, and right in a document window. You can move up one line by clicking the up arrow at the top of the vertical scroll bar. You can move down one line by clicking the down arrow at the bottom of the vertical scroll bar. As you move up and down, Quicken moves the scroll bar marker (it's the square in the scroll bar) up or down the scroll bar. This marker shows your position relative to the entire document.

To move your view of a document window's contents left and right, use the horizontal scroll bar. Mechanically, it works the same way as a vertical scroll bar. You can click the arrows at either end of the horizontal scroll bar to move one column to either the left or the right.

You can also *drag* the scroll bar marker in the direction you want to go. To do this, place the mouse pointer on the scroll bar marker, hold down the left mouse button, and then move the mouse up or down (or right or left). As you drag the mouse, Quicken scrolls the contents of the document window.

There's still another way to scroll through a document window with a mouse. You can click the scroll bar itself. For example, clicking above the vertical scroll bar's marker does the same thing as pressing the PgUp key. Clicking below the vertical scroll bar's marker does the same thing as pressing the PgDn key. Clicking to the right of this marker on the horizontal scroll bar moves to the right one page, and clicking to the left moves to the left one page.

Working with Multiple Document Windows

Quicken displays only one document window at a time, but it allows you to keep multiple document windows open at once. After you open an area, Quicken adds a QuickTab for it along the left side of the Quicken application window so that you can quickly access the area again. When you move to another document window, Quicken displays it on top of any other open document windows.

To move to another open area, you simply click its QuickTab. For example, if you want to schedule a payment, you can choose My Finances ➢ Calendar. Quicken displays the Financial Calendar, as shown in Figure 1.8. The QuickTabs list shows that the Accounts and Checking register areas are also open, in addition to the main areas, which are always open. To redisplay the Accounts or Checking register, just click its QuickTab.

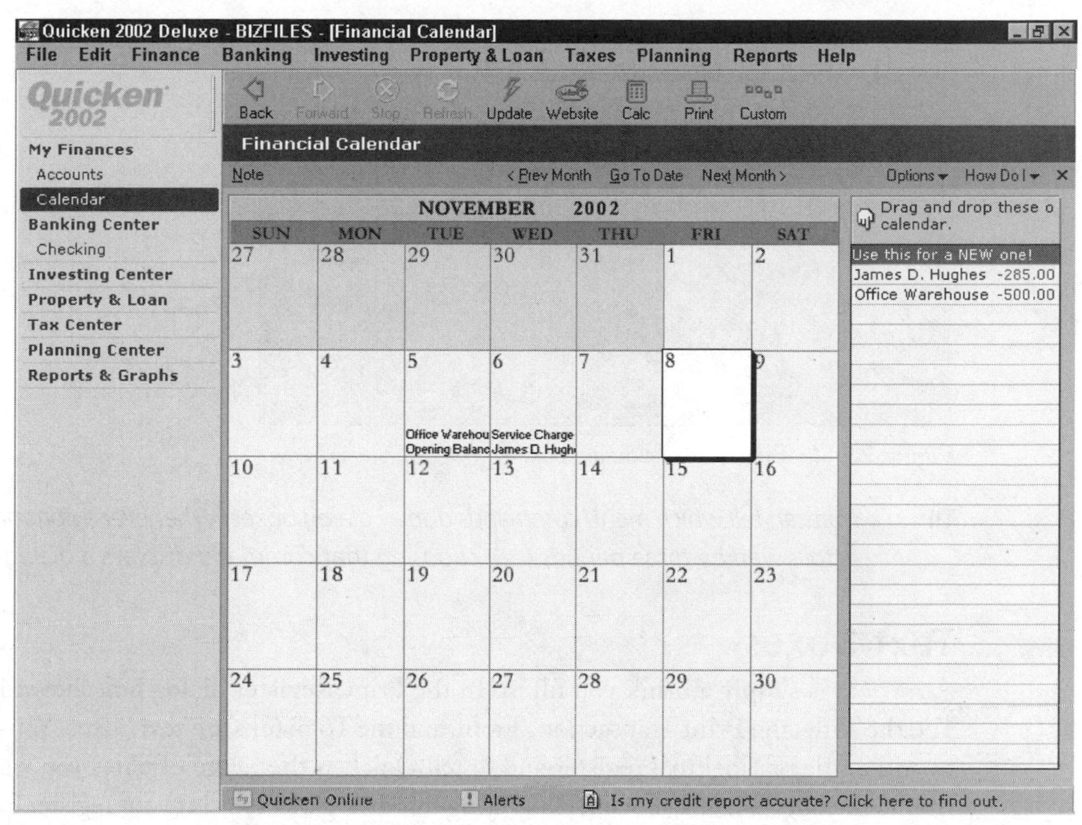

Figure 1.8: The Quicken application with three document windows open: the Accounts document window, the Checking document window, and the Calendar document window.

NOTE *In some applications, you can resize and move the document windows. This isn't the case in Quicken, because Quicken wants to treat document windows like the pages of a book. For this reason, the Window menu you see in other Windows applications is not available in Quicken, and some Control menu commands aren't available (they're disabled).*

Working with Dialog Boxes

Quicken often needs additional information from you when you tell it to execute a particular command. To get that information, the program displays a *dialog box*. Figure 1.9 shows the parts of the Print Register dialog box, which Quicken displays whenever you choose the Print Register command from the File menu. (For the Print Register command to be displayed, the active document window must show an account register such as checking; display the Register document window and then select the File ➤ Print Register command.) Dialog boxes contain boxes, lists, and buttons that allow you to provide additional information.

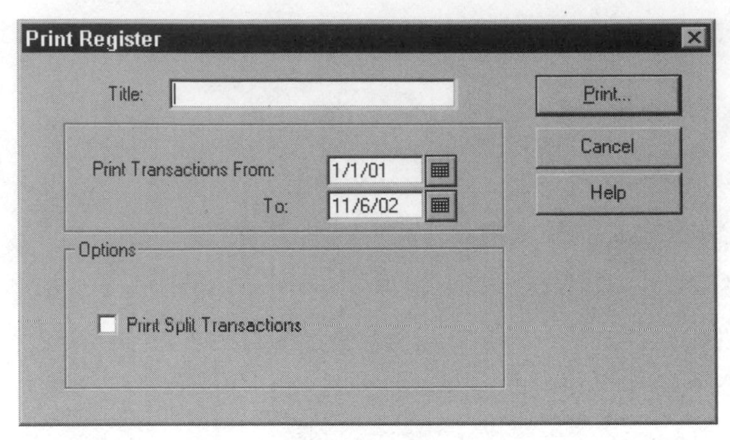

Figure 1.9: Elements of a dialog box.

TIP *You can tell which menu commands display dialog boxes. Whenever a command name is followed by three periods (...), choosing that command displays a dialog box.*

Text Boxes

A *text box* is simply a blank you fill in. In the Print Register dialog box shown in Figure 1.9, the Title, the Print Transactions From, and the To blanks are text boxes. You use them to add a title or label to a register and to tell Quicken the range of dates you want a register to include. (I'll talk about actually using this dialog box to print your register in Chapter 2; for now, just focus on the mechanics of using dialog box elements.)

To enter information into a text box, you first need to activate the text box. You can do this either by clicking the text box with the mouse or by pressing Tab or Shift+Tab until the text box is highlighted.

Once you've activated the text box, you're ready to enter data in it. If a text box is empty (like the Title text box in Figure 1.9), selecting the text box simply causes Quicken to put the insertion bar (a flashing vertical I-beam) at the start of the text box.

If the text box already holds data, Quicken selects and highlights the current contents. When this is the case, you can replace the selected contents of the text box by just typing over.

If you don't want to replace text box contents but instead want to insert or add to the current contents, you position the insertion bar at the position where you want to add new text, as follows:

- To place the insertion bar at the beginning of a text box, press the Home key or click the very first character position in the text box.
- To insert characters into the middle of the text box, you can use the ← and → keys to move the insertion bar to the point where you want to insert characters, or you can click the mouse to move the insertion bar there.
- To place the insertion bar at the end of the text box, press the End key or click after the very last character in the current text box.

Once you've positioned the insertion bar, begin typing.

Command Buttons

Command buttons tell Quicken what you want it to do with the information you've entered into the dialog box. Most dialog boxes have an OK command button, which tells Quicken to proceed to the next step. If a dialog box is displayed to collect information for a command, selecting OK initiates the command.

In some cases, the OK command button is replaced by an equivalent command button that names the action that occurs when the command is executed. For example, the Print Register dialog box doesn't provide an OK command button, but it does provide a Print command button. In this case, the Print command button is equivalent to an OK command button.

Most dialog boxes have a Cancel command button, which tells Quicken not to accept any information you've entered and to return to what you were doing before. Dialog boxes commonly provide other command buttons too.

You can select command buttons in several ways. You can click the command button, or you can highlight the command button using the Tab and Shift+Tab keys and then activate it by pressing Enter. If a command button shows a thick, dark border—and one of the commands usually does—you can select it by pressing Enter. (The command button with the thick, dark border is the *default* command button.) If a command button's name has an underlined letter in it, you can press the Alt key and the underlined letter to select the command button.

Option Buttons

Earlier in the chapter, I mentioned that you can move between the Quicken areas by clicking the QuickTabs. You can choose to display these QuickTabs either on the right of the Quicken area or on the left. When you have a mutually exclusive set of choices such as this, Quicken uses *option buttons* to present your choices. For example, in the QuickTabs tab of the General Options dialog box, shown in Figure 1.10, the option buttons in the Position section of the dialog box let you choose the location of the QuickTabs on your screen. (To display the General Options dialog box, choose Edit ➢ Options ➢ Quicken Program.)

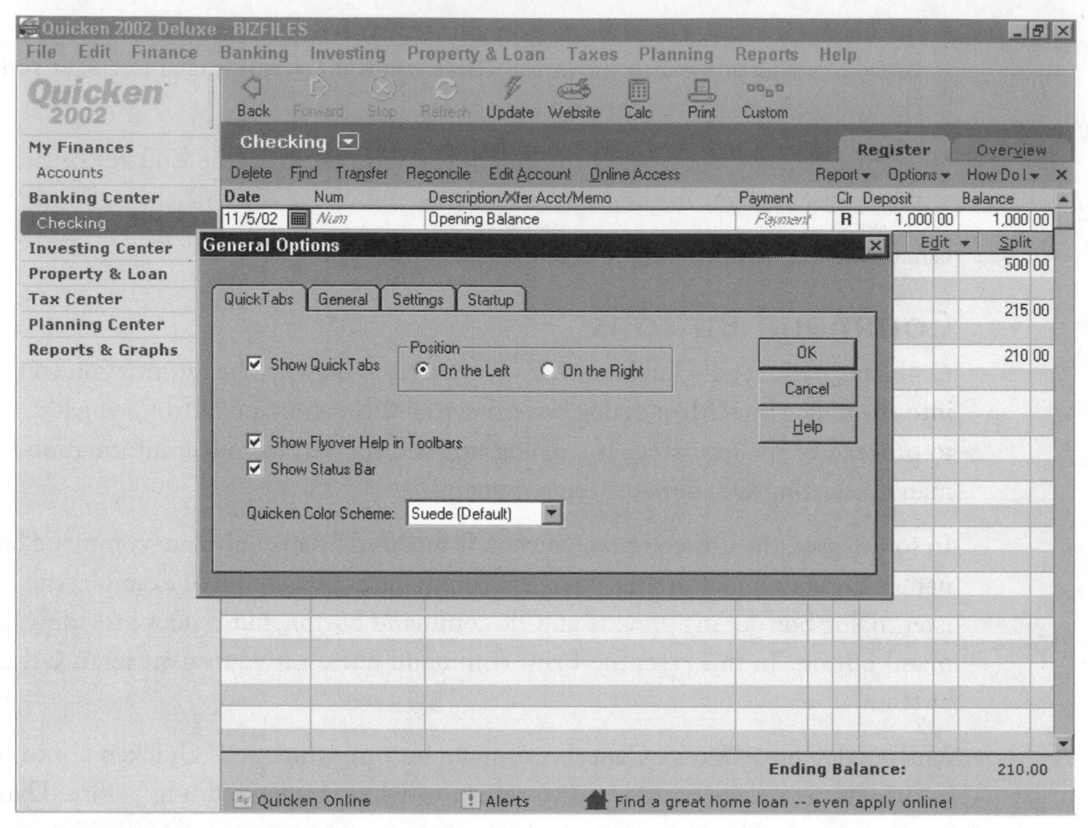

Figure 1.10: The QuickTabs tab in the General Options dialog box.

To mark an option button with the mouse, click it. To indicate your choice, Quicken inserts a black dot, or bullet, in the button you choose. Figure 1.10 shows the On The Left option button marked with the bullet.

To mark an option button with the keyboard, highlight the selected option button by using the Tab or Shift+Tab keys. Then use the ↑ and ↓ keys to move the bullet to one of the other option buttons. Quicken then moves the bullet to mark your choice.

Checkboxes

Checkboxes amount to on/off switches. Figure 1.10 shows three checkboxes: Show QuickTabs, Show Flyover Help In Toolbars, and Show Status Bar. (Don't worry what these checkboxes do right now; I'll talk about them in Chapter 6.)

The easiest way to turn on (or turn off) a checkbox is by clicking the mouse. If you click a checkbox that's turned on—indicated by a checkmark in the box—Quicken turns off the checkbox and removes the checkmark. If you click a checkbox that's turned off—one that is empty—Quicken turns on the checkbox and adds a checkmark to it.

You can also turn checkboxes on and off using the keyboard. For example, you can highlight the checkbox using the Tab and Shift+Tab keys; then you can use the spacebar to alternately turn the checkbox on and off. Or you can press the Alt key and then the underlined letter in the checkbox name to alternately turn the checkbox on and off. Pressing Alt+Q, for example, toggles the Show QuickTabs checkbox on and off.

List Boxes

If you want to choose from a series of items, Quicken uses a *list box* to display your choices. In Figure 1.10, for example, the Quicken Color Scheme box is really a list box. Quicken doesn't display the Quicken Color Scheme list until you tell it to. If you want to change the Quicken Color Scheme option, you display, or *drop down,* the list box's list, and then you select one of the list entries by clicking it.

To drop down a list box, you can click the down arrow at the end of the list box, or you can select it by using the Tab or Shift+Tab keys and then pressing Alt+↓.

To select an entry in a drop-down list, click the entry with the mouse or highlight the entry with the arrow keys and press Enter.

When a list box is active, pressing a letter key, such as S, selects the first entry that starts with the letter. If a list box's entries don't fit within the list box, Quicken adds a vertical scroll bar to it. You can use it to scroll through the list box's entries. A list box's scroll bar works just like a document window's scroll bar.

Combo Boxes

One other element of the Windows user interface bears mentioning: *combo boxes*. Combo boxes are a hybrid. A combo box looks like a text box but works like both a text box and a list box. Everything I've said about text boxes and list boxes is true for combo boxes. For example, you can enter information into a combo box by typing, or you can activate a list box for the combo box and select a list entry that then goes into the combo box. Many of the fields you fill in Quicken are combo boxes, as you'll see in the pages that follow.

Finding Help When You Need It

Quicken provides a couple of easy ways to access help when you need it. One method allows you to find quick answers to pressing questions, while the other allows you to browse through Quicken's extensive online help information.

Getting Quick Answers in an Area

If you're struggling with a task in an area, you can find out how to accomplish it by clicking the How Do I? button. This action displays a drop-down menu of common tasks in the area you're currently in, as shown in Figure 1.11. To find out how to accomplish a task listed in the menu, just select it. Quicken displays the topic in the Quicken Help window.

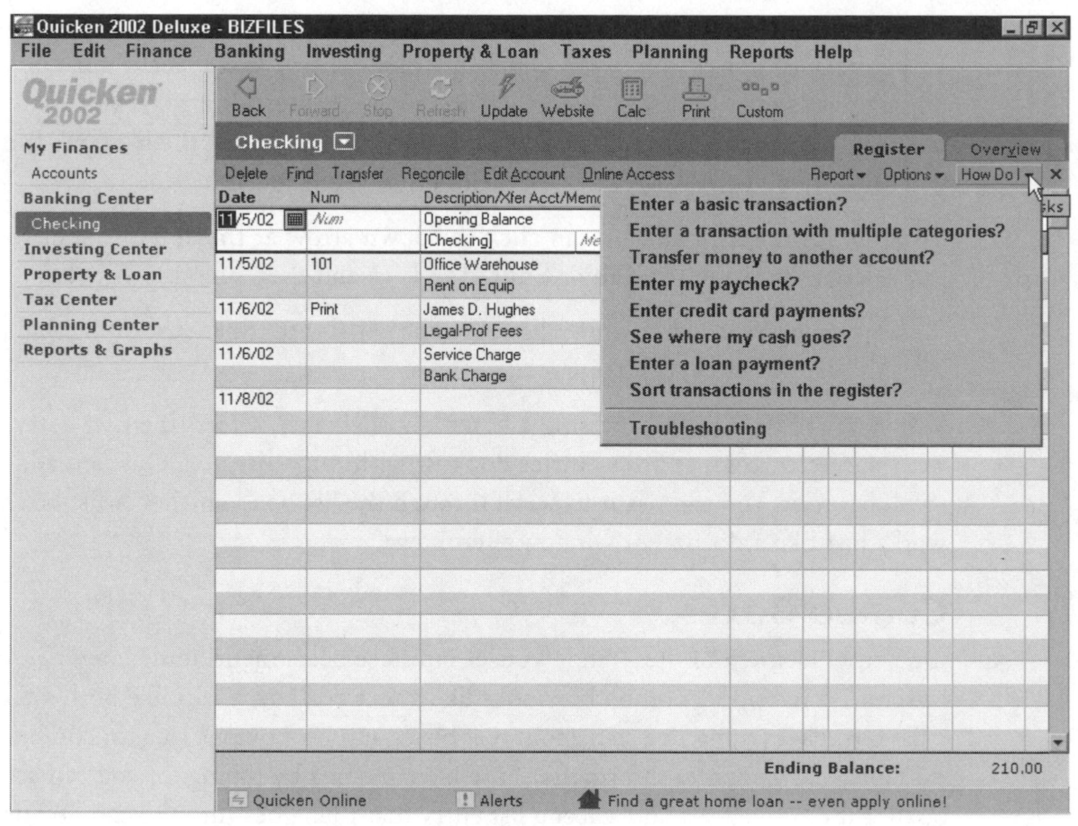

Figure 1.11: The How Do I? menu for an account register.

Browsing the Online Help Information

To browse Quicken's online help information, press the key labeled F1 on your keyboard. Quicken starts the Help application and displays the Help window shown in Figure 1.12, which has three tabs:

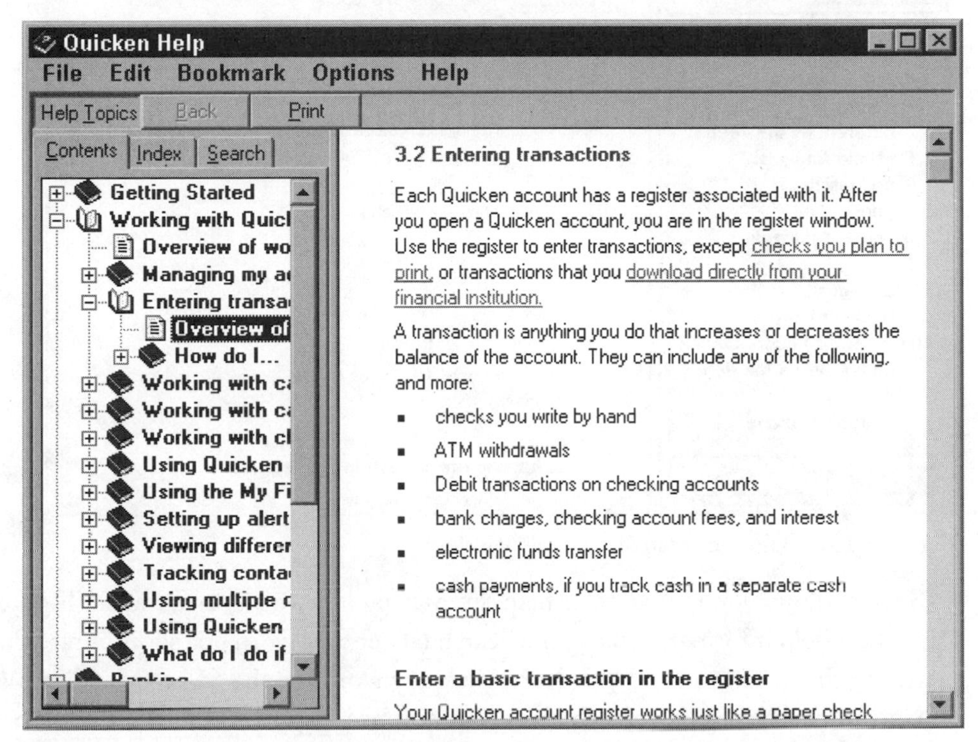

Figure 1.12: The Help application window with the Contents tab displayed.

- Contents lists "books" that provide information about Quicken procedures, examples of how to set up Quicken to suit your financial needs, and expert financial advice, as shown in Figure 1.12. To browse the information provided through the Contents tab, click on books you want to open. Quicken displays the help topic information in the Help window pane. The pane includes hyperlinks you can click to jump to other, related topics.
- Index allows you to scroll through the index of Help topics or search for a term, as shown in Figure 1.13. To look up for help information using the Index tab, enter a word or short phrase that closely ties to the question you have. Quicken displays a list of topics that match what you enter. To display the topic's help information, click it. Quicken displays the help topic in the Help window pane.

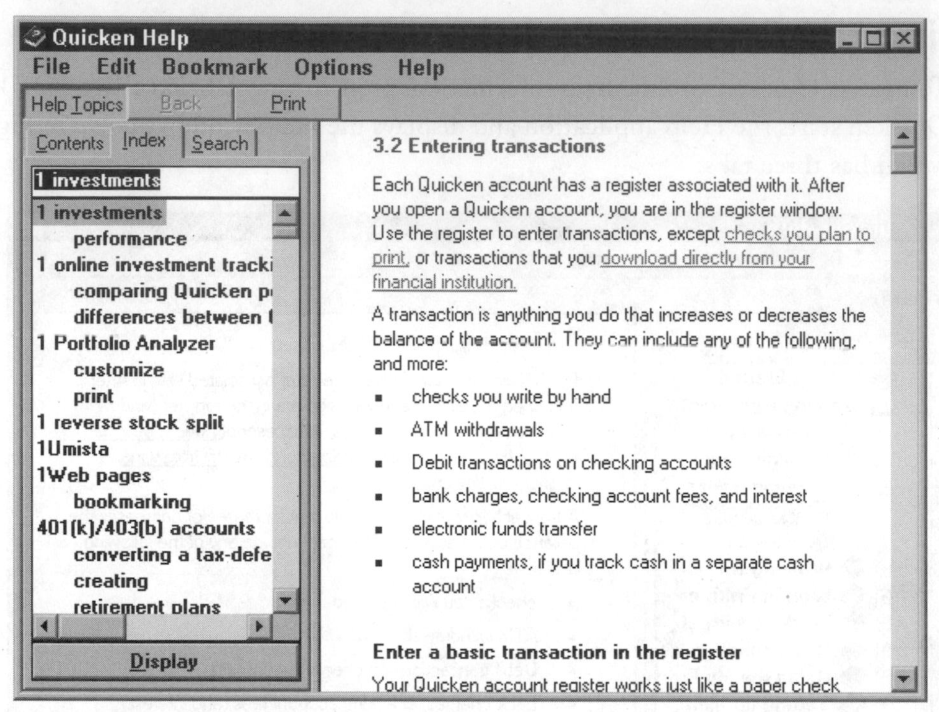

Figure 1.13: The Index tab of the Help window.

- Search allows you to search for help by entering key words, as shown in Figure 1.14 To find for help information using the Search tab, enter a word or a short phrase that closely ties to the question you have. Next, click any words in the Select Matching Words To Narrow Search box that closely tie to your question to pinpoint your search. Finally, select the help topic you want to browse by clicking an entry in the Choose Topic To Display box. Quicken displays the help topic information in the Help window pane.

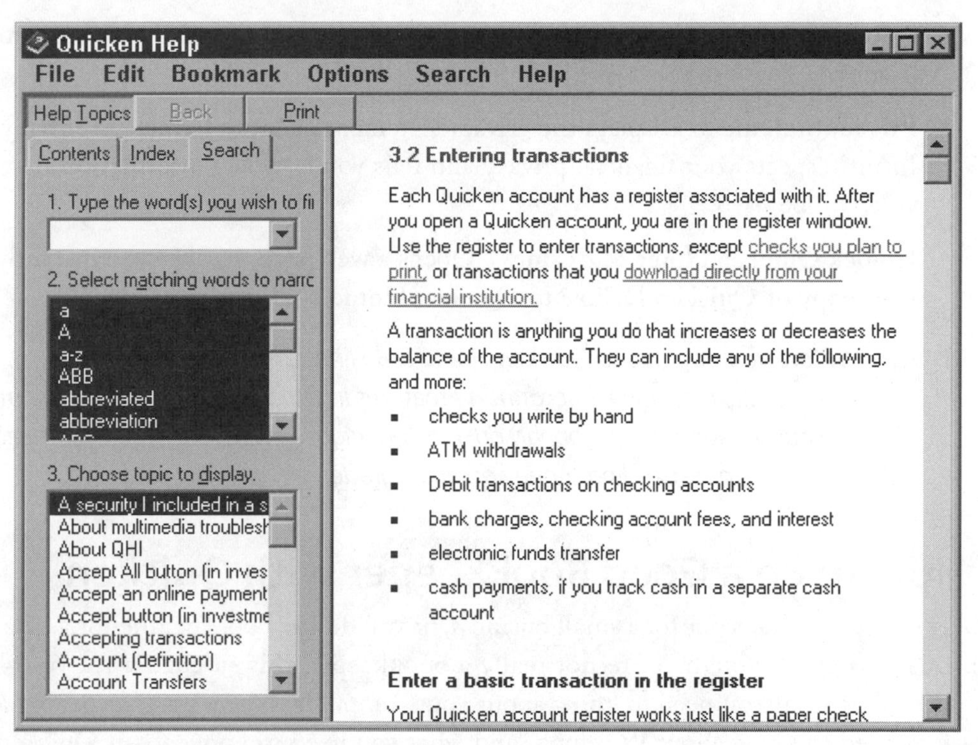

Figure 1.14: The Search tab of the Help window.

You can also access Quicken's help information files by choosing commands from the Help menu. Help menus vary between the different flavors of Quicken, but Quicken Deluxe supplies the following commands on its Help window:

- **Contents** Displays the Help window with the Contents tab selected.
- **Current Window** Displays the Help window with the Contents tab selected and a list of help topics for the open Quicken area. Choosing this command is the same as pressing F1.
- **Troubleshooting This Window** Displays the Help window with the Contents tab selected and a list of help topics that specifically help you resolve common problems.
- **Watch QuickTour Video** Starts the QuickTour video, which shows what Quicken can do and flags features new to Quicken 2002.
- **Show Me Videos** Provides hyperlinks you can click to see what's new in the Quicken 2002 QuickTour video and to view free learning videos available at the Quicken.com web site.
- **Product & Customer Support** Displays the Product & Customer Support Web page. The Web page's hyperlinks provide several options for accessing technical support.

- **About Quicken** Displays the Quicken copyright notice and the version and release numbers. To close the dialog box, just press Esc.
- **Privacy Statement** Displays the privacy statement of Intuit (which essentially says that Intuit respects your financial privacy and tells you how any information that you provide will be used.
- **Unlock Quicken Home & Business** Opens a web page that lets you instantly upgrade your copy of Quicken Deluxe to Quicken Home & Business.

NOTE *Before you upgrade to Quicken Home & Business, review Chapters 13, 16, and 17 to see if the extra business accounting features in Quicken Home & Business make sense in your situation. They probably do, but you might as well verify you really need the extra power before spending money on an upgrade.*

How to Be a Good Bookkeeper with Quicken

If you're a bookkeeper for a small business, or you do the bookkeeping for a small business even though you're not really a bookkeeper, this sidebar is for you. It describes what you need to know about your computer to be a bookkeeper, what you need to know about Windows, and what you need to know about Quicken. It also explains how to perform financial record keeping in a small business and where to get additional help if you need it.

What You Need to Know about Quicken and Windows

Remember that accounting systems do three things: They let you calculate profits, they generate business forms, and they let you keep records of assets and liabilities. Quicken lets you calculate profits by tagging bank account deposits as income and bank account withdrawals as expense. If this approach doesn't work for the small business you're keeping the books for, you need to use another program. Quicken Deluxe, the most common version of Quicken, lets you generate only one business form: a check. Quicken Home & Business, a special version of Quicken especially for small businesses lets you generate invoices and customer statements. If you need other business forms, such as purchase orders or packing slips, you need to use another program. Also, Quicken keeps detailed records of only bank accounts, credit cards, loans, and investments. If you need to keep detailed records of other assets, such as inventory, you need to use another program. (Note that you can keep records of other assets and liabilities—as you'll read about in the pages that follow. What you can't keep with Quicken, however, are detailed records of these items).

You need to know how to work within the Windows operating environment to use Quicken; the more you know about Windows, the easier you'll find using Quicken. This chapter provides most of the information you need, but you might also want to read the Microsoft Windows documentation.

Spend a few days—maybe even a week or two—working with Quicken. Be sure you've entered a series of checks and deposits, and experiment with Quicken's reports. If things still don't click for you, you may be trying to do too much with Quicken.

What You Don't Need to Know

As a bookkeeper, you need to know how to keep financial records that let your employer assess profitability and cash flow; how to keep records for a bank account and reconcile the account; and, in some cases, how to prepare payroll checks and returns. (Most of this work I'll talk about in the chapters that follow.) But there is also a list of things you don't need to know—information that goes beyond the scope of your job:

- You don't need to be an expert on federal or state income taxes. It's helpful if you know a few things, but, for example, your boss shouldn't expect you to understand the income tax rules for employee fringe benefits, asset depreciation, or partnership taxation. Your boss can get this type of information and analysis from a CPA or from an attorney who specializes in income tax planning.
- You don't need to be a computer genius. Yes, you need to know how to work with Windows and Quicken, but you don't need to know how to drop an Ethernet card into a computer or reformat the hard disk. A local computer retail or repair shop can take care of these things.
- You also don't need to (and shouldn't) provide legal advice to your employer. An employer who wants to incorporate, deal with an employee's legal threats, or determine whether a contract is fair should talk to an attorney.

A Weekly Bookkeeping Checklist

Use the following list of tasks as a checklist at the end of each week:

- Enter all the payment and deposit transactions for the week (see Chapter 2).
- Back up the Quicken file to a removable disk so that you won't lose the data in the event of a computer problem or a human error (see Chapter 7).

- Check to see if you should remit any payroll tax deposit money by looking at the payroll tax liability account balances (see Chapter 15).
- Print a copy of the check register for the week and store it as a permanent financial record (see Chapter 2).

A Monthly and Quarterly Bookkeeping Checklist

Here is a checklist of tasks you should usually complete at the end of each month:

- Reconcile all your bank accounts (see Chapter 5).
- Print monthly Cash Flow and Profit & Loss Statement reports. Give a copy to the owner for assessing the month's profitability and cash flow, and put another copy in a permanent financial reports file (see Chapter 4).
- Prepare any monthly or quarterly payroll tax reports. Most businesses prepare the quarterly 941 payroll tax statement (see Chapter 15).
- Make quarterly estimated tax payments for the owner, or remind the owner to make the estimated tax payments. A small business owner is typically required to make quarterly payments of estimated taxes owed on April 15, June 15, September 15, and January 15.

An Annual Checklist

Here are the things you should do at the end of each year:

- Print annual Cash Flow and Profit & Loss Statement reports. Give one copy to the owner for assessing the year's profitability and cash flow, and put another copy in a permanent financial reports file (see Chapters 4 and 19).
- Prepare a Tax Summary and Tax Schedule report (see Chapter 13).
- Consider creating a disk version of the Tax Schedule report so that the Quicken data can be exported to a tax-preparation package (see Chapter 13).
- Prepare any annual payroll tax reports. Most businesses prepare the annual 940 payroll tax statement and W-2 employee wage statements (see Chapter 15).
- Archive a copy of the previous year's financial records (see Chapter 7).

Two Things Bookkeepers Should Never Do

There are a couple of things you should never do. If you're not careful, doing either of these two things can, quite literally, lead to financial ruin.

Don't Borrow Payroll Tax Deposit Money

Don't ever borrow the payroll tax deposit money, and don't ever help the business owner borrow the payroll tax deposit money. Handling payroll tax deposits is discussed in Chapter 15. The important thing is that the Internal Revenue Service (IRS) takes a very dim view of mishandling this money. If you're the bookkeeper and you've actively participated in borrowing the payroll tax deposit money, the IRS can collect the money from you. The IRS assumes that this borrowing amounts to stealing and that, as an accomplice to the theft, you may as well be the one to pay. I should also point out that if you only work someplace and didn't actually have the ability to make or delay payroll tax deposits, the IRS is considerably more lenient.

If you've already been doing this, my advice is that you stop immediately. If the small business you keep the books for owes payroll tax money it can't repay, I suggest you find a new job. You may also want to confer with a tax attorney.

Don't Participate in Misrepresentation

Financial misrepresentation occurs when you (or the business owner with your help) juggle a few of the financial figures to make the business look a little more profitable or a little healthier. Although the practice may seem innocent enough, it's a serious crime. Never participate in misrepresentation.

A business owner might juggle the figures to get a bank or a vendor to lend money or to get an investor to contribute money. When this happens, the bank, vendor, or investor contributes money because of a lie. If the bank, vendor, or investor loses money or discovers you've lied, both you and the business owner can end up in serious trouble. People do go to jail for this.

Income tax evasion is basically just another form of financial misrepresentation. In this case, however, it's the IRS that's being lied to rather than a bank or an investor.

If you've been participating in financial misrepresentation or are being asked to participate, I suggest that you try to find a new job and that you talk with an attorney to see if there is some way you can extricate yourself from the mess.

Chapter 2

USING THE QUICKEN REGISTER

In This Chapter

- Recording checks, other payments, and deposits
- Using the Paycheck Wizard
- Scheduling recurring transactions
- Fixing mistakes in a register
- Using the Quicken calculator
- Setting up additional bank accounts
- Transferring money between accounts
- Splitting transactions
- Register record-keeping tricks
- Printing an account register

First things first: You'll probably want to start using Quicken by tracking the money that flows into and out of the bank account that you use most frequently. You'll be able to summarize your financial affairs in a way that you've never done before, and you'll learn the basics of working with the Quicken program.

Before You Begin

Before you can use the Quicken register to track the money that flows into and out of your bank accounts, you need to do the following:

- Install and set up Quicken, which really means that you need to copy the Quicken application onto your hard disk and set up your first bank account. If you haven't already done these two things, refer to Appendix A.

- Learn how to work with the Windows operating environment. If you don't already know how to do this, take the time to review Chapter 1.

Recording Checks, Other Payments, and Deposits

With Quicken running, you'll need to display the Bank Account Register for the bank account you want to work with. Choose Banking ➢ Bank Accounts to display a menu listing bank accounts and then choose your bank account.

Figure 2.1 shows the Checking register. Quicken highlights the first empty row in the register. (If the next empty row of the register isn't highlighted, you can use the arrow keys to highlight it, or choose Edit ➢ Transaction ➢ New.)

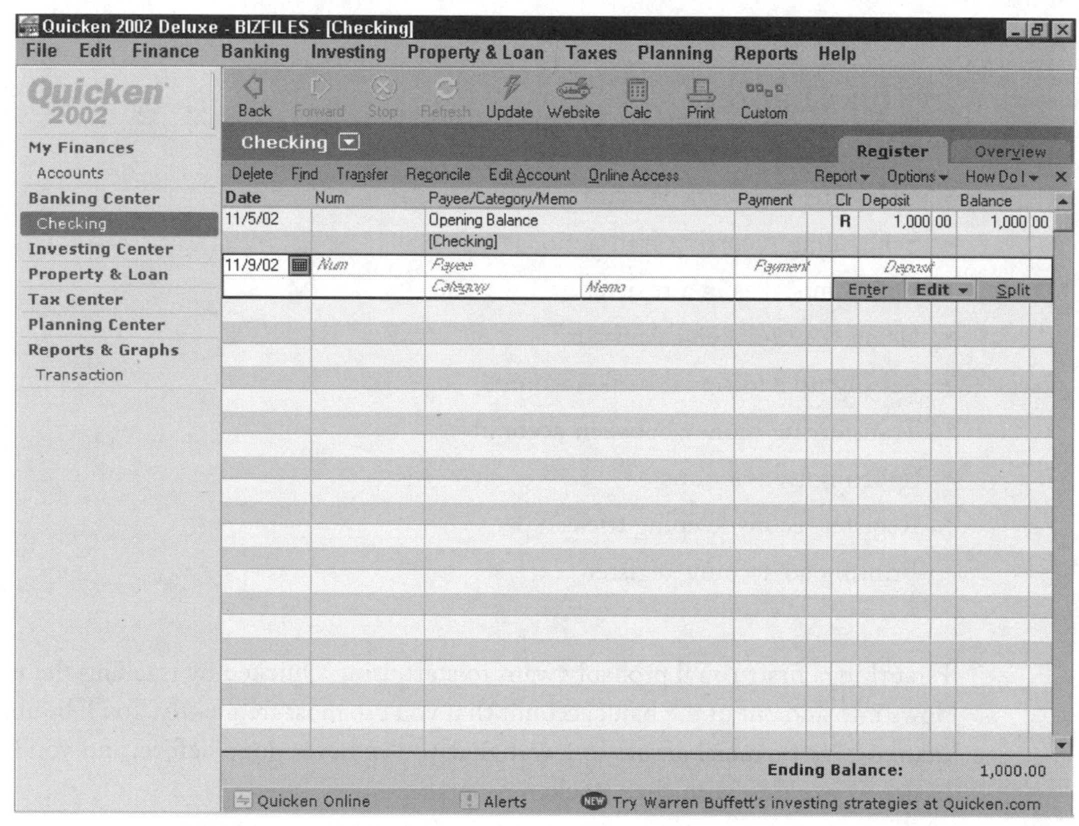

Figure 2.1: The Quicken register showing account information for the bank account named Checking.

To record a payment from an account into the empty register row, follow these steps:

1. Enter the payment date in the Date field (text box). You may need to highlight the Date text box if it isn't already selected. Quicken automatically enters the present date based on your computer's internal clock. If the date shown isn't the transaction date, enter the

date in MM/DD/YY fashion. (You don't need to enter the year number if the one Quicken already shows is correct.) When the Date text box is selected, Quicken provides several shortcuts for quickly changing the display date:

- Press + or – to adjust the date ahead or back one day at a time. (If you press the key that shows the = and the + symbol, you don't need to hold down the Shift key; Quicken assumes you mean +.)
- Press **T** to set the date to today's date. Press **M** to adjust the date to the first day in the month and **H** to adjust the date to the last day in the month. (Quicken uses M and H because *M* is the first letter in the word *month* and *H* is the last letter.) Press **Y** to adjust the date to the first day in the year and **R** to adjust the date to the last date in the year. (*Y* is the first letter in the word *year* and *R* is the last letter.)

NOTE *You can use upper- or lowercase letters. In this case, Quicken is not case-sensitive.*

- Click the button at the right end of the active Date field to open a small calendar. The calendar highlights the current month and day; you can change months by clicking the arrows at the top of the calendar and change dates by clicking the mouse directly on the date.

NOTE *If the current date is not correct, consult your Windows documentation for information about resetting the clock and calendar.*

2. Once the date is correct, press Tab or click the Num field, which is a combo box. Quicken activates a list box that contains abbreviations for the different bank account transactions.

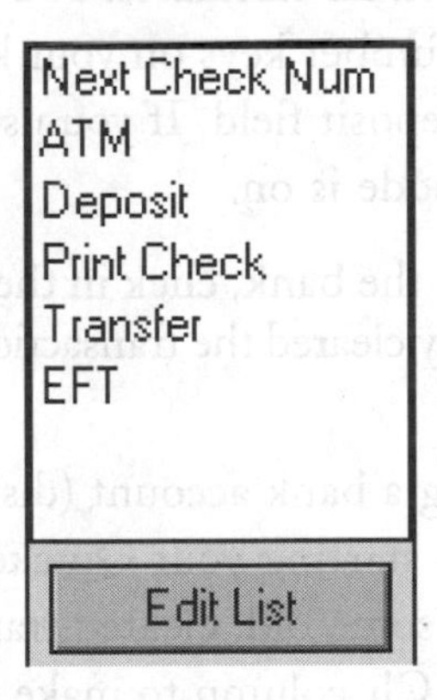

- If you're recording a handwritten check, type the check number, or select the Next Check Num entry to calculate the handwritten check's number by adding one to the previous check number.

- If you're recording a cash machine withdrawal, select the ATM entry from the list box.
- If you're recording a deposit, select the Deposit entry from the list box (discussed later in the chapter).
- If you want to print checks, use the Print Check entry to identify which checks you want to print, as described in Chapter 3.
- If you want to record an account transfer, use the Transfer entry for the transaction (discussed later in the chapter).
- If you're recording an electronic funds transfer, select the EFT entry from the list box.

3. Move to the Payee field by clicking it or pressing Tab until you reach it. Enter the name of the payee. If this is the first time you've recorded a payment to this payee, type the payee's name. If you've paid this payee before, you can select the payee's name from the Payee drop-down list.

TIP *Using the Payee drop-down list makes it easy to use the same exact payee name every time you record a transaction from any given payee. Then you'll find it easy to summarize your spending by payee.*

4. Move to the Payment field and enter the amount of the payment. You don't need to enter dollar signs or commas. You must use a period, however, to identify any cents.

When you enter the Payment or Deposit text box, a small calculator icon appears at the right end of the field. Clicking the calculator icon opens a small calculator. You can enter numbers by clicking the calculator's keys or by using the number keys on your keyboard. The result of the calculation appears in the Payment or Deposit field. If you use the numeric keypad on your keyboard, be sure that NumLock mode is on.

5. If you want to mark the transaction as already cleared by the bank, click in the Clr box, and a C will appear. The C indicates that you have manually cleared the transaction. When Quicken reconciles a transaction, an R appears.

Normally, you mark checks as cleared as part of reconciling a bank account (discussed in Chapter 5). If you're entering old transactions—say you're starting your Quicken record keeping as of the start of the current year and so you have some old, cleared transactions to enter—you can mark these transactions with a C in the Clr column to make your reconciliation easier. (If you do this, Quicken displays a Reconcile This Account dialog box and you need to click No to continue entering transactions. If you click Yes, Quicken starts its account reconciliation process.)

6. Categorize the transaction by moving the cursor to the Category combo box. From the list of existing categories that appears, select the category that best describes the payment.

A check to your landlord for rent, for example, might be categorized as Rent. If you can't find an expense category that describes the payment, you can enter a short category description directly into the Category text box. If you want to create a category named, for example, Software, type ***Software***, and press Tab. When Quicken asks if you want to create a new category, click Yes to open the Set Up Category dialog box, as shown in Figure 2.2. The new category name you entered shows in the Name text box. If you want, enter a description of the category in the Description text box. Verify that the Expense or Subcategory Of option button is marked so Quicken knows this is a category used to track spending. Mark the Spending Is Not Discretionary checkbox if that also describes this expense. Finally, mark the Tax-Related checkbox if this expense category is tax deductible (usually the case with business expenses) and, optionally, identify on which line of your tax return this category gets reported.

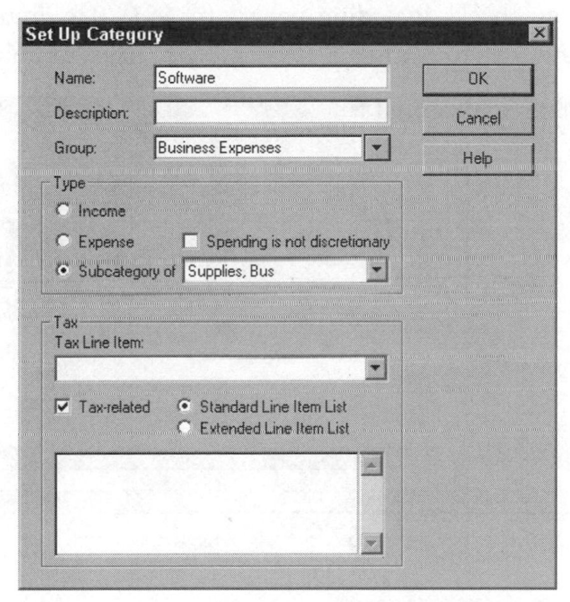

Figure 2.2: The Set Up Category dialog box.

The Subcategory Of drop-down list box allows you to create more detailed categorization. In Figure 2.2, Software is a subcategory of the category Supplies, Bus. (Supplies, Bus is short for Supplies, Business and is an expense category.) When you enter software in the register, Quicken lists the category as Supplies, Bus: Software. When you create reports, the expense accumulates in the Supplies, Bus category. In other words, the definition of the parent category as either expense or income sets the definition for subcategories.

NOTE *I'll talk more about categories in later chapters. See Chapter 13 for help on setting up category lists that support your income tax planning and preparation. See Chapter 14 for a discussion about how to use categories and subcategories as budgeting tools.*

7. If you want to add a memo description of the transaction, highlight the Memo text box by clicking it or by pressing Tab. Then enter a brief description. You can enter anything you want in the Memo text box, but there's no reason to duplicate information you've entered or will enter someplace else.
8. Click the Enter button (it appears just below the Deposit text box) to enter the transaction data into the register.

Quicken updates the bank account balance and highlights the next empty row in the register.

NOTE *Quicken also records transactions into the register if you press Enter when the Memo box is highlighted or if you press Ctrl+Enter when any of the text or combo boxes are highlighted.*

Figure 2.3 shows a register with four checks, including a check for $51.20 to Frank's Place for software and another for $500, written to Armstrong Commons to pay November's rent.

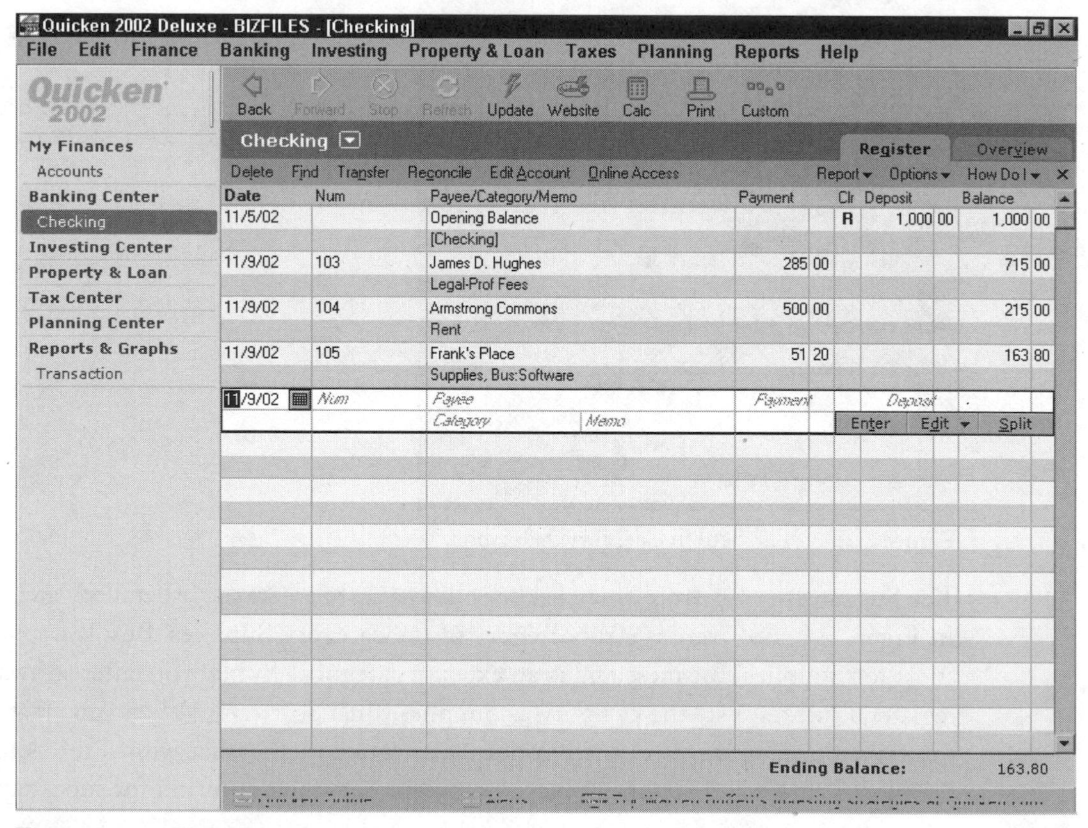

Figure 2.3: Recording checks in the register.

Using QuickFill to Speed Data Entry

Quicken provides QuickFill, a data-entry aid that you run into as soon as you start recording transactions. QuickFill keeps lists of the entries you make in the Payee and Category combo boxes. (In fact, it's QuickFill's list that Quicken displays in the Payee and Category drop-down list boxes.) When you make a new entry in a text box, QuickFill matches your new entry against the first entry that looks similar in its list. Then it fills the text box with this similar-looking entry.

This sounds unwieldy, but it works wonderfully. If, for example, you enter the Payee name Armstrong Commons, the next time you begin typing something into the Payee combo box that starts out with the letters ***Arm***, QuickFill completes the combo box so it shows Armstrong Commons. You can then move to the next field if QuickFill's guess is correct. If you're typing something different from what QuickFill guesses, it's not a problem. Just keep typing. What you type replaces whatever QuickFill supplies.

In the case of a payee name, QuickFill does even more than fill in the Payee field. If you accept the payee name supplied by QuickFill and move to the next field, QuickFill fills in the rest of the transaction's fields using the previous transaction's information. For example, if you let QuickFill fill in the payee name Armstrong Commons, and then you press Tab to move to the Payment text box, QuickFill uses the amount, memo, and category information from the previous Armstrong Commons transaction. Because checks you write to the same payee usually have similar features, QuickFill's automatic completion saves lots of data-entry time.

Recording Deposits

To record the money that flows into an account, you record a deposit transaction into the next empty row of the register. Follow these steps:

1. To enter the deposit date, highlight the Date text box, if necessary. Enter the date in MM/DD/YY fashion. Again, you don't need to enter the year number if it's already correct.
2. To identify the transaction as a deposit, highlight the Num combo box and select the transaction:
   - If you're making a regular deposit into the account, select the Deposit entry from the list box.
   - If you're recording an electronic deposit such as a wire transfer or a direct deposit of a paycheck, select the EFT entry.
3. To enter the person or company from whom you received the money you're depositing, move to the Paid By combo box.

- If this is the first time you've recorded a payment from this person or business, type the person's or firm's name.
- If you've previously recorded a check from the person or business, activate the Paid By drop-down list and select the person's or business's name from it.

4. Highlight the Deposit text box and enter the amount. Don't enter dollar signs or commas. Do enter a period to identify the cents.
5. If the deposit you're entering into the register has already been recorded by the bank, click in the Clr (Clear) text box. You would probably do this only if you're entering an old transaction or the transaction is an automatic deposit, such as an automatic payroll deposit.
6. Categorize the deposit using the Category drop-down list.

A check from a customer, for example, might best be categorized as Gr Sales (the category name for Gross Sales). A check from a consulting client might best be categorized as Consulting. If you can't find an income category that describes the deposit, enter a short category name directly into the Category combo box and press Enter. Quicken asks if you want to create a new category. If you do, click the Yes button. Quicken displays the Set Up Category dialog box (see Figure 2.2). Enter the category name you want to use in the Name text box. If you want, enter a description of the category in the Description text box. Verify that the Income option button is marked so that Quicken knows this is a category used to track income. Finally, mark the Tax-Related checkbox if this income category is taxable (it is if the category is for business income).

7. If you want to add a memo description, click in the Memo text box. Then enter a brief description. If you're depositing a payroll check, you might want to record the customer's check date. Or if you're depositing a customer or client check, you might want to record the invoice being paid.
8. Click the Enter button to record the deposit into the register. Quicken updates the bank account balance and highlights the next empty row in the register.

Figure 2.4 shows a $1,000 customer check from a fictitious customer, The Meteor Group. Note that the check is categorized as Gr Sales.

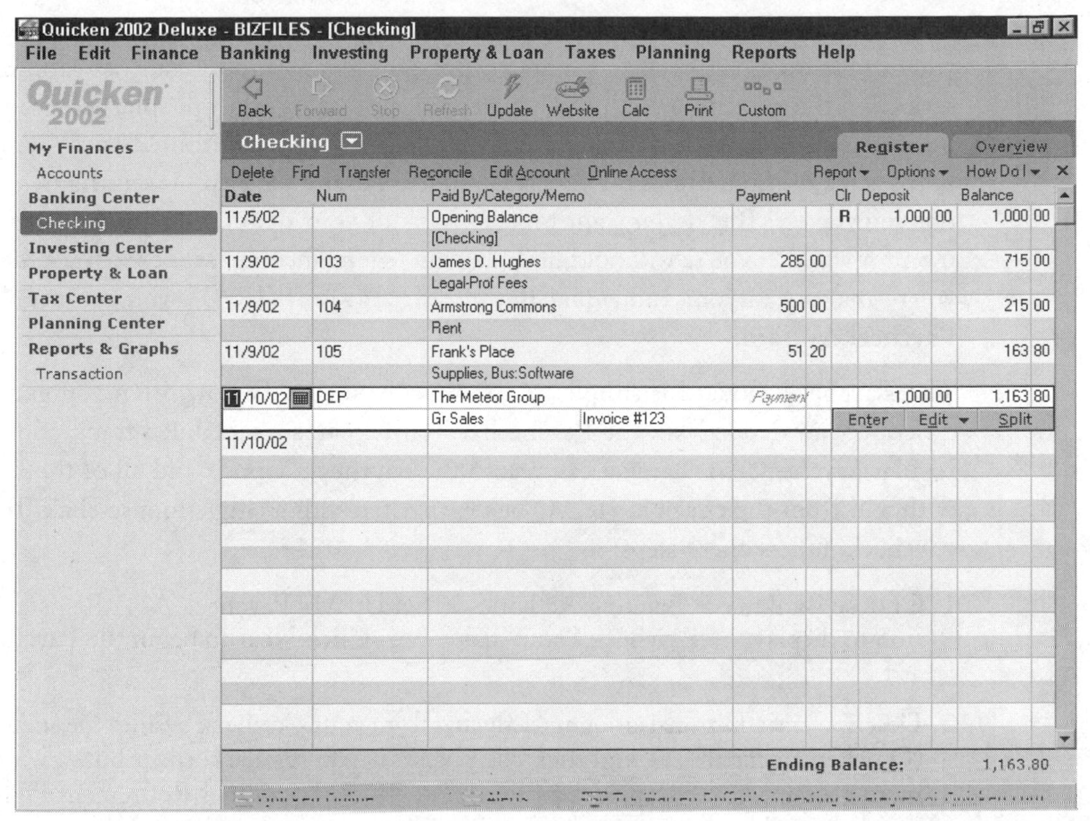

Figure 2.4: The register after categorizing a deposit as Gr Sales.

Using the Paycheck Wizard

Because you will probably use Quicken not just for a business but also for your personal financial record keeping, let me talk for a moment about how to record payroll checks that you receive (or that your spouse receives) as employees.

TIP *You can use the same checking account for both business and personal record keeping if the business is a sole proprietorship. In fact, for very small sole proprietorships, this approach often makes the most sense. Using the same bank account for both personal and business banking activities means you only need to pay one set of banking fees and only need to keep a balance in a single account. The only trick to using an account for both personal and business banking is that you must use different income and expense categories for tracking personal and business transactions. Chapters 13 and 14 discuss this topic in more information.*

You have two options for recording paychecks. If you want to make less work for yourself, you can record a paycheck as a simple deposit in the amount of your net earnings, as described in the preceding section. This method suffices for most people, because you really need to track only your net income, not your deductions and withholding. (Your employer keeps track of these things for you, and you need to use your employer's figures when you file your taxes.) But if you want to keep track of your deductions yourself—perhaps to monitor whether you're withholding enough in federal income taxes or to track the progress you're making in your Individual Retirement Account (IRA)—you can use Quicken's Paycheck Wizard.

The Paycheck Wizard is simple to use. Once you specify how often you get paid and describe your deductions, the Paycheck Wizard creates a scheduled transaction for your regular paychecks so that you can record the paycheck deposit and all of the deductions withheld from the check in your Quicken register with a single mouse click. To set up a paycheck, follow these steps:

1. Choose Banking ➢ Banking Activities ➢ Set Up My Paycheck As A Register Transaction to display the Paycheck Setup dialog box. Click Next to begin the Paycheck Wizard.
2. Describe any additional amounts deducted from your paycheck besides the standard taxes (Quicken tracks those), and then click Next. If you regularly contribute to your retirement account, for example, mark the 401(k)/403(b) or Other Retirement Plan Contributions checkbox, as shown in Figure 2.5.

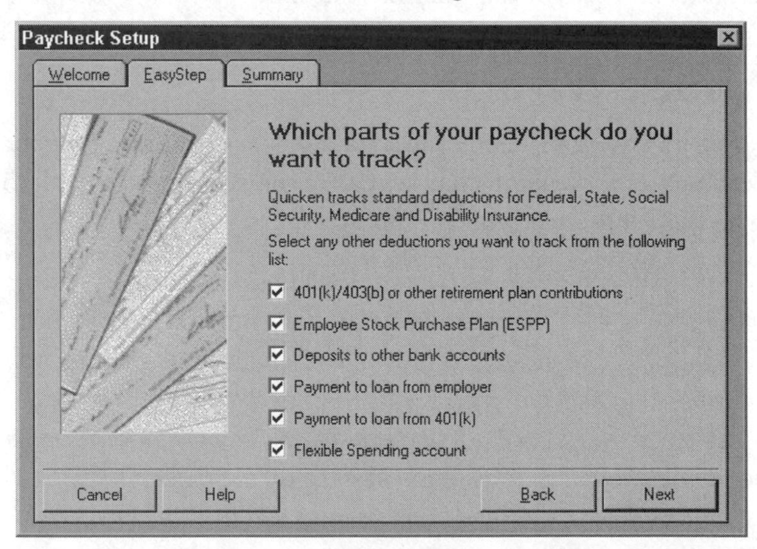

Figure 2.5: The Paycheck Wizard lets you specify which deductions you want to track.

3. Enter a name for the paycheck transaction and specify how often you get paid in the dialog box Quicken provides. Click Next to continue.

4. Enter the date of the first paycheck you want to record and specify the account into which you'll deposit your paychecks. Then click Next.
5. Enter the gross and net pay, and categorize the income from the paycheck, as shown in Figure 2.6, and then click Next.

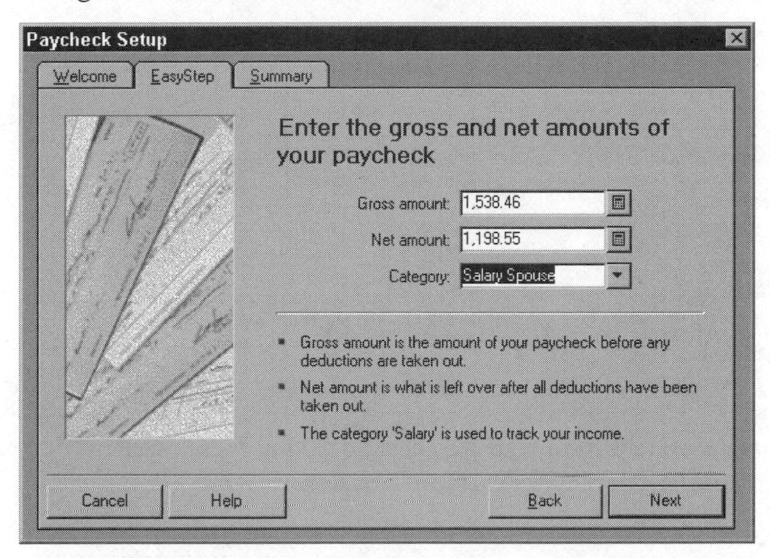

Figure 2.6: Entering the gross and net pay amounts from the paycheck.

6. If you have sources of income other than straight salary (such as bonuses, for example), click the Yes button, categorize them, and enter the amounts. Click Next to begin describing your paycheck deductions.
7. Describe the taxes deducted from your gross pay by entering the amount withheld for each tax in the corresponding Amount text box, as shown in Figure 2.7. If you don't pay a certain tax (if your state doesn't collect income taxes, for instance), leave the amount as zero. Quicken suggests categories for describing the taxes in the Category drop-down list boxes. If you want to select a different category for describing a tax, you can select one from the drop-down list. Click Next to continue.

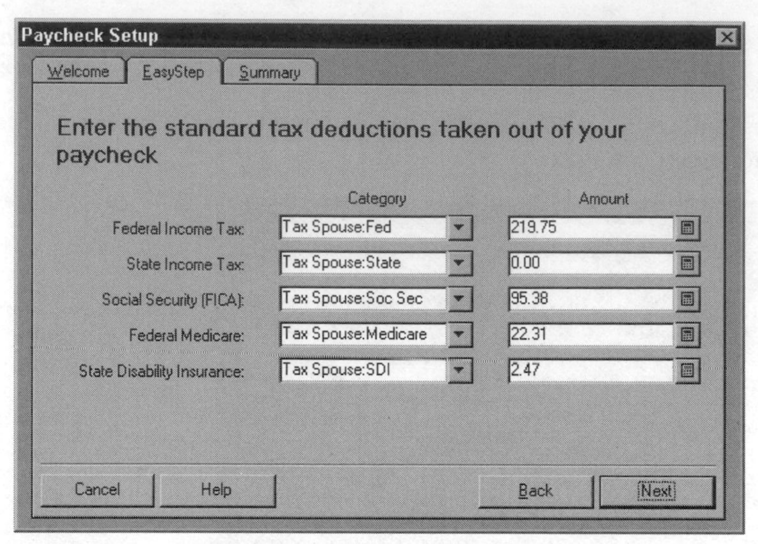

Figure 2.7: Describing the taxes withheld from the paycheck.

8. If other taxes are withheld from your paycheck, describe these taxes in the next dialog box Quicken displays. Then click Next.
9. If you specified in step 2 that you wanted to track any deductions beside the standard taxes, Quicken displays dialog boxes where you can describe these deductions. Click Next to describe each deduction.
10. If you had other amounts deducted from your paycheck that were not listed in step 2 and have not been accounted for, use the dialog boxes Quicken provides to describe these deductions. Then click Next.
11. Specify whether or not you want Quicken to remind you of your paycheck transaction. Then click Next to display a summary of your paycheck transaction, as shown in Figure 2.8.

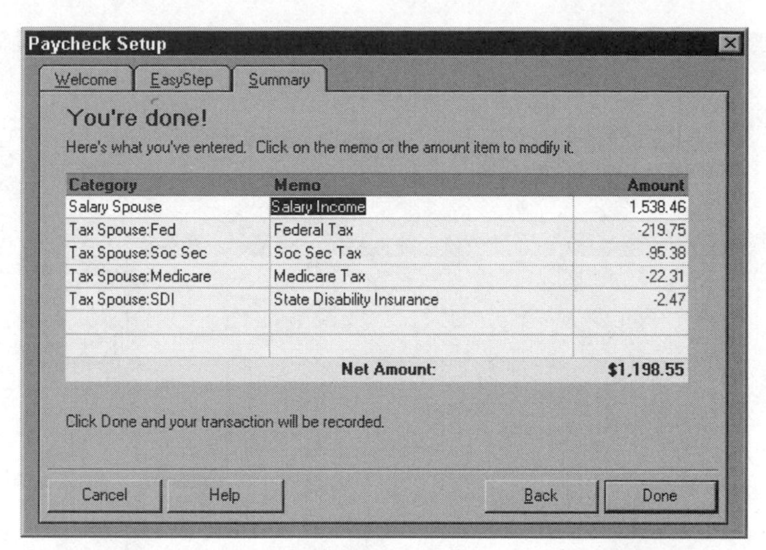

Figure 2.8: Quicken displays a summary of your deductions.

The scheduled paycheck transaction appears in the Alerts window and on the Financial Calendar. The next section of the chapter describes how to use this information to automatically record the paycheck whenever the paycheck deposit approaches.

Scheduling Recurring Transactions

If you have bills you want to pay without fail every month, Quicken's scheduled transactions feature can help you. To tell Quicken that it should automatically record a transaction, you schedule the transaction with the Financial Calendar.

Scheduling a Transaction Using the Financial Calendar

To schedule a transaction using the Financial Calendar, you must first enter the transaction once in the register so that Quicken memorizes it. Then follow these steps:

1. Choose Finance ➢ Calendar to display the Financial Calendar, as shown in Figure 2.9.

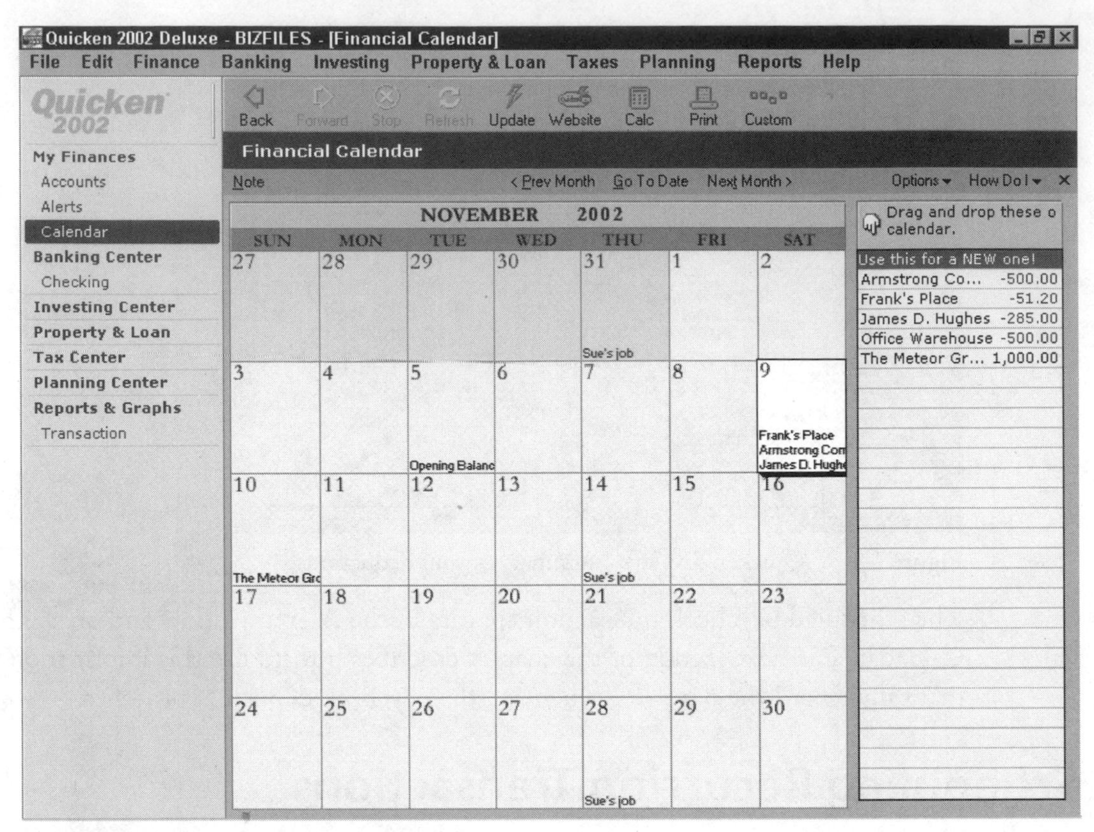

Figure 2.9: The Financial Calendar.

2. Display the first month you want to schedule the transaction by using the Prev Month or Next Month button.

3. Select the transaction from the list box that appears along the right side of the register by clicking it. Then drag the transaction to the first day it should be scheduled. Quicken displays the New Transaction dialog box, as is shown in Figure 2.10. The information displayed in the dialog box describes the transaction you've just dragged.

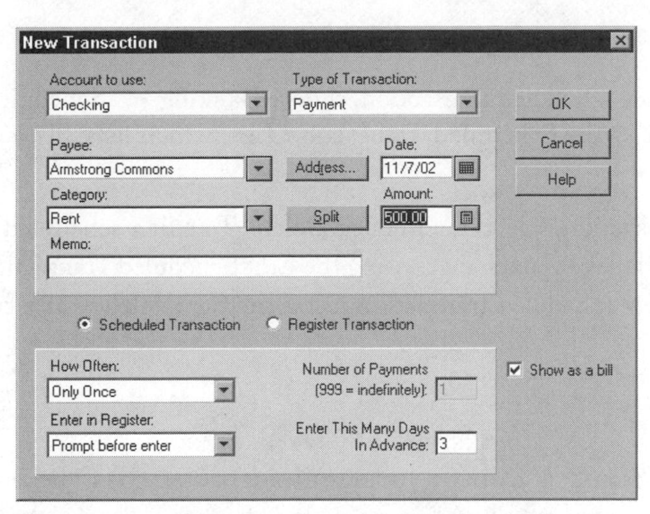

Figure 2.10: The New Transaction dialog box.

4. Activate the Account To Use drop-down list box and choose the account into which the account should be recorded.
5. Activate the Type Of Transaction drop-down list box to indicate whether you want Quicken to record a check, a deposit, or another type of transaction.
6. Use the next section's drop-down lists and text boxes to change any part of the recurring transaction.
7. Mark the Scheduled Transaction option.
8. Activate the How Often drop-down list box to indicate the frequency of the transaction: Only Once, Weekly, Every Two Weeks, Twice a Month, or another time period.
9. Use the Number Of Payments text box to enter the number of payments you want Quicken to enter.
10. Use the Enter In Register drop-down list box to specify whether you want Quicken to automatically enter the transaction or prompt you to enter the transaction.
11. If you want Quicken to remind you of unprinted checks, investment reminder notes, and scheduled transactions, use the Enter This Many Days In Advance text box to specify the number of days of advanced warning you want for this scheduled transaction.

Quicken schedules the transaction. To show the scheduled transaction, it puts the payee name on the calendar for each day the transaction will be recorded. Quicken also reminds you of the scheduled transactions in the Alerts window. You can view the Alerts window by choosing Finance ➢Alerts. With the Alerts window open, you can enter a scheduled transaction by selecting it and clicking the Enter button. Or, you can slip the individual occurrence by clicking the Skip button.

Using the Scheduled Transaction List

If you want to delete or edit a scheduled transaction, choose Banking ➤ Scheduled Transaction List. Quicken displays the Scheduled Transaction List, which lists all your scheduled transactions.

To delete a scheduled transaction, select it, and click Delete. To edit a scheduled transaction, select it, click Edit, and make your changes using the Edit Scheduled Transaction dialog box. You can also add a new scheduled transaction using the Scheduled Transaction List window's New button.

Using QuickEntry

If you need to enter only a transaction or two and don't want to start the Quicken program, you can use QuickEntry, a small, separate program that allows you to enter register transactions. To start QuickEntry, double-click the QuickEntry shortcut, which appears on the Windows Desktop. This displays an empty register for one of your Quicken accounts. You enter transactions in the QuickEntry register the same way you enter transactions in the regular Quicken register, as shown below. If you want to enter transactions into a different account, click the Accounts menu, choose an account group—either Bank Accounts or Property & Loan—from the Accounts menu, and then choose the specific account.

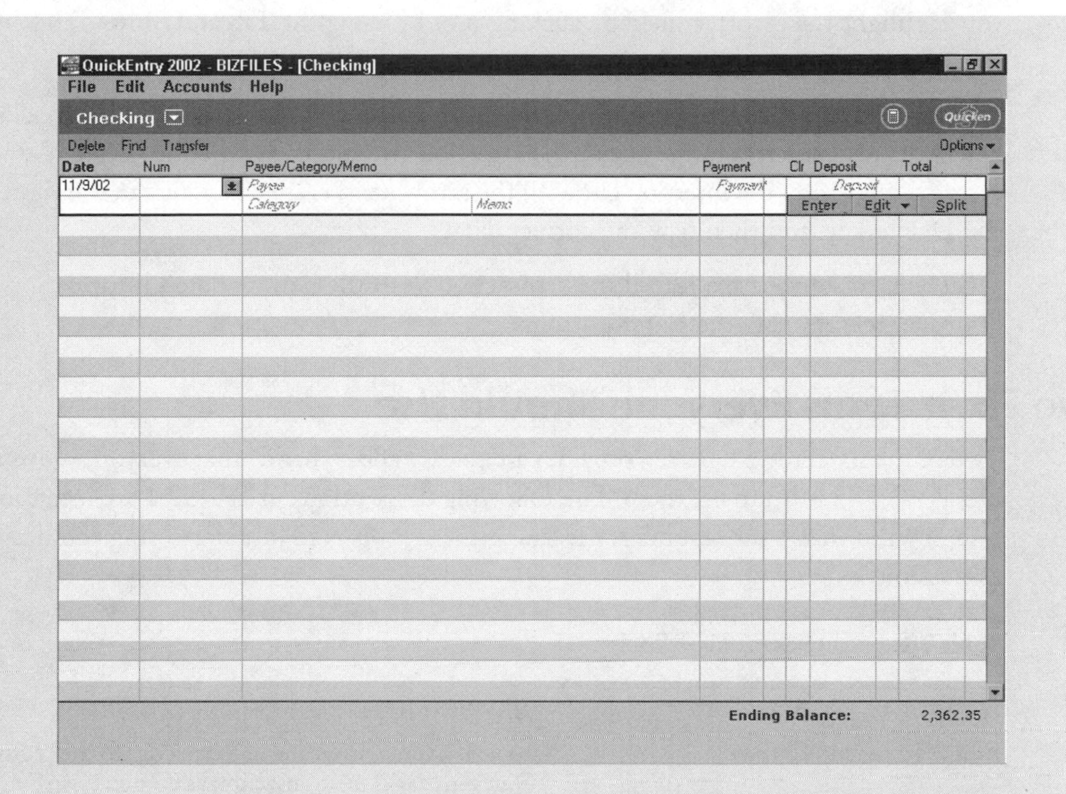

When you finish entering transactions, click the QuickEntry application window's Close button. The next time you display the register for the account, Quicken displays a list of QuickEntry transactions at the bottom of the Register window. To accept the QuickEntry transactions, click Accept All.

Fixing Mistakes in a Register

Your typing skills aren't perfect, of course. What's more, you will sometimes enter transactions into your registers using bad source documents (an erroneous deposit slip, for example). These little errors shouldn't cause you much concern, because Quicken provides a rich set of tools for fixing data-entry mistakes.

Fix-It Basics

If you make a mistake entering a transaction, all you need to do is change the erroneous piece of data. If you haven't yet recorded the transaction, you can move the selection cursor to the incorrect field. If you have recorded the transaction, you need to find the transaction and then highlight it either by clicking it with the mouse or by using the arrow keys. Then, you highlight the incorrect field by clicking it or by using the Tab and Shift+Tab keys. At this point, you can replace the incorrect entry by typing over it.

You can also edit the incorrect entry rather than replacing it altogether. Use the Backspace key to erase characters to the left of the insertion bar and then type the correct data. You can also reposition the insertion bar with the arrow keys, erase characters to the right with the Delete key, and then type the correct data.

Once you make your fix, record the transaction with the new, updated information—for example, by selecting the Enter button.

Two Fix-It Tools Everyone Should Use

Two of the fix-it tools Quicken provides are so easy and so handy that everyone—even new users—should learn to use them. The following descriptions in Table 2.1 are intentionally brief, by the way. Your best bet for learning these tools is to just start using them as soon as possible.

Table 2.1: Quicken's Fix-It Tools

TOOL	WHY YOU USE IT
Edit ➤ Transaction ➤ Void	To void a transaction already entered into the register. Quicken marks the transaction as void so it isn't included in account balances or category titles but leaves the transaction in the register so that you have a record of the transaction's existence.
Edit ➤ Transaction ➤ Delete	To permanently remove a transaction from the register. Quicken asks you to confirm the deletion with a message box. Delete appears as a command button at the top of the Register window and as an Edit menu command, and Delete Transaction appears as a command on the shortcut menu that you see when you click the Edit command button.

NOTE *Alongside the Enter and Edit command buttons, the Register window contains a Split button. I'll talk about how to use this button in the "Split Transactions" section later in this chapter.*

More Editing Tools

Once you're comfortable with the two fix-it tools just described, you may want to use the more powerful fix-it commands Quicken provides: Copy, Cut, Paste, Find, Find/ Replace, and Recategorize.

Cutting, Copying, and Pasting Data

With the Copy, Cut, and Paste commands, you can copy or cut the contents of one text or combo box and paste them into another text or combo box. This means that you can move text easily if you've stuck something into the wrong text box. It also means you can type something once and then copy it (or a portion of it) as many times as you need.

To copy and cut text box contents, you follow the same basic process:

1. Select the text box containing the text.
2. Position the insertion bar at the start of the chunk of text you want to copy.
3. Highlight the rest of the chunk of text by dragging the mouse or by holding down the Shift key and then using the left and right arrow keys.
4. Once you've selected the text, choose the Edit ➢ Copy or Edit ➢ Cut command. Copying duplicates the selected text and stores the duplicate copy in the Windows Clipboard, a temporary storage area. Cutting moves the selected text to the Windows Clipboard.
5. To indicate where you want to place the copied or cut item, first identify the text or combo box by selecting it. Then use the mouse or the arrow keys to move the insertion bar within the text or combo box to the location where you want to place the text.
6. Once you've indicated the destination location, choose Edit ➢ Paste.

NOTE *The Cut, Copy, and Paste commands are supported by the Windows operating environment, and they appear in most Windows applications. This means you can copy and cut chunks of text among different Windows applications. For example, you can select a chunk of text in Quicken, copy or cut the text to store it in the Clipboard, switch to another application such as Microsoft Word, and then use that application's Paste command to move the text stored in the Clipboard to a text box there.*

Finding a Transaction

If you know you made a mistake but don't know where, you can use the Find and Find/ Replace commands. Let's look at the Find command first.

Find locates transactions within a register. To use this command, choose Edit ➢ Find & Replace ➢ Find or click the Find command button at the top of the register. Quicken displays the Quicken Find dialog box, as shown in Figure 2.11. Enter whatever it is you're looking for in the Find text box. In the case of an error, for example, this might be a name you misspelled.

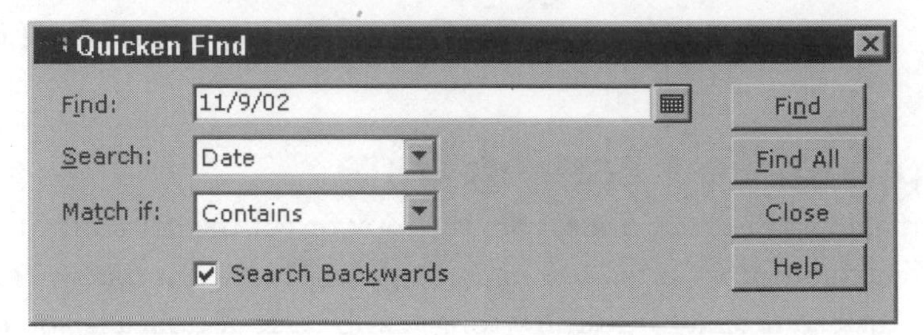

Figure 2.11: Use the Quicken Find dialog box to describe transactions you're looking for.

Use the Search drop-down list box to specify which fields you want to search. If you activate the drop-down list, you can choose any or all of the fields you fill in as part of recording a transaction into your register.

Use the Match If drop-down list box to specify what constitutes a match:

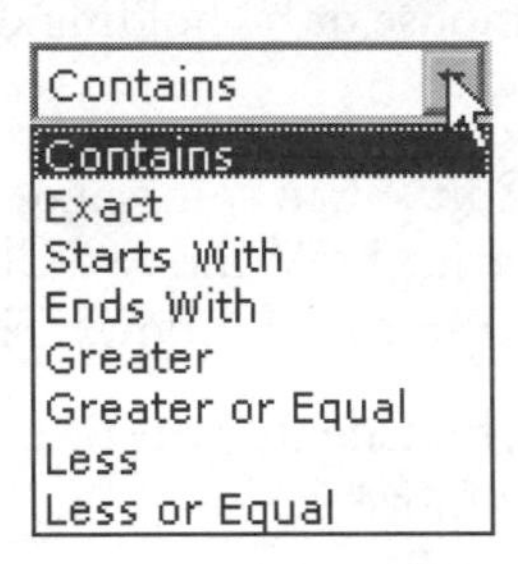

You can specify, for example, that the match be exact—in other words, that the bit of text or the number you entered in the Find text box must exactly match a field's contents in order for Quicken to consider the pair as matched. Or, you can specify that the text you entered in the Find box only match what starts or ends a field's contents. The Match If drop-down list also provides a complete set of mathematical operators such as greater, less, greater or equal, less or equal, and so on, just in case you want to search for an amount.

Quicken also provides three wildcard characters that you can use in the Find text box:

- **A question mark (?)** can stand for any single character. If you specify ***?at***, for example, Quicken will find *bat*, *cat*, *hat*, and so on—any three-letter word that ends with the letters *at*.
- **Two periods (..)** stand for any group of characters. You can use the two periods at the beginning, in the middle, or at the end of the word or text. If you specify ***..ville***, for example, Quicken will find *Marysville*, *Seville*, *Coupe De Ville*, and so on.
- **The tilde character (~)** indicates you want to find a field that doesn't contain an entry. For example, if you want to find a transaction that doesn't use the category Household, enter ***~Household***.

You can also combine wildcard characters. For example, the Find text entry *~?at* will find fields that don't contain three-letter words ending with the letters *at*.

Once you've described the search criteria, select the Find command button. Quicken searches from the selected transaction backward. (You can unmark the Search Backwards checkbox if you want to search from the selected transaction forward.) If Quicken finds a transaction that matches your search criteria, it activates the register but leaves the Quicken Find dialog box open in case you want to use it again. You can click the transaction to make a change to it. You can continue your search by clicking in the Quicken Find dialog box and selecting the Find command button again. When you finish with the Quicken Find dialog box, click its Close button.

If you want to build a list of all the transactions that match the search criteria, select the Quicken Find dialog box's Find All command button. Quicken displays a list of matching transactions in the Quicken Find document window, as shown in Figure 2.12.

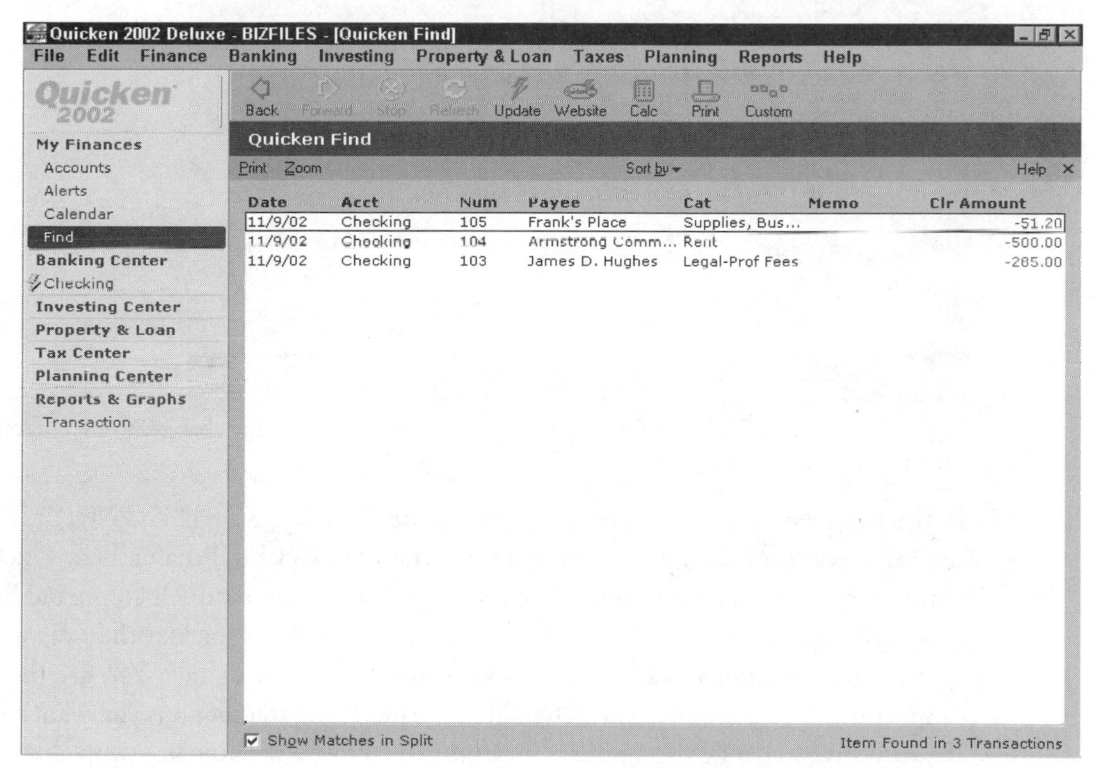

Figure 2.12: When you choose the Find All command button in the Quicken Find dialog box, Quicken builds a list of transactions that match your search criteria.

To edit a transaction or see it in complete detail, double-click it in the list or select it with the arrow keys and then press Enter. (This tells Quicken to select the transaction in the register.) When you're finished, click the Close button to remove the matching transactions list and the Quicken Find document window.

The Find/Replace Command for Making Many Transaction Changes

The Edit ➢ Find & Replace ➢ Find/Replace command is a more powerful version of Edit ➢ Find & Replace ➢ Find. It lets you change a field in all the transactions that match your search criteria. When you choose Edit ➢ Find & Replace ➢ Find/Replace, Quicken displays the Find And Replace dialog box, as shown in Figure 2.13.

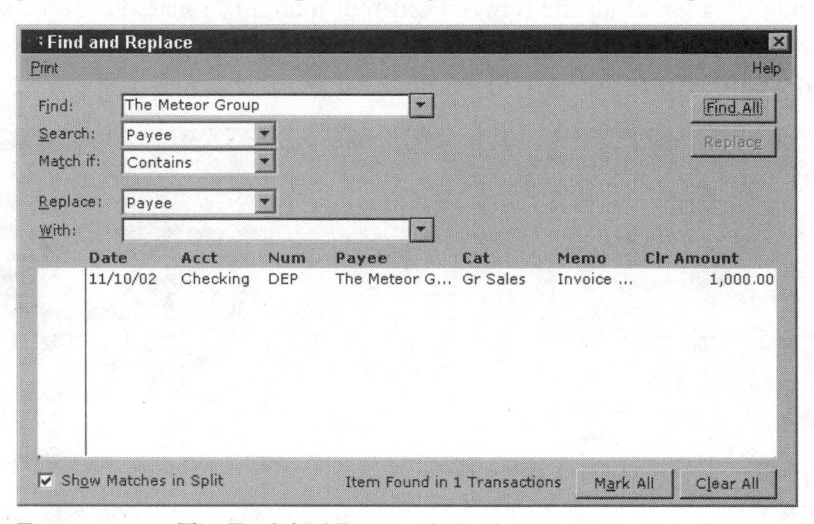

Figure 2.13: The Find And Replace dialog box lets you make editing changes to a set of transactions that match your search criteria.

In the Find And Replace dialog box, you can use the Find, Search, and Match If boxes in the same way you use their counterparts in the Quicken Find dialog box. Once you've entered the search criteria using these boxes, you select the Find All command button to locate all the transactions that match your search criteria. Quicken then displays these matching transactions in a list box at the bottom of the dialog box. You use the Replace drop-down list box to specify which field in the matching transactions you want to change. If you want to change the amount, for example, activate the Replace drop-down list box and select Amount. Use the With text box to specify the replacement text or value.

If you enter a value in the Find text box, Quicken assumes that you are trying to find an amount and makes Amount the default selection in the Replace drop-down list. Once you enter the value in the Find text box, press Enter or click Find All to locate all the Amount transactions.

To specify which matching transactions you actually want to replace with the contents of the With box, click each transaction to mark it with a checkmark. Use the Mark All button to add a checkmark to all the matching transactions. Use the Clear All button to remove checkmarks from all the matching transactions.

When only the transactions you want to change are marked with checkmarks, click the Replace button. Quicken displays a message box asking you to confirm your change. Select OK. Quicken then makes the replacements and displays a message box that tells you the number of replacements made.

The Recategorize Command for Replacing a Category

Quicken also provides a Recategorize command on the Find & Replace submenu. You can use this command to build a list of transactions for which you want to change the category, as shown in Figure 2.14. To build the list of transactions which use a category, select the category from the Search Category drop-down list box and click Find All. To recategorize transactions, mark the transactions you want to check, enter the new category that you want to use in the Replace With drop-down list box, and click Replace.

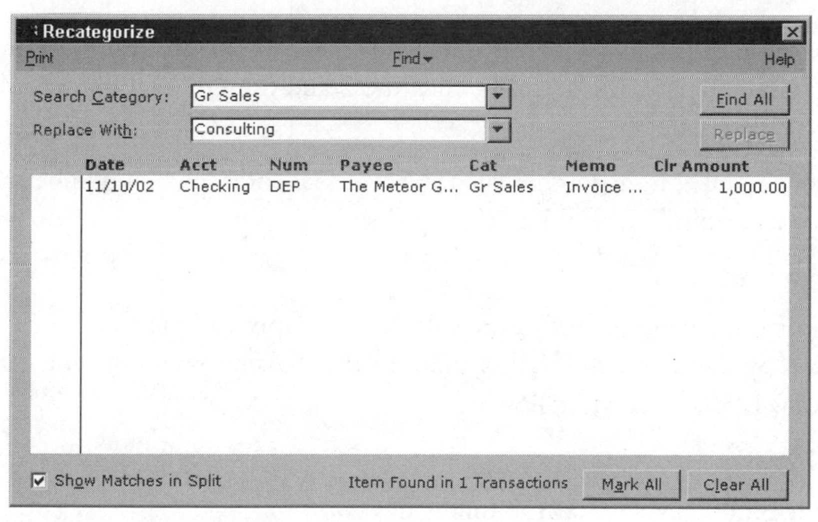

Figure 2.14: The Recategorize dialog box.

Using the Quicken Calculator

Quicken includes a simple pop-up calculator. You can start the calculator by choosing Finance ➢ Calculator. Quicken starts the calculator and displays it on top of the Quicken application window, as shown in Figure 2.15.

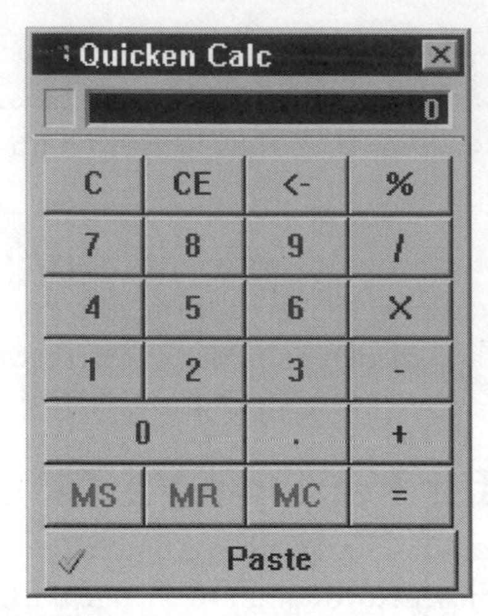

Figure 2.15: The Quicken calculator.

To add two numbers, such as 24 and 93, type the first number, the plus symbol, the second number, and then click the equal sign or press Enter:

24+93=

If you want to use the mouse, click the calculator's keys, which are really command buttons. For example, to enter the value 24, click the 2 and then the 4. (The calculator displays 24 if you do this.)

To subtract one number from another, such as 5 from 25, enter the first number, the minus symbol, the second number, and then the equal sign:

25–5=

To multiply or divide numbers with the calculator, simply use the times symbol as the multiplication operator and the slash symbol as the division operator. For example, to multiply 25 by 1250, enter the following:

25×1250=

And to divide 32,000 by 4, enter the following:

32000/4=

The MR, MS, and MC buttons recall, save, and clear entries from the calculator memory.

When you're finished working with the calculator, you can click the calculator's Close button, or you can click anywhere on the Quicken application window to make it the active window.

If you make the Quicken application window active, the calculator remains visible on your screen. To place the value shown on the calculator display into a text box in the application window, select the text box and then select the calculator's Paste command button.

TIP *Quicken displays a scaled-down version of its calculator when you click the calculator button that appears at the right end of the selected amount field. With the scaled-down calculator, you can calculate amounts on the fly. To enter the calculated amount directly into the selected amount field, simply press Enter.*

Setting Up Additional Bank Accounts

As part of installing Quicken, you set up at least one bank account. (In fact, the preceding discussion assumes you've done so.) You'll want to set up additional accounts in Quicken for each of your other bank accounts so that you can track the account balances and the money flowing into and out of all of them.

Adding a New Bank Account

To set up another bank account, follow these steps:

1. Click the Accounts QuickTab or choose Finance ➤ Account List to display the Account List. This window is just a big list box of the accounts you are using Quicken to track.
2. Click the New button at the top of the Account List document window to display the Create New Account dialog box, as shown in Figure 2.16.

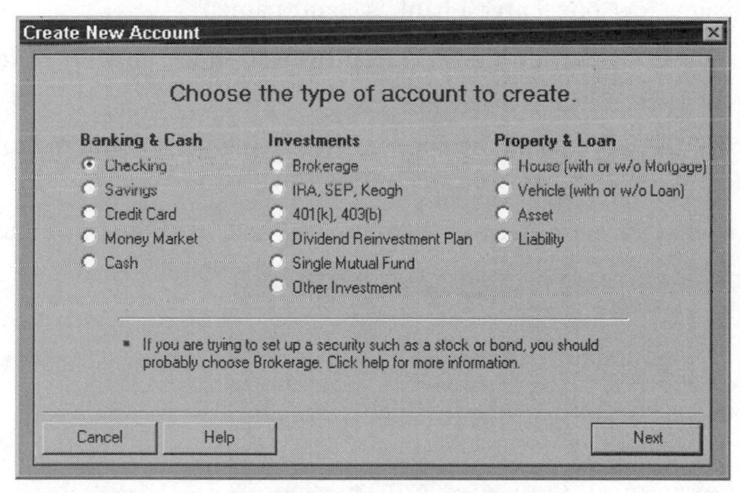

Figure 2.16: The Create New Account dialog box.

NOTE *Later chapters describe how you set up and why you use the other account types shown in Figure 2.16. For now, concentrate on setting up a checking, savings, or money market account.*

3. Click the Checking, Savings, or Money Market option button to tell Quicken that you want to set up another bank account and then click Next. No matter which button you choose, the process works the same: Quicken next displays the Checking Account Setup dialog box, Savings Account Setup dialog box, or Money Market Setup dialog box. Figure 2.17 shows an example of the Checking Account Setup dialog box.

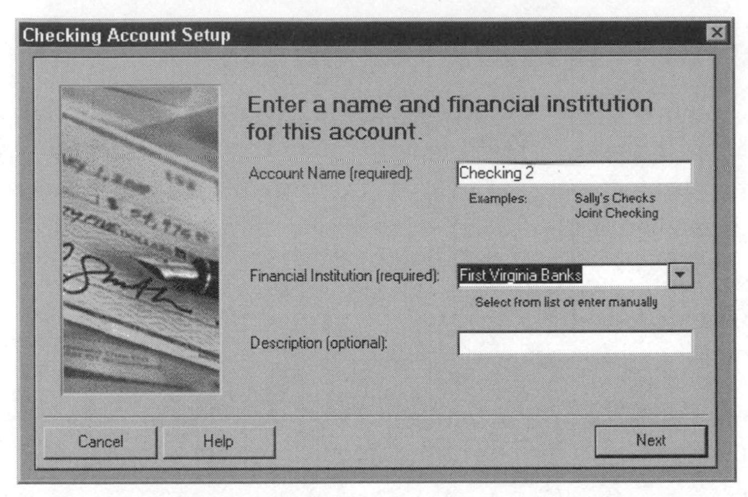

Figure 2.17: The first Checking Account Setup dialog box.

4. In the Account Name text box, enter a bank account name.

5. Select the name of your bank from the Financial Institution list box. Or, if your bank isn't listed, type its name into the Financial Institution list box.

6. In the Description text box, you have the option of describing the account in more detail, such as by providing the bank name or account number.

7. Click Next to move to the next Account Setup dialog box, as shown in Figure 2.18.

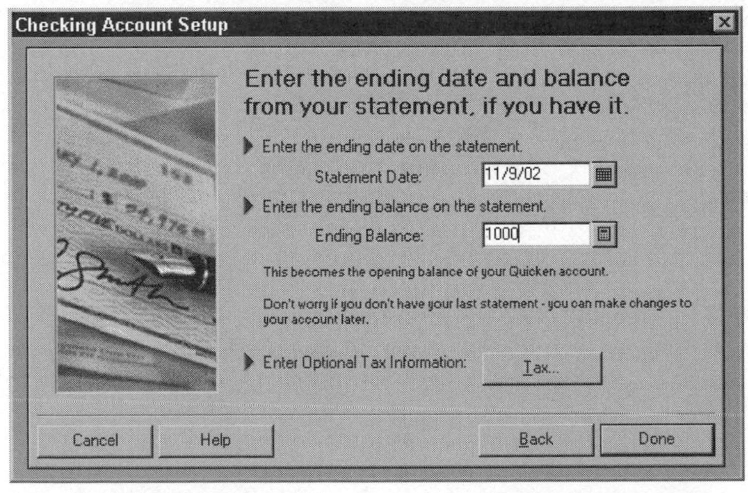

Figure 2.18: The second Checking Account Setup dialog box.

8. Enter the bank account balance and bank statement date information in the text boxes provided. As noted in Appendix A, unless you have meticulous records, the best approach is usually to use the balance from your bank statement and then adjust this balance (so it's correct) by recording any uncleared transactions.
9. If you like, you can also add information about taxes. Click the Tax button in the Account Setup dialog box to display the dialog box shown in Figure 2.19. This lets you tell Quicken that moving money into and out of this checking account has an impact on your income taxes.

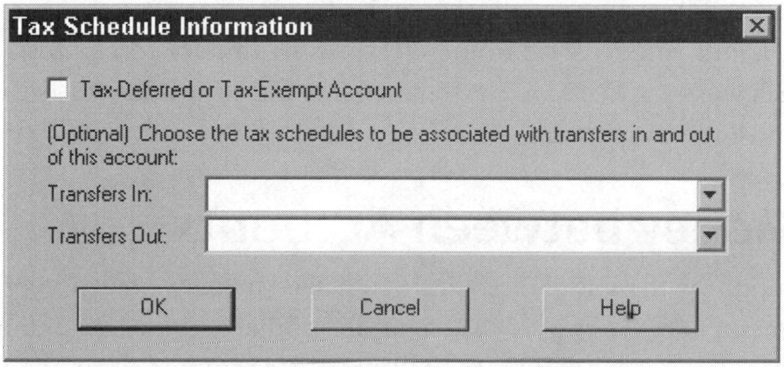

Figure 2.19: The Tax Schedule Information dialog box.

Most people and most businesses won't need to worry about the Tax button. However, if your transactions into and out of the account affect your taxes, you should keep track of that information. For example, if you're keeping IRA money in a checking account or money market account and then writing checks on this account as a way to withdraw money from the IRA account, you probably want to click the Tax button. When Quicken displays the Tax Schedule Information dialog box, mark the Tax Deferred Or Tax-Exempt Account checkbox. Then use the Transfers In drop-down list box to specify which tax form and line transfers into this account should be reported. Use the Transfers Out drop-down list box to specify which tax form and line transfers (or withdrawals) from this account should be reported. When you finish entering this information, click OK.

10. Click Done. Quicken redisplays the Account List.

TIP *When you're displaying an account register, you can click the Overview tab at the top of the register to display and edit the details of the account.*

Copying Transactions into an Account

You can copy transactions from an existing account into a new account (or a new file). If you need to copy only a few transactions, the easiest way is to print a copy of the account register (see "Printing an Account Register" later in this chapter), and then enter the transactions individually into the new account.

When you want to copy a number of transactions, you can save time by exporting the transactions as a QIF file and then importing them back into the new account:

- To export the transactions, choose File ➤ Export ➤ QIF File. In the QIF Export dialog box, enter a name for the QIF file in the QIF File To Export To text box, select the account from which you want to export transactions, and enter the date range of transactions you want to export. Mark the Transactions checkbox, and then click OK.
- To import the transactions into the new account, open the Quicken file containing the account and choose File ➤ Import ➤ QIF File. In the QIF Import dialog box, enter the name of the QIF file you exported in the QIF File To Import To text box, select the account to which you want to import the transactions, and click OK. Quicken copies the transactions into the new account.

Transferring Money between Accounts

Once you start working with multiple accounts, you'll need to know how to record account transfers—movements of money from one account to another account. For example, if you have a business checking account that doesn't pay interest (a common situation), you might have a business savings account or business money market account that does pay interest. In this case, you might commonly be transferring money from one account to the other.

Recording account transfers in the Register window is very easy. Enter the date in the Date field, and then press Tab to move to the Num field. Click the arrow button and select Transfer, and then enter the amount in the Payment or Deposit field, depending on whether you're transferring the money out of or into the account whose register you currently have displayed. Tab to the Xfer Acct field (Quicken replaces the Category field name with Xfer Acct when you choose Transfer in the Num field) and select the account to or from which you wish to transfer the funds from the drop-down list. Figure 2.20 shows an account transfer: $500 deposited into the money market account from the checking account. To identify the transaction as an account transfer, Quicken places brackets around the account name.

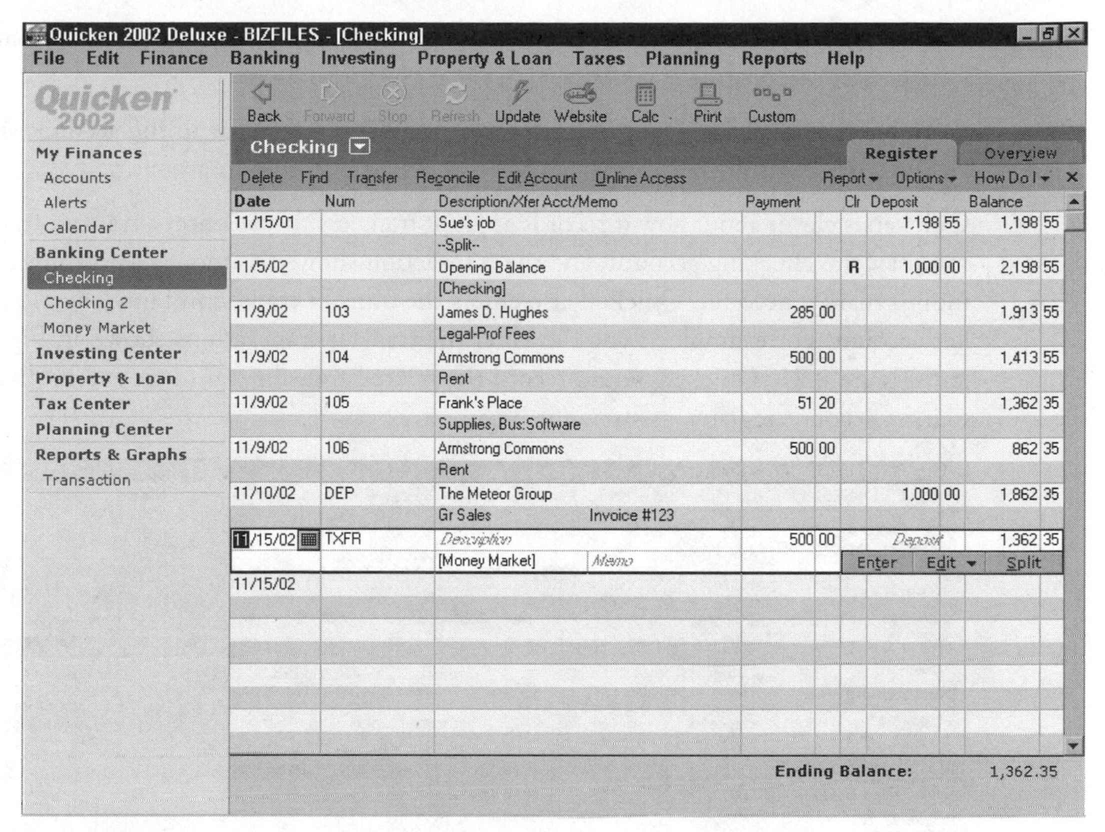

Figure 2.20: A $500 account transfer transaction, with money transferred from the checking account to the money market account.

You can also use the Transfer dialog box, shown in Figure 2.21, to record account transfers. To use the Transfer dialog box, select the Transfer button that appears at the top of the register. Then, use the text and combo boxes it provides to give the transfer date and amount as well as the names of the accounts the money moves between.

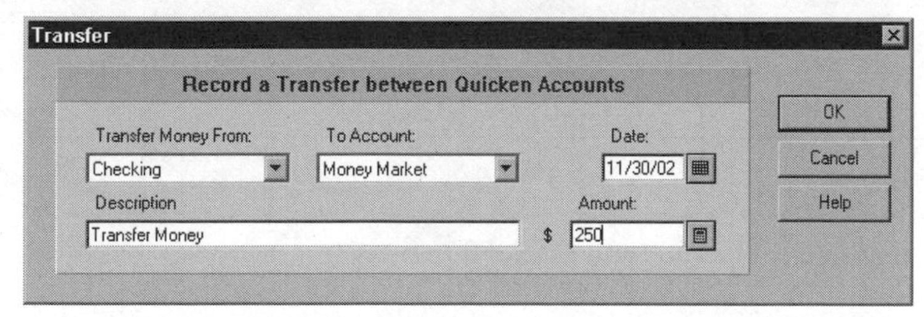

Figure 2.21: The Transfer dialog box recording a $250 transfer.

Using the Transfer dialog box to record transfers has a couple of advantages over using the Register window to record transfers:

- The Transfer dialog box visually shows you that only four pieces of information are necessary to record a transfer.
- You aren't limited to recording a transfer transaction from or to the account shown in the active register. You can specify any source or destination account.

Quicken is clever about how it records account transfers. If you enter a transfer transaction into, say, the checking account, and the transaction shows the money as coming from the money market account, Quicken also enters the transfer transaction into the money market account. For example, if you did enter the transfer transactions shown in Figure 2.20 and Figure 2.21, Quicken would record the related transfer transactions into the money market account register, as shown in Figure 2.22.

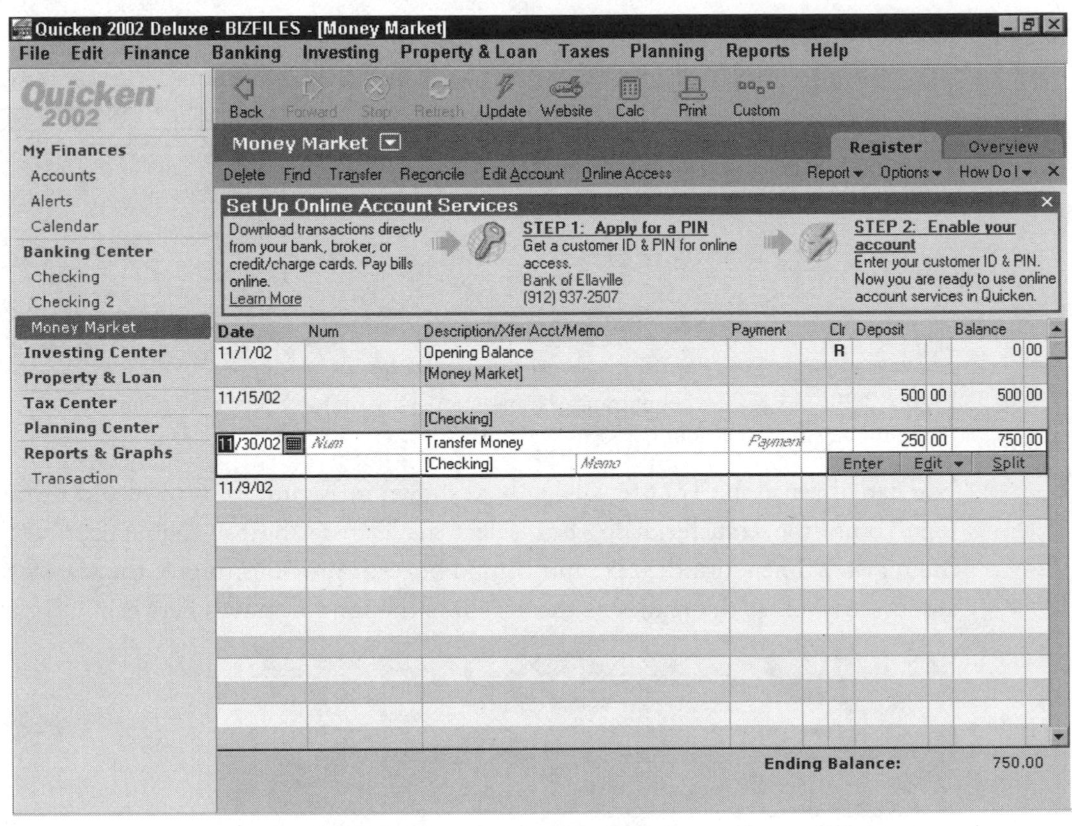

Figure 2.22: The other side of the $500 and the $250 transfer transactions.

If you edit a transfer transaction in one register, Quicken may even update the matching transfer transaction in the other register. Changes to a transfer transaction's date or amount, for example, are made to the matching transfer transaction too. (However, changes to a transfer transaction's other fields—such as its check number, memo description, and cleared status—don't get made to the matching transfer transaction.)

TIP *You can flip between the two sides of a transfer in a couple of ways. If the highlighted transaction in a register is a transfer, choose Edit ➢ Transaction ➢ Go To Transfer to move to the other side of the transfer.*

Splitting Transactions

Not every check you write can be fairly categorized using a single category. For example, a check written to a particular warehouse store might cover office supplies expenses for your business, an equipment purchase for business, and then groceries for your family which would of course be a personal expense. In this sort of situation, you can't create an accurate transaction that uses a single category.

Similarly, not every deposit you make can be fairly categorized using a single category. More commonly, this is the case with personal deposits. A check that includes your regular wages and a reimbursement for travel expenses can't be described entirely as wages (or as expense reimbursement). But there might also be business deposits that can't be fairly described using a single category. For example, if you use two categories to segregate revenues you earn through the sales of a product and those you earn through the sales of a service, a customer check that pays for both products and services can't be described with a single category.

Fortunately, Quicken provides a handy way to deal with this record-keeping reality: split transactions.

Making a Split Transaction

Suppose you want to record a $100 check that pays $75 of office supplies and $25 of groceries. To record this check, you follow the same steps you use to record any other check. But when you get to the step where you're supposed to enter the category, you select the Split button, which appears in the row for the transaction (just below the Balance column) when the transaction is selected. When you select Split, Quicken displays the Split Transaction Window, as shown in Figure 2.23.

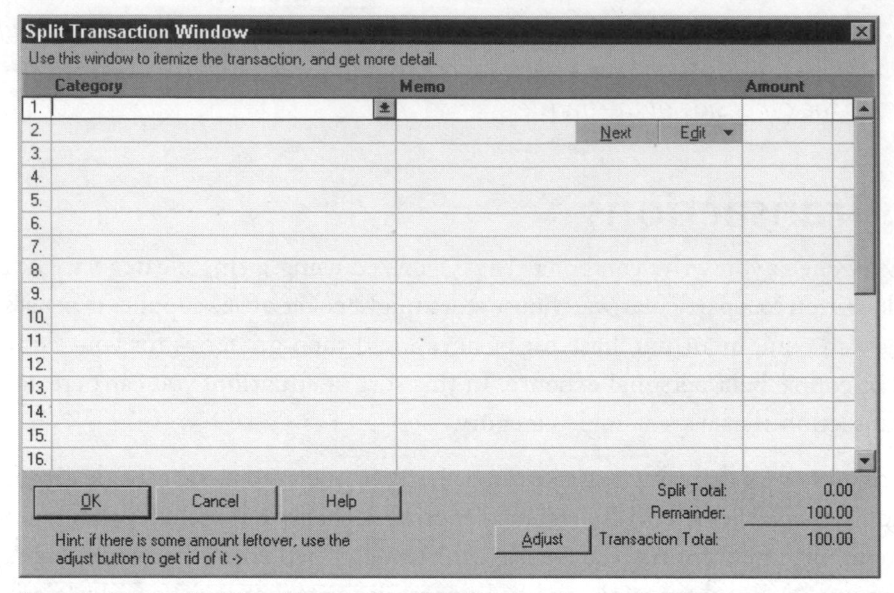

Figure 2.23: The Split Transaction Window.

Here's what you do to use the Split Transaction Window:

1. Categorize the first expense paid with the check: Place the cursor in the first Category combo box. Activate the drop-down list. Then, choose the first spending category—in this case, it's Supplies, Bus—paid with the check.
2. If you want a memo description of the expenditure, place the cursor in the first Memo text box. Then enter a description of the expenditure.
3. Enter the first expense category amount: Place the cursor in the first Amount text box and enter the amount. (Because the first spending category is Supplies, Bus and you spent $75 on business office supplies, type *75*.)

TIP *You don't need to enter split amounts in dollars. If you enter a percentage amount, such as 75%, Quicken calculates the split amount by multiplying the split percentage by the transaction total. If the transaction total is $100 and you enter a split transaction amount as 75%, Quicken calculates 75 percent of 100 and enters $75 as the split transaction amount.*

4. Repeat steps 1 through 3 for the other spending category, Groceries.

To record a transaction with more than two spending categories, repeat steps 1 through 3 as many times as necessary. If you need more than 16 categories to split the transaction, use the vertical scroll bar in the Split Transaction Window to page down to more split transaction lines. You can split a transaction into as many as 30 categories.

5. Verify that the split transaction lines agree with the register.

When you finish describing each of the spending categories for a check, the total of the individual split transaction lines you've entered should agree with the payment you entered. If it doesn't, you can click the Adjust button in the Split Transaction Window to adjust the Payment amount shown in the register to whatever the split transaction lines total. In addition, you can either enter additional split transaction lines or adjust one of the split transaction lines already entered.

TIP *You can easily tell whether the total of the split transaction lines equals the payment amount entered in the register. Quicken uses the empty split transaction line beneath the last split transaction you entered to show the difference between the payment amount and the total of the individual split transaction lines.*

Figure 2.24 shows the Split Transaction Window filled out to record a $100 check that pays $75 for business office supplies and $25 for groceries.

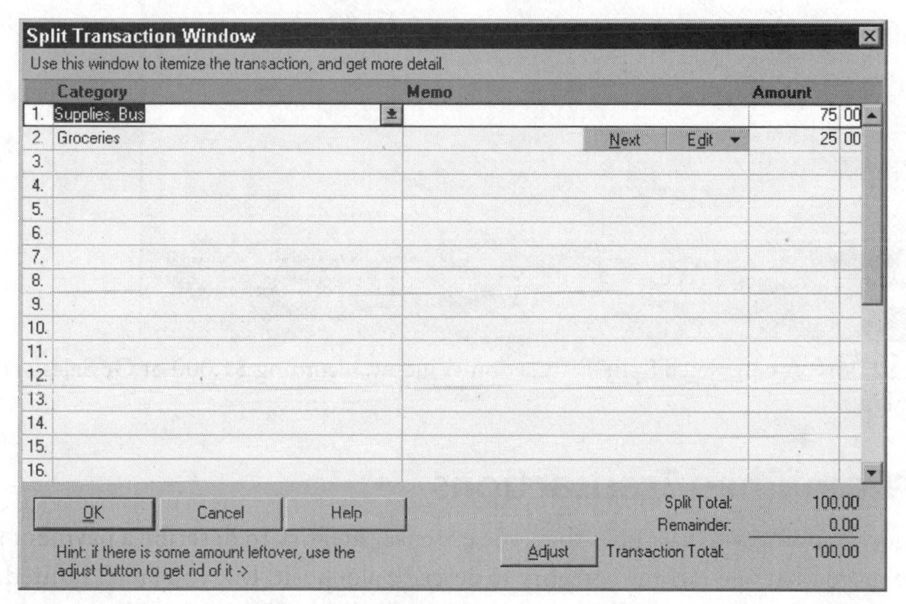

Figure 2.24: A completed Split Transaction Window, recording $75 of supplies expense and $25 of groceries.

Removing a Split Transaction

To remove a split transaction—a split category and amount shown in the Split Transaction Window—select Split in the Category field and click the × button next to it. You might use this technique, for example, to delete an erroneous split transaction line. You can click the checkmark button to go back to the Split Transaction Window.

Splitting Deposit Transactions

Splitting deposit transactions works the same way as splitting payment transactions. You enter the deposit in the usual way, including the deposit amount. Then, when you get to the Category combo box, click the Split command button. Quicken displays the Split Transaction Window, and you describe each of the income categories in a deposit using different split transaction lines. Figure 2.25 shows how you might record a $1,200 deposit that represents $1,000 of Gr Sales and $200 of Consulting.

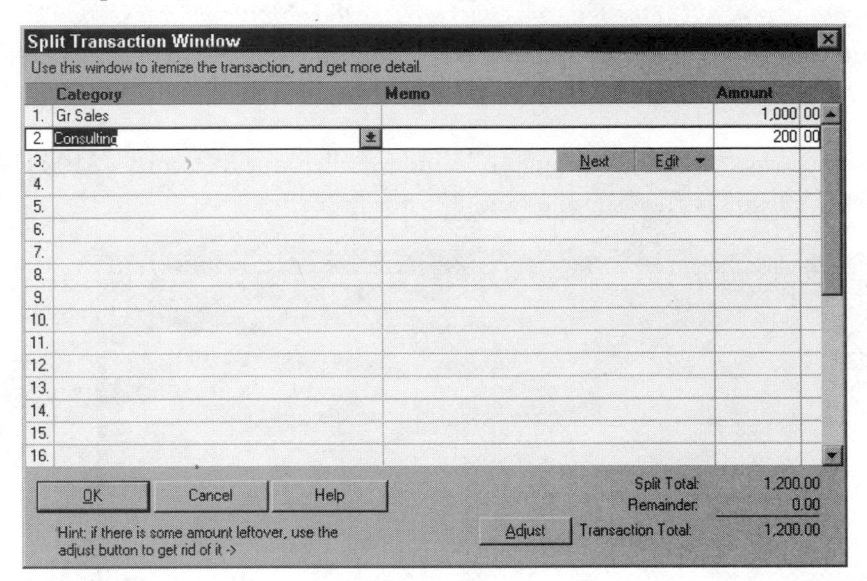

Figure 2.25: A completed Split Transaction Window, recording $1,000 of Gr Sales and $200 of Consulting.

Splitting Combined Transactions

You now know how to use more than one expense category to describe a payment and how to use more than one income category to describe a deposit. But you aren't limited to using just expense or just income categories on a split transaction. You can, in effect, mix and match your categories.

For example, if you go to the bank and deposit your $1,000 payroll check but keep $25 of cash for Friday-night fun, you would fill out the Split Transaction Window as shown in Figure 2.26. Your net deposit is really $975. You would record the deposit amount as $975, of course.

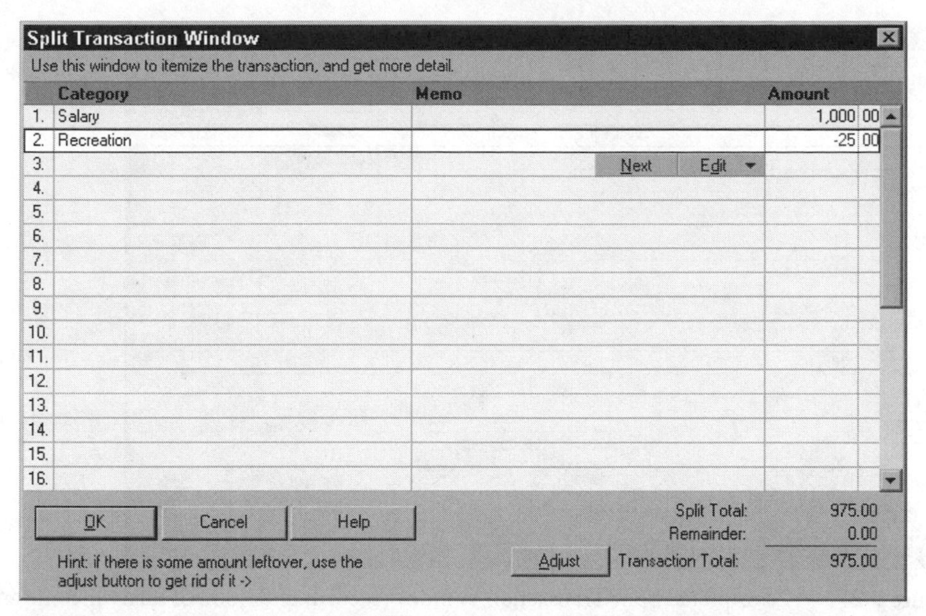

Figure 2.26: A completed Split Transaction Window, recording $1,000 of salary income and $25 of recreation expense.

One thing that's initially tricky about splitting combined income and expense transactions is the sign of the split transaction line amounts. In Figure 2.26, for example, the $1,000 of salary shows as positive and the $25 of recreation shows as negative. (On a color monitor, the negative $25 also shows in red to further identify the value as a negative number.) However, this isn't because salary income increases the account balance or because recreation expense decreases the account balance. Quicken just adds up the amount of the split transaction lines. So you use negative split transaction amounts, such as the $25 of recreation expense, to reduce the total split transaction lines.

Say, for example, you want to record the purchase of an item your spouse's employer manufactures—a new $1,500 hot tub. If you'll pay $500 by writing a check and will also forfeit a $1,000 payroll check, you would record this split transaction as shown in Figure 2.27.

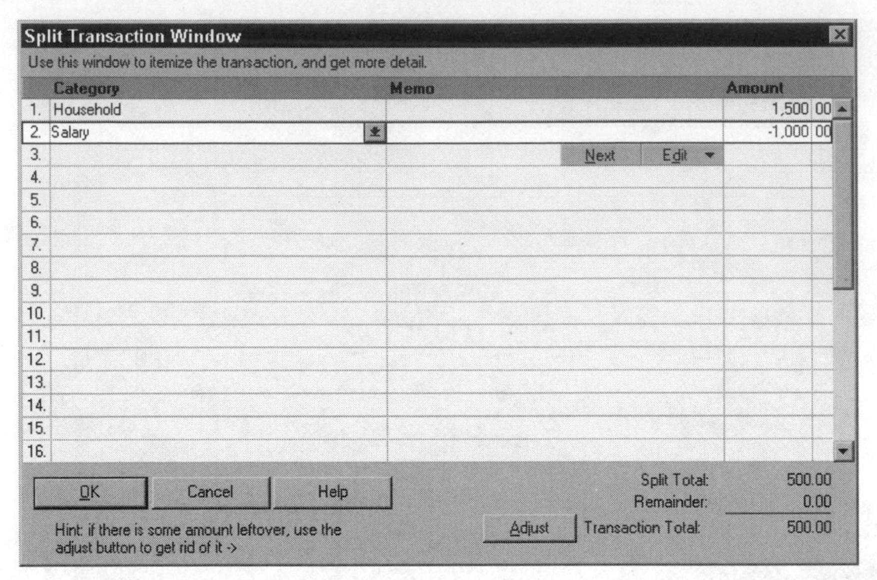

Figure 2.27: A completed Split Transaction Window, recording $1,000 of salary income and $1,500 of household expense.

NOTE *You can also use the Split Transaction Window to describe account transfers. Chapter 15 shows how you split transactions between expense categories and account transfers as part of preparing employee payroll.*

Changing a Split Transaction

Editing the details of a split transaction works very much like you might expect, with one minor exception.

To display the Split Transaction Window so that you can make changes, click the Split button or click the button that has a checkmark. In the Split Transaction Window, you can make whatever changes you want by replacing categories, memo descriptions, or amounts. You make these changes by clicking the text box you want to change and then typing the new information.

You can also remove the splits from a transaction. In other words, you can tell Quicken you want to "unsplit" a transaction. To do this, click the Cancel button—it looks like a small x—that appears next to the Category drop-down list, as you can see in Figure 2.28.

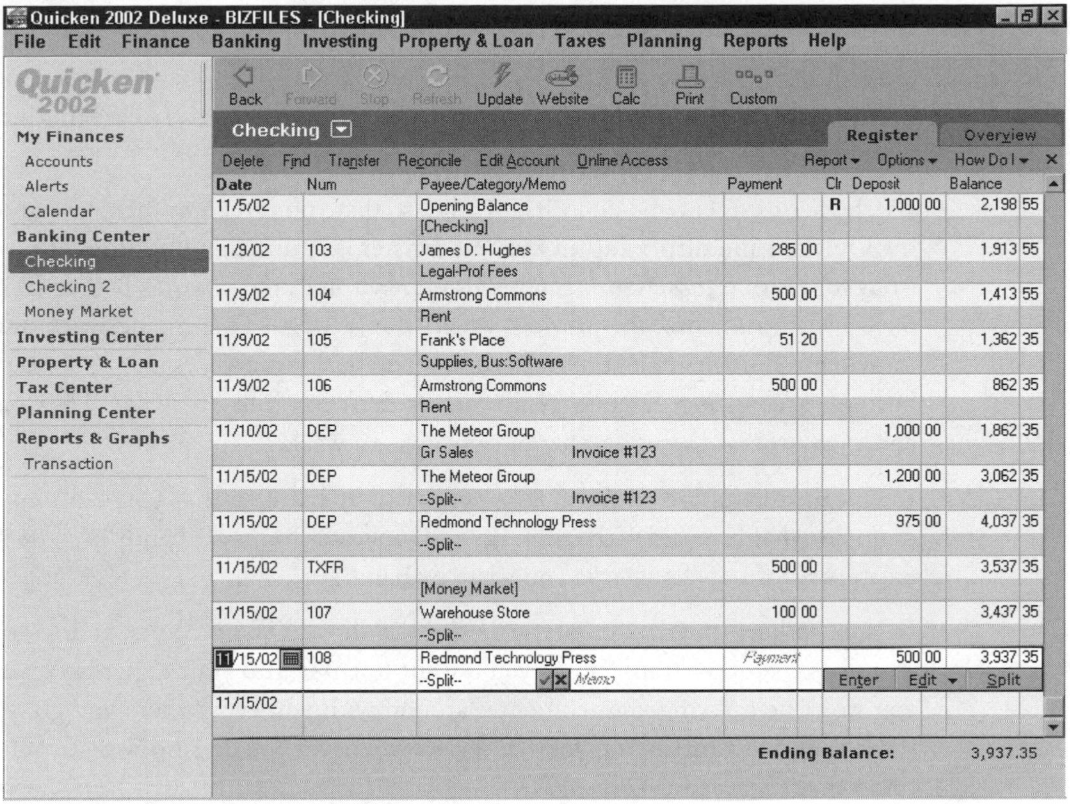

Figure 2.28: Quicken adds buttons next to a split transaction.

The most common reason that you will want to "unsplit" a transaction is that QuickFill has filled out the Split Transaction Window for you even though it shouldn't have. For example, if you write a $100 check to Beeson's Corner Market and split the check as $75 groceries and $25 gifts, Quicken's QuickFill feature memorizes this information. The next time you write a check to Beeson's Corner Market, QuickFill copies all the information you used to describe the last check, including the split-transaction information. If the new check to Beeson's, however, is only for groceries, you'll want to "unsplit" the transaction.

NOTE *There's nothing wrong with having only a single split transaction line. Everything still works correctly within Quicken. The only disadvantage of this single split transaction line is that you need to select the transaction and open the Split Transaction Window to see how a check or a deposit was categorized.*

Register Record-Keeping Tricks

If you're just getting started with a checkbook program like Quicken, incorporating the program into your record-keeping routines can be a little awkward. To ease this process, here is a handful of helpful ideas:

- Batch your payment and deposits together so that you can enter them as a group. Starting Quicken and displaying an account register isn't difficult, but doing it several times a day for every transaction is time-consuming. You'll find it works best to sit down, say, once a week and enter the previous week's transactions. This should work fine for both individuals doing personal record keeping and business owners and bookkeepers doing business accounting. Even large businesses don't pay bills every day. They batch them and then process them together once or twice a week.
- Keep documentation of the checks you write by hand so that you can remember, for example, what you paid with check 1245. (Duplicate checks are handy because you always create a record of the checks you write by hand.)
- Be sure to keep the documentation—deposit slips, ATM receipts, and so forth—that describes the other transactions you'll want to enter into your register. Again, because you won't be carrying your computer around with you everywhere you go, you'll want some paper documentation you can review whenever you do sit down at your computer to do financial record keeping.

Printing an Account Register

It's a good idea to print an account register at the end of the month. This paper record provides a hard copy of the transactions you've entered and acts as a permanent backup copy of your financial records. You can keep this copy with the bank account statement you receive. (You probably won't need the register unless you someday need to restore your financial records from a backup copy.)

To print an account register, first display the account in the register such as clicking the Banking Center QuickTab and then clicking the account name in the Banking Center window. Then follow these steps:

1. Choose File ➢ Print Register to display the Print Register dialog box, as shown in Figure 2.29.

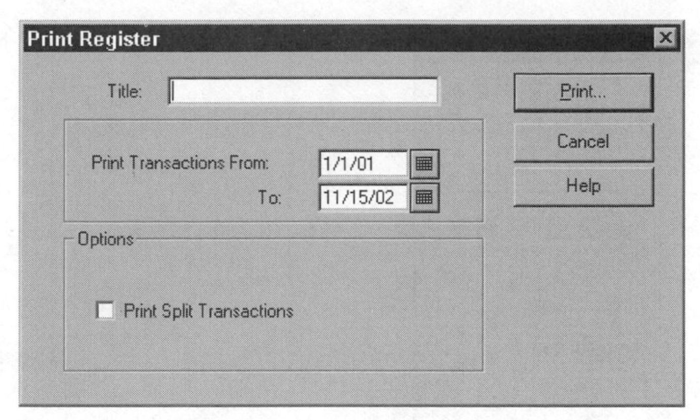

Figure 2.29: The Print Register dialog box.

2. If you want to enter a title for the register, use the Title text box. If you don't enter a title, Quicken uses Account Register for the title.

3. Enter the range of dates you want the register to include using the Print Transactions From and To text boxes.

NOTE *If you look closely at the Print Transactions From and To text boxes, you'll see something that resembles (sort of) a small calendar. Click this calendar to display a pop-up calendar you can use to quickly enter a date into the text box. The calendar highlights the date already shown in the text box, but you can change the month by clicking the arrows at the top of the calendar and change the date by clicking the mouse directly on the date.*

4. If you want to print split transaction information—and you probably do if you've been splitting transactions—mark the Print Split Transactions checkbox.

5. Click the Print command button when you're ready to print. Quicken displays another Print dialog box, as shown in Figure 2.30. (See Chapter 4 for information about how to use the Print dialog box to control the way Quicken prints reports such as the register.)

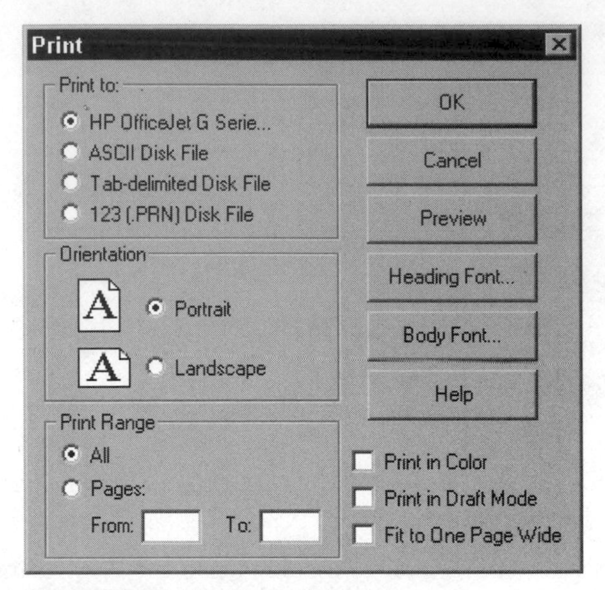

Figure 2.30: The Print dialog box.

6. Click OK. Quicken passes the register information to Windows, and it prints your register. Figure 2.31 shows a printed Quicken check register.

Check Register

Checking
11/9/2001

Page 1

Date	Num	Transaction	Payment	C	Deposit	Balance
11/15/2001		Sue's job cat: --SPLIT--			1,198.55	1,198.55
11/5/2002		Opening Balance cat: [Checking]		R	1,000.00	2,198.55
11/9/2002	103	James D. Hughes cat: Legal-Prof Fees	285.00			1,913.55
11/9/2002	104	Armstrong Commons cat: Rent	500.00			1,413.55
11/9/2002	105	Frank's Place cat: Supplies, Bus:Software	51.20			1,362.35
11/9/2002	106	Armstrong Commons cat: Rent	500.00			862.35
11/10/2002	DEP	The Meteor Group cat: Gr Sales memo: Invoice #123			1,000.00	1,862.35
11/15/2002	DEP	The Meteor Group cat: --SPLIT-- memo: Invoice #123			1,200.00	3,062.35
11/15/2002	DEP	Redmond Technology Press cat: --SPLIT--			975.00	4,037.35
11/15/2002	TXFR	cat: [Money Market]	500.00			3,537.35
11/15/2002	107	Warehouse Store cat: --SPLIT--	100.00			3,437.35
11/15/2002	108	Redmond Technology Press cat: --SPLIT--			500.00	3,937.35

Figure 2.31: A printed Quicken check register.

Chapter 3

PRINTING CHECKS

In This Chapter

- Collecting check information
- Printing your checks
- Check-printing problems

Once you've worked a bit with a Quicken register and used it to track a bank account balance and the money that flows into and out of an account, you'll want to consider printing checks using Quicken. Doing so will save you time, particularly if you now handwrite a lot of checks. What's more, printing checks with Quicken lets you produce professional-looking checks—something that's particularly valuable for business users of Quicken.

Before You Begin

Before you can print checks in Quicken, you need to do the following:

- Install the Quicken program, through Windows, and set up a bank account (see Appendix A).
- Order and receive the check forms you'll print. You'll find check order-form information in your Quicken packaging. You can also order checks online. Choose Banking ➢ Banking Services ➢ Order Checks & Supplies.

Collecting Check Information

Once you've completed the prerequisites, you're ready to begin describing the checks you want to print. You'll find it much easier to print checks if you're already familiar with the Quicken register. If you've been using the Quicken register to track a bank account, you'll notice that many of the steps are identical; the only differences are that Quicken supplies a different document window for you to use and that you also collect address information for the payee.

Telling Quicken You Want to Write Checks on an Account

To tell Quicken you want to write checks, open the register for the account that you want to use, and then choose Banking ➤ Write Checks. Figure 3.1 shows the Write Checks document window for a checking account. At the top of the Write Checks window, you see the name of your bank account—Checking in Figure 3.1. To select another account on which you want to write a check, just click the arrow button to the right of the account name and then select the other bank account.

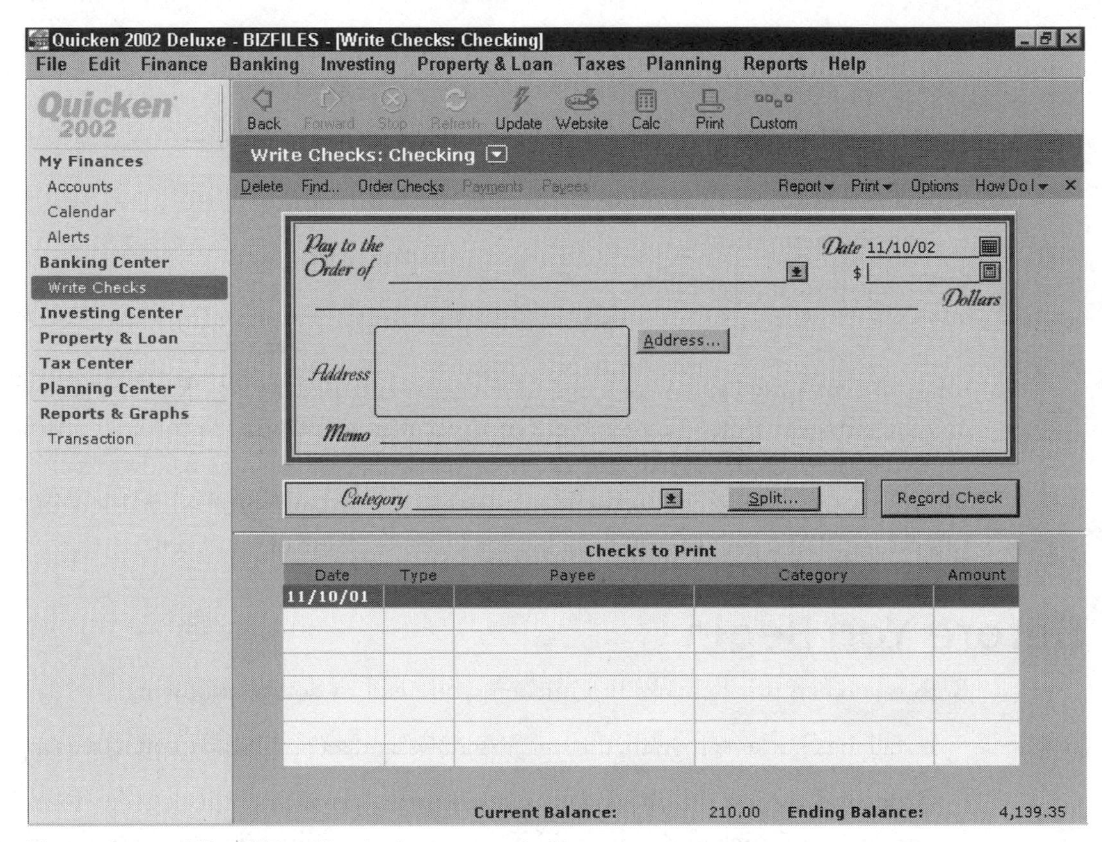

Figure 3.1: The Write Checks document window.

TIP *If you look closely at the Write Checks window shown in Figure 3.1, you'll notice that Quicken reports two account balances at the bottom of the window: Current Balance and Ending Balance. The Current Balance shows the account balance using only transactions through the current date. The Ending Balance shows the account balance using all transactions—including, for example, postdated checks and deposits.*

Describing a Check You Want Quicken to Print

Once you've identified the account and displayed the Write Checks window, you're ready to start writing checks. This process largely mirrors the process you use for recording a handwritten check into the Quicken register.

To describe a check you want Quicken to print, follow these steps:

1. If the date shown in the Date field (which automatically shows the current date) isn't the date that you want to print on the check, highlight the date and enter the correct date in MM/DD/YY format. You don't need to enter the year number unless the one Quicken already shows is not correct.

NOTE *Quicken provides shortcuts you can use to set the date. They are described in Chapter 2.*

2. Enter the name of the payee in the Pay To The Order Of field. If this is the first time you've recorded a payment to this payee, just type the payee's name. If you've written a check to this payee before, you can activate the Pay To The Order Of drop-down list by clicking the button at the right side of the field. Then you can select the payee name from thc list of payees.

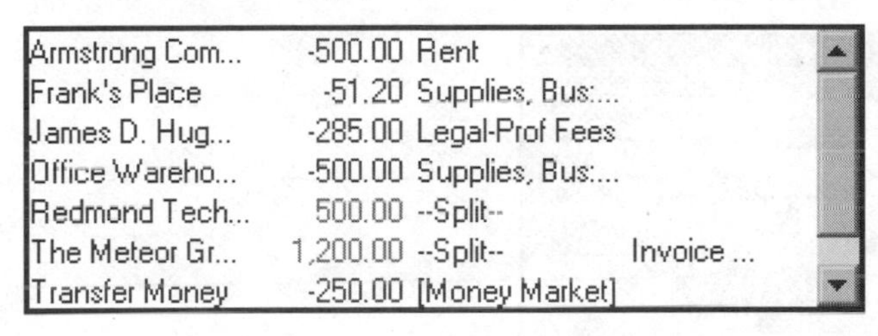

3. Enter the payment amount in the Payment field beneath the date. You don't need to cnter a dollar sign or comma (to separate thousands), but you must include a period to identify cents. After you enter the payment amount, press the Tab key. Quicken writes out the payment amount in words on the line below the Pay To The Order Of field.
4. If you'll use an envelope with a window (the address you enter will show through the envelope window), type the payee name and the address in the Address block.
5. If you want to add a memo description, move to the Memo line and enter a brief description. You can enter anything you want into this field. (Note that there's no reason to duplicate information you've entered or will enter some place else.) If a check pays a particular invoice or involves a specific account, consider using the Memo field to record this bit of information.
6. Categorize the transaction by using the Category drop-down list:

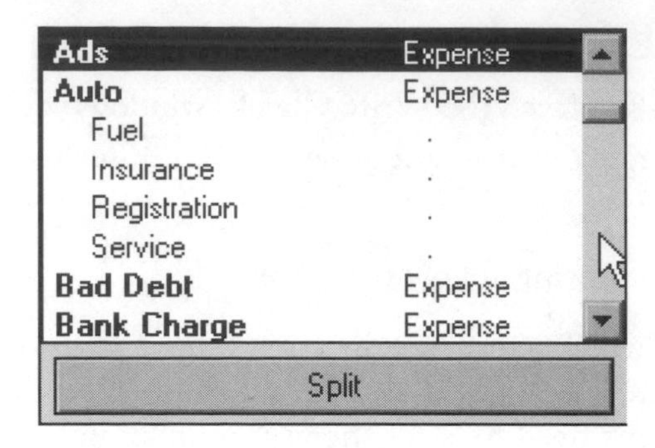

If you can't find an expense category that describes the payment, you can enter a category description directly into the Category field and press Tab. In the New Category dialog box that appears, click Yes to confirm and open the Set Up Category dialog box, as shown in Figure 3.2. You can enter a description of the category in the Description text box. Verify that the Expense option button is marked so Quicken knows this is a category used to track spending. Finally, mark the Tax-Related checkbox if this expense category is tax deductible. (See Chapters 2 and 14 for more information about setting up and using categories.) Click OK when done.

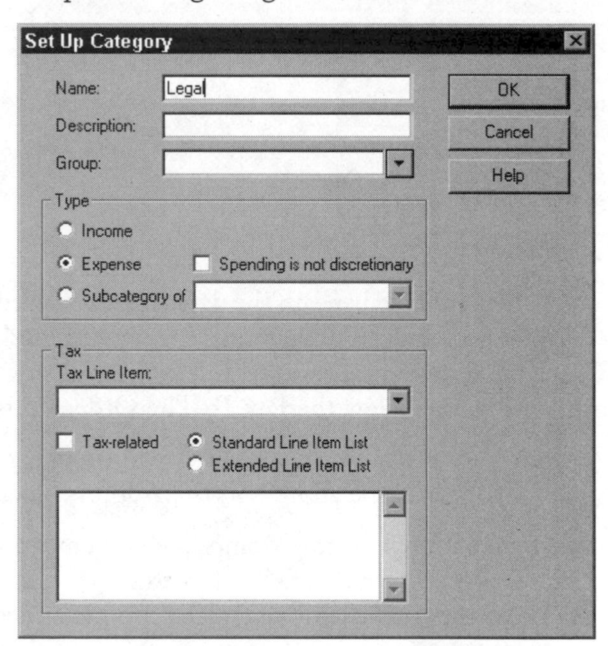

Figure 3.2: The Set Up Category dialog box.

7. Click Record Check to record the check.

Quicken updates the bank account balance, scrolls the completed check form off the window, and then displays another, blank Write Checks window. Quicken also tells you the total value of the checks you have to print on the To Print line at the bottom of the window. And if you've set your display properties of your monitor to a resolution higher than 640 × 480, Quicken even displays a Checks To Print box that lists the important information about each check. Figure 3.3 shows a $285 check written to James D. Hughes, Attorney, to pay a legal bill. The check is categorized as Legal. (A little later in the chapter, you'll see what this check looks like when it's printed.)

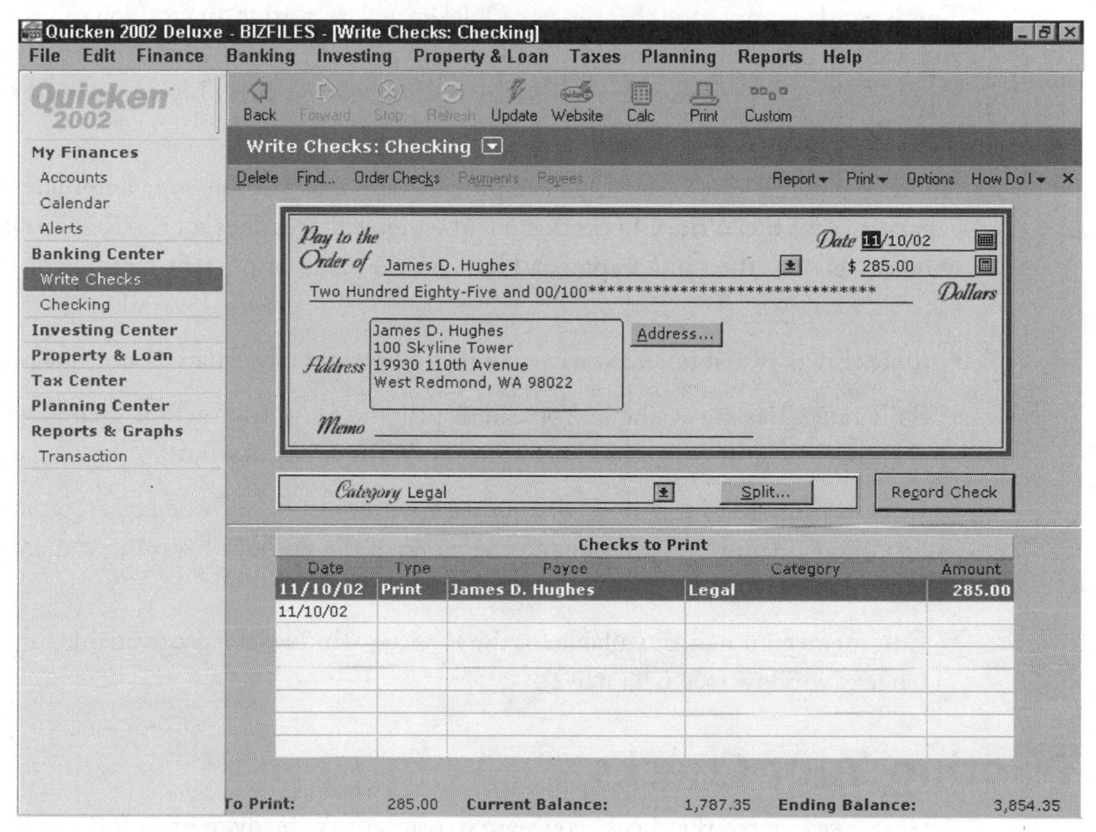

Figure 3.3: A completed check.

TIP *Changing your monitor resolution to 800 × 600 or better allows you to fit more elements on your screen at once. To change your monitor's display properties, minimize all open application windows and right-click on your Desktop. Then choose the shortcut menu's Properties command. Click the Settings tab and move the Desktop Area slider to the right so that it reads 800 x 600 pixels. (If it won't slide past 640 × 480, your monitor cannot work at a higher resolution.) Then click OK twice. Windows resizes your Desktop. Click Yes to keep the new resolution setting.*

Some Notes about Check Writing

When you click the Record Check command button or press Enter to signal to Quicken that you're finished describing a check, Quicken actually records the check into your register. So don't be concerned if you later flip to the Register window and see the check there.

If you do flip to the register, you'll notice that the Num text box for the check shows Print. This is what identifies the check as one Quicken will later print. In fact, you can enter checks you want to print directly into the register by typing ***Print*** in the Num text box. You can't, however, record a payee address into the register, so you probably won't want to use the "directly into the register" approach.

Another thing to note is that Quicken provides almost all of the same helpful features and capabilities for the Write Checks document window that it does for the Register document window, as described in Chapter 2. Here are the most important features of the Write Checks window:

- QuickFill is available, and you can use it to help enter payee names and category names.
- Split categories are available. You can display the Split Transaction Window simply by clicking the Split command button in the Write Checks window.
- Checks you write for deposit to another account can be recorded as account transfers. Just choose Transfer To/From and the name of the account from the Category combo box.
- Edit menu commands available for the Register window are also available for the Write Checks window (see Chapter 2).

Printing Your Checks

After you've entered the checks you want to print, you're ready to print some or all of them. Printing checks on an impact printer works in roughly the same way as printing checks on a laser or ink-jet printer. The only difference is that some of the dialog boxes look slightly different. The following steps are for a laser or ink-jet printer:

1. Load the preprinted check forms into your printer. If you use a laser or ink-jet printer, for example, remove the paper tray and place the appropriate number of check form sheets there. If you use an impact printer with tractor feed, unload the paper you currently have loaded and replace this paper with your check forms.
2. Choose File ➤ Print Checks to display the Select Checks To Print dialog box, as shown in Figure 3.4.

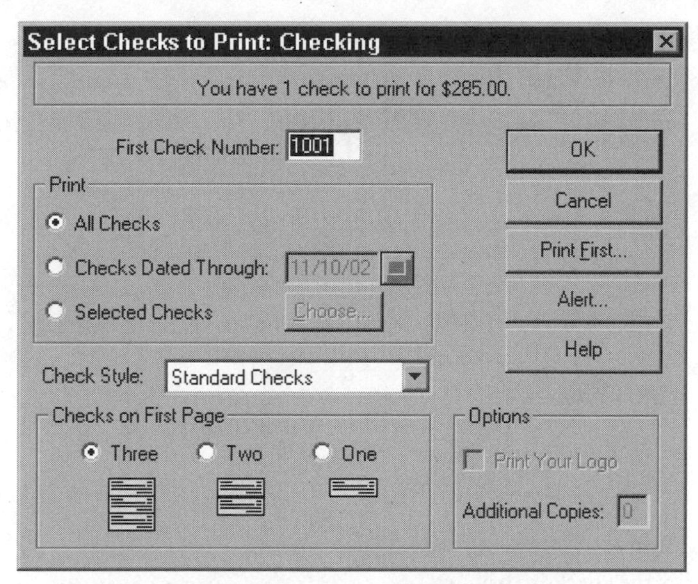

Figure 3.4: The Select Checks To Print dialog box.

3. Move the cursor to the First Check Number text box and enter the number preprinted on the first check form you'll print. This is important! You want to make sure that the way Quicken numbers your checks is the same way that the bank numbers them on your bank statement.

4. Use the option buttons in the Print section to indicate which checks you want to print, as follows:

   - **All Checks** If you want to print all the checks you entered, mark this button.

   - **Checks Dated Through** If you want to print checks only through a specified date, mark this button. Specify this date using the text box that appears to the right of the option button.

   - **Selected Checks** If you want to print some but not all of the checks you entered, mark this button. Then click the Choose command button. Quicken displays the Select Checks To Print dialog box, shown in Figure 3.5, which lists all the checks Quicken can print. Initially, all the checks are marked with a checkmark, meaning Quicken thinks it should print them. To indicate you don't want to print a check, click the check to remove the checkmark. When you've unmarked each of the checks you don't want to print, select Done to return to the dialog box shown in Figure 3.4.

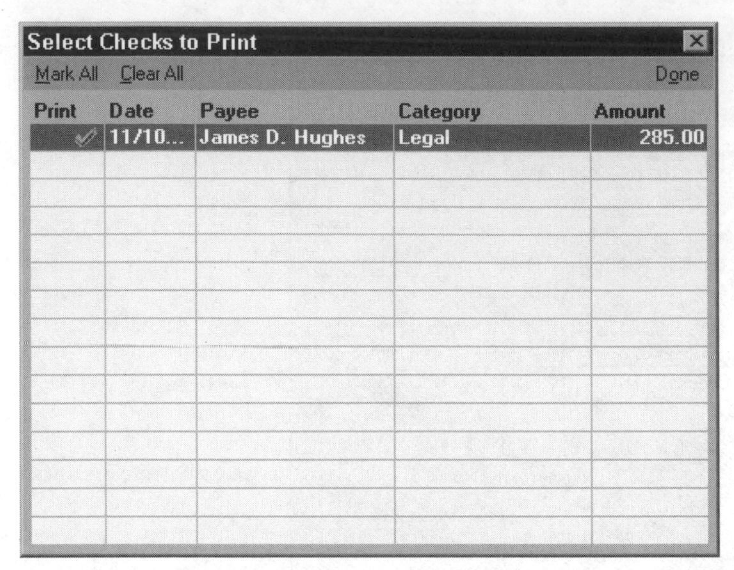

Figure 3.5: Quicken lists the checks to print.

NOTE *If you make a mistake and want to start over, click the Mark All command button to mark the status of all the checks as Print.*

5. To tell Quicken which check form style you'll use, activate the Check Style drop-down list box and choose the check style—the one you ordered and will print on—from the list. If you ordered regular laser printer checks, for example, choose the Standard Checks option.

TIP *For businesses, voucher checks often work best. The voucher, or remittance advice, provides space for you to explain why you're paying some business or individual.*

6. Click the appropriate Checks On First Page button to indicate how many check forms appear on the first page of the laser check forms you loaded into your printer. If there's only one check form per page, only the One button will be enabled. It will be the default—and only possible—choice. If you're using tractor forms on your printer or voucher checks which always put only one check form per page, the Checks On First Page buttons in the Print Checks dialog box will be grayed out (unavailable).
7. If you want a copy of the check forms you print, enter the number of copies you want in the Additional Copies text box.
8. Click OK. Quicken prints the checks and displays a message asking if the checks printed correctly, as shown in Figure 3.6.

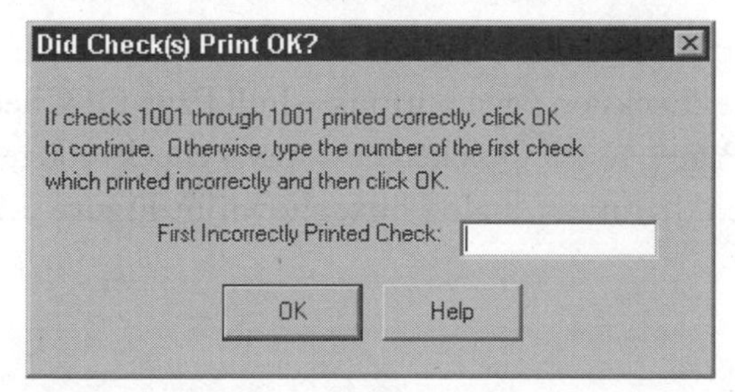

Figure 3.6: The Did Check(s) Print OK? message box.

9. If the checks printed correctly, click OK. If they didn't (for instance, if the forms were misaligned or jammed in your printer), enter the check number of the first check that printed incorrectly in the text box provided in the First Incorrectly Printed Check text box, and click OK. Quicken redisplays the Print Checks dialog box. Then repeat steps 2 through 8 to reprint the checks correctly. (See the next section for information about correcting check-printing problems.)

Check-Printing Problems

One occasional problem you can have with check printing is misaligned forms. It may be that the printed information appears a character or two too far to the left, too high, or too low.

To correct check alignment problems, choose the File ➤ Printer Setup ➤ For Printing Checks command. When Quicken displays the Check Printer Setup dialog box, shown in Figure 3.7, verify that it correctly describes your checks as either Page-Oriented (the case for laser and inkjet printers) or Continous (the case for most impact printers), that it shows the correct check style, and that it identifies how you feed partial pages of checks through the printer.

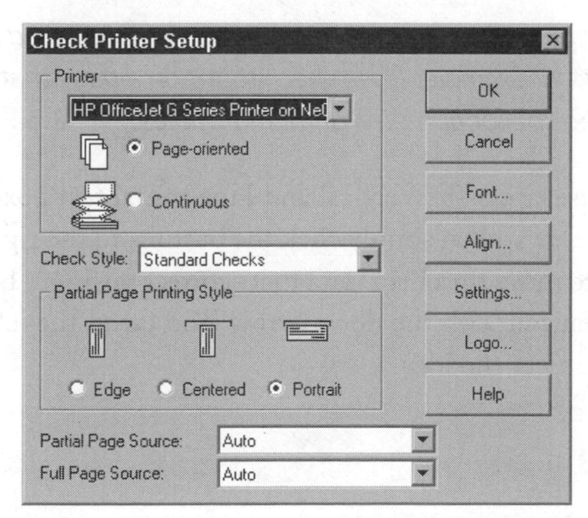

Figure 3.7: The Check Printer Setup dialog box.

Next, select the Align command button. Quicken displays the Align Checks dialog box, shown in Figure 3.8. Select one of the checks on page buttons—Full Page Of Checks, Two Checks On Page, or One Check On Page—to tell Quicken how many checks you're printing per page. Quicken displays the Fine Alignment dialog box, shown in Figure 3.9.

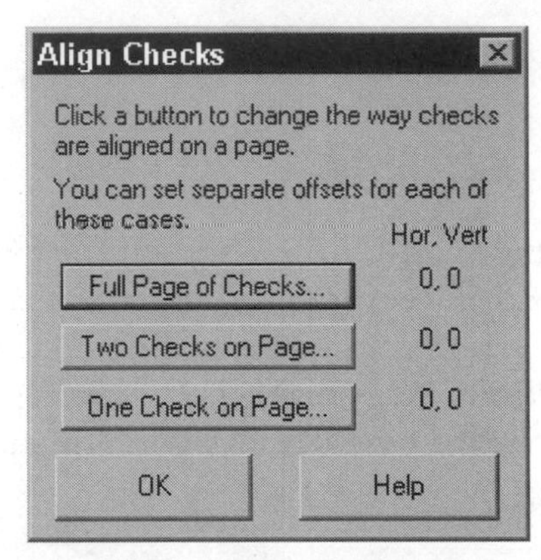

Figure 3.8: The Align Checks dialog box.

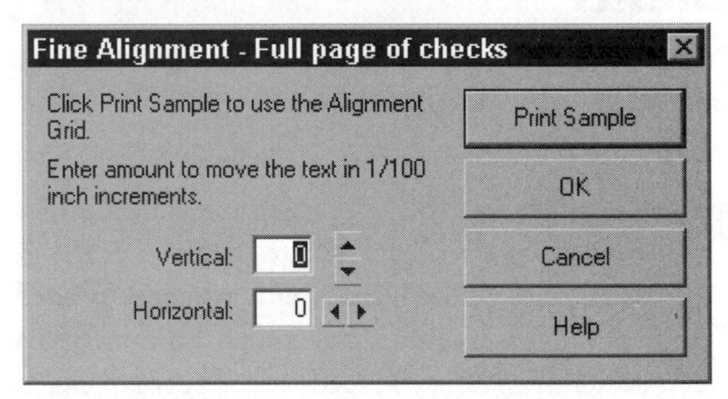

Figure 3.9: The Fine Alignment dialog box.

NOTE *The number of checks on the page is the first, and most basic, thing you need to check. If Quicken thinks it can print, for example, three check forms on a page that has only two check forms, it's a sure recipe for printer-alignment troubles.*

To correct the alignment, you can use either the Vertical and Horizontal text boxes or the mouse. Using the mouse is the easiest way. You simply click the buttons to the right of the Vertical and Horizontal text boxes to move the check data to its correct position. Is the text printing a bit too high? Click the button with the down arrow. Too far to the left? Click the button with the right arrow. You get the idea.

A more precise (but more cumbersome) way to change the alignment is to enter the correct horizontal and vertical alignment values for your printer in the Horizontal and Vertical text boxes. Enter values in hundredths of an inch. Positive values move the text right or up. Negative values (preceding the number with a minus sign) move the text down or to the left.

You can check the alignment by clicking the Print Sample button in the Fine Alignment dialog box. Quicken prints a sample check that fills up each of the fields on a check form. You can use this check to make sure that Quicken is printing the information that it's supposed to print in the right places. When the check's alignment is satisfactory, click OK to save the setup.

NOTE *If you're really having troubles and don't mind using up a few check forms, you can try printing another sample check form. A cheaper way is to print samples on plain paper and then hold them over the real checks to verify the alignment.*

Chapter 4

TRACKING YOUR FINANCES WITH REPORTS

In This Chapter

- Quicken's simple reports
- Quicken's advanced reports
- Report-printing basics
- Zooming in on a report
- Changing the way your reports are printed
- Creating customized reports
- Memorizing your customized reports
- Rules for retaining records

The information you collect using the Quicken Register and Write Checks windows creates a database that describes your personal or business financial affairs. Although you don't ever need to "do anything" with this financial database, Quicken's powerful reporting and charting features let you review, summarize, and organize it in ways that almost surely will provide valuable and interesting insights into your business.

This chapter shows you how to produce and use Quicken reports and how to customize these reports so that they more closely fit your needs. There's only one prerequisite to using Quicken's reporting and charting features: entering transactions into its registers. If you've done this, you're ready to begin producing reports and charts.

NOTE *Chapter 8 explains how you produce charts that can often show you things that reports never will.*

Quicken's Simple Reports

Quicken provides two simple-to-use reports that new users will want to make immediate use of: QuickReports and EasyAnswer Reports. Let's look at these reports first.

QuickReports for Summarizing Register Information

QuickReports summarize information in a register. The easiest way to illustrate how they work is with an example. Suppose that you're reviewing the checks you've received from various customers. You see a large deposit from The Meteor Group, then another, and then you wonder how much money you've received from The Meteor Group over the year.

To answer this question with a QuickReport, select a transaction where the payee is The Meteor Group, and then select the Report button at the top-right of the Register document window. Quicken displays a menu with commands corresponding to the various QuickReport options available for the selected transaction. (In this case, one option will be Payments Received from The Meteor Group.) When you select one of the QuickReport options, Quicken produces the report and displays it in a separate document window on your screen, as shown in Figure 4.1.

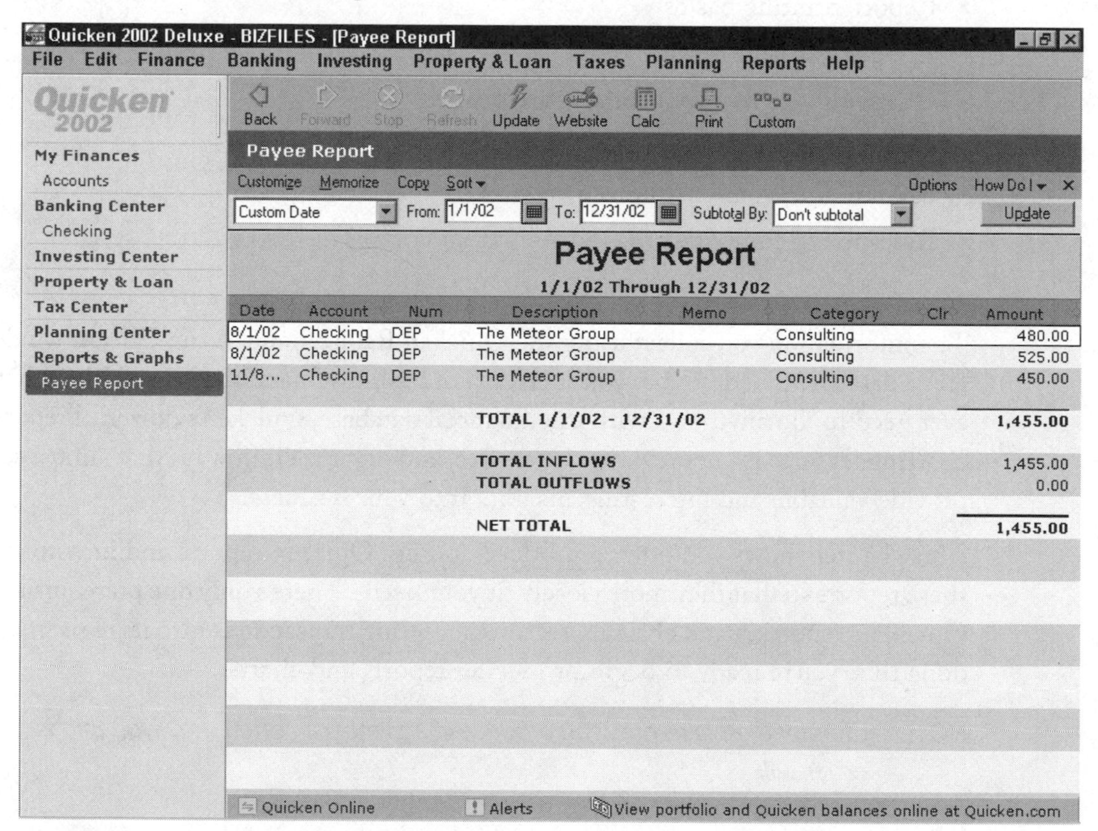

Figure 4.1: QuickReports make it easy to summarize account information.

You can create QuickReports that summarize your information by payee or by category and that plot expense category information in a chart. If you want to print a QuickReport report (but not a chart), select the Print toolbar button at the top of the Quicken application window (see the "Report-Printing Basics" section later in this chapter for details on printing reports). To remove the QuickReport window from your screen, select its Close button. Or, right-click the window in the QuickTabs list and choose the Close command associated with the specific report.

EasyAnswer Reports for Answering Financial Questions

EasyAnswer Reports work by letting you ask a question. Quicken then selects the report that best answers your question.

To use the EasyAnswer Reports, choose the Reports ➤ EasyAnswer Reports And Graphs command. Quicken displays the Reports And Graphs window, as shown in Figure 4.2, with the EasyAnswer Reports And Graphs tab displayed.

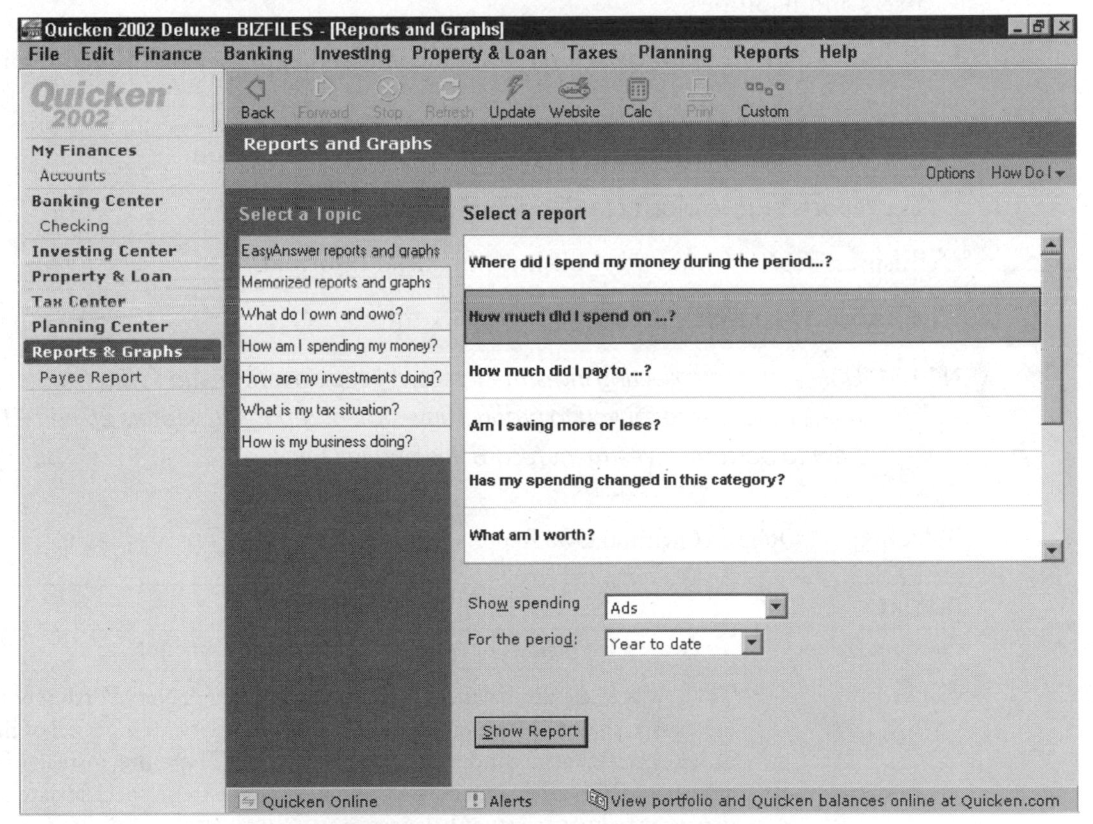

Figure 4.2: The EasyAnswer Reports And Graphs tab of the Reports And Graphs window.

To produce an EasyAnswer Report, click the question you want to ask, and then click the Show Report button. Quicken displays a report that answers the question.

You can change the nature of the question in the report by activating the drop-down list boxes that provide keywords or phrases to further define the question text and then selecting a new keyword or phrase. For example, if you want to ask the first question, "Where did I spend my money?" you can specify the last part of the question in the report as "Last Year," "Last Month," and so on.

Quicken's Advanced Reports

In addition to the simple reports such as QuickReports and EasyAnswer Reports, Quicken also produces dozens of more advanced reports that are preformatted to save you time. On the Reports menu, these advanced reports are grouped into five sets:

- Own and Owe reports summarize account balances, personal net worth, and business assets and liabilities.
- Spending reports summarize cash flow, income and expense, and budgeting information.
- Investing reports summarize investment account information.
- Tax reports summarize tax-related information.
- Business reports summarize business financial information.

These reports are summarized in Tables 4.1 through 4.5.

NOTE *Until you start collecting investment record-keeping information with Quicken, it won't make much sense for you to produce investment reports. Chapters 20 and 21 describe how to perform investment record keeping in Quicken.*

Table 4.1: Quicken Own and Owe Reports

REPORT	WHEN TO USE IT
Account Balances	To create a list of all your assets and liabilities by account.
Net Worth	To show the account balances in all your accounts. A Net Worth report is unusual in that it doesn't summarize financial activity for a period of time, but rather your financial condition at a point in time. Therefore, instead of entering a range of dates when you create the report, you enter a specific date on which you want to know account balances.

Table 4.2: Quicken Spending Reports

REPORT	WHEN TO USE IT
Banking Summary	To summarize transactions by category or some other method that you specify.
Budget	To compare your annual actual income and spending against your budget.
Cash Flow	To summarize the money that flows into and out of bank accounts. If you've set up cash or credit card accounts, the money that flows into and out of these accounts is summarized by category too.
Cash Flow Comparison	To compare transaction totals for two time periods. For example, you can use a Comparison report to compare your spending by category last month with your spending by category this month.
Income/Expense	To summarize all the transactions in all your accounts by income and expense category. The difference between an Itemized Categories report and an Income/Expense report is that Income/Expense reports don't include transactions between accounts.
Income/Expense Comparison	To compare income and expense totals for two time periods. For example, you can use a Comparison report to compare your spending by category last month with your spending by category this month.
Itemized Categories	To summarize all the transactions in all your accounts by income and expense category. The difference between an Itemized Categories report and an Income/Expense report is that the Itemized Categories report includes transfers between accounts.
Missing Checks	To identify checks that have not been cleared. This includes missing and duplicate check numbers.
Monthly Budget	To compare your actual income and spending by category with the budget you've assigned for each income and expense category. This report summarizes income and expense categories for bank, cash, and credit card accounts.
Spending	To summarize spending by expense category. Highlights the top 10 expenses.
Transaction	To create a list of individual transactions and their total according to various classes such as time period, account, or payee.

Table 4.3: Quicken Investment Reports

REPORT	WHEN TO USE IT
Capital Gains	To calculate your long- and short-term realized capital gains and losses.
Investment Asset Allocation	To summarize your investments by asset classes such as stocks, bonds, and so on.
Investment Income	To summarize financial transactions by income such as interest, dividends, capital gains distribution for one or more investment accounts.
Investment Performance	To calculate the average annual total return on the individual securities you own during a specified period.
Investment Transactions	To calculate the effect of investment transactions on the market value or cost basis of an invesment.
Portfolio Value	To summarize the market value of each of the securities you hold in your investment portfolio as of a specified date—individual stocks, bonds, shares of mutual funds, and so on. This information includes the cost basis, market value, and unrealized capital gain or loss of each security.
Portfolio Value and Cost Basis	To summarize the current market value and the cost basis of each of the securities you hold in your investment portfolio.

Table 4.4: Quicken Tax Reports

REPORT	WHEN TO USE IT
Capital Gains	To calculate long- and short-term gains (or losses) on securities that you have sold during a specified period.
Tax Schedule	To summarize your tax-related categories by input line on your personal or business federal income tax return. You don't need to be concerned with which tax return line a category is reported on, unless you're exporting data directly to a tax-preparation package.
Tax Summary	To summarize your taxable income and tax deductions. The difference be tween an Itemized Categories report and a Tax Summary report is that the Tax Summary report includes only those categories you (or Quicken) marked as tax-related.

Table 4.5: Quicken Business Reports

REPORT	WHEN TO USE IT
Accounts Payable	To see the unpaid bills, categorized by person or company. (A/P stands for accounts payable.)
Accounts Receivable	To see the unpaid incoming bills, categorized by person or company. (A/R stands for accounts receivable.)
Balance Sheet	To show the account balances in all your accounts. Like the nearly identical Net Worth report, a Balance Sheet report doesn't summarize financial activity for a period of time, but rather your financial condition at a point in time. You don't enter a range of dates when you create the report, but rather a specific date on which you want to know account balances.
Cash Flow	To summarize the money that flows into and out of bank accounts. If you've set up cash or credit card accounts, the money that flows into and out of these accounts is summarized by category too.
Cash Flow Comparison	To compare transaction totals for two time periods. For example, you can use a Comparison report to compare your spending by category last month with your spending by category this month.
Missing Checks	To identify checks that have not been cleared. Transactions are presented in date order, with uncleared checks highlighted in red on your screen.
Payroll	To summarize payroll transactions by employee. Payroll transactions are those transactions that use special payroll categories.
Profit and Loss Comparison	To compare profit and loss totals for two time periods. For example, you can use a Profit and Loss Comparison report to compare your profits last month with your profits this month.
Profit and Loss Statement	To summarize profit and loss category totals.
Project/Job	To summarize your transactions for a specific project from all your accounts by income and expense categories, and by classes.

Report-Printing Basics

To print any report, follow these steps:

1. Click the Reports And Graphs QuickTab. Quicken displays the Reports And Graphs window, as shown in Figure 4.3. Choose a report group by clicking a tab on the left side of the window.

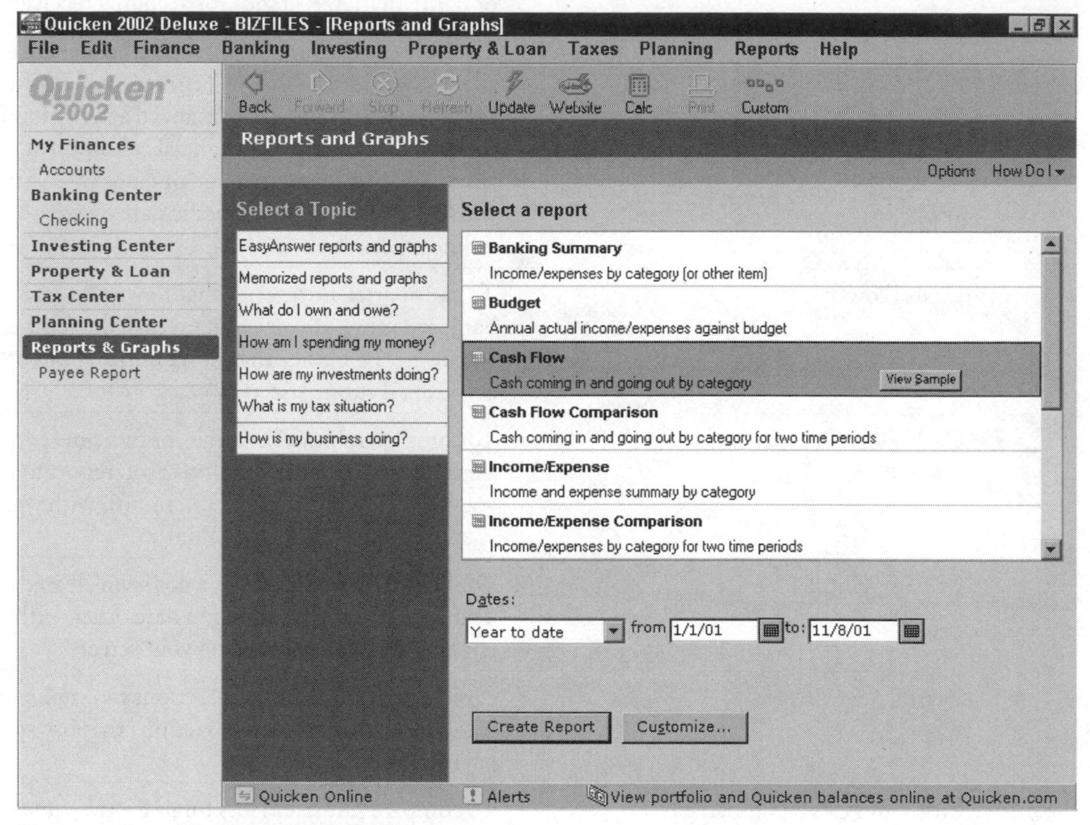

Figure 4.3: The Reports And Graphs window.

2. Select the specific report you want to produce. For example, if you want to print a Cash Flow report, click the How Am I Spending My Money tab? and select Cash Flow report.

3. Quicken assumes that the reports you produce should describe financial activity from the start of the year through the current date. If you want to describe some other period of financial activity, select a different time frame from the Dates drop-down list box or enter custom dates in the From and To boxes. Clicking the calendar icon next to the From and To combo boxes opens small calendars you can use to change to any month and select any date.

4. Click Create Report to produce the report.

Quicken opens a Report window for the report you request. Figure 4.4 shows a business Cash Flow report in a new document window. This is the same report Quicken produces if you choose Reports ➢ Business ➢ Cash Flow.

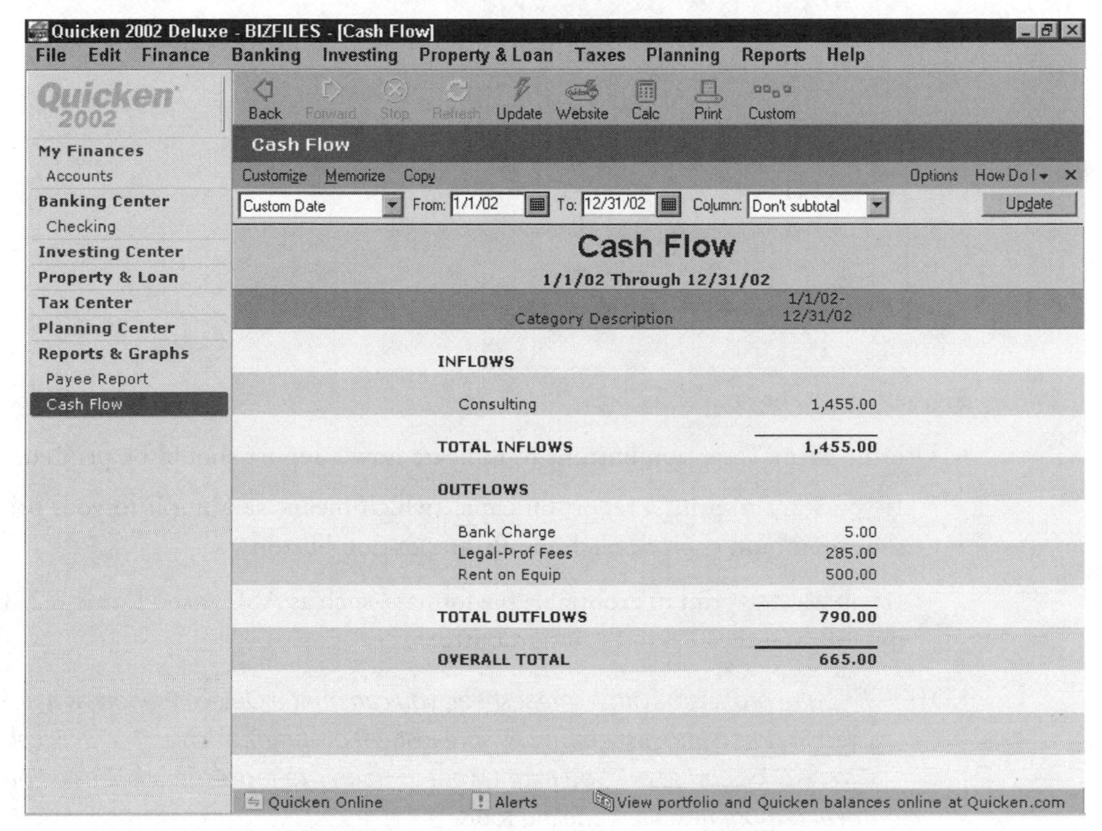

Figure 4.4: A Cash Flow report summarizing data entered in Quicken's registers.

NOTE *To remove a report's QuickTab from the Quicken application window, click the Close button at the top-right corner of the Report document window.*

5. To print a paper copy of the report displayed in the active document window, click the Print toolbar button in the row of command buttons at the top of the Quicken application window. The Print dialog box appears, as shown in Figure 4.5.

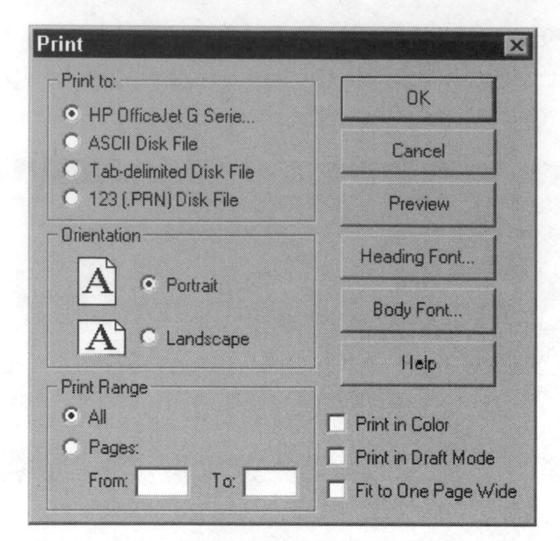

Figure 4.5: The Print dialog box.

6. Use the Print To option buttons to indicate how a report should be printed:
   - If you want to print a report on paper (which means sending it to your printer, the most common choice), click the Printer option button.
   - If you want to print to exportable file formats, such as ASCII and Lotus 1-2-3, choose one of the other Print To option buttons.

NOTE *If you're proficient with a spreadsheet, you can print a Quicken report as a disk file and then import it into just about any spreadsheet program, such as 1-2-3, Excel, Quattro Pro, Works, and so on. You might want to do this to tap a spreadsheet's more powerful and more flexible modeling tools.*

7. Use the Orientation option buttons to specify how Quicken should print the report on the page: Portrait or Landscape.
8. If you want to print only a page or range of pages of the report, mark the Pages option button in the Print Range area. Then use the From and To text boxes to specify the page range.
9. If you are using a color printer, mark the Print In Color checkbox to see your financial red ink in printed red ink or to see other color effects similar to those you see on your screen.
10. If you want to accelerate printing speed when print quality isn't important, mark the Print In Draft Mode checkbox.
11. If you want Quicken to fit the report's information across the width of a single page, mark the Fit To One Page Wide checkbox.

NOTE *To preview what you are about to print, click the Preview button, which displays a screen preview of your paper report.*

12. Select OK when the Print dialog box is complete.

    If you're printing to a printer, Quicken sends the report to Windows, which manages the actual work of printing the report. If you indicate that you want to print a disk file, Quicken displays the Create Disk File dialog box, as shown in Figure 4.6.

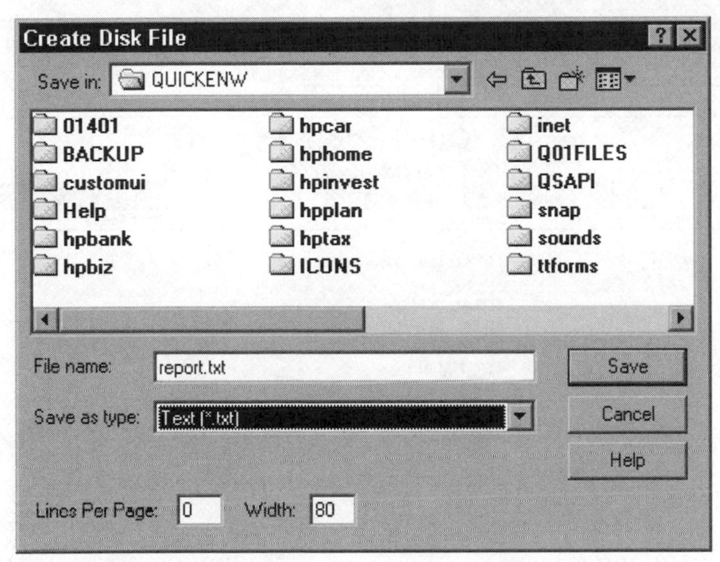

Figure 4.6: The Create Disk File dialog box.

13. If you're printing to disk, use the Create Disk File dialog box to indicate the path and filename for the disk file. For example, to create a file named report.txt in the Quicken directory on your C hard drive, locate the QUICKENW folder from the Directories list box and then enter the name ***report.txt*** in the File Name text box.

Zooming In on a Report

Quicken provides QuickZoom, a handy feature that you can use in any Report window. Here's how it works: Say you have a question about a figure that appears on a report. You simply point to the figure with the mouse. (Quicken changes the mouse pointer to a magnifying glass with a Z where the magnifying glass lens should be.) Then you double-click the mouse. Quicken prepares a list of the individual transactions that, collectively, make up the figure that you've clicked and displays it in its own Report window. (If you wish to look at a transaction underlying the report, you can double-click again to be taken to that specific transaction in the register.)

With QuickZoom, you never need to wonder why some expense category is so high or what income transactions go into a sales figure; a double-click of the mouse produces a report that answers the question. Figure 4.7 shows a QuickZoom report created by double-clicking the Legal-Prof Fees total in Figure 4.4 (the Cash Flow report shown earlier in the chapter).

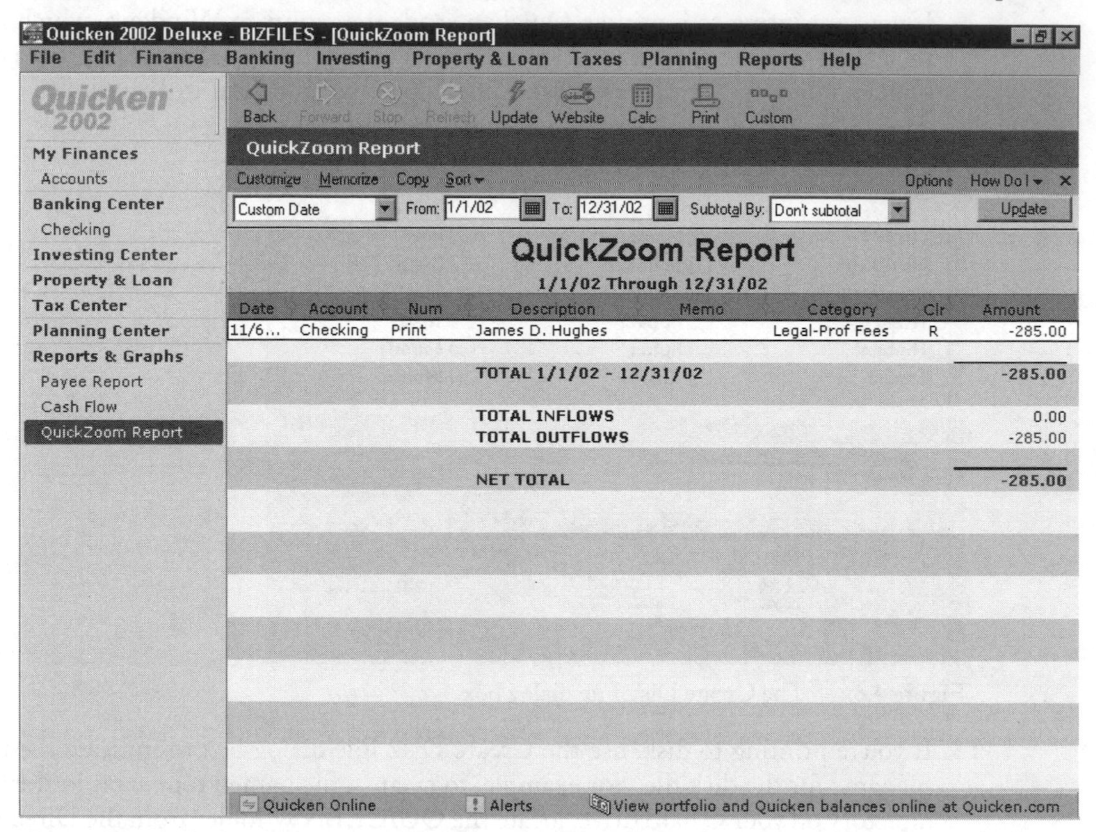

Figure 4.7: A QuickZoom report shows the individual transactions that go together to explain a summary figure on a report.

Changing the Way Your Reports Are Printed

Quicken lets you have it your way when it comes to printing your reports. You can choose the font, font style, and font size for your reports. To make this change, click the Heading Font or Body Font command buttons in the Print dialog box. Quicken displays a dialog box like the one shown in Figure 4.8 (if you click the Heading Font command button) or a similar dialog box (if you click the Body Font command button).

Use the Font text box or list box to select a font or typeface. Use the Font Style text box or list box to add boldfacing or to italicize the report header. Use the Size text box or list box to select a point size (one point equals 1/72 inch). You can see the effect of your font, font style, and point size changes in the Sample box.

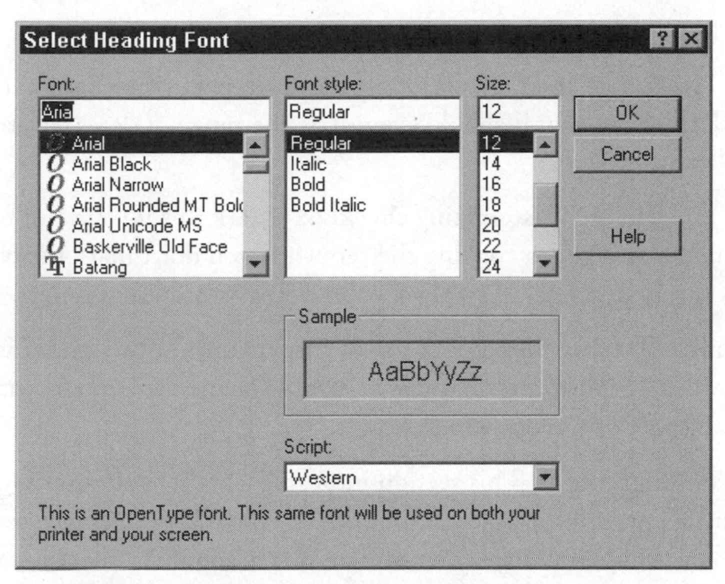

Figure 4.8: The Select Heading Font dialog box.

Describing Your Report Preferences

To customize a report, you change the report preferences settings: Choose Edit ➤ Options ➤ Reports And Graphs. When Quicken displays the Report And Graph Options dialog box, shown in Figure 4.9, make the changes you want.

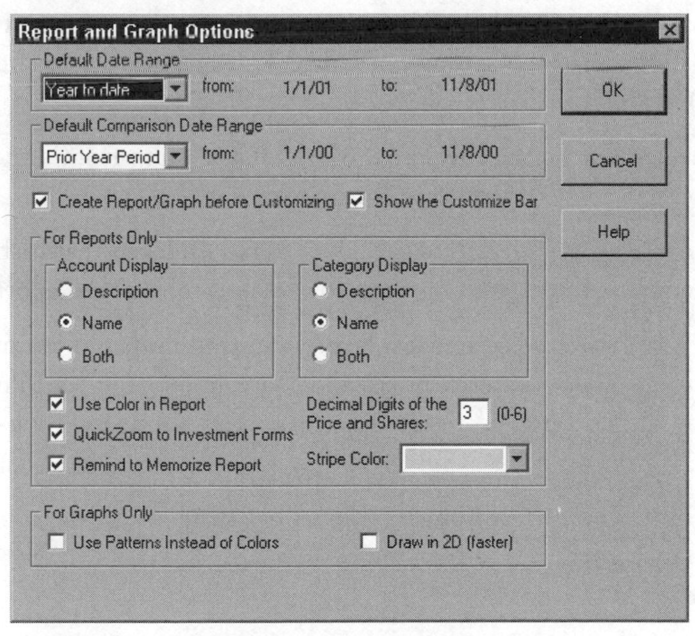

Figure 4.9: The Report And Graph Options dialog box.

The settings in the Report And Graph Options dialog box work as follows:

- **Default Report Date Range** and **Default Comparison Report Date Range text boxes** Here, you can tell Quicken what it should suggest as the range of dates covered in the report.
- **Create Report/Graph Before Customizing checkbox** Mark this if you want to use the default settings and go straight to creating the report. If you don't mark the checkbox, Quicken displays the Reports And Graphs Center when you select a report.
- **Show The Customize Bar checkbox** Mark this to display the Customize bar in Report document windows. The Customize bar allows you to change the report time frame directly from the Report document window.
- **Account Display option buttons** This section indicates whether you want Quicken to display the account name, a description, or both. Note that this preference setting has no effect when you've chosen to display more than one account. In this case, Quicken uses the description All Accounts or Selected Accounts.
- **Category Display option buttons** This section indicates whether, when Quicken summarizes by categories, it should use the shorter 32-character category name, the longer 54-character category description, or both the name and the description. Note that when a category doesn't have a description, Quicken uses the category name, regardless of what the Category Display option buttons show.
- **Use Color In Report checkbox** Mark this if you want Quicken to use color in the Report document windows. (Of course, this setting can't add color to reports printed on a black-and-white printer.)
- **QuickZoom To Investment Forms checkbox** Mark this to jump from a specific investment transaction to an investment form for that transaction.
- **Remind To Memorize Report** Mark this checkbox to tell Quicken that it should ask if you want it to memorize the custom settings you've used to create a report.
- **Decimal Digits Of The Price And Shares text box** Enter the number of decimal places you want Quicken to display for security prices and share amounts in your investment reports. Quicken can display up to six decimal places (prices to one ten thousandth of a cent).
- **Stripe Color** Use this drop-down list box to select a bar stripe color for reports when they appear in the report area.

Creating Customized Reports

The standard reports provided by Quicken almost always provide you with the information you need. But you aren't limited to viewing the information in your financial database (the transactions you've collected in the Quicken registers) using these standard reports. You can customize any of them, and you can change the contents of your report while creating it or while it is displayed on your screen.

Before you begin customizing a report, however, it's helpful if you understand that all Quicken reports derive from one of five basic report types, as shown in the following table:

Table 4.6: Quicken Report Types

REPORT TYPE	WHAT IT DOES
Transaction	Lists register transactions
Summary	Summarizes register transactions
Comparison	Shows two sets of summary numbers, such as last year's category totals and this year's category totals, as well as the difference between the two sets
Budget	Shows actual category totals, budgeted category totals, and the difference between the two
Account Balances	Shows account balance information

NOTE *Although customizing reports in Quicken isn't difficult, you may want to postpone it until you're comfortable entering transactions into registers. Most of what you do when you customize a report is simply describe how you want register information organized and summarized. The more familiar you are with the information that goes into a register, the easier it is to customize.*

Customization is similar for all types, so I'll describe the general procedures and then comment on the items that vary by report type. The action begins from a summary report as discussed in the following section.

Click the Customize button to open the customization dialog box. Figure 4.10 shows the dialog box for customizing a Summary report, which is similar to the other report customization dialog boxes. By clicking the dialog box tabs—Display, Accounts, Include, and Advanced—you reach boxes and option buttons for customizing the reports in various ways. In the following sections, I'll explain the customization options (by tab) for each major type of report.

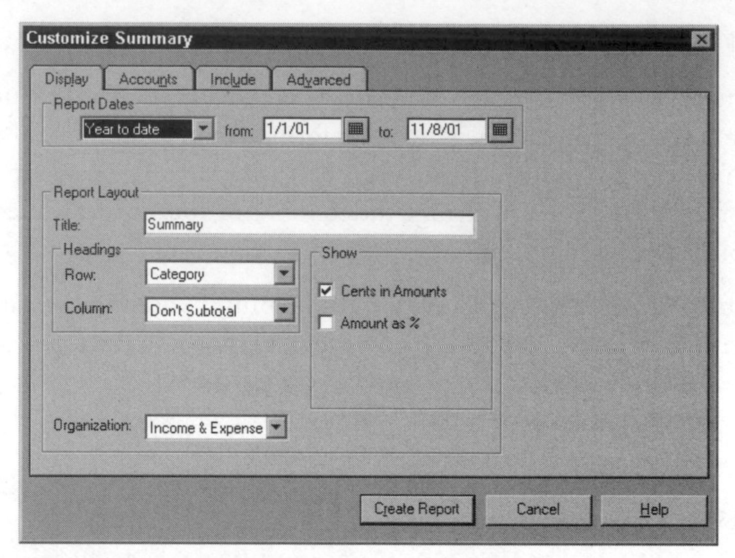

Figure 4.10: The Customize Summary dialog box.

Customizing a Summary Report

To begin customizing a Summary report, choose Reports ➢ Spending ➢ Banking Summary. Click the Customize command button to open the Customize Summary dialog box (see Figure 4.10).

Changing Summary Report Display Settings

In the Customize Summary dialog box, the Report Dates boxes let you specify the range of dates that the report covers. You can specify a date range either by typing a starting and ending date in the From and To boxes or by selecting a report duration from the Report Dates drop-down list box:

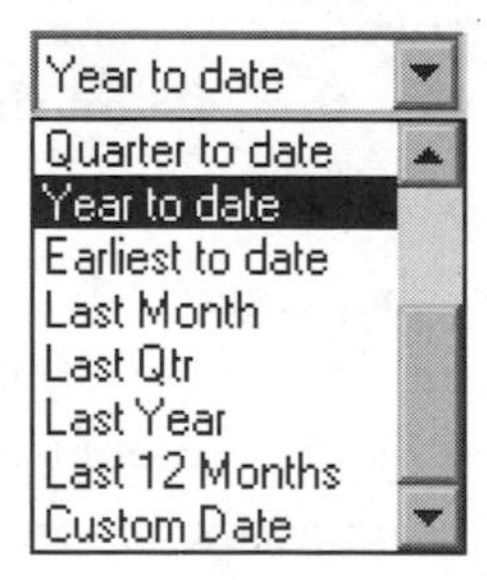

The Report Layout settings let you change the report name, select headings for rows and columns, and reorganize the summary structure of your report.

You can use the Title text box to replace the generic report title with a more specific description. Highlight the text box and enter the desired report title or description.

In the Headings area, the Row drop-down list box offers choices to create a row for each category, class, payee, or account. The Column drop-down list box provides a Don't Subtotal entry, a series of time-related subtotaling entries (a week, two weeks, half a month, and so on), and the Category, Class, Payee, and Account column subtotaling options.

The Show section contains two checkboxes. The Cents In Amounts box, if marked, displays amounts in dollars and cents. If unmarked, the amounts are shown rounded to the nearest dollar. The Amount As % checkbox, if marked, shows amounts as percentages of the total. Leaving the box unmarked shows amounts as dollars and cents.

Use the Organization drop-down list box to tell Quicken how it should arrange the report's information: by income and expense or on a cash-flow basis. Select Income & Expense if you want to organize the report into three parts: income category summaries, expense category summaries, and account transfer summaries. Select Cash Flow Basis if you want to organize the report into two parts, cash inflows and cash outflows. Select Category if you want to group and total report information by categories.

Finally, as appropriate, check or uncheck the Cents In Amounts and Amount As % boxes to tell Quicken how it should show report amounts.

Changing Summary Report Account Settings

Clicking the Accounts tab of the Customize Summary dialog box displays options for specifying which accounts' transactions should be included in the report, as shown in Figure 4.11.

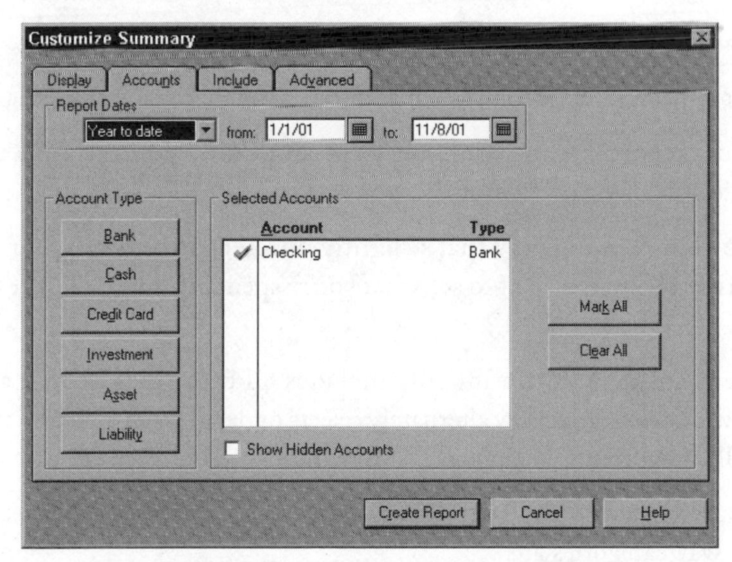

Figure 4.11: The Accounts tab of the Customize Summary dialog box.

If you want to change the account selection, click an Account Type button to include all accounts of that type. Click the Mark All button to put a checkmark next to all listed accounts, or click individual account names to deselect or reselect them until you have the selection you want.

Changing Summary Report Include Settings

The Include tab lets you filter the transactions in a register so that only those that conform to your description appear in the report. The Include tab of the Customize Summary dialog box is shown in Figure 4.12.

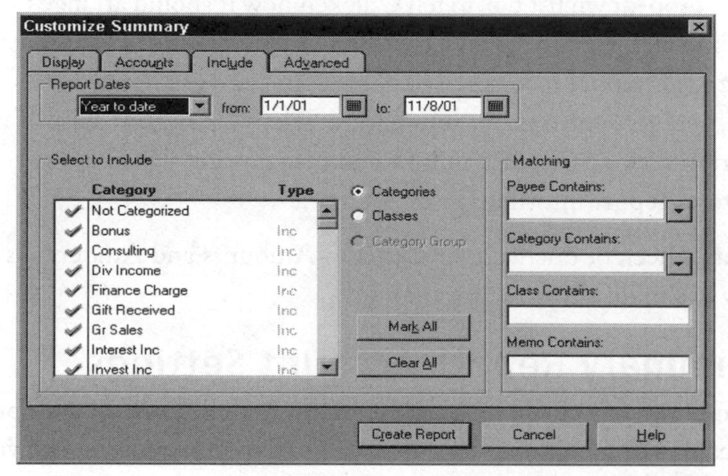

Figure 4.12: The Include tab of the Customize Summary dialog box.

Here are some situations in which you might filter transactions in this way:

- You're looking for a specific transaction (such as deposits or checks for more than $500).
- You want to build a report that includes only a subset of the information in a regular Summary report (perhaps just your travel expenses).
- You want to slice your data in a way that's slightly different from what your existing categories and classes allow (you want to see what you're spending on supplies at the local warehouse store).

The list in the Select To Include area initially includes all categories as well as a Not Categorized category. Clicking a category alternately selects or deselects it. Clicking the Mark All button selects all categories. Clicking the Clear All button deselects all categories.

Click the Classes button to display defined classes in the list. Classes are selected and deselected the same way categories are.

NOTE *If you're confused by this "class" business, don't worry—you haven't missed something. Classes are another tool you can use to summarize financial information. I'll describe how to use classes to track individual real estate investments in Chapters 17 and 21.*

You can also limit, or *filter*, the information included in a Summary report. For example, you might want to see a report that includes only checks categorized as Entertainment if you were reviewing ways to reduce your spending in that area. To limit the information in a Summary report, use the Matching boxes: Payee Contains, Category Contains, Class Contains, and Memo Contains.

To use the Matching boxes, follow these steps:

1. Enter the name of the payee whose transactions you want to show. For example, to include only those transactions with the payee name Armstrong Commons, type ***Armstrong Commons*** into the Payee Contains text box.

NOTE *To include names that start with the word* Armstrong*, type* ***Armstrong..*** *instead. To include payee names that end with the word* Armstrong*, type* ***..Armstrong****. To include payee names that use just the word* Armstrong*, type* ***=Armstrong****. To exclude payee names that show or use Armstrong, you use the tilde (~). For example, to exclude payee names that start with Armstrong, type* ***~Armstrong****. These tricks—using two periods and the tilde, which Quicken calls match characters—also work for the Class Contains, Category Contains, and Memo Contains drop-down boxes.*

2. Enter the category you want included transactions to show. For example, to include only those transactions with the category Salary, type ***Salary*** in the Category Contains text box.
3. Enter the class you want the included transactions to show. For example, to include only those transactions with the class Winston, type ***Winston*** into the Class Contains text box or select it from the drop-down list of classes.
4. Enter the memo description you want the included transactions to show. For example, to include only those transactions with the memo description Payroll, type ***Payroll*** into the Memo Contains text box.

Changing Summary Report Advanced Settings

In addition to the Display, Accounts, and Include settings, Quicken also provides an eclectic set of additional customization options. These options allow you to further filter the transactions appearing on the report by choosing transactions by amount or type. The Advanced tab of the Customize Summary dialog box is shown in Figure 4.13.

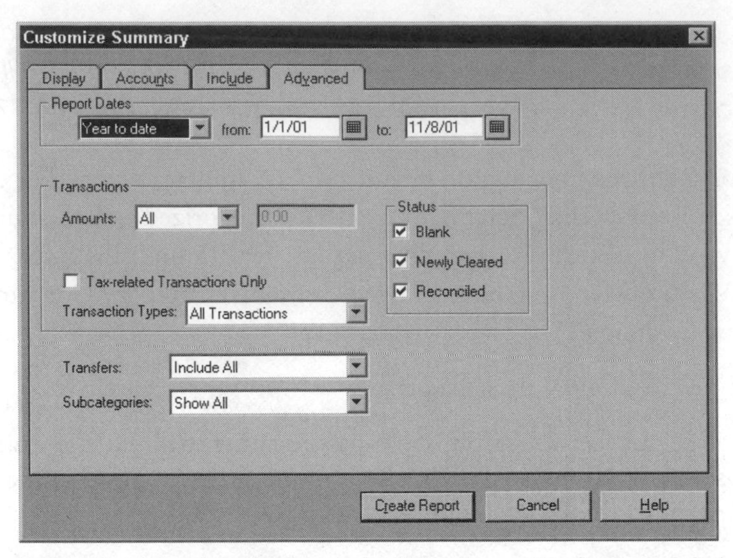

Figure 4.13: The Advanced tab of the Customize Summary dialog box.

- **Amounts drop-down list** Lets you include all transactions or only those less than, equal to, or greater than the number you enter in the adjacent text box.
- **Include Unrealized Gains checkbox** This appears only if you've set up an investment account. If marked, this option adds income rows to your report to document the impact of the increase or decrease in security prices. If you leave the box unmarked, unrealized security gains are not shown.
- **Tax-Related Transactions Only checkbox** If marked, this checkbox shows only transactions you have assigned to tax-related categories in Quicken's category lists. Leaving it unmarked shows all transactions.
- **Transaction Types drop-down list** Lets you choose to include all transactions or to show only payments, deposits, or unprinted checks in your report.
- **Status checkboxes** Allow you to prepare a Summary report that focuses on blank, newly cleared, or reconciled checks. Normally, to show all items in your reports, you leave all three boxes marked (their default state). Selectively unmarking the boxes produces specialized reports focusing on only the marked type of item.
- **Transfers drop-down list** Lets you include all or exclude all transfer transactions from the report. You can also choose Exclude Internal to hide transfers between accounts included in the report.
- **Subcategories drop-down list** Shows all subcategories when Show All is selected. You can also choose Hide All to not display subcategories or Show Reversed to group categories under subcategories, which has the effect of grouping subcategories that are normally separated under different categories.

Customizing a Transaction Report

Like the Summary report, the Transaction report has a variety of customization options.

To begin customization, choose Reports ➤ Spending ➤ Transaction. In the Create Report dialog box, click the Customize command button to open the Customize Transaction dialog box, as shown in Figure 4.14.

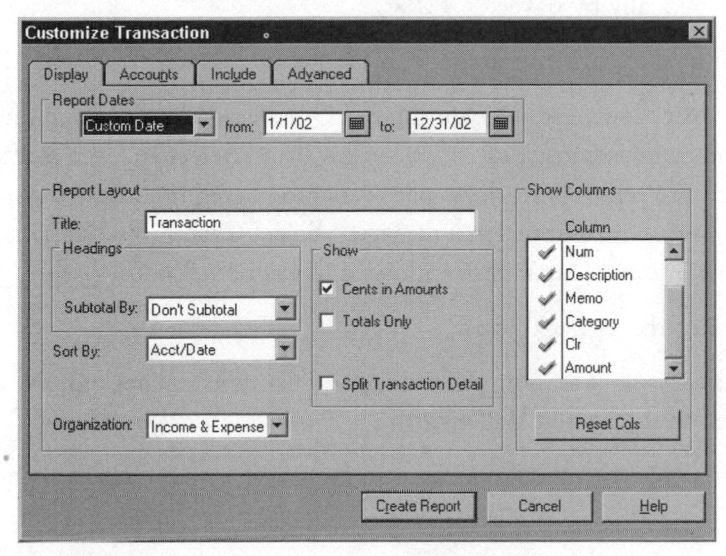

Figure 4.14: The Customize Transaction dialog box.

Changing Transaction Report Display Settings

The Customize Transaction dialog box's Display tab works in the same basic way as the Customize Summary dialog box's Display tab. You can change the report dates, report name, select headings for rows and columns, and reorganize the summary structure of your report.

Use the Report Dates boxes to specify for what period of time you want to report on transactions.

In the Title text box, replace the generic report title with a more specific description: Highlight the text box and enter the desired report title or description.

In the Headings area, the Subtotal By drop-down list provides a Don't Subtotal entry, a series of time-related subtotaling entries (a week, two weeks, half a month, and so on), and the Category, Class, Payee, Account, and Tax Schedule subtotal by heading options. A Don't Subtotal entry creates only a single column.

The Sort By drop-down list contains six options:

- **Acct/Date** Sorts by account type, account name, and date.
- **Date/Acct** Sorts by date and then by account type and account name.
- **Acct/Chk#** Orders entries by account type and then by check number.
- **Amount** Sorts from the smallest to the largest amount.
- **Payee** Sorts alphabetically by payee.
- **Category** Sorts alphabetically by category.

In the Organization drop-down list box, you can tell Quicken how to arrange the report's information: by income and expense or on a cash-flow basis. Select Income & Expense if you want to organize the report into three parts: income category summaries, expense category summaries, and account transfer summaries. Select Cash Flow Basis if you want to organize the report into two parts: cash inflows and cash outflows.

The Show area contains three checkboxes:

- **Cents In Amounts** Displays amounts in dollars and cents. If unchecked, the amounts are shown rounded to the nearest dollar.
- **Totals Only** Shows only the total amount of the transactions meeting the other report criteria.
- **Split Transaction Detail** Includes details from split transactions.

The Show Columns box lets you select which columns appear in the report. Mark the columns you want on your report. Unmark the columns you don't want. To mark and unmark columns, click them.

Changing Other Transaction Report Settings

With the exception of the layout settings noted in the previous section, the procedures and options for customizing a Transaction report are similar to the procedures described for customizing a Summary report. Refer to the Summary report sections earlier in this chapter that discuss the Accounts, Include, and Advanced customization options.

Customizing Other Reports

You can customize three other types of basic reports:

- Comparison
- Budget
- Account Balances

If you've reviewed the options described in the preceding discussion of customizing a Summary report, you will have no surprises as you approach these three. They're all somewhat simpler than either the Summary or Transaction type of report; in many cases, you have fewer options to deal with.

There are one or two wrinkles, though. The Comparison report has Difference As % and Difference In $ checkboxes in its Display tab. Marking these boxes generates columns that show the percentage and dollar differences between the categories chosen for the report.

The Account Balances report has a setting called Interval, which creates a column with totals for the time period you select from a drop-down list. Note that for business balance sheets, you should set the interval to None.

Memorizing Your Customized Reports

You can go to quite a bit of effort to create customized reports that summarize the information you've collected in the Quicken registers. Sometimes, you'll be creating a customized report for one-time use. However, other times you will be creating a customized report that you'll want to use repeatedly. In these cases, you can *memorize* the customization settings, filters, and options. This means that when you want to produce the report, you can reuse the memorized report.

Memorizing a Report

Memorizing a report is simple. After you've generated the report, click the Memorize command button, which appears in the command button row at the top of every Report document window. Quicken displays the Memorize Report dialog box, shown in Figure 4.15.

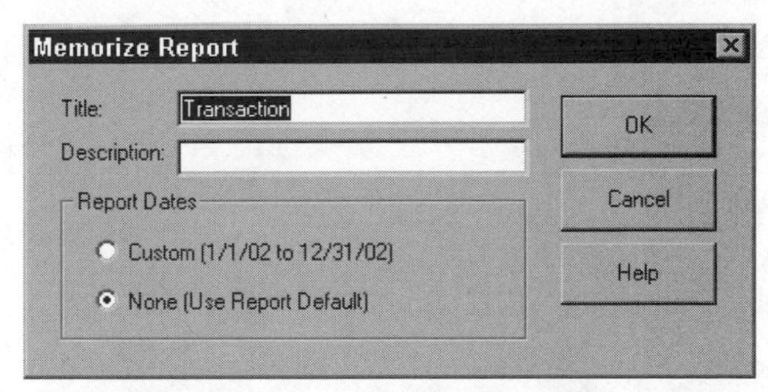

Figure 4.15: The Memorize Report dialog box.

Enter a name for the report to be memorized in the Title text box. Then use the Report Dates option buttons to indicate whether you want to use the textual description of the report date range (the Named Range option button) or the actual fixed date description (the Custom option button). Or click None to use the default report date ranges. (You can specify and change this range using the Edit ➤ Options ➤ Reports And Graphs command, as described earlier in this chapter.)

Optionally, use the Description box to provide additional information about the report, such as why you've created the memorized report or when it should be used.

The Icon option lets you assign an icon to the memorized report. This icon will appear next to the report name and description in the window from which you select the report (selecting a memorized report is discussed next).

Using a Memorized Report

Once you have Quicken memorize a report, you can produce a new copy of the memorized report any time by selecting it from the Memorized Reports menu. To display this menu, choose Reports ➤ Memorized Reports And Graphs. Alternatively, Figure 4.16 shows what the Memorized Reports And Graphs tab of the Reports And Graphs window looks like with two memorized reports named Income/Expense and Transaction.

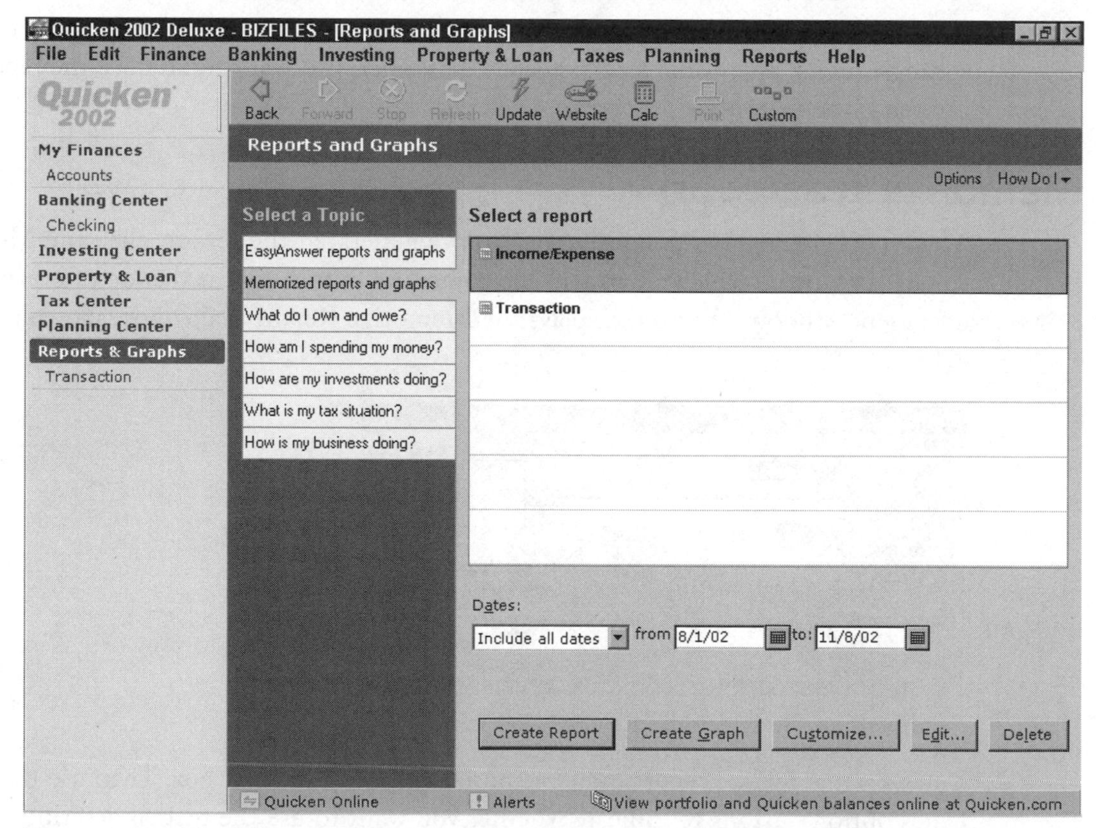

Figure 4.16: The Memorized Reports And Graphs tab of the Reports And Graphs window.

NOTE *Printing a report that appears on the Memorized Reports menu works just like printing a report that appears on the Banking, Planning, Business, Taxes, or Investments Report menu.*

Rules for Retaining Documents

You've probably wondered how long you should keep your canceled checks and how long it makes sense to hang onto old tax returns. Now that you have Quicken producing all these handy reports, see Table 4.7 for some useful guidelines for determining how long you should hold onto these things. This table summarizes the usual document-retention rules for Quicken reports and for several other business documents and forms as well. These rules are based on conservative applications of the relevant statutory and regulatory requirements, as well as statutes of limitations.

Table 4.7: Document-Retention Rules and Guidelines

DOCUMENT OR FORM	YEARS RETAINED
Asset purchase records	Seven years after asset is sold or disposed (including investment registers)
Backup files	One year
Checks, canceled	Permanently
Check registers	Permanently
Monthly home tax summaries and schedules	Three years
Yearly home tax summaries and schedules	Seven years after filing a return based on report
Other home reports (including investment reports)	One year
Monthly business P&L and tax reports	Three years
Yearly business P&L and tax reports	Seven years
Other business reports	One year

Chapter 5

BALANCING BANK ACCOUNTS

In This Chapter

- Understanding the reconciliation process
- Balancing an account in Quicken
- Troubleshooting accounts that won't balance

From time to time, you'll need to balance the bank accounts you track with Quicken. Balancing an account entails explaining the difference between what your records say you have in a bank account and what the bank says you have in that bank account. By regularly balancing bank accounts, you catch both the errors you've made and the errors the bank has made, and you can thereby ensure the accuracy of your financial record keeping.

There's no magic in this, of course. All Quicken does is automate and expedite the balancing you would (or should) normally do by hand. With Quicken, balancing a bank account takes only minutes.

Before You Begin

To balance a bank account with Quicken, you must have your most recent bank statements. In addition, you must have the following:

- A record of the bank account's activity—your payments and deposits—stored in Quicken.
- An accurate starting balance for the bank account when you originally set it up.

NOTE *If you didn't provide an accurate starting balance when you originally set up the bank account, all is not lost. You can still balance your account, as explained later in the chapter.*

Understanding the Reconciliation Process

Balancing a bank account has a simple premise: The difference between what your records show as an account balance and what the bank's records show as an account balance should equal the sum of your uncleared payments and deposits.

Let's set up a simple example to show how the reconciliation process works. Suppose your records of a bank account show the account balance as $50, and the bank's records show the account balance as $95. Furthermore, suppose your records show a $50 check that you've written but which has not yet cleared the bank, and suppose the bank's records show a $5 monthly service charge that you haven't yet recorded into the Quicken register.

Clearly, the $50 balance in your register doesn't equal the $95 balance shown on the bank account statement. But this will almost always be the case. The real question is whether the difference between the two balances can be explained. If it can, the account balances. If the difference can't be explained, the account doesn't balance.

Determining whether an account balances requires four simple steps:

1. Record any transactions shown on the bank statement that should be but aren't shown in your register. For example, if the bank statement shows a $5 monthly service charge, you'll need to record this payment in your register. In the simple example we're using, recording this transaction adjusts the balance shown in your records to $45, because $50 minus $5 equals $45.

NOTE *Your bank statement may show other transactions that your records don't: payments for bank services, credit card fees, and deposits for items like monthly interest income. Your bank statement may also show transactions that you initiated but forgot to record, such as automated teller machine (ATM) withdrawals.*

2. Add up the uncleared transactions. (Subtract the total of the uncleared deposits from the total of the uncleared checks.) In our example, there's just one uncleared transaction—the $50 check—so the sum of the uncleared transactions is $50. In a more typical case, you might have recorded numerous checks that the bank hasn't recorded, or there might be deposits that you've recorded but that the bank hasn't.
3. Determine the difference between what your records show as the account balance and what the bank's records show as the account balance. In the example, your records now show $45 as the account balance. The bank's records show $95, so there's a $50 difference between your records and the bank's.
4. Verify that the uncleared transactions total (calculated in step 2) equals the difference between your records and the bank's records (calculated in step 3). In our example, we know that $50 equals $50; so we've now explained the difference between the two accounts.

When an Account Won't Balance

Sometimes, of course, an account won't balance. Although an account that doesn't balance can be perplexing and even infuriating, the basic reasons for imbalance are usually straightforward:

- The bank's balance is wrong because its starting balance is wrong or because one or more transactions are wrong or missing.
- Your account balance is wrong for one of the same reasons.
- The uncleared transaction total is incorrect.

In my experience, it's unlikely that the bank's balance is wrong or that the bank missed or incorrectly recorded a transaction. Whatever else may be true about banks, they generally do a very good job of financial record keeping.

So when there's a problem with a bank account, it usually stems from one of two situations: either you've come up with an incorrect uncleared transaction total, or your records' account balance is wrong. To get the account to balance, you need to find the error in your records or the error in the uncleared transaction total. A little later in the chapter, I'll describe tricks for finding errors in your record keeping.

Balancing an Account in Quicken

To balance a bank account in Quicken, display the bank account in the active document window. Usually, the active document window is the Register window, as shown in Figure 5.1, but it could also be the Write Checks window.

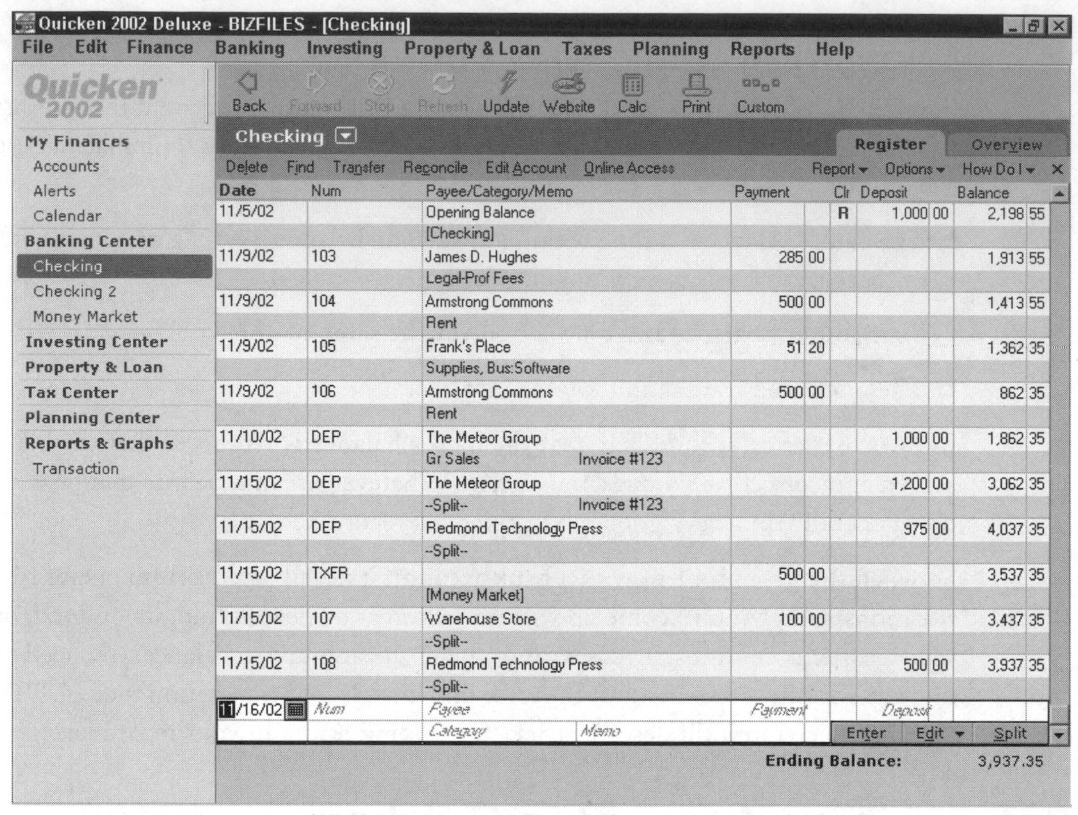

Figure 5.1: Getting ready to balance a bank account.

As discussed in the previous section, be sure that the bank statement doesn't show any payments or deposits that you need to record in the register. The only bank account transactions you don't need to record are the monthly service charge and the interest income; Quicken lets you record these as part of reconciling the account. Any other new transactions that the bank account statement shows need to be recorded.

Crime-Stopper's Textbook: Catching Forgers

When you reconcile your bank accounts, review the canceled checks to be sure that they haven't been altered and that whoever was supposed to sign the check really did sign it. Fraudulently altering or marking a document (such as a check form) to change another person's liability constitutes forgery, and reviewing canceled checks may be the only way you'll catch a forger.

As long as you immediately report forgery to the bank, you probably won't suffer any losses. This may not be true, however, if you've been careless (for example, you left a checkbook on the dashboard of your car and left your car's windows open, or you hired someone whom you knew to be a convicted check-forging felon) or if you delay reviewing the canceled checks or reporting forgery you've discovered to the bank.

Here's an example from personal experience: Long after I began telling people to review their canceled checks, a new employee of mine stole a sheet of blank checks and wrote himself extra weekly payroll checks. I caught him when I reviewed my canceled checks and realized that he had forged my signature.

Reconciling the Account

Once you've entered the missing transactions shown on the statement, follow these steps:

1. Click the Reconcile button to display the Reconcile Bank Statement dialog box, as shown in Figure 5.2 (for balancing a checking account).

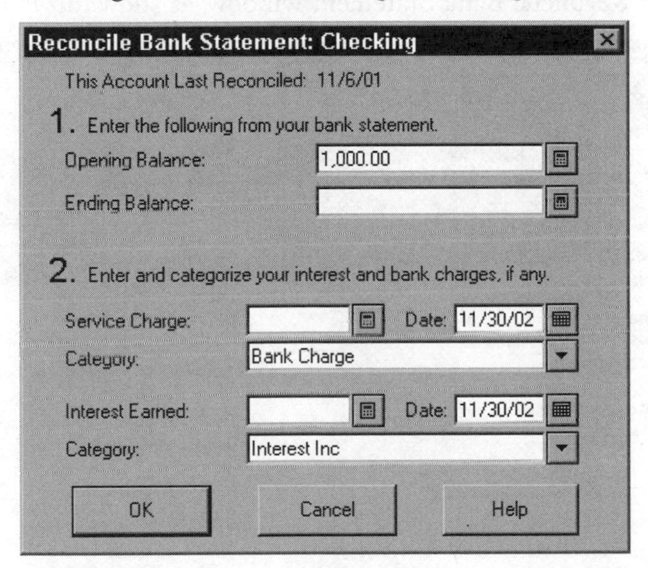

Figure 5.2: The Reconcile Bank Statement dialog box.

2. Verify that the figure shown in the Opening Balance text box is the starting bank account balance on your bank statement. If it isn't, correct it.

The first time you reconcile an account, Quicken uses your starting account balance. The subsequent times you reconcile an account, Quicken uses the Ending Balance from the previous reconciliation.

3. Enter the ending bank account balance from your bank statement in the Ending Balance text box. Simply place the cursor in the text box and type the figure.

4. In the Service Charge box, enter the monthly service charge shown on the bank statement (if you haven't already entered this directly in the register).
5. In the Service Charge Date box, tell Quicken when the service charge occurred.
6. In the Category box, Quicken categorized the service charge as Bank Charge. If you want to use a different category, click the arrow at the right of the box and select the category you want from the drop-down list.
7. In the Interest Earned box, enter the monthly interest income shown on the bank statement (if you haven't entered this directly in the register).
8. In the Interest Earned Date box, enter the date the bank added the interest to your account.
9. In the Category box, Quicken categorizes the interest as Interest Inc. If you want to use a different category, click the arrow at the right of the box and select a category from the drop-down list.
10. Click OK. You'll see the Reconcile Bank Statement window, as shown in Figure 5.3.

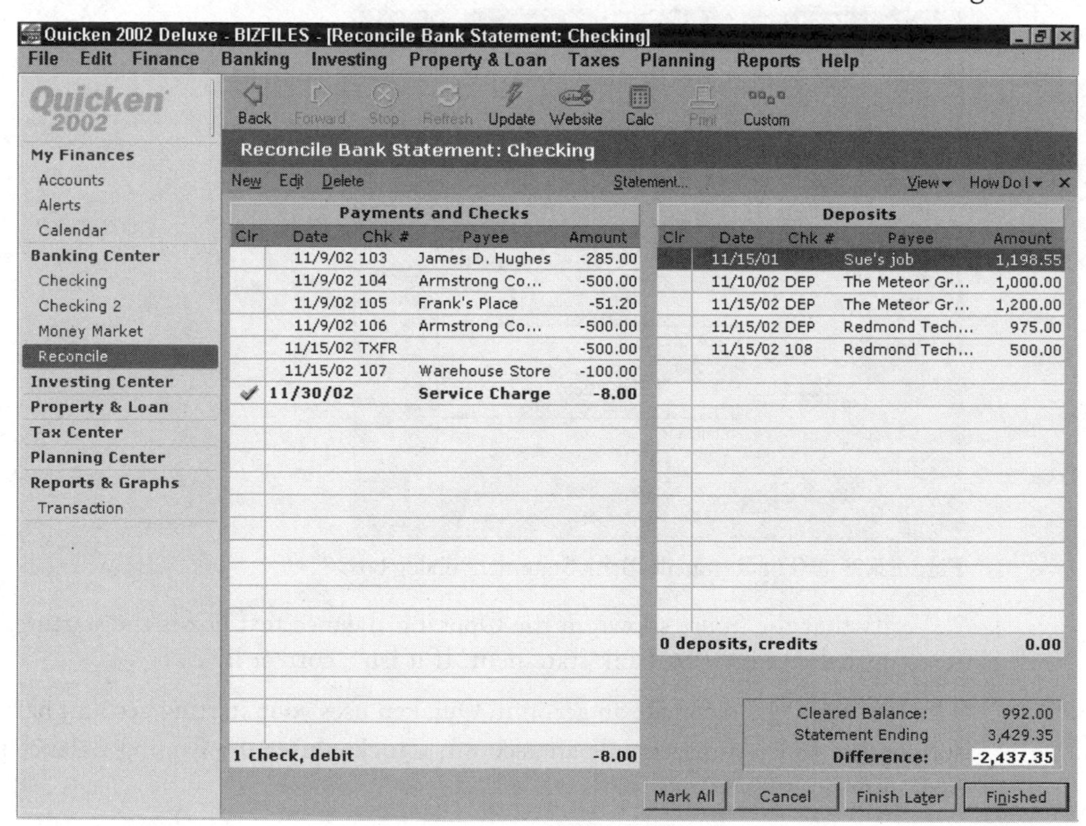

Figure 5.3: The Reconcile Bank Statement window.

11. If you have a question about a transaction shown in the Reconcile Bank Statement window, select the transaction either by using the arrow keys or by clicking the mouse. Then select the Edit command button. (It's the second button from the left.) Quicken displays the bank account's register in its document window, with the cursor in the transaction. You can examine the transaction in more detail, including the split transaction lines. When you're ready to return to the Reconcile Bank Statement window, click the Return To Reconcile button, which appears at the right end of the transaction.
12. Review the list of transactions shown in the Reconcile Bank Statement window and mark each transaction that has cleared by clicking it. Quicken places a checkmark next to it. (If you accidentally mark a transaction as cleared when it shouldn't be, click it with the mouse or press the spacebar.)

As you indicate which transactions have cleared, Quicken continually calculates a Cleared Balance figure at the bottom of the screen. The Cleared Balance is just your records' bank account balance minus all the uncleared transactions. When this Cleared Balance equals the bank statement balance, your account balances, because the uncleared transactions total explains the difference between your records and the bank's records.

NOTE *You can rearrange the entries in the reconciliation lists by date, payee, or amount rather than by check number. To do so, choose one of these options from the View menu.*

13. Select Finished when the difference between the cleared balance and the bank statement balance is zero. Figure 5.4 shows how the Reconcile Bank Statement window should look when you've successfully reconciled an account.

NOTE *If you made a mistake entering your ending bank account balance, you can return to the Reconcile Bank Statement dialog box (Figure 5.2) by selecting the Statement button.*

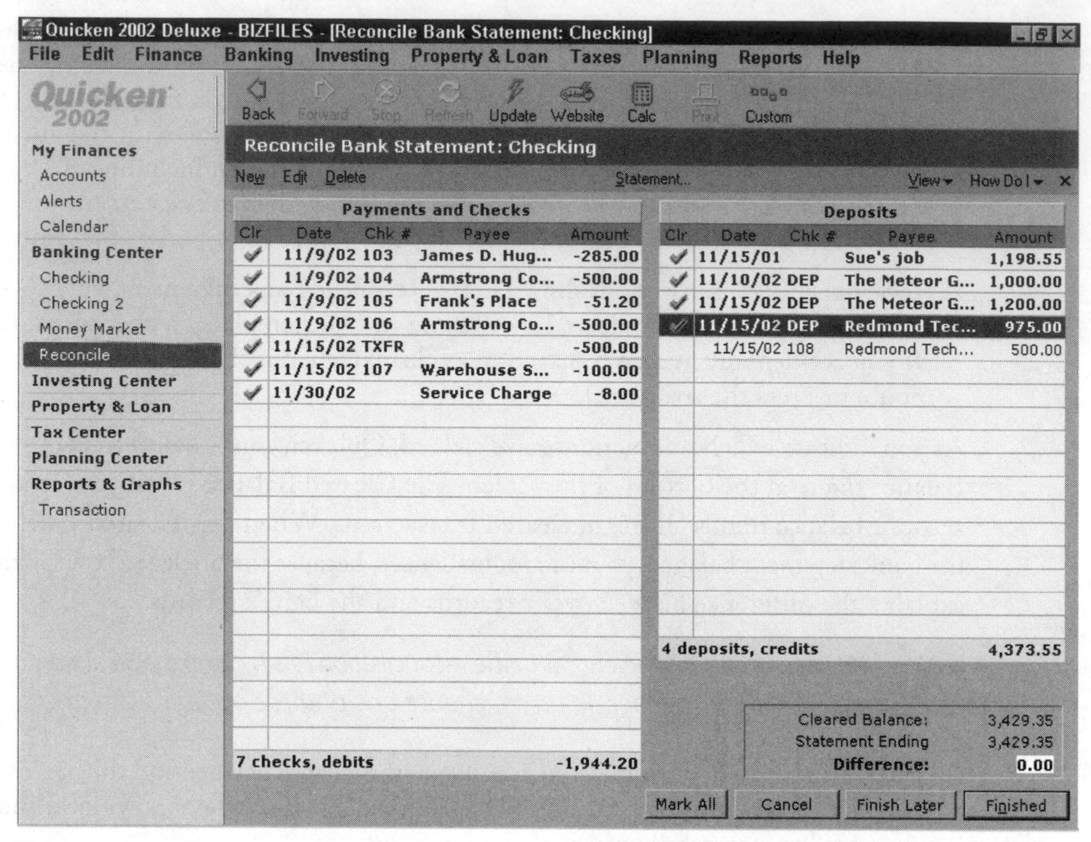

Figure 5.4: The Reconcile Bank Statement window showing a difference of zero.

When you select the Finished button, Quicken updates the status of the transactions you marked as cleared by placing an R in the Clr column of the Register window. Then it displays a message box congratulating you on finishing the reconciliation and asking you if you want to print a report describing the reconciliation. The message box is shown in Figure 5.5.

Figure 5.5: The Congratulations message.

The reconciliation report simply documents the fact that you reconciled an account. For this reason, you probably don't need a reconciliation report for either personal record keeping or business record keeping performed by you as the owner. And after all, you already know that you reconciled the account. In these cases, select No in the Reconciliation Complete dialog box.

The one time it probably does make sense to print a reconciliation report is when you're reconciling an account for someone else. For example, if you're a bookkeeper and you use Quicken in your work, it makes sense for you to document that you've completed a reconciliation so that you can show your employer that you've balanced the account. Continue with the instructions in the next section to create this report.

Producing a Reconciliation Report

If you want to produce a report that summarizes the reconciliation, follow these steps:

1. Select Yes in the Reconciliation Complete dialog box to display the Reconciliation Report Setup dialog box, shown in Figure 5.6.

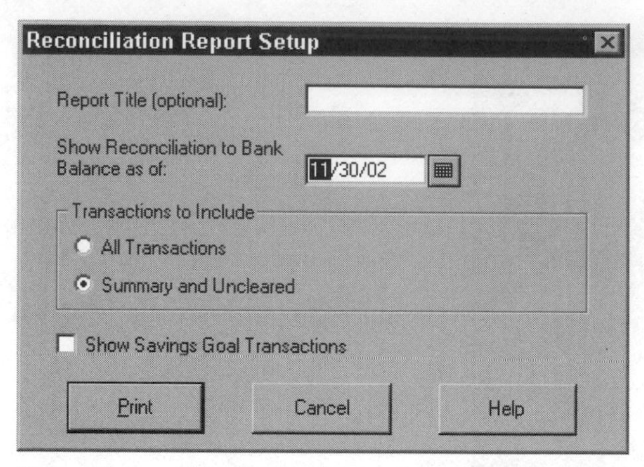

Figure 5.6: The Reconciliation Report Setup dialog box.

NOTE *If you don't want to print a report immediately after reconciling an account, you can do so later by choosing Reports ➢ Spending ➢ Reconciliation.*

2. If you want to record a title or description for the report, enter it in the Report Title text box.
3. In the Show Reconciliation To Bank Balance As Of text box, enter the date (in *MM/DD/YY* format) through which cleared and uncleared transactions should be reported.
4. Use the Transactions To Include option buttons to indicate what you want to show on the report:
   - Mark the All Transactions option button if you want all the transactions from the last reconciliation through the Show Reconciliation To Bank Balance As Of [date] to show on the report. (You usually won't need to show this level of detail.)
   - Mark the Summary And Uncleared option button if you want summary information and the individual uncleared transactions to show. (This is the option you'll usually want; it individually lists the uncleared transactions that explain the difference between your records and the bank's.)
5. Select Print to produce the reconciliation report, and use the Print To option buttons to indicate where Quicken should send the reconciliation report. Quicken sends the reconciliation report to Windows so that your report can be printed, or if you clicked any of the three Disk option buttons, Quicken prompts you for the complete path name of the reconciliation report disk file.

Troubleshooting Accounts that Won't Balance

If you can't get a bank account to reconcile, you have a choice: You can tell Quicken to force your records to agree with the bank's (this isn't a very good idea), or you can suspend the reconciliation, attempt to find the error that's causing you problems, and then restart the reconciliation. I'll describe both approaches here, although the former should be used only as a last resort or when you haven't been able to get an account to reconcile for several months in a row.

Postponing a Reconciliation so You Can Find Your Error

If you diligently entered each of the new transactions your bank statement showed and carefully marked each cleared transaction in the Reconcile Bank Statement window, and your account won't reconcile, here's what you should do:

First, click Finish Later in the Reconcile Bank Statement window. This tells Quicken not to complete the reconciliation. Quicken closes the window but leaves intact the transactions you've marked as cleared. (It does this by putting an R in the Clr text box in the account register.)

Next, review your records—particularly the transactions you entered since the last reconciliation—for any errors. The most common causes of reconciliation problems are transactions that you haven't yet entered into the register and transactions that you incorrectly marked as cleared or uncleared. If you've double-checked your records for these errors, consider these other potential errors:

- **Backward numbers** Look for transactions you may have entered backward—deposits you entered as payments or vice versa. These can be tricky to spot because every transaction looks right except for one tiny thing: the sign of the amount is wrong. But you can often find backward transactions by dividing the unexplained difference by two and then looking for a transaction equal to the result. If the unexplained difference is $101.50, for example, it may be that you entered a $50.75 transaction backward.
- **Transposed numbers** Look for amounts with transposed numbers. These errors are also tricky to locate because all the digits appear correct, but they aren't in the right order: $46.25 might have been entered as $42.65, for example. If the difference is evenly divisible by nine, look for transposed numbers in the amount. For example, if you did enter 42.65 instead of 46.25, the difference in the Reconcile Bank Account window will equal $3.60. The $3.60 amount is evenly divisible by nine, so the difference suggests a transposition error.

- **Transactions entered twice** Look for transactions you've erroneously entered twice. These are usually pretty easy to spot. A telltale sign is that the difference shown equals the amount of a transaction correctly marked as cleared or left as uncleared.

Once you find and correct the error causing the discrepancy, restart the reconciliation process by clicking the Reconcile button. Fill out the Reconcile Bank Statement dialog box and the Reconcile Bank Statement window to continue marking transactions as cleared (or uncleared). Then, when the difference equals zero, select Finished.

Forcing Your Records to Agree with the Bank's

If you can't get an account to reconcile, you can force your records to agree with the bank's. The one time it is reasonable (at least in my opinion) to force your records to agree with the bank's is when you've attempted to reconcile your account for two or three or (better yet) four months and find that you always have the same unexplained difference. In this case, you know that the uncleared transactions total explains the difference; so the problem you can't find is either in the bank's records (which is unlikely) or yours. By forcing your records to agree with the bank's, you implicitly admit that the problem is yours and not the bank's.

To make this adjustment, just click the Finished command button in the Reconcile Bank Statement window, even though the difference doesn't equal zero. Quicken displays the Adjust Balance dialog box, as shown in Figure 5.7.

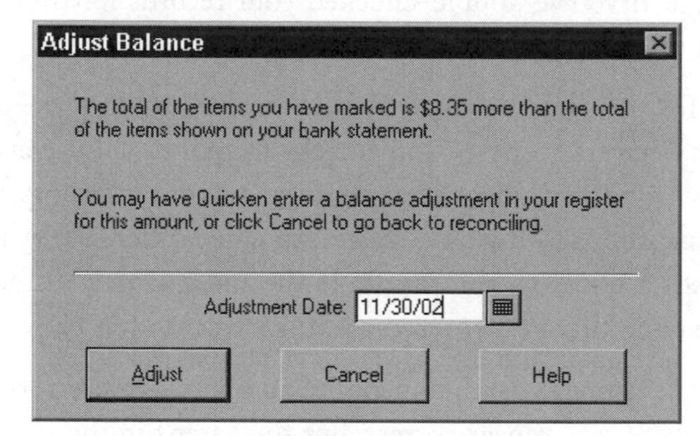

Figure 5.7: The Adjust Balance dialog box.

To make the adjustment, simply enter the date on which the adjustment transaction should be recorded, and then click Adjust. Quicken records an adjustment transaction that forces your records to agree with the bank's. For example, if your records show the account balance as $3 too high, Quicken just adds a payment transaction for $3 and marks the transaction as cleared.

Quicken doesn't categorize adjustment transactions, but you may want to do so. Because you never found the error, you don't actually know which category should be used. Here are two things you can do:

- You can use the category you use for the largest share of your spending. As a practical matter, the adjustment transaction will then have the least effect on this category's totals (because this category will show the largest category totals). What's more, there's a pretty good chance the record-keeping error affects this category.
- You can set up a Balance Adjustment category that you can use to summarize your reconciliation balance adjustments. This doesn't actually make your category reporting any better, but it does make it easy to see just what portion of your spending is unknown.

Chapter 6

CUSTOMIZING THE WAY QUICKEN WORKS

In This Chapter

- Three easy changes you can make
- Changing the way the Write Checks window works
- Changing Quicken's general options
- Using alerts and reminders
- Customizing the toolbar
- Changing the way the register looks and works

You can make a whole series of changes to the way Quicken works. Many of the changes are largely cosmetic; they affect only the way Quicken appears. But some of the changes are more structural; they affect either the way Quicken works or the way you work with Quicken. I'll describe each of these sets of possible changes in this chapter.

NOTE *The only prerequisite for this chapter is to know how to work with Windows.*

Three Easy Changes You Can Make

Three of the changes you can make are so easy you can (and should) consider making them as soon as you're comfortable working with Quicken and entering transactions into a register. These include customizing your My Finances window, switching to a one-line view of the register, and saving your Desktop arrangement.

Customizing Your My Finances Window

When you start Quicken the first time, you see a screen similar to the one in Figure 6.1. These lists, tables, and charts are colorful and attractive, but these particular representations sometimes won't make any sense to you, and it's often the case that they'll be of little use to you. You can tell Quicken that you don't want to see this window by following the instructions in the "Saving a Desktop" section or in the "Changing Quicken's General Options" section found later in this chapter.

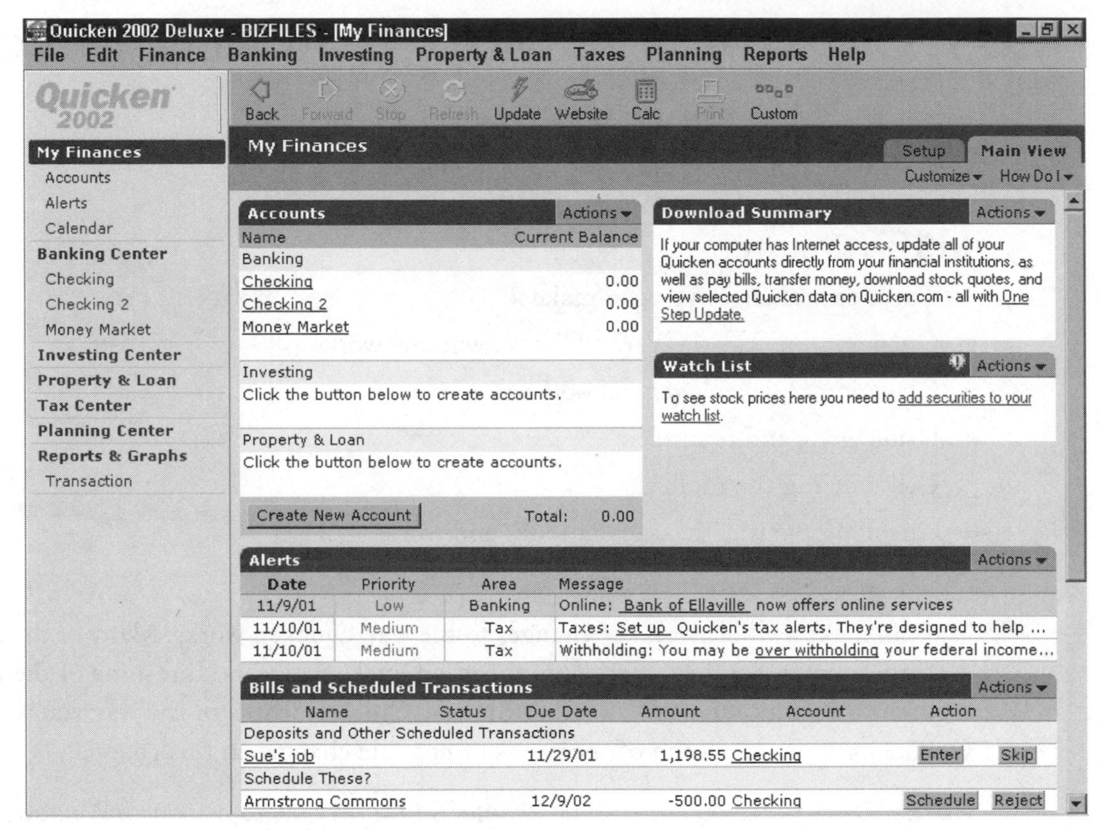

Figure 6.1: The default My Finances window.

If you like this page, though, you can customize what it contains so that it is meaningful to you. To customize the current view, follow these steps:

1. From the My Finances window, click the Customize button, and from the drop-down menu, choose Customize This View to open the Customize View dialog box, as shown in Figure 6.2.

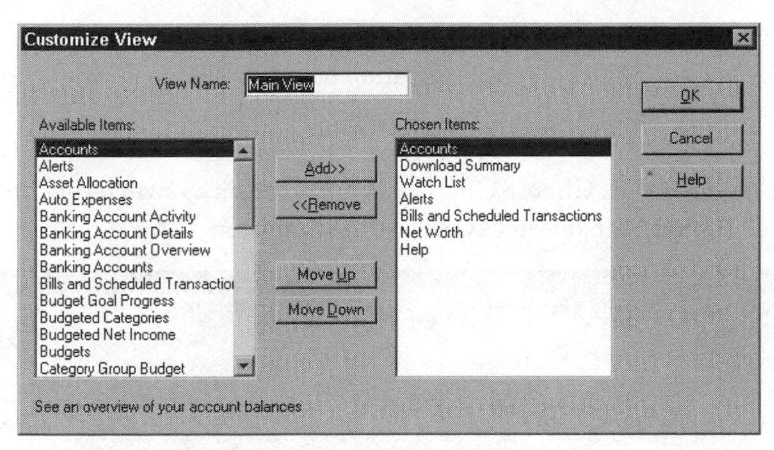

Figure 6.2: The Customize View dialog box.

2. To remove an item from the display, select it in the Chosen Items list and click Remove.
3. To add an item to the display, select it in the Available Items list and click Add.
4. To change the order in which items are displayed, select an item in the Chosen Items list and click either Move Up or Move Down.
5. When the arrangement suits you, click OK.

NOTE *By default, your view is named Main View. To rename it, simply type a new name in the View Name box.*

To create an entirely new view, click Customize, and from the drop-down menu choose Create A New View to open the Customize View dialog box. Select items from the Available Items list, click Add to add them to the Chosen Items list, arrange them to suit your fancy, name your view if you want, and click OK.

After you add a view, click the new view's tab on the My Finances page to see the view. Or, click Customize and choose the view from the drop-down menu.

If you later decide that you want to remove a view, click that view's tab, click Customize, and from the drop-down menu choose Delete This View.

Changing Views of the Register

The Options button in the top-right corner of the Register window provides several commands for changing the information shown in the Register window and for reorganizing that information.

Switching to a one-line view of the register is another change you may want to make. This lets you pack more information into the Register window. To switch to a one-line view, just click the Options button in the top right of the Register window and then choose One-Line Display. Quicken condenses all the information normally shown in two lines into one line by using shorter text boxes and omitting the Memo text box. If you click the Options button again, you will find that Quicken has placed a checkmark next to One-Line Display to indicate that it is active. Choose One-Line Display again to switch back to the two-line view. Figure 6.3 shows the one-line version of the register.

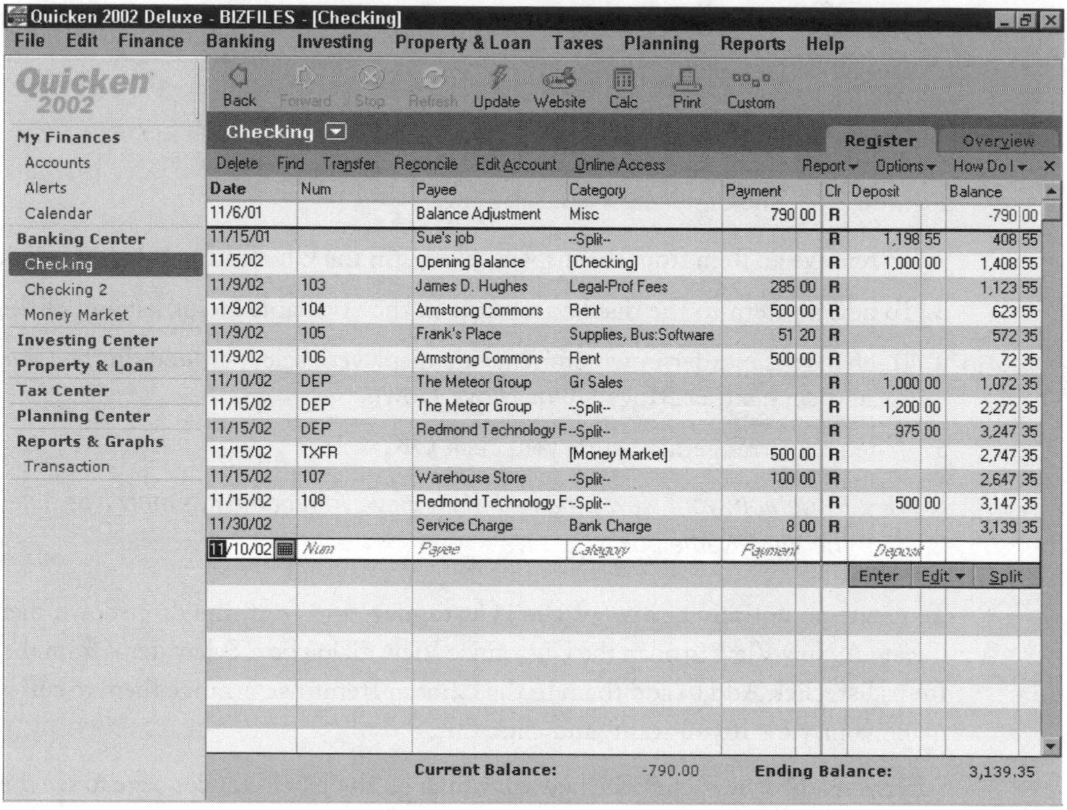

Figure 6.3: The one-line view of a Quicken register.

The Options menu provides View commands for specifying that information should appear in the Register window. For example, choose the View Online Setup command to display the information and hyperlinks that let you set up online banking for a bank account. Choose the View Scheduled Transactions command to display a list of bills and scheduled transactions. Choose the View Compare To Register command to tell Quicken to display a portion of the register during an account reconciliation. (This command is only available when you're reconciling an account.) Choose View Register Only to display only the register. Quicken marks the view you've selected with a checkmark on the menu.

The Options menu also provides Sort commands for organizing the transactions that appear in the register: Sort By Date/Amount, Sort By Amount (Largest First), Sort By Amount (Smallest First), Sort By Check Number, Sort By Payee, and so on. If you're reviewing the contents of your register (rather than entering data into it), you can often use these sorting commands to more easily locate specific transactions.

Saving a Desktop

As mentioned in Chapter 1, Quicken calls the application window area beneath the menu bar the *Desktop*. Whenever you start Quicken, it displays the Desktop just the way you left it. Windows will be the same size and in the same location as when you last exited Quicken. You can change this, however, and have Quicken use a standard Desktop whenever you start.

First arrange the Desktop exactly the way you want it to appear. Select the document windows you want displayed and arrange the windows the way you want. Then choose the Edit ➢ Options ➢ Desktop command. Quicken displays the Save Desktop dialog box, as shown in Figure 6.4.

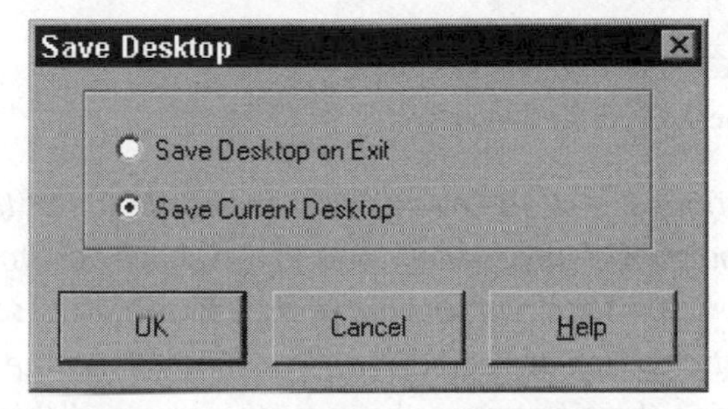

Figure 6.4: The Save Desktop dialog box.

Marking the Save Current Desktop option button tells Quicken to preserve the arrangement of the Desktop as it is. If you prefer to start with the Desktop looking as you left it upon exit, mark the Save Desktop On Exit option button. When you quit Quicken, the window arrangement is saved and will be restored when you return.

Changing the Way the Write Checks Window Works

You can make several changes in the way the Write Checks window works. For example, you can fine-tune aspects of check printing, control QuickFill's operation, and tell Quicken how it should validate the transactions you enter.

Fine-Tuning the Write Checks Window

You can control which information Quicken displays in the Write Checks window and the appearance of that information. To do this, display the Write Checks window (by choosing the Banking ➤ Write Checks command), and then click the Options button. Quicken will display the Check Options dialog box, as shown in Figure 6.5.

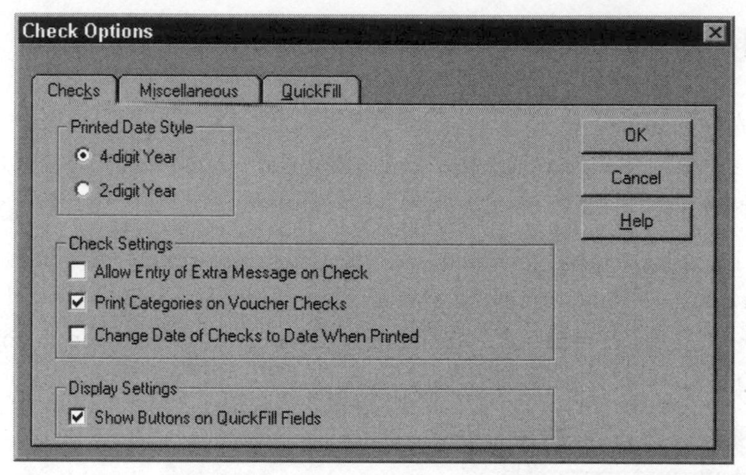

Figure 6.5: The Checks tab of the Check Options dialog box.

TIP *The Options button is on the right side of the row of buttons at the top of the Write Checks window. This row of buttons changes according to the active document window. Although the buttons correspond to menu commands, you can often save yourself a few steps by using the buttons. That can add up to a lot of saved time after a while, so try to get in the habit of using these buttons whenever they are available.*

Use the Printed Date Style option buttons to specify how you would like Quicken to print the year on your check forms. The two option buttons show how a particular year appears. If the check date is July 4, 2002, for example, you have these choices:

BUTTON	WHAT YOU SEE
4-Digit Year	7/4/2002
2-Digit Year	7/4/02

The Allow Entry Of Extra Message On Check checkbox tells Quicken to add another text box to the Write Checks window so that you can include another piece of data on the check form. Figure 6.6 shows the Write Checks window after this checkbox has been marked. The extra message will appear on the printed check in roughly the same position as the message box shown in the Write Checks window.

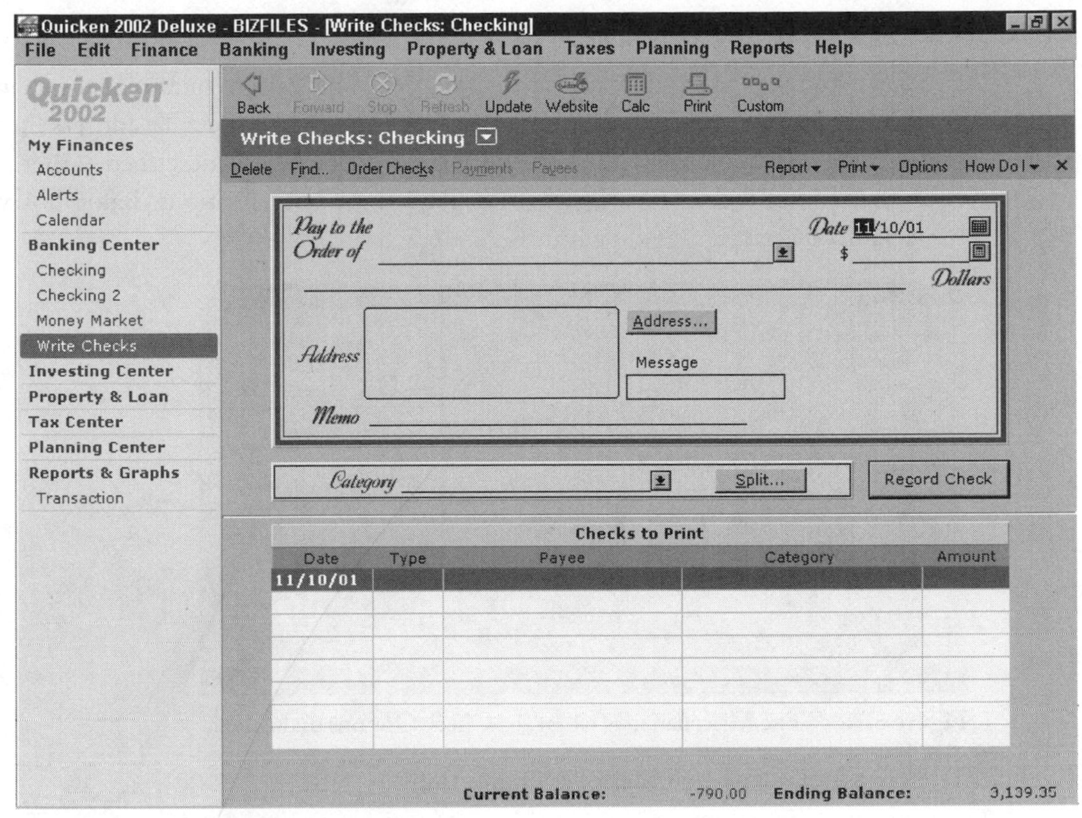

Figure 6.6: The Write Checks window with an extra message box added.

The remaining checkboxes give you the following options:

- **Print Categories On Voucher Checks** Tells Quicken to print what you've entered as a check's category or split category information on the voucher portion of a check. You'll want to mark this box if you use Quicken to prepare employee payroll checks or checks that pay multiple invoices. In the case of payroll checks, for example, you can use the split category information to describe an employee's gross wages and payroll deductions. And in the case of checks paying multiple invoices—common in business bookkeeping—you can identify each of the invoices.

- **Change Date Of Checks To Date When Printed** Lets you exercise control over which date is printed on a check: the system date at the time you print the check or the date you (or someone else) entered in the check register. To use the system date as the date printed on the check, mark this checkbox. To use the date you entered in the Write Checks window, leave the checkbox unmarked.

- **Show Buttons On QuickFill Fields** Lets you remove the down arrows, calculator, and calendar buttons at the end of the Pay To The Order Of, Date, Amount, and Category fields.

Error-Checking Transactions

You can determine what safety measures Quicken should take to minimize the chances that you'll enter erroneous transactions into the Write Checks window. To address these information safety issues, display the Check Options dialog box as described earlier and then click the Miscellaneous tab. Quicken displays the Check Options dialog box with the Miscellaneous settings, as shown in Figure 6.7.

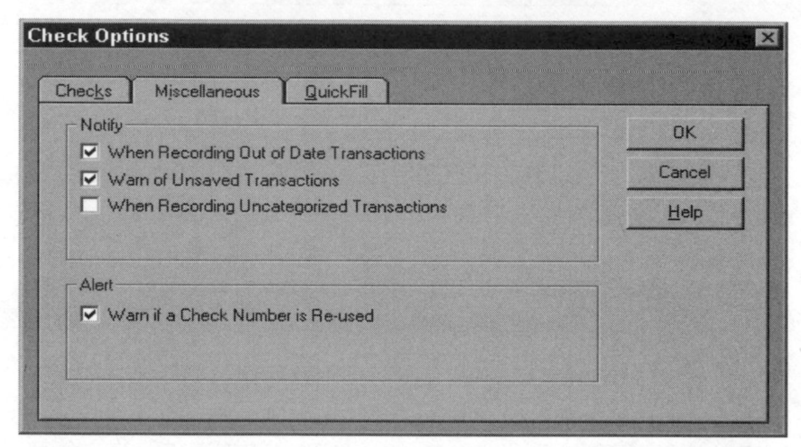

Figure 6.7: The Miscellaneous tab of the Check Options dialog box.

The checkboxes give you the following options:

- **When Recording Out Of Date Transactions** Displays a warning message if you try to record a transaction for a different year.
- **Warn Of Unsaved Transactions** Displays a message box that asks you to confirm you want to discard transactions you don't save by clicking the Record button.
- **When Recording Uncategorized Transactions** To make sure you categorize all your transactions, mark this checkbox. If you later try to record a transaction that doesn't show a category, Quicken displays a message box asking you to confirm that you want to record the transaction without a category. (You can still record transactions without categories if you mark this checkbox, but it will be more work.)
- **Warn If A Check Number Is Re-Used** Tells Quicken to display a message box that warns you whenever you enter a check number that has already appeared in the register. Because a check number should uniquely identify a check, you should use a given check number only once, so leave this checkbox marked.

Controlling How QuickFill Works

To change the way QuickFill works, display the Check Options dialog box as described earlier and click the QuickFill tab. Quicken displays the Check Options dialog box with the QuickFill settings, as shown in Figure 6.8.

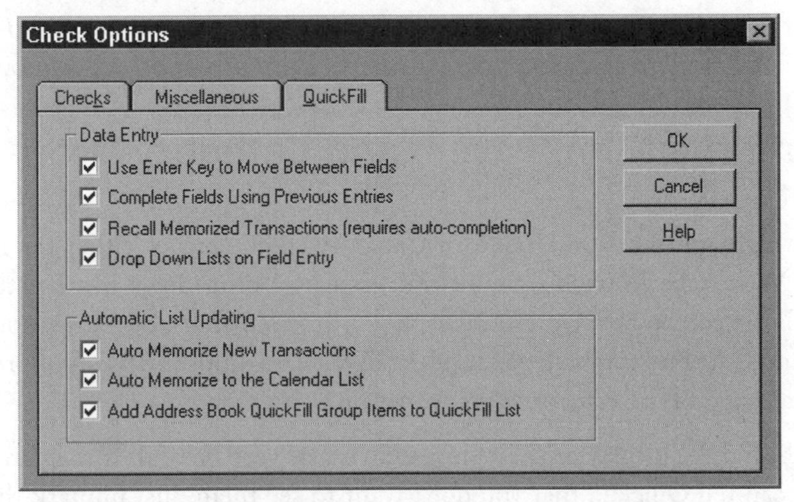

Figure 6.8: The QuickFill tab of the Check Options dialog box.

Turning QuickFill On and Off

QuickFill is such a handy feature and time-saver that I can't imagine not using it. When the Complete Fields Using Previous Entries checkbox is marked, QuickFill automatically fills in the payee, category, amount, address, and memo if what you're typing looks like it might be the start of a payee or category that you've used before. However, if you don't want QuickFill to fill in these fields automatically, unmark the checkbox. QuickFill is a valuable feature, but it can be a little overzealous. If you want, you can limit when and how QuickFill works.

TIP *The Use Enter Key To Move Between Fields checkbox tells Quicken that it should treat the Enter key like the Tab key. When this checkbox is marked, pressing Enter will highlight the next text box—just as pressing Tab does.*

Using Memorized Transactions

To tell QuickFill to find a memorized transaction with the same payee that you entered into the Payee text box and to then use this memorized transaction to fill the rest of the transaction's text boxes, leave the Recall Memorized Transactions checkbox marked. If you don't want QuickFill to retrieve memorized transactions, remove the checkmark.

NOTE *To use a memorized transaction's data to enter a new transaction quickly, just display the Memorized Transaction List window (choose Banking ➢ Memorized Transaction List), select the memorized transaction you want to enter on the check, and click the Use button. You can enter memorized transactions in another account in the same way. Just display the account you want to use, click the Register tab (if required), select the next empty row of the register, click Banking ➢ Memorized Transactions List and then select the memorized transaction from the Memorized Transaction List window*

Controlling the Num, Payee, and Category Drop-Down Lists

Whenever you highlight the Num, Payee, or Category combo box in either the Register window or the Write Checks window, QuickFill displays a drop-down list. For the Register window's Num combo box, QuickFill displays a drop-down list of transaction codes. For the Payee and Category combo boxes, QuickFill displays drop-down lists of previously used payee names and of the categories you've set up.

Normally, you'll find the display of these drop-down lists very helpful. If they aren't useful to you, you can tell Quicken that you don't want to see them. Just unmark the Drop Down Lists On Field Entry checkbox.

Memorizing Transactions Automatically

Unless you tell it otherwise, QuickFill copies every new transaction's information to a list called, appropriately enough, the Memorized Transactions List. You can then set up QuickFill to automatically use memorized transactions to enter new transactions. If you don't want QuickFill to automatically memorize transactions—for example, because you want to conserve memory and disk space—unmark the Auto Memorize New Transactions checkbox.

For the average Quicken user, it's easiest to let QuickFill memorize transactions. But you can also memorize an individual transaction by choosing the Edit ➢ Transaction ➢ Memorize command.

Adding Transactions to the Financial Calendar

If you mark the Auto Memorize To The Calendar List checkbox, Quicken adds check transactions to the Financial Calendar's list of transactions. (Chapter 15 describes how you can use the Financial Calendar for monitoring important payroll transactions.)

Retrieving Names and Addresses from the Address Book

If you place a checkmark in the Add Address Book QuickFill Items To QuickFill List checkbox, Quicken will "QuickFill" the Payee and Pay To The Order Of fields using the names and addresses that you've stored in the Address Book that comes with Quicken Deluxe.

Changing Quicken's General Options

You can make several additional preference-setting changes through the General Options dialog box. To display this dialog box, choose Edit ➢ Options ➢ Quicken Program. The General Options dialog box has four tabs: QuickTabs, General, Settings, and Startup. If it is not already showing, click the QuickTabs tab to display the options shown in Figure 6.9.

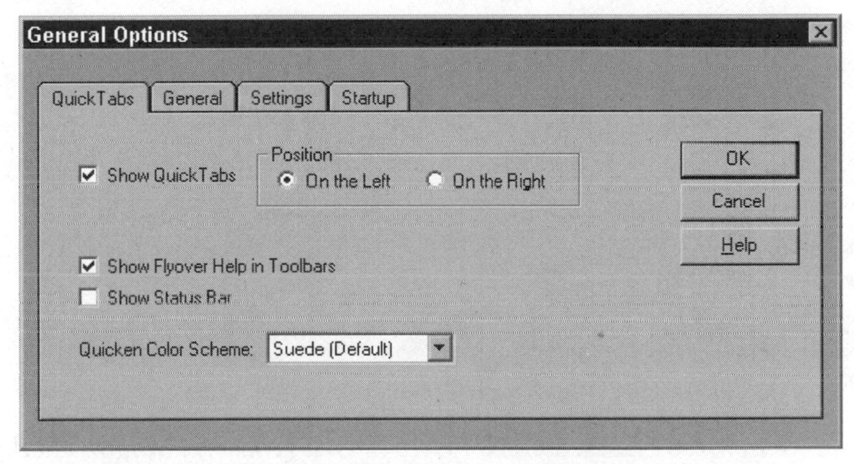

Figure 6.9: The QuickTabs tab of the General Options dialog box.

Controlling the Display of Document Windows

You use the QuickTabs options to specify how Quicken will arrange the QuickTabs and its document windows. Initially, QuickTabs appear to the side of the document window and allow you to page through the open windows quickly.

By unmarking the Show QuickTabs checkbox, you can instruct Quicken to remove the QuickTabs.

If you are using the QuickTabs, you can tell Quicken whether to place them on the left side or the right side of the document window by clicking the appropriate option button in the Position box.

When you check Show Flyover Help In Toolbars, Quicken displays a short description of the button's function whenever you leave the pointer over a toolbar button. You probably want to leave this checkbox marked, unless you know Quicken extremely well.

If the Show Status Bar checkbox is marked, Quicken displays a status bar of information across the bottom of the Quicken application window.

The Quicken Color Scheme drop-down list offers choices for the colors of Quicken's screen elements. From this drop-down list, you can change the color scheme to something that you find visually pleasing. For instance, if you don't like the default Suede color scheme, you can choose a theme such as Denim or Moss.

Changing General Settings

As you can see in Figure 6.10, clicking the General tab of the General Options dialog box displays even more options for customizing Quicken.

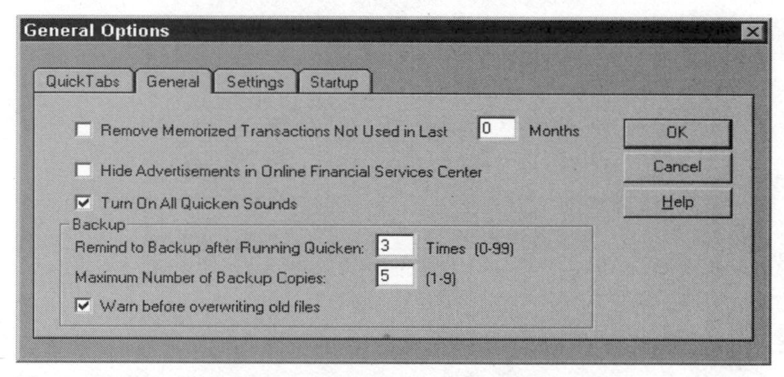

Figure 6.10: The General tab of the General Options dialog box.

The Remove Memorized Transactions Not Used in Last [*Number*] Months checkbox and text box let you clean up and reduce the size of your memorized transactions list. To remove old memorized transactions, mark the checkbox and then, in the text box, enter the number of months after which an unused memorized transaction should be deleted.

If you use Quicken's online services and don't want to be bombarded with commercial messages, check the Hide Advertisements In Online Financial Services Center checkbox.

By default, the sounds associated with actions you take in Quicken are turned on. If you want to turn them off, uncheck the Turn On All Quicken Sounds checkbox.

When you first install Quicken, Quicken asks you after every third time you exit the program if you want to back up your files. To be reminded more or less often (or never), enter a number in the Remind To Backup After Running Quicken box.

TIP *It's a good idea to back up your data files frequently. The more often you change your data, the more often you should back up your changes.*

By default, Quicken automatically makes five copies of your data files every seven days and stores these backup files on your hard drive in the \BACKUP directory. To change this, type a number in the range 1 through 9 in the Maximum Number Of Backup Copies box.

The Warn Before Overwriting Old Files checkbox specifies whether Quicken should warn you if, as part of backing up or restoring a file, you attempt to overwrite an existing file.

Changing Keyboard and Calendar Settings

You can also adjust some of Quicken's keyboard and calendar settings. Click the Settings tab to view the set of options shown in Figure 6.11.

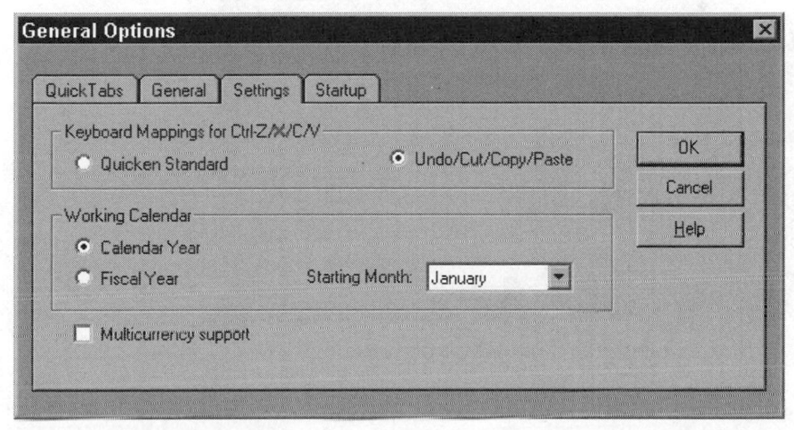

Figure 6.11: The Settings tab of the General Options dialog box.

The Keyboard Mappings For Ctrl-Z/X/C/V options tell Quicken whether you want to use the command shortcuts Ctrl+Z, Ctrl+X, Ctrl+C, and Ctrl+V in the Quicken way or in the Windows way. If you want to adjust this setting, you'll know it. If you're someone who uses command shortcuts regularly (either in Quicken or in other Windows applications), you'll want the shortcuts to work the way you expect.

The Working Calendar option buttons let you use a fiscal (or accounting) year that's different from the calendar year. Individuals who use Quicken probably don't need to worry about this, but some businesses and many nonprofit organizations use a non-calendar fiscal year. If you want to do this, mark the Fiscal Year option button, and then use the Starting Month drop-down list to indicate when your fiscal year starts.

If you have accounts that use a foreign currency, check the Multicurrency Support checkbox. When you then click OK, Quicken places the currency symbols for all your accounts in the Balance field.

TIP *For much more information on using foreign currencies, choose Help ➢ Contents, click the Index tab, and search on currencies. If you set up multiple currencies, see your Windows documentation for how to view or change your default currency.*

Changing the Way Quicken Starts

As I mentioned earlier, by default Quicken displays the My Finances window when you open the program. To change this, you use the Startup tab of the General Options dialog box, as shown in Figure 6.12.

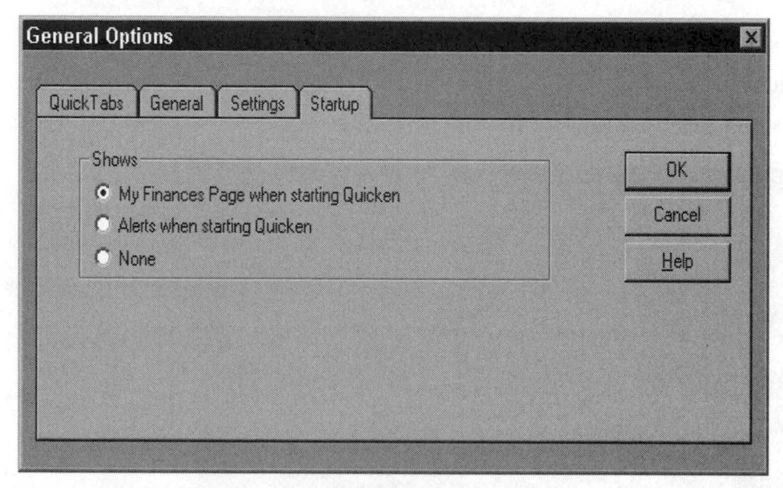

Figure 6.12: The Startup tab of the General Options dialog box.

If you don't want to display the My Finances window, select an option besides the My Finances Page When Starting Quicken button. To display alerts instead (as discussed in the next section), mark the Alerts When Starting Quicken option button. Choose None if you don't want to display either.

Using Alerts and Reminders

An important feature of financial record keeping for both individuals and businesses is keeping a to-do list of future tasks: bills that need to be paid, tax returns that need to filed, customers that need to be invoiced, and so forth. Quicken provides tools for managing this work called Reminders and Alerts.

Working with Alerts

Alerts are warnings and financial announcements that Quicken supplies. To see Quicken's alerts, choose Finance ➢ Alerts. Quicken displays the Alerts window, as shown in Figure 6.13. As the figure shows, the Alerts window lists announcements and warnings in the top half of the window and any bills or scheduled transactions in the bottom half of the window.

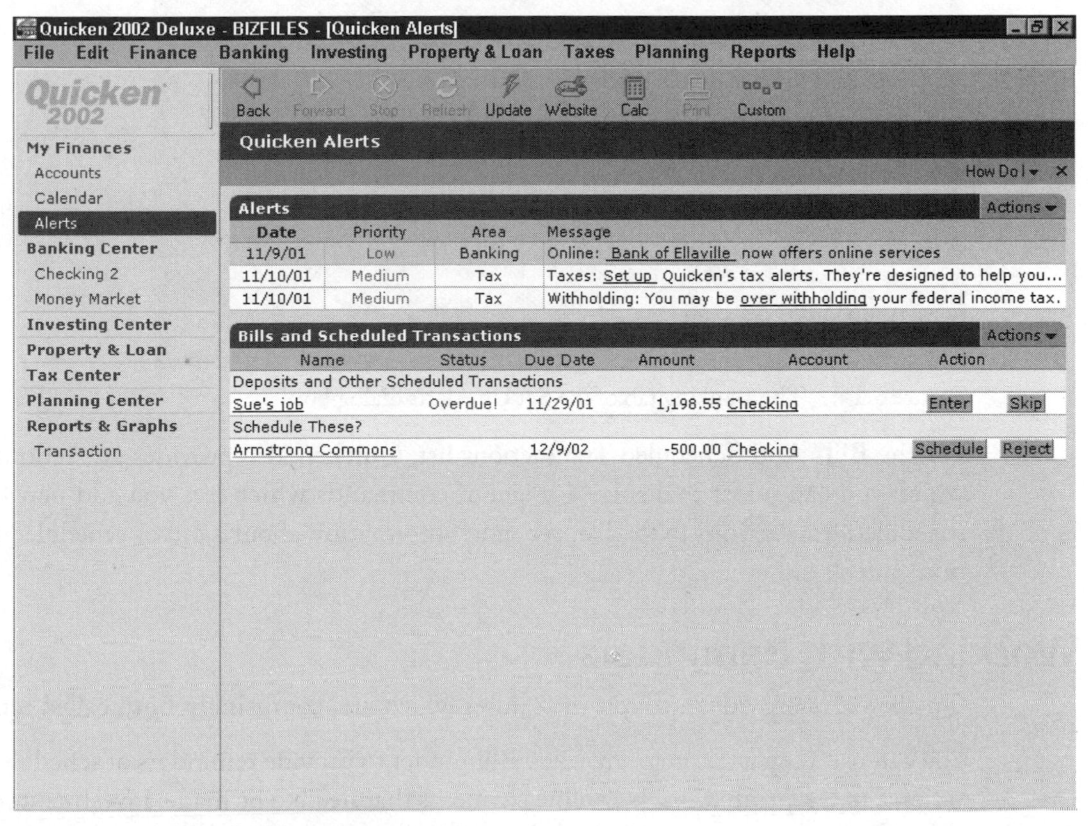

Figure 6.13: The Quicken Alerts window.

For the Alerts list, Quicken provides an Actions button which you can select to display a menu of commands that let you delete an item, delay the alert by some amount of time (a day, a week, a month and so on), filter the Alerts list so that it shows only items with a specified priority, and even customize the Alerts list. If you click the Alerts list's Actions button and choose Set Up Alerts, Quicken displays the Set Up Alerts dialog box, as shown in Figure 6.14. This dialog box provides tabs that let you describe new alerts you want to add to the Alerts window—such as an alert that your bank account balance has fallen under some minimum balance.

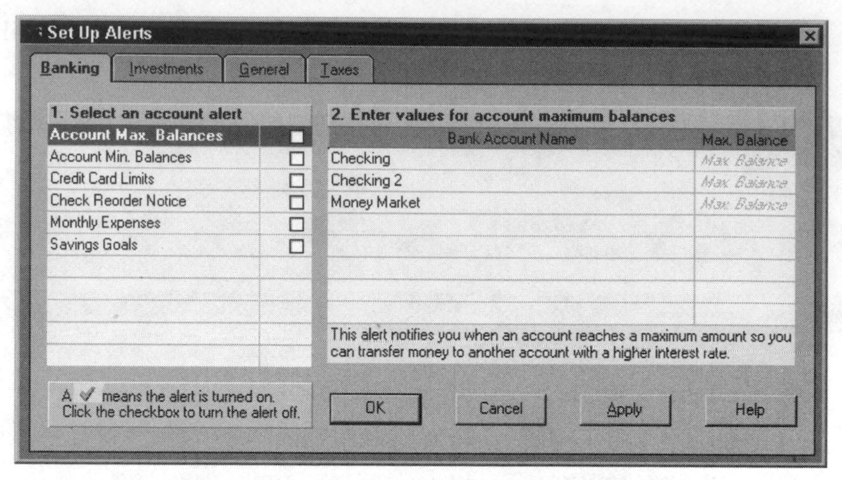

Figure 6.14: The Banking tab of the Set Up Alerts dialog box.

For the Bills And Scheduled Transactions list, Quicken also provides an Actions button which you can select to display a menu of commands which lets you add new bills and scheduled transactions to the list, see more information about a bill or scheduled transaction, and so on.

Working with Reminders

Quicken also provides a couple of features which are, confusingly, both called reminders.

You can use a separate program called Billminder to provide reminders of scheduled transactions, to-be-printed checks, online payments that need to be made, investment reminder notes, and calendar notes. Billminder runs in the background on your computer when Quicken isn't running. In this way, Billminder tracks financial tasks you should perform using Quicken.

To use Billminder, close the Quicken program and then start the Billminder program. How you start Billminder depends on your version of Windows, but in most recent versions you click the Start button, click Programs, click Quicken, and then click Billminder. After Billminder starts, click Options. When Billminder displays the Billminder Options dialog box, check the Enable Billminder On Windows Startup box. Then check the boxes that correspond to the Quicken items you want to be reminded of.

Customizing the Toolbar

Quicken's toolbar provides buttons that you can click instead of activating menus and then selecting commands. Normally, the toolbar automatically appears when you first install Quicken. However, if it doesn't appear, you can add it by choosing Edit ➢ Options ➢

Customize Toolbar. Quicken displays the Customize Toolbar dialog box, shown in Figure 6.15.

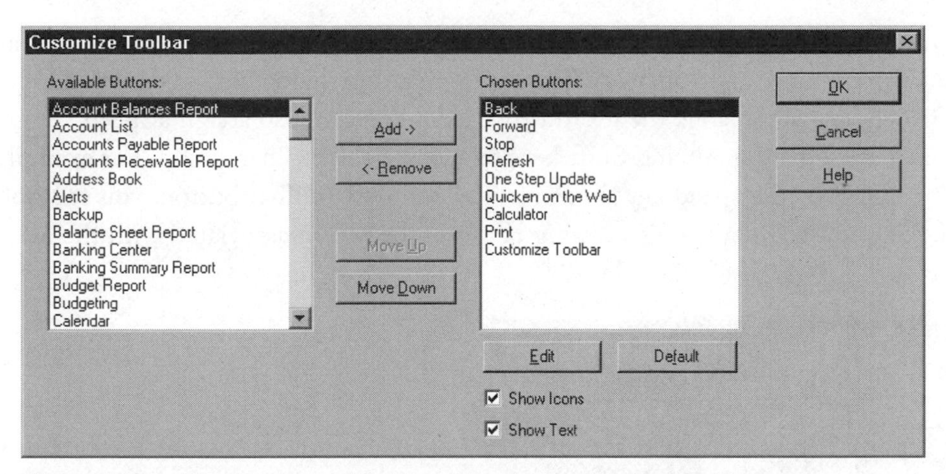

Figure 6.15: The Customize Toolbar dialog box.

To add the toolbar to the Quicken application window, mark the Show Icons checkbox. You'll probably also appreciate it if the buttons are labeled, so mark the Show Text checkbox too.

The icons on the toolbar can be tremendous time-savers. Instead of opening a menu and choosing a command, you can just click an icon and go directly to the activity you want. The standard toolbar contains a selection of the most useful buttons, but as you develop your own style of using Quicken, you may want to tailor the buttons to fit your needs. The Customize Toolbar dialog box contains tools for editing and adding icons.

The simplest change to make is to unmark either of the two checkboxes in the dialog box to turn off either the icon images or the icon text. Turning off the text below the images narrows the toolbar and leaves a bit more space for the application screen, but you need to memorize the meaning of the icons before doing this. Turning off the image but leaving the text narrows the toolbar even more; although the resulting toolbar isn't very attractive, it's still helpful, since the buttons are labeled with text. Mark or unmark the appropriate boxes to adjust the toolbar's appearance. If you want to turn the toolbar off completely, simply unmark both boxes.

Adding New Icons to the Toolbar

To add a new toolbar button, select the button from the Available Buttons list in the Customize Toolbar dialog box. Then click the Add button. Quicken places the button on the toolbar. To remove a toolbar button, select the button from the Chosen Buttons list and then click the Remove button. Quicken removes the button from the toolbar. To reorder the buttons on the toolbar, click a button listed in the Chosen Buttons list and then select the Move Up and Move Down buttons.

If you want to customize further, select a button from the Chosen Buttons list and then click the Edit button to open the Edit Toolbar Button dialog box, as shown in Figure 6.16, in which you can change the text on your icon. You can also assign a speed key combination to use with the Alt and Shift keys to activate the toolbar action. For example, if you designate **K** as the speed key for activating your new toolbar button, you can hold down the Alt and Shift keys while pressing **K** to run the action associated with the new toolbar button.

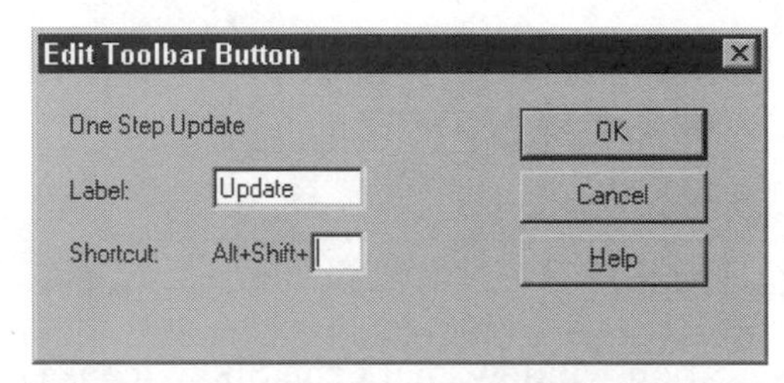

Figure 6.16: The Edit Toolbar Button dialog box.

Changing the Way the Register Looks and Works

Quicken lets you change the way the account register looks and works. Many of the changes you can make are identical to the changes you can make in the Write Checks window.

Changing the Register Display Options

To make changes to the register preferences, choose Edit ➢ Options ➢ Register to open the Register Options dialog box, shown in Figure 6.17.

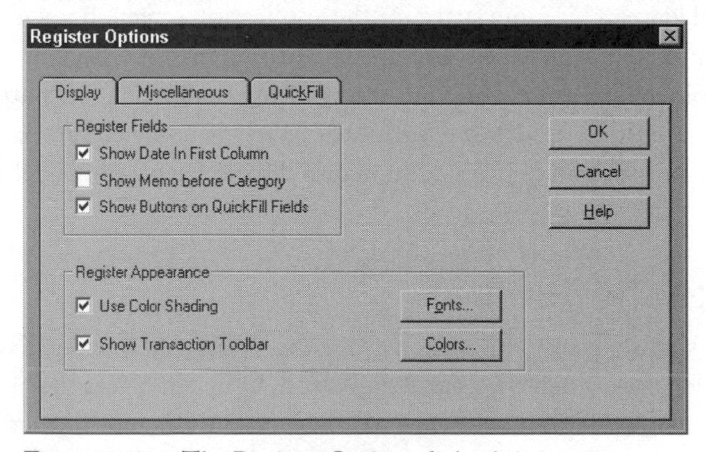

Figure 6.17: The Register Options dialog box.

The checkboxes in the Display tab work as follows:

- **Show Date In First Column** Acts as a toggle switch. Mark this checkbox if you want to see the Date field first and the Num (transaction number) field second. Unmark this checkbox if you want to see the transaction number first and the date second.
- **Show Memo Before Category** Also acts as a toggle switch, flip-flopping the position of the Memo and Category boxes in the register.
- **Show Buttons On QuickFill Fields** Turns on and off the drop-down list that appears at the end of all fields that work with QuickFill.
- **Use Color Shading** Turns on and off the shading that appears on the second line of each transaction.
- **Show Transaction Toolbar** If marked, tells Quicken to display the Enter, Edit, and Split buttons in the selected transaction's row of the register.

The checkboxes in the Miscellaneous tab work as follows:

- **When Recording Out Of Date Transactions** Warns when you record transactions for a different year.
- **Warn Of Unsaved Transactions** Warns when you attempt to leave the register without saving a transaction.
- **When Recording Uncategorized Transactions** Warns when you record transactions without a category. (You definitely want this warning for business record keeping!)
- **To Run A Reconcile Report After Reconcile** Suggests you create an account reconciliation report after you successfully reconcile an account.
- **Automatically Enter Split Data** Lets you record a transaction from the Split Transaction Window.
- **Show Transaction History In QuickEntry** Tells Quicken you want transactions you've already recorded to appear in the QuickEntry window.
- **Use File Password to Restrict QuickEntry Access** Tells Quicken to require a file password when using QuickEntry.

NOTE *Mark the Use Automatic Categorization checkbox to tell Quicken that it should suggest categories for transactions.*

The QuickFill options for the Register window, shown on the QuickFill tab of the Register Options dialog box, work the same way as the QuickFill options for the Write Checks window. Refer to the earlier chapter section, "Controlling How QuickFill Works," for information.

Changing Font Preferences

Quicken adds the ability to change font and font size for the screen display of registers and lists.

Choose Edit ➢ Options ➢ Register and click the Display tab to display the Display tab of the Register Options dialog box. Then click the Fonts button. Quicken displays the Choose Register Font dialog box, as shown in Figure 6.18. Scroll through the font list and highlight a font to select it. Choose a size and, if desired, mark the Bold checkbox. Choose carefully, with regard to legibility. You can see how your choices look in the preview box at the bottom of the dialog box. Click OK to set a new default. If you do not like the new default, you can later return to MS Sans Serif by choosing the Reset button in this dialog box.

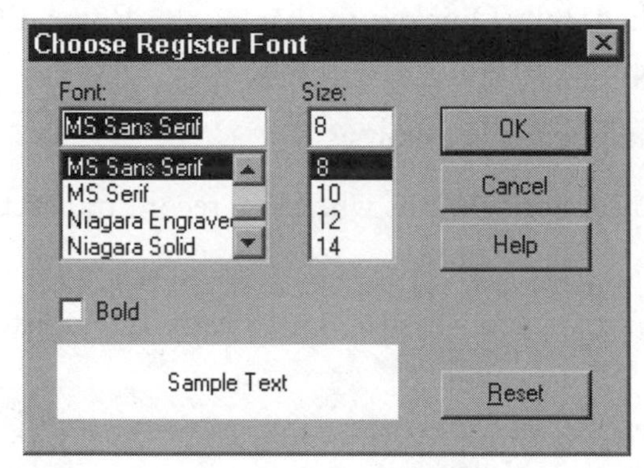

Figure 6.18: The Choose Register Font dialog box.

WARNING *Again, be careful when you make changes, because this option can leave you worse off than when you began. The default font is MS Sans Serif, a Windows font created for legibility on the computer screen. Other fonts, which may look elegant on paper, can be difficult to read on the screen.*

Changing Register Colors

Another button on the Display tab of the Register Options dialog box (choose Edit ➢ Options ➢ Register and click the Display tab) lets you change register colors. Click the Colors button to display the Choose Register Colors dialog box, shown in Figure 6.19. There are six possible account types in Quicken. Assigning colors to registers can help you distinguish them from one another and prevent mistaken entries in the wrong register.

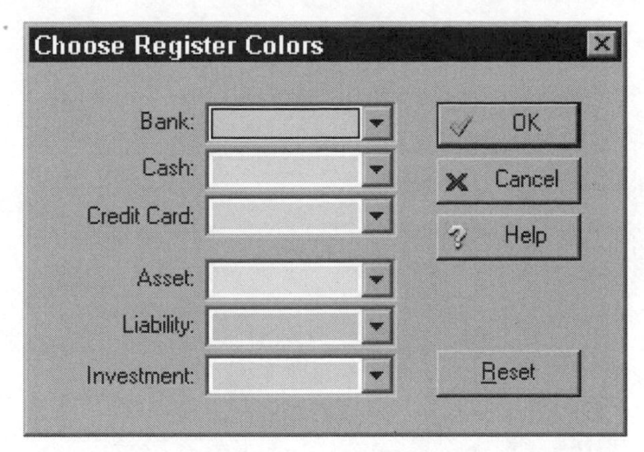

Figure 6.19: The Choose Register Colors dialog box.

To set a color for an account type, activate one of the drop-down list boxes—Bank, Cash, Credit Card, Asset, Liability, or Investment—and click your color of choice. Click OK to complete the selection. The Reset button allows you to return to Quicken's preset color scheme.

Chapter 7

PROTECTING YOUR FINANCIAL RECORDS

In This Chapter

- Backing up and restoring your data
- Using passwords to restrict access to financial data
- Physical security measures

If the information you're collecting with Quicken is important—and it almost certainly is—you'll want to take steps to protect that information. After all, if you're using Quicken as a personal financial record-keeping system, the Quicken data files may describe things such as your net worth, the cash you have available for things like retirement and next week's groceries, and which tax deductions you're entitled to. If you're using Quicken as a business record-keeping tool, the Quicken data files describe the assets you own and the liabilities you owe. They also contain the information necessary to calculate your profits.

Backing Up and Restoring Your Data

You've heard it perhaps a hundred times before, but I'm going to say it again: You need to back up your data files. You don't want to lose your financial records just because your hard disk fails or someone accidentally or intentionally deletes or corrupts the data files.

Quicken's "Hidden" Backup

Quicken has an elegant feature you may never be aware of unless you suffer a data loss disaster or are the type who likes to poke around on your hard disk. When Quicken is installed, it creates a subfolder named Backup. Periodically, as you leave a session with Quicken, your data is copied to the Backup folder without any notice to you.

This is a fine feature for those who delay or forget to make backups. If you lose or damage your main data file, you can use the File Ø Restore Backup File command, as described later in this chapter, to copy the Backup data to your Quicken folder. Remember, however, that this data will not survive the loss of your hard disk or computer. Keep on making backups to removable media so the data won't be lost if the computer is damaged or destroyed.

When you look at the Backup folder, you'll notice several different copies of your files there. If you're running low on disk space, you might want to delete all but the most recent copy of your files.

Backing Up Your Files

It's easy to back up the Quicken data files that contain your financial records. All you need to do is copy the data files to a floppy disk and store the floppy disk in a safe place.

WARNING *Store the backup disk at another location. You don't want whatever corrupts or destroys your original Quicken data files—a fire, a nefarious employee, a burglar, or whatever—to also corrupt or destroy your backup copy of the data files.*

To back up your Quicken data files, follow these steps:

1. Start Quicken and open the data file you want to back up. (If you've only created a single data file, you don't need to worry about first opening this file. Quicken automatically opens the file for you whenever it starts.)
2. Insert a removable disk into the drive you will use to create the backup. Floppy disks work for small Quicken data files. For large data files, you need to either use multiple floppy disks or a large removable disk such as a ZIP disk or recordable CD.
3. Choose File ➤ Backup to display the Quicken Backup dialog box, as shown in Figure 7.1.

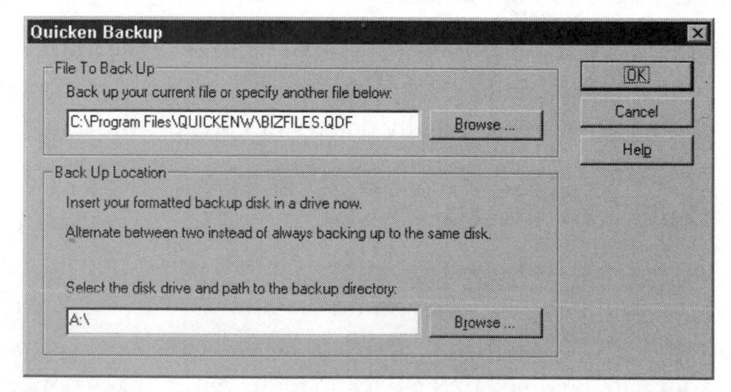

Figure 7.1: The Quicken Backup dialog box showing drive A as the backup drive.

4. In the Select The Disk Drive And Path To The Backup Directory field, select the drive you'll use to create the backup. You can either enter the drive letter or click the Browse button and then select the drive from the dialog box that Quicken displays.
5. Click OK to tell Quicken to begin backing up.

As Quicken backs up the data files, it displays a message box to tell you what it's doing. When it finishes, it displays another message box to tell you it has completed the backup. Click OK in this dialog box.

TIP *It's a good idea to have "backup backups"—in other words, different copies of files you've backed up. Let's say you back up every week and something (perhaps a power surge) happens that damages your Quicken data files. If you try to use the most recent week's backup disk to restore your financial records, you may find that it also has a problem. (Removable disks are more unreliable than hard disks.) But if you also have a backup copy from the previous week's backup operation, you can try it as a last resort. You can make backup backups by using two or three disks for your backups and then alternating your use of these disks. Use one disk for week 1, a second disk for week 2, and a third disk for week 3, and then start the cycle over again by using the first disk for week 4.*

Backup Reminder Messages

If you haven't recently backed up your file, Quicken displays a reminder message when you choose File ➤ Exit, as shown in Figure 7.2.

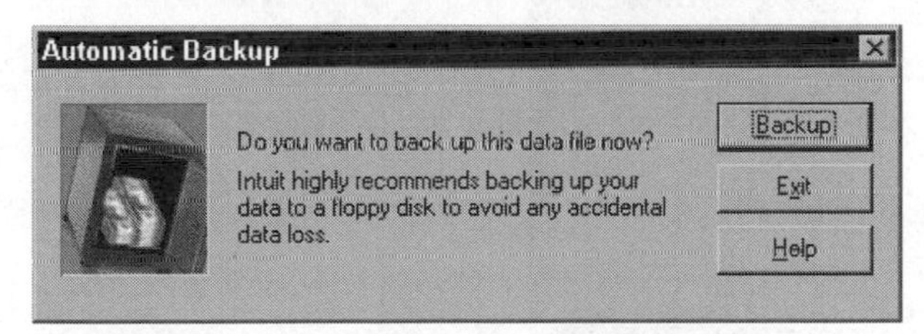

Figure 7.2: The backup reminder message.

You can choose to start the backup process described in the preceding paragraphs by selecting the Backup command button, which appears in the message box. Or you can exit without backing up by choosing the Exit command button, which also appears in the message box.

NOTE *One common data file problem is corruption of the index file that Quicken uses to organize your transaction data. Fortunately, if this index file becomes corrupted—if, for example, your computer loses power while Quicken is running—Quicken automatically rebuilds the index for you without requiring you to restore the entire set of Quicken data files. You will know if this happens; Quicken displays a message box telling you the index file is damaged and that it is rebuilding the file for you.*

How to Restore from a Backup in Seven Easy Steps

If your Quicken data files are corrupted, your problems are pretty minor as long as you have a recent backup copy of the data files to work with.

WARNING *If you don't back up your data and you lose your Quicken data files, you'll need to reenter all your transactions.*

To restore Quicken data files from the backup copy of the files, follow these steps:

1. Insert the disk with the backup copy of the Quicken data file into your floppy drive.
2. Choose File ➤ Restore Backup File. In the Select Restore Drive dialog box, choose the letter of the drive containing the backup disk. Click OK to display the Restore Quicken File dialog box, as shown in Figure 7.3.

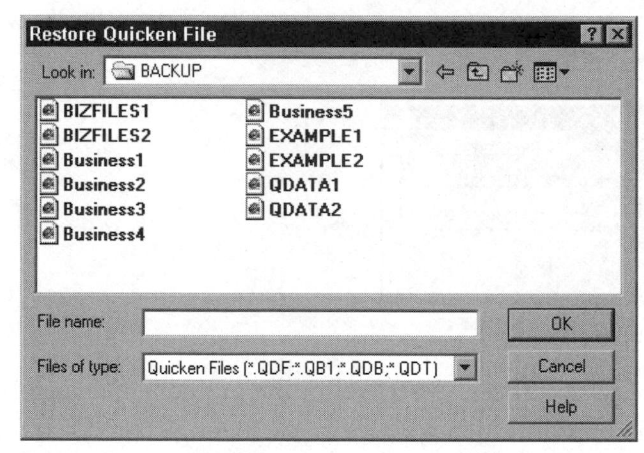

Figure 7.3: The Restore Quicken File dialog box.

3. If necessary, activate the Look In drop-down list box and select the drive and/or folder containing the backup disk.
4. Click the data file you want to restore.
5. Click OK. Quicken displays a message box asking you to confirm that you want to overwrite the current version of the file.

6. To restore the data file by replacing the current, hard-disk version of the data file with the backup copy stored on the floppy disk, click OK. Quicken displays a message box telling you that it's restoring the data file.
7. When the restoration is complete, click OK in the message box telling you that the file has been restored successfully.

Once you've copied the contents of the backup data files to your hard disk, you'll need to reenter each transaction that you recorded after you last backed up. If you've been printing registers, you can use them to get the information you need to reenter the transactions. If you haven't been printing registers, you'll need to use whatever other source documentation you have, such as bank statements, invoices, canceled checks, and so on.

TIP *Back up your Quicken data files immediately after you finish the restoration. It may be that whatever corrupted or damaged the original data file will again corrupt or damage it. This would be a good opportunity to start that second backup disk I suggested earlier in this chapter.*

Using Other Backup Utilities

You can use other backup utilities, such as the Windows Backup utility, to back up your Quicken data files. Simply follow the specific utility's instructions.

If you use another utility, keep in mind that you don't need to back up any of the Quicken program files (any files with the extension .BAT, .EXE, or .DLL). Just back up the Quicken data files—several individual files that make up the complete set of data files Quicken uses to store your financial records. Quicken uses the same filename as it uses for the Quicken program files, such as QDATA, but different extensions, such as .ABD, .QDB, .QDF, .QEL, .QSD, and so on. Therefore, make sure that you back up all the files that have either the QDATA filename Quicken supplies or the filename you've supplied.

Using Passwords to Restrict Access to Financial Data

Quicken also lets you assign passwords to files. Once you've done so, a person can neither use a file nor view its contents without first supplying the password. Quicken also lets you create a special type of password that limits the transaction dates that a person can use when entering transactions.

Locking Up a File by Assigning a Password

To lock up a file so no person without the password can access that file, assign a file-level password to the file. Simply follow these steps:

1. Choose File ➤ Passwords ➤ File to open the Quicken File Password dialog box, shown in Figure 7.4.

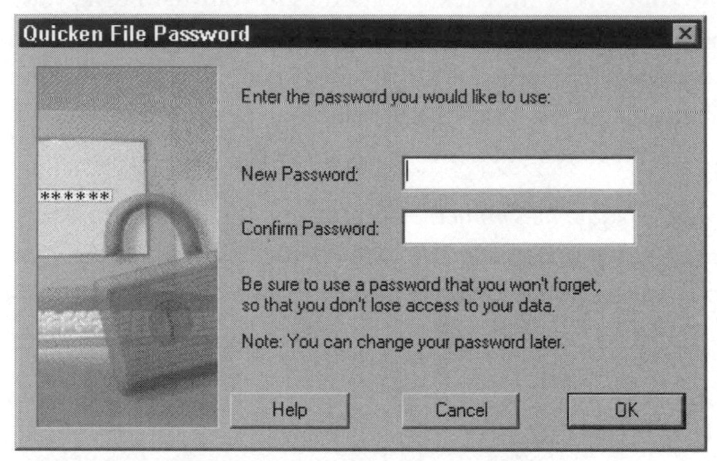

Figure 7.4: The Quicken File Password dialog box.

2. Enter the password you want to use in the New Password text box, enter the same password in the Confirm Password text box, and then click OK.

You can use any combination of characters. Be careful; Quicken 2002 differentiates between uppercase and lowercase characters. From Quicken's perspective, GLADIOLA, Gladiola, and gLADiola are all different passwords.

As you type the password, Quicken displays asterisks instead of the actual characters you type. This helps to prevent someone from looking over your shoulder and learning your password. But you should still be careful, because someone might be able to learn your password by watching which keys you type on your keyboard.

Quicken compares what you entered in the New Password text box with what you entered in the Confirm Password text box. As long as the two passwords are identical, Quicken closes the Quicken File Password dialog box. You now have a password.

If the two entries aren't identical, Quicken displays a message box alerting you to the error, and then Quicken redisplays the Quicken File Password dialog box. You'll need to enter the same password in both the New Password and Confirm Password text boxes.

WARNING *Don't forget your password! Forgetting a password has the same consequences as losing or corrupting your data files and not having a backup copy of the file: You will need to start all over from scratch. Keep a copy of your file password someplace safe. For example, if you use Quicken at work, you might want to keep a record of your password at home.*

You won't need to use the password as part of the current session. But the next time you or someone else tries to access the file (probably the next time you start Quicken), Quicken will display a dialog box like the one shown in Figure 7.5. You'll need to enter your password in order to access the file.

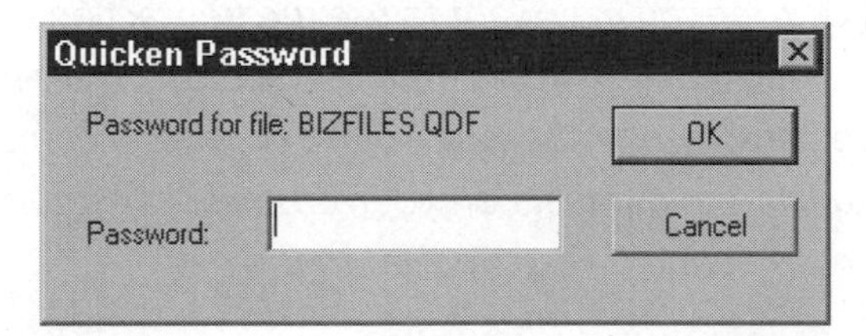

Figure 7.5: The Quicken Password dialog box.

Using a Transaction Password

Quicken also supplies another type of password, called a *transaction password.* This password prevents people who don't have the transaction password from entering transactions that fall before a certain date. For example, you might use a transaction password so that a new user can't accidentally foul up last year's financial records while entering this year's transactions.

To set up a transaction-level password, follow these steps:

1. Choose File ➤ Passwords ➤ Transaction. Quicken displays the Password To Modify Existing Transactions dialog box, shown in Figure 7.6.

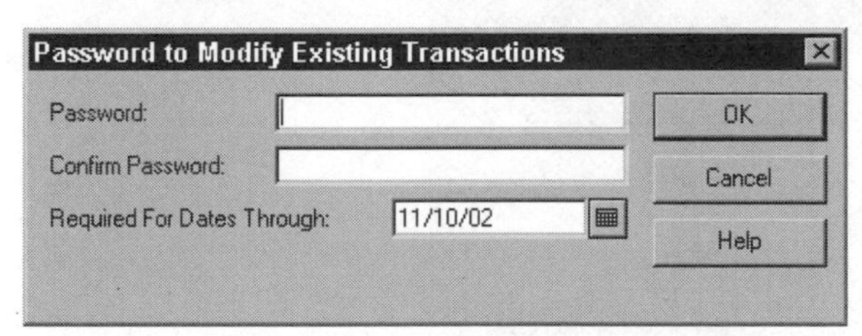

Figure 7.6: The Password To Modify Existing Transactions dialog box.

2. Enter the password you want to use in both the Password and Confirm Password text boxes. Unlike with file-level passwords Quicken doesn't differentiate between uppercase and lowercase characters for transaction passwords.

3. Enter the transaction date on or before which the user must supply the transaction-level password. Clicking the button at the right end of the text box opens a pop-up calendar you can use to choose a date. Click OK.

Quicken compares what you entered in the Password text box with what you entered in the Confirm Password text box. As long as the two passwords are identical, Quicken closes the Password To Modify Existing Transactions dialog box. Now Quicken will require you (and anyone else) to enter the transaction password before recording or editing a transaction dated on or before the specified transaction date.

TIP *For personal record keeping, the Transaction Password probably doesn't make sense. For business record keeping, however, you may want to use the transaction password to prevent inadvertent changes to the previous year's business records. "Freezing" your books in this way means that you or someone else won't make changes that mean your financial records no longer explain the numbers on your business tax return or the numbers on some profit and loss statement you supplied to the bank.*

Changing File-Level and Transaction-Level Passwords

You can change file-level and transaction-level passwords in the same way you add them. One change you can make is to replace a password with a blank password, which is the same as telling Quicken you no longer want to use a password.

Changing a File-Level Password

To change the file-level password, follow these steps:

1. Choose File ➤ Passwords ➤ File to display the Quicken File Password dialog box, shown in Figure 7.7.

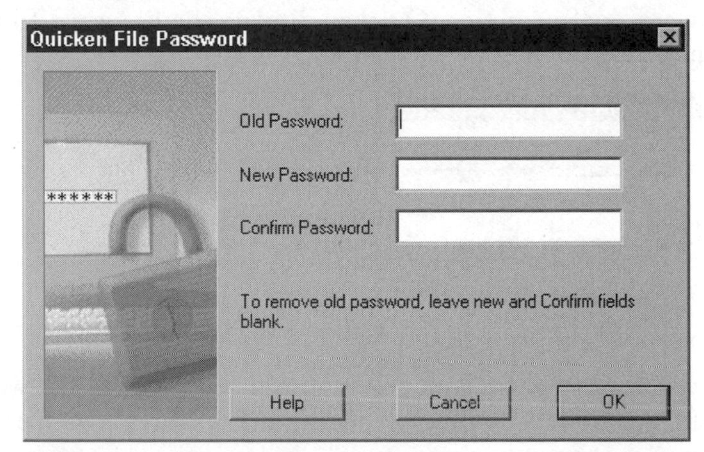

Figure 7.7: The Quicken File Password dialog box.

2. Enter the current file-level password in the Old Password text box.
3. Enter the replacement file-level password in the New Password text box and the Confirm Password text box. (If you want to just get rid of the file-level password and not supply a replacement, leave the New Password and the Confirm Password text boxes blank.) Click OK.

From this point forward, the new replacement password will control access to the file.

Changing a Transaction-Level Password

To change the transaction-level password, follow these steps:

1. Choose File ➢ Passwords ➢ Transaction to display the Change Transaction Password dialog box, shown in Figure 7.8.

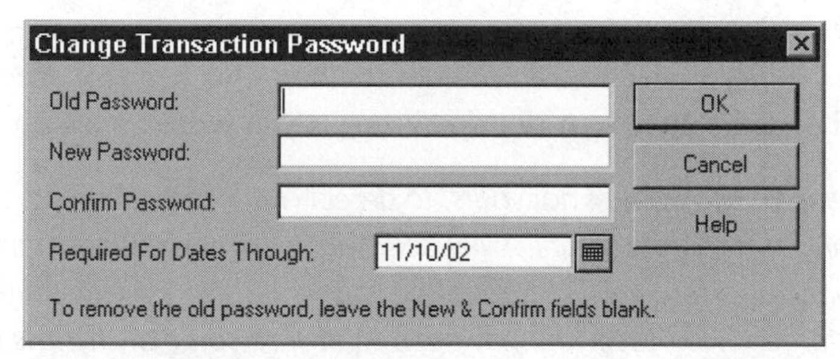

Figure 7.8 The Change Transaction Password dialog box.

2. Enter the current transaction-level password in the Old Password text box.
3. Enter the replacement transaction-level password in the New Password text box and in the Confirm Password text box. (If you want to just get rid of the transaction-level password and not supply a replacement, leave the New Password and Confirm Password text boxes blank.)
4. In the Required For Dates Through text box, enter the date that determines when a transaction-level password is required.
5. Click OK.

From this point forward, Quicken will require the new transaction password whenever anyone attempts to enter a transaction or modify a transaction that falls on or before the cut-off date you specified in step 4.

Physical Security Measures

In terms of computer security, it's easy to focus on things like file backups and passwords. But don't forget about other physical security measures.

If you're using Quicken in a business, for example, it's a good idea to restrict access to the computer that runs the Quicken program and on which the Quicken data files are stored. With computers as relatively inexpensive as they are, for example, you might want to dedicate a computer to Quicken and prohibit people from using the computer for other things. (Large businesses routinely restrict access to their computer systems by providing tighter security and controlled access to their management information systems areas.)

You might want to put the computer that runs Quicken and stores the data files in a locked office. This deterrent wouldn't stop a determined criminal, of course; but with every obstacle you put in the path of a thief, you decrease your chances of becoming a victim.

Another physical measure relates to the check forms you use. Be sure to use a signature that's not easily duplicated (forged). Signatures that consist of a wavy line and a couple of i-dots (or are those t-crosses?) aren't going to be easily detected as forgeries by anyone—including yourself. And while you don't need to worry about the way Quicken fills out a check, be sure to carefully and completely fill out the check forms you write by hand.

NOTE *It's usually the bank's responsibility, not yours, to detect check forgeries. Forgery is any altering or marking that changes your liability, so filling in extra words and numbers on a check form constitutes forgery. It might not be you who suffers the loss if you are a victim of check forgery. However, you may need to absorb some of the loss if you're negligent or if you delay reporting a forgery to the bank.*

Chapter 8

GRAPHING YOUR FINANCES

In This Chapter

- How to create your first graph in 60 seconds
- Memorizing the graph
- Printing the active graph
- QuickZooming on a graph's data markers
- Looking at the other graphs
- Customizing Quicken's graphing

Tabular presentations of quantitative information, such as the Quicken reports with their rows and columns of data, work well when you want access to the details or when you want to-the-dollar or to-the-penny precision. Sometimes, though, a graph works better. Graphs summarize your financial data in a picture, often display trends you might otherwise miss, and sometimes let you see—or at least detect—relationships in the graphed data that otherwise would remain hidden.

NOTE *You don't need any special skills or knowledge to graph data with Quicken. You do, however, need to have collected the data you want to graph by keeping records of your financial affairs using the Quicken registers.*

How to Create Your First Graph in 60 Seconds

To create a graph, you simply choose a few commands from menus and tell Quicken which information you want it to graph. To illustrate how this approach works, suppose that you want to plot a graph that shows your income and expenses over several months.

The Income/Expense Graph

To create an Income/Expense graph, follow these steps:

1. Choose Reports ➢ Reports And Graphs Center to display the Reports And Graphs window, as shown in Figure 8.1.

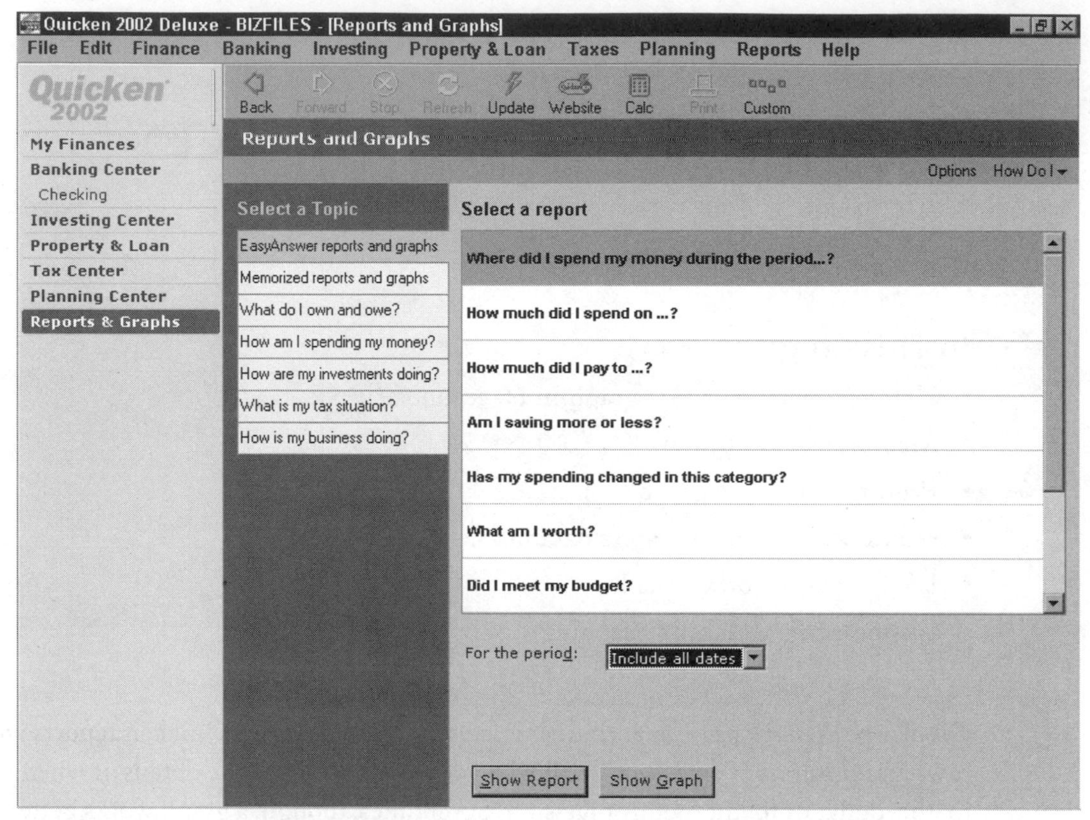

Figure 8.1: The Reports And Graphs window.

2. If necessary, click the EasyAnswer Reports And Graphs tab so that Quicken displays its list of EasyAnswer reports.
3. Verify that the Where Did I Spend My Money During The Period? tab is selected.
4. Tell Quicken for what time period it should graph, using the For The Period drop-down list box. The drop-down list box contains descriptions such as Year To Date or Current Quarter.
5. Click the Show Graph button. Quicken plots your spending in a bar graph, as shown in Figure 8.2.

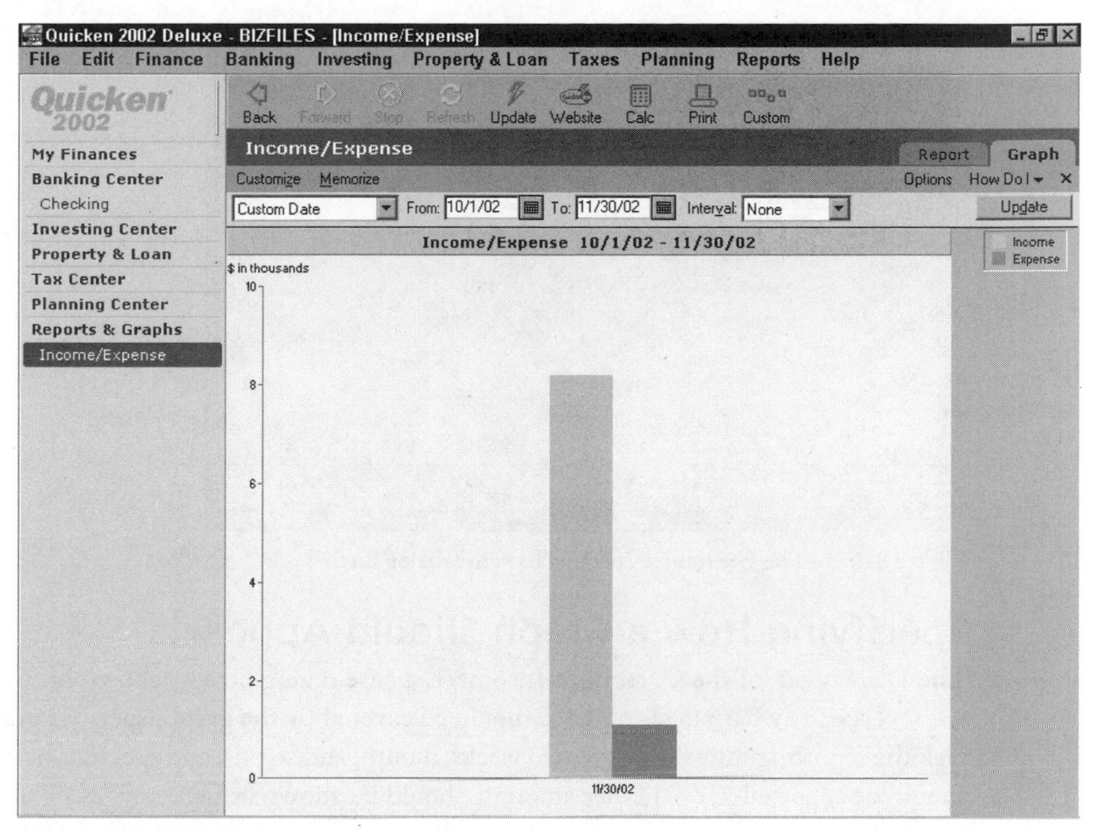

Figure 8.2: The Income/Expense graph.

TIP *If you want to use more precision in the time period than was possible in step 3, use the From and To boxes to provide specific starting and ending dates. For example, to plot income and expense data from November 26, 1999, through April 8, 2002, enter 11/26/99 into the From text box and 4/8/02 into the To box.*

Customizing the Graph

The Customize button, which appears in the top-left corner of the Graph window, displays a Customize dialog box in which you can make changes to the graph. If you've created an Income/Expense graph and you click Customize, you see the Customize Income/Expense dialog box, as shown in Figure 8.3. This version of the Customize dialog box works similarly to the other versions of the Customize dialog box, so let me briefly describe each of the options it provides.

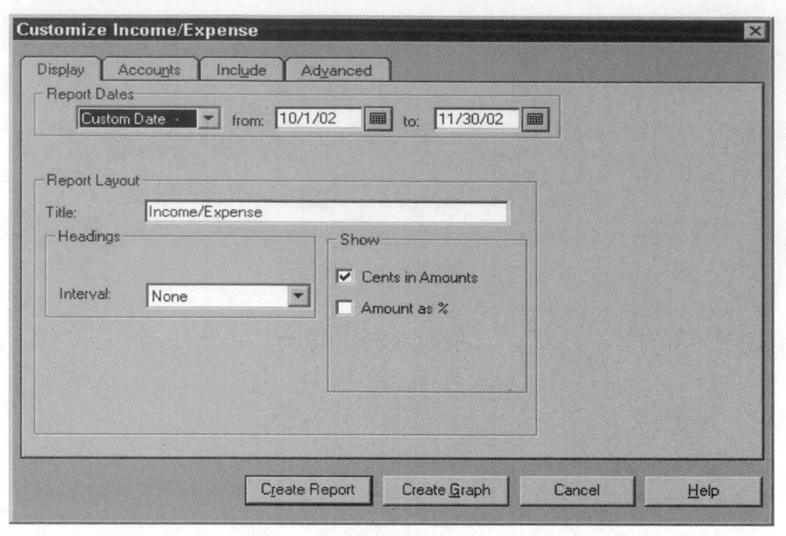

Figure 8.3: The Customize Income/Expense dialog box.

Specifying How a Graph Should Appear

The Display tab of the Customize Income/Expense dialog box, as shown in Figure 8.3, lets you specify what ranges of dates should be covered by the graph, specify a graph title, pick the reporting interval (week, two weeks, month, and so on), and specify whether cents should be reported and whether amounts should be shown as percentages.

Choosing Which Accounts to Graph

The Accounts tab lets you specify which accounts should have their transactions included in a graph. Quicken assumes that all the accounts in a file should be included in a graph. If you want to select specific accounts, click the Customize button in the Create Graph window to open the Customize Income/Expense dialog box. If it is not already showing, click the Accounts tab, which is shown in Figure 8.4. Select an account category by clicking the Bank, Cash, Credit Card, Investment, Asset, or Liability buttons. Select and deselect the accounts to use within an account category by clicking each account or pressing the spacebar. The spacebar and clicking act as toggle switches: they alternately mark an account to be included and then not to be included.

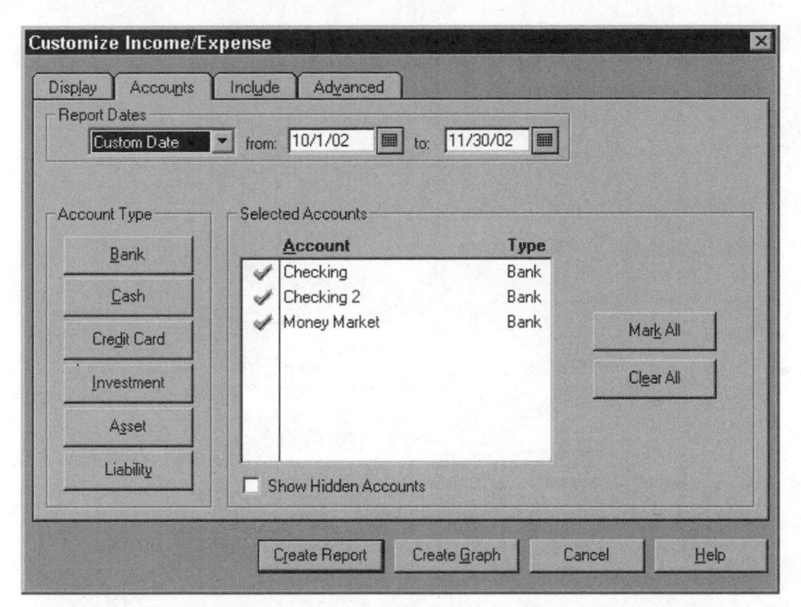

Figure 8.4: The Accounts tab of the Customize Income/Expense dialog box.

Choosing Categories, Classes, and Payees to Graph

The Include tab lets you specify which categories you want plotted in a graph. Quicken assumes that all your categories should be included in a report. If you want to designate categories to plot, mark the Categories option button in the Customize Income/Expense dialog box, which is shown in Figure 8.5. Select and deselect the categories to use by clicking each category in the Category list or pressing the spacebar.

If you want to filter the transactions based on the payee name, category, class or memo, enter the criteria you want to use in the Payee Contains, Category Contains, Class Contains, or Memo Contains boxes. As described in Chapter 2, Quicken lets you use wildcard characters that you can use in your filter criteria.

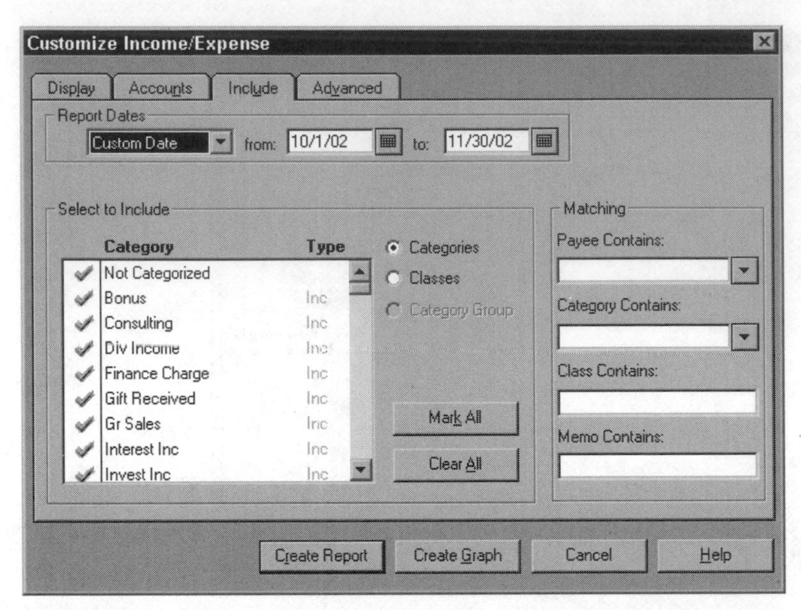

Figure 8.5: The Include tab of the Customize Income/Expense dialog box.

Quicken assumes that you want to graph data from all classes. If you want to designate classes to graph, mark the Classes option button. Designate classes in the same way that you select specific accounts or categories.

Other Graph Customization Options

The Advanced tab of the Customize Income/Expense dialog box supplies still another set of customization options for your graphs, as shown in Figure 8.6. Like the other tabs, the Advanced tab lets you specify a reporting date. The Advanced tab lets you select transactions based on the transaction amount (use the Amounts boxes), the taxable status (use the Tax-Related Transactions Only checkbox), type of transaction (use the Transaction Types drop-down list box), and the transaction status (use the Blank, Newly Cleared, and Reconciled checkboxes). The Advanced tab also lets you specify which transfer transactions get included or excluded from the graph (use the Transfers drop-down list box) and whether subcategories should appear (use the Subcategories drop-down list box).

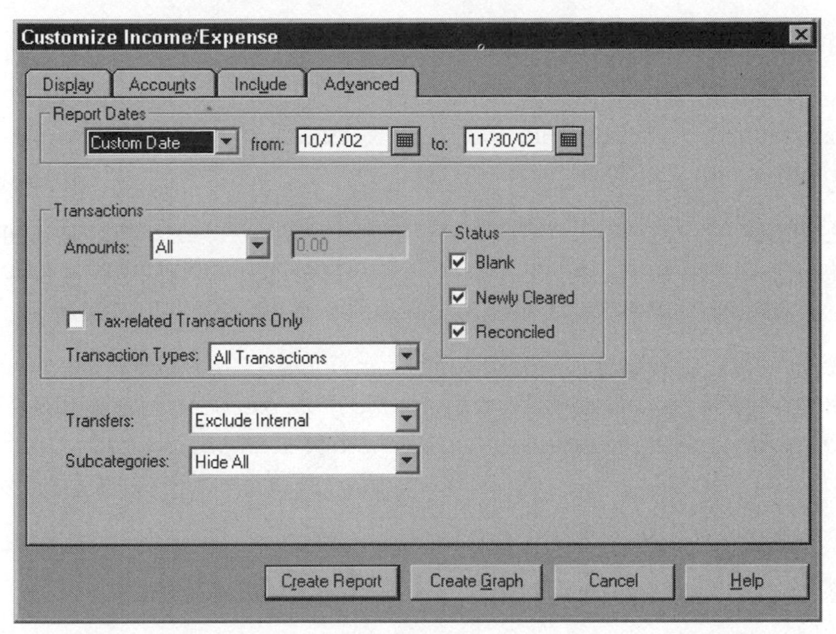

Figure 8.6: The Advanced tab of the Customize Income/Expense dialog box.

Memorizing the Graph

Just as you can "memorize" reports, you can memorize graphs. By doing so, you can save any special graph creation settings, such as the accounts or categories you want to use. The graph-memorization process works in the same way as the report-memorization process. Once you've produced a graph you want to save for future use, click the Memorize button in the Graph document window. When Quicken displays the Memorize Graph dialog box, as shown in Figure 8.7, give the memorized graph a name and click OK.

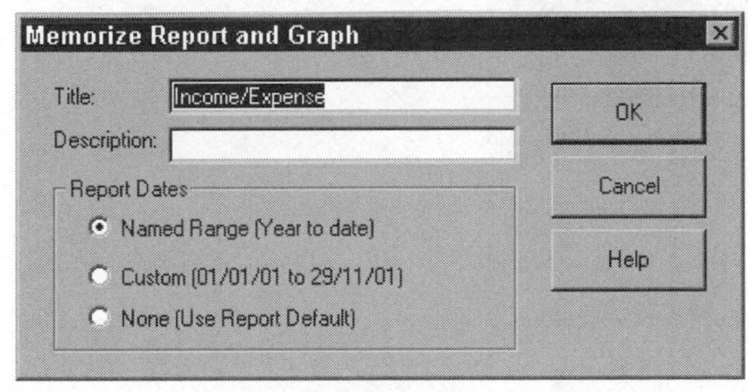

Figure 8.7: The Memorize Graph dialog box.

The next time you want to display the graph, choose Reports ➢ Memorized Reports And Graphs and select the name of the memorized graph from the menu that Quicken displays.

Printing the Active Graph

To print the graph shown in the Quicken window, choose File ➢ Print Report/Graph or click the Print button. Quicken sends the graph to Windows to begin the work of printing your graph.

Graphs are more work to print than text, so it takes longer to print a page of graphs than a page of report information. As Quicken and Windows work to print your graph, you'll see a message box on your screen telling you that the graph is being printed.

NOTE *Two-dimensional graphs like the one shown in Figure 8.2 may look less interesting than the three-dimensional variety, but they are also more precise visually. If you want to add interest (perhaps at the expense of precision) to your graphs by plotting them in three dimensions, see the last section of this chapter, "Customizing Quicken's Graphing."*

QuickZooming on a Graph's Data Markers

Data markers are the symbols that a graph (or chart) uses to show its information. These include the bars in a bar chart, the slices in a pie chart, and so on. If you want more information about a particular data marker's data—say, you want to see another graph that further describes a slice of a pie chart—you can use QuickZoom. The cursor changes to a magnifying glass when it points to a data marker. Just double-click the data marker you want to further explore. Quicken draws another graph, which shows information about the selected data marker. If you use QuickZoom on an Income/Expense bar graph to get more information about your income, for example, QuickZoom produces a report that details your income, as shown in Figure 8.8.

Income Comparison (10/1/02 - 11/30/02)

Category	Amount	Percentage
Consulting	6,200.00	75.61%
Gr Sales	2,000.00	24.39%

Figure 8.8: A QuickZoom report lets you see details of the graph data.

TIP *Sometimes when you QuickZoom on a data marker, Quicken produces a QuickZoom graph. In this case, you can even QuickZoom on a QuickZoom graph.*

TIP *If you begin using QuickZoom to create QuickZoom reports, you'll very quickly create a collection of Graph document windows. Remember that you can individually close windows by clicking the Close button. This is the little x button in the upper-right corner.*

Looking at the Other Graphs

Quicken produces several graphs in addition to the Income/Expense graph just described. If you choose one of the reports from the Reports And Graphs Center, and you have the option of producing a graphic version of the report (rather than the usual tabular version), Quicken places a Create Graph button at the bottom of the Reports And Graphs window, as shown in Figure 8.9.

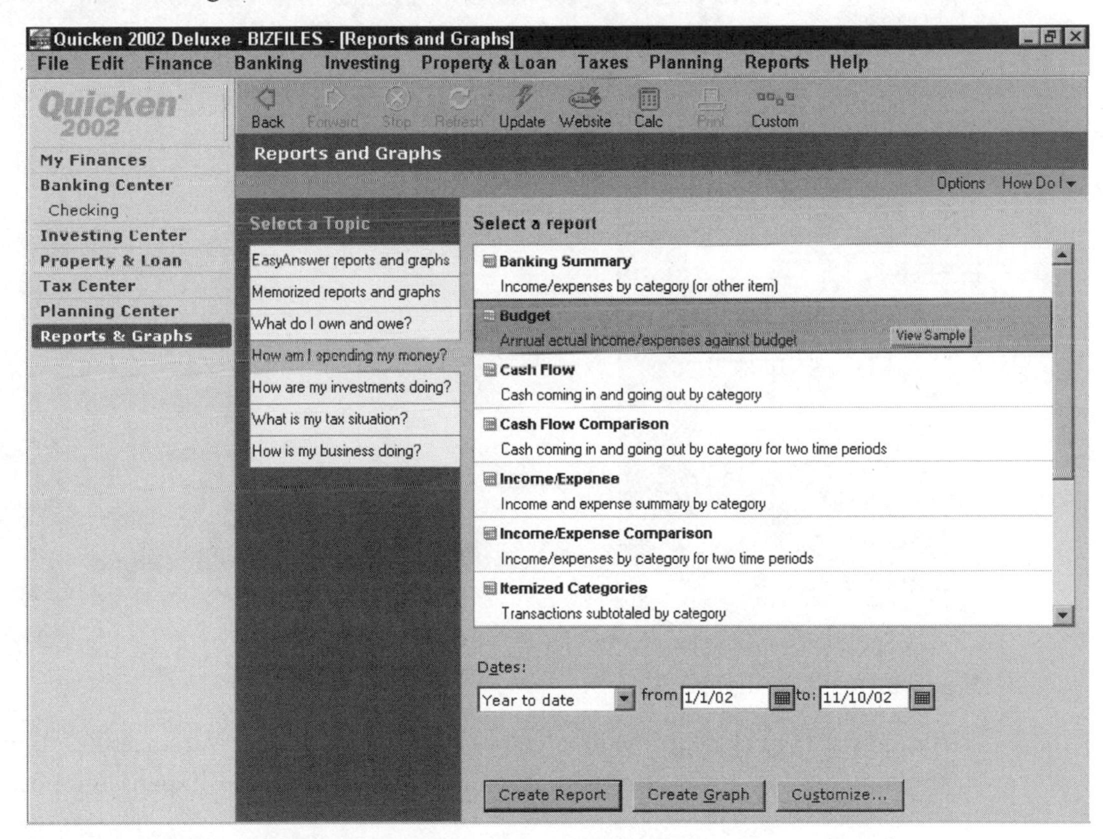

Figure 8.9: The Reports And Graphs window with the Budget report selected.

The Budget Variance Graph

A Budget Variance graph compares your actual income and expense to your budgeted income and expense. To create this graph, you must first have created a budget (see Chapter 14, which explains how to create budgets). Then you follow a procedure similar to that used for creating an Income and Expense graph. Choose Reports ➢ Reports And Graphs Center. Select the How Am I Spending My Money? tab, select the Budget report, and then click the Create button.

Figure 8.10 shows the Budget graph. The graph shows the monthly actual income and budgeted income.

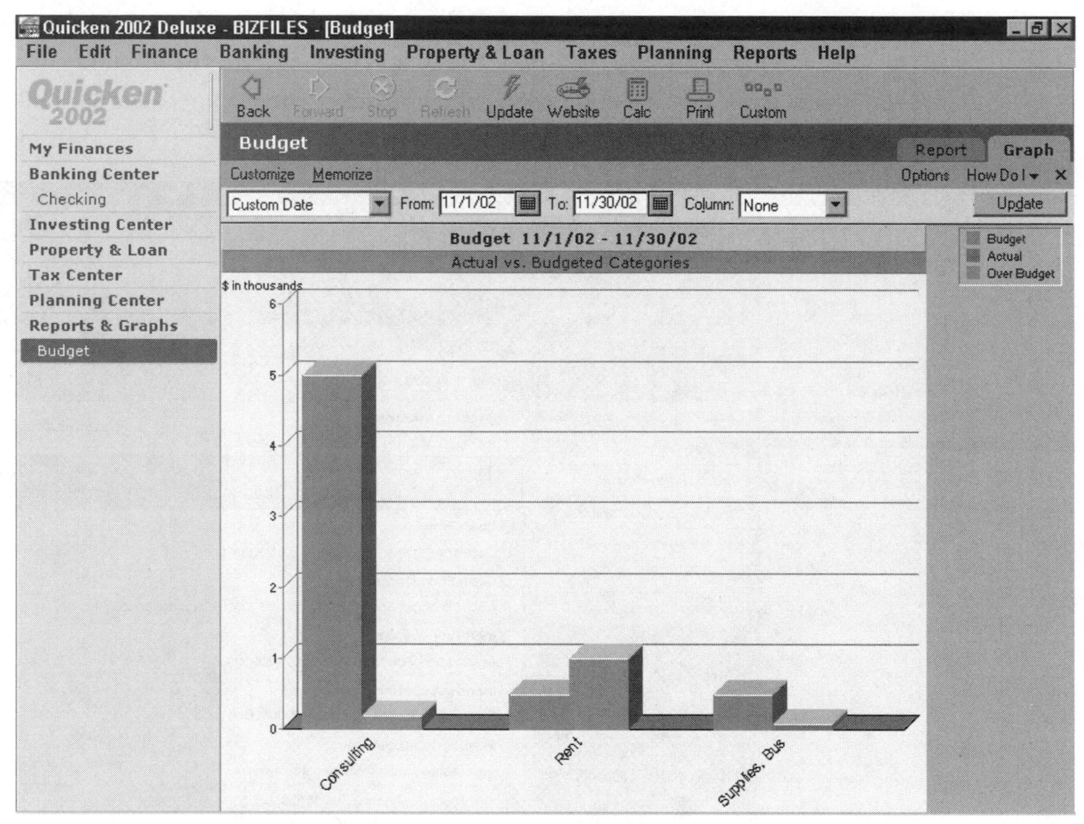

Figure 8.10: A Budget graph.

You can print, QuickZoom on data markers, and close Budget Variance Graph windows in the same way that you print, QuickZoom, and close Income/Expense graphs.

The Net Worth Graph

A Net Worth graph shows your total assets, total liabilities, and resulting net worth on a month-to-month basis. To create this graph, follow the same basic procedure you use to create Income/Expense and Budget Variance graphs. First, choose Reports ➢ Reports And Graphs Center and select the What do I Own and Owe? tab. Then select the Net Worth report and click the Create Graph button. Quicken displays the Net Worth graph. Figure 8.11 shows an example Net Worth graph. Quicken uses bars to show your total assets and your total liabilities. It uses a small square to represent the net value, or your net worth, within each bar. It then draws a line to plot your net worth.

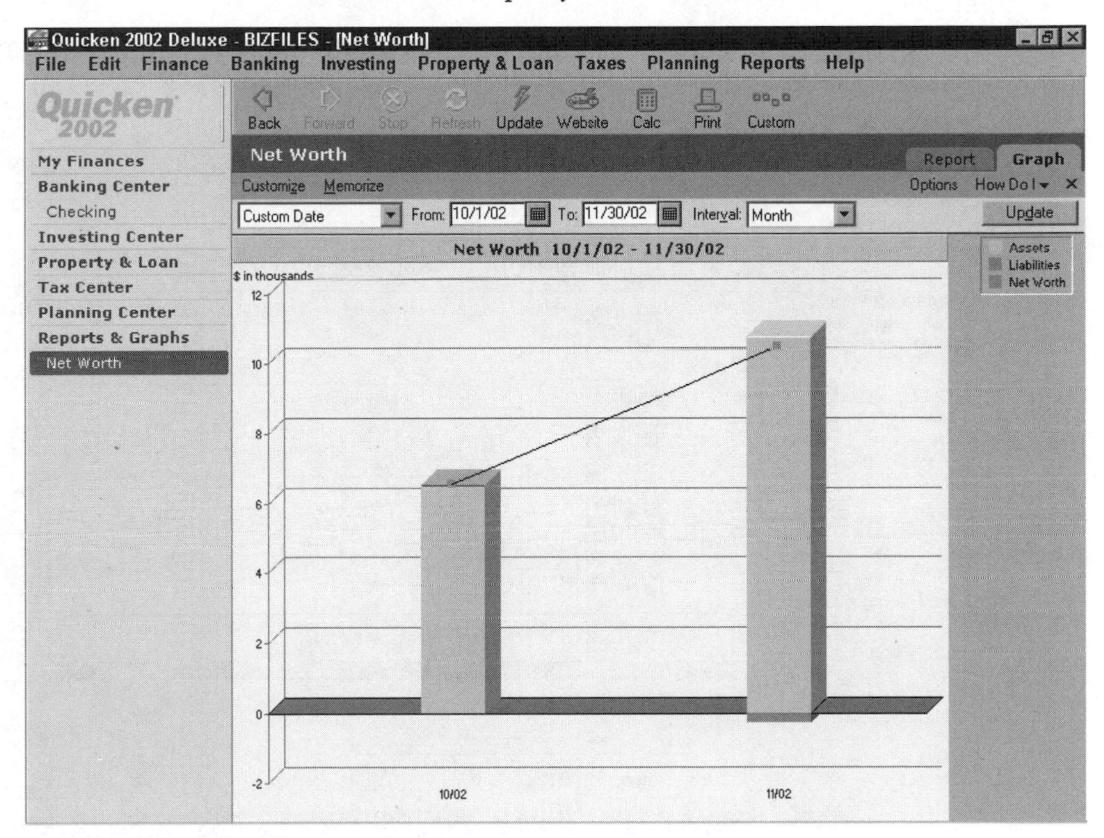

Figure 8.11: A Net Worth graph.

TIP *You can click any area of a graph to display the exact amount of the data being plotted.*

You can print, QuickZoom on data markers, and close the Net Worth Graph window in the same way that you print, QuickZoom, and close other Graph document windows.

The Investment Graphs

If you're using Quicken for your investment record keeping, you can produce a bar chart that shows your investment allocations, investment performance, and portfolio values. To produce these sorts of graphs, you need to have begun using Quicken for investment record keeping to produce an investment graph, as explained in Chapters 20, 21, and 22.)

To produce an investment graph, choose Reports ➢ Reports And Graphs Center and select the How Are My Investments Doing? tab. Select the investment report you want to produce and click the Create Graph button. Figure 8.12 shows an Investment Performance graph.

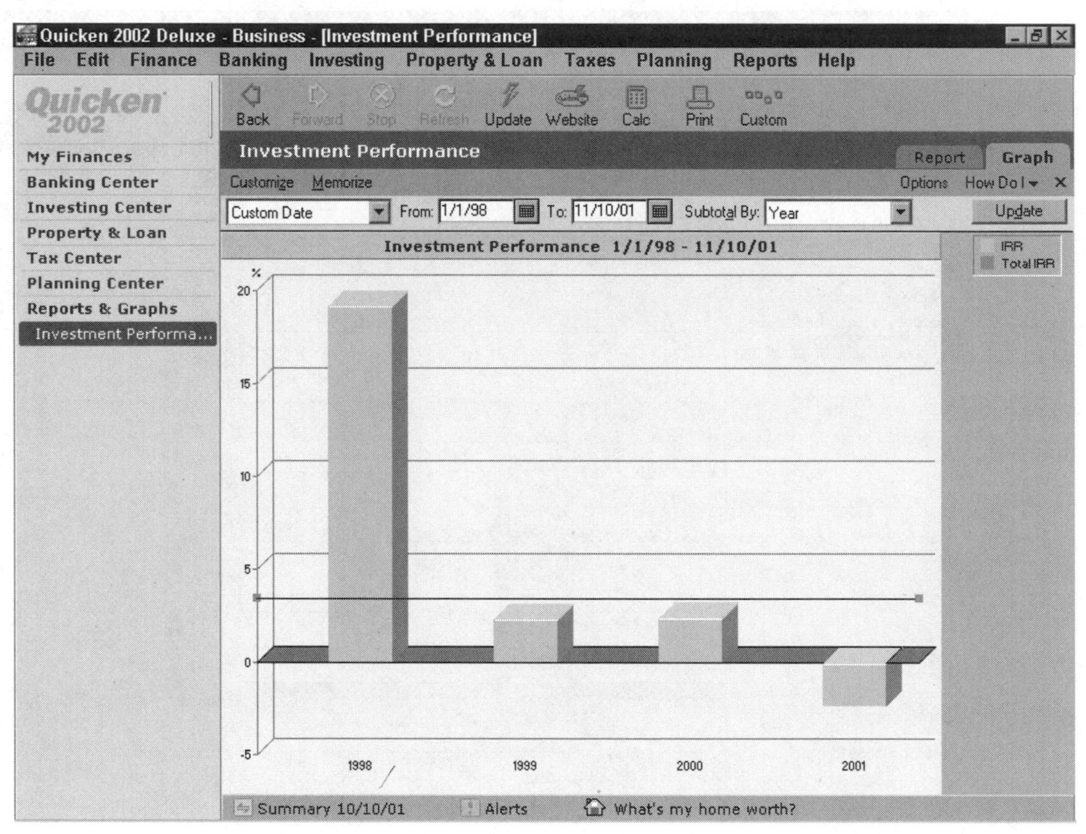

Figure 8.12: An Investment Performance graph.

Customizing Quicken's Graphing

Once you're comfortable using Quicken graphs, you can change the way Quicken draws and prints your graphs. To change the way Quicken draws many of the graphs you see and the way it prints them, click the Options button in the Graph window. Quicken displays the Reports And Graph Options dialog box, as shown in Figure 8.13.

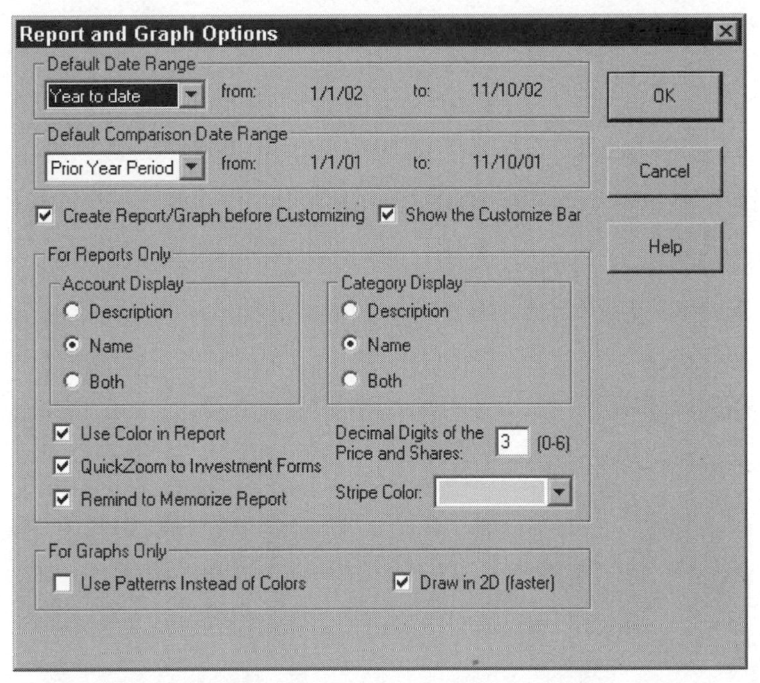

Figure 8.13: The Report And Graph Options dialog box.

Near the bottom of this dialog box, Quicken provides two checkboxes that let you control how graphs get plotted:

- **Use Patterns Instead Of Colors** By default, Quicken displays graphs on screen with colored segments. When you select this option, Quicken displays all graphs using black-and-white patterns on the screen.
- **Draw In 2D (Faster)** If you want to use more precise, two-dimensional pie and bar graphs, select this option.

NOTE *Some people feel that pie charts don't do a very good job of summarizing data because they can be used to visually depict only small data sets. A report is usually a much better way to show a small data set. Also, making pie charts three-dimensional distorts the slices of the pie; those in the background appear smaller than they are, while those in the foreground appear larger.*

Chapter 9

ONLINE PAYMENTS AND BANKING

In This Chapter

- Online Payment
- Online Account Access

Quicken lets you simplify your financial affairs using its Online Payment and Online Account Access features. With Online Payment, you can automatically make payments for items you record in your Quicken registers. In essence, you tell either Intuit's computer or a bank's computer to use the information you've recorded about a particular payment to actually make the disbursement. With Online Account Access, you can transfer money between accounts set up for online banking and download account transaction information. This chapter describes both Online Payment and Online Account Access.

Before You Begin

To use Quicken's Online Payment and Online Account Access features, you need the following:

- Your computer must have a connection to the Internet. (This means you need to have signed up for and set up dial-up Internet access with a service provider such as America Online or Microsoft's MSN or have set up an always-on, high-bandwidth connection such as with a cable modem or DSL adapter.)
- To use the Online Account Access feature, your bank must support Quicken's online banking functions.

NOTE *Currently, several dozen banks support online banking. To see if your bank supports online banking, choose Finance ➢ Online Financial Institutions List.*

Online Payment

Quicken lets you pay bills electronically using Online Payment. With Online Payment, you use the Internet to transmit information to another computer about the bills that you need to pay. Then the computer writes a check from your account to pay your bills for you.

Is Online Bill Payment for You?

Why would you use a service like Online Payment? Online bill payment delivers a major benefit. For the same work you go through to record payments in a Quicken register, you can also pay a bill. If you pay a bill with a check, you still need to print or handwrite that check, and then stuff, address, and mail the envelope.

NOTE *The cost of the online bill payment service varies, depending on your bank. Currently, my bank charges $9.95 a month. Does the price of the service seem expensive? If you consider how much it costs to mail in a payment ($.34 at this writing), it's not so bad. And the check form you use to pay a bill may not be cheap. (For business checks and computer checks, you can easily pay a dime a form.) Using Online Payment can actually save you money.*

There are only two potential drawbacks to using an online bill payment service. One is that it does require you to be a bit more organized in your bill paying. You need to transmit electronic payment information to the online bill payment service a few days early so that the service has time to process your payment. If you're always juggling those last few bills, this might not work. If you pay the mortgage with a handwritten check, for example, you may want the option of paying the mortgage on the last day and personally running the check down to the bank.

Another potential drawback is that some merchants don't like to deal with electronic payments. Reportedly, some banks with their own online bill payment services have balked at accepting electronic bill payments through Intuit or another financial institution. To be quite candid, I have had trouble paying some of my bills electronically, which is somewhat understandable. Electronic payments can be a little confusing to merchants. The checks don't look exactly like regular checks. (They aren't signed, for example.) And there's no way to include a remittance advice or payment coupon.

An Online Bill Payment Service Choice

As of this writing, Quicken 2002 also supports CheckFree, another online bill payment service. Intuit (the company that makes and sells Quicken) has said that Online Payment is a better value for customers. Here are a few reasons why Online Payment might be the better choice:

- The financial transactions may be handled directly by your bank, rather than by the CheckFree Corporation. If you are also using Online Account Access, this makes one less company to deal with. It also means that you work with a local service.
- Online Payment implements several helpful details in the service, such as automatic confirmation of payments and automatic adjustment of lead time, depending on the method of payment.

Note, however, that Intuit recently sold the Online Payment service to the same company that owns and runs CheckFree. So, in practice, there probably will be less and less difference between the two services as time goes by. CheckFree operates in a manner very similar to Online Payment. You can use CheckFree by choosing the Banking Ø Banking Services Ø Set Up CheckFree command.

Signing Up for Online Bill Payment Services

You sign up for an online bill payment service by filling out the Online Services Agreement that comes in the Quicken package or by filling out forms that are available through your bank. You may need to include a voided check with your sign-up paperwork.

For information and instructions about this process, display the register for the account you want to set up for online payment or banking. Click the Options button and then choose View Online Setup. When Quicken displays the Set Up Quicken Online Account Services information, as shown in Figure 9.1, click the hyperlinks provided to research the service, apply for a PIN, and set up online bill payment for your account.

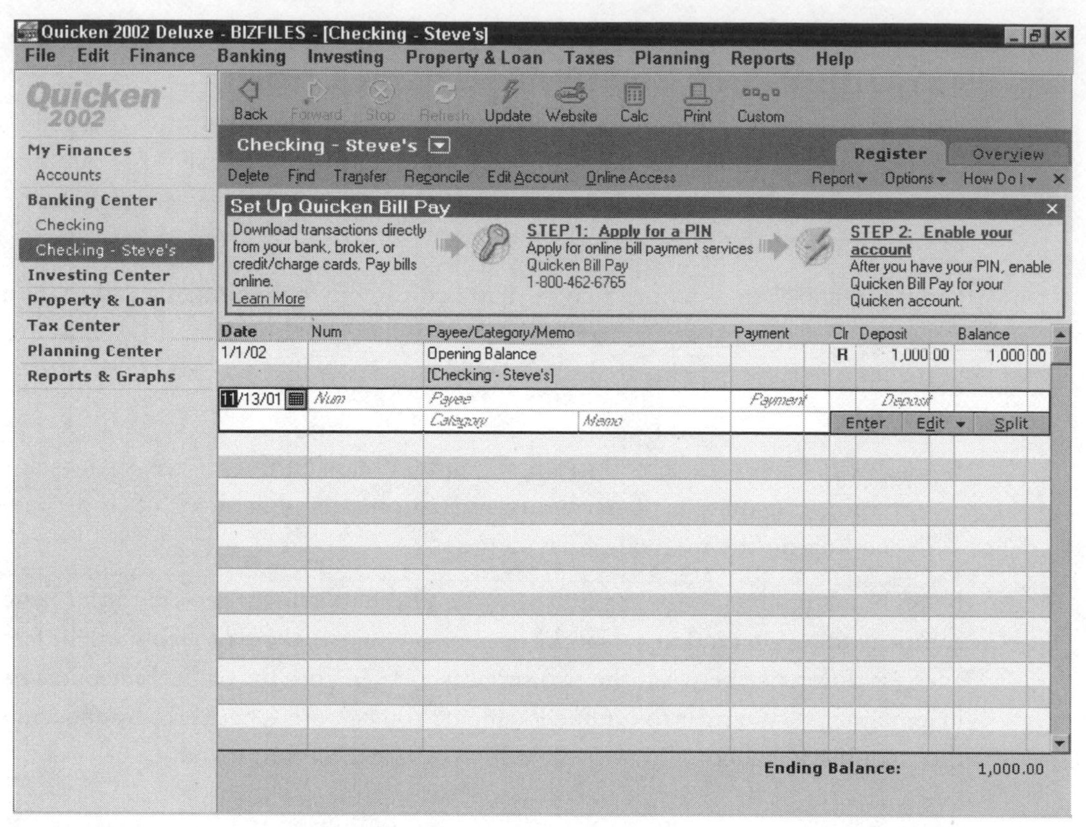

Figure 9.1: The account register showing Quicken online payment setup information.

A few days after you sign up for service, you will get a welcome letter from either your bank or Intuit Services Corporation. The letter provides the information you need to set up Quicken for the online bill payment service.

Using Online Bill Payment

If you know how Quicken works, you'll have no trouble with Online Bill Pay. Once you've told Quicken that you want to use the Online Bill Pay feature with a particular account, the only extra tasks you need to complete are building a list of electronic payees (the merchants, banks, and individuals that the online bill payment service pays) and learning to electronically transmit payment instructions to the online bill payment service center.

Marking an Account for Online Bill Pay

To tell Quicken you want to use Online Bill Pay with an account, follow these steps:

1. Display the account's register and click the Overview tab.
2. Click the Available, Not Enabled hyperlink beside Quicken Bill Pay. This displays the Edit Bank Account dialog box shown in Figure 9.2.

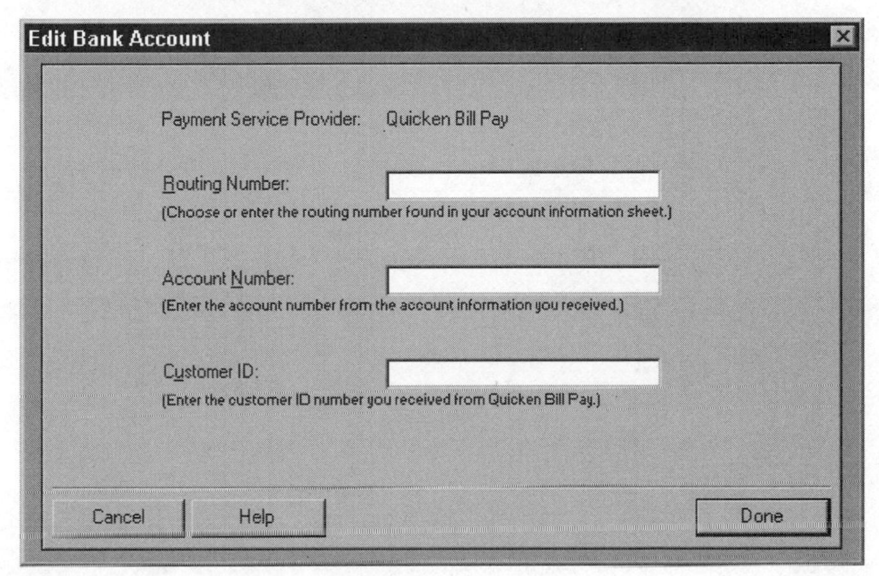

Figure 9.2: The Edit Bank Account dialog box.

3. Enter your bank's routing number. The welcome letter that you got from your bank or Intuit supplies this information.
4. Enter your account number.
5. Enter your customer ID number (this is usually your Social Security number).
6. Click Done.

Describing Electronic Payees

To set up Online Payment, you need to create a list of the merchants you pay regularly. To do this, choose Banking ➤ Online Payees List. Quicken displays the Online Payee List window, as shown in Figure 9.3.

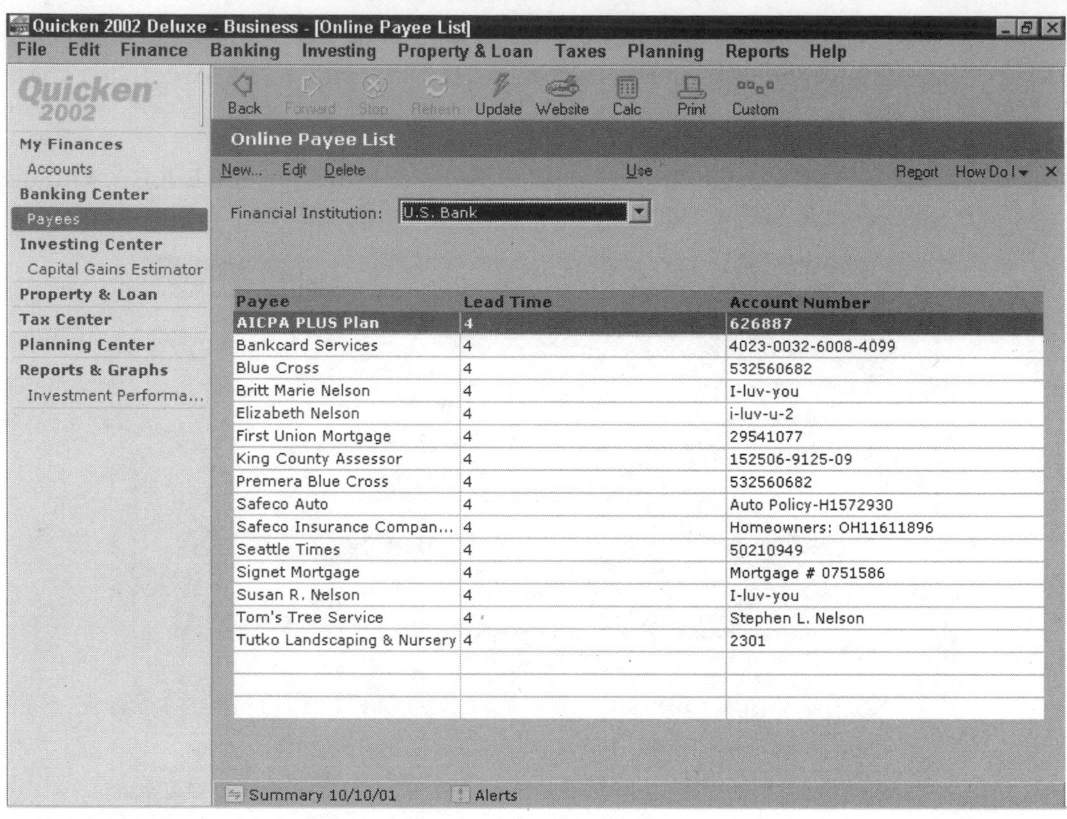

Payee	Lead Time	Account Number
AICPA PLUS Plan	4	626887
Bankcard Services	4	4023-0032-6008-4099
Blue Cross	4	532560682
Britt Marie Nelson	4	I-luv-you
Elizabeth Nelson	4	i-luv-u-2
First Union Mortgage	4	29541077
King County Assessor	4	152506-9125-09
Premera Blue Cross	4	532560682
Safeco Auto	4	Auto Policy-H1572930
Safeco Insurance Compan...	4	Homeowners: OH11611896
Seattle Times	4	50210949
Signet Mortgage	4	Mortgage # 0751586
Susan R. Nelson	4	I-luv-you
Tom's Tree Service	4	Stephen L. Nelson
Tutko Landscaping & Nursery	4	2301

Figure 9.3: The Online Payee List window.

To describe an electronic payee, click the New button. Quicken displays the Set Up Online Payee dialog box, as shown in Figure 9.4.

Set Up Online Payee
Name and Address
Name:
Description: (Optional)
Street:
City:
State:
Zip:
Payee Numbers
Account #:
Phone:
OK
Cancel
Help

Figure 9.4: The Set Up Online Payee dialog box.

Follow these steps to fill in the dialog box:

1. In the Name text box, enter the name of the electronic payee as shown on the last billing statement or invoice.
2. Optionally, enter a brief description of the payee.
3. Enter the street address in the first Street text box and the post office box in the second text box. Be sure to enter the exact same address here that you use when you're mailing payments to the payee.
4. Enter the city, state, and zip code into the text boxes provided.
5. Enter the account number the payee uses to identify your account into the Account # text box. You should be able to get this number from your last bill or statement.
6. In the Phone text box, enter the telephone number you're supposed to call if you have a billing question. When I don't have a telephone number for the online payee, I just enter my own telephone number. What this means is that if the online bill payment service has problems making the payment and calls this number, at least I'll learn of the problem.
7. Click OK.
8. Review the information in the Confirm Online Payee Information dialog box and click Accept.

If you have additional payees to describe, click the New button in the Online Payee List window and repeat steps 1 through 8.

Paying a Bill with Online Payment

To pay a bill with Online Payment, choose Banking ➢ Online Banking. When Quicken displays the Online Center window, click the Payments tab. Figure 9.5 shows this tab.

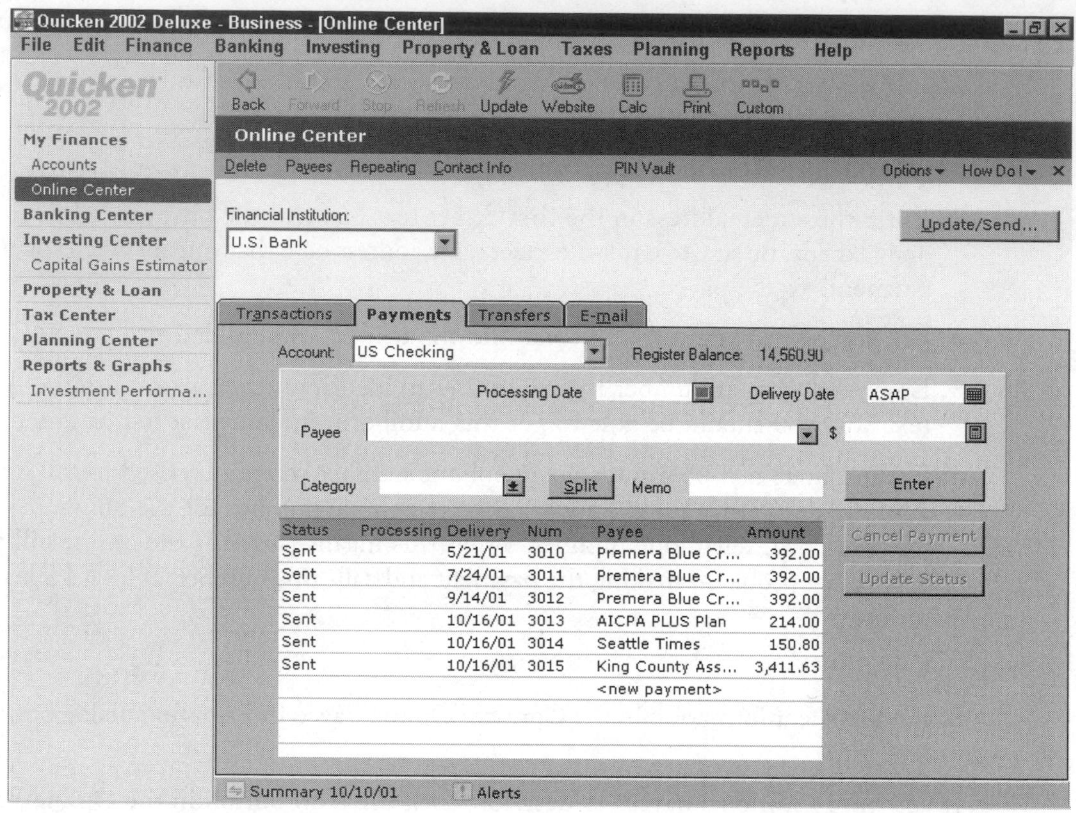

Figure 9.5: The Payments tab of the Online Center window.

Notice that the form is very similar to a check, with a few important differences: There is a drop-down list box for selecting the account that you're using, the Delivery Date is automatically shown as ASAP, and the Pay To The Order Of line is labeled Payee.

You enter an electronic payment in almost the same way that you enter a regular check, with two differences: you must select which bank account you're using for the payment, and when you get to the Payee line, you must specify an electronic payee.

You can specify an electronic payee by entering a name into the Payee text box. As you type, if the payee is on your Online Payee list, Quicken will attempt to automatically fill in the rest of the name. If the name is not on your list, when you click Enter, Quicken displays the Set Up Online Payee dialog box (see Figure 9.4) so you can supply the information necessary to make an electronic payment. Figure 9.6 shows the Online Center window describing an electronic payment. As you can see, you fill in an electronic payment form in the same way that you complete a check that you want to print.

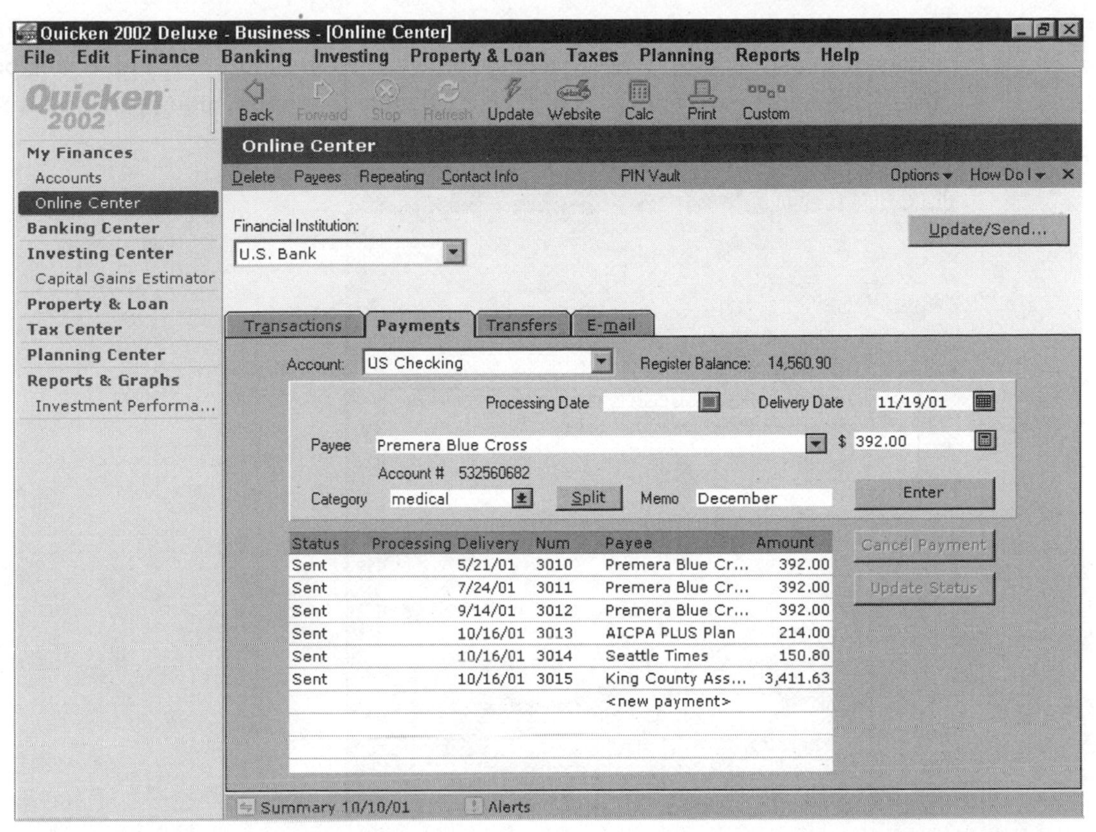

Figure 9.6: The Online Center describing an electronic payment.

After you have filled out the form, click the Enter button. Quicken adds your payment to the list and displays its current status in the text box at the bottom of the window. Note that Quicken has not sent the payment to your bank yet. It is stored on your computer until you send your transactions to the bank by clicking Update/Send, as explained in the next section.

TIP *Before you start using Online Bill Pay to pay your bills, experiment with the feature by sending yourself an electronic payment for some nominal amount, such as $1.00. You'll learn how long the online bill payment service takes to get payments to the payee. And you'll understand how the service uses the electronic payee information you provide.*

Sending Electronic Payments

Once you've described all of your electronic payments, making the actual payments is a snap. Simply display the Online Center (by choosing Banking ➢ Online Banking), and then click the Update/Send command button at the top right of the window. Quicken connects to the Internet; as it does so, you will see a series of message boxes.

Through the Internet, Quicken connects to the online bill payment service computer and displays the Instructions To Send dialog box, as shown in Figure 9.7. This dialog box shows a list of the online payments you have recorded up to that point, along with any other online transactions waiting to be sent.

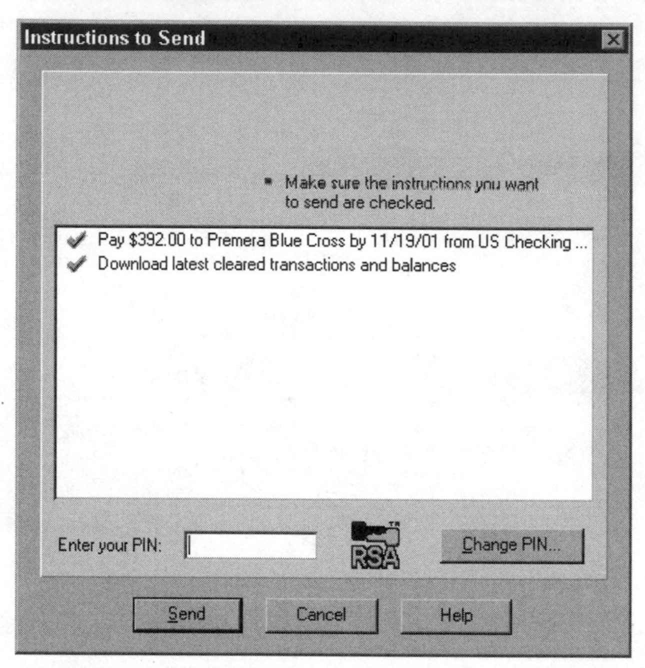

Figure 9.7: The Instructions To Send dialog box.

If you see an electronic payment in the Instructions To Send dialog box that you don't want to transmit—or at least not yet—click it. This unmarks the electronic payment so Quicken won't send it. When you want Quicken to send an unmarked electronic payment, click that payment to mark it again.

Just type your PIN in the Enter Your PIN text box, and then click Send. Quicken sends your payment instructions. After the transmission is complete, Quicken displays the Online Transmission Summary dialog box.

NOTE *The first time you using Online Payment, the Instructions To Send dialog box may look different from the one shown in Figure 9.7, depending on your bank. It may not show a PIN text box. In this case, you first click Send. Quicken asks you for your existing PIN (Personal Identification Number) and prompts you to change it to a new PIN for your Online Payment account. (Usually, on your first call-in, you use your ATM card PIN.)*

PINs for Security

Online Bill Pay and Online Banking (described in the next section of the chapter) use a PIN as a way to keep your account information private. When you instruct the online bill payment service computer to actually process payments, Quicken supplies your account number and you supply your PIN. The online bill payment service computer then verifies the numbers you and Quicken provided and lets you transmit payment instructions. While this process may sound dangerous—after all, someone only needs to know your account number and PIN to start tapping your account—this security system is the same one you now use with your automated teller machine (ATM) card.

As an extra measure of security, some of the banks that provide online bill payment services require you to change your PIN every time you transmit payment information. This little gambit means that even if someone discovered the PIN that you were using last week, it wouldn't be any help this week. What's more, if a miscreant did access your Online Payment account, he or she would need to change your PIN. And in that case, the next time you tried to send payments, you would find that someone had accessed your account and changed your PIN. The bottom line is that PINs work very well as long as you keep the number a secret and don't forget it.

Making Regular Payments with Online Payment

You most likely pay some bills regularly, such as on a monthly basis. For example, mortgage, rent, car loan, and medical insurance payments are made regularly. To make it easier to pay this type of repeating transaction, Quicken lets you schedule a transaction so that it is paid automatically until you tell the Online Payment service to stop paying it. For example, if you're supposed to pay, say, a $1,000-per-month mortgage payment by the tenth of every month and you have 30 years of these monthly payments, you can tell Online Payment to send in your $1,000 every month by the tenth of the month.

To create such a repeating transaction, follow these steps:

1. Display the Online Center window by choosing Banking ➤ Online Banking. Make sure the Payments tab is displayed.
2. Click the Repeating button. Quicken displays the Create Repeating Online Payment dialog box, as shown in Figure 9.8.

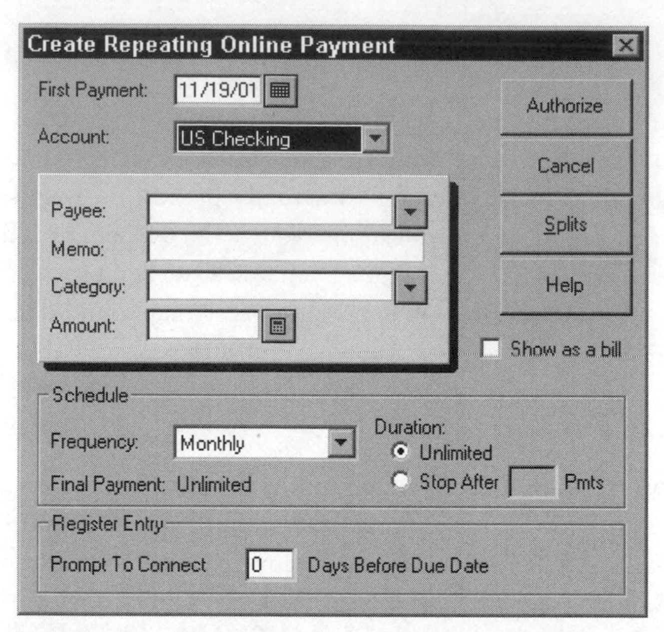

Figure 9.8: The Create Repeating Online Payment dialog box.

3. In the First Payment text box, enter the date of the first repeating payment you'll make using the Online Payment service.
4. If you have more than one account set up for Online Payment, select the account that will be used for the payment from the Account drop-down list box.
5. Select the electronic payee from the Payee drop-down list box.
6. Optionally, provide a memo description of the payment using the Memo text box.
7. Use the Category drop-down list box to describe the payment as falling into some expense category. If you want to split the payment, click the Splits command button and then fill out the Split Transaction Window. (See Chapter 2 for information about splitting transactions.)
8. In the Amount text box, provide the payment amount.
9. Activate the Frequency drop-down list and select a payment frequency: every two weeks, twice a month, monthly, every two months, and so on.
10. Use the Duration option buttons and the Stop After [*x*] Pmts text box to describe how many payments you'll make. For example, if you have a $500 rent check you'll pay each month indefinitely, mark the Unlimited option button. If you have a $1,000 mortgage payment you'll pay monthly for 30 years, mark the Stop After option button and enter *360* in the text box.

11. Use the Prompt To Connect text box to specify how far in advance Quicken should remind you to transmit this payment. In general, you should transmit payments about five days before they're due.

12. Click the Authorize command button. Quicken closes the Create Repeating Online Payment dialog box.

To create additional online repeating payments, repeat steps 2 through 12.

If You Have Problems with Electronic Payments

When you have problems with an electronic payment, you do the same things you would do if the payment had been made with a paper check. If you've transmitted an electronic payment by mistake, you can try to stop payment. If you have questions about a particular payment, you can contact the bank or the Online Payment service.

Stopping a Payment

To stop payment, open the Online Center by choosing Banking ➤ Online Banking. Check the status of your payment in the list at the bottom of your screen. If it says Unsent in the Status column, highlight the transaction by clicking it, then click the Delete button. When Quicken asks you to confirm the deletion, click Yes.

If it says Sent, click the transaction to highlight it, then click the Cancel Payment button. Quicken asks you to confirm your stop payment request, then adds the payment cancellation to your list of instructions to send. The next time you connect to your bank, Quicken sends the instruction to cancel the payment. (This works only if the payment hasn't already been made by your bank, of course.) If the stop payment request works, Quicken voids the electronic payment.

Getting Electronic Payment Information

To see electronic payment information, open the Online Center window by choosing Banking ➤ Online Banking. The list box at the bottom of the screen lists any current online transactions.

To inquire about an earlier payment, click the Payments tab of the Online Center. Select a payment from the list and click the Update Status button to get the current status of a payment.

Getting Help from Your Bank

There are two ways you can get help from your bank regarding electronic payments:

- Call the bank at the number listed on your bank's welcome letter.
- Send the bank an e-mail message.

To send an e-mail message to your bank, follow these steps:

1. Choose Banking ➤ Online Banking to open the Online Center and click the E-Mail tab, which is shown in Figure 9.9.

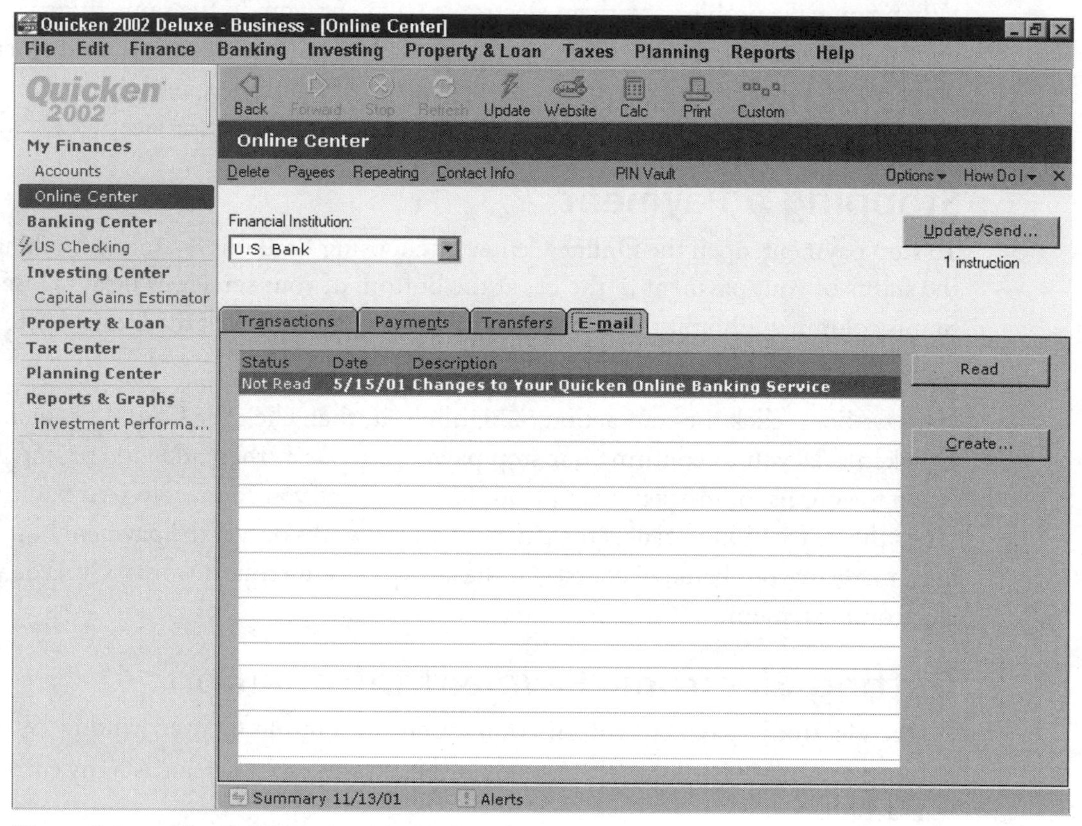

Figure 9.9: The E-Mail tab of the Online Center window.

2. Click Create. Quicken opens the Create dialog box.
3. Mark the E-Mail About An Online Payment option button.
4. Select the Online Payment account on which you made the payment from the drop-down list box.
5. Select the individual online payment from the list box.

6. Click OK. Quicken opens the Payment Inquiry dialog box.
7. Mark the E-Mail Message option button to open a form for sending an e-mail to your bank, as shown in Figure 9.10.

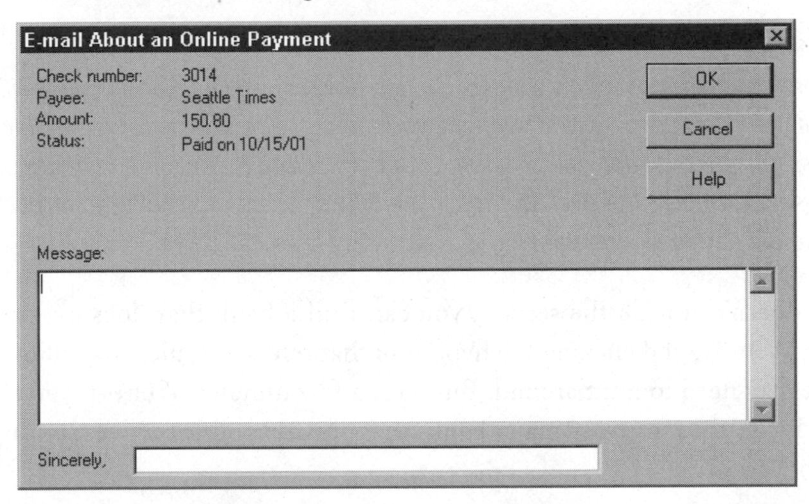

Figure 9.10: Sending an e-mail inquiry to a bank.

8. Write your message in the Message text box, and then click OK to add the message to the list of instructions to send to your bank.

Replies to your inquiries and any other e-mail messages from your bank are automatically "mailed" to you whenever you connect to your bank to do your online banking. Incoming messages are listed on the E-Mail tab of the Online Center window.

To read a mail message listed on the E-Mail tab, select it in the first list box by clicking it and then click the Read button. Quicken displays the message text in the Message box. To delete a message after you've read it, select the message and click the Delete command button.

Online Account Access

With Online Account Access, you can move money between accounts and even pay a credit card bill, if the credit card is issued by the bank with which you do your online banking. You can also receive your bank statement electronically.

There aren't any hard-and-fast prerequisites for using Online Account Access. However, you'll find Online Account Access easiest if you've been using Quicken for at least a few weeks and have performed one or two reconciliations on the accounts that you want to use. Of course, you'll also need to sign up for online banking services with your bank and have an Internet connection.

Signing Up for Online Banking Services

Signing up for online banking isn't difficult, but you do need to work with a bank that supports Quicken's Online Account Access feature. Telephone your bank and ask whether your bank provides online banking services using Quicken.

NOTE *The previous sections in this chapter explain how to use Quicken's Online Bill Pay feature. If you're set up for Online Payment, you can probably sign up for the Online Account Access feature by simply telephoning your bank. Note that Online Banking provides a superset of the features available to Online Bill Pay users. Accordingly, upgrading from Online Bill Pay to Online Banking is a very easy learning curve.*

If your bank doesn't provide the service, you can find a bank that does by visiting the Quicken.com Web site and clicking the hyperlink that refers to Quicken's online banking services. You may need to hunt around. But with a few minutes of effort, you should be able to find a list of the numerous major banks that provide online services in cooperation with Quicken.

Setting Up Quicken for Online Account Access

To tell Quicken you want to use Online Account Access with an account, follow these steps:

1. Display the account's register and click the Overview tab.
2. Click the Available, Not Enabled hyperlink beside Online Account Access. Quicken connects to the bank's web site. Follow the online instructions provided there. Note that the process varies from financial institution to financial institution, which is why I'm not providing detailed, step-by-step instructions here.

Using Online Account Access

Using Online Account Access is quite simple as long as you're comfortable entering transactions into a bank account register. When you want to get account balance information or move money between accounts, choose Banking ➢ Online Center. Quicken displays the Online Center window.

Retrieving Account Statements

To retrieve your account balance and cleared transactions for all your online accounts, including bank accounts and credit card accounts, follow these steps:

1. Click the Update/Send button in the upper right of the window. Quicken opens the Instructions To Send dialog box (see Figure 9.7).

2. The Instructions To Send dialog box shows all of the transactions that Online Account Access will send once it goes online. (Quicken automatically assumes that you will want to send any transactions.) If you do not want Quicken to send a particular transaction while online, click the transaction. Quicken removes the checkmark to indicate that the transaction will not be sent.
3. Click in the Enter Your PIN text box and type in your PIN. (The bank included your PIN with the information it sent when you activated Online Account Access.)
4. Click Send. Quicken connects to the bank and transfers the information from your computer to the bank. At the same time, Online Account Access retrieves transactions from your bank and picks up any new transactions it can't find in your register. Online Account Access also marks transactions that have cleared the bank as cleared.

Approving Online Transactions

Quicken holds the transactions that it has downloaded so you can approve them before you put them in your account registers. To examine the transactions, click OK in the Online Transmission Summary dialog box, and then click the Transactions tab in the Online Center. This tab is shown in Figure 9.11.

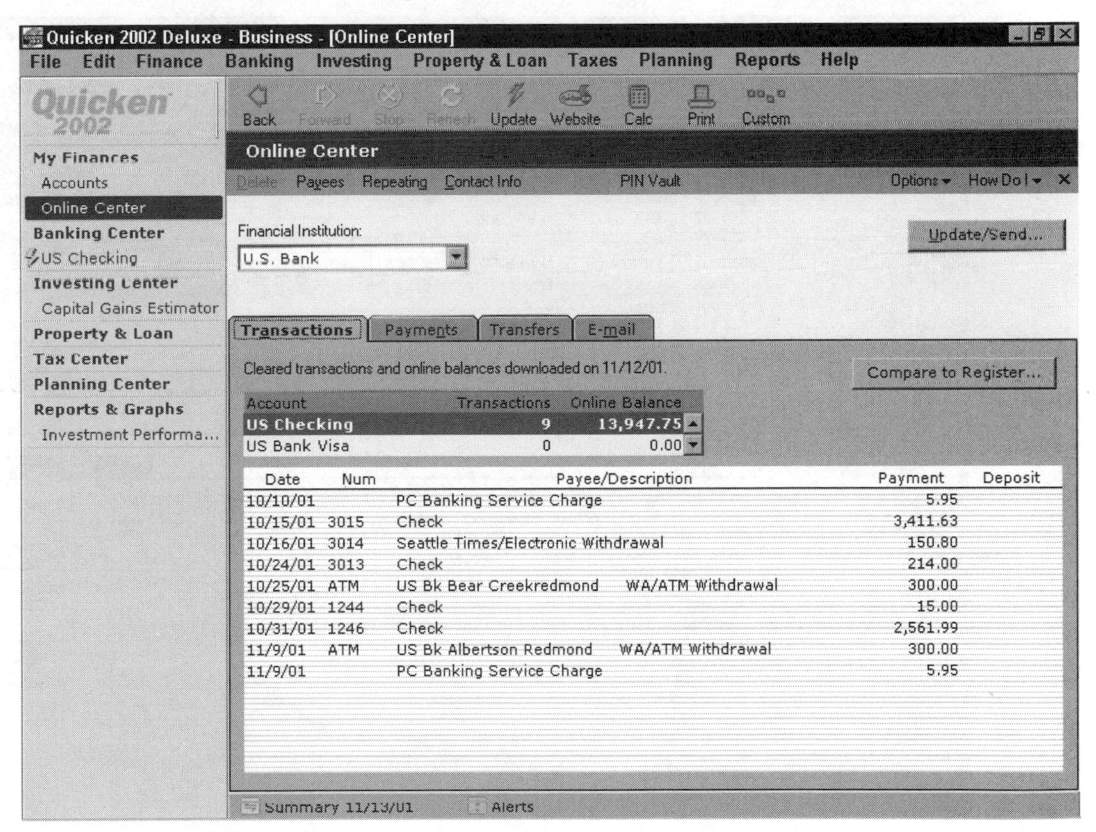

Figure 9.11: The Transactions tab of the Online Center.

If you have more than one account at the financial institution, you can use the list box at the top of the tab to choose an account. Click the name of the account that you want to examine, and Quicken will display the data in the window below the list box.

NOTE *In Figure 9.11, you can see one disadvantage of online banking. Because banks don't keep track of the names on all the checks, some checks (like check number 3015 in Figure 9.11) look as though they're made out to Check. As you compare the downloaded information to your register, you can update the Payee name and assign the category. Online Account Access does supply the Payee name for your credit card accounts or for debit purchases. Different banks handle the register details differently, however.*

To compare the downloaded data with your register, click the Compare To Register button. Quicken splits the window, with the register showing in the top half and the list of downloaded transactions that Quicken recognizes underneath, as shown in Figure 9.12. Use the scroll bars in each section to move through the lists and compare transactions. To accept a single transaction and add it to your register, highlight the transaction by clicking it, and then click the Accept button. To accept all of the transactions at once, click Accept All.

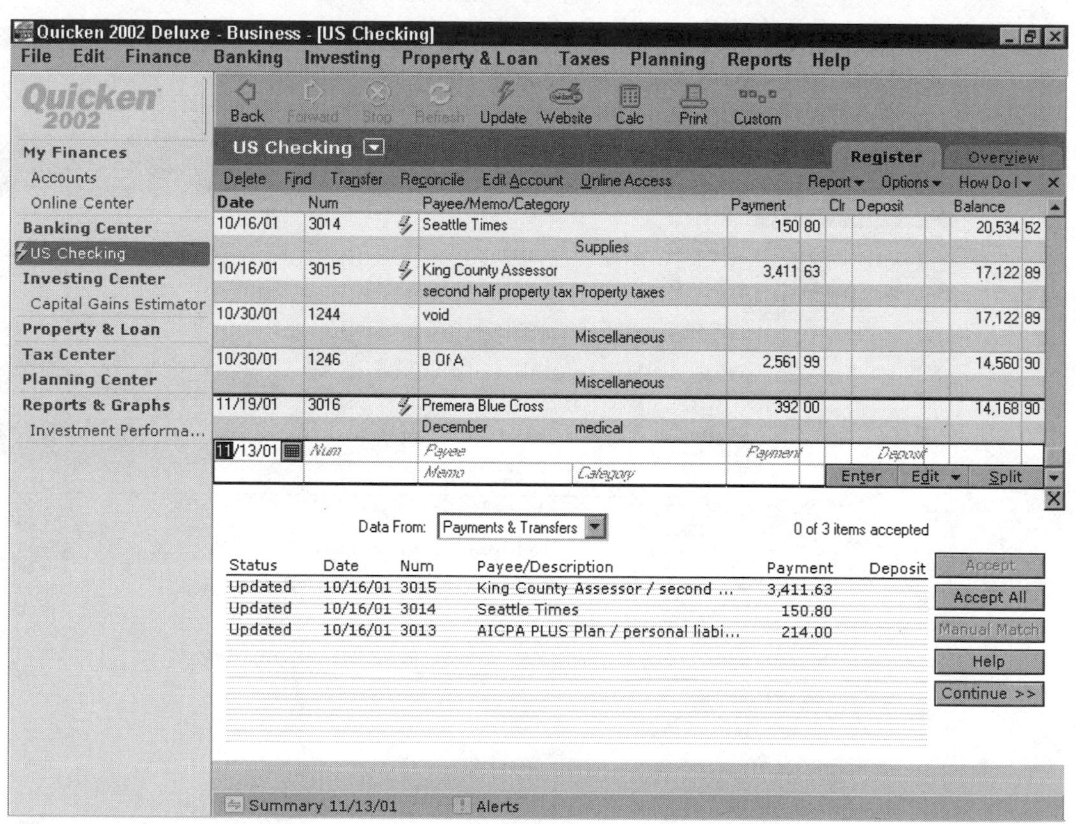

Figure 9.12: Comparing the online transactions and the account register.

After you accept recognized transactions, click the Continue button. Quicken updates the list of downloaded transactions to show new transactions which it can't find in your register. You can accept these new transactions in the same way that you accepted the first set of recognizable transactions—by clicking the Accept and Accept All buttons. Quicken enters the new transactions into your register, prompting you to supply any missing information. To remove a transaction without adding it to your register, click the transaction, and then click Delete. When you finish, click Done.

Transferring Funds between Accounts

If you have two or more accounts at the same institution and you want to transfer money between accounts, open the Online Center window (by choosing Banking ➤ Online Banking), and then click the Transfers tab. Quicken displays the dialog box shown in Figure 9.13.

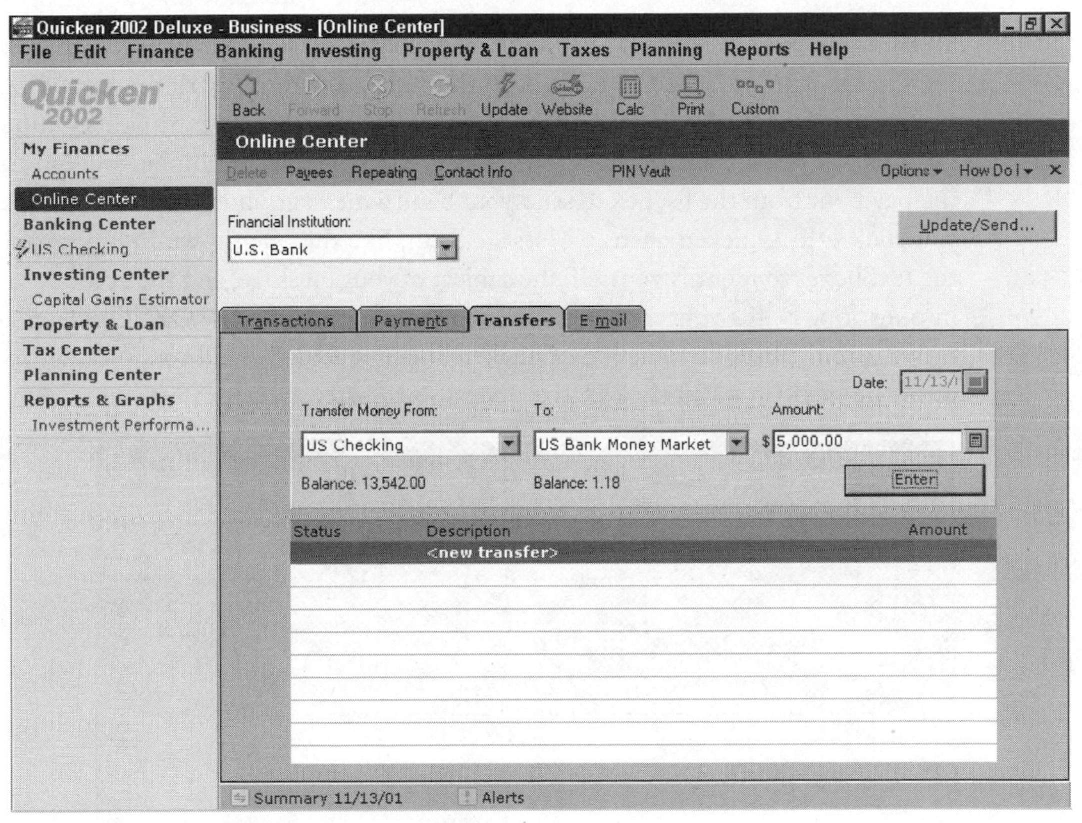

Figure 9.13: The Transfers tab of the Online Center.

Use the Transfer Money From and To drop-down list boxes to identify the accounts you're moving money between. Use the Amount text box to give the amount of the transfer. Click the Enter button to add the transfer to the list of transactions to be sent to the financial institution.

The text box at the bottom of the tab lists all of the transfers you have recorded. To remove a transfer, click the transaction and then click Delete.

NOTE *Some financial institutions do not process transfers electronically; instead, they process the transfers manually at central clearinghouses. This procedure may cause a time lag between the time you send your transfer in and the time the bank actually processes it.*

Corresponding with the Bank

As with Online Payment, if you have any questions, comments, or problems about your Online Account Access transactions, you can correspond directly with your bank via e-mail. Your messages are automatically transferred with your transactions.

To begin, click the E-Mail tab of the Online Center. To send a message to your bank, click the Create button in the E-Mail tab. In the next dialog box, mark the E-Mail About An Online Account option button to send your bank a message regarding its online banking services. Or mark the E-Mail About An Online Payment option button and then select the payment from the list box to send your bank a message about a specific payment. After you click OK, Quicken opens a Message form, like the one shown in Figure 9.14. Fill in the text boxes to identify yourself, the subject of your message, and the account or payment in question. Enter your message. To send your message, click OK. Quicken adds your message to the list of transactions. Quicken does not actually send your message to the bank until the next time you click Update/Send to transfer your transactions.

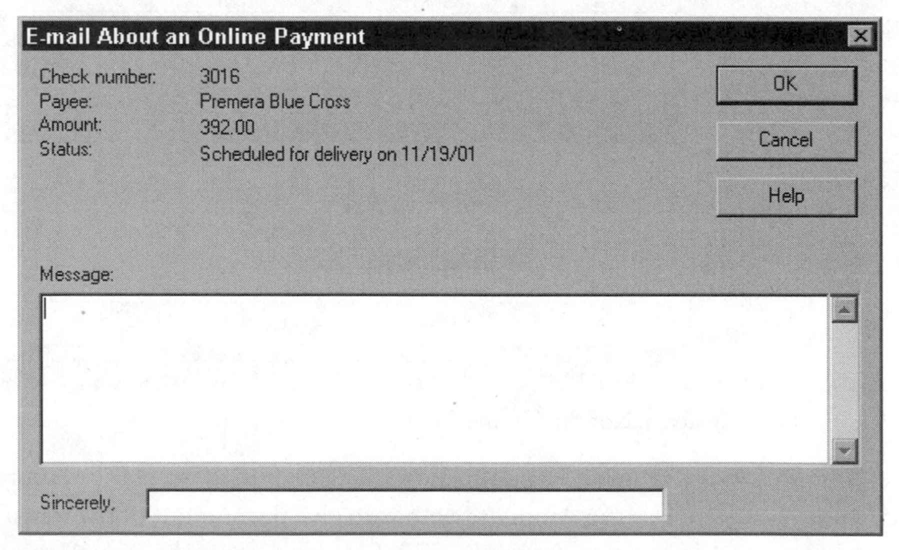

Figure 9.14: Writing a message to your financial institution.

Replies to your inquiries and any other e-mail messages from your bank are automatically "mailed" to you whenever you connect to your bank to do your online banking. Incoming messages are listed on the E-Mail tab of the Online Center window. Quicken displays a window that lists any messages you have received. To read a message, highlight it by clicking it and then click Read. Quicken opens a window containing your message. You can print the message by clicking the Print button.

Reconciling an Online Bank Account

You reconcile, or balance, online bank accounts in a manner very similar to the way you balance other bank accounts. For example, you can display the account's register and click the Reconcile button at the top of the register. When Quicken then displays the Reconcile Online Account dialog box, as shown in Figure 9.15, you indicate whether you want to balance against a paper statement you've received through the mail or against the most recent online balance you've retrieved.

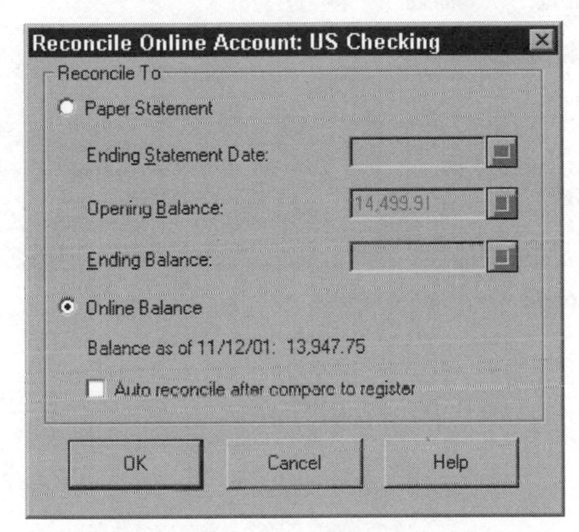

Figure 9.15: The Reconcile Online Account dialog box.

Once you choose which balance you want to reconcile against, Quicken displays the Reconcile Bank Statement window, as shown in Figure 9.16. You use this window to indicate which transactions have cleared the bank. As you do, Quicken calculates a cleared balance figure at the bottom of the screen. When this amount equals the statement balance, you've reconciled your account and should click Finished. Note that the steps you take to reconcile, or balance, a bank account are described in detail in Chapter 5. Chapter 5 also describes what to do when an account won't balance.

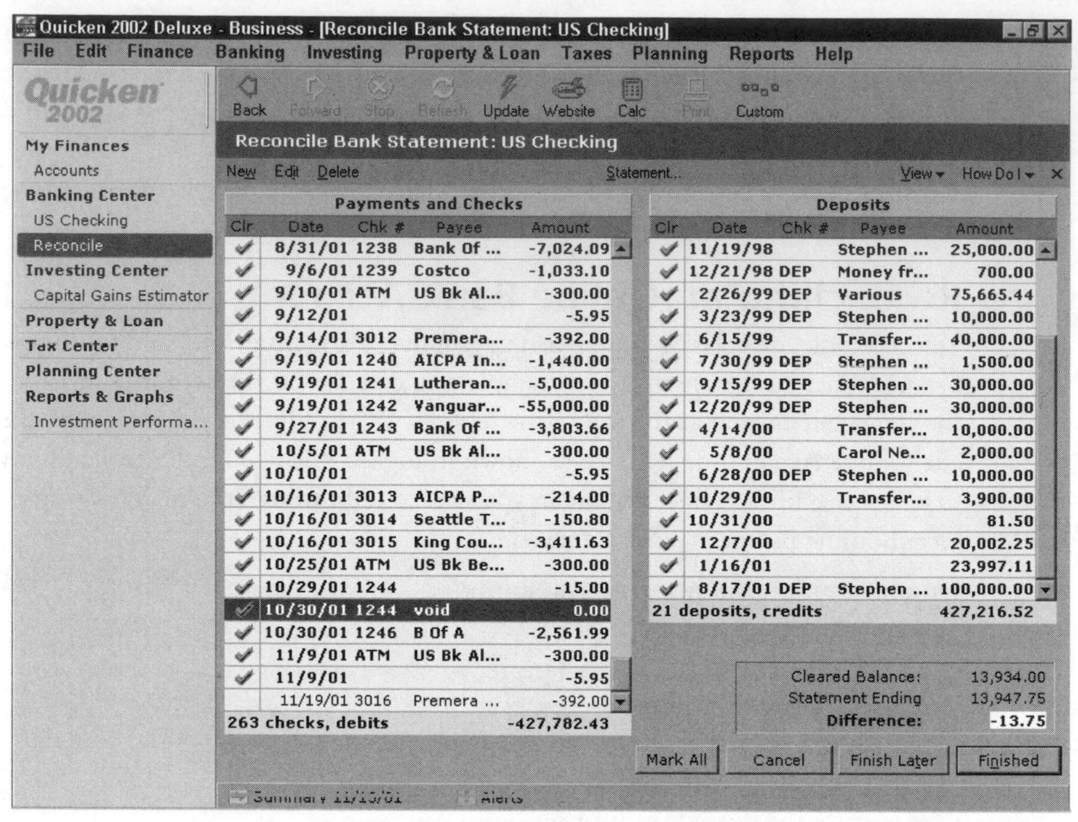

Figure 9.16: The Reconcile Bank Statement window.

Part 2

QUICKEN IN A SMALL BUSINESS

In This Part

Chapter 10

TRACKING CREDIT CARDS

In This Chapter

- Paying off credit card debt
- Tracking credit cards
- Accepting credit cards from customers

You can use Quicken not only to track bank accounts but also to track just about any personal asset, most business assets, and just about any liability. This chapter describes how to use Quicken to track one such liability, your personal and business credit cards. This chapter also describes how you can use the Quicken Loan Planner to calculate how long it will take you to pay off credit card balances.

Before You Begin

Here are the prerequisites for using Quicken for credit card tracking:

- Know how the Quicken register works and how to record payments and deposits into it (see Chapter 2).
- Know your current credit card balance and, ideally, your credit limit. You should be able to get some of this information from your most recent credit card statement. If you've saved your transaction slips since the most recent credit card or debit card statement, these will be useful too.
- Have applied for a credit card with a bank that supports Quicken's online banking feature, if you want to retrieve your credit card statements over the Internet. You'll also need Internet access, of course.

Paying Off Credit Card Debt

Credit cards can simplify and improve your financial life. You don't need to carry large sums of cash around, just a tiny rectangle of plastic. If you need a short-term loan—say a delivery truck breaks down or you need to purchase a larger-than-usual quantity of whatever you sell your customers—you have immediate funding at your fingertips.

Despite all the positive ways credit cards influence our lives, it's easy for too much of a good thing to turn bad. And this can be especially true in the case of a business where it's often easy to justify the charge on a credit card because, after all, it's for "the business." To get into trouble, simply make that tempting minimum payment a few times on a credit card with a painfully high annual interest rate. Before you know it, you have hefty credit card balances, and you're paying hundreds or even thousands of dollars in annual interest charges.

If you find yourself in this predicament and want to get out of the credit card trap, you can use the Loan Planner to estimate what size payment will pay off a credit card over a specified number of years. Just follow these steps:

1. Choose Planning ➢ Financial Calculators ➢ Loan to display the Loan Calculator dialog box, as shown in Figure 10.1.

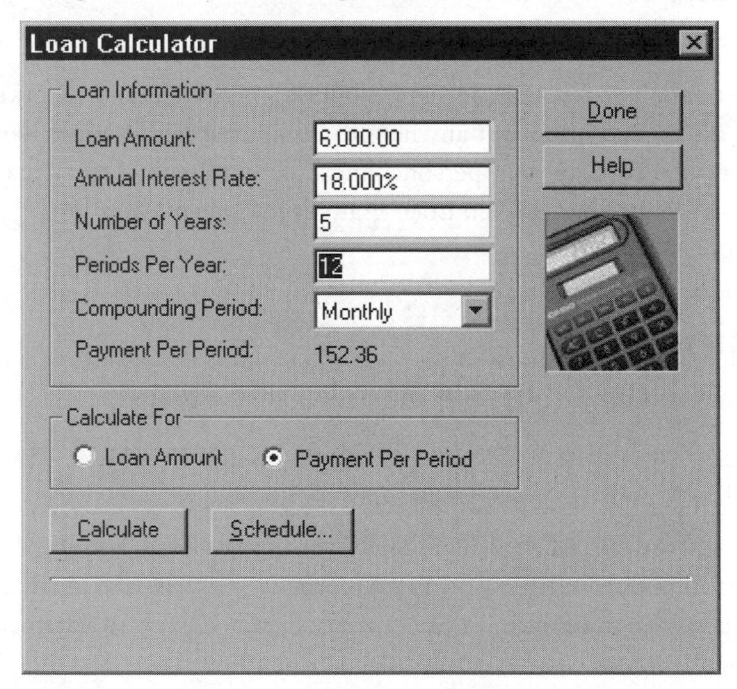

Figure 10.1: The Loan Calculator dialog box.

2. Mark the Payment Per Period option button in the Calculate For section at the bottom of the dialog box, and use the Loan Amount text box at the top of the dialog box to enter the amount you currently owe on a credit card.
3. In the Annual Interest Rate text box, enter the annual interest rate charged on the card balance. If a card charges 18 percent annually, for example, type *18*.
4. In the Number Of Years text box, enter the number of years over which you want to pay off the credit card balance. If you want to have the balance paid off in five years, for example, type *5*.
5. Verify that the Periods Per Year text box shows 12, which indicates that you'll be making monthly payments.
6. Click the Calculate button.

Quicken calculates the monthly payment that repays the credit card balance over the specified number of years and displays it at the bottom of the Loan Information section. If you currently owe $6,000 on a credit card charging 18 percent annual interest, for example, paying off the $6,000 over five years will require monthly payments of $152.36.

If you want to see a breakdown of payments to principal and interest, click the Schedule command button to display a schedule of payments based on your figures. Figure 10.2 shows an example of a schedule of future payments.

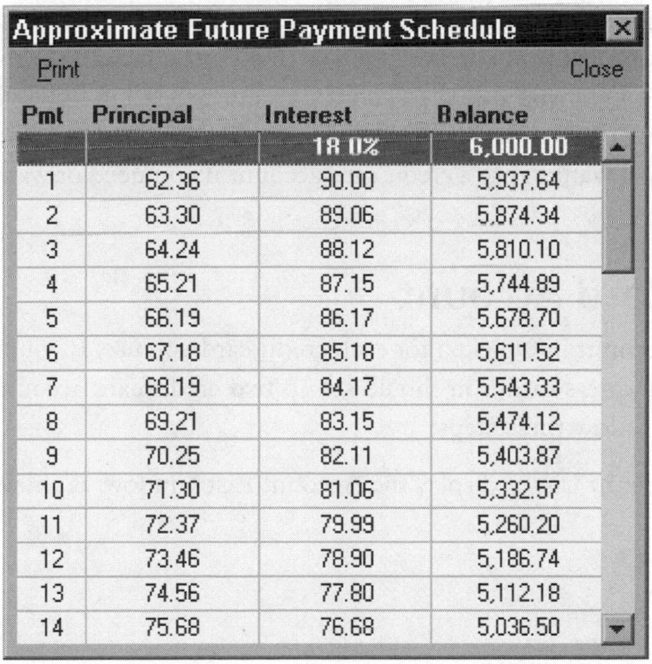

Approximate Future Payment Schedule

Print — Close

Pmt	Principal	Interest	Balance
		18.0%	6,000.00
1	62.36	90.00	5,937.64
2	63.30	89.06	5,874.34
3	64.24	88.12	5,810.10
4	65.21	87.15	5,744.89
5	66.19	86.17	5,678.70
6	67.18	85.18	5,611.52
7	68.19	84.17	5,543.33
8	69.21	83.15	5,474.12
9	70.25	82.11	5,403.87
10	71.30	81.06	5,332.57
11	72.37	79.99	5,260.20
12	73.46	78.90	5,186.74
13	74.56	77.80	5,112.18
14	75.68	76.68	5,036.50

Figure 10.2: The Approximate Future Payment Schedule window shows how your regular monthly payment will repay the credit card debt.

TIP *If a credit card issuer charges you interest from the date of the charge transaction, you also pay interest on the charges you make over a month rather than only the balance outstanding at the start of the month. It will take longer to repay the credit card balance than the Loan Calculator computes if you continue to use the credit card.*

Tracking Credit Cards

To track a credit card in Quicken, you need to set up an account for the credit card, and then you need to record the charges and payments you make. If you've set up bank accounts before and worked with these accounts, you'll find credit card accounts easy to set up and to use.

When to Set Up a Credit Card Account

Do you need to set up a credit card account? Even if you use a credit card, you may not need to track it with Quicken. If you pay off your credit card in full every month, you can categorize your credit bill when you write the check to pay the credit company by using the Split Transaction Window. And if you always charge nominal amounts that you don't need to keep careful track of, you probably don't need to set up a credit card balance.

On the other hand, if you carry a substantial credit card balance, you'll want to set up a credit card account to categorize your credit card spending. You'll also want to set up a credit card account if you want to track your spending by merchant—the businesses that accept your credit card charges—even if you always pay off the credit card bill in full each month. Merchant information can't be recorded anywhere as part of writing a check to the credit card company. Finally, you'll want to use a credit card account if you need or want to track your credit card balance.

Setting Up a Credit Card Account

You set up a credit card account in Quicken for each credit card you use. If you have both a Visa and an American Express card, you should set up two credit card accounts. To set up a credit card account, follow these steps:

1. Choose Finance ➢ Account List to display the Account List window, as shown in Figure 10.3.

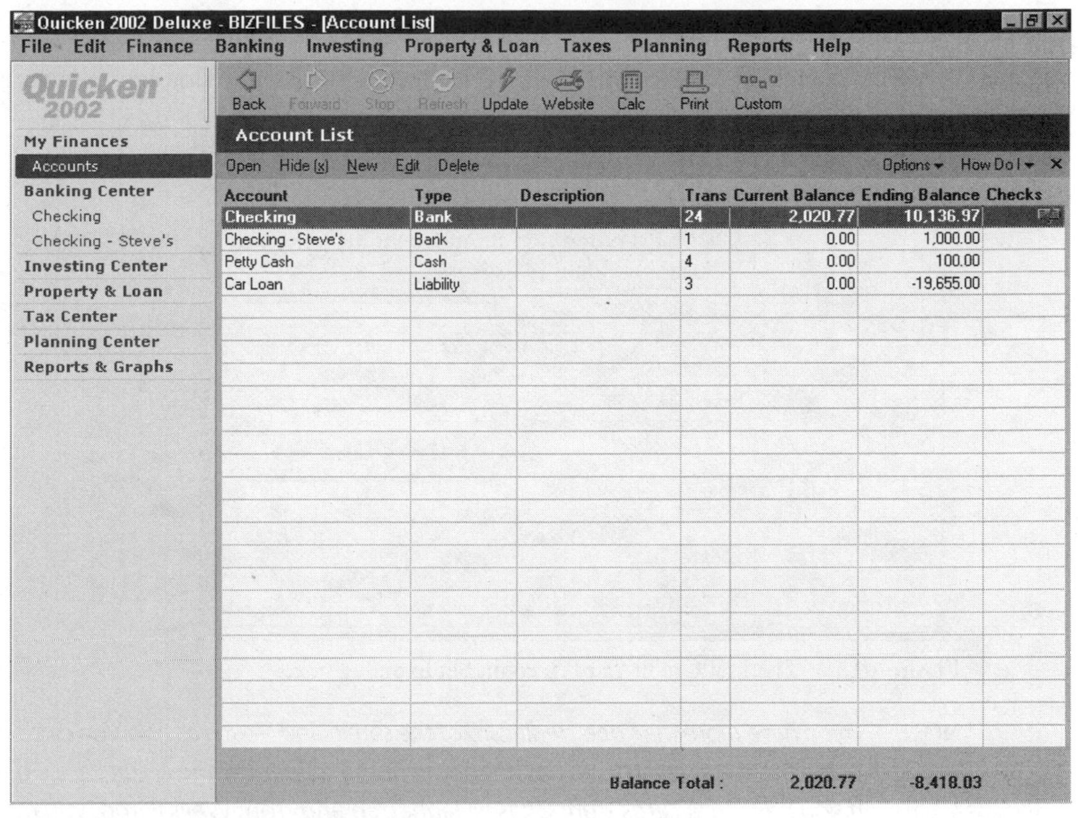

Figure 10.3: The Account List.

2. Click the New command button in the Account List window to display the dialog box you use to set up a new account, as shown in Figure 10.4.

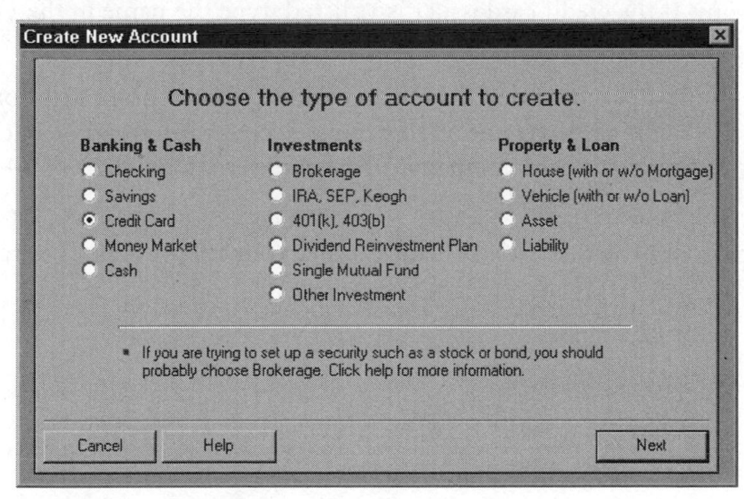

Figure 10.4: Setting up a new account.

3. Mark the Credit Card option button, and then click Next.
4. When Quicken displays the Credit Card Account Setup dialog box, shown in Figure 10.5, enter a name for the account such as *Visa* or *AMEX*.

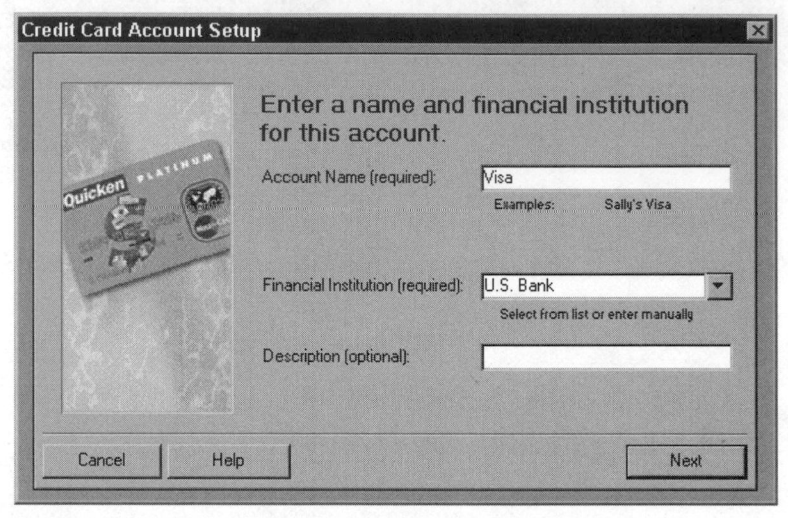

Figure 10.5: The first Credit Card Account Setup dialog box.

NOTE *If you have more than one credit card of the same kind—such as two Visa cards—consider using the credit card name and the issuer name to identify the credit card. For example, if you have Visa cards from Chase Manhattan and from Wells Fargo, you might name one credit card* Visa–Chase *and the other* Visa–Wells.

5. Use the Financial Institution drop-down list box to identify the name of the bank or credit card company. If the credit card issuer isn't listed, type the name in the Financial Institution text box.
6. If you want to provide an account description, click in the Description text box. Enter a description of the credit card account or additional account information, such as the account number or the credit card company. You can enter a maximum of 54 characters.
7. Click Next. Quicken displays the second Credit Card Account Setup dialog box, as shown in Figure 10.6.

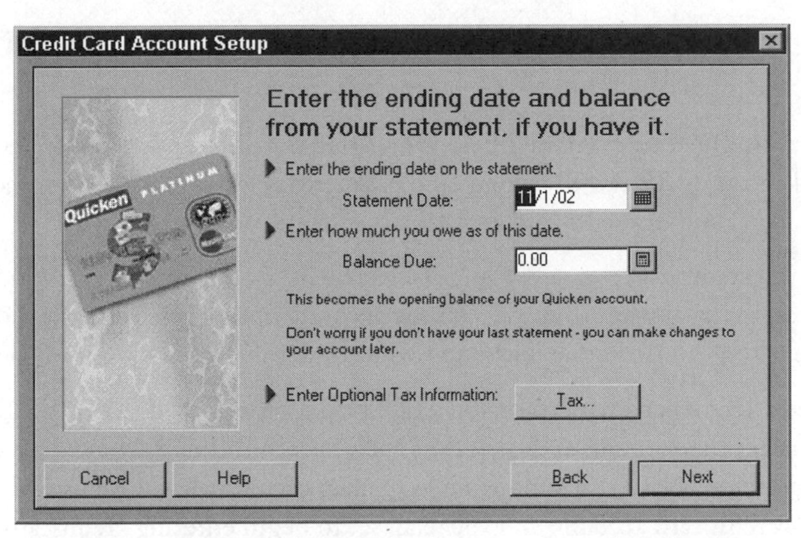

Figure 10.6: The second Credit Card Account Setup dialog box.

NOTE *You can enter the credit card balance as of the last statement date, but this figure won't include the payments you've made since the last statement or any charges you've incurred. Therefore, if you do enter the balance as of the last statement date, be sure to enter the transactions that have occurred since the last statement date when it is time to reconcile.*

8. In the As Of Date text box, enter the date on which you want to start keeping records for this account, in MM/DD/YY fashion. For example, type July 4, 2002, as *7/4/02*.
9. In the Balance text box, enter the account balance on the day that you'll start keeping records for the credit card.
10. Click Next. When Quicken displays the third and final Credit Card Account Setup dialog box, which I don't show here, use the Credit Limit text box to identify the card's credit limit.
11. Click Done to tell Quicken that the Credit Card Account Setup dialog box is complete. Quicken displays the Account List window, and this time it includes your new credit card account. You're finished, and you can skip the rest of the steps described here.
12. If your credit card comes from a bank or credit card company that supports online account access, display the credit card's register, click the Overview tab, and then click the Available, Not Enabled hyperlink beside Online Account Access. Quicken should connect to the credit card issuer's web site, and this web site should walk you through the steps to setting up the credit card account for online account access.

Telling Quicken Which Credit Card Account You Want to Work With

As you may know, Quicken displays different registers for different accounts and different credit card accounts. To record charges and payments related to a specific credit card, you'll need to activate that credit card register's document window.

If you can see the credit card register's QuickTab in the Quicken application window, you can tell Quicken that you want to work with the account simply by making its document window active. (You can make the document window active by clicking its QuickTab.)

If you can't see a credit card register's QuickTab, display the Account List window (see Figure 10.3), select the account, and click the Open button in the Account List window. (You can also double-click the account name.) Quicken then displays a Register document window for the credit card account, and you're all set to begin entering credit card charges and payments. Figure 10.7 shows a sample credit card register.

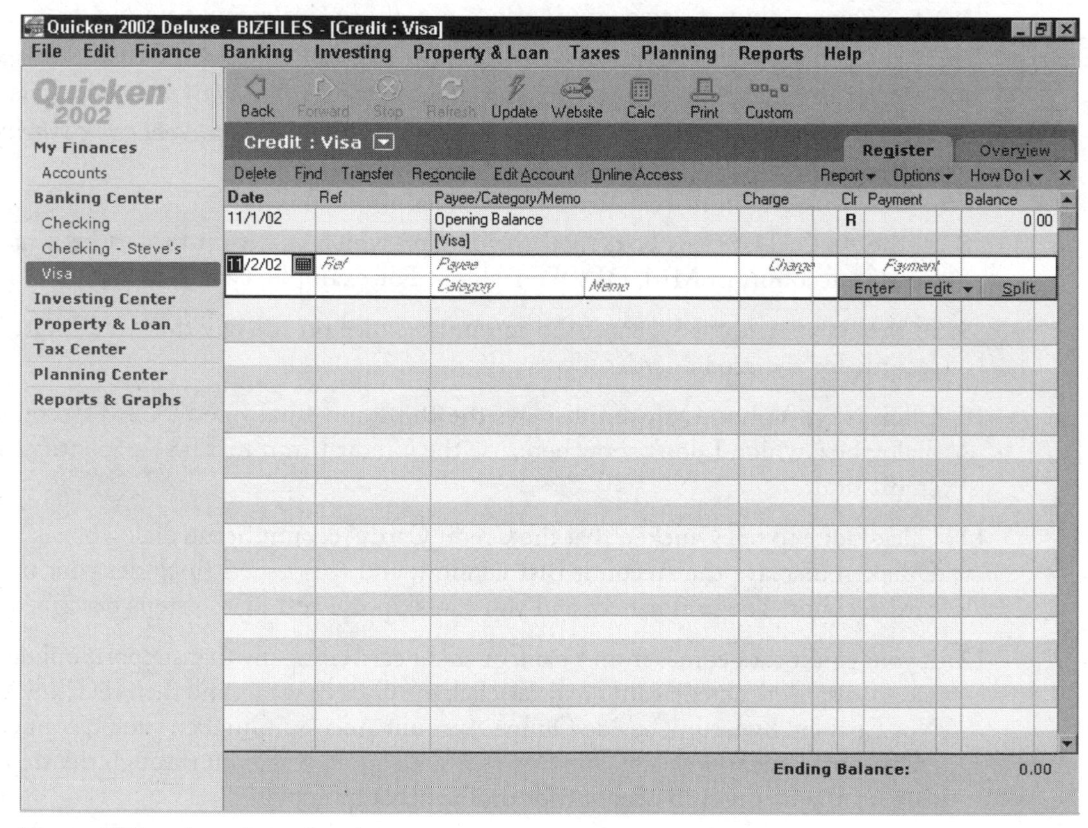

Figure 10.7: A credit card register.

Recording Credit Card Charges

As long as you're not working with an online banking account, you record credit card charges in the same way you record payments made from a bank account. (Because recording transactions into an online account is a little different, I'll describe that later in this chapter.)

To record a credit card charge, use the arrow keys or the mouse, or choose Edit ➤ Transaction ➤ New to move to the next empty row of the register. Then follow these steps:

1. Enter the credit card charge date in the Date text box. If the date shown isn't the correct transaction date, enter the date in *MM/DD/YY* format. You typically don't need to enter the year number; the one Quicken already shows is usually correct.
2. If you want to enter a credit card reference number, enter the number in the Ref text box. You can do this in the same way that you enter check numbers. (You might choose, for example, to enter a portion of the credit card transaction number.)
3. Enter the name of the merchant who accepted the credit card charge. Place the cursor in the Payee combo box. If this is the first time you've recorded a charge with the merchant, type the payee's name. If you've recorded a charge before or written a check, you can activate the Payee drop-down list and select the merchant's name from it.
4. Enter the amount in the Charge or Payment text box. You don't need to enter currency punctuation—such as dollar signs or commas—but you should include a decimal point to identify any cents.
5. If you want to mark cleared transactions manually and the transaction you're entering into the register has already cleared or been recorded by the credit card company, click in the Clr text box to place an R there.

Normally, you won't mark cleared transactions. Marking charges and payments as cleared is something you do as part of reconciling a credit card account, which is discussed a little later in this chapter. If you're entering old transactions—say you're starting your record keeping as of the previous credit card statement—you can mark cleared transactions to make your reconciliation easier.

6. To categorize the transaction, highlight the Category combo box and activate the Category drop-down list. Then select the category that best describes the charge. A charge at the office supplies store, for example, might fall into the Office category.

A payment will usually be recorded as a transfer from the bank account you'll use to write the check that pays the bill (see Chapter 2). If you can't find an expense category that describes the charge, you can enter a short category description directly into the Category combo box. If you want to create a category named Office Supplies, for example, type ***Office Supplies***. (See Chapter 13 for information about setting up category lists that easily support your income tax planning and preparation.)

7. If you want to enter a short description, click in the Memo text box and enter the description. You can enter anything you want in this field, but there's no reason to duplicate information that you've entered or will enter some place else.
8. Select Enter to record the credit card charge or payment.

Quicken updates the credit card balance and the remaining credit limit and then highlights the next empty row in the Register window. Figure 10.8 shows several credit card charge transactions.

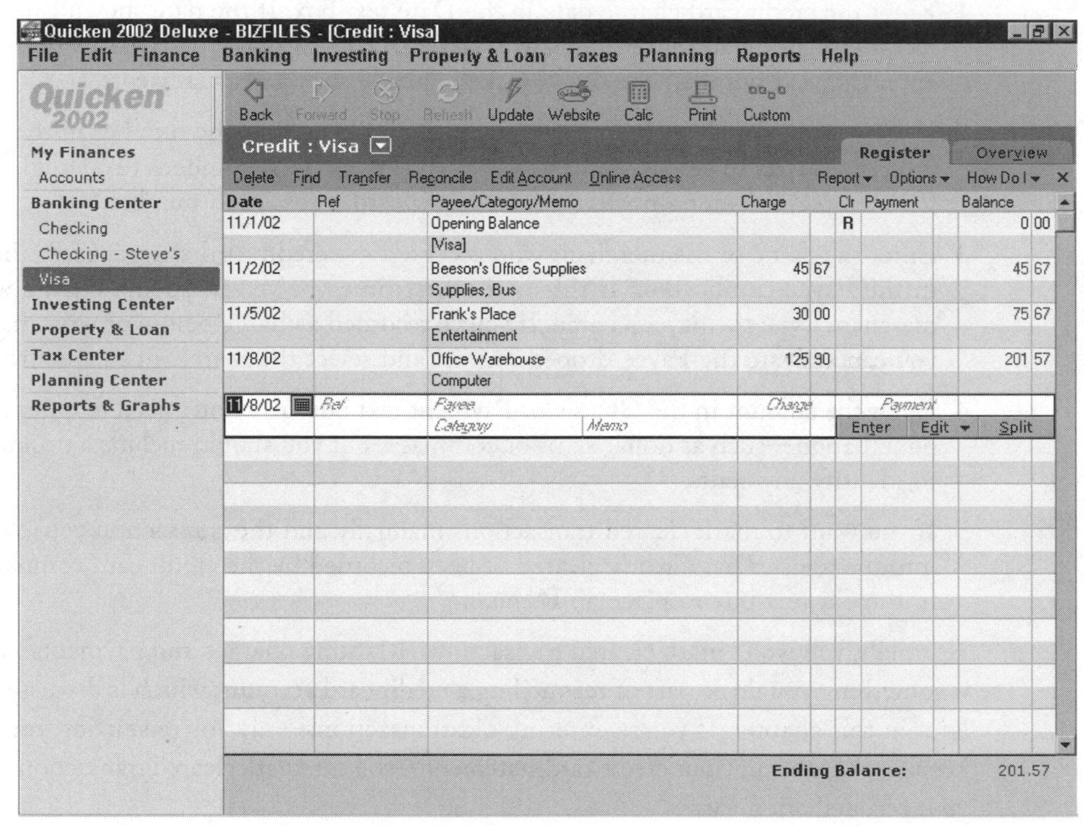

Figure 10.8: A credit card register with several charges.

Paying a Credit Card Bill the Easy Way

The easiest way to pay a credit card bill is to just record a payment transaction into the register. If you write a check, for example, the payment shows as a transfer from your bank account to the credit card account, like the last transaction in the register in Figure 10.9. (Chapter 2 explains how transfer transactions work.)

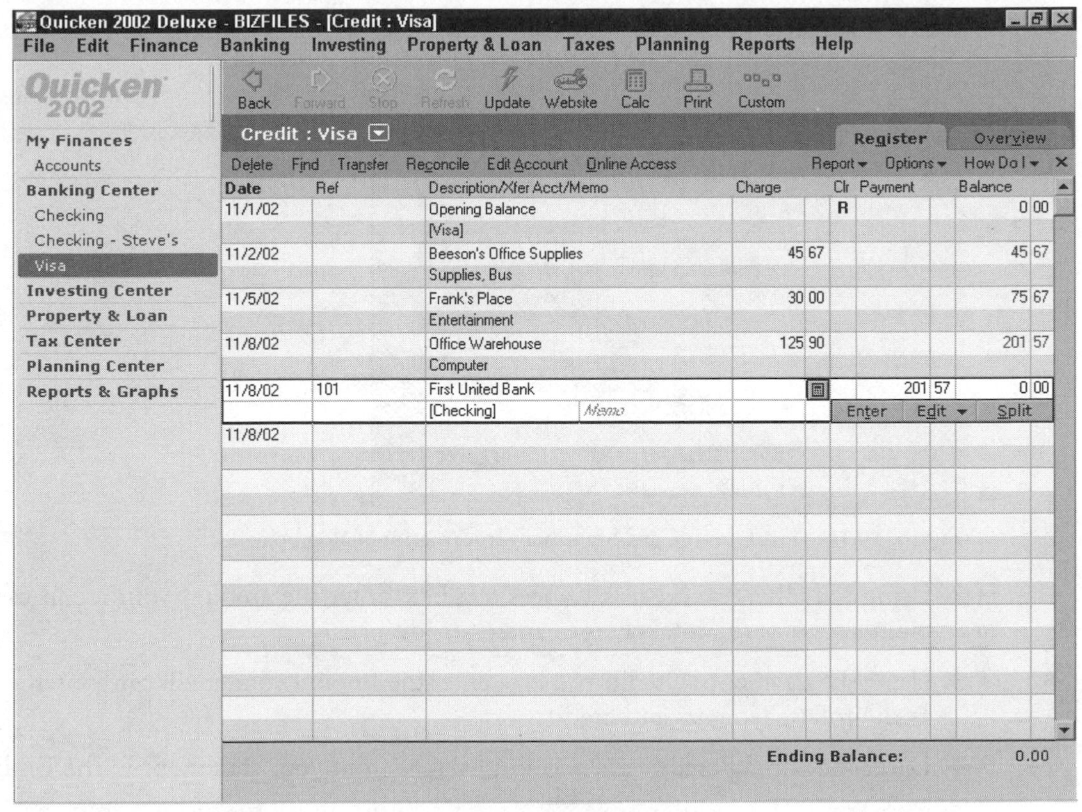

Figure 10.9: A credit card register with several charges and a payment.

Paying and Reconciling a Credit Card Bill

You can also pay a credit card bill as part of reconciling a credit card statement. To do so, you go through the steps for analyzing the difference between your credit card records and the credit card company's records. (This process works just like a bank account reconciliation.) Then, at the end, you tell Quicken how much you want to pay.

To reconcile and pay a credit card bill, display the Register window for the credit card account. Then follow these steps:

1. Click Reconcile to display the Credit Card Statement Information dialog box, as shown in Figure 10.10.

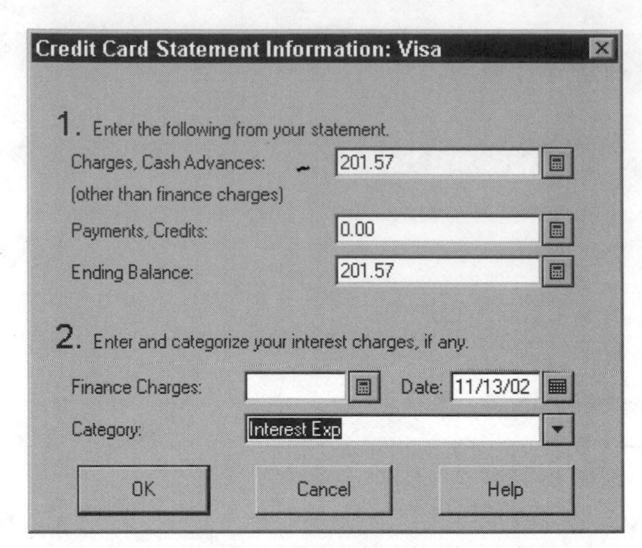

Figure 10.10: The Credit Card Statement Information dialog box.

2. Using the Charges, Cash Advances text box, enter the amount your credit card statement shows as the total charges and cash advances.
3. Using the Payments, Credits text box, enter the amount your credit card statement shows as the total payments and credits.
4. Enter the ending credit card account balance from your statement in the Ending Balance text box.
5. Enter the monthly finance charge shown on the statement (if you haven't done so already) in the Finance Charges text box.
6. Tell Quicken when the finance charge occurred using the Date text box.
7. Categorize the finance charge by using the Category text box. (If you don't remember which category you want to use, click the down arrow on the Category drop-down list box to display a list of categories.)
8. Click OK to display the Reconcile Credit Statement window, as shown in Figure 10.11.

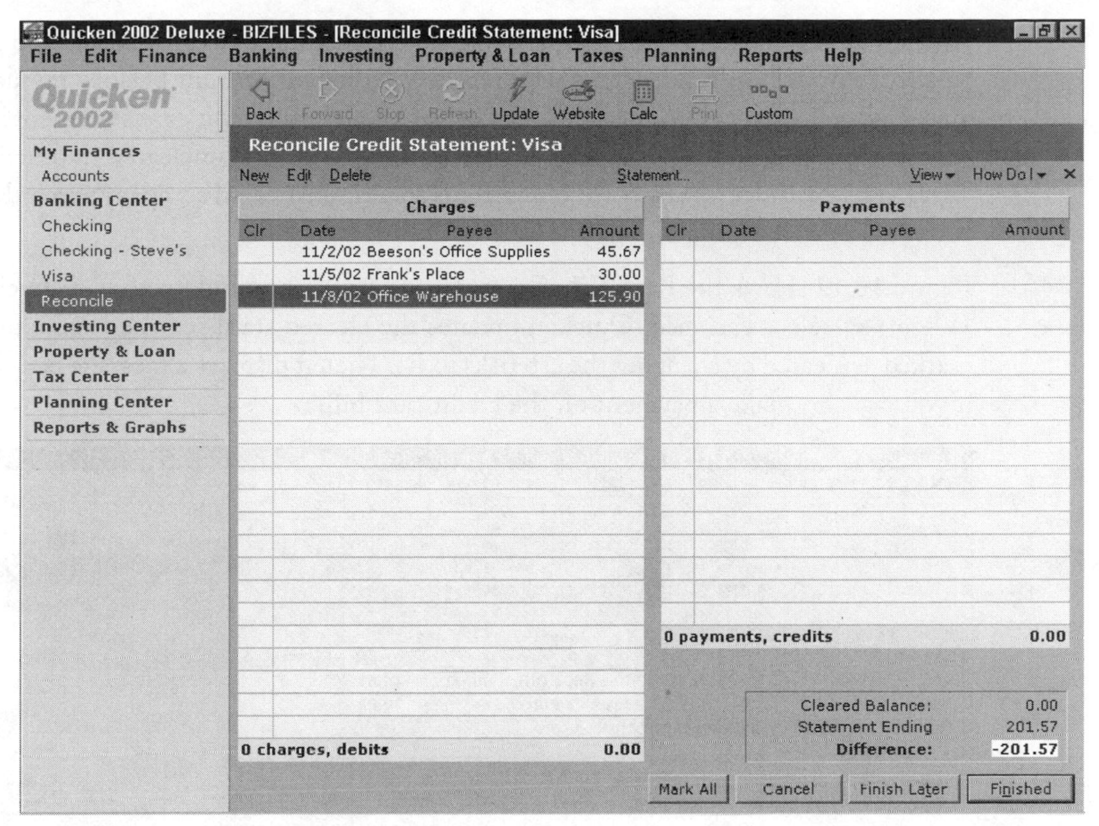

Figure 10.11: The Reconcile Credit Statement window.

TIP *If you have a question about a transaction shown in the Reconcile Credit Statement window, double-click the transaction to display the credit card account's register with the transaction highlighted. You can examine the transaction in more detail—for example, by reviewing the split transaction information. When you're ready to return to the Reconcile Credit Statement window, click the Return To Reconcile command button.*

9. Review the list of transactions shown in the Reconcile Credit Statement window, and highlight each of the transactions that has cleared. Quicken places a checkmark by each transaction you highlight. If you accidentally mark a transaction as cleared when it shouldn't be, click it again or press the spacebar to unmark it.
10. Select Finished when the difference between the cleared balance and the credit card statement balance is zero. Or click Finish Later if you would rather finish reconciling the credit card account at a later time.

As you indicate which transactions have cleared, Quicken continually recalculates a "cleared balance" figure. This figure is just your records' credit card account balance minus all the uncleared transactions. When the cleared balance equals the credit card statement balance, your account balances, or reconciles. In other words, when the uncleared transactions total explains the difference between your records and the credit card company's records, you've reconciled the account.

Figure 10.12 shows the Reconcile Credit Card Statement window after reconciliation. When you select Finished, Quicken updates the cleared status of the transactions you marked as cleared by changing the asterisks to Rs. Then it displays a message box that asks if you want to make a payment on the credit card bill.

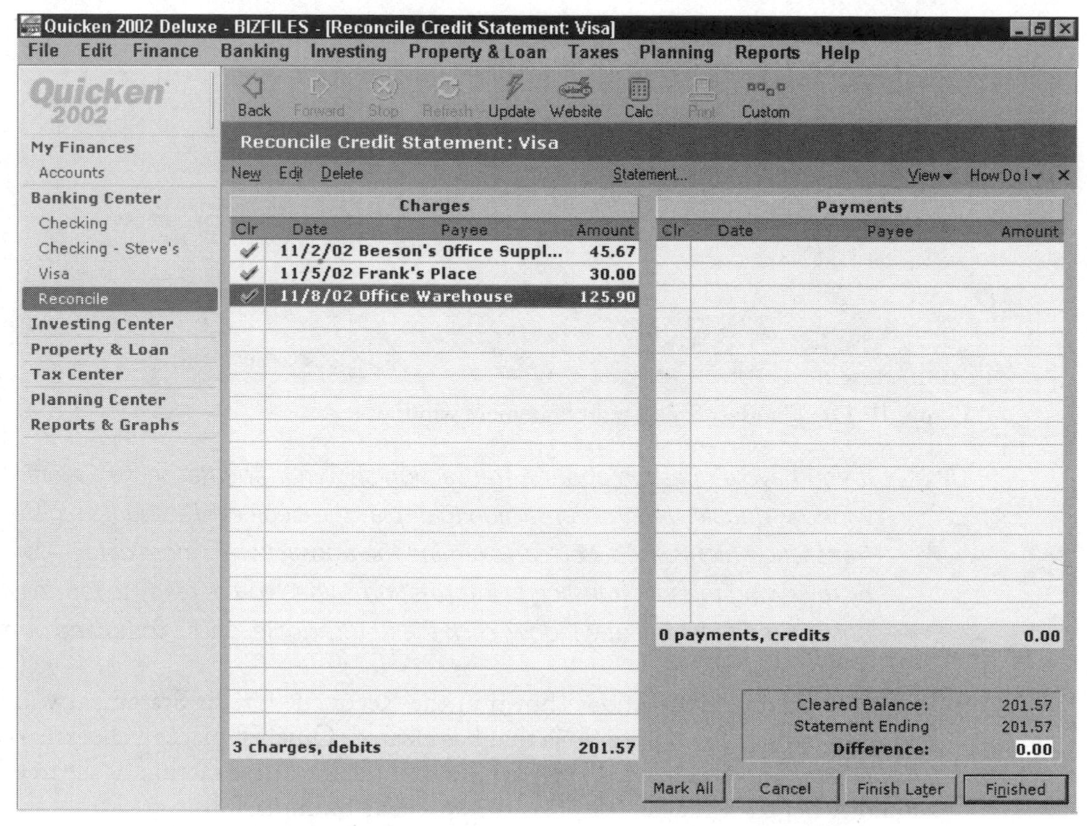

Figure 10.12: The Reconcile Credit Statement window showing a cleared balance figure.

11. If you want to make a payment on the credit card bill, choose the bank account on which you'll write the check from the Bank Account drop-down list box.
12. Use the Payment Method option buttons to indicate whether you will handwrite the check or use Quicken to print it:

- Mark the Printed Check option button to display the Write Checks window for the account you selected in step 11. Describe the check by filling out the text boxes in this window, and select Record Check.
- Mark the Hand Written Check option button, then Yes to display the bank account register for the account you selected in step 11. Complete the transaction as you would normally, and then select Enter.

Quicken also fills in the Category text box with the credit card account name; don't change this. When you pay off a portion of a credit card balance, you actually are transferring money from your bank account to the credit card company. Click Enter when you finish describing the payment transaction.

Recording Credit Card Charges with Online Banking

As long as you have either the Quicken credit card or a credit card issued by one of the banks that supports Quicken's Online Payment feature, you can retrieve your credit card transactions from the credit card company through an online connection.

Retrieving a Credit Card Statement

Whenever you want to, you can retrieve your most recent credit card transactions from the credit card issuer.

To update your credit card register, choose Banking ➤ Open Center and click Update/Send. Quicken retrieves the data. You can then click the Compare To Register button to compare your register's transactions to those the online credit card statement shows. When you do this, Quicken displays a list of the transactions shown in the online credit card statement. To accept all of the transactions shown on the online statement, click the Accept All button. To individually review transactions, select a transaction and then click either Accept or Delete. Note that when you review the online credit card statements by comparing them to what your register already shows, you're effectively reconciling the credit card statement.

What about Debit Cards?

You can also track debit cards in Quicken. The process varies from that used for tracking credit cards because a debit card isn't actually a liability. Rather, it's an asset, which makes it more analogous to a bank account, so you treat a debit card like another bank account. You can record debit card charges on the account in the same way that you record payments on a regular checking account. And you treat additions to the debit card account balance in the same way as deposits into a regular checking account.

NOTE *A debit card attached to a regular bank account doesn't need a separate bank account. The debit card transactions can be recorded directly into the bank account's register.*

Accepting Credit Cards from Customers

Quicken doesn't provide a clean way for businesses to accept credit cards from their customers. This means that if you want to accept credit cards, you'll need to use whatever tools are provided by the bank with whom you've set up a merchant account.

When you receive money from the bank for credit card transactions, you'll need to record this cash inflow as a bank account deposit. For information on recording bank account deposits, refer to Chapter 2.

TIP *Accepting credit cards from customers is well-supported by Quicken's "big-brother" product, QuickBooks. If you want to or need to accept credit cards and find yourself struggling with one or two other shortcomings in Quicken (perhaps you need to track inventory or perhaps you have complicated payroll) you may want to look at upgrading to QuickBooks.*

How to Choose and Use Credit Cards

Credit cards are convenient, but they're also dangerous. A lot of people ruin their financial lives by turning the phrase "charge it" into a reflex. It's a real problem, and for that reason the rest of this chapter explains how to make good use of credit cards and how to choose a good credit card. This information, by the way, applies both to using a credit card for personal expenses and to using a credit card for business expenses.

Selecting the Right Credit Card

Selecting a credit card is easy. If you don't carry charges forward from month to month, choose the card with the lowest annual fee. It doesn't matter to you if the credit card company charges a painfully high interest rate, since you pay only the annual fee if you pay your monthly credit card bill on time.

If you do carry a balance, it makes sense to choose the card with the lowest interest rate. Some credit card issuers play interest rate calculation tricks that make it very difficult to make apples-to-apples comparisons of credit cards. But if you choose the credit card rate with the lowest annual percentage rate, you're doing about as well as you can.

The Right Way to Use a Credit Card

You shouldn't use a credit card as a way to borrow money. That means always repaying the charges within the grace period. You want to be what the bank calls "a revolver," which is a person who always pays his or her credit card bills on time.

After investments in a profitable business, a 401(k), and a deductible IRA, the next best investment you can make is to pay off credit cards that charge a high interest rate. Earning a tax-free interest rate of, say, 14 percent, which is what a 401(k) and deductible IRA pay (and probably only slightly less than investments in your business should pay) is too good to pass up.

NOTE *While credit card interest on personal charges would not be deductible for income tax purposes, credit card interest on business charges should be deductible as business interest expense. Therefore, the worst kind of credit card debt is personal credit card debt. Business debt isn't quite as bad.*

Do Affinity Cards Make Sense?

An *affinity card* is a credit card that's issued by someone other than a bank—such as a car manufacturer, an airline, a professional group, and so forth. Affinity cards typically combine the usual features of a credit card with some extra benefit connected to the issuer. In the case of a General Motors card, for example, you accumulate dollars in a rebate account by virtue of what you spend with the affinity card.

In general, an affinity card—especially one that doesn't charge a fee—is a good deal as long as the interest rate is competitive. For example, I have a General Motors credit card that includes a 5 percent rebate account. In other words, five cents of every dollar I charge on the card goes into a rebate account that I can use toward purchasing a new General Motors car. How big your rebate gets depends on the type of affinity card you have. For example, as of this writing the regular General Motors credit card lets you accumulate up to $500 a year to a maximum of $3,500. The General Motors gold credit card lets you accumulate up to $1,000 a year to a maximum of $7,000.

There are many different affinity cards. Ford has one. Most of the major airlines have them too. Airline affinity cards let you accumulate frequent flier miles based on the credit card charges. In the plans I've seen, you usually get a mile per dollar.

The one sticky part of using affinity cards, however, is that getting even a 5 percent rebate isn't worth it if having the card makes you spend more money. Some studies show that you spend 23 percent more when you use a credit card. The same is very likely true of affinity cards.

If you're one of those people who spends more when you have a card in hand, you won't save any money by using an affinity card. Even if you get a new General Motors car for free or a handful of free airline tickets to Europe, you pay indirectly for your new car or airline tickets with all the extra charging you do. If you don't make use of the rebate, the situation is even worse. You've charged more, perhaps paid hefty annual fees, and you've received nothing in return.

NOTE *One other point to consider argues in favor of using affinity cards for business charges. In many businesses, you will have large business credit card charges—much larger than an individual making personal charges will have. In this case, assuming you don't overcharge and don't overspend, you may find that an affinity charge card produces big benefits. In my case, because many of my business expenses can be charged on my frequent flier credit card, I probably get two free airline tickets a year.*

How to Save Money on Credit Cards

Fortunately, you can use a bunch of different tactics to save money on credit cards. Some suggestions follow:

Leave Home without It

If you're like most people, you spend more money if you carry a credit card around. As I mentioned, some studies show that credit card holders spend 23 percent more on average even if they don't carry a balance on the credit cards. No investment pays an instantaneous 23 percent rate after taxes. Even business investments. Despite what American Express says, you're really better off if you leave home *without* it.

Cancel Unnecessary Credit Cards

If you don't carry credit card balances, cancel credit cards that charge an annual maintenance fee. Lighten your wallet by canceling all the cards you don't use, for that matter. You'll only spend more if you use them, anyway.

Ask Your Bank to Waive Its Annual Fee

Call your bank and explain that, because of the annual fee, you might cancel your credit card. Tell the bank you think it should waive its annual fee. Your current credit card issuer will probably gulp and then waive the fee. For a two-minute telephone call, you'll be ahead by $20 or $30. (By the way, most credit card issuers don't waive the fee on a gold card.)

Consider an Affinity Card

If you travel on business a lot, you can easily run up $10,000 or more on a credit card as you pay for airline tickets, hotels, and rental cars. In this case, it's well worth it to pay $50 for an affinity card. Once you have the card, charge all your personal and business purchases on it.

One caution here, however: Talk to your tax advisor, because there's a good chance your rebate will be considered taxable income if you go this route. On the other hand, if you only charge personal purchases on the affinity card, you can make a good case that the rebate isn't taxable income but is an adjustment in the price of the goods you bought.

Cancel Credit Insurance If You Have Any

Credit life insurance is usually a big waste of money. You only need credit life insurance if you know your estate will collect and you can't get a better kind of insurance.

Credit disability insurance is usually another big waste of money. But, as with credit life insurance, you may need this insurance if you require disability insurance and you can't get better insurance.

Cancel Credit Card Protection Insurance If You Have It

Credit card protection insurance is another waste of money. If some nefarious type steals your credit card and runs up huge charges, you are probably only liable for the first $50 or so as long as you immediately tell the credit card issuer that the credit card was stolen.

Never Make the Minimum Payment

Pay more than the minimum payment. Paying off high-interest-rate credit cards is one of the best investments you can make. (The others are typically investing in a profitable business and contributing money to a 401(k) plan in which the employer matches a portion of the contribution.) If you make minimum payments only, your credit card debt quickly balloons. *Very* quickly balloons, I should say. Soon you are paying massive monthly finance charges.

Get Rid of Your Gold Card

You're paying for the privilege and prestige of that gold card. But you knew that, right? You can probably save yourself at least $40 or $50 just by having a boring, regular Visa or MasterCard.

Chapter 11

TRACKING CASH

In This Chapter

- Setting up a cash account
- Recording receipts and disbursements
- Working with a petty cash box
- Working with a cash drawer

Most people won't need to track the cash they hold (like what's in a wallet) or the cash they spend and receive. It's usually easy enough to monitor cash balances by looking in your pocket. And it's often possible to record the income and expense categories associated with cash receipts and disbursements as part of cashing the check you use to get the cash or as part of withdrawing money from the bank. If you withdraw $100 from a bank account to spend on groceries, for example, you can categorize the $100 withdrawal as a Groceries expense.

Businesses, however, encounter two situations where they do need to track cash: petty cash boxes and cash drawers. In this chapter, I'll describe how to use Quicken's cash account for these two items.

NOTE *A petty cash box is a box—usually a small locked box—that a business keeps to make small cash purchases and disbursements. A cash drawer is the drawer—perhaps the drawer in a cash register into which a business places cash from customer sales and from which a business makes change.*

Before You Begin

Here are the prerequisites for using Quicken for cash account tracking:

- Know how the Quicken register works and how to record payments and deposits into it (see Chapter 2).
- Know your current cash account balance. (You can get this information by counting the cash in the petty cash box or in the cash drawer.)

Setting Up a Cash Account

You set up a cash account in Quicken for each petty cash or cash drawer you use. To set up a cash account, follow these steps:

1. Choose Finance ➢ Account List to display the Account List window, as shown in Figure 11.1.

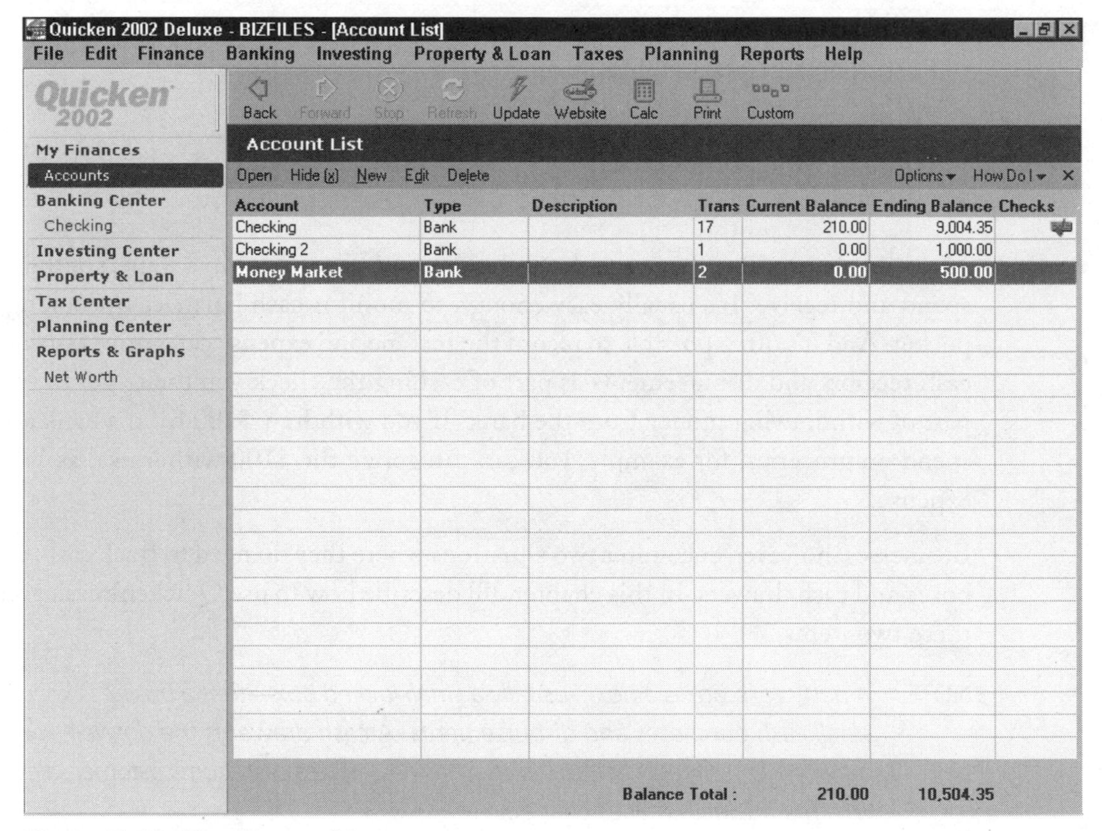

Figure 11.1: The Account List.

2. Click the New command button in the Account List window to display the dialog box you use to set up a new account, as shown in Figure 11.2.

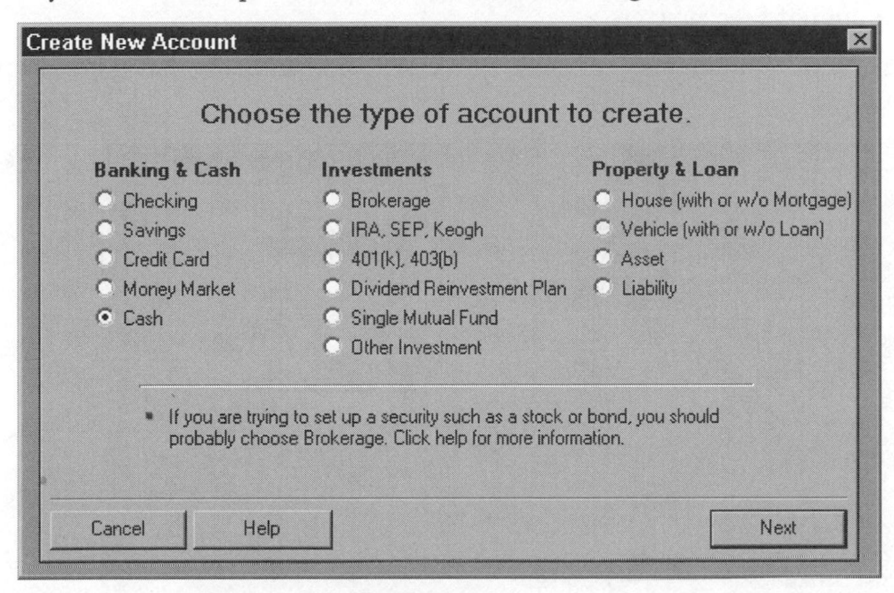

Figure 11.2: Setting up a new account.

3. Mark the Cash option button, and then click Next.
4. When Quicken displays the Cash Account Setup dialog box, shown in Figure 11.3, enter a name for the account such as ***Petty Cash*** or ***Cash Drawer***.

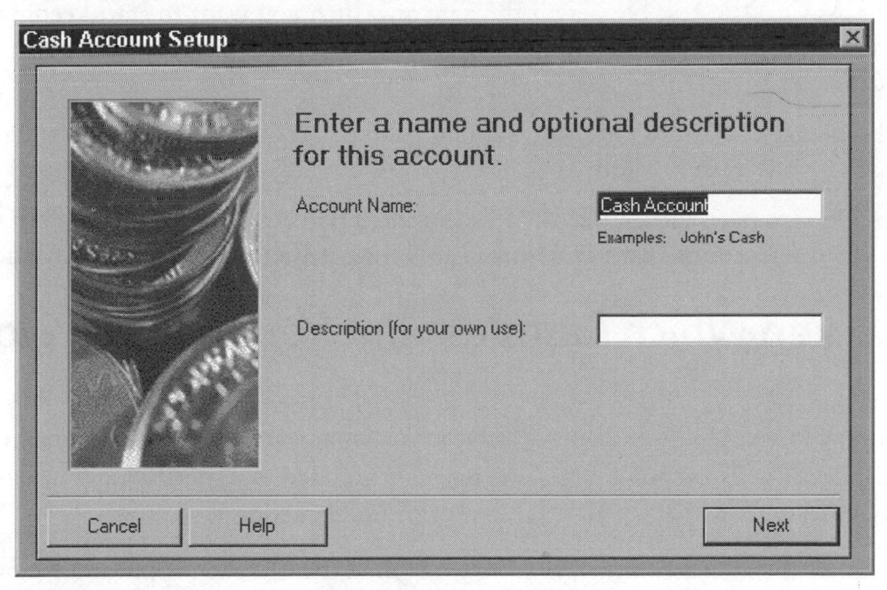

Figure 11.3: The first Cash Account Setup dialog box.

5. If you want to provide an account description, click in the Description text box. Enter a description of the cash account or additional account information. You can enter a maximum of 54 characters.
6. Click Next. Quicken displays the second Cash Account Setup dialog box, as shown in Figure 11.4.

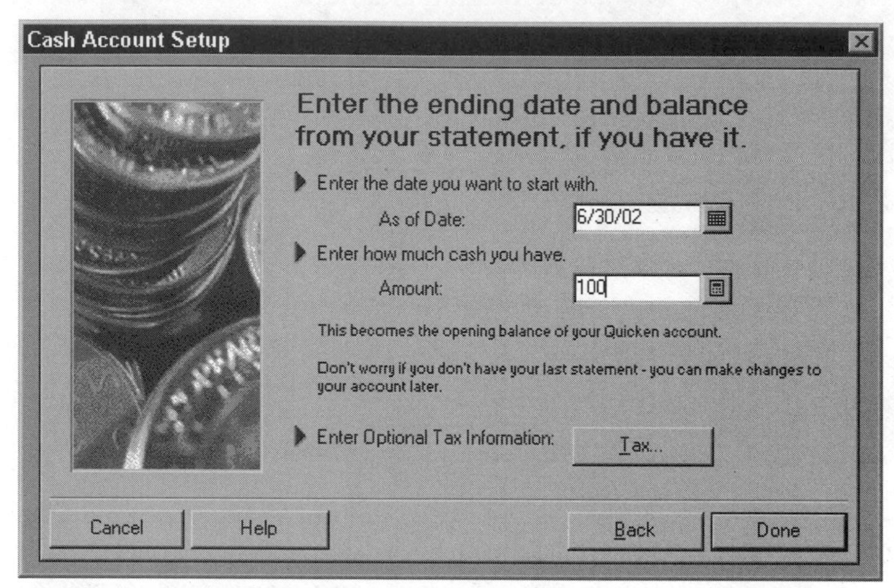

Figure 11.4: The second Cash Account Setup dialog box.

7. In the As Of Date text box, enter the date on which you want to start keeping records for this cash account, in *MM/DD/YY* fashion. For example, type June 30, 2002, as *6/30/02*.
8. In the Balance text box, enter the account balance on the day that you'll start keeping records for the cash account.
9. Click Done to tell Quicken that the Cash Account Setup dialog box is complete. Quicken displays the Account List window, and this time it includes your new cash account.

Telling Quicken Which Cash Account You Want to Work With

As you may know, Quicken displays different registers for different accounts and different cash accounts. To record charges and payments related to a specific cash account, you'll need to activate that cash account register's document window.

If you can see the cash account register's QuickTab in the Quicken application window, you can tell Quicken that you want to work with the account simply by making its document window active. (You can make the document window active by clicking its QuickTab.)

If you can't see a cash account register's QuickTab, display the Account List window (see Figure 11.1), select the account, and click the Open button in the Account List window. (You can also double-click the account name.) Quicken then displays a Register document window for the cash account, and you're all set to begin entering cash disbursements and receipts. Figure 11.5 shows a sample cash account register.

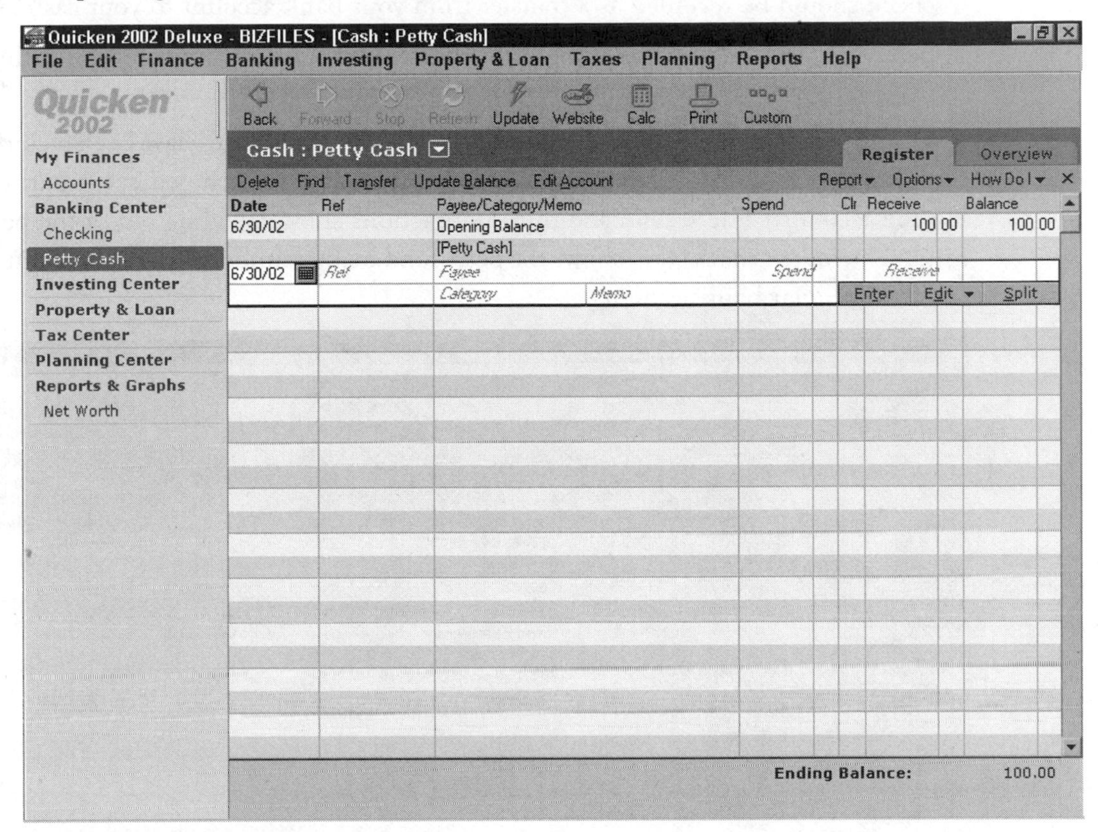

Figure 11.5: The cash account register.

Recording Receipts and Disbursements

Recording cash receipts and disbursements is similar to recording bank account withdrawals and deposits. You begin by placing the cursor in the next empty row of the register or choosing Edit ➤ Transaction ➤ New. Then follow these steps:

1. Enter the cash receipt or disbursement date.
2. If you want a more detailed record, enter a cash receipt or disbursement reference number.
3. Name the person from whom you received or to whom you disbursed the cash.

4. Enter the receipt or disbursement amount. Use the Spend column for disbursements and the Receive column for receipts.
5. If you want to add more details, enter a memo description.
6. Categorize the receipt or disbursement transaction. (Increases in cash when you cash a check should be recorded as a transfer from your bank account to your cash account.)
7. Select Enter to record the receipt or disbursement. Quicken updates the cash balance and highlights the next empty row in the Register window.

Figure 11.6 shows a cash account register after several transactions have been recorded. The first transaction shows the opening cash account balance (which gets set as part of creating the account.) The second and third transactions show spending out of the petty cash fund. The fourth transaction shows the petty fund being reimbursed by an account transfer from the regular bank account.

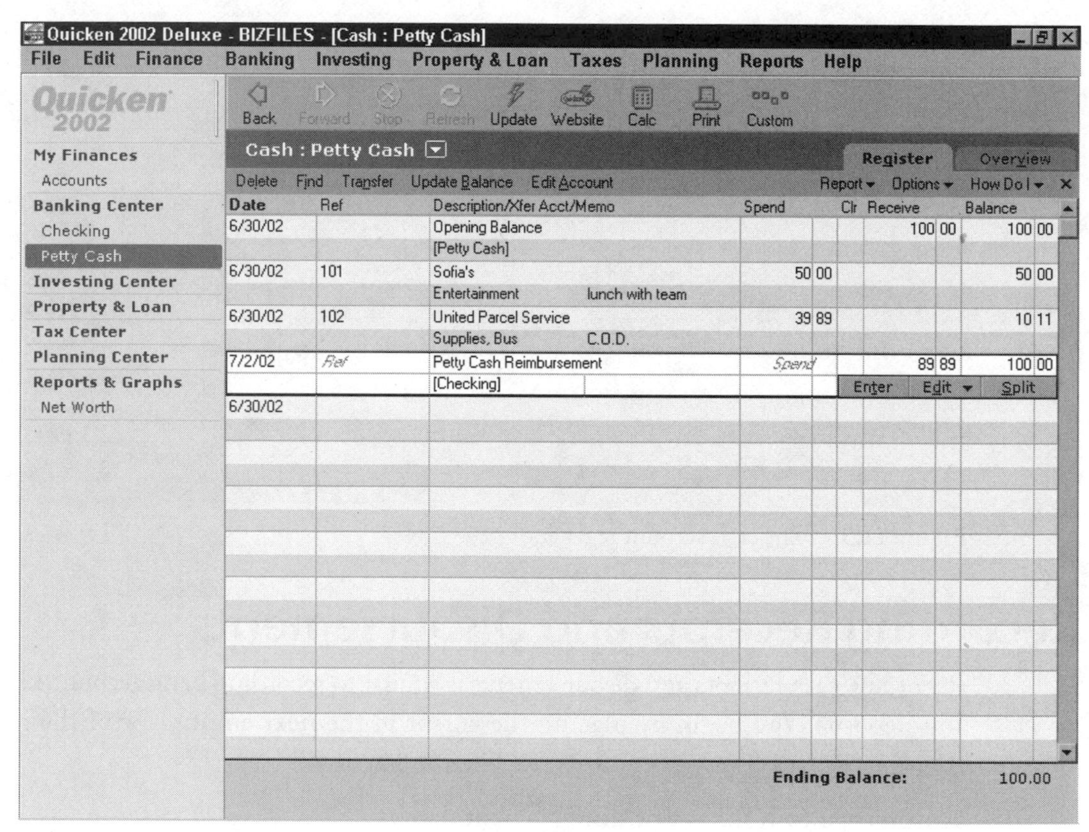

Figure 11.6: A cash account register with several transactions.

TIP *To reimburse the petty cash account, you can't simply transfer money the same way you transfer money from a checking account to a savings account. You presumably need to visit the bank, write a check for cash, and use that cash to replenish the petty cash box.*

Updating the Cash Account Balance

When a cash account is displayed in the active document window, click the Update Balance command button, and Quicken displays the Update Account Balance dialog box, as shown in Figure 11.7. You can use it to enter a cash transaction that adjusts the current balance to whatever actual cash you hold. The Update Account Balance dialog box provides text boxes for entering the correct account balance, the category to use for the adjustment transaction, and the adjustment date. You just fill in the blanks and click OK.

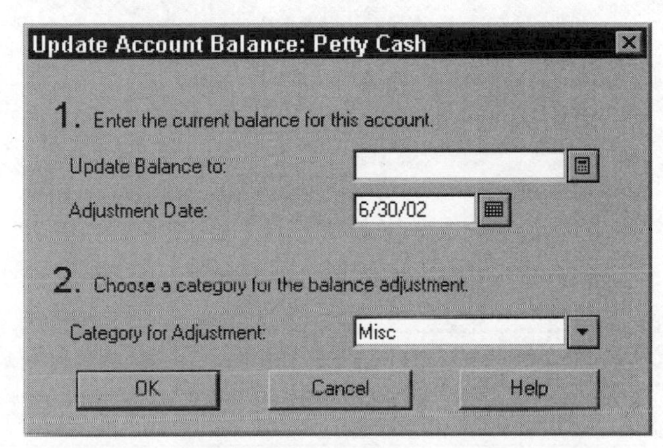

Figure 11.7: The Update Account Balance dialog box.

Working with a Petty Cash Box

Quicken's cash account feature and documentation suggests that you work in the fashion described in the preceding paragraphs. In other words, Quicken assumes that to track something like petty cash you will set up a cash account and then record transactions into the Quicken register every time you spend money and receive money.

This approach works fine, although it requires you to record transactions every time you spend or receive money. For this reason, you should know that there's a handy variation to the obvious method. What you can do is set up a cash account (as described earlier), and then spend money out of the petty cash account as needed, placing receipts for the spending back into the petty cash box. Periodically, you reimburse the petty cash account by writing a check to petty cash on the regular bank account. To categorize this check, you use the spending receipts stored in the petty cash box.

Here's an example of how this works. To return to the situation shown in Figure 11.6, suppose that you have a $100 petty cash fund and that from this fund you disburse two amounts: $50 to Sofia's, a local restaurant, for an employee luncheon and $39.89 to United Parcel Service for a C.O.D. delivery of some business supplies. Figure 11.6 shows the way that Quicken expects you to record these transactions. But what you could do instead is to write a check on your regular banking account for $89.89 and categorize this check as $50 of Entertainment and $39.89 of Supplies, Bus, as shown in Figure 11.8.

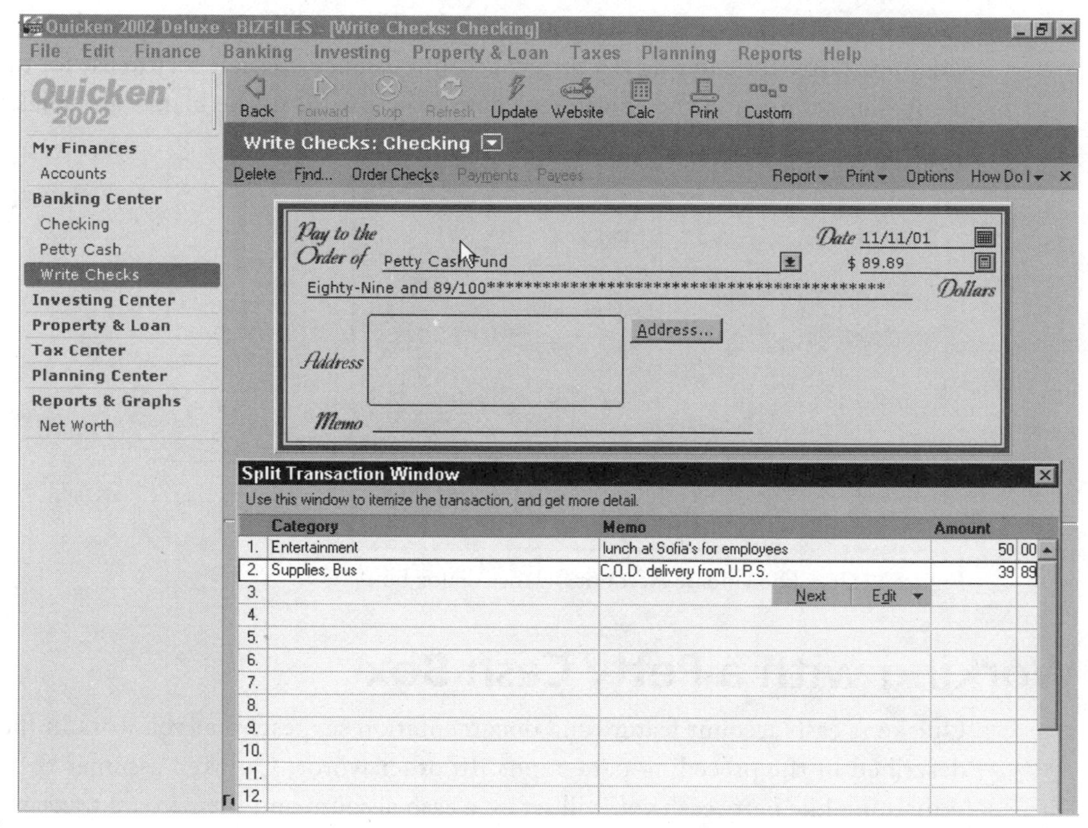

Figure 11.8: Reimbursing your petty cash fund by writing a check on your bank account.

When you reimburse petty cash by writing a check to petty cash, petty cash spending doesn't appear in the petty cash account. It appears in the bank account you're using to record the replenishment checks. The petty cash fund account balance doesn't change and, then, is frequently in error. Anytime, in fact, that you've spent some of the petty cash money and haven't yet reimbursed the petty cash fund, Quicken's records overstate the petty cash fund account balance. But as a practical matter, this error is usually immaterial. Another way to think about this error is that it's a tradeoff: You get to simplify your petty cash record-keeping, but for the simplicity you trade away a bit of accuracy.

TIP *The one trick to using this simplified approach to petty cash accounting is that you need to religiously store unreimbursed receipts from petty cash spending in the petty cash box. The total of the cash and the receipts in the petty cash box should always equal your petty cash fund account balance as shown in Quicken.*

Working with a Cash Drawer

Quicken isn't set up very well to work with a cash drawer or cash register till. In fact, if you use a cash drawer or cash register, this condition indicates that you may want to step up to Quicken's big-brother product, QuickBooks. QuickBooks supports point-of-sale accounting, which means it works with cash registers to record sales.

In simple situations, however, you can use Quicken for cash drawer accounting. What you want to do first, is set up a cash account (as described earlier in the chapter) for your cash drawer balance.

As you collect money from customers, you store the cash or checks in the cash drawer. At the end of the day, you take the following steps:

1. Remove and then count your cash drawer balance. This balance includes both your starting cash drawer balance and the money you received from customers during the day.
2. Replenish your cash drawer balance by replacing the original, start-of-the-day cash balance.
3. Tally the sales for the day and then record a deposit into your bank account register for the sales proceeds that you received for the day.
4. If you have some way to audit your sales for the day—say, as by comparing the day's sales receipts to the actual total daily sales—attempt to do so. If there's a discrepancy, explore whether the discrepancy stems from an honest error in collecting cash from or in making change for a customer (which is very common) or from employee or customer theft (which is also, unfortunately, very common).

Preventing Cash Drawer Embezzlement

If you're a business owner and you'll be manning the cash drawer, you don't have to be as careful in tracking your sales and receipts. By definition, you can't steal from yourself and all of your mistakes will be honest.

If, however, you'll have employees manning the cash drawer, you need to create some method for reducing the opportunities for employee theft. One of the most common ways to do this is to require the person keeping the cash drawer to issue receipts to customers. As long as you keep a copy of any receipts issued to customers, you can total these receipts and compare them to the sales for the day. One tactic that businesses use to ensure employees issue receipts is putting up a sign that says, "If you don't get a receipt, your purchase is free." This gambit tends to force even dishonest employees to prepare receipts if, as part of preparing a receipt for the customer, the employee also prepares a copy of the receipt for you.

Note also that cash registers typically prepare two receipts as part of every sale—one that's given to the customer and the other that's safely locked inside the register. You can also use a simpler method—those pads of receipts sold by office supply stores. However, you want to make sure that a dishonest employee can't easily obtain a duplicate pad of receipts. Why? A duplicate pad of receipts could be used by a dishonest employee to issue fake receipts for occasional sales.

Chapter 12

BUSINESS LOANS AND MORTGAGES

In This Chapter

- Using the Loan Calculator
- Saving money with early repayment
- Tracking loans and mortgages
- How to borrow and repay money

Earlier chapters described how you can use Quicken to track items such as bank accounts and credit cards and the ways you earn and spend your money. You can also use Quicken to track your debts and what they cost you. Performing this record keeping lets you more closely monitor your liabilities. And if you keep records of all your assets, Quicken lets you track your net worth as well.

NOTE *Everything I talk about in this chapter applies to both personal and business accounting. Don't let the fact that I use business examples and situations make you think otherwise.*

Before You Begin

What you need to know to track loans and mortgages depends on what you want to do:

- To track any loan or mortgage, you need to know the current loan balance. You can probably get this information from your most recent loan statement or by telephoning the lender.
- To have Quicken break down loan payments into the interest and principal components, you need to know the loan's annual interest rate and the remaining number of payments. You can get this information from the loan contract or perhaps by telephoning the lender.

Using the Loan Calculator

The Loan Calculator works well for experimenting with possible loan balances and payments. You can use this tool to see, for example, what the loan payment would be on that car you're eyeing or what size mortgage you can afford, given a specific payment amount.

To use the Loan Calculator for these tasks, follow these steps:

1. Choose Planning ➢ Financial Calculators ➢ Loan to display the Loan Calculator dialog box, as shown in Figure 12.1.

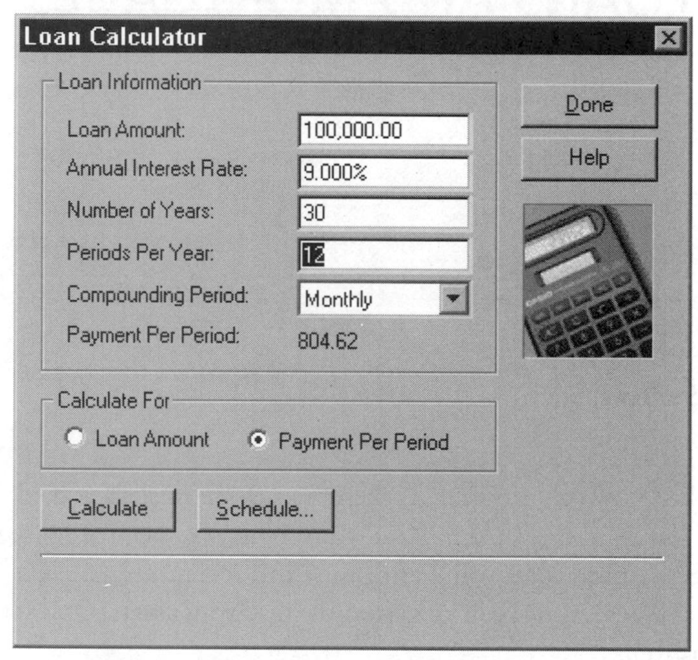

Figure 12.1: The Loan Calculator dialog box can calculate either the loan amount or the payment.

2. Tell Quicken which loan variable you want to calculate: Mark the Loan Amount option button in the Calculate For section to calculate a loan payment given the loan amount, or mark the Payment Per Period option button to calculate the loan amount given a loan payment.
3. If you've indicated you want to calculate a loan payment, enter the loan balance in the Loan Amount text box.
4. Enter the loan's annual interest rate in the Annual Interest Rate text box. If a loan charges 9 percent annually, for example, type *9*.
5. Using the Number Of Years text box, enter the number of years over which you will repay the loan. For a 30-year mortgage, for example, type *30*.
6. Enter the number of payments you'll make each year into the Periods Per Year text box. In Figure 12.1, this text box shows 12, which indicates monthly payments.

7. If you indicated in step 2 that you want to calculate a loan balance, enter the loan payment you want to or will make in the Payment Per Period text box.

Once you complete these steps, click the Calculate button, and Quicken calculates the variable you said you wanted to calculate. Figure 12.1, for example, shows that the monthly payment on a $100,000 30-year mortgage bearing 9 percent annual interest equals $804.62.

To create an amortization schedule that shows the periodic payments, the interest and principal portions of these payments, and the loan balance after each payment, click the Schedule command button. Quicken produces an amortization schedule report and displays it in its own dialog box, as shown in Figure 12.2. You can print the amortization schedule by clicking the dialog box's Print command button.

Approximate Future Payment Schedule

Print Close

Pmt	Principal	Interest	Balance
		9.0%	100,000.00
1	54.62	750.00	99,945.38
2	55.03	749.59	99,890.35
3	55.44	749.18	99,834.91
4	55.86	748.76	99,779.05
5	56.28	748.34	99,722.77
6	56.70	747.92	99,666.07
7	57.12	747.50	99,608.95
8	57.55	747.07	99,551.40
9	57.98	746.64	99,493.42
10	58.42	746.20	99,435.00
11	58.86	745.76	99,376.14
12	59.30	745.32	99,316.84
13	59.74	744.88	99,257.10
14	60.19	744.43	99,196.91

Figure 12.2: The Approximate Future Payment Schedule dialog box.

Saving Money with Early Repayment

You can often save enormous sums by repaying a loan early. In the preceding section, for example, I referred to a $100,000 30-year mortgage bearing 9 percent annual interest. Although such a mortgage loan would call for monthly payments of $804.62, suppose a borrower could afford to increase the payment amount by $20 to $824.62—and the lender doesn't charge prepayment penalties. By making the larger payment each month, the borrower would save $24,135.56. No, you didn't misread the amount. An extra $20 a month results in roughly $24,000 of interest savings!

You can calculate how much money you'll save by early repayment of a loan such as a mortgage. To do this, calculate the total regular-sized payments you would have made according to the loan contract and the total new-but-bigger payments you're now planning to make. The difference between these two amounts equals the interest savings from the new payment.

Making the Early Repayment Calculations

The calculations just described require several steps, so I've created a simple worksheet you can use to work through the numbers. It is shown in Table 13.1. The worksheet's left column of numbers shows how you would calculate the interest rate savings by adding an extra $20 to a monthly payment of $804.62 when you have a $100,000, 30-year mortgage bearing 9 percent interest. The worksheet's right column provides blank spaces that you can use to calculate the actual interest rate savings you would receive via early loan repayment.

Table 13.1: The Early Loan Repayment Savings Worksheet.

INPUT DESCRIPTION	EXAMPLE LOAN	YOUR LOAN
Line 1: Regular payment amount	804.62	
Line 2: Number of remaining regular payments	360	
Line 3: Total regular payments (line 1 × line 2)	289,663.20	
Line 4: New payment amount	823.12	
Line 5: Number of remaining new payments	324	
Line 6: Total new payments (line 4 × line 5)	266,690.88	
Line 7: Repayment savings (line 3 – line 6)	22,969.08	

To complete the worksheet, follow these steps:

1. Enter the regular payment amount on line 1.
2. Enter the remaining number of payments on line 2. If you've just closed on a 30-year mortgage with monthly payments, for example, you have 360 monthly payments remaining. If you're halfway through repaying the same loan, you have 180 monthly payments remaining.
3. Multiply line 1 by line 2 to calculate the total remaining payments (you can use the Quicken calculator) and enter the result on line 3. To calculate the total remaining

payments when the regular monthly payment equals $804.62 and there are 360 months of payments left, for example, multiply $804.62 by 360 months for a result of $289,663.20.

4. To set up the Loan Calculator so it's ready for calculating the number of new, larger payments you'll need to make, display the Loan Calculator dialog box and mark the Payment Per Period option button. Enter the remaining loan balance in the Loan Amount text box, the loan's interest rate in the Annual Interest Rate text box, and the number of payments per year (probably 12) in the Payments Per Year text box.

5. To estimate the number of years you'll make the new, larger payment, just keep entering new, smaller values in the Number Of Years text box until you find the Number Of Years value that results in a calculated loan payment that's close to your new payment; you probably won't be able to get a Number Of Years value that produces a payment amount exactly equal to your new planned payment. In the example, setting the Number Of Years to 27 produces a payment amount equal to $823.13 even though I've indicated that $824.62 is really the new payment planned. This means I need to calculate the early repayment savings stemming from a monthly payment of $823.13, not $824.62.

6. Enter the new payment in the Loan Calculator dialog box on line 4 of the worksheet. In this case, this amount is $823.13. Actually, you will probably make the $824.62 payment because that figure equals the extra $20 plus the regular payment of $804.62. Unfortunately, you can't calculate the early repayment savings that stem from an $824.62 payment, only from an $823.13 payment.

7. Calculate the number of new, larger payments you'll need to make, and enter this value on line 5 of the worksheet. Do this by multiplying the value in the Number Of Years text box by 12. If you'll make 27 years of monthly payments, for example, you calculate the number of payments as 324 (27 × 12).

8. Calculate the total new payments you'll make and enter this value on line 6 of the worksheet. To calculate the total remaining payments when the new monthly payment equals $823.13 and there are 324 months of payments left, for example, multiply the monthly payment of $823.13 by 324 months for a result of $266,694.12.

9. Calculate the difference between the total regular payments and the total new payments, and enter this value on line 7 of the worksheet.

In the example, this difference of $22,969.08 represents the interest savings stemming from early repayment of the loan using the payment amount shown on line 4. If a borrower actually paid an amount larger than the monthly payment shown on line 4, the early repayment savings would exceed those shown in the worksheet.

Should You Always Repay Early?

When you work through the numbers, the savings that stem from early repayment of a loan can seem almost too good to be true. Can a few dollars a month really add up to, for example, $25,000 of savings?

When you save money over long periods of time and let the interest compound, the amount of interest you ultimately earn becomes very large. In effect, when you pay an extra $20 a month on a 9 percent mortgage, you're saving $20 each month in a savings account that pays 9 percent. By "saving" this $20 over more than 25 years, you earn a lot of interest. In the earlier example, this monthly $20 really would add up to roughly $23,000.

But you can't look just at the interest savings. If you placed the same $20 a month into a money market fund, purchased savings bonds, or invested in a stock market mutual fund, you would also accumulate interest or investment income.

How can you know whether early repayment of a loan makes sense? Simply compare the interest rate on the loan with the interest rate (or investment rate of return) you would earn on alternative investments. If you can place money in a money market fund that earns 6 percent or repay a mortgage charging you 9 percent, you'll do better by repaying the mortgage. Its interest rate exceeds the interest rate of the money market account. But if you can stick money in a small company stock fund and earn 12 percent or repay a mortgage charging you 9 percent, you'll do better by putting your money in the stock fund.

One complicating factor, however, relates to income taxes. Some interest expense, such as mortgage interest, is tax-deductible. What's more, some interest income is tax-exempt, and some interest income isn't tax-deferred. Income taxes make early repayment decisions a little bit complicated, but here are four rules of thumb:

- If you're a business owner with the ability to invest additional funds in the business—and that investment will produce extra profits—you should usually make this investment first. Investments in small businesses often return 20 percent to 30 percent annually. If you can get that sort of return, every other opportunity pales in comparison. Note that in Chapter 14, I describe how to estimate the returns you receive from business investments.
- Usually, if you have extra money that you can tie up for a long time and can't invest additional money profitably in your business, you'll make the most money by saving your money in a way that provides you with an initial tax deduction and where the interest compounds tax free, such as a 401(k) plan or an IRA. (Opportunities in which an employer kicks in an extra amount by matching a portion of your contribution are usually too good to pass up—if you can afford them.)

- If you've taken advantage of investment options that give you tax breaks and you want to save additional money, your next best bet is usually to pay off any loans or credit cards that charge interest you can't deduct, such as credit card debt. Start with the loan or credit card charging the highest interest rate and then work your way down to the loan or credit card charging the lowest interest rate. For this to really work, of course, you can't go out and charge a credit card back up to its limit after you repay it.
- If you repay loans with nondeductible interest and you still have additional money you want to save, you can begin repaying loans that charge tax-deductible interest. Again, you should start with the loan charging the highest interest rate first.

Understanding the Mechanics

Successful saving relies on a simple financial truth: You should save money in a way that results in the highest annual interest, including all the income tax effects.

It's tricky to include income taxes in the calculations, however. They affect your savings in two ways. One way is that they may reduce the interest income you receive or the interest expense you save. If interest income is taxed, for example, you need to multiply the pretax interest rate by the factor (1–*marginal tax rate*) to calculate the after-income-taxes interest rate. And if interest expense is tax-deductible, you need to multiply the interest rate by the factor (1–*marginal tax rate*) to calculate the after-income-taxes interest rate.

NOTE *The marginal tax rate is the tax rate you pay on your last dollars of income.*

For example, suppose you have four savings options: a credit card charging 12 percent nondeductible interest, a mortgage charging 6 percent tax-deductible interest, a tax-exempt money market fund earning 4 percent; and a mutual fund earning 9 percent taxable interest income. To know which of these savings opportunities is best, you need to calculate the after-income-taxes interest rates. If your marginal income tax rate equals 33 percent—meaning you pay $.33 in income taxes on your last dollars of income—the after-income-taxes interest rates are as follows:

- 12 percent interest on the credit card
- 6 percent interest on the mutual fund
- 4 percent interest on the mortgage
- 4 percent interest on the tax-exempt money market fund

In this case, your best savings opportunity is the credit card; by repaying it you save 12 percent. Next best is the mutual fund because even after paying the income taxes, you'll earn 6 percent. Finally, the mortgage and tax-exempt money market fund savings opportunities produce 4 percent after you deduct the effect of income taxes.

TIP *The difference between percentages such as 12 percent and 6 percent may not seem all that large. But choosing the savings opportunity with the highest after-income-taxes rate delivers big benefits. If you invest $20 each month in something paying 6 percent after income taxes, you'll accumulate $5,107 over 25 years. But if you invest $20 each month in something paying 12 percent after income taxes, you'll accumulate $13,848 over 25 years.*

The second complicating factor stems from the tax deduction you sometimes get for certain kinds of investments, such as IRAs and 401(k) plans. When you get an immediate tax deduction, you actually get to boost your savings amount by the tax deduction. This effectively boosts the interest rate.

For example, if you have an extra $1,000 to save and use it to repay a credit card charging 12 percent, you will save $120 of interest expense (12% × $1,000).

If you save the $1,000 in a way that results in a tax deduction, such as through an IRA, things can change quite a bit. Say your marginal income tax rate is 33 percent. In this case, you can actually contribute $1,500. ($1,000 / the factor [1–*marginal tax rate*]). The arithmetic might not make sense, but the result should. If you have $1,000 to save but you get a 33 percent tax deduction, you can actually save $1,500, because you'll get a $500 tax deduction ($1,500 × 33%).

What's more, by investing in a tax-deferred opportunity, you avoid paying income taxes while you're earning interest. (A tax-deferred investment just lets you postpone paying the income taxes.) If you invest in a stock mutual fund earning 10 percent, for example, you can keep the whole 10 percent as long as you leave the money in the stock mutual fund. If you work out the interest income calculations, you would find that you earn 10 percent on $1,500, or $150. So the tax deduction and the tax-deferred interest income mean you'll earn more annually on the stock mutual fund paying 10 percent than you will save on the credit card charging 12 percent.

Be aware that ultimately you pay income taxes on the money you take out of a tax-deferred investment opportunity, such as an IRA. In the example, you would need to pay back the $500 income tax deduction, and you would also need to pay income taxes on the $150. (At 33 percent, you would pay $50 of taxes on the $150 of interest income, too.)

In general, however, if you're saving for retirement, it usually still makes sense to go with a savings opportunity that produces a tax deduction and lets you postpone your income taxes. The reason is that the income taxes you postpone also boost your savings—and thereby boost your interest rate. (It's also possible that your marginal income tax rate will be lower when you withdraw money from a tax-deferred savings opportunity.)

Tracking Loans and Mortgages

You can keep detailed records of loan balances and the payments you make on the loan. First, however, you'll need to set up an account in Quicken. To create an account for a car loan, mortgage, or any other debt you owe, follow these steps:

1. Choose Lists ➢ Account to display the Account List window, as shown in Figure 12.3.

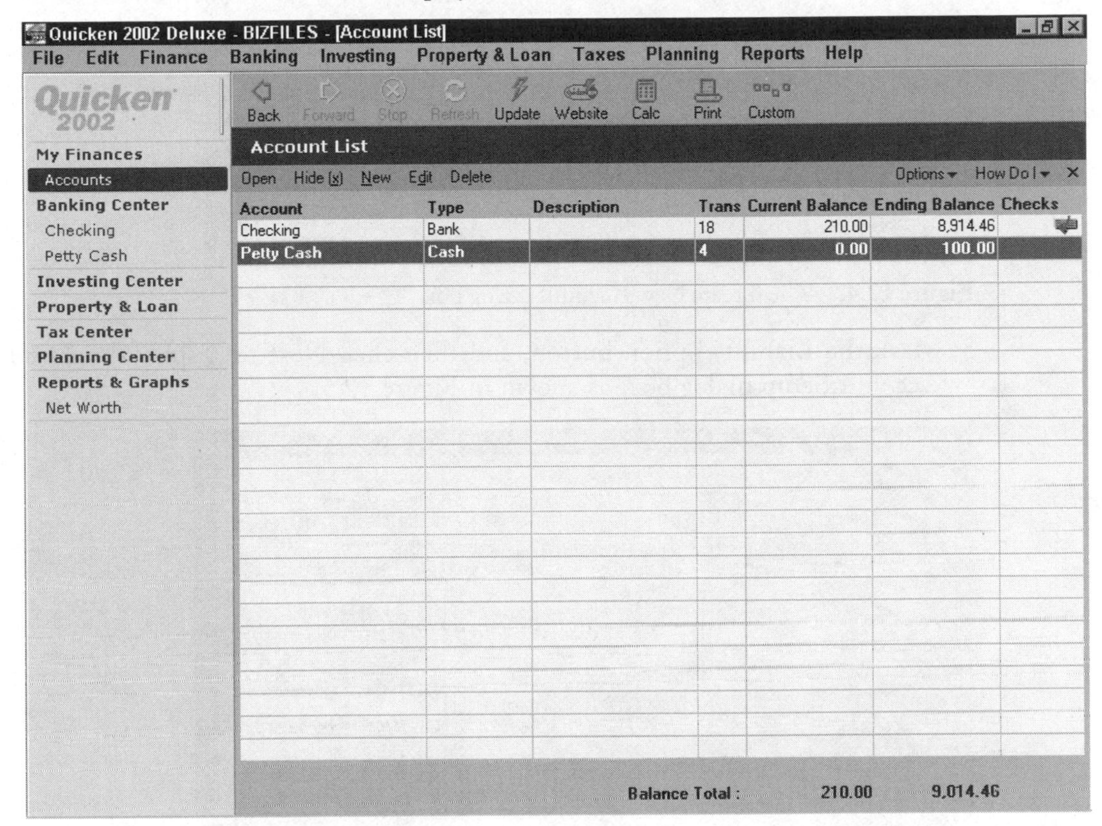

Figure 12.3: The Account List window.

2. Click the New command button to display the Create New Account dialog box, as shown in Figure 12.4.

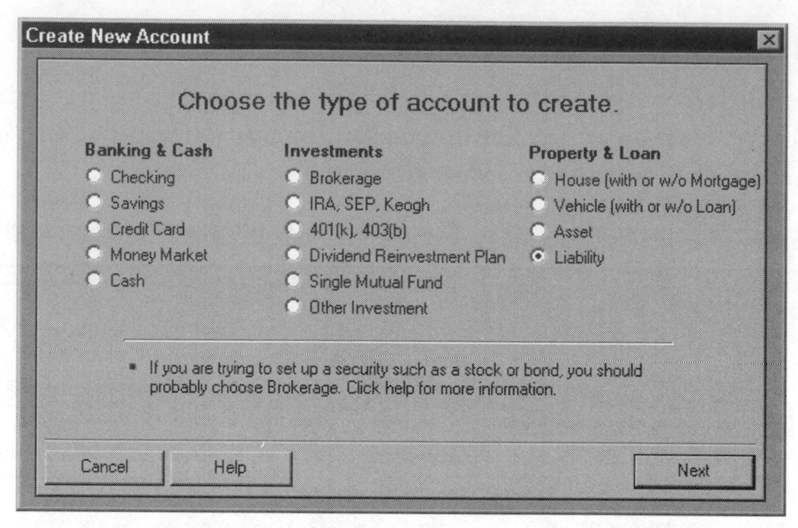

Figure 12.4: The Create New Account dialog box.

3. Mark the Liability option button, and then click Next to display the first Liability Account Setup dialog box, as shown in Figure 12.5.

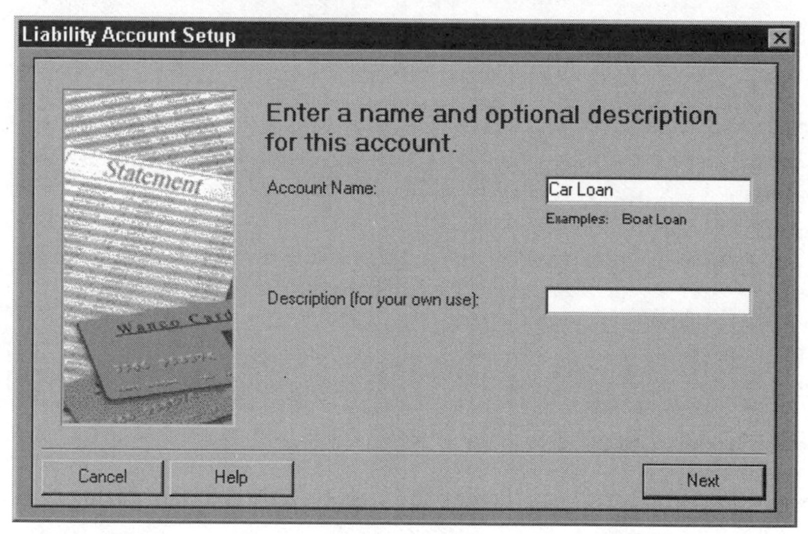

Figure 12.5: The first Liability Account Setup dialog box.

4. In the Account Name text box, enter an account name, such as ***Mortgage*** or ***Car Loan***.
5. In the Description text box, enter a description of the loan or mortgage or additional information, such as the loan number or the lender's name.
6. Click Next to display the second Liability Account Setup dialog box, as shown in Figure 12.6.

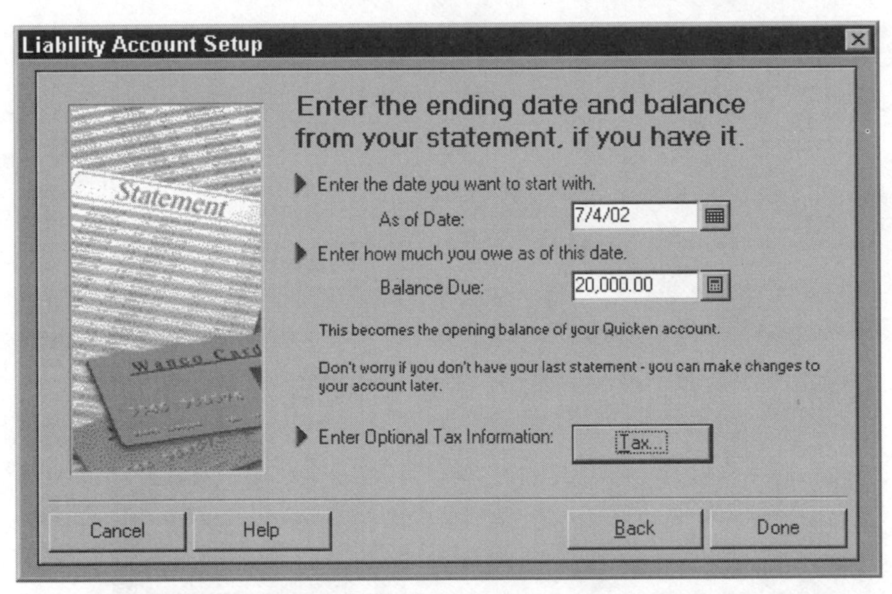

Figure 12.6: The second Liability Account Setup dialog box.

7. In the Balance text box, enter the account balance on the day you'll start keeping records for the loan.

NOTE *You can enter the loan balance as of the last statement date, but this figure won't include the payments made since the last statement. You will need to enter any transactions that have occurred since then.*

8. Enter the date on which you start keeping records for the loan in *MM/DD/YY* format. For example, enter July 4, 2002, as *7/4/02*.
9. Click Done to tell Quicken that the Liability Account Setup dialog box is complete.
10. When Quicken asks if you would like to set up an amortized loan, answer the question by clicking either the Yes or No command button.
    - If you answer this question with the No button, you're finished with the liability account setup and can skip the rest of the steps listed here.
    - If you answer this question with the Yes button, be sure to click the Summary tab. Quicken displays the Loan Setup dialog box, as shown in Figure 12.7.

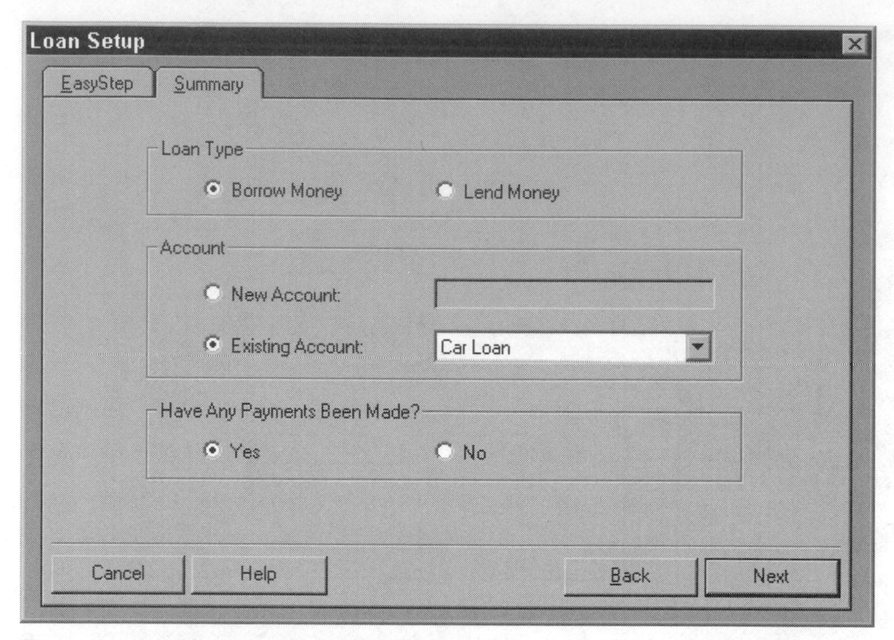

Figure 12.7: The Loan Setup dialog box.

11. Because our example is set up as a Car Loan account, the Loan Type is Borrow Money, and the account is an existing car loan account. Since the account is new, no payments have been made; so mark the No option button. Click Next, and Quicken displays the next stage of the Loan Setup dialog box, as shown in Figure 12.8.

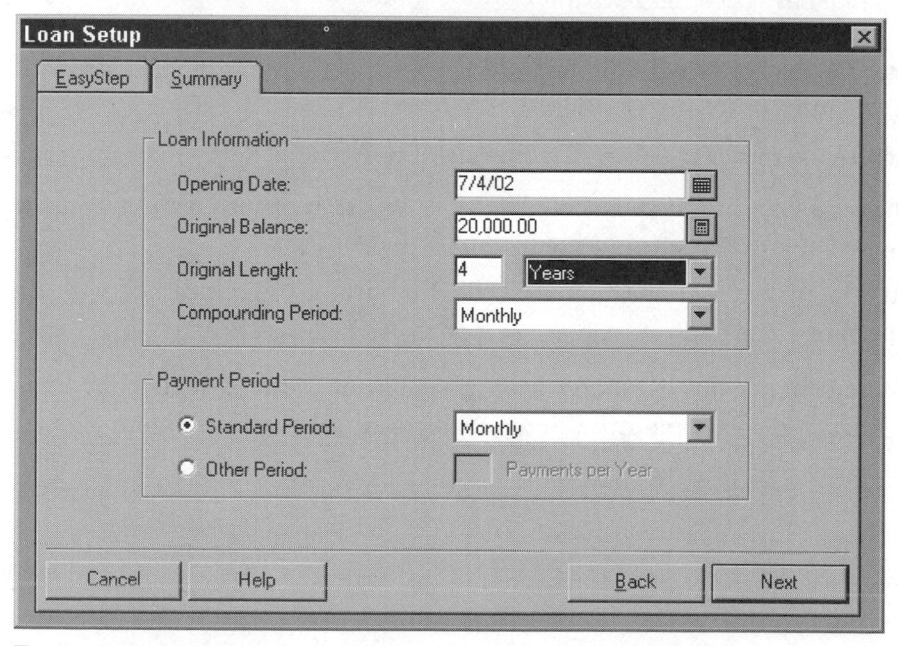

Figure 12.8: Part 2 of the Loan Setup dialog box.

12. The Opening Date text box shows the date you entered in the Create New Account window. Confirm the original amount of the loan in the Original Balance text box. Note that you can display a pop-up calculator by clicking the button at the right end of the Original Balance text box.

13. Use the Original Length boxes to specify how long you'll make payments on the loan. Enter the number of years or months in the first text box. Then use the second box (a combo box) to specify whether you've entered the length in years or months.

14. Use the Payment Period option buttons and boxes to indicate how often you'll make loan payments. The default payment period is a standard payment made monthly. You can select another payment period by selecting another period from the Standard Period drop-down list box—Monthly, Bi-Monthly, Semi-Monthly, and so on. You can also use the Other Period option button and box to specify a different period.

15. Click Next when you finish providing Quicken with the Loan Information and Payment Period information. Quicken displays a new set of buttons and boxes, as shown in Figure 12.9.

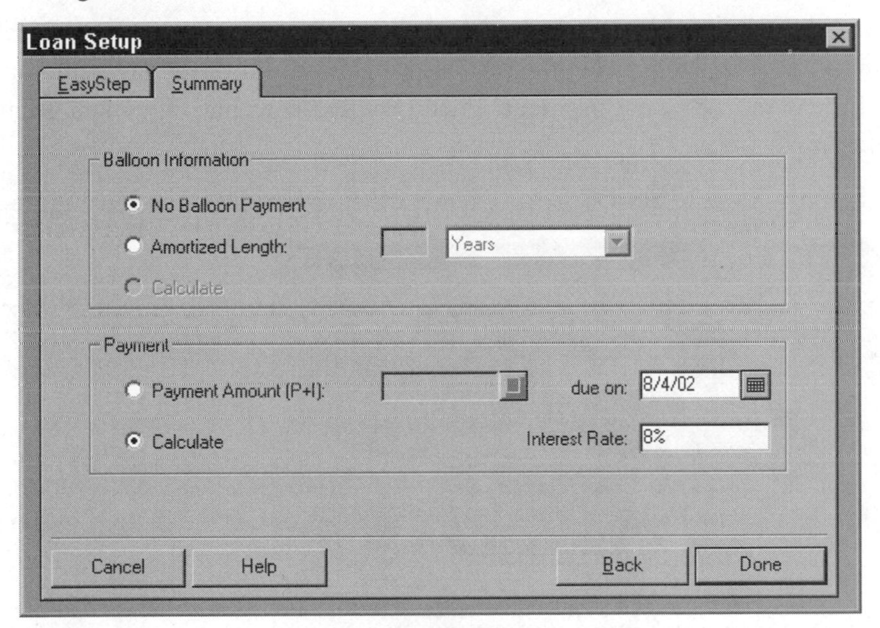

Figure 12.9: Part 3 of the Loan Setup dialog box.

16. If your loan includes a balloon payment, use the Balloon Information options to describe the loan's balloon payment. Enter the number of months or years (or some other time period) that the lender used to amortize the loan balance and to calculate the regular payments. Then indicate how you've specified this amortization term: months, years, or some other time period. (If your loan includes a balloon payment and you don't know the amortization term but you do know the regular payment amount, you can mark the Calculate button in the Balloon Information options to have Quicken determine the balloon payment for you.)

17. Enter the loan's interest rate in the Interest Rate text box.

NOTE *Don't use the annual percentage rate figure as the annual interest rate, even though it is required by truth-in-lending laws in the United States and the United Kingdom (and maybe elsewhere). The annual percentage rate (APR) expresses all the costs of obtaining credit, including the loan interest, any fees, things like loan origination costs, and so on. APRs are an excellent way to compare the overall costs of one loan with another. But you can't use an APR to calculate loan payments because it's not the loan interest rate. The annual interest rate is documented in your loan agreement.*

18. What you do next depends on whether you will make a balloon payment:
    - If you haven't specified that Quicken should calculate the balloon payment, mark the Payment option's Calculate button. Then click Done to have Quicken calculate the loan payment. Quicken presents a dialog box saying that it has estimated the amount of the payment and asking you to click OK and then Done to accept the estimate.
    - If you did tell Quicken to calculate the balloon payment, use the Payment Amount button and boxes to provide the regular principal and interest payment you'll make and the date of the first payment. Then click Done to have Quicken calculate the balloon payment.
19. Quicken displays the Set Up Loan Payment dialog box, as shown in Figure 12.10.

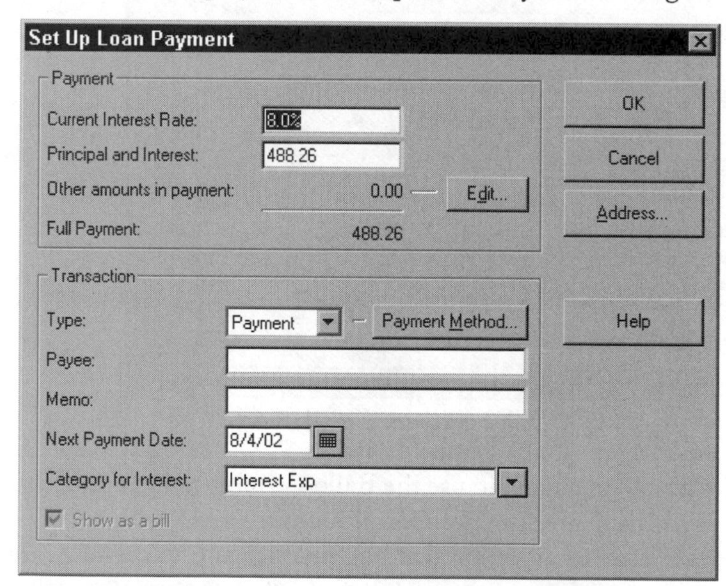

Figure 12.10: The Set Up Loan Payment dialog box.

20. If you'll pay other amounts with the loan payment, such as $100 a month for insurance, click the Edit command button to display the Split Transaction Window, as shown in Figure 12.11. This is the same window you see whenever you split a transaction among multiple categories.

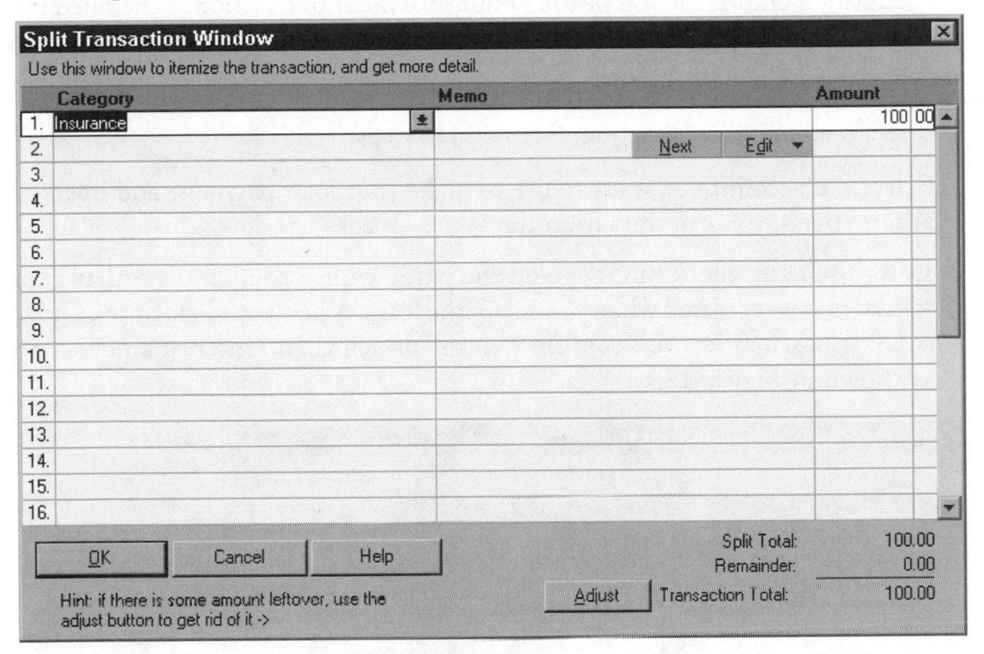

Figure 12.11: The Split Transaction Window.

21. Enter the category and amount of any other expenses you'll pay with the loan payment. For example, $100 of car insurance might be categorized as Insurance. Click OK, and Quicken redisplays the Set Up Loan Payment dialog box.

22. In the Transaction area of the Set Up Loan Payment dialog box, enter the information that will be used to complete the payment. In the Type drop-down list, choose Payment if you plan to write the payment from your checkbook, choose Print Check if you plan to use a Quicken memorized transaction to write the check, or select Online Pmt if you will use Quicken's online banking feature to make this payment. Enter the Payee for this payment.

23. If you want Quicken to print a check for this payment, click the Address command button to open a dialog box you can use to enter the address to be printed. Click OK.

24. Click OK again. Quicken displays a message asking if you would like to associate an asset with this loan. For now, click No. You're finished.

You have done a lot of work, but you won't need to do anything further except to make an occasional "tweak" if some element of your loan changes. Ways to maintain and alter your loan are discussed in the following sections.

Making Payments

One of the final steps of setting up your new loan transaction is to use the Type drop-down list in the Set Up Loan Payment dialog box to specify whether your payment should be a scheduled, memorized, or repeating online payment transaction. Scheduled transactions are entered automatically on the date you specify. (Repeating online payment transactions are covered in Chapter 9.)

To use a memorized transaction, follow these steps:

1. Select the account you want to use to make your loan payment and open its register. Alternatively, you can start from the Write Checks window.
2. Enter the date, check number, and the payee name. You will find that a memorized transaction was created when you set up the loan. When you click Enter, Quicken opens a dialog box that lets you confirm that the principal and interest amounts are correct, as shown in Figure 12.12.

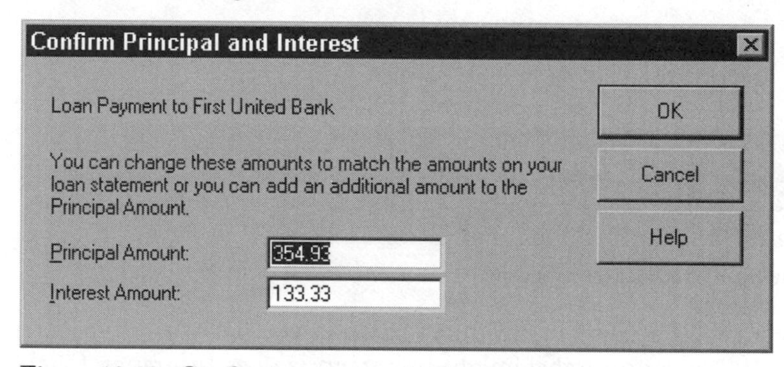

Figure 12.12: Confirming a memorized transaction.

3. Confirm or change the amounts shown in the dialog box. Click OK to close the dialog box.

Maintaining Your Loan

Once you've set up a loan, you will want to track its progress and, if it is a variable-rate loan, change the interest rate from time to time. The View Loans window shown in Figure 12.13 is the key to these activities.

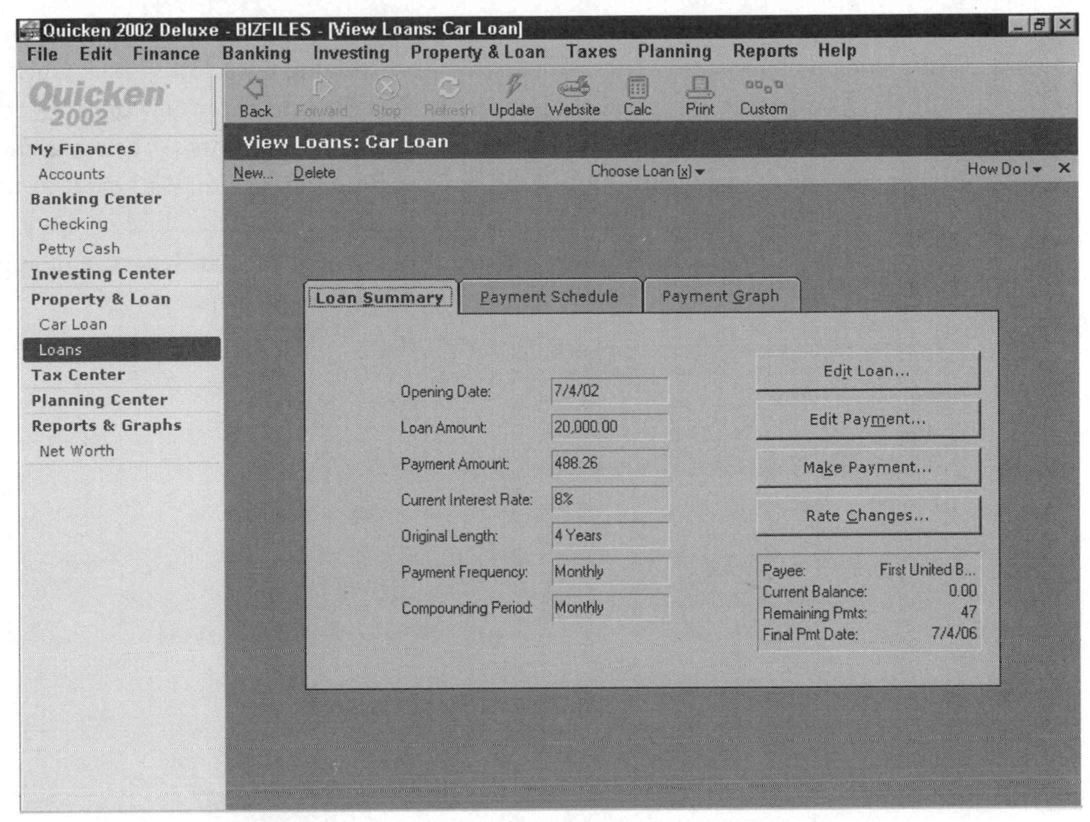

Figure 12.13: The Loan Summary tab of the View Loans window.

To display the View Loans window, choose Property & Loan ➢ Loans. You can choose the loan to view from the drop-down list that appears when you click the Choose Loan command button at the top of the window. The Loan Summary tab of the View Loans window shows the specifications of the loan, such as payee, term, and interest rate.

The Payment Schedule tab shows details about payments, and the Payment Graph tab shows a line graph that plots the loan balance.

Along the right edge of the View Loans window are four command buttons: Edit Loan, Edit Payment, Make Payment, and Rate Changes. Choosing the Edit Loan button opens the Edit Loan dialog box containing the details of the active loan. You can edit the loan information, retracing the steps covered in the preceding section on setting up a loan. If you choose the Edit Payment button, Quicken opens the Edit Loan Payment dialog box, in which you can edit the payment information. If you choose Make Payment, Quicken enters the next loan payment for you and then asks if you want to record the transaction.

Choosing Rate Changes opens the Loan Rate Changes dialog box shown in Figure 12.14. This dialog box displays a history of rate changes involving the selected loan. Click the Edit command button to change existing rates, or click New to enter new ones. Quicken will calculate the necessary change in payment based on the new rate. When you change the interest rate or the payment in the Edit Interest Rate Change dialog box or in the Insert An Interest Rate Change dialog box, click OK, and then click Close in the Loan Rate Changes dialog box. Quicken recalculates the payment or loan length and applies the changes to the payment history section in the View Loans window.

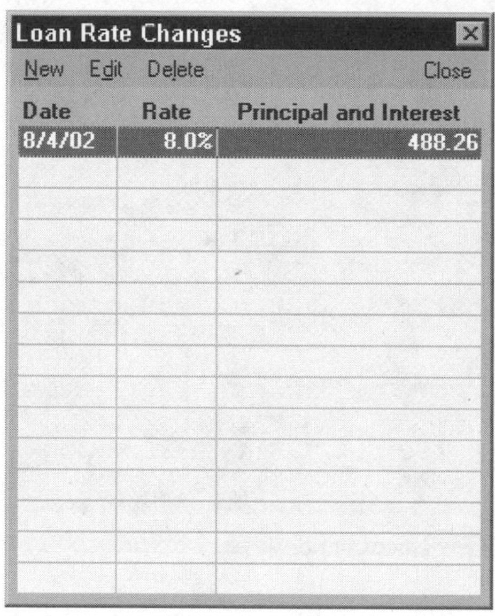

Figure 12.14: The Loan Rate Changes dialog box.

Adjusting Interest Calculations

It's possible that the interest calculation Quicken makes won't agree with the interest calculation a lender makes. Such discrepancies are common when you're talking about loans other than mortgages: car loans, business loans, and so on. If you make a payment a few days early or a few days late, for example, or if there's a delay in the mail, the number of days of interest you calculate will differ from the number of days of interest the lender calculates.

NOTE *Interest calculation discrepancies aren't as much a problem with mortgage interest calculations because your lender probably calculates a month's worth of interest even if you pay early or pay late. Of course, if you pay too late, the mortgage lender may also assess a late-payment penalty.*

To adjust the Quicken interest calculations so that they agree with the lender's, display the loan's register in the active document window, and then click on its Update Balance command button. When Quicken displays the Update Account Balance dialog box, you enter the loan balance as of the date you're making the correction (often the loan statement date), the interest expense category you're using to summarize interest expense on this loan, and the date you're making the correction.

Figure 12.15 shows the Update Account Balance dialog box with entries to adjust a loan balance to $19,655 on September 4, 2002. If the loan balance before this adjustment was shown as $19,652.30, Quicken will add an adjustment transaction to the loan's register that reduces the loan balance by $2.70 and categorizes this change as interest expense.

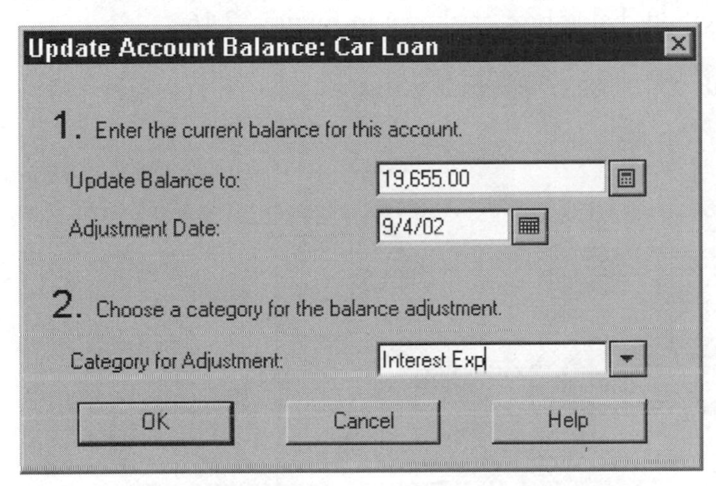

Figure 12.15: The Update Account Balance dialog box allows you to make adjustments to the account.

If it's confusing to you that the adjustment transaction is categorized as interest expense, remember this: When you set up an amortized transaction, Quicken splits all your loan payments between a principal category (which is actually a transfer to the liability account) and an interest category. If the liability account balance is wrong, it's because the split between principal and interest was wrong. And if the total principal splits are too low by, say, $2.70, it also means the total interest splits are too high by $2.70.

WARNING *If the interest expense you're recording in Quicken is tax deductible—because it's interest charged on a business loan or on a qualifying mortgage on a residence—you need to use the lender's total interest expense figure for your tax deduction, not the figure shown in your Quicken records. So, if you export Quicken's tax-deduction information to a tax-preparation package, be sure to adjust your loan balance and interest category total to whatever the mortgage lender shows on the annual loan statement information.*

Scheduling a Transaction Using the View Loans Window

If you have certain payments automatically deducted from a bank account, you set these up using the View Loans window. For example, you might well have your monthly mortgage payment automatically deducted from your checking account. To schedule these types of transactions, follow these steps:

1. Choose Property & Loan ➢ Loans to open the View Loans window.
2. Select the Payment Schedule tab, and click Edit Payment.
3. In the Edit Loan Payment dialog box, click the Payment Method button to open the Select Payment Method dialog box, as shown in Figure 12.16.

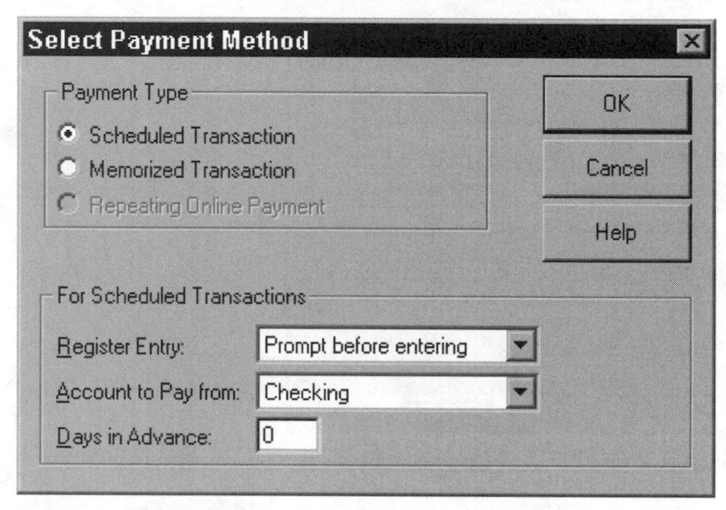

Figure 12.16: The Select Payment Method dialog box.

4. Mark the Scheduled Transaction option button and then record your preference for when to enter the transaction in the register, the account to use, and the number of days in advance you want to be reminded of the transaction.
5. Click OK.

At the appointed time, Quicken enters the transaction in the account. This happens as soon as you start Quicken on or following the next scheduled date.

Refinancing a Mortgage

There's one final loan transaction that's often tricky for people new to financial record keeping: recording a mortgage refinancing.

First, you need to set up a new liability account. The only difference is that you don't enter a balance for the new liability. You initially set the liability balance to zero by entering *0* into the Balance text box in the Liability Account Setup dialog box.

To record the starting loan balance, enter a transaction into the loan register. The amount of the transaction should be the loan amount. If the new loan equals the old loan, enter the category as the old, now-refinanced loan. If the new loan doesn't equal the old loan amount—say you borrowed a little more money as part of refinancing—you need to use the Split Transaction Window. One of the split transaction lines should show the old loan's account balance being transferred to the new loan's account balance. (This is really what you're doing—transferring a debt from one loan to another loan.) Any additional new loan amount you spend on items such as loan fees should be categorized using the appropriate expense. Finally, any cash you receive as part of the refinancing should be recorded as a transfer to the bank account into which you deposited the cash.

The rules of thumb people use in deciding whether or not to refinance are often useless. Calculating whether it makes sense to refinance a loan actually requires some very complicated analysis. Nevertheless, you can use some general rules in specific situations to easily determine when refinancing makes sense. First, you want to swap lower interest rate debt for higher interest rate. You can tell whether a new loan truly costs less when you include all the costs of obtaining credit by comparing its annual percentage rate (APR) with your existing loan's interest rate. The APR is the cost of borrowing money as a percentage of the loan. It includes not only the loan interest, but most of the other costs as well, including loan-origination charges, credit reports, escrow fees, and all the other ways the lender increases the cost of borrowing. If the new loan's APR is less than the old loan's interest rate, you will save interest—at least on a monthly basis—by swapping the new loan for the old loan.

You also want to make sure that you don't pay a lot more in interest on the new loan because its term is longer. For example, even in the case where you can refinance for free, it doesn't make sense to swap a 9 percent, 15-year mortgage for an 8 7/8 percent, 30-year mortgage; even though with the new 30-year mortgage you'll pay a little less interest for the first 15 years, you'll make payments for an extra 15 years. To deal with this "years' interest is charged" issue, ask the lender to calculate the APR on the new loan assuming that you'll have the new loan paid off by the same time you would have had the old loan paid off. (This will make the APR higher, by the way.) You'll also want to make payments that are large enough to have the new loan paid off by the same time you would have had the old loan paid off.

NOTE *If you are interested in refinancing your mortgage, Quicken's Refinance Planner can compute the potential savings and time to recover the refinancing costs.*

How to Borrow and Repay Money

Get smart about the way you borrow and repay money, and you can dramatically improve both your business and personal finances. Smart borrowing, however, is tricky. Dozens of big-dollar traps are out there waiting to snare you, and you have only a handful of money-saving tricks at your disposal.

Two Simple Rules

The following two simple rules for handling debt will take you a long way toward staying in the black.

Rule 1: Choose the Cheapest Debt You Can Find

By choosing the cheapest debt you can find—in other words, by finding the least expensive loan—you save money. It's that simple. Surprisingly, even small differences in interest rates can add up to big savings over time.

In the case of a fixed-interest-rate loan, choosing cheap debt is pretty easy to do. All you need to do is look for the loan with the lowest APR.

Finding a cheap loan is also relatively easy to do in the case of adjustable-interest-rate debt. With this type of debt, the interest rate is readjusted periodically, usually every six months or every year. Again, you can focus on the APR, but there is a slight problem with doing that: you want to make sure that you can bear the added risk of borrowing money at an unknown interest rate.

Rule 2: Repay the Loan before the Item You're Buying Wears Out

You should repay a loan before the item you're buying wears out. By doing so, you pay off the loan you borrowed to buy the first item before you buy the second item. A side benefit of this "quick repayment" approach is that you save substantial amounts in interest payments because you're not paying interest for two items, only one.

A debt, or loan, is a way to spread out the cost of something over the years that you use it, and it should be treated as such. By taking out a loan, you can purchase a house, purchase a delivery truck, or go to college, even though you don't have the cold, hard cash right now. For this privilege, you pay interest. But that doesn't have to be a bad situation as long as you're careful.

Thirty-year home mortgages are, for example, perfectly reasonable. You pay off a 30-year mortgage for most of your adult life, but that's okay, because you're using the loan to buy something that will hold its value and will benefit you for the entire

30 years. Homes built today, if they are well-maintained, can last for 100 years or more. Student loans, although they can take 10 or more years to pay off, are reasonable, because they provide long-term benefits such as preparation for a lifetime of employment.

To my mind, a five-year car loan is pretty reasonable as long as the car lasts five or more years. Again, the car loan payments end long before the car wears out. An even better deal is saving the money first and then buying a car with cash, but often that can't be done.

Ways of Borrowing Money

Money is usually borrowed in one of two ways: with revolving credit debt or amortizing debt.

Revolving Credit Debt

Revolving credit debt is the simpler approach. You probably have credit cards that fit into the revolving credit category. You borrow money on your credit card, interest is calculated on the amount you've borrowed, and at the end of the month, you pay the entire balance, a portion of the balance, or the interest for the month.

As a borrower, revolving credit offers more flexibility—and for this reason it is the most popular way to borrow money. The bank or credit card company sets minimum payment amounts and maximum credit limits, but within those guidelines, you borrow and repay as you please. Unfortunately, besides being the most flexible way to borrow money, revolving credit debt is also the most expensive.

Amortizing Debt

The other type of borrowing is *amortizing debt*. *Amortization* means paying off the balance on a loan in little increments over a period of time. Most home mortgages are of the amortizing variety: Each month you send the bank or mortgage company a check for the same amount. In the beginning, most of your payment goes toward reducing the balance of the loan. Over time, however, the little reductions in the loan balance begin to add up and thereby reduce the interest you're charged.

Assuming you make regular payments, this amortization of the loan's balance results in a larger and larger portion of each month's payment going to pay off the loan balance. Home mortgages aren't the only types of debt that are amortizing. Most car loans are amortizing, and so are student loans.

Which Type of Debt Is Better?

Which type of debt is better, revolving credit debt or amortizing debt? This is a good question. Certainly, revolving credit is more flexible. It's easy to borrow money the instant you need it. Putting aside the convenience angle, however, you can almost always do better by using amortizing debt. It provides three important advantages:

- Amortizing debt is much tougher to use for impulse purchases. When you get the urge for a new car or item of clothing, you can't simply pull out your wallet or purse and, five minutes later, be even deeper in debt. Impulse purchases are a problem for some people. If you're one of them, you should definitely stay away from revolving credit cards.
- The lender makes sure you pay off the debt before the item you're buying wears out.
- Amortizing debts almost always have lower interest rates than revolving credit debts, and that is their chief advantage.

Vehicle Loans and Leases

A vehicle is usually the second largest purchase that people need to finance (the largest purchase, of course, is a home). Not surprisingly, vehicle loans and leases are an area where borrowing decisions dramatically affect financial progress.

Choosing a Vehicle

The first decision to make concerning a vehicle loan is which vehicle to buy. Choosing transportation is largely a personal decision, not a financial one, but two points are worth noting about buying a car, truck, minivan, or sport utility vehicle:

- Check the insurance and, if applicable, state and city taxes. (These can end up being big, unhappy surprises if you're not careful.)
- Reforecast your budget once you've picked a vehicle to make sure that you can afford to spend as much money as you're planning to spend. (Remember that you can calculate a loan payment, including a car loan payment, by using the Loan Planner, as described in this chapter.)

If you absolutely must have a luxury German or Italian import, consider getting a two-year-old car instead of a new one. Try to get a car that someone else owned for two years and then discovered he or she couldn't afford. New cars take the biggest drop in value over the first two years of their lives, even though most of their lives are still left. This advice, by the way, applies to just about any car. Buying a reasonably priced used car is usually an excellent way to purchase a car. Do have a mechanic you trust check the car first, however.

If you want a new car and you don't need it immediately, you can usually get a better deal by waiting until the start of the new model year and buying one of last year's models.

Finally, be sure to "comparison-shop." Take notes. Don't go to just one dealer. And get whatever deal you're offered in writing. As a general rule, you can't rely on a promise made by a car salesman (or anyone else) unless the promise is made in writing.

Picking a Vehicle Loan or Lease

Vehicle loans work just like other loans. For this reason, all you need to do is pick the loan with the lowest APR.

Call a couple of banks before you head on down to the car dealer's showroom. Most car dealers offer financing for the cars on their lots. To know whether or not you're getting a good offer, you need to be able to compare what the dealer offers with what the bank offers.

You probably shouldn't lease a car. Almost always, it's a better deal to purchase one. The reason is that when you are finally finished making your car loan payments, you still have your car, but when you are finished making car lease payments, you don't. It's that simple.

More about Vehicle Leases

Why do people lease cars if it's such a bad deal? There are two big reasons: The inception fee you pay to get into a lease usually isn't as big as the down payment you're required to make on a regular car loan, and the monthly lease payment is usually less than the monthly loan payment. This makes sense, if you think about it for a minute. With a lease, you're really only renting the car for a couple years—maybe three. With a loan, you're buying the car.

Is there a good reason for leasing a car? You probably pay more money for automobile expenses if you do. Acquiring a car by means of a lease is inherently more expensive than getting a regular car loan. Another factor that makes leases more expensive—and this is just my intuition, since I haven't done a rigorous statistical study—is that people tend to get expensive cars when they lease.

These criticisms aside, however, I can think of several reasons why it makes sense to lease that shiny new car you've been eyeing. First, if you really, truly, absolutely must have a new car, leasing may be your only option if you're low on cash. If your business or job requires having a better-than-average late model car, it probably does make sense to spend, say, an extra $10,000 on a lease so you can keep your $50,000-a-year business or your $50,000 sales job.

Unless you're independently wealthy, your biggest investment is what you do for your living, no matter whether that's a job or a business. Doing things that help you keep your business going or that let you keep a good job or that let you get a better job can be very worthwhile.

How Vehicle Leases Work

Vehicle leases, in essence, amount to long-term rental agreements. To get into a lease, you need to pay an inception fee and probably a deposit. Then, over the course of the lease, you make monthly lease, or rental, payments.

When the lease expires, you usually give the vehicle back to the leasing company. There are a couple of possible catches, however. Most lease agreements state that you can't run up 100,000 miles on the car. If you put, say, ten years' worth of mileage on a car that you've leased for only two or three years, you must pay an extra charge for the extra miles you drove.

Another catch concerns damage done to the vehicle: dings and dents, spilled milkshakes, and excess wear and tear. In all likelihood, you also need to pay extra for damages.

There's also usually one other complicating factor: Most leases give you the option of either releasing the vehicle or purchasing the vehicle at the end of the lease. Sometimes this is a great deal, and sometimes it isn't.

Picking a Mortgage

By making smart decisions about a mortgage, you can easily add tens of thousands of dollars to your net worth—and do it almost effortlessly. But to capture this easy source of wealth, you need to understand much more than most people do about choosing, refinancing, and ultimately repaying a mortgage. (The "How to Choose a Home and a Mortgage" sidebar at the end of Chapter 22 describes the general rules that most mortgage companies and banks use to determine mortgage affordability.)

Perhaps the most important thing to do when you search for a mortgage is comparison shop. Borrowing money for a home is just like borrowing money for anything else. The main thing to do is find a mortgage lender that offers inexpensive loans. It's important to shop around and find the lowest APR.

Just for fun, I kept tabs on all the 30-year fixed mortgage interest rates that were available as I was writing this. The thing that struck me is how much the rates vary. From the lowest rate to the highest rate, there's a difference of roughly half a percent. On a $100,000 mortgage, that's equivalent to around $500 a year in payments for the first few years.

Fifteen-year and biweekly mortgages usually save you interest because you repay the mortgage earlier. (Usually, you save thousands of dollars.) But you shouldn't pay anything extra for these types of mortgages. In fact, because you've reduced the lender's risk by paying biweekly or paying off the mortgage in 15 years, you should get a lower interest rate. You certainly don't need to pay some third party a special processing or handling fee, either, which is sometimes the case with a biweekly mortgage. If you want to get a 30-year mortgage paid off as quickly as you would pay off a biweekly mortgage, just add one-twelfth of your usual payment to your regular monthly payment. For example, if you're usually paying $1,200 a month in mortgage and interest, add another $100 a month to that payment. You can use Quicken's Loan Planner to see how much money you save by repaying a loan early, as described earlier in the chapter.

Why You Should Consider an Adjustable-Rate Mortgage

With an adjustable-rate mortgage (ARM), the interest rate on the loan is adjusted every 6 months or every 12 months, and as a result, the amount you pay is adjusted too. The lender adjusts the rate by pegging, or tying, the mortgage interest rate to a well-known and respected interest rate *index.* For example, one such index is the 6-month or 1-year Treasury Bill rate. A typical ARM might adjust your mortgage interest rate to the 6-month Treasury Bill rate plus 2 percentage points. In other words, if the 6-month Treasury Bill rate is 4 percent, the interest rate on your loan is 6 percent.

The extra amount that gets added to the index (2 percent in this example) is called the *spread.* If interest rates rise or fall, the lender recalculates your payment by using the new interest rate plus the spread.

Tying the interest rate on a loan to an index sounds risky, but it's not quite as bad as it sounds, provided ARM interest rates are substantially lower than fixed-mortgage interest rates. In this situation, ARM payments are lower to begin with. The prospect of having your ARM payment bounce between $600 a month and $1,000 a month sounds risky indeed, but it isn't actually as risky as it seems if the alternative is an $800-a-month payment on a fixed-interest rate mortgage. What's more, there's usually a *cap,* or maximum amount, above which rates on an ARM can't rise. If interest rates drop, then your mortgage interest rate drops too. However, mortgage interest rates don't drop as often as you might think because of teaser interest rates.

Teaser interest rates are artificially low starting interest rates. Teasers aren't bad, really. They save you money. But with a teaser interest rate, your payment often rises at the next adjustment date. Be sure to recalculate your loan payment using the current index and spread. You can do this by using Quicken's Loan Planner, as explained in this chapter.

Do ARMs make sense? Despite the risk of interest rates and payments climbing and dropping, ARMs can be good deals for borrowers when interest rates are high. They usually save borrowers money because they charge a lower interest rate in the long run. What's more, if the index rate drops, your mortgage rate and monthly payment drop as well, and you don't need to go through the rigmarole and cost of refinancing your mortgage.

The only problem with an ARM is that you bear extra risk: When interest rates rise, your monthly payment is adjusted upward.

Common sense says that you shouldn't take an ARM unless you know you can make the maximum payment. To find out what a maximum payment is, calculate your monthly payment using the interest rate cap—the highest interest rate you are forced to pay—on your ARM. If the payment looks pretty ugly, it probably doesn't pay to pick an ARM.

Here is a financial trick that an ARM borrower can use to reduce (and often reduce completely!) the risk of rising payments. Get an ARM but make the same payment you would make if you had a fixed-rate mortgage. In other words, if the ARM payment is $600 per month and the fixed-rate mortgage payment would be $800 per month, get the ARM and pay $800 a month. The extra amount that you pay each month quickly reduces the mortgage balance. What's more, you get accustomed to making larger payments in case the ARM interest rate does go up. If you're lucky and interest rates don't jump up dramatically in the first few years, you may never see your payment increase. The reason is that if you pay, say, an extra $100 to $200 a month over a five- or six-year period, the effect of the extra principal payments may more than offset the effect of a rise in interest rates.

Tips for Picking an ARM

If I've convinced you that an ARM is something you should look into, here are some smart shopping tips for picking one:

- Make sure the ARM has an annual adjustment limit, or interest rate cap. There should be a cap on how much the mortgage lender can adjust your payments upward in a year. If the cap is a percent a year or half a percent every 6 months (these are the figures I look for), you won't get caught in a budget crunch if interest rates rise quickly. Instead, your payment will be adjusted over several adjustment dates.
- Make sure there's no possibility of negative amortization. *Negative amortization* means your loan balance increases because your payment doesn't cover all of the loan interest. You shouldn't have a problem with negative amortization on a fixed-rate loan as long as the lender doesn't calculate your payment incorrectly. But negative amortization is a possibility when interest rate adjustments are made to an ARM more frequently than payment adjustments are made. Don't sign up for an ARM if this is the case.
- Compare spreads. If two ARMs are tied to the same index, go with the one that has the lower spread. Remember that the spread is the percentage point amount added to the index to calculate the ARM interest rate.
- Calculate the maximum payment. I know this isn't any fun. I know it may cause a big argument with your spouse about whether buying a house is a good decision. But you need to consider the risk of rising interest rates before, and not after, you're locked into them.
- Don't use an ARM to get a bigger house. The reason that most people get an ARM, or so an honest mortgage lender will tell you, is so they can buy a bigger home. I think this is a mistake. If you need to stretch yourself by getting an ARM, you're setting yourself up for trouble when interest rates rise. And rates always rise at some point in the future.
- Consider getting an ARM with annual adjustments. With annual adjustments, the chances of your getting a raise in salary or wages between adjustments is higher, and that raise could help with the increased payment. I should point out, however, that you usually pay a bit more in interest over the life of the loan if you go with annual adjustments. That's fair, however, since you're bearing less risk.

Chapter 13

BUSINESS INCOME TAXES

In This Chapter

- Building appropriate category lists
- Using Quicken's tax reports
- Exporting to a tax-preparation program
- Using TurboTax to prepare your taxes
- Using the Tax Planner
- Finding tax deductions
- Reviewing Quicken's other tax tools
- Solving common tax-preparation problems
- What to do if you get audited
- Common tax-saving opportunities for businesses

Because Quicken largely (and perhaps completely) summarizes your business and personal financial affairs, much of the information you'll need to prepare your business and personal income tax returns can and should be extracted from your Quicken accounts. What's more, Quicken Deluxe provides an income tax estimator that you can use to plan for your income tax expenses.

Building Appropriate Category Lists

There's only one real trick to using Quicken as a tool for income tax preparation: Use category lists that neatly tie to the tax form lines you need to fill in when you file your income tax return.

Although you won't actually know which tax form lines you'll use for the current year until the year is almost over, in Quicken you track your tax-related transactions throughout the year. Then, at the end of the year, you can create a report listing the category totals and use it to fill out your tax return forms and schedules.

Determining Which Categories You Need

In case you don't have last year's forms handy, you can take a look at the tax schedule in Figures 13.1 through 13.7. Use these forms as guides for indicating which categories you need to complete in the 2001 forms. Each input line on each form that you'll use should have its own category or set of categories.

TIP *U.S. taxpayers can download up-to-date versions of your tax forms from the Internal Revenue Service web site at* http://www.irs.gov/forms_pubs/index.html.

NOTE *Despite what some people say, the business income tax laws don't actually have very many "gray areas." You need to know two basic rules. First, all business income is taxed—unless it's specifically excluded. Second, any business expense that's ordinary and necessary is deductible. The bottom line is that it's pretty clear whether a particular amount that flows into the business needs to be counted as income. (It almost always does.) And it's pretty clear whether a particular expenditure is deductible. (Ask yourself the question, "Is this expense ordinary and necessary for the business?")*

Form **1040** Department of the Treasury—Internal Revenue Service
U.S. Individual Income Tax Return **2000** (99) IRS Use Only—Do not write or staple in this space.

For the year Jan. 1–Dec. 31, 2000, or other tax year beginning , 2000, ending , 20 OMB No. 1545-0074

Label

(See instructions on page 19.)

Use the IRS label. Otherwise, please print or type.

LABEL HERE

Your first name and initial	Last name	Your social security number
If a joint return, spouse's first name and initial	Last name	Spouse's social security number
Home address (number and street). If you have a P.O. box, see page 19.	Apt. no.	▲ **Important!** ▲ You **must** enter your SSN(s) above.
City, town or post office, state, and ZIP code. If you have a foreign address, see page 19.		

Presidential Election Campaign (See page 19.)

Note. Checking "Yes" will not change your tax or reduce your refund.
Do you, or your spouse if filing a joint return, want $3 to go to this fund? . . . ▶ You ☐ Yes ☐ No Spouse ☐ Yes ☐ No

Filing Status

Check only one box.

1 ☐ Single
2 ☐ Married filing joint return (even if only one had income)
3 ☐ Married filing separate return. Enter spouse's social security no. above and full name here. ▶
4 ☐ Head of household (with qualifying person). (See page 19.) If the qualifying person is a child but not your dependent, enter this child's name here. ▶
5 ☐ Qualifying widow(er) with dependent child (year spouse died ▶). (See page 19.)

Exemptions

6a ☐ **Yourself.** If your parent (or someone else) can claim you as a dependent on his or her tax return, **do not** check box 6a
b ☐ **Spouse**
c **Dependents:**

(1) First name Last name	(2) Dependent's social security number	(3) Dependent's relationship to you	(4) ✓ if qualifying child for child tax credit (see page 20)
			☐
			☐
			☐
			☐
			☐
			☐

If more than six dependents, see page 20.

d Total number of exemptions claimed

No. of boxes checked on 6a and 6b ____
No. of your children on 6c who:
• lived with you ____
• did not live with you due to divorce or separation (see page 20) ____
Dependents on 6c not entered above ____
Add numbers entered on lines above ▶ ☐

Income

Attach Forms W-2 and W-2G here. Also attach Form(s) 1099-R if tax was withheld.

If you did not get a W-2, see page 21.

Enclose, but do not attach, any payment. Also, please use **Form 1040-V.**

7 Wages, salaries, tips, etc. Attach Form(s) W-2 . . . 7
8a **Taxable** interest. Attach Schedule B if required . . . 8a
b **Tax-exempt** interest. **Do not** include on line 8a . . . 8b
9 Ordinary dividends. Attach Schedule B if required . . . 9
10 Taxable refunds, credits, or offsets of state and local income taxes (see page 22) . . 10
11 Alimony received . . . 11
12 Business income or (loss). Attach Schedule C or C-EZ . . . 12
13 Capital gain or (loss). Attach Schedule D if required. If not required, check here ▶ ☐ 13
14 Other gains or (losses). Attach Form 4797 . . . 14
15a Total IRA distributions . 15a | b Taxable amount (see page 23) 15b
16a Total pensions and annuities 16a | b Taxable amount (see page 23) 16b
17 Rental real estate, royalties, partnerships, S corporations, trusts, etc. Attach Schedule E 17
18 Farm income or (loss). Attach Schedule F . . . 18
19 Unemployment compensation . . . 19
20a Social security benefits . 20a | b Taxable amount (see page 25) 20b
21 Other income. List type and amount (see page 25) 21
22 Add the amounts in the far right column for lines 7 through 21. This is your **total income** ▶ 22

Adjusted Gross Income

23 IRA deduction (see page 27) . . . 23
24 Student loan interest deduction (see page 27) . . . 24
25 Medical savings account deduction. Attach Form 8853 . 25
26 Moving expenses. Attach Form 3903 . . . 26
27 One-half of self-employment tax. Attach Schedule SE . 27
28 Self-employed health insurance deduction (see page 29) 28
29 Self-employed SEP, SIMPLE, and qualified plans . . 29
30 Penalty on early withdrawal of savings . . . 30
31a Alimony paid b Recipient's SSN ▶ 31a
32 Add lines 23 through 31a . . . 32
33 Subtract line 32 from line 22. This is your **adjusted gross income** . . . ▶ 33

For Disclosure, Privacy Act, and Paperwork Reduction Act Notice, see page 56. Cat. No. 11320B Form **1040** (2000)

Figure 13.1: The 1040 form.

Tax and Credits

Standard Deduction for Most People
Single: $4,400
Head of household: $6,450
Married filing jointly or Qualifying widow(er): $7,350
Married filing separately: $3,675

34 Amount from line 33 (adjusted gross income) . . . 34
35a Check if: ☐ You were 65 or older, ☐ Blind; ☐ Spouse was 65 or older, ☐ Blind.
Add the number of boxes checked above and enter the total here . . . . ▶ 35a
b If you are married filing separately and your spouse itemizes deductions, or you were a dual-status alien, see page 31 and check here . . . ▶ 35b ☐
36 Enter your **itemized deductions** from Schedule A, line 28, **or standard deduction** shown on the left. **But** see page 31 to find your standard deduction if you checked any box on line 35a or 35b **or** if someone can claim you as a dependent . . . 36
37 Subtract line 36 from line 34 . . . 37
38 If line 34 is $96,700 or less, multiply $2,800 by the total number of exemptions claimed on line 6d. If line 34 is over $96,700, see the worksheet on page 32 for the amount to enter . 38
39 **Taxable income.** Subtract line 38 from line 37. If line 38 is more than line 37, enter -0- . 39
40 **Tax** (see page 32). Check if any tax is from **a** ☐ Form(s) 8814 **b** ☐ Form 4972 . . . 40
41 Alternative minimum tax. Attach Form 6251 . . . 41
42 Add lines 40 and 41 . . . ▶ 42
43 Foreign tax credit. Attach Form 1116 if required . . . 43
44 Credit for child and dependent care expenses. Attach Form 2441 44
45 Credit for the elderly or the disabled. Attach Schedule R . . 45
46 Education credits. Attach Form 8863 . . . 46
47 Child tax credit (see page 36) . . . 47
48 Adoption credit. Attach Form 8839 . . . 48
49 Other. Check if from **a** ☐ Form 3800 **b** ☐ Form 8396 **c** ☐ Form 8801 **d** ☐ Form (specify) ________ 49
50 Add lines 43 through 49. These are your **total credits** . . . 50
51 Subtract line 50 from line 42. If line 50 is more than line 42, enter -0- . . . ▶ 51

Other Taxes

52 Self-employment tax. Attach Schedule SE . . . 52
53 Social security and Medicare tax on tip income not reported to employer. Attach Form 4137 53
54 Tax on IRAs, other retirement plans, and MSAs. Attach Form 5329 if required . . . 54
55 Advance earned income credit payments from Form(s) W-2 . . . 55
56 Household employment taxes. Attach Schedule H . . . 56
57 Add lines 51 through 56. This is your **total tax** . . . ▶ 57

Payments

If you have a qualifying child, attach Schedule EIC.

58 Federal income tax withheld from Forms W-2 and 1099 . . 58
59 2000 estimated tax payments and amount applied from 1999 return 59
60a **Earned income credit (EIC)** . . . 60a
b Nontaxable earned income: amount . . ▶ ________ and type ▶ ________
61 Excess social security and RRTA tax withheld (see page 50) 61
62 Additional child tax credit. Attach Form 8812 . . . 62
63 Amount paid with request for extension to file (see page 50) 63
64 Other payments. Check if from **a** ☐ Form 2439 **b** ☐ Form 4136 64
65 Add lines 58, 59, 60a, and 61 through 64. These are your **total payments** . . . ▶ 65

Refund

Have it directly deposited! See page 50 and fill in 67b, 67c, and 67d.

66 If line 65 is more than line 57, subtract line 57 from line 65. This is the amount you **overpaid** 66
67a Amount of line 66 you want **refunded to you** . . . ▶ 67a
▶ b Routing number ▶ c Type: ☐ Checking ☐ Savings
▶ d Account number
68 Amount of line 66 you want **applied to your 2001 estimated tax** . ▶ 68

Amount You Owe

69 If line 57 is more than line 65, subtract line 65 from line 57. This is the **amount you owe**. For details on how to pay, see page 51 . . . ▶ 69
70 Estimated tax penalty. Also include on line 69 . . . 70

Sign Here

Joint return? See page 19. Keep a copy for your records.

Under penalties of perjury, I declare that I have examined this return and accompanying schedules and statements, and to the best of my knowledge and belief, they are true, correct, and complete. Declaration of preparer (other than taxpayer) is based on all information of which preparer has any knowledge.

Your signature	Date	Your occupation	Daytime phone number ( )
Spouse's signature. If a joint return, **both** must sign.	Date	Spouse's occupation	May the IRS discuss this return with the preparer shown below (see page 52)? ☐ **Yes** ☐ **No**

Paid Preparer's Use Only

Preparer's signature	Date	Check if self-employed ☐	Preparer's SSN or PTIN
Firm's name (or yours if self-employed), address, and ZIP code		EIN	
		Phone no. ( )	

Form **1040** (2000)

SCHEDULES A&B
(Form 1040)

Department of the Treasury
Internal Revenue Service (99)

Schedule A—Itemized Deductions

(Schedule B is on back)

▶ Attach to Form 1040. ▶ See Instructions for Schedules A and B (Form 1040).

OMB No. 1545-0074

2000

Attachment Sequence No. 07

Name(s) shown on Form 1040 | Your social security number

Section	Line	Description	Box	Amount	Line	Amount
Medical and Dental Expenses		**Caution.** Do not include expenses reimbursed or paid by others.				
	1	Medical and dental expenses (see page A-2)	1			
	2	Enter amount from Form 1040, line 34. [2]				
	3	Multiply line 2 above by 7.5% (.075)	3			
	4	Subtract line 3 from line 1. If line 3 is more than line 1, enter -0-			4	
Taxes You Paid (See page A-2.)	5	State and local income taxes	5			
	6	Real estate taxes (see page A-2)	6			
	7	Personal property taxes	7			
	8	Other taxes. List type and amount ▶	8			
	9	Add lines 5 through 8			9	
Interest You Paid (See page A-3.)	10	Home mortgage interest and points reported to you on Form 1098	10			
	11	Home mortgage interest not reported to you on Form 1098. If paid to the person from whom you bought the home, see page A-3 and show that person's name, identifying no., and address ▶	11			
Note. Personal interest is not deductible.	12	Points not reported to you on Form 1098. See page A-3 for special rules	12			
	13	Investment interest. Attach Form 4952 if required. (See page A-3.)	13			
	14	Add lines 10 through 13			14	
Gifts to Charity If you made a gift and got a benefit for it, see page A-4.	15	Gifts by cash or check. If you made any gift of $250 or more, see page A-4	15			
	16	Other than by cash or check. If any gift of $250 or more, see page A-4. You **must** attach Form 8283 if over $500	16			
	17	Carryover from prior year	17			
	18	Add lines 15 through 17			18	
Casualty and Theft Losses	19	Casualty or theft loss(es). Attach Form 4684. (See page A-5.)			19	
Job Expenses and Most Other Miscellaneous Deductions	20	Unreimbursed employee expenses—job travel, union dues, job education, etc. You **must** attach Form 2106 or 2106-EZ if required. (See page A-5.) ▶	20			
	21	Tax preparation fees	21			
(See page A-5 for expenses to deduct here.)	22	Other expenses—investment, safe deposit box, etc. List type and amount ▶	22			
	23	Add lines 20 through 22	23			
	24	Enter amount from Form 1040, line 34. [24]				
	25	Multiply line 24 above by 2% (.02)	25			
	26	Subtract line 25 from line 23. If line 25 is more than line 23, enter -0-			26	
Other Miscellaneous Deductions	27	Other—from list on page A-6. List type and amount ▶			27	
Total Itemized Deductions	28	Is Form 1040, line 34, over $128,950 (over $64,475 if married filing separately)? ☐ **No.** Your deduction is not limited. Add the amounts in the far right column for lines 4 through 27. Also, enter this amount on Form 1040, line 36. ☐ **Yes.** Your deduction may be limited. See page A-6 for the amount to enter.			▶ 28	

For Paperwork Reduction Act Notice, see Form 1040 instructions. Cat. No. 11330X Schedule A (Form 1040) 2000

Figure 13.2: Schedule A.

Schedules A&B (Form 1040) 2000 OMB No. 1545-0074 Page **2**

Name(s) shown on Form 1040. Do not enter name and social security number if shown on other side. | **Your social security number**

Schedule B—Interest and Ordinary Dividends

Attachment Sequence No. **08**

Part I Interest

(See page B-1 and the instructions for Form 1040, line 8a.)

Note. If you received a Form 1099-INT, Form 1099-OID, or substitute statement from a brokerage firm, list the firm's name as the payer and enter the total interest shown on that form.

Note. If you had over $400 in taxable interest, you must also complete Part III.

			Amount
1	List name of payer. If any interest is from a seller-financed mortgage and the buyer used the property as a personal residence, see page B-1 and list this interest first. Also, show that buyer's social security number and address ▶	1	
2	Add the amounts on line 1	2	
3	Excludable interest on series EE and I U.S. savings bonds issued after 1989 from Form 8815, line 14. You **must** attach Form 8815	3	
4	Subtract line 3 from line 2. Enter the result here and on Form 1040, line 8a ▶	4	

Part II Ordinary Dividends

(See page B-1 and the instructions for Form 1040, line 9.)

Note. If you received a Form 1099-DIV or substitute statement from a brokerage firm, list the firm's name as the payer and enter the ordinary dividends shown on that form.

Note. If you had over $400 in ordinary dividends, you must also complete Part III.

			Amount
5	List name of payer. Include only ordinary dividends. If you received any capital gain distributions, see the instructions for Form 1040, line 13 ▶	5	
6	Add the amounts on line 5. Enter the total here and on Form 1040, line 9 ▶	6	

Part III Foreign Accounts and Trusts

(See page B-2.)

	You must complete this part if you **(a)** had over $400 of interest or ordinary dividends; **(b)** had a foreign account; or **(c)** received a distribution from, or were a grantor of, or a transferor to, a foreign trust.	Yes	No
7a	At any time during 2000, did you have an interest in or a signature or other authority over a financial account in a foreign country, such as a bank account, securities account, or other financial account? See page B-2 for exceptions and filing requirements for Form TD F 90-22.1		
b	If "Yes," enter the name of the foreign country ▶		
8	During 2000, did you receive a distribution from, or were you the grantor of, or transferor to, a foreign trust? If "Yes," you may have to file Form 3520. See page B-2		

For Paperwork Reduction Act Notice, see Form 1040 instructions. **Schedule B (Form 1040) 2000**

Figure 13.3: Schedule B.

SCHEDULE C (Form 1040)

Department of the Treasury Internal Revenue Service (99)

Profit or Loss From Business

(Sole Proprietorship)

► Partnerships, joint ventures, etc., must file Form 1065 or Form 1065-B.

► Attach to Form 1040 or Form 1041. ► See Instructions for Schedule C (Form 1040).

OMB No. 1545-0074

2000

Attachment Sequence No. **09**

Name of proprietor | **Social security number (SSN)**

A Principal business or profession, including product or service (see page C-1 of the instructions) | **B Enter code from pages C-7 & 8** ►

C Business name. If no separate business name, leave blank. | **D Employer ID number (EIN), if any**

E Business address (including suite or room no.) ►
City, town or post office, state, and ZIP code

F Accounting method: (1) ☐ Cash (2) ☐ Accrual (3) ☐ Other (specify) ►

G Did you "materially participate" in the operation of this business during 2000? If "No," see page C-2 for limit on losses . ☐ Yes ☐ No

H If you started or acquired this business during 2000, check here . . . . ► ☐

Part I Income

1	Gross receipts or sales. **Caution.** If this income was reported to you on Form W-2 and the "Statutory employee" box on that form was checked, see page C-2 and check here . . . . . . ► ☐	1	
2	Returns and allowances	2	
3	Subtract line 2 from line 1	3	
4	Cost of goods sold (from line 42 on page 2)	4	
5	**Gross profit.** Subtract line 4 from line 3	5	
6	Other income, including Federal and state gasoline or fuel tax credit or refund (see page C-2) . . .	6	
7	**Gross income.** Add lines 5 and 6 . . . . ►	7	

Part II Expenses. Enter expenses for business use of your home only on line 30.

8	Advertising	8		19	Pension and profit-sharing plans	19	
9	Bad debts from sales or services (see page C-3) . .	9		20	Rent or lease (see page C-4):		
				a	Vehicles, machinery, and equipment .	20a	
10	Car and truck expenses (see page C-3)	10		b	Other business property . .	20b	
				21	Repairs and maintenance . .	21	
11	Commissions and fees . .	11		22	Supplies (not included in Part III) .	22	
12	Depletion	12		23	Taxes and licenses	23	
13	Depreciation and section 179 expense deduction (not included in Part III) (see page C-3) . .	13		24	Travel, meals, and entertainment:		
				a	Travel	24a	
				b	Meals and entertainment		
14	Employee benefit programs (other than on line 19) . . .	14		c	Enter nondeductible amount included on line 24b (see page C-5) .		
15	Insurance (other than health) .	15					
16	Interest:						
a	Mortgage (paid to banks, etc.) .	16a		d	Subtract line 24c from line 24b .	24d	
b	Other	16b		25	Utilities	25	
17	Legal and professional services	17		26	Wages (less employment credits) .	26	
18	Office expense	18		27	Other expenses (from line 48 on page 2)	27	

28	**Total expenses** before expenses for business use of home. Add lines 8 through 27 in columns . ►	28	
29	Tentative profit (loss). Subtract line 28 from line 7	29	
30	Expenses for business use of your home. Attach **Form 8829**	30	
31	**Net profit or (loss).** Subtract line 30 from line 29. • If a profit, enter on **Form 1040, line 12,** and **also** on **Schedule SE, line 2** (statutory employees, see page C-5). Estates and trusts, enter on Form 1041, line 3. • If a loss, you **must** go to line 32.	31	

32 If you have a loss, check the box that describes your investment in this activity (see page C-5).
- If you checked 32a, enter the loss on **Form 1040, line 12,** and **also** on **Schedule SE, line 2** (statutory employees, see page C-5). Estates and trusts, enter on Form 1041, line 3.
- If you checked 32b, you **must** attach **Form 6198.**

32a ☐ All investment is at risk.
32b ☐ Some investment is not at risk.

For Paperwork Reduction Act Notice, see Form 1040 instructions. Cat. No. 11334P **Schedule C (Form 1040) 2000**

Figure 13.4: Schedule C.

SCHEDULE C (Form 1040)

Department of the Treasury
Internal Revenue Service (99)

Profit or Loss From Business

(Sole Proprietorship)

▶ **Partnerships, joint ventures, etc., must file Form 1065 or Form 1065-B.**

▶ **Attach to Form 1040 or Form 1041.** ▶ **See Instructions for Schedule C (Form 1040).**

OMB No. 1545-0074

2000

Attachment Sequence No. **09**

Name of proprietor | **Social security number (SSN)**

A Principal business or profession, including product or service (see page C-1 of the instructions) | **B Enter code from pages C-7 & 8** ▶

C Business name. If no separate business name, leave blank. | **D Employer ID number (EIN), if any**

E Business address (including suite or room no.) ▶
City, town or post office, state, and ZIP code

F Accounting method: **(1)** ☐ Cash **(2)** ☐ Accrual **(3)** ☐ Other (specify) ▶

G Did you "materially participate" in the operation of this business during 2000? If "No," see page C-2 for limit on losses . ☐ **Yes** ☐ **No**

H If you started or acquired this business during 2000, check here . . . . ▶ ☐

Part I Income

1	Gross receipts or sales. **Caution.** If this income was reported to you on Form W-2 and the "Statutory employee" box on that form was checked, see page C-2 and check here . . . ▶ ☐	1	
2	Returns and allowances	2	
3	Subtract line 2 from line 1	3	
4	Cost of goods sold (from line 42 on page 2)	4	
5	**Gross profit.** Subtract line 4 from line 3	5	
6	Other income, including Federal and state gasoline or fuel tax credit or refund (see page C-2)	6	
7	**Gross income.** Add lines 5 and 6 . . . ▶	7	

Part II Expenses. Enter expenses for business use of your home **only** on line 30.

8	Advertising	8		19	Pension and profit-sharing plans	19	
9	Bad debts from sales or services (see page C-3)	9		20	Rent or lease (see page C-4):		
10	Car and truck expenses (see page C-3)	10			**a** Vehicles, machinery, and equipment	20a	
11	Commissions and fees	11			**b** Other business property	20b	
12	Depletion	12		21	Repairs and maintenance	21	
13	Depreciation and section 179 expense deduction (not included in Part III) (see page C-3)	13		22	Supplies (not included in Part III)	22	
14	Employee benefit programs (other than on line 19)	14		23	Taxes and licenses	23	
15	Insurance (other than health)	15		24	Travel, meals, and entertainment:		
16	Interest:				**a** Travel	24a	
	a Mortgage (paid to banks, etc.)	16a			**b** Meals and entertainment		
	b Other	16b			**c** Enter nondeductible amount included on line 24b (see page C-5)		
17	Legal and professional services	17			**d** Subtract line 24c from line 24b	24d	
18	Office expense	18		25	Utilities	25	
				26	Wages (less employment credits)	26	
				27	Other expenses (from line 48 on page 2)	27	

28	**Total expenses** before expenses for business use of home. Add lines 8 through 27 in columns . ▶	28	
29	Tentative profit (loss). Subtract line 28 from line 7	29	
30	Expenses for business use of your home. Attach **Form 8829**	30	
31	**Net profit or (loss).** Subtract line 30 from line 29. • If a profit, enter on **Form 1040, line 12,** and **also** on **Schedule SE, line 2** (statutory employees, see page C-5). Estates and trusts, enter on Form 1041, line 3. • If a loss, you **must** go to line 32.	31	
32	If you have a loss, check the box that describes your investment in this activity (see page C-5). • If you checked 32a, enter the loss on **Form 1040, line 12,** and **also** on **Schedule SE, line 2** (statutory employees, see page C-5). Estates and trusts, enter on Form 1041, line 3. • If you checked 32b, you **must** attach **Form 6198.**	32a ☐ All investment is at risk. 32b ☐ Some investment is not at risk.	

For Paperwork Reduction Act Notice, see Form 1040 instructions. Cat. No. 11334P **Schedule C (Form 1040) 2000**

SCHEDULE C-EZ (Form 1040)

Department of the Treasury
Internal Revenue Service (99)

Net Profit From Business

(Sole Proprietorship)

▶ Partnerships, joint ventures, etc., must file Form 1065 or 1065-B.

▶ Attach to Form 1040 or Form 1041. ▶ See instructions on back.

OMB No. 1545-0074

2000

Attachment Sequence No. **09A**

Name of proprietor | **Social security number (SSN)**

Part I **General Information**

You May Use Schedule C-EZ Instead of Schedule C Only If You:

- Had business expenses of $2,500 or less.
- Use the cash method of accounting.
- Did not have an inventory at any time during the year.
- Did not have a net loss from your business.
- Had only one business as a sole proprietor.

And You:

- Had no employees during the year.
- Are not required to file **Form 4562,** Depreciation and Amortization, for this business. See the instructions for Schedule C, line 13, on page C-3 to find out if you must file.
- Do not deduct expenses for business use of your home.
- Do not have prior year unallowed passive activity losses from this business.

A Principal business or profession, including product or service | **B Enter code from pages C-7 & 8** ▶

C Business name. If no separate business name, leave blank. | **D Employer ID number (EIN), if any**

E Business address (including suite or room no.). Address not required if same as on Form 1040, page 1.

City, town or post office, state, and ZIP code

Part II **Figure Your Net Profit**

1 **Gross receipts. Caution:** *If this income was reported to you on Form W-2 and the "Statutory employee" box on that form was checked, see* **Statutory Employees** *in the instructions for Schedule C, line 1, on page C-2 and check here* . . . . ▶ ☐ | **1**

2 **Total expenses.** If more than $2,500, you **must** use Schedule C. See instructions . . . . . | **2**

3 **Net profit.** Subtract line 2 from line 1. If less than zero, you **must** use Schedule C. Enter on **Form 1040, line 12,** and **also** on **Schedule SE, line 2.** (Statutory employees **do not** report this amount on Schedule SE, line 2. Estates and trusts, enter on Form 1041, line 3.) . . . . . | **3**

Part III **Information on Your Vehicle.** Complete this part **only** if you are claiming car or truck expenses on line 2.

4 When did you place your vehicle in service for business purposes? (month, day, year) ▶ ...../...../.....

5 Of the total number of miles you drove your vehicle during 2000, enter the number of miles you used your vehicle for:

a Business .... **b** Commuting .... **c** Other ....

6 Do you (or your spouse) have another vehicle available for personal use? . . . . ☐ **Yes** ☐ **No**

7 Was your vehicle available for use during off-duty hours? . . . . ☐ **Yes** ☐ **No**

8a Do you have evidence to support your deduction? . . . . ☐ **Yes** ☐ **No**

b If "Yes," is the evidence written? . . . . ☐ **Yes** ☐ **No**

For Paperwork Reduction Act Notice, see Form 1040 instructions. Cat. No. 14374D **Schedule C-EZ (Form 1040) 2000**

Figure 13.5: Schedule C-EZ.

Instructions

You may use Schedule C-EZ instead of Schedule C if you operated a business or practiced a profession as a sole proprietorship and you have met all the requirements listed in Part I of Schedule C-EZ.

Line A

Describe the business or professional activity that provided your principal source of income reported on line 1. Give the general field or activity and the type of product or service.

Line B

Enter the six-digit code that identifies your principal business or professional activity. See pages C-7 and C-8 of the Instructions for Schedule C for the list of codes.

Line D

You need an employer identification number (EIN) only if you had a qualified retirement plan or were required to file an employment, excise, estate, trust, or alcohol, tobacco, and firearms tax return. If you need an EIN, file **Form SS-4,** Application for Employer Identification Number. If you do not have an EIN, leave line D blank. **Do not** enter your SSN.

Line E

Enter your business address. Show a street address instead of a box number. Include the suite or room number, if any.

Line 1

Enter gross receipts from your trade or business. Include amounts you received in your trade or business that were properly shown on **Forms 1099-MISC.** If the total amounts that were reported in box 7 of Forms 1099-MISC are more than the total you are reporting on line 1, attach a statement explaining the difference. You must show all items of taxable income actually or constructively received during the year (in cash, property, or services). Income is constructively received when it is credited to your account or set aside for you to use. Do not offset this amount by any losses.

Line 2

Enter the total amount of all deductible business expenses you actually paid during the year. Examples of these expenses include advertising, car and truck expenses, commissions and fees, insurance, interest, legal and professional services, office expense, rent or lease expenses, repairs and maintenance, supplies, taxes, travel, the allowable percentage of business meals and entertainment, and utilities (including telephone). For details, see the instructions for Schedule C, Parts II and V, on pages C-3 through C-6. If you wish, you may use the optional worksheet below to record your expenses.

If you claim car or truck expenses, be sure to complete Part III of Schedule C-EZ.

Optional Worksheet for Line 2 (keep a copy for your records)

a Business meals and entertainment	a		
b Enter nondeductible amount included on line **a** (see the instructions for lines 24b and 24c on page C-5)	b		
c Deductible business meals and entertainment. Subtract line **b** from line **a**		c	
d		d	
e		e	
f		f	
g		g	
h		h	
i		i	
j **Total.** Add lines **c** through **i.** Enter here and on line 2		j	

Schedule C-EZ (Form 1040) 2000

SCHEDULE D (Form 1040)

Department of the Treasury Internal Revenue Service (99)

Capital Gains and Losses

▶ Attach to Form 1040. ▶ See Instructions for Schedule D (Form 1040).

▶ Use Schedule D-1 for more space to list transactions for lines 1 and 8.

OMB No. 1545-0074

2000

Attachment Sequence No. 12

Name(s) shown on Form 1040 | Your social security number

Part I Short-Term Capital Gains and Losses—Assets Held One Year or Less

	(a) Description of property (Example: 100 sh. XYZ Co.)	(b) Date acquired (Mo., day, yr.)	(c) Date sold (Mo., day, yr.)	(d) Sales price (see page D-6)	(e) Cost or other basis (see page D-6)	(f) Gain or (loss) Subtract (e) from (d)
1						

2 Enter your short-term totals, if any, from Schedule D-1, line 2 . . . . **2**

3 **Total short-term sales price amounts.** Add column (d) of lines 1 and 2 . . . . . . **3**

4 Short-term gain from Form 6252 and short-term gain or (loss) from Forms 4684, 6781, and 8824 . . . . **4**

5 Net short-term gain or (loss) from partnerships, S corporations, estates, and trusts from Schedule(s) K-1 . . . . **5**

6 Short-term capital loss carryover. Enter the amount, if any, from line 8 of your 1999 Capital Loss Carryover Worksheet . . . . **6** ( )

7 **Net short-term capital gain or (loss).** Combine column (f) of lines 1 through 6 ▶ **7**

Part II Long-Term Capital Gains and Losses—Assets Held More Than One Year

	(a) Description of property (Example: 100 sh. XYZ Co.)	(b) Date acquired (Mo., day, yr.)	(c) Date sold (Mo., day, yr.)	(d) Sales price (see page D-6)	(e) Cost or other basis (see page D-6)	(f) Gain or (loss) Subtract (e) from (d)	(g) 28% rate gain or (loss) * (see instr. below)
8							

9 Enter your long-term totals, if any, from Schedule D-1, line 9 . . . . **9**

10 **Total long-term sales price amounts.** Add column (d) of lines 8 and 9 . . . . . . **10**

11 Gain from Form 4797, Part I; long-term gain from Forms 2439 and 6252; and long-term gain or (loss) from Forms 4684, 6781, and 8824 . . . . **11**

12 Net long-term gain or (loss) from partnerships, S corporations, estates, and trusts from Schedule(s) K-1. . . . . **12**

13 Capital gain distributions. See page D-1 . . . . **13**

14 Long-term capital loss carryover. Enter in both columns (f) and (g) the amount, if any, from line 13 of your 1999 Capital Loss Carryover Worksheet . . . . . . **14** ( ) ( )

15 Combine column (g) of lines 8 through 14. . . . . **15**

16 **Net long-term capital gain or (loss).** Combine column (f) of lines 8 through 14 ▶ **16**
Next: Go to Part III on the back.

* **28% rate gain or loss** includes **all** "collectibles gains and losses" (as defined on page D-6) and up to 50% of the eligible gain on qualified small business stock (see page D-4).

For Paperwork Reduction Act Notice, see Form 1040 instructions. Cat. No. 11338H **Schedule D (Form 1040) 2000**

Figure 13.6: Schedule D.

Part III Summary of Parts I and II

17 Combine lines 7 and 16. If a loss, go to line 18. If a gain, enter the gain on Form 1040, line 13 — **17**

Next: Complete Form 1040 through line 39. Then, go to **Part IV** to figure your tax if:

- Both lines 16 and 17 are gains **and**
- Form 1040, line 39, is more than zero.

Otherwise, **stop here.**

18 If line 17 is a loss, enter here and as a (loss) on Form 1040, line 13, the **smaller** of these losses:

- The loss on line 17 **or**
- ($3,000) or, if married filing separately, ($1,500) . . . . — **18** ( )

Next: Skip **Part IV** below. Instead, complete Form 1040 through line 37. Then, complete the **Capital Loss Carryover Worksheet** on page D-6 if:

- The loss on line 17 exceeds the loss on line 18 **or**
- Form 1040, line 37, is a loss.

Part IV Tax Computation Using Maximum Capital Gains Rates

19 Enter your taxable income from Form 1040, line 39 . . . . — **19**

20 Enter the **smaller** of line 16 or line 17 of Schedule D . . . . . — **20**

21 If you are filing Form 4952, enter the amount from Form 4952, line 4e — **21**

22 Subtract line 21 from line 20. If zero or less, enter -0- . . . . . — **22**

23 Combine lines 7 and 15. If zero or less, enter -0- . . . . — **23**

24 Enter the **smaller** of line 15 or line 23, but not less than zero . . . — **24**

25 Enter your unrecaptured section 1250 gain, if any, from line 17 of the worksheet on page D-8 . . . . — **25**

26 Add lines 24 and 25 . . . . — **26**

27 Subtract line 26 from line 22. If zero or less, enter -0- . . . . — **27**

28 Subtract line 27 from line 19. If zero or less, enter -0- . . . . — **28**

29 Enter the **smaller** of:

- The amount on line 19 **or**
- $26,250 if single; $43,850 if married filing jointly or qualifying widow(er); $21,925 if married filing separately; or $35,150 if head of household } . . . . — **29**

30 Enter the **smaller** of line 28 or line 29 . . . . — **30**

31 Subtract line 22 from line 19. If zero or less, enter -0- . . . . . — **31**

32 Enter the **larger** of line 30 or line 31 . . . . ▶ — **32**

33 Figure the tax on the amount on line 32. Use the Tax Table or Tax Rate Schedules, whichever applies — **33**

Note. If the amounts on lines 29 and 30 are the same, skip lines 34 through 37 and go to line 38.

34 Enter the amount from line 29 . . . . — **34**

35 Enter the amount from line 30 . . . . — **35**

36 Subtract line 35 from line 34 . . . . ▶ — **36**

37 Multiply line 36 by 10% (.10) . . . . — **37**

Note. If the amounts on lines 19 and 29 are the same, skip lines 38 through 51 and go to line 52.

38 Enter the **smaller** of line 19 or line 27 . . . . — **38**

39 Enter the amount from line 36 . . . . — **39**

40 Subtract line 39 from line 38 . . . . ▶ — **40**

41 Multiply line 40 by 20% (.20) . . . . — **41**

Note. If line 26 is zero or blank, skip lines 42 through 51 and go to line 52.

42 Enter the **smaller** of line 22 or line 25 . . . . — **42**

43 Add lines 22 and 32 . . . . — **43**

44 Enter the amount from line 19 . . . . — **44**

45 Subtract line 44 from line 43. If zero or less, enter -0- . . . . . — **45**

46 Subtract line 45 from line 42. If zero or less, enter -0- . . . . ▶ — **46**

47 Multiply line 46 by 25% (.25) . . . . — **47**

Note. If line 24 is zero or blank, skip lines 48 through 51 and go to line 52.

48 Enter the amount from line 19 . . . . — **48**

49 Add lines 32, 36, 40, and 46 . . . . — **49**

50 Subtract line 49 from line 48 . . . . — **50**

51 Multiply line 50 by 28% (.28) . . . . — **51**

52 Add lines 33, 37, 41, 47, and 51. . . . . — **52**

53 Figure the tax on the amount on line 19. Use the Tax Table or Tax Rate Schedules, whichever applies — **53**

54 **Tax on all taxable income (including capital gains).** Enter the **smaller** of line 52 or line 53 here and on Form 1040, line 40. . . . . — **54**

Schedule D (Form 1040) 2000

SCHEDULE E (Form 1040)

Department of the Treasury
Internal Revenue Service (99)

Supplemental Income and Loss

(From rental real estate, royalties, partnerships, S corporations, estates, trusts, REMICs, etc.)

▶ Attach to Form 1040 or Form 1041. ▶ See Instructions for Schedule E (Form 1040).

OMB No. 1545-0074

2000

Attachment Sequence No. **13**

Name(s) shown on return | **Your social security number**

Part I **Income or Loss From Rental Real Estate and Royalties** **Note.** Report income and expenses from your business of renting personal property on **Schedule C** or **C-EZ** (see page E-1). Report farm rental income or loss from **Form 4835** on page 2, line 39.

1	Show the kind and location of each **rental real estate property:**	2 For each rental real estate property listed on line 1, did you or your family use it during the tax year for personal purposes for more than the greater of: • 14 days **or** • 10% of the total days rented at fair rental value? (See page E-1.)		Yes	No
A			A		
B			B		
C			C		

Income:		Properties A	Properties B	Properties C		Totals (Add columns A, B, and C.)
3 Rents received	3				3	
4 Royalties received	4				4	
Expenses:						
5 Advertising	5					
6 Auto and travel (see page E-2)	6					
7 Cleaning and maintenance	7					
8 Commissions	8					
9 Insurance	9					
10 Legal and other professional fees	10					
11 Management fees	11					
12 Mortgage interest paid to banks, etc. (see page E-2)	12				12	
13 Other interest	13					
14 Repairs	14					
15 Supplies	15					
16 Taxes	16					
17 Utilities	17					
18 Other (list) ▶	18					
19 Add lines 5 through 18	19				19	
20 Depreciation expense or depletion (see page E-3)	20				20	
21 Total expenses. Add lines 19 and 20	21					
22 Income or (loss) from rental real estate or royalty properties. Subtract line 21 from line 3 (rents) or line 4 (royalties). If the result is a (loss), see page E-3 to find out if you must file **Form 6198**	22					
23 Deductible rental real estate loss. **Caution.** Your rental real estate loss on line 22 may be limited. See page E-3 to find out if you must file **Form 8582.** Real estate professionals must complete line 42 on page 2	23	( )	( )	( )		

24 **Income.** Add positive amounts shown on line 22. **Do not** include any losses	24	
25 **Losses.** Add royalty losses from line 22 and rental real estate losses from line 23. Enter total losses here	25	( )
26 Total rental real estate and royalty income or (loss). Combine lines 24 and 25. Enter the result here. If Parts II, III, IV, and line 39 on page 2 do not apply to you, also enter this amount on Form 1040, line 17. Otherwise, include this amount in the total on line 40 on page 2	26	

For Paperwork Reduction Act Notice, see Form 1040 instructions. Cat. No. 11344L **Schedule E (Form 1040) 2000**

Figure 13.7: Schedule E.

Name(s) shown on return. Do not enter name and social security number if shown on other side. | **Your social security number**

Note. If you report amounts from farming or fishing on Schedule E, you must enter your gross income from those activities on line 41 below. Real estate professionals must complete line 42 below.

Part II Income or Loss From Partnerships and S Corporations

Note. If you report a loss from an at-risk activity, you **must** check either column **(e)** or **(f)** on line 27 to describe your investment in the activity. See page E-5. If you check column **(f)**, you must attach **Form 6198.**

27	**(a)** Name	**(b)** Enter **P** for partnership; **S** for S corporation	**(c)** Check if foreign partnership	**(d)** Employer identification number	Investment At Risk? **(e)** All is at risk	**(f)** Some is not at risk
A						
B						
C						
D						
E						

	Passive Income and Loss		Nonpassive Income and Loss		
	(g) Passive loss allowed (attach **Form 8582** if required)	**(h)** Passive income from **Schedule K-1**	**(i)** Nonpassive loss from **Schedule K-1**	**(j)** Section 179 expense deduction from **Form 4562**	**(k)** Nonpassive income from **Schedule K-1**
A					
B					
C					
D					
E					
28a Totals					
b Totals					

29	Add columns (h) and (k) of line 28a	29	
30	Add columns (g), (i), and (j) of line 28b	30	( )
31	Total partnership and S corporation income or (loss). Combine lines 29 and 30. Enter the result here and include in the total on line 40 below	31	

Part III Income or Loss From Estates and Trusts

32	**(a)** Name	**(b)** Employer identification number
A		
B		

	Passive Income and Loss		Nonpassive Income and Loss	
	(c) Passive deduction or loss allowed (attach **Form 8582** if required)	**(d)** Passive income from **Schedule K-1**	**(e)** Deduction or loss from **Schedule K-1**	**(f)** Other income from **Schedule K-1**
A				
B				
33a Totals				
b Totals				

34	Add columns (d) and (f) of line 33a	34	
35	Add columns (c) and (e) of line 33b	35	( )
36	Total estate and trust income or (loss). Combine lines 34 and 35. Enter the result here and include in the total on line 40 below	36	

Part IV Income or Loss From Real Estate Mortgage Investment Conduits (REMICs)—Residual Holder

37	**(a)** Name	**(b)** Employer identification number	**(c)** Excess inclusion from **Schedules Q,** line 2c (see page E-6)	**(d)** Taxable income (net loss) from **Schedules Q,** line 1b	**(e)** Income from **Schedules Q,** line 3b

38	Combine columns (d) and (e) only. Enter the result here and include in the total on line 40 below	38	

Part V Summary

39	Net farm rental income or (loss) from **Form 4835**. Also, complete line 41 below	39	
40	**Total** income or (loss). Combine lines 26, 31, 36, 38, and 39. Enter the result here and on Form 1040, line 17 ▶	40	
41	**Reconciliation of Farming and Fishing Income.** Enter your **gross** farming and fishing income reported on Form 4835, line 7; Schedule K-1 (Form 1065), line 15b; Schedule K-1 (Form 1120S), line 23; and Schedule K-1 (Form 1041), line 14 (see page E-6)	41	
42	**Reconciliation for Real Estate Professionals.** If you were a real estate professional (see page E-4), enter the net income or (loss) you reported anywhere on Form 1040 from all rental real estate activities in which you materially participated under the passive activity loss rules	42	

Schedule E (Form 1040) 2000

Modifying the Category List

When you create a new Quicken file, Quicken sets up a category list for you based on the general information you provide. You may need to make changes to this original category list in order to better support your income tax preparation. You can make changes to the list from the Category & Transfer List window, as shown in Figure 13.8. To display this window, choose Finance ➤ Category & Transfer List. From this window, you can add, edit, and delete categories, as described in the following sections.

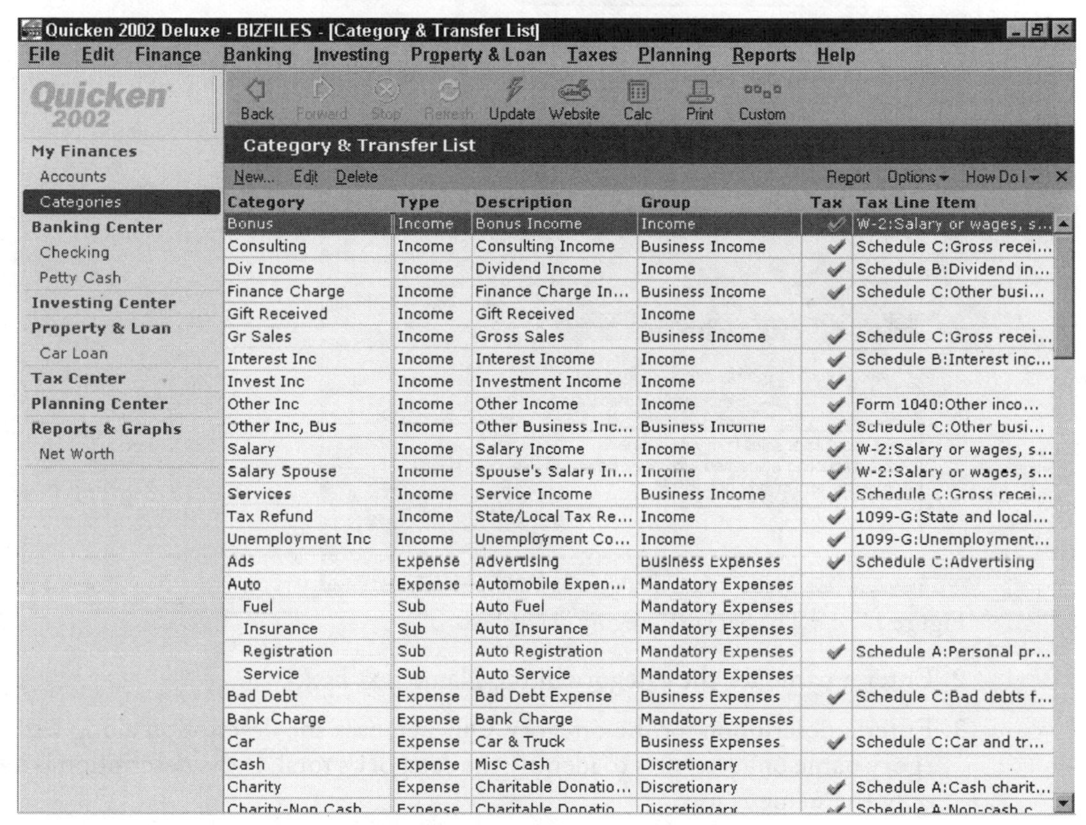

Figure 13.8: The Category & Transfer List window.

WARNING *Quicken sets up special categories for tracking investments when you create your first investment account. To identify these categories, Quicken starts each category name with an underscore character. You shouldn't change any of the investment categories.*

Adding a Category for Income Taxes

To add a new category to the Category & Transfer List, follow these steps:

1. Click the New command button in the Category & Transfer List window to display the Set Up Category dialog box, as shown in Figure 13.9.

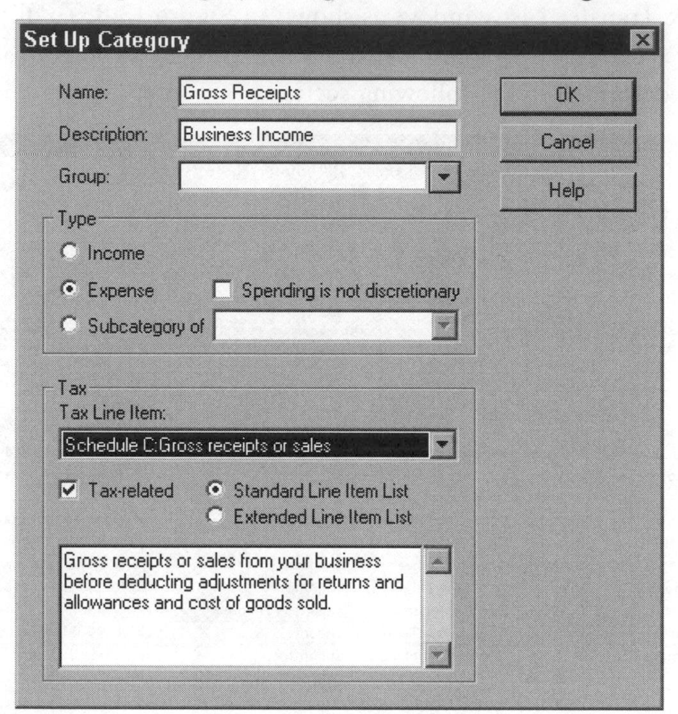

Figure 13.9: The Set Up Category dialog box.

2. Enter a name for the category in the Name text box.
3. Enter a description for the category. Quicken uses the description along with the category name on its reports to identify the category's total. If the description is left blank, only the name is used.
4. Use the Type option buttons to indicate whether the new category tracks income or expense or is a subcategory of a category that tracks income or expense.
5. If you marked the Subcategory Of option button, activate the Subcategory drop-down list box and select the category that the subcategory's total gets rolled up into. You can have subcategories that roll up into other subcategories. To do this, select as a primary category the subcategory that the new subcategory's total will get rolled up into from the Subcategory drop-down list.
6. Mark the Tax-Related checkbox to indicate that you'll use this category for tracking taxable income or tax-deductible expense items. This tells Quicken that the category total should appear on a Tax Summary report.

7. Indicate on which tax form and tax form line the category total is reported: Activate the Tax Line Item drop-down list box and select the list entry that names the correct form (or schedule) and the form (or schedule) line. For example, if you want to set up a category for tracking the gross sales figure that will ultimately be entered on line 1 of the Schedule C form, select the Schedule C: Gross Receipts entry.

NOTE *Quicken Deluxe doesn't display the Form drop-down list box in the Set Up Category dialog box until you mark the Use Tax Schedules With Categories checkbox in the General Options dialog box.*

8. Click OK. Quicken adds the category you described to the Category & Transfer List window and closes the dialog box.
9. Repeat steps 1 through 8 for each tax category you want to add.

Editing a Category for Income Taxes

To edit an existing category so it works (or works better) for tracking taxable income and tax-deductible expenses, follow these steps:

1. Select the category in the Category & Transfer List window and click the Edit command button to display the Edit Category dialog box, as shown in Figure 13.10.

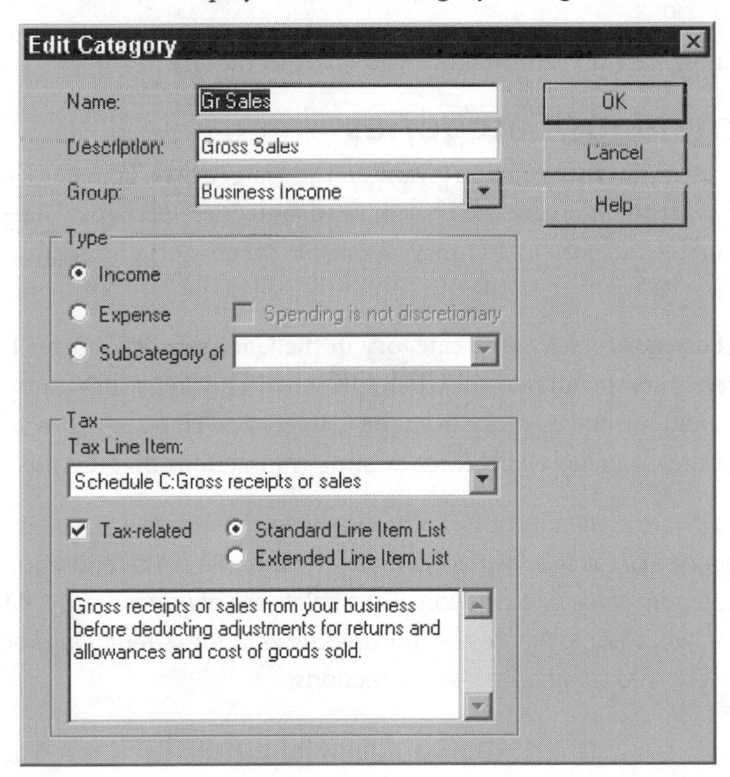

Figure 13.10: Alter existing categories in the Edit Category dialog box.

2. If you need to, change the category name. Quicken will update the transactions that used the old category name so they show the new category name.
3. If you need to, edit the description for the category.
4. Use the Type option buttons to indicate whether the category tracks income or expense or is a subcategory of a category that tracks income or expense.

TIP *You can change a category into a subcategory and a subcategory into a category using the Type option buttons. If you demote a category, you must also complete step 5.*

5. If you mark the Subcategory option, select the parent category in which you want the subcategory included from the Subcategory drop-down list box.
6. Mark the Tax-Related checkbox to indicate that you'll use this category for tracking taxable income or tax-deductible expense items, or unmark the checkbox if the category is currently being treated as taxable or tax-deductible but shouldn't be.
7. If the category is tax-related, indicate on which tax form and tax form line the category total is reported: From the Form drop-down list box, select the list entry that names the correct form (or schedule) and the form (or schedule) line.
8. Click OK when the Edit Category dialog box is complete. Quicken makes the changes and closes the dialog box.
9. Repeat steps 1 through 8 for each category you want to modify.

Deleting Extraneous Categories

You can remove any categories that you don't want on the Category & Transfer List. (This is a good idea if you want to eliminate the chance that someone—perhaps you—will accidentally use an incorrect category to summarize taxable income or a tax-deductible expense.)

To remove unneeded categories, select the category in the Category & Transfer List window and click the Delete command button. Click OK when Quicken asks you to confirm the deletion. Quicken removes the category from the Category & Transfer List window and erases the contents of the Category text box for existing transactions that use the category.

TIP *If you want to delete a category but want transactions that use the old category to use another category—I'll call this the new category—make the old category you want to delete a subcategory of the new category. Then delete the old category. Click Yes when Quicken asks if you want to merge the subcategory with the parent. Quicken will use the parent category to summarize the transactions.*

Using Quicken's Tax Reports

Quicken provides two reports for helping you prepare your income tax returns more easily: the Tax Summary and Tax Schedule reports (see Chapter 4 for details about viewing, printing, and customizing Quicken's reports).

If you haven't connected taxable income categories and tax-deductible expense categories to tax schedule lines, use the Tax Summary report (choose Reports ➢ Taxes ➢ Tax Summary). Use the data in this report to enter the taxable income and tax-deductible expense category totals into the appropriate tax form or schedule input lines. If your business is a sole proprietorship, for example, you would enter the Total Supplies, Bus figure shown in Figure 13.11 on the "Supplies" line (line 22) of the Schedule C form (see Figure 13.4).

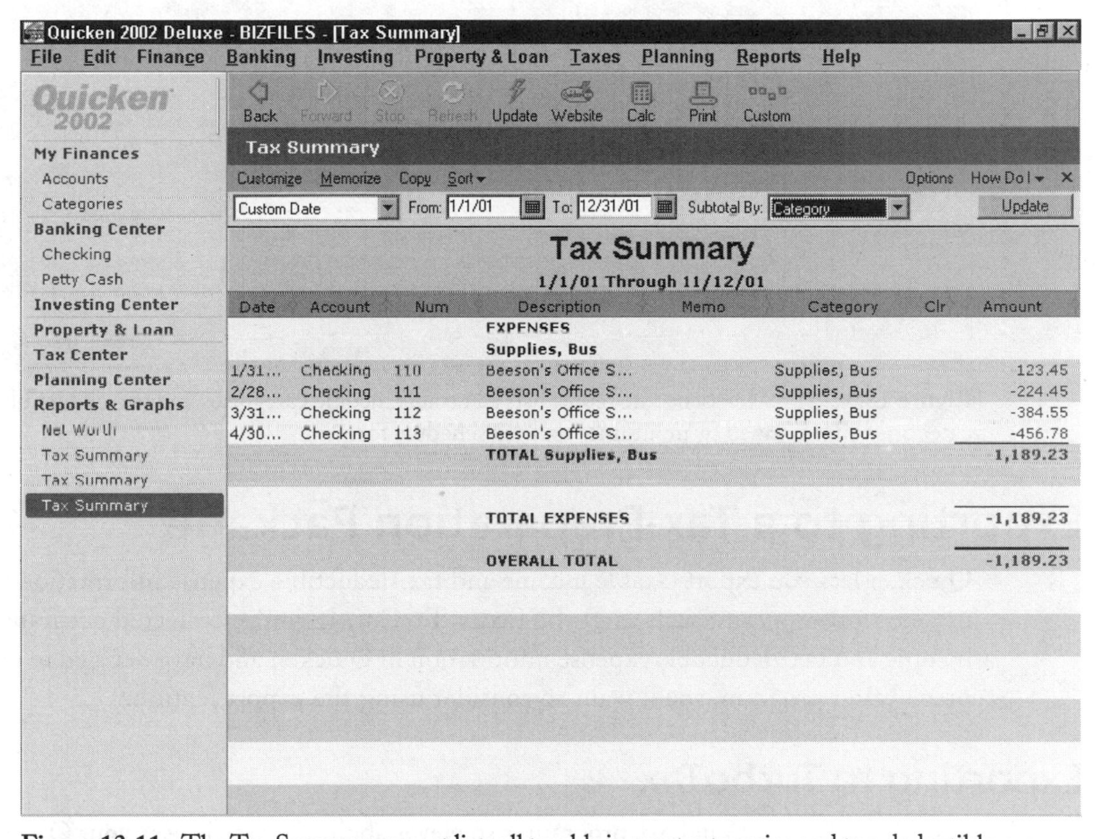

Figure 13.11: The Tax Summary report lists all taxable income categories and tax-deductible expense categories (as long as you've set up your category list correctly).

If you have connected taxable income categories and tax-deductible expense categories to tax schedule lines, use the Tax Schedule report (choose Reports ➢ Taxes ➢ Tax Schedule). Enter the report's tax schedule line totals on the corresponding tax schedule lines. Figure 13.12 shows a portion of a Tax Schedule report.

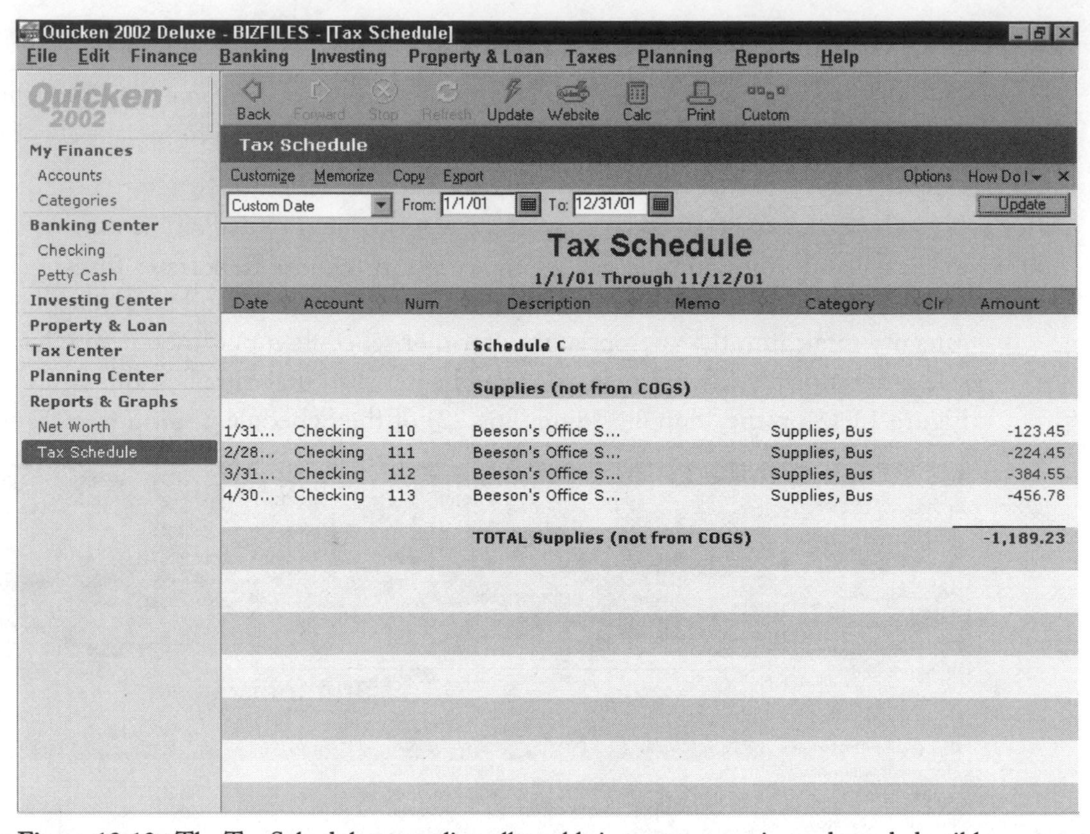

Figure 13.12: The Tax Schedule report lists all taxable income categories and tax-deductible expense categories summarized by input lines on a tax schedule form.

Exporting to a Tax-Preparation Package

Quicken lets you export taxable income and tax-deductible expense information to a tax-preparation program, such as TurboTax or TaxCut. If you've collected accurate taxable income and tax-deductible expense information in Quicken and have decided to use a tax-preparation program, you'll want to consider using the export feature.

Exporting to TurboTax

The TurboTax for Windows program is so clever about the way it uses your Quicken data that all you need to do is start TurboTax and tell it you want to import data from Quicken. (If you've installed TurboTax, you can start it by choosing Taxes ➢ TurboTax.) TurboTax then starts Quicken, tells it to create a Tax Schedule report for the appropriate year, and uses the Tax Schedule report information to fill in the open tax return.

There are only two tricks to exporting Quicken data to TurboTax:

- The Quicken file with the tax information you want to use needs to be the active Quicken file, so that when TurboTax starts Quicken, it gets the correct file. If you're using only one Quicken file—and you probably are—this isn't a problem. But if you have more than one Quicken file, TurboTax gives you a chance to specify which one you want to use. It will display the name of the active Quicken file and ask you if it's correct, before it imports the data. You can indicate that the active file isn't correct and then tell TurboTax which Quicken file it should have Quicken open.

NOTE *TurboTax can look at the Q3.DIR file in the Quicken directory to determine which Quicken data file was last used and, therefore, is active. It's also possible to include a command-line parameter that names the active file when starting Quicken. If you indicate that your tax information is in another Quicken file, TurboTax tells Quicken to make that file active when TurboTax starts Quicken.*

- Make sure that you use the correct version of TurboTax. If you use the 2001 version of TurboTax, for example, the Tax Schedule report that TurboTax has Quicken produce includes the transaction date range January 1, 2001, through December 31, 2001.

This rigid transaction date range feature makes perfect sense, of course. Because the tax laws and tax tables change, you can't use the 2001 version of TurboTax to do your 2000 or your 2002 taxes. (You can't, for example, use this automatic importing feature to "guesstimate" what your 2002 income taxes will be using 2002 data and the 2001 version of TurboTax.)

Exporting to Other Tax-Preparation Programs

You can export the information shown in a Tax Schedule report to a Tax Exchange Format, or TXF, file. Almost any tax-preparation program you work with, including TurboTax, will import the data contained in this file and use it to fill in the lines of a tax return.

NOTE *You don't need to first export your Quicken data to a TXF file if you're working with TurboTax. TurboTax will retrieve Quicken data automatically.*

To export the information shown in a Tax Schedule report, you first produce the report: Choose Reports ➢ Taxes ➢ Tax Schedule. (Figure 13.12 shows a Tax Schedule report.)

Once you've created the Tax Schedule report and it appears in a document window, take these steps to export the tax schedule information to a TXF file:

1. Click the Export command button on the button bar of the report to display the Create Tax Export File dialog box, as shown in Figure 13.13.

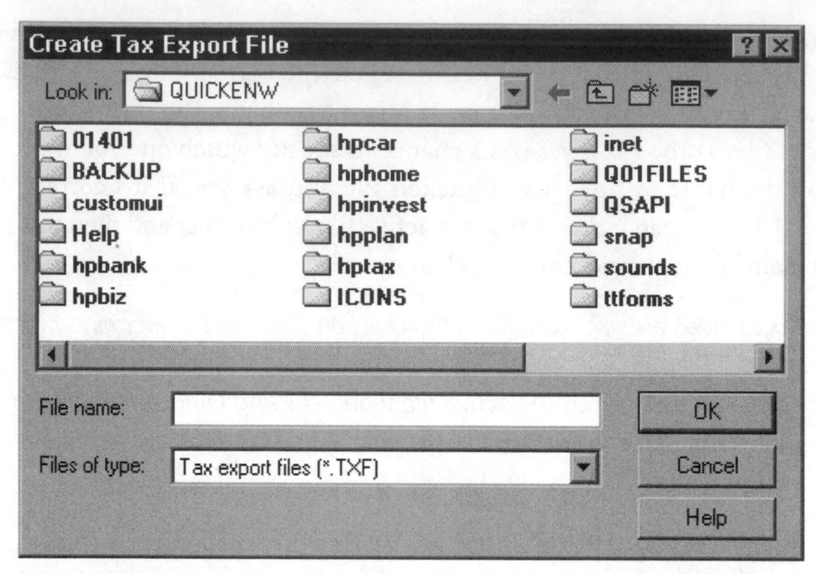

Figure 13.13: Name the export file in the Create Tax Export File dialog box.

2. Use the File Name text box to name the TXF file. You don't need to specify TXF as the file extension; Quicken adds it for you. If you don't specify a path, Quicken puts the file in the current directory, which is probably the Quicken data directory.
3. If you want to put the file in some other folder, such as the TurboTax folder, use the Look In drop-down list in the dialog box to navigate to the destination folder. Then click OK. Quicken creates the TXF file.

To use the TXF file, import it into the tax-preparation package you'll use to complete your return. Refer to that product's documentation or user's guide for information about how you do this. If you're working with TaxCut, for example, choose File ➤ Import In TaxCut. Then complete the dialog boxes supplied by the tax-preparation program to answer questions about where the TXF file is located.

Quicken and Tax-Preparation Programs

You need to be careful when you export Quicken data to a tax-preparation program for a couple of reasons:

- The numbers you enter on your tax form need to match the numbers shown on the W-2, 1099, or 1098 forms that you receive—even if your Quicken reports show different numbers. (If the information on one of these forms is wrong, you need to have the issuer of the information correct the return.)
- To determine which taxable income or tax-deduction transactions should be counted for a particular year, Quicken and the tax-preparation program can look

only at the transaction date. If the transaction date shows the income or deduction amount falling in the tax year, it gets counted for that year. This sounds correct, but it often isn't. Usually, some transactions you enter at the very beginning of the calendar year really relate to the previous year's tax return.

Using TurboTax to Prepare Your Taxes

TurboTax, as mentioned earlier in the chapter, is an income tax-preparation program. Because TurboTax is another Intuit program and because many Quicken users will be interested in knowing just a bit more about this program, let's take a closer look at its features and suitability for different situations.

NOTE *You might be curious as to how TurboTax compares with other tax-preparation programs. I can give you some helpful information in this area. For several years in a row, I reviewed income tax-preparation packages for Home Office Computing magazine. TurboTax always ranked near the top.*

TurboTax is relatively easy to use (although not as easy as Quicken). You can use it in a couple of ways. If you're familiar with what forms you need to fill out to complete your federal and state income tax returns, you can display on-screen forms that mirror the actual forms you file. Using this approach, you just fill in the blanks.

If you're not sure about income tax laws and accounting, you can tell TurboTax you want to be "interviewed." The program will ask you a series of questions that you answer by filling in text boxes and clicking buttons. Based on your answers, TurboTax then fills out your tax return. You can print a copy of your tax return directly from TurboTax, and you can file your federal tax return electronically if you want.

The Benefits of Using TurboTax

Is TurboTax a good product? Yes, it is. In fact, I do my own personal tax returns with TurboTax and my own business tax returns with TurboTax for Business, so I really like the programs. You benefit in a couple of big ways from using a tax-preparation package. First, being able to print an entire return with TurboTax means never having to worry about whether you have all the right tax forms and schedules. If you need to file a particular form or schedule, TurboTax can print it. (Before TurboTax, I always found myself running over to the local public library or calling the IRS to get some obscure form or schedule I needed.)

NOTE *If you have an Internet connection and a web browser, you can get almost any tax form you need from the IRS web site at* www.irs.gov. *You can download tax forms in a variety of formats.*

A second benefit of TurboTax is that you can easily make changes to your return. For example, when I used to prepare my return manually, I would invariably complete the entire return, think I was finished, and then find a missing deduction or income amount I needed to report. Because of this, I would need to input the new figure and then recalculate a bunch of different figures. With TurboTax, redoing your return for last-minute input is a breeze. You just start up TurboTax, input the new figure, and then tell the program to recalculate the return.

Who Should Use TurboTax?

Does this mean everyone should go out and buy a tax-preparation program? No, I don't think so.

If you pay a tax preparer to do your taxes now, I don't think you can use TurboTax as a substitute for that professional. TurboTax automates and expedites the tax-preparation process, but it still requires you to answer a series of questions having to do with your income taxes.

If you file a really simple return, you probably don't need TurboTax. For example, if you're a single taxpayer with no itemized deductions whose only income is from a job, your taxes are fairly simple in the first place. It wouldn't make sense in your situation to get TurboTax only to have it make a few calculations automatically. You won't actually save any tax-return preparation time, because you'll need to install the program and learn the ropes.

If you have a business but can file your business return using the very simple Schedule C-EZ, again, you probably don't need TurboTax. You can easily prepare your tax return manually.

In any other situation, however, you'll probably find TurboTax and TurboTax for Business invaluable.

NOTE *TurboTax for Business typically comes in several versions. Each version works for a specific business form: For example, there's a version of TurboTax for sole proprietors, a version of partnerships, a version for corporations, and so on. When you buy TurboTax, you actually purchase a CD with each of the versions on the disk, but you can use only one version—usually the version you register.*

Purchasing TurboTax

You need to buy a new copy of tax-preparation programs such as TurboTax every year because the tax rates and, sometimes, the tax laws change. Unfortunately, tax rate changes and tax law changes usually don't occur until the very end of the year. For this reason, there are always two versions of tax-preparation programs: an early-bird version that's available late in the year and useful only for making estimates, and a final version that you need to actually prepare and print your return. Early-bird purchasers always get a free upgrade to the final version, but you still need to be aware of the difference between the two versions. You don't, for example, want to purchase an early-bird version on April 15, thinking you'll have time to install the software and then prepare the return.

Using the Tax Planner

Quicken comes with a handy income tax expense estimator, built by the same people who produce TurboTax. This tool is called the Tax Planner. Based either on inputs you enter directly into a worksheet or on Quicken data, the Tax Planner gives you an accurate estimate of what you'll pay in income taxes for a particular year.

You may want to print a copy of the Tax Schedule report before you estimate your income taxes. To do this, choose Reports ➤ Taxes ➤ Tax Schedule and then click the Print button to print the report.

Estimating Your Income Taxes

To use the Tax Planner, follow these steps:

1. Choose Taxes ➤ Tax Planner. Quicken asks whether you want it to import tax deduction information from your registers and from the previous year's TurboTax files. When you answer these questions by clicking the Yes and No buttons, Quicken displays the Tax Planner window, as shown in Figure 13.14.

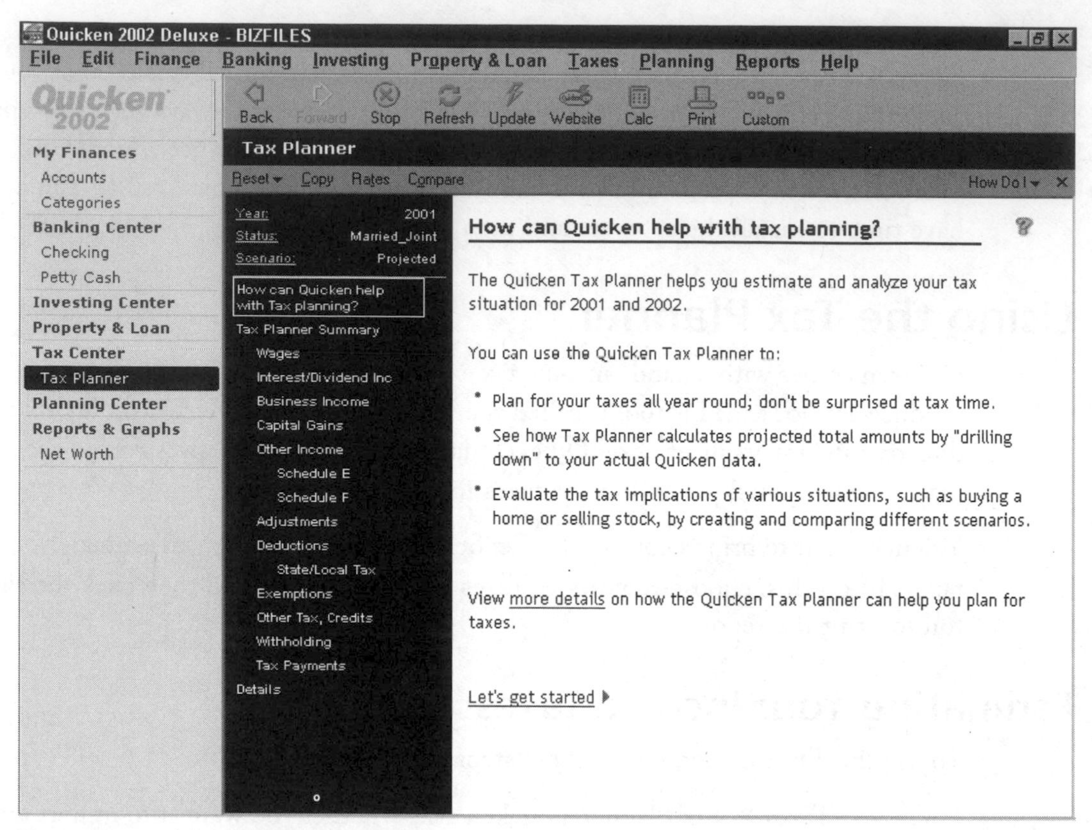

Figure 13.14: The Tax Planner window displaying its introductory message.

2. Click the Year hyperlink to display drop-down list boxes that ask for the year, filing status, and scenario for which you're estimating income taxes, as shown in Figure 13.15.

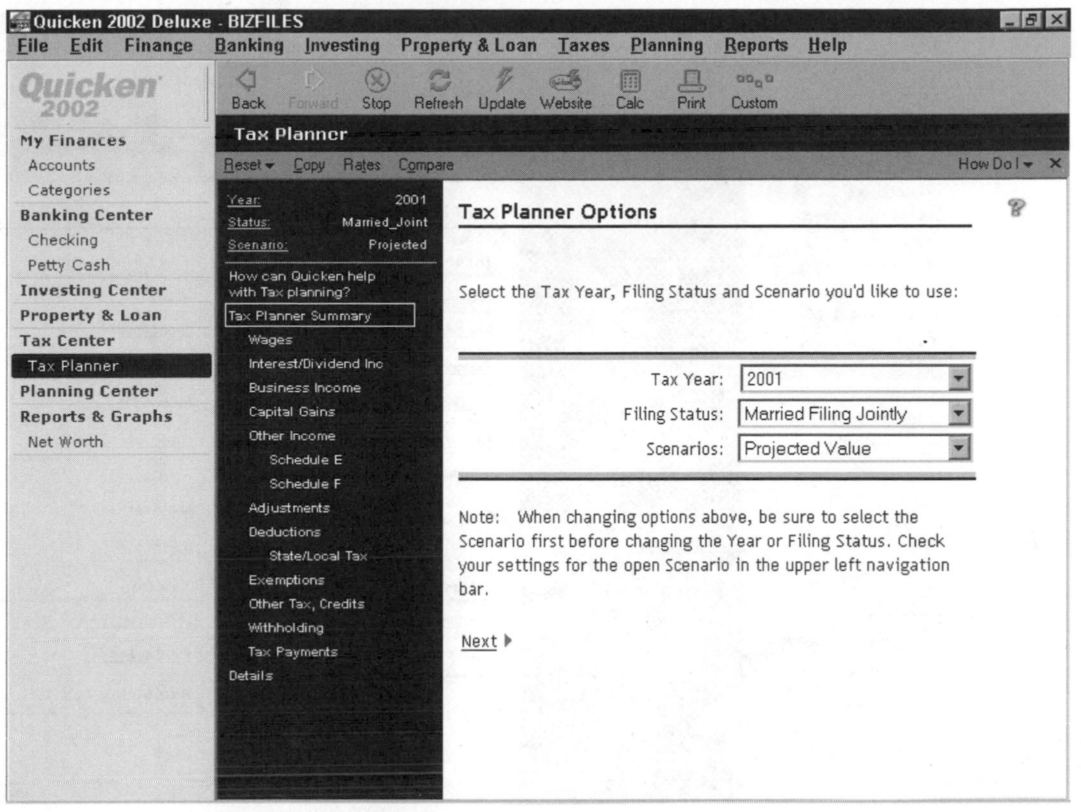

Figure 13.15: The Tax Planner window collecting year and filing status information.

3. Select the year for which you're estimating your income tax expenses. (Picking the right year is important because the tax rate schedules are annually adjusted for things like tax law changes and inflation.)
4. Activate the Status drop-down list box and select the appropriate filing status: Single, Married Filing Jointly, Married Filing Separately, Head of Household, or Qualifying Widow. (If you have questions about your filing status, refer to the IRS instructions that came with last year's return.)

NOTE *The Scenarios choices in the Tax Planner window let you store up to three sets, or scenarios, of inputs to the Tax Planner and compare them. See the "Comparing Different Income Tax Scenarios" section later in the chapter for more information.*

5. Click Next. Quicken displays the Tax Planner Summary information in the Tax Planner window, as shown in Figure 13.16.

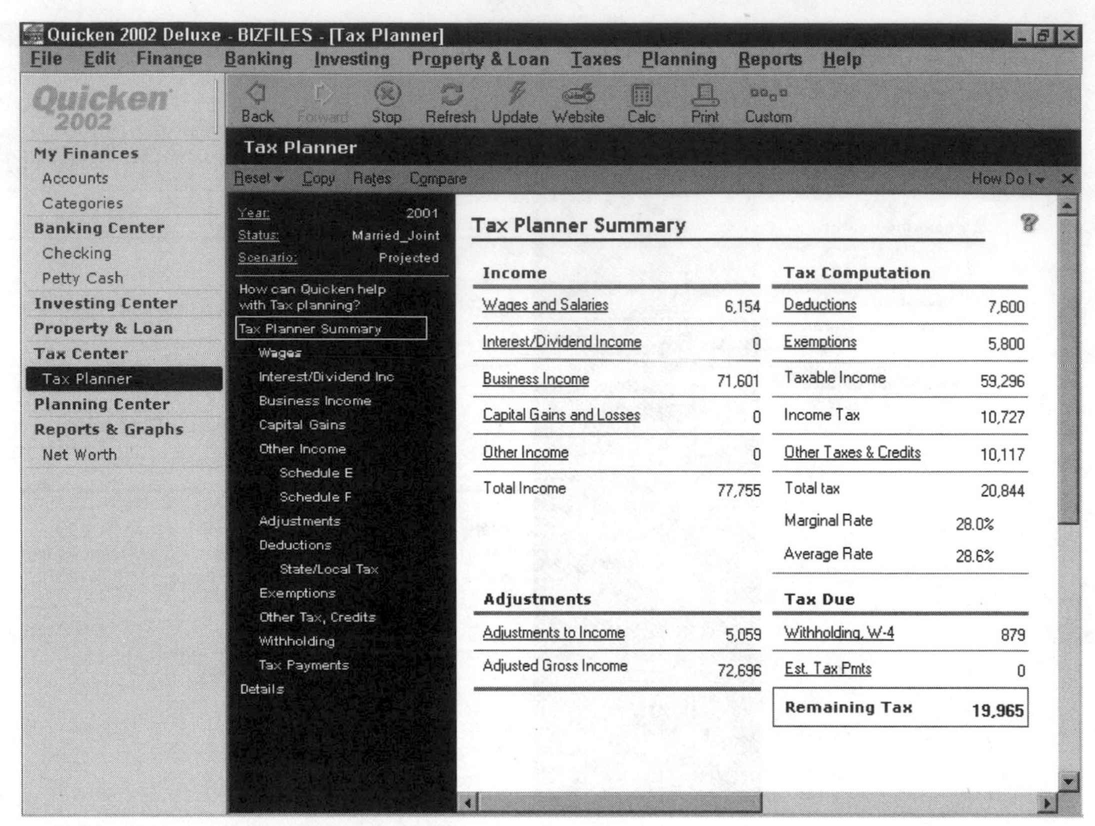

Figure 13.16: The Tax Planner Summary information.

6. Click the Wages hyperlink. When Quicken displays the Wages And Salaries boxes, as shown in Figure 13.17, enter your total wages in the Wages And Salaries-Self text box and enter your spouse's total wages in the Wages And Salaries-Spouse text box.

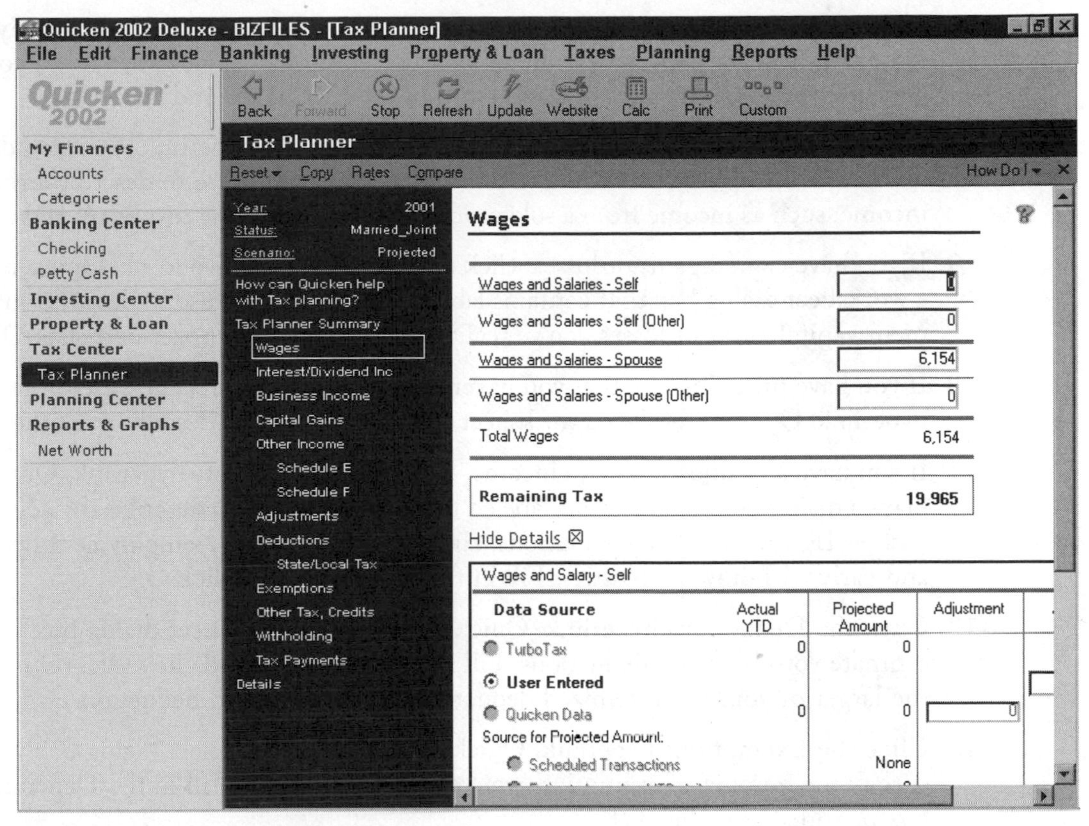

Figure 13.17: The Wages And Salaries boxes.

TIP *You can also move to the next tax planning step by clicking the Next button, which appears at the bottom of the Tax Planner window, and to the previous tax planning step by clicking the Previous button. You may need to scroll down to see these buttons.*

NOTE *To hide the extra detail shown beneath the Wages And Salaries boxes, mark the Hide Details checkbox. To later show this detail, click the Show Details box. Other collections of input boxes provide this same level of detail, which can be alternatively hidden and displayed by marking the Hide Details and Show Details checkboxes.*

7. If you have interest or dividend income, click the Interest/Dividend Inc hyperlink. Quicken displays a worksheet dialog box that contains labeled text boxes you use to describe your interest and dividends. Fill in the text boxes and click OK.
8. If you have business income, click the Business Income hyperlink. Quicken displays a worksheet dialog box that contains labeled text boxes you use to describe any business income, such as income from a sole proprietorship. Fill in the text boxes and click OK.
9. If you have capital gains or losses, click the Capital Gains hyperlink. Quicken displays a worksheet dialog box that contains labeled text boxes you use to describe any investment capital gains or losses you've realized. Fill in the text boxes and click OK.
10. If you have other income that you haven't recorded elsewhere, click the Other Income hyperlink. Quicken displays a worksheet dialog box. Use it to describe this other income.
11. If you have any adjustments to income, click the Adjustments hyperlink. Quicken displays a dialog box that contains labeled text boxes you use to describe any adjustments, such as IRA or Keogh contributions, alimony payments, self-employment deductions, and early withdrawal penalties. Fill in the text boxes and click OK.
12. Click the Deductions hyperlink. Quicken displays a worksheet dialog box you use to estimate your itemized deductions. Fill in the text boxes and click OK. (Quicken uses the larger of your total itemized deductions or the standard deduction.)
13. Click the Exemptions hyperlink. Quicken displays a worksheet dialog box you use to specify the number of exemptions you're entitled to claim. Fill in the Dependents text box provided and click OK.
14. If you pay other federal taxes or are entitled to claim any income tax credits, click the Other Tax, Credits hyperlink. Quicken displays a worksheet dialog box you use to specify any other taxes you pay, such as self-employment income tax, or any income tax credits. Fill in the text boxes and click OK.

With the information you provide in steps 2 through 14, the Tax Planner estimates your total federal tax bill and also calculates both your marginal income tax rate and your average income tax rate.

TIP *Your marginal income tax rate is a useful piece of information. It allows you to convert pre-tax investment yields and interest rates to after-tax investment yields and interest rates. All you do is multiply the pre-tax rate by 1 minus the marginal income tax rate. For example, to convert a 10 percent pre-tax rate to an after-tax rate if the marginal tax rate is 28 percent, make the following calculation: 10 percent x (1 – 28 percent). This formula returns 7.2 percent.*

TIP *Quicken lets you view the tax rates by clicking the Rates button. Quicken displays a window that you can use to see the tax rates for the selected filing statutes.*

15. Click the Withholding hyperlink. Quicken displays a worksheet dialog box you use to describe the federal income taxes you (and your spouse if you're married) have already had withheld, and how much you'll probably have withheld over the remaining payroll periods in the year. Fill in the text boxes and click OK.
16. Click the Tax Payments hyperlink. Quicken displays a worksheet dialog box you use to describe any estimated taxes you (and your spouse if you're married) have made and will make. Fill in the text boxes and click OK.

With the completion of steps 15 and 16, the Tax Planner calculates the remaining federal taxes you'll still owe at the end of the year after all your estimated withholding and any estimated income taxes.

To print a summary of the tax-planning calculations, choose File ➤ Print Report. Quicken displays a Print dialog box, which mirrors the Print dialog boxes you use to print reports. If you've printed a report or two—presumably you have by this point—you'll have no trouble completing the Tax Planner's version. (See Chapter 4 if you need more information about printing reports.)

Comparing Different Income Tax Scenarios

You can store as many as four sets, or scenarios, of inputs to the Tax Planner: projected value, 1, 2, and 3. You first create the projected value scenario. You can create alternative scenarios by clicking the Scenarios hyperlink and then selecting the scenario you want to create from the Scenarios drop-down list box. When you select 1, 2, or 3 from the Scenarios drop-down list box, Quicken asks if you want to copy the projected value scenario inputs as a starting point for the new scenario. If you want to do this—and you probably do—click Yes.

You can compare the inputs and the income tax calculations for two scenarios by clicking the Compare button. Quicken displays a dialog box that summarizes the filing status, tax year, adjusted gross income, deductions and exemptions, taxable income, total tax, and tax rates for each scenario.

Finding Tax Deductions

Quicken Deluxe and Quicken Home and Business help you find tax deductions that you may have missed in your planning. They also check your eligibility for the deductions. Choose Taxes ➤ Deduction Finder and the Introduction To Deduction Finder dialog box appears. Click OK to move to the Deduction Finder window, as shown in Figure 13.18.

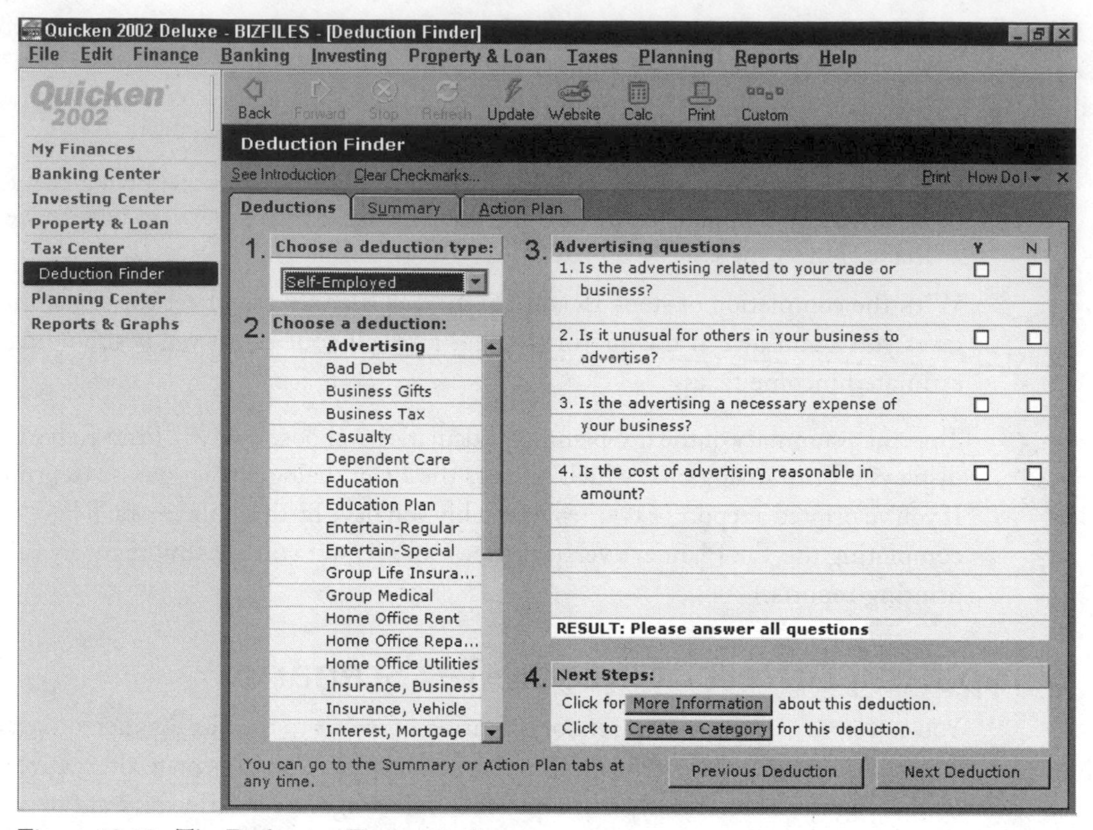

Figure 13.18: The Deduction Finder window.

You begin by choosing a deduction type in the drop-down list box, then clicking a possible deduction in the Choose A Deduction list. Answer the Yes or No questions in the third section by clicking the appropriate checkboxes. When you answer all of the questions, the Deduction Finder tells you whether or not you may be eligible for that particular deduction.

WARNING *After you have consulted the Deduction Finder, be sure to talk over the information with your tax advisor before making any final decisions.*

The Deduction Finder also keeps track of the deductions you have tried and develops an action plan for you, based on the results. Click the Summary and Action Plan tabs to see Deduction Finder's records.

Reviewing Quicken's Other Tax Tools

Up to this point, this chapter has described the most important and commonly used tax features of Quicken. However, as even a quick review of the Tax menu indicates, Quicken provides several other noteworthy tax tools. There isn't space here to describe each of these tools in detail, but before I move on to a discussion of how you solve common tax and tax-preparation problems, let me quickly review these other features:

- **Tax Center** The Tax Center command displays Quicken's Tax Center window. The Tax Center provides hyperlinks to other tax-planning tools, a calendar of tax-related deadlines (especially useful for small businesses!), and hyperlinks to reports and graphs that summarize your current tax situation. It's well worth your time to spend a few minutes exploring this self-explanatory window.
- **Tax Line Assignment** The Tax Line Assignment command displays a version of the Category & Transfer List window that shows how your income and expense categories map to tax form lines. You can use this window to review your tax line assignments.
- **Tax Category Audit** The Tax Category Audit command reviews your tax categories to see if there are any that, to Quicken, look incorrect or suspicious. If Quicken identifies any suspicious tax categories, it reports them to you.
- **Itemized Deduction Estimator** The Itemized Deduction Estimator command displays a window of information that steps you through the process of identifying and estimating any itemized deductions to which you're entitled.
- **Tax Withholding Estimator** The Tax Withholding Estimator command displays a window of information that steps you through the process of estimating how much you should and will have withheld in income taxes.
- **Tax Activities** The Tax Activities command displays a submenu of about a half a dozen commands that amount to a grab bag of tax planning tools. The Tax Activities submenu supplies commands for setting up a paycheck, for importing TurboTax data, for accessing the Capital Gains Estimator, for comparing the yields of taxable and tax-exempt investments, and so on.

TIP *You can use Quicken's Capital Gains Estimator to estimate capital gains you'll owe if you sell investments. In order to use the Capital Gains Estimator, you might have an investment account set up in Quicken. To start the Capital Gains Estimator, click the Let's Get Started hyperlink. Quicken walks you through the steps for estimating the capital gains taxes on securities in your investment accounts.*

- **Tax Services** The Tax Services command displays a submenu with commands for viewing any special offers related to the TurboTax product and for viewing a web page that describes other related Quicken services.

Solving Common Tax-Preparation Problems

There are some potential pitfalls to using your Quicken data as the one and only source of all your taxable income and tax-deductible expense information. This doesn't mean you shouldn't use Quicken; it just means that you need to be careful—you can't blindly automate the process.

Discrepancies between Your Records and Informational Returns

When the IRS processes your return, one of the things the processors will do is verify that any informational returns they've received match up with your return. They will compare the W-2 information provided by your employer (or employers) with what you enter on the "Wages, Salaries, Tips, etc." line, and they will compare the 1099-INT and 1099-OID statements provided by almost anyone who has paid you interest with what you enter on your 1040 or Schedule B. (Schedule B summarizes your dividend and interest income when you have more substantial amounts of either.)

Any difference between what one of these informational returns shows and what you enter on a line of a tax schedule of your income tax return will almost certainly trigger a review of your return. In this case, the IRS will write you a letter asking for an explanation of the discrepancy. You'll then need to review your records to determine whether your return's number was the correct one or—and this is probably more likely—the informational return's number was the correct one. Then you'll need to fix the mistake.

This sequence of events points out a potential trouble spot. You can use Quicken to collect your taxable income and, in some cases, your tax-deductible expense information. But it may just be that there's another, more accurate source of the taxable income or tax-deductible expense numbers you need to enter on your tax return. When this is the case, it makes the most sense to use this other source for preparing your tax return. And even if you do record the information provided by this other source into Quicken, you may make an error entering the data.

For this reason, it's easiest and most accurate to get your salaries and wages information from employer-provided W-2s and to get interest and dividend information from the 1099 informational returns your broker or bank prepares.

Timing Differences

Another opportunity for error concerns timing differences. You may be required to report some item of income or deduct some expense in one year, although you did not record the information into a Quicken register until a subsequent year. For example, if you're a partner in a business, you may be required to include in your taxable income a share of partnership profits earned in one year but paid in the following year. Or if you've invested in a long-term certificate of deposit (CD), you may be required to report any accrued interest for the year as income. (The CD issuer may send you a 1099-OID statement of your interest earnings.)

To use Quicken to keep records of taxable income and tax-deductible expenses like this, you need to use a transaction date that places the transaction in the year that the transaction affects taxable income or tax-deductible expenses, which won't necessarily be the same year you make a deposit or write a check.

What to Do If You Get Audited

Although your chances of being audited are probably remote, some of the people who read this chapter will be audited. Here are some things you should do—and shouldn't do—if you get audited.

Quicken Tasks You Should Complete

The Quicken Tax Summary report lists and tallies each of the taxable and tax-deductible transactions included on your return. Since the audit will probably consist of the agent reviewing these transactions and deductions, you'll want to have a listing of the transactions. A Tax Summary report gives this information.

If you know beforehand that a specific tax deduction is being questioned, be sure to bring all the source documents that evidence the pertinent transactions. For example, if the IRS is questioning your charitable contributions deduction, bring any canceled checks you used to make your contributions.

WARNING *Don't bring a laptop computer with Quicken to the audit. The IRS agent may appreciate your enthusiasm, but remember that your Quicken file largely summarizes your financial life. And Quicken's reports make it easy for the agent to quickly review every nook and cranny, searching for income you may have missed or deductions you shouldn't have taken.*

Other Audit Preparation Tasks

There are a couple of other things you should be sure to do before you attend the audit:

- Make sure that you understand all the numbers on your return, and remember that you signed it under penalty of perjury.
- You may want to consider asking your tax preparer to represent you at the audit. There are a variety of reasons for doing this. If you don't understand your return but your preparer does, it makes sense to have the preparer at the audit.

NOTE *Sometimes it also makes more sense to have a tax preparer represent you because he or she knows (or should know) quite a lot about the income tax laws but relatively little about your financial life. I know a tax attorney who follows this approach because the tax preparer can honestly answer many IRS questions by saying, "I don't know." The tax attorney feels that the "I don't knows" tend to terminate many spontaneous inquiries.*

Things to Do during the Audit

An audit doesn't have to be a bad experience. All that really happens is that the IRS agent will ask you to explain and document items that the IRS doesn't understand.

Nevertheless, let me provide you with two final suggestions. First, if the agent identifies himself or herself as a special agent, ask to terminate the interview so you can reschedule it. A special agent investigates criminal tax code violations, so you'll probably want a tax attorney present at any meetings.

Another thing I suggest is that you be very reserved in your comments. Don't lie, of course, but don't volunteer extra information. If you have questions about some deduction or how to treat some income item, ask a tax preparer or telephone the IRS's taxpayer assistance line, but don't expect the IRS agent auditing your return to answer tax-preparation questions. (My feeling is that there's a very strong tendency for the auditor to look only for things that increase your income tax bill, and not for things that decrease your bill.)

Common Tax-Savings Opportunities for Businesses

One of the hidden benefits of owning your own business is the tax savings opportunities. Small business owners get three significant tax benefits not available or not as generously available to individual taxpayers and large businesses. In the following sections, I'll introduce the opportunities and provide you with enough information to let you determine whether you want to do more research.

NOTE *U.S. taxpayers can get more information about all of the topics discussed in the following paragraphs at the Internal Revenue Service web site at* www.irs.gov.

Pension Plans

Pension plans don't seem like much of a benefit at first. You probably already know that you can put money away into an IRA. You may also know that by putting money into something like an IRA you get a tax deduction. If you pay a marginal tax rate of 15 percent, for example, you might save $300 by making a $2,000 IRA contribution.

What you may not know is that small business owners can select pension plans that let them save large sums into pension plans. With an IRA, for example, an individual is limited to contributing $2,000 a year. But with other pension funds, the business owner can contribute much larger sums. For example, by setting up a Simplified Employee Pension, or SEP, plan, you may be able to contribute 15 percent of your income up to as much as $30,000. By setting up a SIMPLE plan, which is essentially a 401(k) plan for small businesses, you can contribute 100 percent of your income up to $6,000. And by setting up a qualified defined benefit plan, you might be able to contribute $50,000 annually or even more (based on complicated formulas that require a pension consultant's help).

As a small business owner, then, you can probably pick a pension plan that lets you save large sums of money tax-free, creating a huge tax-savings opportunity.

A couple of other quick, related points should be made. At the point when you have a successful small business, you may be paying a very burdensome marginal income tax rate—especially if you live in a state with high income taxes. It's possible, for example, for small business people to find themselves paying 40 percent of the last part of their income in income taxes. With a 40 percent marginal tax rate, a $10,000 contribution to a pension plan produces $4,000 in tax savings. Often, with small business pension plans, the business owner finds that a large percentage of the contribution is funded through tax savings.

Another more sobering point about pension plans should be made, too. Money you've stored in a pension plan often isn't available to creditors. This means that you can usually keep any money you've stored in a pension plan no matter what happens in your business. How secure pension plan money is depends on the state in which you live, so you'll need to consult your attorney for specific details. Know, however, that you may be able to keep your pension plan even if you go through a bankruptcy or even if someone successfully sues you.

Section 179 Depreciation

Large businesses must spread out, or depreciate, the cost of a long-lived asset such as a truck or computer over the years the item will be used. In comparison, most small businesses shouldn't need to depreciate the equipment and furniture they purchase. They can instead write off the complete amount of a computer or new furniture in the year the item or items are purchased.

Most small business owners reading this book, for example, can write off up to $24,000 of equipment in the years 2001 and 2002 and up to $25,000 of equipment in the years 2003 and beyond. However, special rules limit your Section 179 write-off if you're purchasing a car or when you buy more than $200,000 of equipment. Because these rules quickly get complex, you'll want to consult your tax advisor when you have questions.

Incorporate Your Business

You shouldn't make the decision to incorporate your business lightly. Incorporation greatly complicates your tax accounting. For example, you probably won't be able to use Quicken anymore. You'll probably want to step up to QuickBooks.

However, the extra work of incorporation may be worth it to you because corporations offer two significant tax-savings opportunities to small business owners.

The first tax-savings opportunity concerns fringe benefits provided to corporate employees. As you may remember if you've ever worked for a corporation, a corporation can provide many fringe benefits to its employees. While the corporation typically gets a tax deduction for these fringe benefits, the employee doesn't get taxed on the benefits. One common example of such a fringe benefit is medical insurance. The corporate employer can write off as a business expense the cost of any medical insurance premiums, but the employees don't have to count this benefit as income.

This curious feature of corporation-provided employee fringe benefits creates an opportunity for small businesses that employ the owners. For example, if you are a small business owner and incorporate, you can provide fringe benefits to *all* employees, including yourself, your spouse, and your children, and then deduct the cost of those fringe benefits on your corporation's tax return.

The only wrinkle is that you can't discriminate in favor of yourself in distributing the fringe benefits. In other words, you can't set up a fringe benefits plan that benefits only yourself as the owner. However, as is common, many small businesses employ only the owner and the owner's family. In this case, you, as the owner, may be able to incorporate and then set up a very rich fringe benefits program.

WARNING *There's one potential problem with incorporating, however. You must pay yourself a fair salary. That sounds fine, at first blush. But this fair salary may be less than the business makes. And in the case of a regular corporation—what's called a "C" corporation—this extra money creates accounting and tax problems. Technically, the extra money is corporate profit, which means the corporation needs to pay income taxes on the money. That taxation may be okay if you want to leave the money in the corporation so that you can grow the business. But if you want to take the money out of the business, the money comes to you in the form of a corporate dividend on which you pay taxes again. For this reason, you'll want to ask your attorney or C.P.A. about the problem of this double-taxation before you decide to incorporate. Note that any amounts the corporation pays you in the form of salary gets taxed only once—when it's counted as your wages.*

A second tax-savings opportunity concerns self-employment taxes. As a sole proprietor, you pay self-employment taxes of 15.3 percent on roughly the first $80,000 of your income and then Medicare taxes of 2.9 percent on amounts in excess of $80,000. These taxes are in addition to the amounts you pay in the form of income taxes.

There's a way around paying some of these taxes, however. You can incorporate your business and then elect what's called Sub S status. When you elect Sub S status, you tell the IRS that even though you're a corporation you want to be treated like a partnership on any corporate profits. This means that the corporation doesn't get taxed on the profits but rather the profits flow through and are taxed to the corporate shareholders as if they're simply partners.

This election, though, produces a funny opportunity. And the best way to explain this is to compare what happens in a sole proprietorship with what happens in a Sub S corporation. Let's say, for the sake of illustration, that your business makes $80,000 a year. Let's further suppose that the fair salary someone gets paid to do what you do is $40,000. The other thing you need to know if you don't already is that self-employment is just the Social Security tax and Medicare tax that self-employed people pay.

If you're a sole proprietor, you will pay 15.3 percent in self-employment taxes on the $80,000 of business profits. That equals roughly $12,000.

If you're a Sub S corporation and you set your salary at $40,000, you'll pay 15.3 percent of Social Security and Medicare tax on the $40,000 of salary. That equals roughly $6,000.

In this example, by incorporating and then electing Sub S status, you save about $6,000 of self-employment taxes.

Note that you would still receive the same $80,000 of profit in both cases. When you're a sole proprietor, you get paid in the form of sole proprietorship profits—all of which are subject to self-employment taxes. When you're a Sub S corporation, you get paid in two ways: in wages, which are subject to Social Security and Medicare taxes, and in dividends, which aren't subject to Social Security and Medicare taxes.

The self-employment tax savings from Sub S status accrue because you can avoid paying self-employment taxes on some of the business's profits.

WARNING *When operating as a Sub S corporation, business owners are tempted to pick an artificially low salary since that maximizes the self-employment tax savings. Predictably, however, you must set a fair salary for yourself.*

Chapter 14

BUDGETING AND FINANCIAL PLANNING

- Setting savings goals
- Monitoring finances with Category Groups
- Setting up a budget
- Quicken's tools for strategic planning
- Reviewing the Planning menu's other tools
- How to achieve financial independence

Quicken's record-keeping abilities are fabulous. In fact, that's probably the reason Quicken is so popular. But both personal and business financial success requires more than just good record keeping. You need to intelligently monitor and plan your finances. This chapter describes the tools that Quicken provides to help you plan.

NOTE *To use many of the planning tools described in this chapter, you must have the Deluxe or Home and Business version of Quicken. Most of the planners are not available in Quicken Basic.*

Setting Savings Goals

Quicken lets you set savings goal amounts, calculate the periodic saving required to reach the goal, and track your progress toward the goal. While you don't need to use Quicken to achieve your savings goals, it can make the whole process much easier (by quantifying exactly what you need to do) and increase your chances of success (by focusing attention on your progress).

Creating a Savings Goal

To create a savings goal, choose Planning ➤ Savings Goals. Quicken displays the Savings Goals window. The window won't list any savings goals because you have not yet described any. To set up a goal, click the New command button. Quicken displays the Create New Savings Goal dialog box, as shown in Figure 14.1.

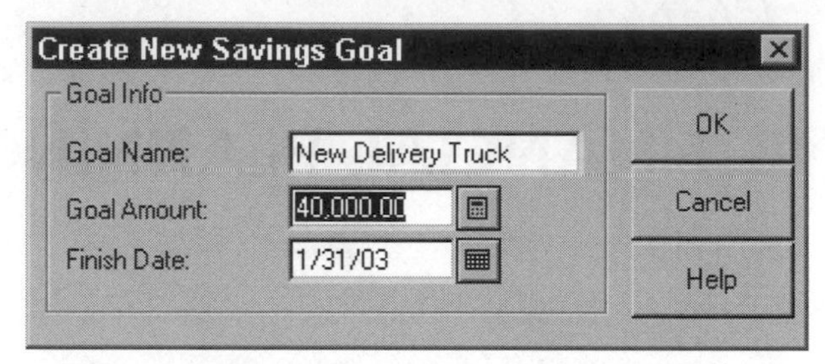

Figure 14.1: The Create New Savings Goal dialog box.

NOTE *If you don't find the Savings Goals item on your Planning menu, this planner is not implemented in your version of Quicken.*

Describe your savings goal by filling in the text boxes in the Create New Savings Goal dialog box. Enter a name for the goal (perhaps the item you're saving for) in the Goal Name text box. In the Goal Amount text box, enter the amount you want to accumulate. Using the Finish Date combo box, give the date by which you want to reach your goal. Figure 14.1 shows an example. When you enter your information and click OK, Quicken returns you to the Savings Goals window, which now lists the goal you described. Figure 14.2 shows an example.

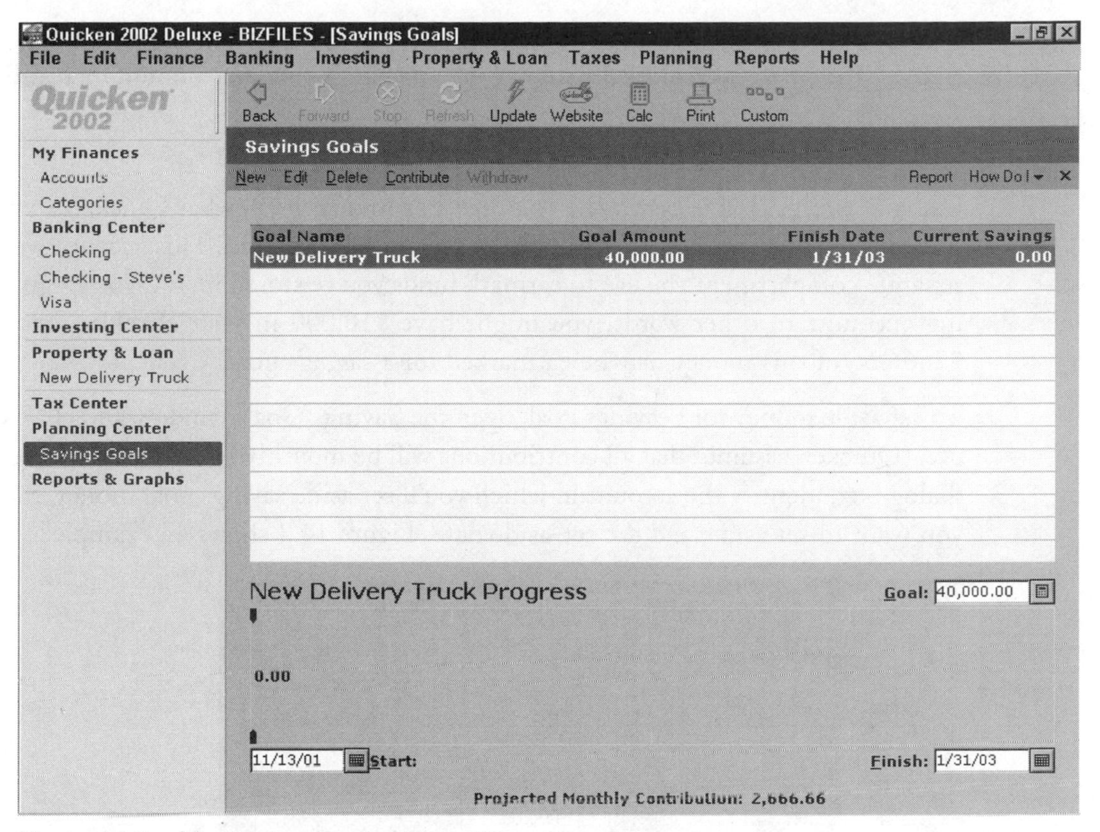

Figure 14.2: The Savings Goals window lists your savings goals.

In the box in the top half of the Savings Goals window, Quicken lists each of the savings goals you've described. (In Figure 14.2, the list shows only one goal: New Delivery Truck.) In the box in the bottom half of the Savings Goals window, Quicken draws a bar chart that depicts your progress toward the goal. (In Figure 14.2, the bar doesn't appear because zero progress has been made toward the goal.)

At the bottom of the Savings Goals window, a number appears ($2666.66 in Figure 14.2). This is the monthly amount you need to save in order to reach your goal by the finish date. Quicken calculates this figure by dividing the savings goal amount by the number of payments. (Quicken assumes that you won't earn any interest on your savings.)

From the Savings Goals window, you can take the following actions:

- You can print your savings goals by displaying the Savings Goals window and choosing File ➢ Print Goal.
- By clicking Report, you can get a printable report that shows your progress toward your goals.

- You can change a savings goal's description by selecting the goal and clicking Edit. In the Edit Savings Goals dialog box, you can change the goal amount or finish date.

Saving Money toward a Goal

Using a savings goal is easy. When you set up a savings goal, what Quicken actually does is create a special type of account called a savings goal account. This account works like a separate compartment you use to earmark funds you've stored in, say, your regular checking account. In other words, you might have $10,000 in your checking account, but $2666.66 of this money may be earmarked for a savings goal.

To set aside money for a savings goal, open the Savings Goals window and click Contribute. (Quicken assumes that all contributions will be monthly.) In the Contribute To Goal dialog box, identify the account in which you'll set aside savings goal money, the amount you want to set aside, and the set-aside date. Figure 14.3 shows an example.

Figure 14.3: The Contribute To Goal dialog box lets you describe amounts you want to set aside for a savings goal.

The transaction will appear as a transfer in the register of whatever account you have chosen. The money will remain in the account but will not be shown in your balance figure. Figure 14.4 shows a transaction recording a transfer to the New Delivery Truck account.

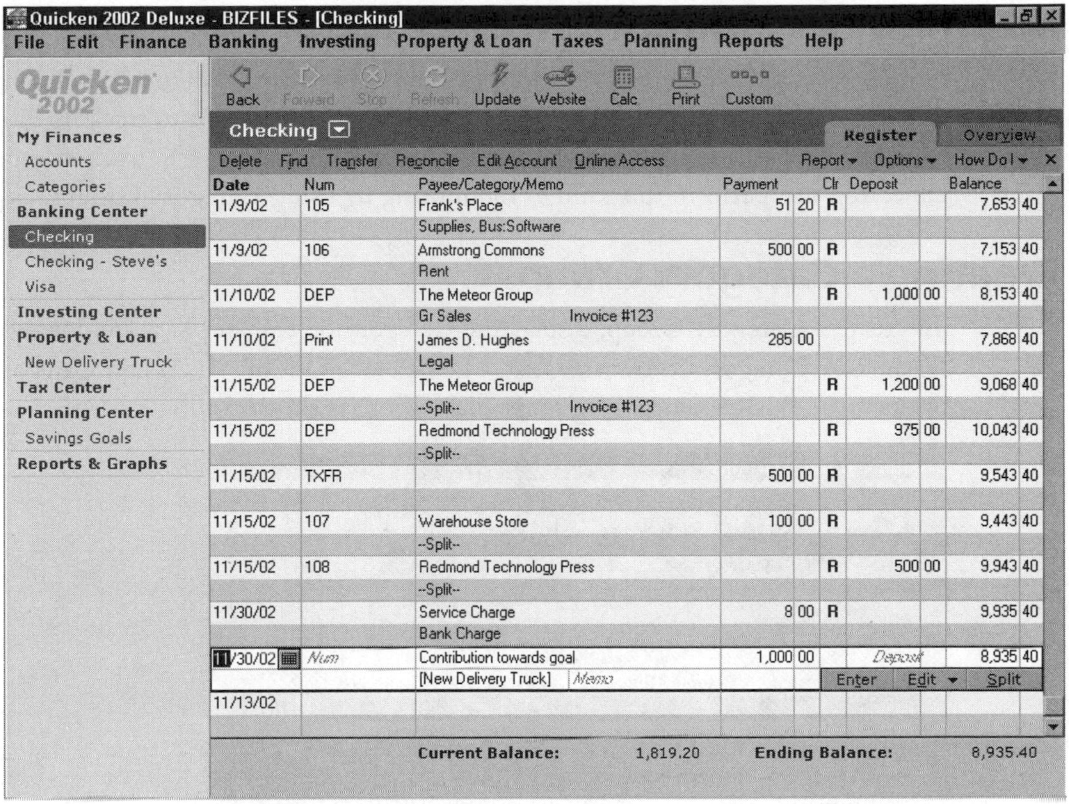

Figure 14.4: The last transaction in this account register transfers money to a savings goal account.

NOTE *Savings goal transactions don't have any effect on bank account reconciliations. When you reconcile a bank account with savings goals transactions, Quicken hides all the savings goal transactions.*

Deleting a Savings Goal

To delete a savings goal, display the Savings Goals window (choose Planning ➢ Savings Goals), select the goal, and click Delete.

Quicken returns the money to the source account and asks what to do with the account it created for the savings goal. You can tell Quicken to delete the account or to save the account. You might want to save the account, for example, if you really did purchase the item you were saving for and now you want to keep the account for tracking the appreciation or depreciation of that item (Quicken creates an asset account for the item).

Monitoring Finances with Category Groups

Category Groups are just groups of categories you want to monitor especially closely. A family that's closely monitoring its finances and cash flow might want to track its discretionary spending. A business with several sources of income might want to track its monthly revenue. You can perform this kind of monitoring by using Category Groups.

Creating a Category Group

To create a Category Group, display the Category & Transfer List window by choosing Finance ➢ Category & Transfer List. Then choose Options ➢ Assign Category Groups to open the Assign Category Groups dialog box, as shown in Figure 14.5.

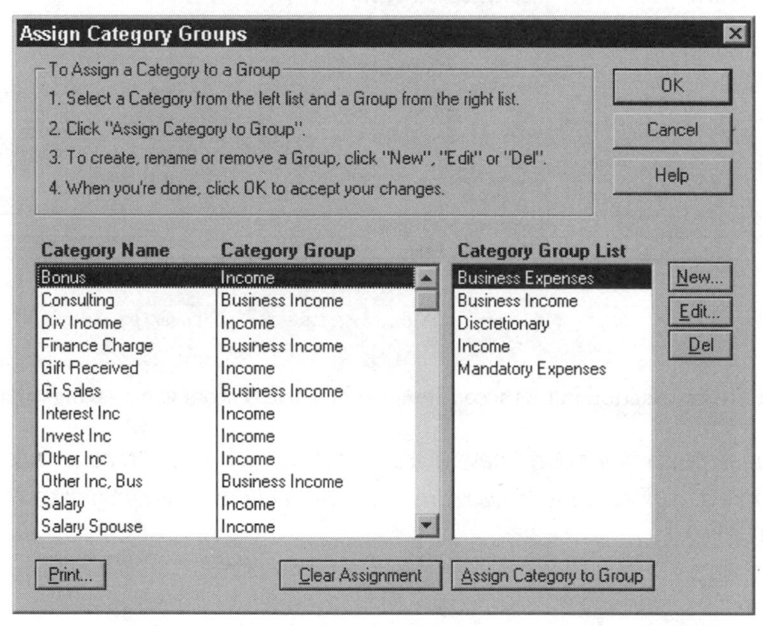

Figure 14.5: The Assign Category Groups dialog box lets you create groups of categories to monitor.

In this dialog box, click the New button. When Quicken prompts you with the Create Category Group dialog box, enter a name and click OK.

To assign categories to a Category Group, follow these steps:

1. Select the categories you want to place into a Category Group by clicking each one. To select more than one category at a time, hold down the Ctrl key as you click the categories.
2. Select the Category Group you want to use to tally and track these categories.
3. Click the Assign Category To Group button.
4. Click OK.

Monitoring a Category Group

Quicken lets you summarize your financial data by category groups. Chapter 4 describes how you prepare reports. Quicken also lets you budget by categories, as described later in this chapter in the section "Setting Up a Budget."

Using Category Groups for ABC Management

Activity-based cost (ABC) management can give you powerful insights into your business. Simple ABC management can be performed with category groups.

Let me start by explaining what ABC management is. In a nutshell, ABC management attempts to group the costs of different business activities so these activities' costs can be more closely monitored and better understood.

This sounds abstract, but in practice, especially for small businesses, ABC management is very straightforward. Take the example of an interior decorator, for instance. Suppose this individual's work consists of teaching an interior design course at the local community college, providing hourly design consulting services to businesses, and reselling furniture and accessories to homeowners. What you could say—and I'm obviously simplifying this to make the example easier—is that everything this business owner does is either teaching, consulting, or retailing.

In this case, it might be useful to create category groups for teaching income and expenses, consulting income and expenses, and retailing income and expenses. By creating these category groups, the interior decorator could easily see the income, expenses, and profits of her different activities.

Two practical points about ABC management should be made:

1. A business may need to expand its category list in order to implement an ABC management system. For example, if the interior decorator incurs supplies expenses for both the consulting and retailing activities, each activity needs its own supplies expense category.

2. You usually don't have to be particularly precise in order to gain real insights into the costs of your various activities. If you monitor just the largest and most expensive activities and are only roughly accurate in breaking down costs across activities, you'll probably still gain insights into the costs and profits of your activities.

NOTE *As described here, ABC management closely resembles job and project costing, which Quicken lets you do using classes. As a practical matter, for small businesses, ABC management and job costing look and work very similar. The differences between the two account techniques, in fact, really don't become apparent until you use them for larger businesses with high overhead. For more information about job and project costing, refer to Chapter 19.*

Setting Up a Budget

There's a lot written about budgeting, and most of the advice isn't all that bad—although it may not be too insightful. Mostly, the process is mechanical. You sit down, look at what you'll make, and then come up with a plan for spending the money that meets your needs. The process works this way for both businesses and individuals.

Two Tricks for Successful Budgeting

You can read an entire book about budgeting, but I'm assuming you would prefer some quick tips on how to use budgets and budgeting to make it easier to manage your personal and business financial affairs, as described in the following sections.

NOTE *Much of the information discussed at the end of this chapter in the sidebar "How to Achieve Financial Independence" directly relates to personal budgeting.*

Start with a Categorized Report

You need to start some place, and the best place is with an itemized list of what you've already been making and spending. In fact, it's probably most accurate to start by planning to spend in the future what you've been spending in the past.

If you've already been tracking your income and spending with Quicken, you can print an itemized category report to get the information you need.

TIP *If you can, look at an entire year's income and spending. It's too easy for an individual month's category total to be significantly higher or lower than average. Note that seasonal affects are often striking for both personal and business budgets. Retailers do most of their business during the Christmas season, for example. Employees often have periods when earnings are higher—perhaps because of overtime or bonuses. And both businesses and individuals pay more for heating costs in the winter.*

Don't Plan to Spend Every Dollar You Make

One of the bigger mistakes you can make in your budgeting is to plan how you'll spend every dollar that you'll make. Two problems exist with this approach:

- You probably will have some unexpected expenses during the year—the water pump on your truck or car may need to be replaced, you may need a new computer, or you may have some unexpected medical expenses not covered by insurance.
- You probably will find some new ways you want to spend money during the year (if you're an individual) or some new ways you want to invest money during the year (if you're a business). You might see something six months from now that you need or want.

If you leave yourself some extra money to pay for these things, they don't have to be financial emergencies. To do this, you might want to set up an Unbudgeted Expenses or Miscellaneous Emergencies category to track and tally just these sorts of expenditures. Then you'll be able to take the extra $150 needed for the car repair out of the Unbudgeted Expenses category.

Using a Budgeting Spreadsheet

Once you've figured out or estimated what you'll make and what you'll want to spend, you can record this information in Quicken in a budgeting spreadsheet. In fact, since Quicken will do a lot of the math for you, you may want to use this budgeting spreadsheet as a tool for building your budget.

To get to the Quicken budgeting spreadsheet so you can begin entering your budget, choose Planning ➤ Budgeting and click the Setup tab. Quicken displays the Setup tab of the Budgeting window, as shown in Figure 14.6. You'll use this window to describe the income and expenses you plan by category.

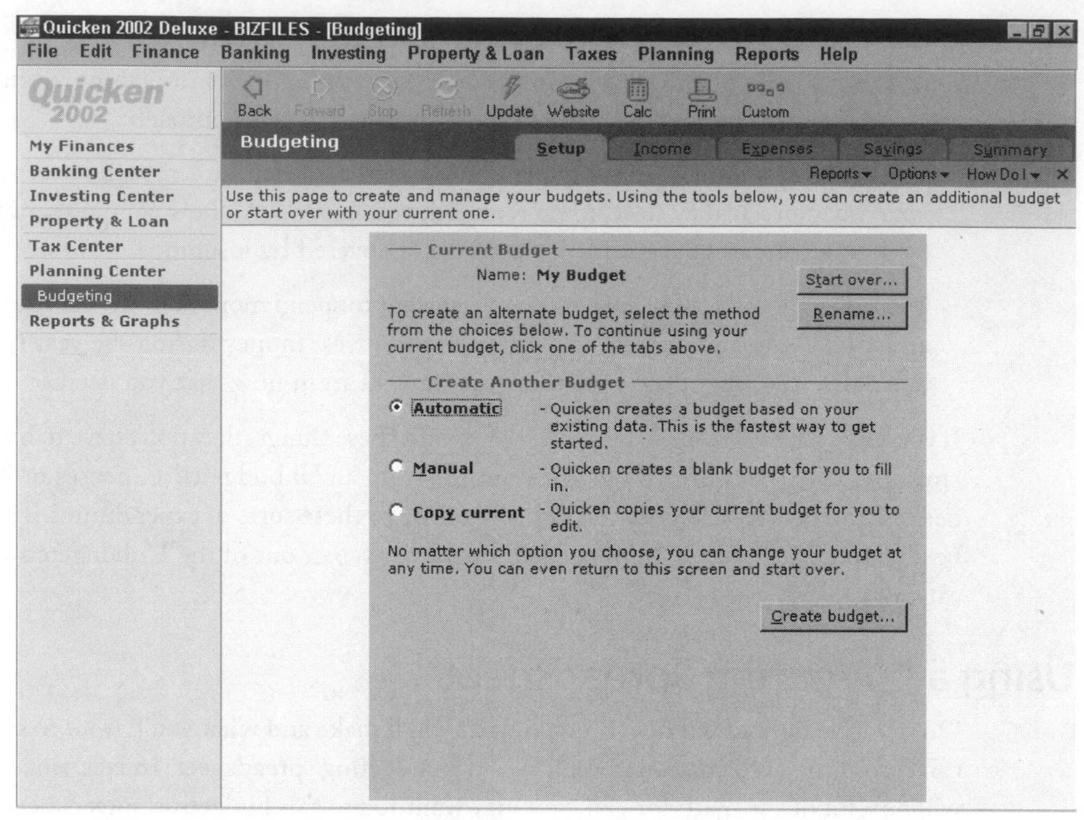

Figure 14.6: The Setup tab of the Budgeting window.

Setting Up Your Budget

Your first task in creating a budget is telling Quicken whether you want to create a budget from scratch or automatically. To create a budget based on the data you've collected with Quicken, mark the Automatic option button. To create a budget from scratch, mark the Manual option button. To create a new budget by copying an old, existing budget, mark the Copy Current option button. After you indicate how you want to create the new budget, click the Create Budget button and then, when prompted by Quicken, name the budget.

Entering Income Budget Data

To budget your income amounts, click the Income tab and then click the Choose Categories button. When Quicken displays the Choose Categories dialog box, shown in Figure 14.7, select the income categories you want to budget by clicking them. Then click OK.

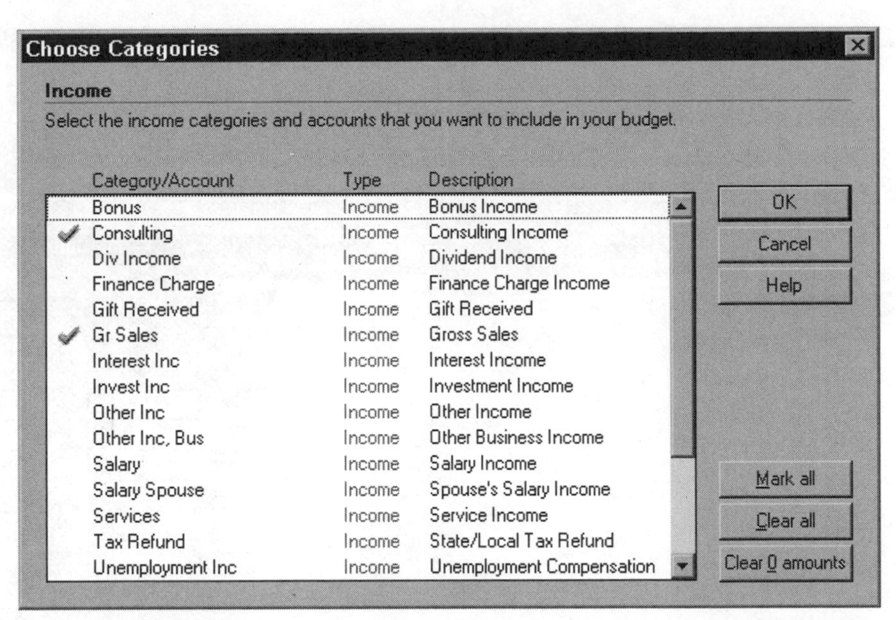

Figure 14.7 The Choose Categories dialog box.

TIP *You need to maximize the Quicken application window in order to see all the buttons and boxes you'll need for budgeting. To maximize the application window, click the Maximize button, which appears in the top-right corner of the window. If you don't maximize the application, you must click an Edit button (which doesn't appear in Figures 14.8 and 14.9) in order to display a dialog box that lets you enter budgeted amounts.*

To budget an income category, select it. To budget the same amount for each month, mark the Average Amount option button and then enter the monthly budget amount. To budget different amounts for different months, mark the Monthly Detail option button and then enter the amounts for each month. To budget amounts for each quarter, mark the Quarterly Detail option button and then enter the amounts for each quarter. Figure 14.8 shows the Income tab as it might look after entering income budget amounts.

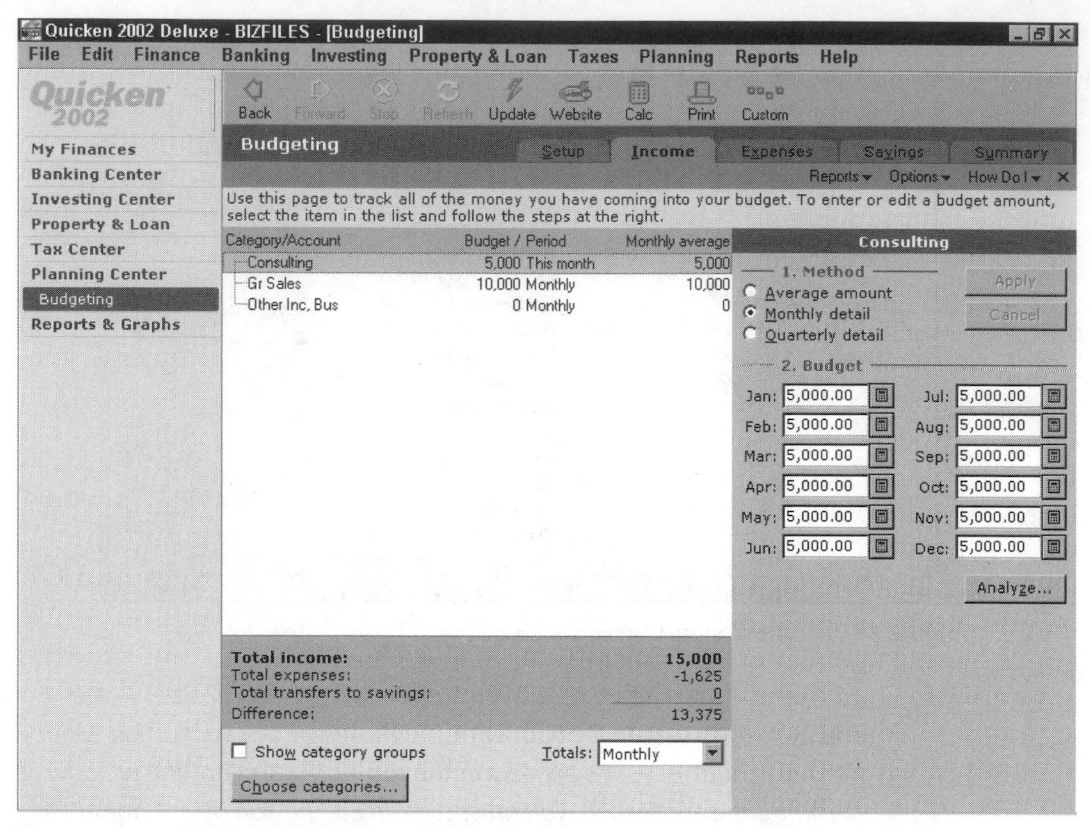

Figure 14.8 The Income tab of the Budgeting window.

TIP *To see actual amounts for the selected category over the last year, click the Analyze button. Quicken displays the Analyze dialog box, which displays a graph showing the category over the preceding months.*

Entering Expense Budget Data

Budgeting expenses works the same way as budgeting income. To budget your expense amounts, click the Expenses tab and then click the Choose Categories button. When Quicken displays the Choose Categories dialog box, select the expense categories you want to budget by clicking them. Then click OK.

To budget an expense category, select it. To budget the same amount for each month, mark the Average Amount option button and then enter the monthly budget amount. To budget different amounts for different months, mark the Monthly Detail option button and then enter the amounts for each month. To budget amounts for each quarter, mark the Quarterly Detail option button and then enter the amounts for each quarter. Figure 14.9 shows the Expenses tab as it might look after entering expenses budget amounts.

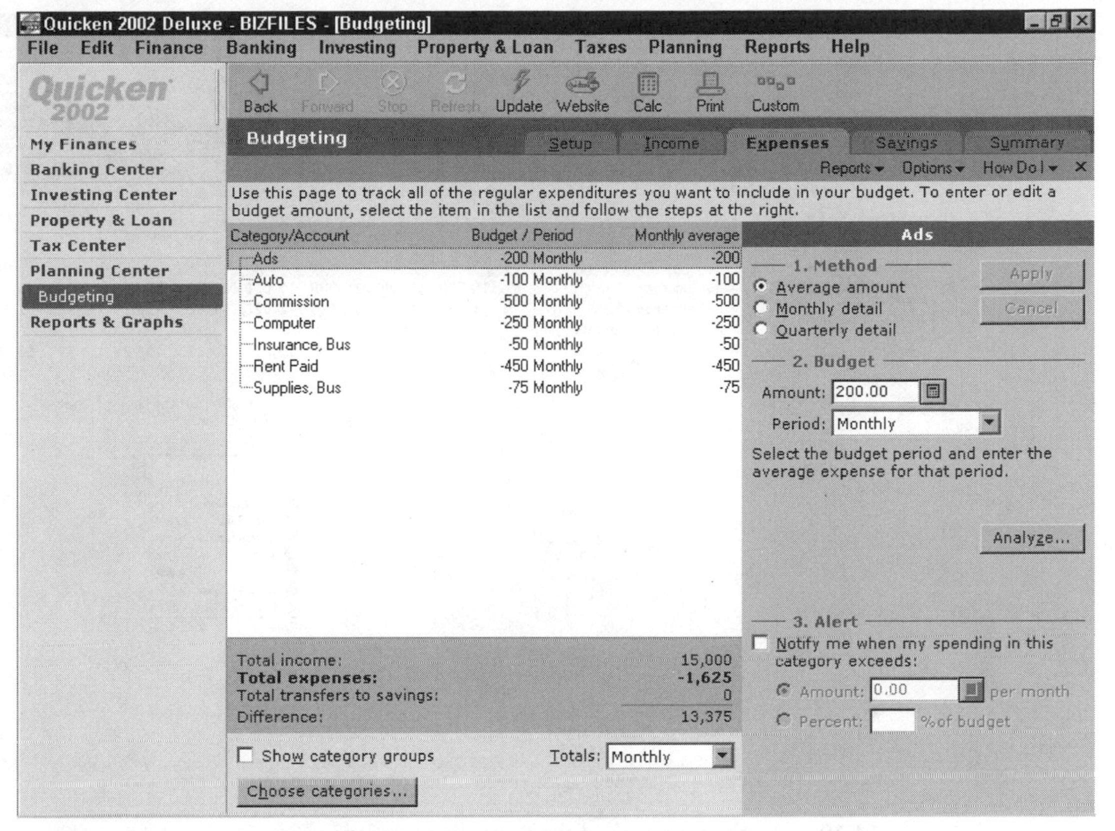

Figure 14.9 The Expenses tab of the Budgeting window.

Entering Savings Budget Data

The Savings tab of the Budgeting window lets you budget account transfers. To budget an account transfer, click the Savings tab and then click the Choose Accounts button. When Quicken displays the Choose Accounts dialog box, select the accounts for which you want to budget transfers by clicking them. Then click OK. To budget transfers for an account, select the account and then enter the budgeting account transfer.

Reviewing a Budget

After you collect income, expense, and savings budget amounts, you can view a high-level snapshot of the budget by clicking the Summary tab, as shown in Figure 14.10.

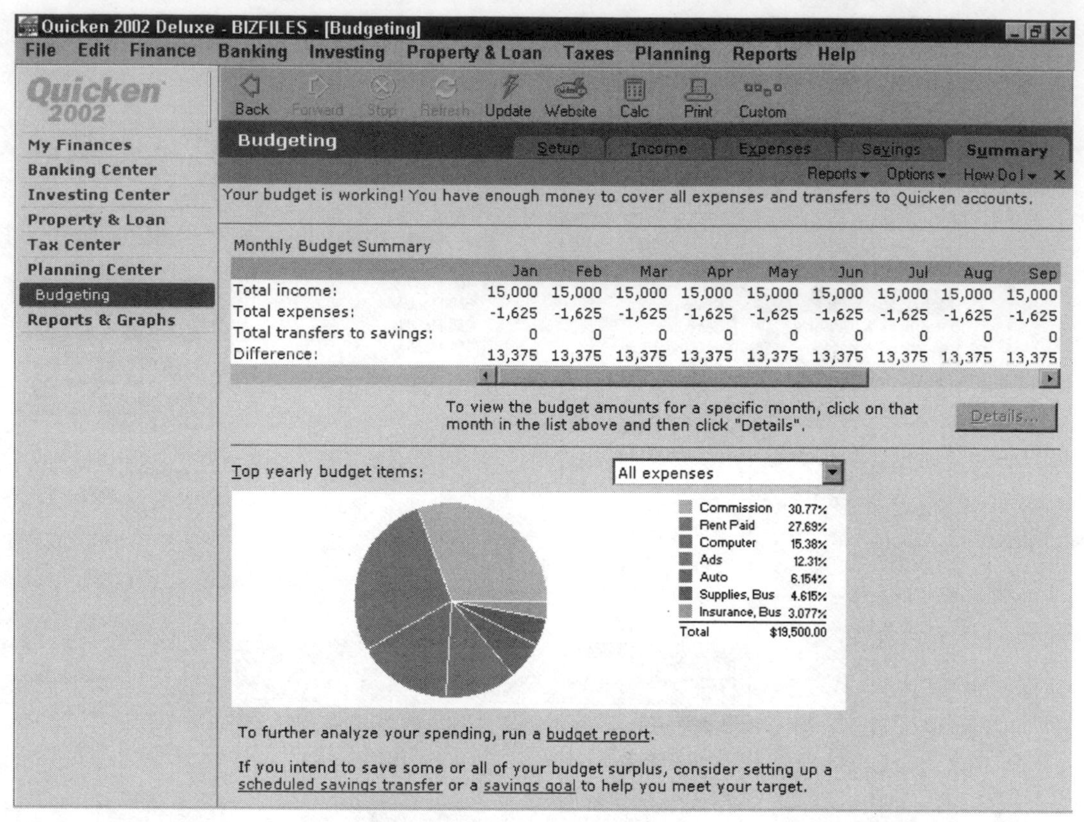

Figure 14.10: The Summary tab of the Budgeting window.

To view the detailed budget amounts for a particular month, select that month and then click the Details button. Quicken displays a Monthly Summary dialog box, as shown in Figure 14.11.

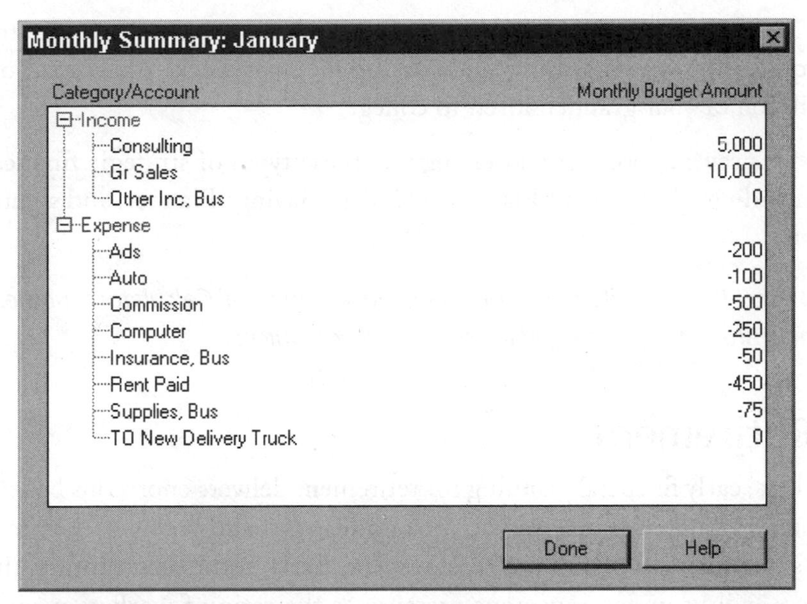

Figure 14.11: The Monthly Summary dialog box.

Saving Your Budget

Choose Options ➢ Save Budget to save your budget entries to a file on your computer's hard disk. Clicking the Close button does the same thing, but it also closes the Budget window.

Monitoring Your Success in Achieving a Budget

The information you enter into the budgeting spreadsheet is valuable in its own right. You can use it to plan your income and spending in a way that makes the most sense for you, your business, and your family.

But this budget information can be even more valuable. You can use it to compare your actual income and spending with the budget. To do this, you produce a Budget report using the Reports ➢ Spending ➢ Budget command. For information about creating and printing Quicken reports, see Chapter 4.

Quicken's Tools for Strategic Planning

Savings goals, Category Groups, and budgeting are important elements of successful personal and business financial planning. But while such budgeting improves your financial affairs on a short-term basis, it doesn't address your long-term, or strategic, personal financial objectives.

Presumably, there are financial objectives you want to achieve. Some day, for example, you may want to quit working—or at least quit working for a paycheck. You may also want to send your children or your grandchildren to college.

Quicken provides several tools for addressing just these types of strategic financial planning issues, including a Retirement Planner, a College Savings Planner, and a generalized Savings Planner.

NOTE *If you don't find these items on your Planning ➤ Financial Calculators submenu, these planners are not implemented in your version of Quicken.*

Planning for Retirement

For most workers, early financial planning for retirement delivers enormous benefits. And for today's younger workers—people who are middle-aged and younger—it's imperative to do at least some financial planning for retirement. Early in the next century, the Social Security system will be under enormous pressure as the ratio of workers paying Social Security to retirees receiving Social Security drops to two-to-one. (Currently the ratio is more than three-to-one.) And the growth in federal entitlement programs like Social Security almost dictates that at some point in the future upper–middle-class recipients will lose benefits.

What's more, with a shift from defined benefit plans to defined contribution plans, thoughtful workers will benefit by making forecasts of future total retirement savings and the investment income generated by those savings. Quicken's Retirement Planner lets you do this.

NOTE *A defined benefit retirement plan pays a specified benefit—for example, 50 percent of your last year's salary. A defined contribution plan contributes specified amounts to a retirement account—such as $2,000 a year.*

Using the Retirement Planner to Forecast Your Retirement Income

To use Quicken's Retirement Calculator to estimate the retirement income you'll have, given your current savings plans, follow these steps:

1. Choose Planning ➤ Financial Calculators ➤ Retirement to display the Retirement Calculator dialog box, as shown in Figure 14.12.

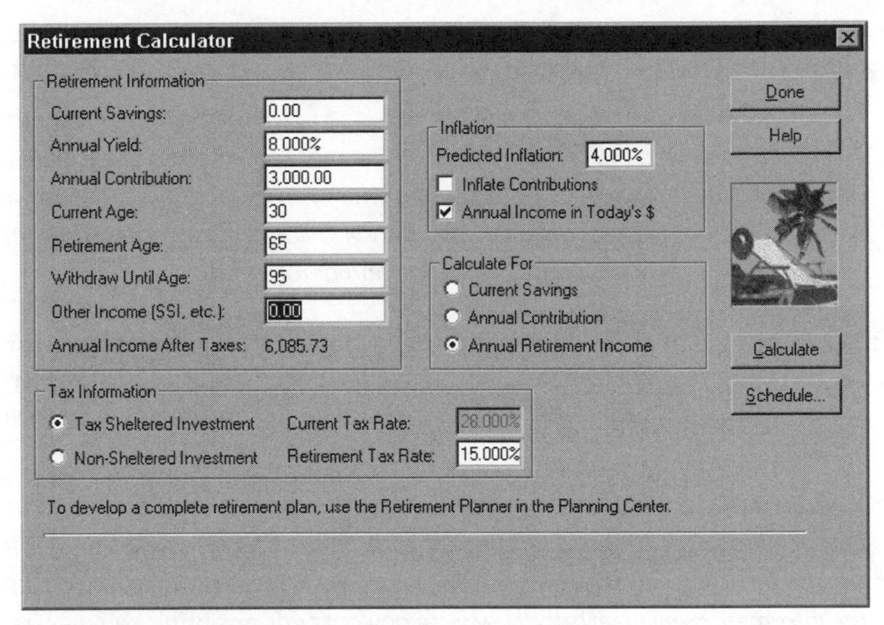

Figure 14.12: The Retirement Calculator dialog box.

2. Make sure the Annual Retirement Income option button is marked in the Calculate For area of the dialog box.

3. Enter the amount you've already saved for retirement in the Current Savings text box. Include amounts saved in employer-defined contribution retirement plans, such as deferred compensation programs and 401(k) plans, as well as amounts you've saved in things such as IRAs and Keogh plans.

4. In the Annual Yield box, enter the average annual yield you expect your investment portfolio to generate over your working years.

TIP *As a frame of reference, the stock market's annual return over the last 60 years or so is about 10 percent, the average annual return on long-term corporate bonds over roughly the same period of time is just shy of 6 percent, and the average annual return on long-term government bonds is about 5 percent. These are gross return numbers, so if you invest in a way that results in investment expenses—such as a mutual fund that charges fees—you may want to adjust the historical return.*

5. Enter the annual amount you'll contribute in the Annual Contribution text box. For example, if you plan to contribute $2,000 a year to an employer's 401(k) plan, type ***2000***. If someone else, such as your employer, will contribute to your retirement savings, include this extra amount. Some employers, for example, match 401(k) contributions as a way to encourage employee retirement saving. If your employer will add 50 percent to your $2,000-per-year contribution, the total annual contribution you enter should be $3,000.

6. Enter your age in the Current Age box, the age you want to retire in the Retirement Age box, and the age through which you want to withdraw money in the Withdraw Until Age box.

TIP *A reasonable way to build in a financial cushion for retirement is to assign a Withdraw Until Age value that's several years beyond when you expect to live. I do my retirement planning calculations, for example, assuming I will withdraw money through age 95, even though I may well run out of steam long before that.*

7. Use the Other Income text box to indicate how much other retirement income you'll have available. For example, you may be eligible for Social Security benefits, or you may have invested in a defined-benefit retirement plan that promises to pay you some monthly amount.

TIP *You can get an estimate of your future Social Security benefits by filling out a simple form (called an SS-700) and sending the form to the Social Security Administration. To get the form you need, you can call the local Social Security office, or you can request the information online at* http://www.ssa.gov/online/forms.html. *You may be surprised by the Social Security benefit you're slated to receive. Social Security benefits are paid according to a complicated formula that allows people with modest incomes (or only a few years of earnings) to get a benefit that's a much larger percentage of their current earnings than people who make a lot of money.*

8. Use the Tax Information settings and Current Tax Rate text box to describe the income taxes you'll pay on your retirement savings. If you will use investment options like IRAs and 401(k)s that allow for deferral of income taxes, mark the Tax Sheltered Investment option button. If you will use investment options that result in your paying taxes on the investment income earned by your savings, mark the Non-Sheltered Investment option button. Then enter the marginal tax rate you'll pay on the investment income in the Current Tax Rate text box.

9. If you want to estimate your after-income-taxes retirement savings account withdrawals, you can estimate the income tax rate in effect over the years you're retired and enter the figure in the Retirement Tax Rate text box. Alternatively, enter the Retirement Tax Rate as *0*. With this input, the Planner calculates the pre-tax withdrawal you'll make. (This is simpler and will probably work better for you anyway.)

10. Enter the inflation rate you expect over the years you'll work and be retired. As a frame of reference, the inflation rate over the last 60 years or so has averaged slightly over 3 percent.

11. If you will make annual contributions and will adjust these amounts for inflation over the years you work, mark the Inflate Contributions checkbox. With 4 percent inflation and $1,000-per-year contributions, for example, Quicken assumes you contribute $1,000

the first year, $1,040 the second year ($1,040 is 104 percent of $1,000), $1,081.60 the third year ($1081.60 is 104 percent of $1,040), and so on.

12. Make sure the Annual Income In Today's $ checkbox is marked to tell Quicken to estimate an annual retirement income figure that uses the same size dollars you make and spend today. (If you don't mark this checkbox, Quicken estimates an annual retirement income figure using inflated dollars you'll actually receive, say, in 30 years.)
13. Click the Calculate button.
14. Click the Schedule command button to see a scrollable list of the annual amounts you'll contribute or withdraw, the annual interest earnings, and the retirement savings balance. Figure 14.13 shows a Deposit Schedule depicting retirement savings activity in a schedule.

Deposit Schedule

Print — Close

This deposit schedule assumes that your retirement income keeps pace with a 4.0% annual inflation rate. Note that income is in future, pre-tax dollars.

Age	Deposit	Income	Balance
0	0.00	0.00	0.00
30	3,000.00	0.00	3,000.00
31	3,000.00	0.00	6,240.00
32	3,000.00	0.00	9,739.20
33	3,000.00	0.00	13,518.34
34	3,000.00	0.00	17,599.80
35	3,000.00	0.00	22,007.79
36	3,000.00	0.00	26,768.41
37	3,000.00	0.00	31,909.88
38	3,000.00	0.00	37,462.67
39	3,000.00	0.00	43,459.69

Figure 14.13: The Deposit Schedule details the progress of your plan.

15. Once you've entered all the needed information and told Quicken how it should make the calculations, you can scroll down and look at the Income column for your indicated retirement age. It shows the estimated annual retirement income you'll receive based on your forecasting assumptions.
16. To close the Deposit Schedule box, click the Close button. To remove the Retirement Calculator dialog box when you're finished with it, select Done.

Figuring Out How Much You Should Save

The preceding discussion calculates how much you'll have in the way of retirement income, given your current savings and your plans about how you'll save in the future. If instead you want to provide for a specific level of retirement income, you can calculate the current savings you must already have accumulated in order to reach your retirement income goal.

Or you can calculate how much you need to be saving on a regular basis in order to reach that income goal.

To calculate how much you already need to have saved, given all the other retirement information, go back to the Retirement Calculator (see Figure 14.12) and mark the Current Savings option button. To calculate how much you need to save on an annual basis, given all the other retirement information, mark the Annual Contribution option button. Once you've indicated what savings figure you want to accumulate, enter the annual retirement income you want in the Annual Income After Taxes text box. Then fill in each of the remaining text boxes and mark the appropriate option buttons and checkboxes.

Finding the Money You Need to Save for Retirement

It can be more than a little discouraging to start making retirement planning calculations. You'll usually find that to achieve the annual retirement income you want, you need to be saving a lot more than is practical.

Suppose, for example, that the Retirement Calculator calculates an annual savings amount equal to $5,200 a year—which is the same as $450 a month. (This savings amount will produce roughly $15,000 a year of retirement income if you start with $0 savings, increase your annual contributions 3 percent each year because of inflation, and earn 9 percent over 20 years of contributions.)

While $450 a month seems like a lot of money, you may be able to come up with this figure more readily than you might think. Say, for example, that you work for an employer who's generous enough to match your 401(k) contributions by 50 percent. In other words, for every dollar you contribute, your employer contributes $.50. Also suppose that you pay federal and state income taxes of 33 percent and that you can deduct your 401(k) contributions from your income. In this case, the actual monthly out-of-pocket amount you need to come up with equals $200, not $450.

Here's how the arithmetic works. You need to come up with $300 a month to have $450 a month added to your retirement savings because of your employer's 50 percent matching, as shown here:

Amount you contribute	$300
Employer's matching amount	$150
Total 401(k) contribution	$450

However, if your last dollars of income are taxed at 33 percent, the $300 tax deduction you'll receive because of your $300 401(k) contribution will save you $100 in income taxes. So the actual amount you need to come up with on a monthly basis equals $200, as shown here:

Amount you contribute	$300
Income taxes saved	(100)
After-tax contribution	$200

Admittedly, $200 a month is still a lot of money. But it's also a lot less than the $450-per-month savings figure that the Retirement Calculator calculations suggest.

These calculations also suggest a couple of tactics to consider using when you save for retirement. If an employer offers to match your contributions to something like a 401(k) plan, it will almost always make sense to accept the offer—unless your employer is trying to force you to make an investment that is not appropriate for you.

TIP *If you do want to contribute $300 a month to a 401(k) plan and need to reduce your income taxes withheld by $100 a month to do so, talk to your employer's payroll department for instructions. You may need to file a new W-4 statement and increase the number of personal exemptions claimed.*

What's more, any time you get a tax deduction for contributing money to your retirement savings, it's almost certainly too good a deal to pass up. As described in the preceding example, you can use the income tax savings because of the deduction to boost your savings so they provide for the desired level of retirement income.

While people often have an emotional aversion to locking money away in tax-sheltered investments, there are only three situations in which it may be a poor idea to use tax-sheltered investments:

- You need (or may need) the money before retirement. In this case, it may not be a good idea to lock away money you may need before retirement because there is usually a 10 percent early-withdrawal penalty paid on money retrieved from a retirement account before age 59 1/2. But you will also need money after you retire, so the "What if I need the money?" argument is more than a little weak. Yes, you may need the money before you retire, but you will absolutely need money after you retire.
- You've already saved enough money for retirement. Using retirement planning vehicles, such as IRAs, may be a reasonable way to accumulate wealth. And the deferred taxes on your investment income do make your savings grow much more quickly. Nevertheless, if you've already saved enough money for retirement, it's possible that you should consider other investment options as well as estate planning issues. This special case is beyond the scope of this book, but if it applies to you, I encourage you to consult a good personal financial planner—preferably one who charges you an hourly fee, not one who earns a commission by selling you financial products you may not need.

- You'll pay more income taxes when you're retired than you do now. The calculations get tricky, but if you're only a few years away from retirement and you believe income tax rates will be going up because you'll be paying a new state income tax, it may not make sense for you to save, say, 15 percent now but pay 45 percent later.

NOTE *This chapter assumes that you'll save for retirement using tax-deductible retirement savings options like IRAs and pension plans like 401(k)s, SEP-IRAs, and SIMPLE-IRAs. Some people can also invest through Roth-IRAs, however. And in some cases, a Roth-IRA is very attractive. Note though that Roth-IRAs don't actually deliver tax benefits in most situations. In fact, if you work out the mathematics, Roth-IRA's produce no additional financial benefit for retirement except in the case where your marginal tax rate will rise in retirement.*

Read This If You Can't Possibly Save Enough for Retirement

It's relatively easy to save for retirement when you're still young. Five thousand dollars set aside for a new baby grows to an amount that generates over a $100,000 a year in current-day dollars if the money earns 12 percent annually and inflation runs at 3 percent.

NOTE *The data is a little sketchy, but small-company stocks probably deliver average returns of around 12 to 13 percent over long periods of time. Small-company stocks are, however, very risky over shorter periods of time.*

The flip side of this is that it becomes difficult to save for retirement if you start thinking (and saving) late in your working years. If you're 60, haven't started saving, and want $25,000 a year in income from your retirement savings at age 65, you probably need to contribute annually more than you make.

Say you're in your 50s—or even a bit older. With the kids' college expenses, or perhaps a divorce, you don't have any money saved for retirement. What should you do? What can you do? This situation, though unfortunate, doesn't need to be untenable. There are some things you can do.

One tactic is not to retire—or at least, not yet. After all, you save for retirement so the earnings from those savings can replace your salary and wages. If you don't stop working, you don't need retirement savings to produce investment income.

Note, too, that "not retiring" doesn't mean you need to keep the same job. If you've been selling computers your whole life and you're sick of it, do something else. Get a job teaching at the community college. (Maybe you'll get summers off.) Join the Peace Corps and go to South America. Get a job in a daycare center and help shape the future.

A second tactic is to postpone retirement a few extra years, which, of course, also reduces the number of years you're retired. Rather than working to age 62 or 65, for example, working until age 67 or 69—a few more years of contributions and compound interest income—will make a surprising difference, and you'll boost substantially the money you receive from defined-benefit retirement plans. If you're paying a mortgage, maybe you can pay that off in those few extra years, too.

A third and more unconventional tactic is to decide that less is more and tune into the art and philosophy of frugality. A good book on this subject is *Your Money or Your Life* by Joe Dominquez and Vicki Robin (Viking Penguin, 1992). And if you decide to live on less while you're still working, you'll end up saving a lot more over the remaining years you work.

NOTE *Quicken Deluxe also supplies a retirement planning wizard, which walks you through roughly the same retirement planning steps described here. It doesn't make sense for me to provide a step-by-step description of how you use a wizard because the wizard itself provides good explanations of how you use it. Don't mistake my lack of coverage as an editorial comment. The Retirement Planner, which you access by choosing Planning ➢ Retirement Planner, can be a wonderful aid to planning.*

Planning for a Child's College Expenses

Quicken provides another financial calculator, similar to the Retirement Calculator, which helps you prepare for the expenses of a child attending college.

Calculating the Amount You Need to Save

To use the College Calculator, follow these steps:

1. Choose Planning ➢ Financial Calculators ➢ College to display the College Calculator dialog box, as shown in Figure 14.14.

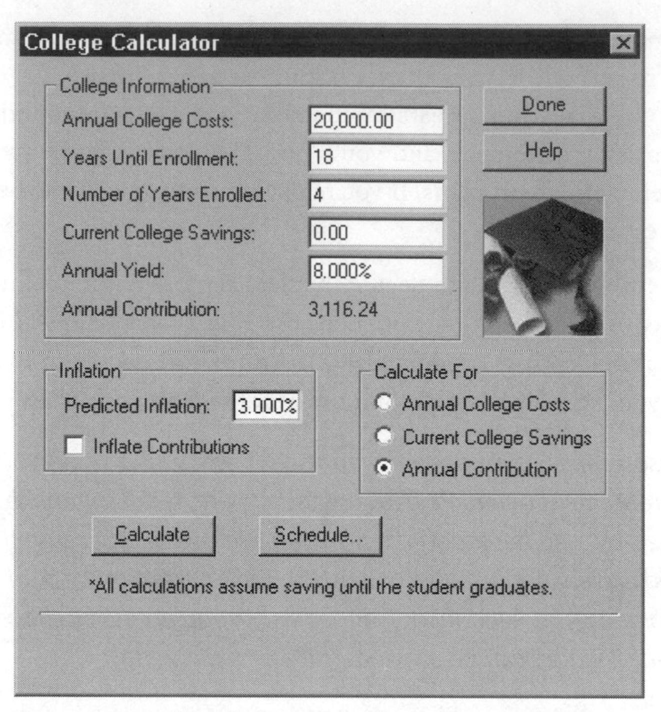

Figure 14.14: The College Calculator dialog box.

2. Make sure the Annual Contribution option button is marked in the Calculate For area in the lower-right corner of the dialog box.
3. Enter the current annual costs of college in the Annual College Costs text box. (If you don't know for sure which college your child will attend, enter a figure that's representative.)
4. Enter the number of years until the child enrolls in college in the Years Until Enrollment text box.
5. Indicate how many years the child will attend college. For example, if you assume the child will enroll in a regular four-year undergraduate program, type *4*.
6. Enter the amount you've already saved for college in the Current College Savings text box.
7. In the Annual Yield box, enter the annual average yield you expect the college savings money to generate and the inflation rate you expect.

NOTE *As noted earlier, the inflation rate over the last 60 years or so has averaged slightly over 3 percent. College tuition, however, has risen much faster than inflation. (Some recent studies show average tuition hikes in the 7 percent neighborhood!) It seems unlikely that college costs will continue to outpace inflation because few people will be able to afford college if the percentage increases continue to be more than double the inflation rate. For this reason, I use a 3 percent inflation rate in my calculations—and cross my fingers.*

8. If you will adjust your college-savings contributions for inflation, mark the Inflate Contributions checkbox. For example, with 4 percent inflation and $1,000-per-year contributions, Quicken assumes you contribute $1,000 the first year, $1,040 the second year, $1,081.60 the third year, and so on.
9. Click the Calculate button.
10. Click the Schedule command button to see a summary of the annual amounts you'll contribute or withdraw, the annual interest earnings, and the college-savings balance.

Once you've entered all the needed information and told Quicken how it should make the calculations, you can look at the Annual Contribution field. It shows the estimated annual contribution you'll need to make each year until your child finishes college, based on your forecasting assumption.

The preceding discussion calculates how much you need to save annually to be able to pay for college. You can also calculate the current savings you must already have accumulated in order to pay for college. And you can calculate the college costs you can afford given your current and planned savings.

To calculate how much you need to have already saved, click the Current College Savings option button, and then click Calculate. To calculate what college costs you can afford, click the Annual College Costs option button. Indicate what figure you want to calculate, fill in the dialog box's remaining text boxes, and mark the appropriate option buttons and checkboxes. Then click Calculate. (For help with a text box entry or in deciding whether to mark an option button or checkbox, see the discussion about using the Retirement Calculator earlier in this chapter.)

What You Should Know About Income Taxes and College Savings

There's a minor flaw in the way the college-savings calculations work: The College Calculator doesn't make any allowance for income taxes, but the interest income the college savings earn will be subject to income taxes.

To deal with this deficiency, you can increase your annual contributions to pay the income taxes (or assume the child pays the income taxes). For example, if you have $10,000 of college savings earning a respectable 9 percent, you'll be taxed on $900 of investment income. If the marginal income tax rate is 33 percent, you'll need to come up with an extra $300 for income taxes (33 percent of $900 is $300), so you would need to contribute an extra $25 a month.

You can also consider giving the money to the child in the form of a trust account so the child is taxed, not you. The benefit is that much, and perhaps all, of the investment income earned probably won't be taxed because of the standard deduction the child gets. In 2001, for example, a child claimed as a dependent on someone else's return gets a standard deduction of at least $750, which allows the child to escape taxes on at least the first $750 of investment income.

There is a drawback to having the child rather than the parent pay the income taxes: The savings need to be given to the child for the investment income earned by the savings to be taxed to the child. This means, for example, that the $8,000 you've scrimped and saved for and put into an account for college may ultimately get spent on what the child decides—which might be a sports car instead of a college education. By putting the money in a trust, you, as the custodian of the trust, retain control of the trust as long as the child is a minor. But when the child reaches the age of majority, the child can spend the money any way he or she wants.

NOTE *Depending on income, some families may be eligible for Education IRAs, which allow saving up to $500 a year into an IRA in 2001 and more in 2002. The neat thing about Education IRAs is that students can later withdraw this money tax-free for educational expenses. Education IRAs aren't discussed here, however, because they don't allow a parent to save enough money for a child's college expenses except in the special case where a parent begins saving for a child's educational expenses very early.*

Using the College Planner

Quicken Deluxe also supplies a College Planner. The College Planner, which you start by choosing the Planning ➤ College Planner command, discusses many of the same issues I've just covered in the preceding paragraphs. I'm not going to provide step-by-step descriptions of how to use the College Planner here. Simply follow the on-screen instructions.

Planning for Other Savings Goals

Quicken provides another financial planning tool you'll sometimes find helpful: the Savings Calculator. The Quicken Savings Calculator works like a regular financial calculator. It calculates future value, present value, and payment amounts.

Calculating a Future Value

One of the most common financial calculations you make when you plan savings is the *future value,* which is the amount your savings or investment will be worth at some point in the future—including any profits you've reinvested or left invested. For example, if you plan to save $2,000 a year in a mutual fund for 25 years and expect to earn 9 percent annually, you can forecast the future value of the mutual fund investment.

To perform a future-value calculation, follow these steps:

1. Choose Planning ➤ Financial Calculators ➤ Savings to display the Investment Savings Calculator dialog box, as shown in Figure 14.15.

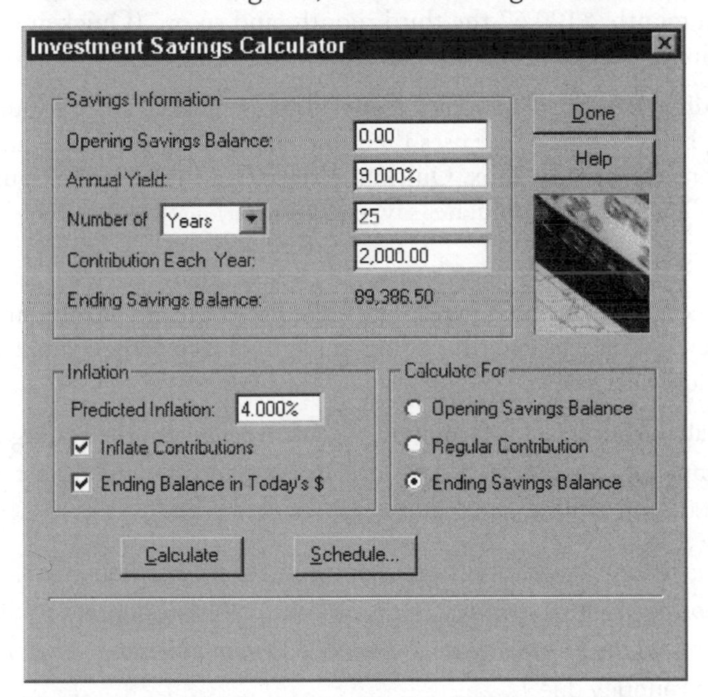

Figure 14.15: The Investment Savings Calculator dialog box.

2. Click the Ending Savings Balance option button in the Calculate For area in the lower right of the dialog box.
3. Enter the starting savings balance in the Opening Savings Balance text box. If you haven't yet saved anything because you're just starting, type *0*.

4. In the Annual Yield box, enter the annual yield you expect your savings to earn. If you've invested in a mutual fund you expect will earn 9 percent, type *9*.
5. Use the Number Of drop-down list box to indicate how often you'll add to the investment—each week, each month, each quarter, or each year—and use the Number Of text box to indicate the number of terms you'll make contributions. For example, if you'll contribute $2,000 to an IRA for 25 years, select Years from the Number Of drop-down list box and type *25* in the Number Of text box.
6. Use the Contribution Each text box to indicate how much you'll contribute. For example, if you'll contribute $2,000 to an IRA for 25 years, type *2000* in the Contribution Each text box.
7. Enter the annual inflation rate you expect over the years you will save in the Predicted Inflation text box.
8. If you will increase your contributions for inflation over the years you save, mark the Inflate Contributions checkbox. With 4 percent annual inflation, for example, and $100-per-month contributions, Quicken assumes you contribute $100 the first month, $100.33 the second month, $100.67 the third month, and so on. (Quicken calculates the monthly inflation by dividing the annual inflation by 12.)
9. Make sure the Ending Balance In Today's $ checkbox is marked to tell Quicken to estimate an ending balance figure that uses the same size dollars you make and spend today. (If you don't mark this checkbox, Quicken estimates a future-value figure using inflated dollars you'll actually accumulate, say, in 25 years.)
10. Click Calculate.
11. Click the Schedule command button to see a scrollable list of the annual amounts you'll save, the annual interest earnings, and the ending savings balance. When you're finished viewing the schedule, select Close.

Once you've collected all the necessary information, Quicken calculates the ending balance. Figure 14.15, for example, shows that in today's dollars, you accumulate almost $90,000 by contributing $2,000 annually.

NOTE *The Savings Calculator calculations assume that you make your contributions at the end of the year, quarter, month, or week. (This is called an* ordinary annuity.*) If you make your contributions at the beginning of the period, you earn an extra period of interest. (This is called an* annuity due.*)*

Calculating a Contribution

If you don't know the regular savings, or contribution, amount, you can calculate it by setting the ending savings balance. To do this, you follow the same basic steps you use for calculating a future value, with just a couple of exceptions. In this case, you mark the Regular Contribution option button rather than the Ending Savings Balance option button, and you enter the ending savings balance, not the regular contribution amount. When you click Calculate, Quicken calculates the regular contribution amount.

When do you calculate the regular contribution? You calculate the contribution when you want to accumulate a specific future-value amount—say $1,000,000—and you want to know how much you need to be contributing to achieve your future-value goal.

NOTE *If you don't know the opening savings balance but you know everything else, you can calculate the opening savings balance, too. To do this, mark the Opening Savings Balance option button.*

Planning a Mortgage Refinancing

Favorable mortgage rates in recent years have prompted a rush of mortgage refinancing. If you find yourself in a position to refinance, Quicken's Refinance Calculator can rapidly compute the potential savings and time to recover the refinancing costs. When you fill in the text boxes, Quicken calculates the costs and savings automatically.

To use this feature, follow these steps:

1. Choose Planning ➢ Financial Calculators ➢ Refinance to display the Refinance Calculator dialog box, as shown in Figure 14.16.

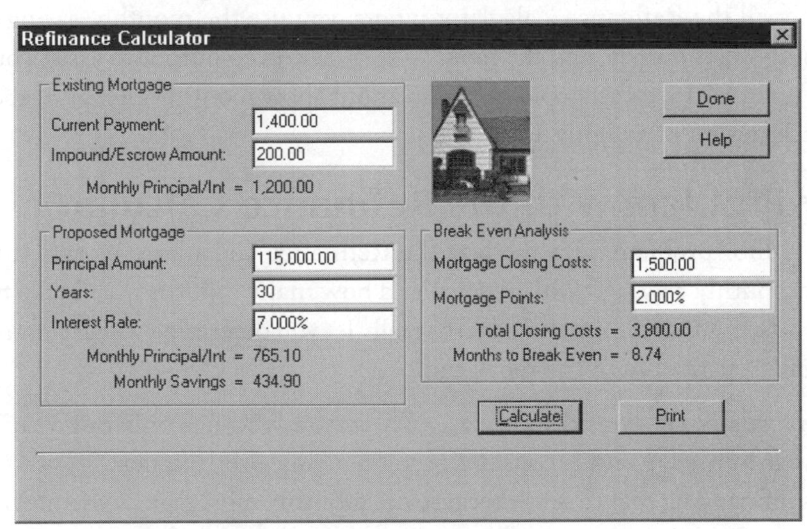

Figure 14.16: The Refinance Calculator dialog box.

2. Enter your current monthly principal and interest payment in the Current Payment text box.
3. Enter any additional amounts you pay into an escrow or impound account each month in the Impound/Escrow Amount text box. (These amounts might include property taxes and insurance, for example.)
4. Enter the new, refinanced mortgage amount in the Principal Amount text box. For example, if the new mortgage balance will equal $115,000, enter that figure into the Principal Amount text box.
5. Enter the number of years you'll be making the mortgage payments in the Years text box. For a 30-year mortgage, for example, you need to enter ***30***.
6. Enter the annual interest rate in the Interest Rate text box.

NOTE *The annual interest rate isn't the same thing as the annual percentage rate, or APR. The annual interest rate is what the lender uses to calculate your monthly payments. The annual percentage rate is a rate that lets you compare the total costs of borrowing between lenders. An annual percentage rate includes the interest costs of borrowing as well as all the other costs of borrowing, such as loan fees and discount points.*

7. Enter the closing costs—appraisals, loan processing fees, and the like—into the Mortgage Closing Costs text box.
8. Enter the total loan fee and discount points in the Mortgage Points text box. If the loan fee is 2 percent and you'll pay 2 percent in discount points, for example, enter *4* in the Mortgage Points text box.
9. Click Calculate.

Once you enter all the Refinance Calculator inputs, you use the monthly-savings output, the total-closing-costs output, and the months-to-break-even output to assist you in your decision. In Figure 14.16, for example, the calculations show monthly savings of about $350 and a pay-back period of roughly 15 months.

A Minor Problem with the Refinance Calculator

There is one minor problem with the way the Refinance Calculator works: It tells you whether your monthly payment will go down and how many months it will take to recoup your closing costs, but that information doesn't really let you determine whether or not you're saving monthly over the life of the mortgage.

To understand this point, consider the case of a person who has only one year left on a $20,000 30-year mortgage and is considering refinancing over the next 30 years. On the face of it, this refinancing makes sense because the monthly mortgage payment will go way down and it will take only a month or two to recoup the closing costs. But by refinancing, the homeowner has 29 extra years of payments! That means, over the long haul, the homeowner pays much more interest by refinancing. In this case, the imprudence of refinancing is clear, but the reasonableness of refinancing gets rather murky if you're considering whether to refinance a mortgage for which you have 24 years of payments.

Fortunately, you can apply a couple of rules to make sure you save money by refinancing. You need to make sure that the annual percentage rate on the new loan is lower than the interest rate on the old loan. You also need to get the new loan paid off just as quickly.

Reviewing the Planning Menu's Other Tools

In the preceding paragraphs of this chapter, I describe or introduce many of the Planning menu's tools. What I tried to do is discuss those tools that are most useful to people—especially people running their own business. Therefore, I skipped or only briefly mentioned those tools that, to me, seem to go overboard. Before this chapter ends, however, it makes sense to quickly go over the other Planning menu commands.

Planning Center The Planning ➢ Planner Center command displays the Planning Window. It provides hyperlinks to many of the other Planning menu commands. It also summarizes some of the information you've collected about your personal financial plans.

Retirement Planner As briefly noted in the discussion of the Retirement Calculator, the Planning ➢ Retirement Planner command walks you through the steps for building a detailed retirement plan. The process takes about 30 minutes, uses your Quicken data and other personal information you supply, and builds a very detailed plan. I personally think it's considerably easier and just as accurate to use the Retirement Calculator in the manner discussed earlier in the chapter, but you will definitely benefit by working through the Retirement Planner's steps and reviewing the information it provides.

College Planner As briefly noted in the discussion of the College Calculator, the Planning ➢ College Planner command helps you plan for attending college or for sending a child to college. The College Planner provides a great deal of useful information about the costs and choices associated with attending college. It also includes hyperlinks to online Web sites that supply great information about colleges and universities. However, if you've read any recent, detailed articles about sending a child to college (for example, the annual feature that *U.S. News and World Report* does), you'll already have reviewed the same basic information.

Home Purchase Planner The Planning ➢ Home Purchase Planner command helps you determine how much house you can afford and provides hyperlinks to the Realtor web site so you can look for a home in your area. The home affordability worksheet is useful, too.

You can often find a better local web site than the one provided, however. In the Seattle area where I live, for example, I think the web sites provided by the large local real estate brokers are the best tools for finding a home.

Debt Reduction Planner The Planning ➢ Debt Reduction Planner command collects information about your debts and then helps you map a route out of debt. If you're in over your head, you can use this tool to see how you might get out of debt. The one comment I'll make, however, is that this tool unfortunately provides no magic pill. To get out of debt, you'll need to spend less than you make. And the obvious way to climb out of the hole is to pay down your most expensive debts first (usually your personal credit cards).

Save More Planner The Planning ➢ Save More Planner command purports to help you plan your savings. If you're trying to get started with a savings program, take the time to walk through this wizard's steps. If you've already figured out how to save money, however, you're not going to get any new great ideas from this.

Special Purchase Planner The Planning ➢ Special Purchase Planner command helps you plan for some future major purchase, such as a new car or a home remodeling job. The planner's calculations are modestly useful because the planner includes both inflation and compound interest in its analysis. However, my feeling is that people usually don't need or truly benefit from the extra complexity that this planner includes.

Assumptions The Planning ➢ Assumptions command collects personal and financial information about you and your family. If you use the Assumptions command to collect this information, the information is available to the various planners identified in the preceding paragraphs of this list.

Plan Results The Planning ➢ Plan Results command provides hyperlinks to the personal financial data you've collected using the Planning ➢ Assumptions command and to the financial plans you've made using the planners.

Professional Planning Resources The Planning ➢ Professional Planning Resources command provides information about the types of personal financial planners you can use to help you with your own plans. Recognize, however, that the information is provided by the Financial Planning Association, the Certified Financial Planners' professional organization. This means the information is not, in my opinion, really objective. As you would expect, anytime someone compares their relative strengths and weaknesses to those of their competitors, well, you need to look at that information with a critical eye.

Professional Planner Summary The Planning ➢ Professional Planner Summary command provides a form you use to collect the information that a Certified Financial Planner expects in order to help you create a personal financial plan.

What-If Scenarios The Planning ➢ What-If Scenarios command lets you change assumptions used for the planners' calculations to see the effects of the change. For example, you can experiment with the effect of a change in the rate of return that your investments earn or a change in the inflation rate.

Planning Services The Planning ➢ Planning Services command displays a submenu of commands: Quicken MasterCard, Learn More About Business Planning, and More Quicken Services. The most interesting and useful item here is the Learn More About Business Planning command. This command displays a window that describes and then gives you access to a business planning tool from PaloAlto Software, a firm that makes business planning tools. A business plan, essentially, is a longer-range budget that helps you plot a course for your business.

How to Achieve Financial Independence

For most people, wealth doesn't have to be an impossible dream. With the right strategies and the appropriate tools, you can achieve financial independence. In fact, I truly believe that many, and maybe most, of the people who buy this book can become millionaires if they want to.

Building a fortune, however, is very similar to building a house. You need time. You need a plan. Of course, you also need the right tools. In most cases, people have the time. And if you have Quicken, you have all the tools you need. All you need after that to enjoy financial independence is a plan.

The Three Routes to Riches

Let me talk for a minute about the various ways you can achieve financial independence. In a nutshell, there are really only three routes to riches: instant wealth, entrepreneurial wealth, and investment wealth.

Instant wealth is the wealth one acquires by winning a lottery, receiving a monstrous inheritance, or making an overnight killing on some wildly speculative investment. Everyone has heard stories about people who have become rich this way: the factory worker who wins a $20 million state lottery, the woman who receives an unexpected inheritance from an uncle she never knew she had, or the neighbor who repeatedly tells how he made an overnight killing on a shady real-estate deal.

Unfortunately, there aren't any guaranteed "get-rich-quick" schemes. You know that. Very few people actually get rich playing the lottery. Even if you have a rich uncle or aunt, you can't be sure that your name is in the will. And wildly speculative investments produce losses more often than they produce profits.

NOTE *People spend more on postage to enter the Publishers' Clearing House sweepstakes than the sweepstakes sponsor gives away in prizes.*

Despite what some would-be entrepreneurs think, entrepreneurial wealth amounts to a "get-rich-slow" scheme. Sometimes, of course, it can work out very well. A couple of bright kids start, say, a software company. They get a couple of lucky breaks and plow the profits back into their company. They work terribly hard. Fifteen or twenty years go by, the business prospers, and bang! The world has a couple of newly minted billionaires. It happens. The preceding is, in a nutshell, the story of Bill Gates and Paul Allen, the founders of the Microsoft Corporation.

I don't want to discourage you from pursuing the entrepreneurial wealth route. If you have the temperament and the skills, the entrepreneurial wealth route represents a way to accumulate a tremendous amount of money. However, entrepreneurial wealth isn't the best route to riches for most people—even if you've already got a successful small business. There's a much simpler, safer way to achieve financial independence if your financial aspirations are more modest.

This simpler, safer way is to invest prudently and wisely. You need to become a disciplined saver and a smart investor. If you do these things, you will become rich by taking the third path to financial independence—the investment-wealth route.

No doubt, at this point, you're thinking one of two things. If you're a bit of a cynic, you're thinking, "If it's so easy, how come everybody isn't doing it?" Well, my response is that many, many people are—some of them without realizing it. What's more, a surprising number of people have already become millionaires.

NOTE *The best figures available estimate that there are more than 7 million millionaires in the United States.*

Another point is that it's a lot easier to say, "Oh, you just need to save religiously and invest smartly," than it is to actually do it. I want to be candid with you: You need to be a disciplined saver. And the older you are, the more serious you need to be about saving. But with time and discipline, it's truly amazing what you can accumulate.

What's more, to earn really impressive investment profits, you need to become a savvy, street-smart investor. You need to learn about taxes, inflation, and the right way to measure investment profits. You need to learn about stocks and bonds and real estate. And you need to make sure that once you start making money you don't start losing it.

NOTE *If a "pack-a-day" 20-year-old quits smoking and stashes the cigarette money in a savings account, he or she can accumulate roughly $150,000 by age 65. If the same "pack-a-day" smoker invests the cigarette money in an employer-sponsored 401(k) plan, he or she can accumulate as much as $1,000,000 in uninflated dollars.*

No, it isn't easy to accumulate a personal fortune. But it isn't all that difficult, either. The trick is to take the necessary time, have a plan, and use the right tools.

Obstacles to Attaining Wealth

I should point out that there are some major obstacles to achieving financial independence. The biggest obstacle, at least in my opinion, is the looking-rich trap. The very first thing you need to realize if you do choose the investment route to riches is that looking rich is far different than becoming or actually being rich. Looking rich requires you to live in a fancy neighborhood. Looking rich requires you to drive an expensive car. Looking rich requires you to wear designer clothes. But looking rich isn't the same as being rich. Most millionaires drive American cars and live in middle-class neighborhoods.

Television and the movies show the rich jetting to places like Paris to shop, sipping champagne, and gorging themselves on caviar. Here's the problem with this patently false image: This sort of consumption invariably prevents you from ever becoming rich. You end up spending all your money trying to look rich and there isn't any leftover money for saving and investing.

False affluence isn't the only obstacle to becoming rich. Another is the "I may die tomorrow" syndrome. People who fall into this trap generally don't think it's worthwhile to postpone enjoying the finer things in life. "Don't put off until tomorrow what you can enjoy today," is their motto and philosophy. I'll be the first to admit that you can't always live for the future. But there is a problem with this business of focusing just on today: Chances are, you won't die tomorrow, and that means that you need to prepare for the future. If you have children, you probably want them to attend college. Some day, presumably, you will retire. To do these sorts of things, you need to prepare financially by accumulating wealth.

Most of the obstacles to acquiring riches are illusory, but one obstacle is almost insurmountable: You may not have enough time. The problem is that the engine that powers wealth creation is something called compound interest. (I explain compound interest at the end of Chapter 20, which covers mutual fund investments.)

You need time for the compound-interest engine to work its magic. You can't use the compound-interest engine to become rich in a year or two.

This doesn't mean that you can't enjoy the benefits of financial success in the coming weeks and months, though. Rather, it means that years must pass before your wealth gives you complete independence from a job. Meanwhile, you have to settle for things like financial peace of mind, financial progress, and a worry-free financial future.

How Much Is Enough: Picking a Wealth Target

All this talk leads quite naturally to a discussion about how much is enough. People always throw around the figure of a million dollars. But do you really need a million dollars? It depends. Usually, you don't need that much money. Let's take a hypothetical case to illustrate why. Say you're 40 years old and that you're making $40,000 a year. Further, suppose that you want to achieve financial independence by age 65. Do you need enough investment wealth to generate $40,000 of income? Probably not. You may currently be spending money on a mortgage that will be paid off by the time you retire. Presumably, you'll receive some money in Social Security or pension benefits. If that is the case, you won't need $40,000 a year by the time you retire.

Here is another example to make the whole thing clearer: Say you are making $40,000 a year; you currently pay $7,500 a year in mortgage payments, but your mortgage will be paid off by the time you retire; and you will receive $7,500 a year in Social Security and pension benefits. Once your mortgage is paid and you're eligible for pension benefits, you can live as well on $25,000 of investment income as you currently live on $40,000 in wages. What you need is enough wealth to produce an investment income of $25,000, because the $25,000 of investment income will make you financially independent.

NOTE *As noted previously, you can find out exactly how much Social Security you'll receive by calling your local Social Security office, asking them to send you an SS-7004 form, and then filling out and returning the form. You can also request the form online at* http://www.ssa.gov/online/ssa-7004.pdf

Your next step is to determine how much wealth you need to produce $25,000 a year of investment income. In general, you need 20 dollars of investment wealth to produce a dollar of investment income. To generate $25,000 of income, therefore, you need $500,000 of investment wealth, because 20 times $25,000 equals $500,000. But you can and should make a more precise determination with the

Retirement Planner. (I described the Retirement Planner earlier in this chapter in the section "Planning for Retirement.")

Looking at the Big Picture

I want to conclude this discussion about financial independence with what will seem like a digression but with what is really the most important point of all. I honestly believe you will be happier if you prepare for and eventually achieve financial independence, but I also believe wealth should not be an end-all, be-all goal. I respectfully suggest that you consider financial independence one of your minor life objectives. It certainly shouldn't be your only objective.

This may seem like strange advice coming from someone who makes his living by writing, thinking, and advising people about money. But my activities give me a rather unique vantage point. Because of the work I do, I get to meet a number of very wealthy individuals. I'll let you in on a little secret: having stacks of money doesn't make the difference you might think. All that will happen, if you do accumulate these great sums of money, is that you'll acquire more expensive habits, hobbies, and friends. You'll still argue with your spouse or children about how you should spend money. You'll still encounter rude neighbors, dangerous drivers, and incompetent sales clerks. And you'll still have to answer all the big questions about life and love and death.

I don't think this perspective conflicts with the idea that you should accumulate a certain amount of wealth. Having a million dollars in wealth isn't essential to your happiness. I don't think it's bad, either. If you want to make financial independence your goal in life, great. My point is that, when you get right down to the specifics of your situation, $200,000 may be as good a target as $1,000,000 or $2,000,000. In any case, $200,000 is a lot easier to achieve.

Chapter 15

PAYROLL

In This Chapter

- Setting up payroll categories and accounts
- Preparing a payroll check
- Using memorized and scheduled transactions
- Preparing payroll tax returns and paying payroll taxes
- Saving payroll tax deposit money
- How to handle federal and state payroll paperwork

You can use Quicken to prepare payroll checks, calculate payroll taxes, and expedite the preparation of federal and state payroll and payroll tax returns. In this chapter, you'll learn how to set up payroll categories and liability accounts for your record keeping. You'll also learn how to prepare payroll checks and payroll tax returns and how to memorize and schedule payroll-related transactions.

NOTE *At the end of this chapter, you'll find information about what you need to do before you hire your first employee to address federal and state payroll tax collection and reporting requirements. Be sure to read that material to make sure that you're ready to start processing a payroll with Quicken.*

TIP *Intuit, the maker of Quicken, also sells another program called QuickPay, which automates many of the payroll tasks described in this chapter. If your payroll needs aren't easily handled using the techniques described here, you may want to consider using QuickPay. For more information, visit the Quicken.com web site.*

Setting Up Payroll Categories and Accounts

Once you take care of the federal and state payroll and employment prerequisites (and you do need to take care of these items first), you're ready to set up Quicken to prepare payroll checks and tax returns. To do this, you set up categories (or subcategories) for each payroll expense that you, the employer, pay. For example, you set up a Payroll Expense category to track wages, Social Security, Medicare, and federal unemployment taxes, as well as any state payroll taxes you pay (such as state unemployment and workers' compensation).

You also need liability accounts for every payroll tax liability (amount you owe someone) you incur, such as the amounts you owe the IRS for the federal income, Social Security, and Medicare taxes you withhold from the employee's payroll check, as well as the federal payroll taxes, Social Security, and Medicare taxes you pay as an employer. (Social Security and Medicare taxes are paid by both the employer and the employee.)

Setting Up Payroll Categories

The easiest way to set up payroll categories is to first set up a Payroll expense category and then create subcategories for each of the types of payroll expense you actually pay: wages, Social Security, Medicare, federal unemployment, state unemployment, and so on. The following sections explain how to create the main category and subcategories.

NOTE *Quicken's category list includes a wages category as well as wages subcategories for federal income taxes, Social Security taxes, Medicare taxes, and state disability insurance. You don't use these for business payroll accounting, however. These categories let you record wages you or your spouse receives.*

Setting Up a Payroll Expense Category

To set up an expense category for payroll, follow these steps:

1. Choose Finance ➢ Category & Transfer List to open the Category & Transfer List window. Click the New command button to display the Set Up Category dialog box, as shown in Figure 15.1.

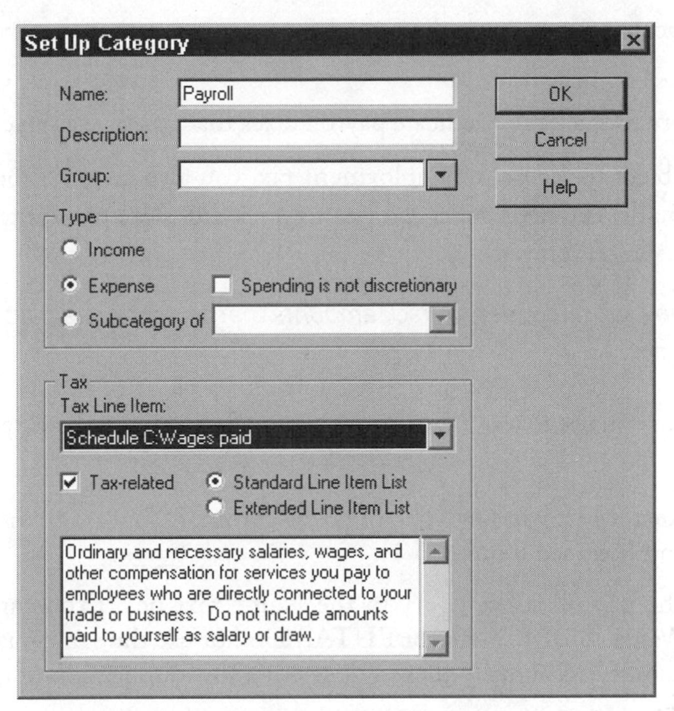

Figure 15.1: The Set Up Category dialog box.

2. Enter ***Payroll*** in the Name text box. (You'll use this as the main expense category for payroll.)
3. If you want to describe the payroll expense category in more detail, use the Description text box.
4. Be sure the Expense option button is marked.
5. If you're going to be processing payroll that is or may be a tax-deductible expense, mark the Tax-Related checkbox and choose the appropriate entry from the Form drop-down list box. Here are some suggestions:
   - If you're a sole proprietor who uses Schedule C, select Schedule C: Wages Paid.
   - If you're a farmer who uses Schedule F, select Schedule F: Labor Hired.
   - If you're a parent preparing to process payroll for an employee providing childcare, select 2441: Qualifying Childcare Expenses.
6. Click OK. Quicken adds the Payroll expense to the Category & Transfer List window.

Setting Up Payroll Expense Subcategories

You need at least three payroll subcategories to handle the payroll:

- A gross wages subcategory to track what an employee really earns

- A Social Security subcategory to track the Social Security taxes that you owe as an employer
- A Medicare subcategory to track the Medicare payroll taxes that you owe as an employer

If your employees are subject to federal unemployment tax, you also need a subcategory to track that expense. Finally, you need subcategories to track any state payroll taxes that you are required to pay as an employer.

NOTE *You don't need any subcategories to track amounts that an employee pays through payroll deductions.*

To set up the subcategories you use to track the various types of payroll expenses, take these steps:

1. In the Category & Transfer List window, click the New command button to display the Set Up Category dialog box (see Figure 15.1).
2. Enter the name for the payroll subcategory in the Name text box. (You can use an abbreviation such as Wages, SS, MCARE, or FUTA.) Do not use the same names that you will use for your liability accounts. Quicken does not allow duplication of names in accounts and categories.
3. If you want to describe the payroll expense subcategory, use the Description text box. For example, if you abbreviated the payroll expense in the Name text box, you can enter the full payroll expense subcategory name in the Description next box. You might describe the Wages subcategory as Gross Wages, the SS subcategory as Social Security, the MCARE subcategory as Medicare, the FUTA subcategory as Federal Unemployment Taxes, and so on.
4. Click the Subcategory Of option button and enter the name of the Payroll expense category into the text box. (If you've followed the instructions so far, the expense category's name will be Payroll.)
5. If you're going to process payroll that is or may be a tax-deductible expense, mark the Tax-Related checkbox.
6. Click OK. Quicken adds the payroll expense subcategory to the Category & Transfer List window.

Repeat steps 2 through 6 for each of the payroll expense subcategories that you need to create. Figure 15.2 shows the Set Up Category dialog box filled out to set up the Wages subcategory.

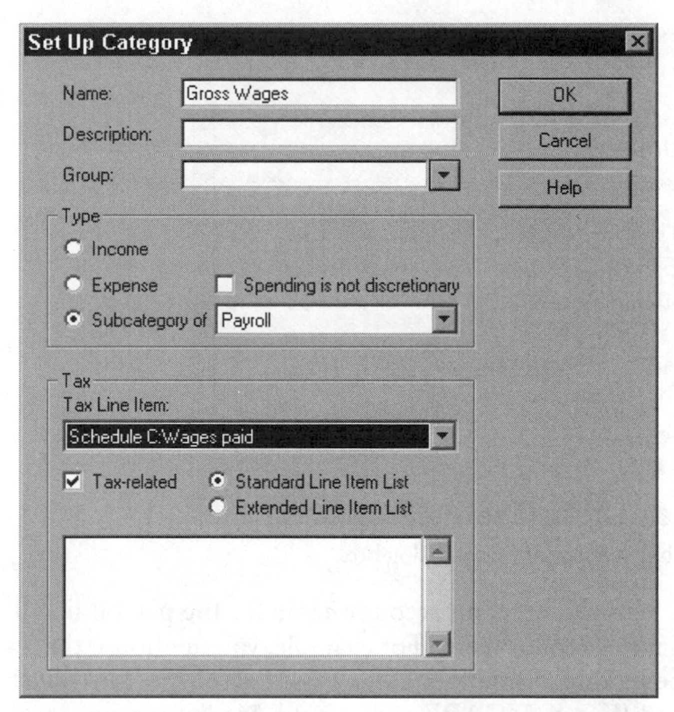

Figure 15.2: The Set Up Category dialog box filled out to set up a subcategory.

Setting Up Payroll Liability Accounts

The next task is to set up liability accounts to track the amounts you owe the federal and state governments. You should set up payroll tax liability accounts for federal income taxes withheld, state income taxes withheld, Social Security owed, and Medicare taxes owed. If there are other significant payroll tax liabilities, set up payroll-tax liability accounts for these too. If a payroll tax liability is very small (federal unemployment taxes, for example, can equal 0.08 percent), you may want to skip tracking the liability. In this case, just categorize the check that pays the tax using a payroll tax category.

To set up the payroll liability accounts you need, follow these steps:

1. Display the Account List window by choosing Finance ➤ Account List.
2. Click the New button. Quicken displays the dialog box for creating new accounts.
3. Click the Liability button, and then click Next. Quicken displays the first Liability Account Setup dialog box, as shown in Figure 15.3.

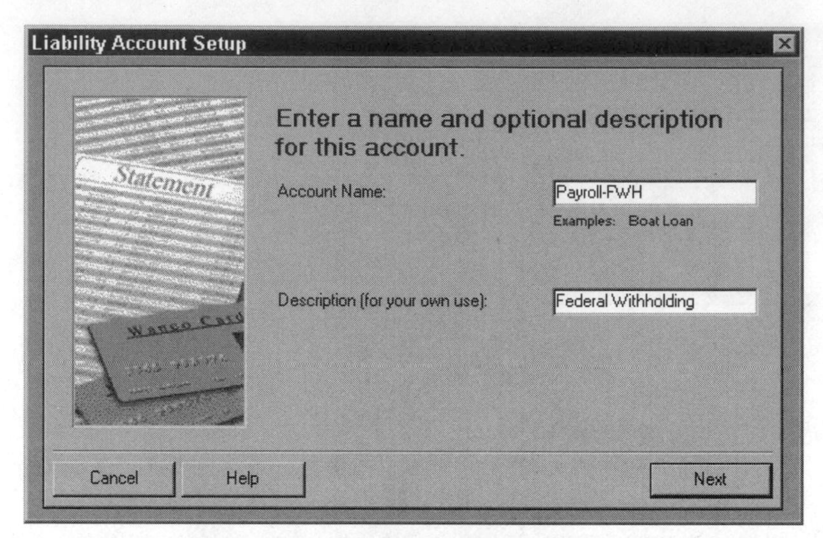

Figure 15.3: The first Liability Account Setup dialog box.

4. In the Account Name text box, enter an account name for the payroll liability. Make *Payroll* the first word in the account name. For example, you might use the name Payroll-FWH to track the federal withholding amounts, Payroll-SS to track the Social Security taxes owed, and Payroll-MCARE to track the Medicare taxes owed.

TIP *You should start each payroll liability account's name with the word* Payroll *so that you can easily prepare a report of payroll transactions and account balances. The Payroll report on the Business submenu does just this; it summarizes transactions that use categories and accounts starting with the word* Payroll.

5. If you want to describe the payroll liability account in more detail, use the Description text box. For example, if you abbreviated the liability name for the account name, you might enter the full payroll liability name as the description.
6. Click Next. Quicken displays the second liability Account Setup dialog box, as shown in Figure 15.4.

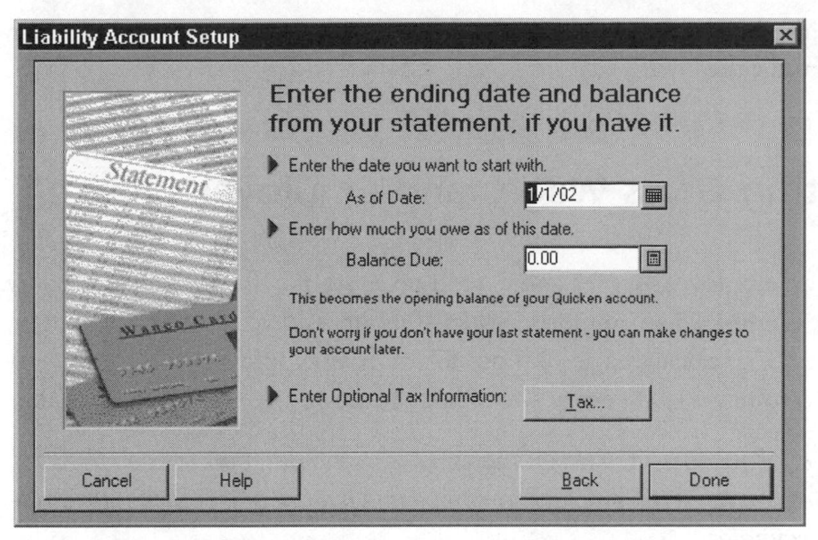

Figure 15.4: The second Liability Account Setup dialog box.

7. In the Balance text box, enter the amount you currently owe on the payroll liability.
8. In the As Of Date text box, enter the date for which you owe the amount entered in step 7.
9. Click Done.
10. When Quicken asks if you want to set up an amortized loan for the account, select No. Quicken adds the new payroll liability account and then opens a register window for the account. Close this register window by clicking its Close button.

Repeat steps 2 through 10 for each of the other payroll tax liability accounts you want to add. At a minimum, you typically need to set up payroll liability accounts for federal income taxes withheld, Social Security and Medicare.

Preparing a Payroll Check

Once you've set up your payroll categories and accounts, you're ready to use Quicken to prepare employee payroll checks. To do this, you first calculate the employee's wages and the payroll taxes you and the employee pay based on those wages. Second, you record a transaction in the Quicken register that summarizes the payroll check and the related payroll taxes.

Calculating an Employee's Wages and Payroll Taxes

There are really two parts to figuring out what a payroll transaction is supposed to look like:

- Calculate the employee's gross wages and the payroll taxes you, the employer, owe. (This is usually the easiest part.)
- Describe the payroll deductions you withhold from the check.

Calculating Gross Wages and Employer's Payroll Taxes

Calculating an employee's wages and payroll taxes starts with the actual gross wages calculation. For example, if an employee works 40 hours and you pay $7.50 an hour, you owe the employee $300, calculated as 40 times $7.50. If an employee works for two weeks and you've agreed to pay $1,000 every two weeks, you owe the employee $1,000.

NOTE *In the following payroll tax examples, I use round numbers to keep things simple. The wages you pay as an employer might be much more or less than the numbers used in the examples.*

Once you know the employee's gross wages, you can calculate the payroll taxes you owe as a result of wages. Just multiply the payroll tax rate by the gross wages amount. (You can start the Quicken calculator by choosing Finance ➢ Calculator.)

Suppose, for example, you owe an employee $1,000 for two weeks of work. To calculate the Social Security taxes you owe because of the $1,000, multiply the $1,000 by the Social Security taxes percentage, which is currently 6.2 percent. (The *Employer's Tax Guide* usually prints this information on the first or second page of the *Guide*, but you can also consult a table in the *Guide* to find out what number is 6.2 percent of $1,000.)

NOTE *To order a printed copy of the* Employer's Tax Guide *or to access it online, go to the Internal Revenue Service (IRS) site at* www.irs.gov.

To calculate the Medicare taxes you owe because of the $1,000, either multiply the $1,000 by the Medicare taxes percentage, which is currently 1.45 percent, or consult the table in the *Guide* to find out what number is 1.45 percent of $1,000.

If you owe an employee $1,000 in gross wages but need to pay 6.2 percent in Social Security taxes and 1.45 percent in Medicare taxes, the total payroll expenses you incur are equal to those shown in Table 15.1.

Table 15.1: Sample Payroll Expenses

DESCRIPTION	AMOUNT
Gross wages	$1,000.00
Social Security	$62.00
Medicare	$14.50
Total payroll expenses	$1,076.50

NOTE *Each of the payroll expenses in Table 15.1 should be recorded using a separate payroll expense subcategory.*

If you owe other federal and state payroll taxes, such as a 1 percent state unemployment tax paid by the employer, calculate them in the same way, obtaining the data you need from your state's equivalent of the *Employer's Tax Guide.*

Calculating the Payroll Deductions

An employee doesn't get paid the gross wages amount. You, the employer, are required to deduct from the employee's gross wages amount for federal income taxes, Social Security, and Medicare. You may also be required or allowed to deduct amounts for other payroll taxes.

The amount an employee pays for Social Security and Medicare taxes through a payroll deduction is calculated in the same way as the amount an employer pays for Social Security and Medicare taxes: You just multiply the appropriate tax rate by the gross wages amount. In the case of a $1,000 biweekly paycheck, Social Security taxes equal $62.00 (calculated as 6.2 percent of $1,000), and Medicare taxes equal $14.50 (calculated as 1.45 percent of $1,000). If there are other payroll taxes paid by the employee, you calculate these in the same way.

The amount of federal income taxes you withhold is dictated by the IRS. You look at the employee's W-4 to obtain the filing status and the number of personal exemptions claimed. Then you look up (in the *Employer's Tax Guide*) the employee's gross wages amount in the appropriate pay-period table for the employee's filing status. For example, to determine the amount of federal income taxes to withhold for an employee who makes $1,000 every two weeks and files a tax return using the Married Filing Jointly status, you use the Married Persons—Biweekly Payroll Period table. Figure 15.5 shows this page from the *Employer's Tax Guide.*

MARRIED Persons- **BIWEEKLY** Payroll Period

(For Wages Paid in 2001)

If the wages are-		And the number of withholding allowances claimed is-										
At least	But less than	0	1	2	3	4	5	6	7	8	9	10
		The amount of income tax to be withheld is-										
$0	**$250**	0	0	0	0	0	0	0	0	0	0	0
250	**260**	1	0	0	0	0	0	0	0	0	0	0
260	**270**	3	0	0	0	0	0	0	0	0	0	0
270	**280**	4	0	0	0	0	0	0	0	0	0	0
280	**290**	6	0	0	0	0	0	0	0	0	0	0
290	**300**	7	0	0	0	0	0	0	0	0	0	0
300	**310**	9	0	0	0	0	0	0	0	0	0	0
310	**320**	10	0	0	0	0	0	0	0	0	0	0
320	**330**	12	0	0	0	0	0	0	0	0	0	0
330	**340**	13	0	0	0	0	0	0	0	0	0	0
340	**350**	15	0	0	0	0	0	0	0	0	0	0
350	**360**	16	0	0	0	0	0	0	0	0	0	0
360	**370**	18	1	0	0	0	0	0	0	0	0	0
370	**380**	19	2	0	0	0	0	0	0	0	0	0
380	**390**	21	4	0	0	0	0	0	0	0	0	0
390	**400**	22	5	0	0	0	0	0	0	0	0	0
400	**410**	24	7	0	0	0	0	0	0	0	0	0
410	**420**	25	8	0	0	0	0	0	0	0	0	0
420	**430**	27	10	0	0	0	0	0	0	0	0	0
430	**440**	28	11	0	0	0	0	0	0	0	0	0
440	**450**	30	13	0	0	0	0	0	0	0	0	0
450	**460**	31	14	0	0	0	0	0	0	0	0	0
460	**470**	33	16	0	0	0	0	0	0	0	0	0
470	**480**	34	17	1	0	0	0	0	0	0	0	0
480	**490**	36	19	2	0	0	0	0	0	0	0	0
490	**500**	37	20	4	0	0	0	0	0	0	0	0
500	**520**	39	23	6	0	0	0	0	0	0	0	0
520	**540**	42	26	9	0	0	0	0	0	0	0	0
540	**560**	45	29	12	0	0	0	0	0	0	0	0
560	**580**	48	32	15	0	0	0	0	0	0	0	0
580	**600**	51	35	18	1	0	0	0	0	0	0	0
600	**620**	54	38	21	4	0	0	0	0	0	0	0
620	**640**	57	41	24	7	0	0	0	0	0	0	0
640	**660**	60	44	27	10	0	0	0	0	0	0	0
660	**680**	63	47	30	13	0	0	0	0	0	0	0
680	**700**	66	50	33	16	0	0	0	0	0	0	0
700	**720**	69	53	36	19	2	0	0	0	0	0	0
720	**740**	72	56	39	22	5	0	0	0	0	0	0
740	**760**	75	59	42	25	8	0	0	0	0	0	0
760	**780**	78	62	45	28	11	0	0	0	0	0	0
780	**800**	81	65	48	31	14	0	0	0	0	0	0
800	**820**	84	68	51	34	17	1	0	0	0	0	0
820	**840**	87	71	54	37	20	4	0	0	0	0	0
840	**860**	90	74	57	40	23	7	0	0	0	0	0
860	**880**	93	77	60	43	26	10	0	0	0	0	0
880	**900**	96	80	63	46	29	13	0	0	0	0	0
900	**920**	99	83	66	49	32	16	0	0	0	0	0
920	**940**	102	86	69	52	35	19	2	0	0	0	0
940	**960**	105	89	72	55	38	22	5	0	0	0	0
960	**980**	108	92	75	58	41	25	8	0	0	0	0
980	**1,000**	111	95	78	61	44	28	11	0	0	0	0
1,000	**1,020**	114	98	81	64	47	31	14	0	0	0	0
1,020	**1,040**	117	101	84	67	50	34	17	0	0	0	0
1,040	**1,060**	120	104	87	70	53	37	20	3	0	0	0
1,060	**1,080**	123	107	90	73	56	40	23	6	0	0	0
1,080	**1,100**	126	110	93	76	59	43	26	9	0	0	0
1,100	**1,120**	129	113	96	79	62	46	29	12	0	0	0
1,120	**1,140**	132	116	99	82	65	49	32	15	0	0	0
1,140	**1,160**	135	119	102	85	68	52	35	18	1	0	0
1,160	**1,180**	138	122	105	88	71	55	38	21	4	0	0
1,180	**1,200**	141	125	108	91	74	58	41	24	7	0	0
1,200	**1,220**	144	128	111	94	77	61	44	27	10	0	0
1,220	**1,240**	147	131	114	97	80	64	47	30	13	0	0
1,240	**1,260**	150	134	117	100	83	67	50	33	16	0	0
1,260	**1,280**	153	137	120	103	86	70	53	36	19	3	0
1,280	**1,300**	156	140	123	106	89	73	56	39	22	6	0
1,300	**1,320**	159	143	126	109	92	76	59	42	25	9	0
1,320	**1,340**	162	146	129	112	95	79	62	45	28	12	0
1,340	**1,360**	165	149	132	115	98	82	65	48	31	15	0
1,360	**1,380**	168	152	135	118	101	85	68	51	34	18	1

Page 42

Figure 15.5: The Married Persons—Biweekly Payroll Period table from the *Employer's Tax Guide.*

WARNING *Don't use the information shown in Figure 15.5! You need to get your own* Employer's Tax Guide *to make sure you're using the most up-to-date income tax rates.*

Look down the first column of the table until you find the gross wages row for monthly wages equal to $1,000. Then look across that row until you get to the withholding amount specified for the claimed number of withholding allowances. For example, if the employee claimed two exemptions on the W-4 form, the table in Figure 15.3 says you should withhold $81 in federal income taxes. Table 15.2 summarizes the calculation.

Table 15.2: A Sample Net Wages Calculation

DESCRIPTION	AMOUNT
Gross wages	$1,000.00
Social Security	$(62.00)
Medicare	$(14.50)
Federal income taxes	$(81.00)
Net wages	$ 842.50

Producing the Payroll Check

Now you're ready to prepare the payroll check and record it. The instructions here assume that you'll print the check in Quicken by using the Write Checks window to record it. If you don't want to print the check, you can record it directly in the Register window.

To record gross wages, deductions, and net wages, follow these steps:

1. In the Write Checks window, enter the payroll date in the Date text box, the employee's name in the Pay To The Order Of text box, and the net wages amount in the $ text box.
2. If you'll mail the check in a windowed envelope, type the employee's address in the Address block.
3. If it will help you or the employee identify the payroll period, enter additional information in the Memo text box.
4. Click the Split command button to display the Split Transaction Window.
5. Enter the gross wages amount on the first split transaction line. In the Category field, type ***Payroll*** followed by a colon (:) and the name of the gross wages subcategory. (If you use Gross Wages as the name of the gross wages subcategory, for example, type ***Payroll:Gross Wages***.) Then type the gross wages amount in the Amount field.
6. Enter the federal income taxes withheld from the employee's payroll check on the second split transaction line. In the Category field, type the name of the payroll liability account you set up to track what you owe for federal income taxes withheld. Then enter the federal income taxes withheld as a negative number in the Amount field.

7. Enter the Social Security tax deduction on the third split transaction line. In the Category field, type the name of the payroll liability account you set up to track what you owe for Social Security. In the Amount field, enter the Social Security taxes paid by the employee as a negative number.

WARNING *Be sure that you use payroll liability accounts in steps 6, 7, and 8. You don't want to use payroll subcategories. By using the payroll liability accounts, you show that it's the employee who is paying these amounts. If you incorrectly use payroll subcategories, you show that it's you, not the employee, who is paying these amounts.*

8. Enter the Medicare tax deduction on the fourth split transaction line. In the Category field, type the name of the payroll liability account you set up to track what you owe for Medicare. In the Amount field, enter the Medicare taxes paid by the employee as a negative number.

Figure 15.6 shows an example of the Split Transaction Window after entering the gross wages, federal income taxes, Social Security, and Medicare deductions information. If the employee pays other payroll taxes through deductions, you record these in the same way as you record federal income taxes.

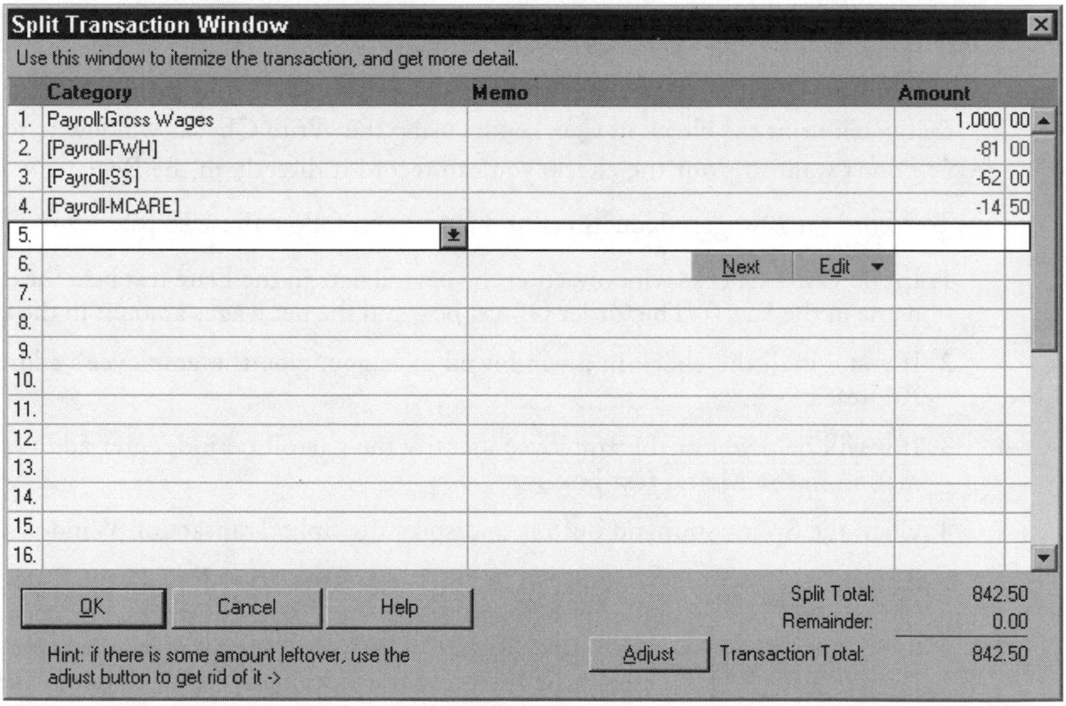

Split Transaction Window

Use this window to itemize the transaction, and get more detail.

	Category	Memo	Amount
1.	Payroll:Gross Wages		1,000 00
2.	[Payroll-FWH]		-81 00
3.	[Payroll-SS]		-62 00
4.	[Payroll-MCARE]		-14 50
5.			
6.		Next Edit	
7.			
8.			
9.			
10.			
11.			
12.			
13.			
14.			
15.			
16.			

OK Cancel Help

Split Total: 842.50
Remainder: 0.00
Transaction Total: 842.50

Hint: if there is some amount leftover, use the adjust button to get rid of it -> Adjust

Figure 15.6: The Split Transaction Window with gross wages and tax withholding information.

NOTE *In steps 9 through 12, you record the Social Security and Medicare payroll taxes that you as the employer must pay. This is the information shown in Table 15.1.*

9. Move to the seventeenth line of the Split Transaction Window (since only the first 15 lines of the split transaction detail appear on check stubs, the employer's payroll taxes won't appear there) and enter the employer's Social Security taxes expense on that line. In the Category field, type ***Payroll*** followed by a colon (:) and the name of the Social Security taxes subcategory. (For example, if you use SS as the Social Security subcategory name, type ***Payroll:SS***.) Then enter the Social Security taxes amount in the Amount field.

10. Enter the employer's Social Security taxes liability (because of the Social Security taxes expense) on the eighteenth split transaction line. In the Category drop-down list box, select Transfer To [the Social Security liability account]. Then enter the Social Security taxes amount as a negative number in the Amount field.

Figure 15.7 shows an example of the Split Transaction Window after entering the employer's Social Security taxes expense and Social Security taxes liability.

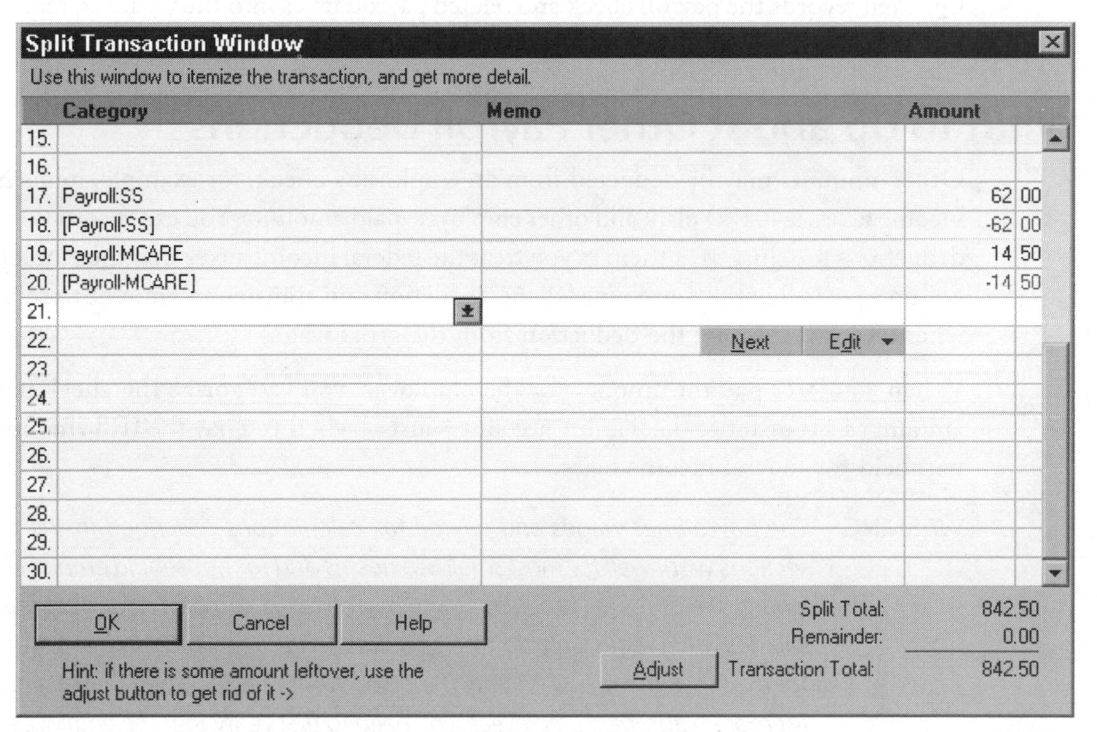

Figure 15.7: The Split Transaction Window with Social Security taxes expense and liability information.

NOTE *You use the same liability account to track both the amounts you owe for Social Security because you withheld money from an employee's check and the amounts you owe for Social Security because of the Social Security payroll tax.*

11. Enter the employer's Medicare taxes expense on the nineteenth split transaction line. For example, if you use MCARE as the Medicare subcategory name, type ***Payroll:MCARE*** in the Category field. Then enter the Medicare taxes amount in the Amount field.
12. Enter the employer's Medicare taxes liability (because of the Medicare taxes expense) on the twentieth split transaction line. In the Category drop-down list box, select Transfer Funds To [the Medicare liability account]. Then enter the Medicare taxes amount as a negative number in the Amount field.

NOTE *You use the same liability account to track both the amounts you owe for Medicare because you withheld money from an employee's check and the amounts you owe for Medicare because of the Medicare payroll tax.*

13. Click OK to close the Split Transaction Window, and then click Record Check.

Quicken records the payroll check and related payroll taxes into the Quicken register. Then it scrolls the just-completed check off your screen so you can write another one.

What to Do about Other Payroll Deductions

Other amounts may be deducted from an employee's check, for example, items like state income taxes, a 401(k) plan, and other employee-paid amounts. You can record these payroll deductions too. Just treat them as you treat the federal income taxes that the employee pays: Set up a payroll liability account for the deduction and transfer an amount to this account whenever you subtract the deduction from the gross wages.

When you later pay the amount for the employee, you categorize the check paying the amount as a transfer to the liability account—just as when you pay the IRS amounts you've withheld for federal income taxes.

WARNING *The payroll net wages and payroll tax calculations described in the preceding sections work well for most small businesses and for household employees. But be aware of a potential problem: Some payroll taxes and payroll deductions apply to salaries and wages only up to a specified limit. Year 2001 Social Security taxes, for example, are levied on only the first $80,400 of income. This rule means that for more highly paid employees, you need to first verify that the employee still owes or that you, the employer, still owe the tax. You can do this manually (with a pencil and a scratch pad), but if you need to track things like the net wages subject to Social Security, get a full-featured payroll program or go to an outside service bureau.*

Using Memorized and Scheduled Transactions

You can memorize the payroll transactions you regularly record. Then, the next time you want to record the same or almost the same transaction, you can recall the transaction from the memorized transactions list. Quicken uses the memorized transaction's information to fill in the text boxes of the transaction.

Memorizing a Transaction

To memorize a transaction, you can start from either the Write Checks window or the Register window. In the Write Checks window, display the payroll check you want to memorize. In the Register window, select the payroll check (or any other transaction). Then choose Edit ➤ Transaction ➤ Memorize to display a message box asking if you want to memorize the split amounts as percentages of the transaction total shown in the Write Checks window. Since you want to memorize the split amounts and not the split percentages, select No. When the "This transaction is about to be memorized" message appears, click OK. Quicken adds the selected payroll transaction to its memorized transactions list.

TIP *It's likely that Quicken is automatically memorizing transactions as you create them. To check on this, click the Options button to display the Check Options dialog box and then click the QuickFill tab. If the Auto Memorize New Transactions checkbox is marked, Quicken is automatically memorizing all your transactions as you record them.*

Reusing a Memorized Transaction

To reuse a memorized transaction, follow these steps:

1. Display an empty check in the Write Checks window or select the new empty row in the Register window.
2. Choose Banking ➤ Memorized Transaction List to display the Memorized Transaction List window, as shown in Figure 15.8.

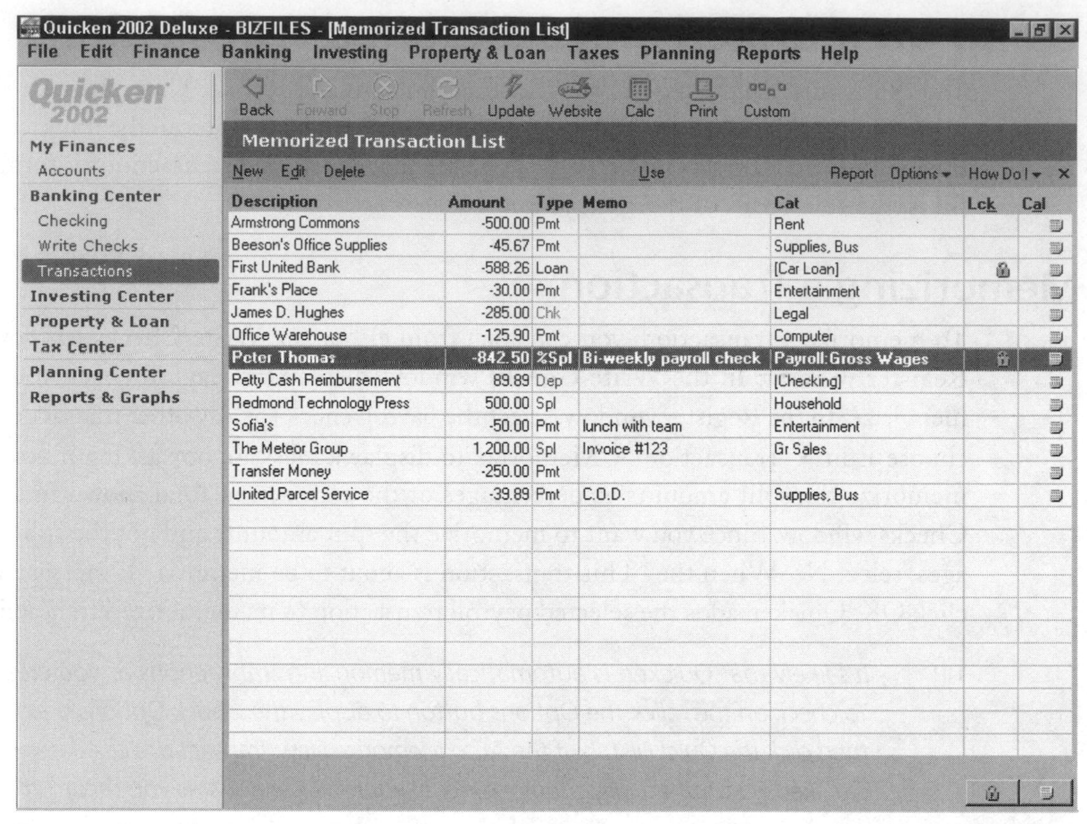

Figure 15.8: The Memorized Transaction List window.

3. Select the memorized transaction you want to reuse and click the Use command button. Quicken uses the memorized transaction to fill in the text boxes in the Write Checks window or in the selected row of the Register window.

TIP *Quicken automatically reuses a memorized transaction if you haven't turned off that option in the QuickFill tab. To check this, choose Edit ➢ Options ➢ Register and click the QuickFill tab. If the Recall Memorized Transactions checkbox is marked, Quicken is automatically recalling transactions. All you need to do is enter the payee name and press Tab.*

Using Scheduled Transactions to Speed Payroll

If you have employees whom you pay, without fail, every week, Quicken's scheduled transactions feature can help you. To tell Quicken that it should automatically record a memorized transaction, you *schedule* the transaction in one of two ways: with the Banking ➢ Scheduled Transaction List command or by using the Financial Calendar.

Scheduling a Transaction Using the Financial Calendar

To schedule one of the memorized transactions shown in the Financial Calendar window, follow these steps:

1. Choose Finance ➢ Calendar to display the Financial Calendar window, as shown in Figure 15.9.

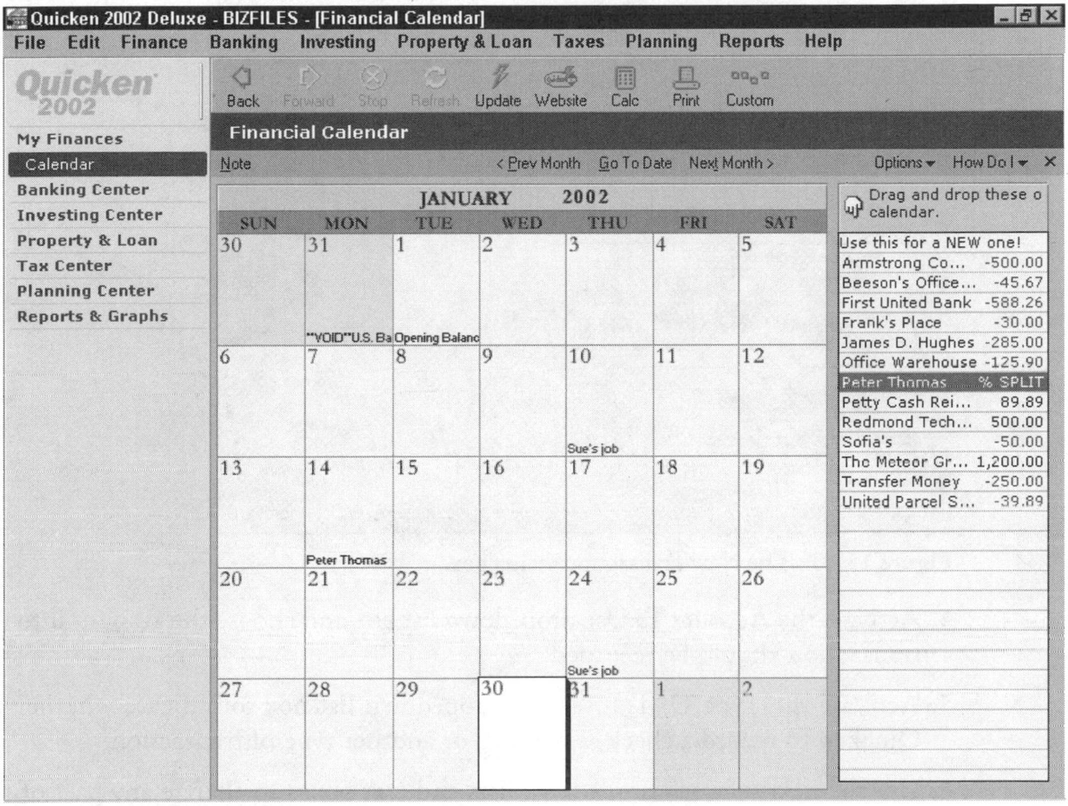

Figure 15.9: The Financial Calendar.

The main part of the Financial Calendar window shows the current month's calendar. You can move backward and forward a month at a time by clicking the Prev Month and Next Month buttons. The list box on the right half of the window shows the memorized transactions.

NOTE *If you want to show transactions from only a selected group of accounts, choose Options ➢ Calendar Accounts to display the Calendar Options dialog box, and then mark and unmark the accounts you want to see by clicking them.*

2. Display the first month you want to schedule the transaction by using the Prev Month or Next Month buttons.
3. Select the memorized transaction by clicking it. Then drag the transaction to the first day it should be scheduled. Quicken displays the New Transaction dialog box, as shown in Figure 15.10. The information displayed in the dialog box describes the transaction you've just dragged.

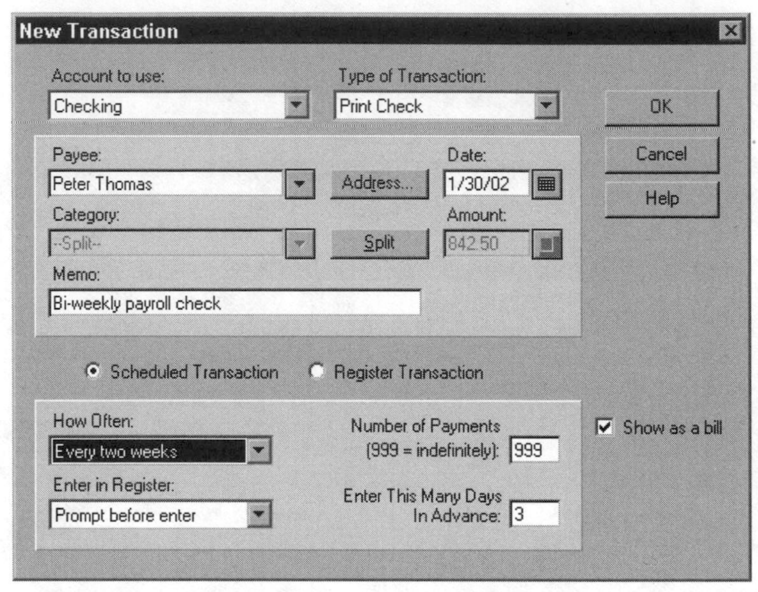

Figure 15.10: The New Transaction dialog box.

4. Activate the Account To Use drop-down list box and choose the account into which the transaction should be recorded.
5. Activate the Type Of Transaction drop-down list box to indicate whether you want Quicken to record a check, a deposit, or another type of transaction.
6. Use the next section's drop-down lists and text boxes to change any part of the recurring transaction.
7. Mark either Scheduled Transaction for a repeating transaction or Register Transaction for a one-time-only transaction.

NOTE *If you mark the Scheduled Transaction option button, other options are displayed in the lower half of the New Transaction dialog box.*

8. Activate the How Often drop-down list box to indicate the frequency of the transaction: Only Once, Weekly, Every Two Weeks, Twice A Month, or another time period.
9. If you want to schedule more than one occurrence of this payment, use the Number Of Payments text box to enter the number of payments you want Quicken to enter.

10. Use the Enter In Register drop-down list box to specify whether you want Quicken to automatically enter the transaction or prompt you to enter the transaction.
11. If you want Quicken to remind you of unprinted checks, investment reminder notices, and scheduled transactions, use the Enter This Many Days In Advance text box to specify the number of days of advance warning you want for this scheduled transaction.
12. Click OK.

NOTE *Quicken automatically displays the Reminder window when you start Quicken if there's something it wants to remind you about. You can also display this window by choosing Finance ➢ Alerts.*

Quicken schedules the transaction. To show the scheduled transaction, it puts the payee name on the calendar for each day the transaction will be recorded.

Using the Scheduled Transaction List Window

If you want to delete or edit a scheduled transaction, choose Banking ➢ Scheduled Transaction List. Quicken displays the Scheduled Transaction List window, which lists all your scheduled transactions.

To delete a scheduled transaction, select it, click Delete, and click OK. To edit a scheduled transaction, select it, click Edit, and make your changes using the Edit Scheduled Transaction dialog box. You can also add new scheduled transactions using the Scheduled Transaction List window's New command button.

Using the Financial Calendar's Reminder Notes

The Financial Calendar provides one other useful feature for managing and monitoring your payroll activities. You can post notes on calendar days. For example, you might add a note that says, "Payroll tax deposit due." Quicken then uses the note text to remind you that the payroll tax deposit is due.

To post a note, follow these steps:

1. In the Financial Calendar window, select the day you want to be reminded.
2. Click the Note command button to display the Note dialog box.
3. Type your note, and then click Save.

Quicken saves your note and adds a yellow square to the calendar day to show that you have a calendar note for the date. (To see the note, click the yellow square.)

TIP *Yellow is the traditional color for reminder notes, but you can change the color Quicken uses. To pick another color, select one from the Note Color drop-down list box in the Note dialog box.*

Customizing the Financial Calendar

When you click the Options down arrow in the upper-right corner of the Financial Calendar window, you have six choices.

To display a graph beneath the Calendar that shows your daily account balances, choose Options ➢ Show Account Graph. To display or hide the Memorized Transaction List, choose Options ➢ Show Memorized Transaction List. To edit the Memorized Transaction List, choose Options ➢ Edit Memorized Transaction List to open the Memorized Transaction List window.

To display recorded or scheduled transactions or both in the Calendar, choose Options ➢ Show Recorded Transactions In Calendar or Options ➢ Show Scheduled Transactions In Calendar.

Preparing Payroll Tax Returns and Paying Payroll Taxes

There are two other payroll tasks that you need to complete on a regular basis:

- You need to pay the IRS both the amounts you've withheld from employee checks and the amounts you owe for payroll taxes.
- You need to prepare payroll tax returns, usually on both a quarterly and an annual basis.

What to Do When You Write the Check

The rules for remitting federal tax deposits change frequently, but one useful piece of information concerns how much you owe. For example, as I'm writing this, if you owe less than $500, you are not required to pay a tax deposit until the end of the quarter. (If you owe more than $500, your best bet is to pay what you owe immediately.)

But how do you know how much you owe the IRS? It's simple: You know by looking at the payroll liability accounts. The balances in these accounts are the amounts you owe for various employer payroll taxes and employee payroll deductions.

Read through the section in the *Employer's Tax Guide* that describes the rules for depositing taxes. It describes how quickly you'll need to make deposits, including information such as the fact that you should allow time for the check to clear. It also describes the penalty you must pay if you're delinquent.

Along with your check, you need to send a Federal Tax Deposit (Form 8109) coupon. This coupon gives your Federal Tax Identification number. The IRS should send you a booklet of these forms a few weeks after you apply for your employer identification number. The booklet of Federal Tax Deposit coupons has instructions about how you fill out the form and where you mail it.

As an example, let's say you currently owe the amounts shown in Table 15.3. The payroll tax liability account balances shown in Table 15.3 equal the amounts you will owe if you have prepared one payroll check for $1,000 of gross wages, as described earlier in the chapter. The $81 in federal taxes is the amount withheld from the employee's check. The $124 is the total Social Security owed, including both the $62 paid by the employee as a payroll deduction and the $62 Social Security payroll tax paid by the employer. The $29 is the total Medicare tax owed, including both the $14.50 paid by the employee as a payroll deduction and the $14.50 Medicare payroll tax paid by the employer.

Table 15.3: Sample Payroll Liability Account Balances

DESCRIPTION	AMOUNT
Social Security	$124.00
Medicare	$29.00
Federal income taxes	$81.00
Total taxes owed	$234.00

To record a check that makes the federal tax deposit for the payroll tax liabilities shown in Table 15.3, write a check for $234. To show that your payment reduces the payroll tax liability account balances, use the Split Transaction Window to record transfers to the liability accounts in the amount shown in Table 15.3. Figure 15.11 shows the Split Transaction Window that records this federal tax deposit.

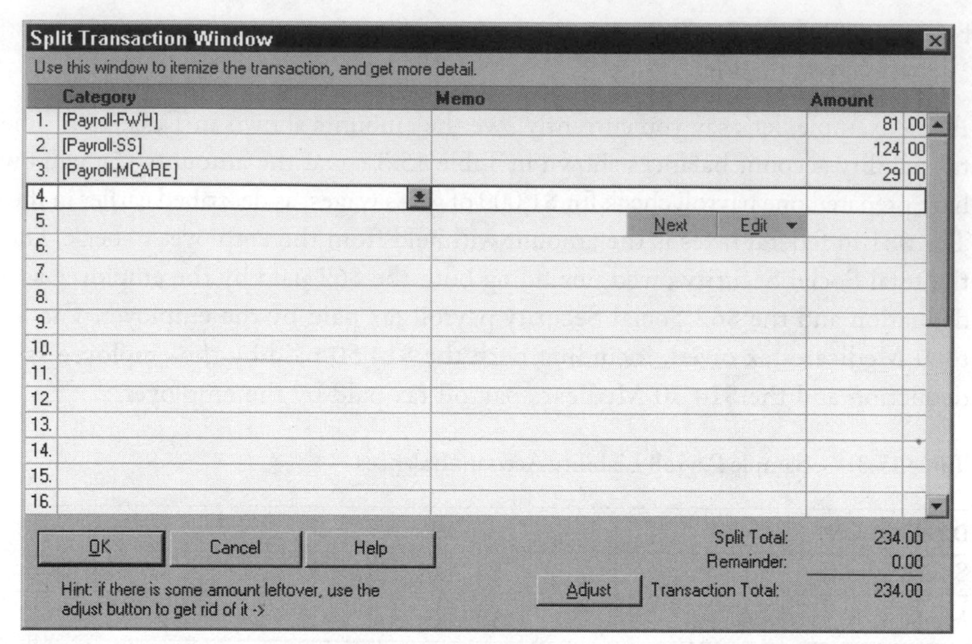

Figure 15.11: The Split Transaction Window that records a federal tax deposit.

NOTE *When you make a federal tax deposit, you use the depository's name for the payee.*

Preparing Payroll Tax Returns

To get the payroll information you need to fill out a payroll tax return, produce the Business Payroll report by choosing Reports ➢ Business ➢ Payroll. Figure 15.12 shows an example of the Payroll report. (For more information about how to produce and customize Quicken's reports, see Chapter 4.)

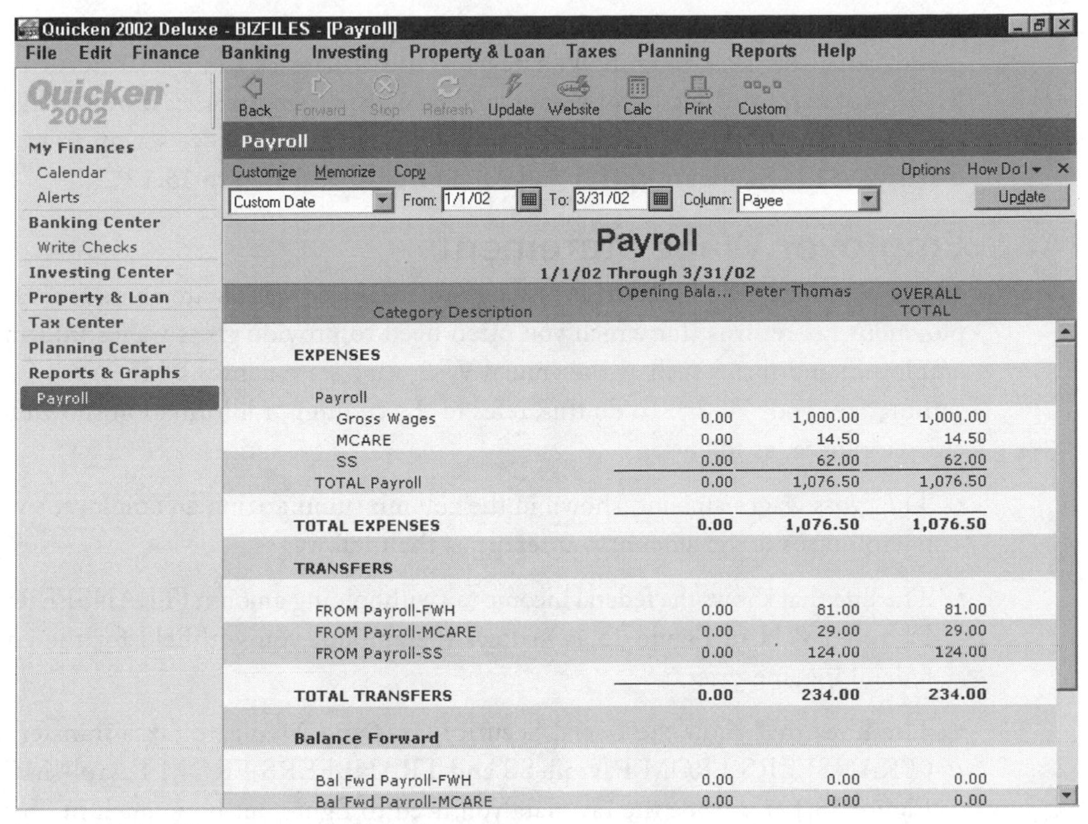

Figure 15.12: First page of the Payroll report.

Quarterly and Federal Payroll Tax Returns

Most, and maybe all, of the quarterly and federal payroll tax returns you file will simply ask for the total gross wages you've paid for the quarter or for the year. In Figure 15.12, you get this number from the Wages (for gross wages) row in the Overall Total column. (This is $1,000 in Figure 15.12, and it includes only the $1,000 paid to one employee.) The trick to getting a quarterly or annual gross wages total is using the appropriate Report From and To date ranges.

You can tell the total federal income taxes you've withheld by looking at the TRANSFERS FROM Payroll-FWH row in the Overall Total column. (It is $81 in Figure 15.12.)

Most of the other numbers you fill in on a quarterly or an annual report for items like Social Security taxes, Medicare, and unemployment taxes are calculated by multiplying the tax rate by the gross wages total. For example, if you fill out the quarterly 941 form (which you use to show Social Security and Medicare taxes for business employees), you multiply the gross wages total by 12.4 percent to calculate the total Social Security taxes owed, and you multiply the gross wages total by 2.9 percent to calculate the total Medicare taxes owed.

You'll probably get a rounding error of a few pennies, but you can double-check your calculations—at least roughly. Whatever you calculate as the Social Security tax and Medicare tax for the quarter or year should be within a few pennies of the TRANSFERS FROM amounts shown for the payroll liability accounts you've set up to track Social Security ($124 in Figure 15.12) and Medicare ($29 in Figure 15.12).

Employer Wage Statements

You also use the Payroll report for filling out employee wage statements for state unemployment tax returns (for which you often need to provide gross wages information by employee) and forms such as the annual W-2 wage statements and the W-3 (which just summarizes your W-2s). To do this, refer to the column of information shown for a specific employee, as follows:

- The gross wages amount shown in the column summarizing an employee's wages and payroll taxes is the amount you report as the total wages.
- The line that shows the federal income tax withholding amount (TRANSFERS FROM Payroll-FWH in Figure 15.12) shows the amount you withheld for the employee's federal income taxes.
- The lines that show the Social Security taxes and Medicare taxes transfer amounts (TRANSFERS FROM Payroll-SS and TRANSFERS FROM Payroll-MCARE in Figure 15.12) provide the raw data you need to figure out how much in Social Security and Medicare taxes to withhold from an employee's gross wages. Simply take one-half of these amounts.

NOTE *Both the employer and employee pay equal amounts for Social Security and Medicare taxes, so one-half of the total Social Security taxes and one-half of the Medicare taxes equal the amount withheld from the employee's payroll check.*

Saving Payroll Tax Deposit Money

You may want to set aside the payroll tax money you owe and the amounts you deduct from employee wages. You can do this by using another bank account or a savings goal account. Which type of account you use depends on the way you actually save, or set aside, the money.

If you will save the money in another bank account, such as a savings account, just set up another bank account in Quicken. Then, when you deposit money into this other account, you record an account transfer transaction (see Chapter 2).

If you won't save money in another bank account but want to show that some of the money you have in, say, your checking account is really payroll tax deposit money, set up a savings goal account (see Chapter 14). Then, whenever you want to set aside money for the payroll tax deposits, you transfer the money to this savings goal account in the same way that you record any transfer. Quicken then records the decrease in your bank account and the increase in your savings goal account, so your account records show the bank account balance minus the payroll tax deposit money. The savings goal account will show the payroll tax deposit money you've accumulated.

There is one big difference about using a savings goal account: Account transfers to and from a savings goal account don't show up as real transactions during a reconciliation, nor do they show up as account transfers on Quicken reports. For purposes of reconciling and reporting, Quicken just ignores any transfers to a savings goal account.

How to Handle Federal and State Payroll Paperwork

Few things are as exciting—or as scary—as hiring your first employee. Whether you're a small business that is doubling its work force (from one employee to two employees!) or a busy professional hiring your first household employee, it's a big step to suddenly assume the responsibility of regularly meeting a payroll.

Unfortunately, in addition to all the other issues that you now need to address—whether you can afford new employees, picking the best person for a job, and so on—you also have mounds of new paperwork to deal with.

I can't describe all this new paperwork, but I can give you an overview of what you need to collect and prepare for the federal and state governments. If you have questions about all this, I suggest you confer with an accountant or a bookkeeper who specializes in helping small businesses prepare their payroll and payroll tax returns.

When You Become an Employer...

As an employer, you need to do the following:

- Request and receive a Federal Tax Identification number from the IRS. To do this, fill out IRS form SS-4 (call the IRS to request one or visit the IRS web site at *www.irs.gov* to download one) and return it to the IRS. The IRS will send you a Federal Tax Identification number.

NOTE *You can also receive a Federal Tax Identification number over the telephone. Just tell the IRS agent how you filled out the SS-4 form, and he or she will enter it into the IRS computer and give you the number. You still need to send or fax in the SS-4 form, however.*

- Obtain a copy of the *Employer's Tax Guide,* commonly referred to as a Circular E, from the IRS. This pamphlet tells you how much federal income tax you need to withhold from a person's check and what Social Security and Medicare taxes you and the employee pay. (As noted earlier, you can download this document from the IRS web site.)
- If your state requires it, get an employer identification number from your state for filing state payroll tax returns, such as unemployment taxes, workers' compensation, and so on.
- If you intend to withhold state income taxes, obtain your state's equivalent of Circular E. It tells how much state income tax to withhold from an employee's payroll check.
- Obtain federal and perhaps state tax deposit coupons so that you can remit federal and state tax deposits to the IRS and the equivalent state revenue agency. (Ask for these if you don't get them automatically.)
- At the end of the first quarter during which you employ people, obtain the appropriate federal and state quarterly payroll tax return forms. For federal payroll taxes, businesses should use the 941 form. You also probably need to file equivalent state quarterly payroll tax returns.
- At the end of the year, obtain the appropriate federal and state annual payroll tax returns. For federal unemployment tax returns, for example, you need the 940 or the 940EZ form, and again, you probably need the equivalent state form for annual payroll tax returns.

When You Hire a New Employee...

Whenever you hire a new employee, the employee must fill out a W-4 form. This form provides you with the employee's Social Security number, filing status, and personal exemptions. You need both the filing status and the personal exemptions to determine the amount of federal income taxes to withhold, and you need the employee's Social Security number so you can prepare a year-end W-2 statement.

You will very likely have other requirements, which are not related to income taxes, to meet. For example, you may need to verify to the Immigration and Naturalization Service (INS) that the person you're employing either is a U.S. citizen or has a valid work permit. Be sure to check for this type of requirement. The IRS's *Employer's Tax Guide* and the equivalent state information guide can supply most of the information you need.

Chapter 16

ACCOUNTS PAYABLE

In This Chapter

- Tracking accounts payable with Quicken
- Tracking accounts payable manually
- Understanding early payment discounts
- Tracking accounts payable using Quicken Home & Business

Accounts payable are the amounts you owe your vendors. Because Quicken is basically a checkbook-on-a-computer program, it doesn't provide the same tools for managing accounts payable that a full-featured accounting package provides. But you can still use Quicken to track the amounts you owe vendors. To use Quicken for tracking accounts payable, you simply need to know how to work with the Quicken register.

NOTE *Most of this chapter assumes that you'll track your accounts payable through the use of unprinted checks. This simple approach works with any version of Quicken 2002. However, Quicken 2002 Home & Business includes a slightly more sophisticated accounts payable tracking system, which some businesses will want to use. This more sophisticated approach lets you track expenses for which you later want to be reimbursed for from customers. Because some Quicken Home & Business users may want to use this more sophisticated approach, at the very end of the chapter, I also describe how to use Quicken Home & Business's special accounts payable and vendor tracking tools.*

Tracking Accounts Payable with Quicken

Tracking accounts payable with Quicken is easy. You simply enter payment transactions for the amounts you owe using the Write Checks window. You enter the check date as the date the payment is due. Then, whenever you want to see what you owe your vendors, you can produce an A/P by Vendor report

Figures 16.1 and 16.2 illustrate how accounts payable tracking works in Quicken. Figure 16.1 shows a Register window with several unprinted checks. Notice that Quicken identifies the unprinted check transactions as checks by putting Print in the Num field. Quicken assigns a number when you print the checks.

Date	Num	Payee/Category/Memo	Payment	Clr	Deposit	Balance
11/10/02	Print	James D. Hughes Legal	285 00			6,791 90
11/15/02	DEP	The Meteor Group --Split-- Invoice #123		R	1,200 00	7,991 90
11/15/02	DEP	Redmond Technology Press --Split--		R	975 00	8,966 90
11/15/02	TXFR		500 00	R		8,466 90
11/15/02	107	Warehouse Store --Split--	100 00	R		8,366 90
11/15/02	108	Redmond Technology Press --Split--		R	500 00	8,866 90
11/30/02		Service Charge Bank Charge	8 00	R		8,858 90
11/30/02		Contribution towards goal [New Delivery Truck]	1,000 00			7,858 90
12/1/02	Print	James D. Hughes Legal	285 00			7,573 90
12/4/02	Print	Beeson's Office Supplies Supplies, Bus	45 67			7,528 23
12/4/02	Print	Office Warehouse Computer	125 90			7,402 33

Current Balance: 2,783.75 Ending Balance: 7,402.33

Figure 16.1: The Quicken register with unprinted check transactions.

Figure 16.2 shows an A/P by Vendor report that summarizes the unprinted check information from Figure 16.1. To create this report, choose the Reports ➤ Business ➤ Accounts Payable command. (See Chapters 3 and 4 if you need help using the Write Checks window or producing a report.)

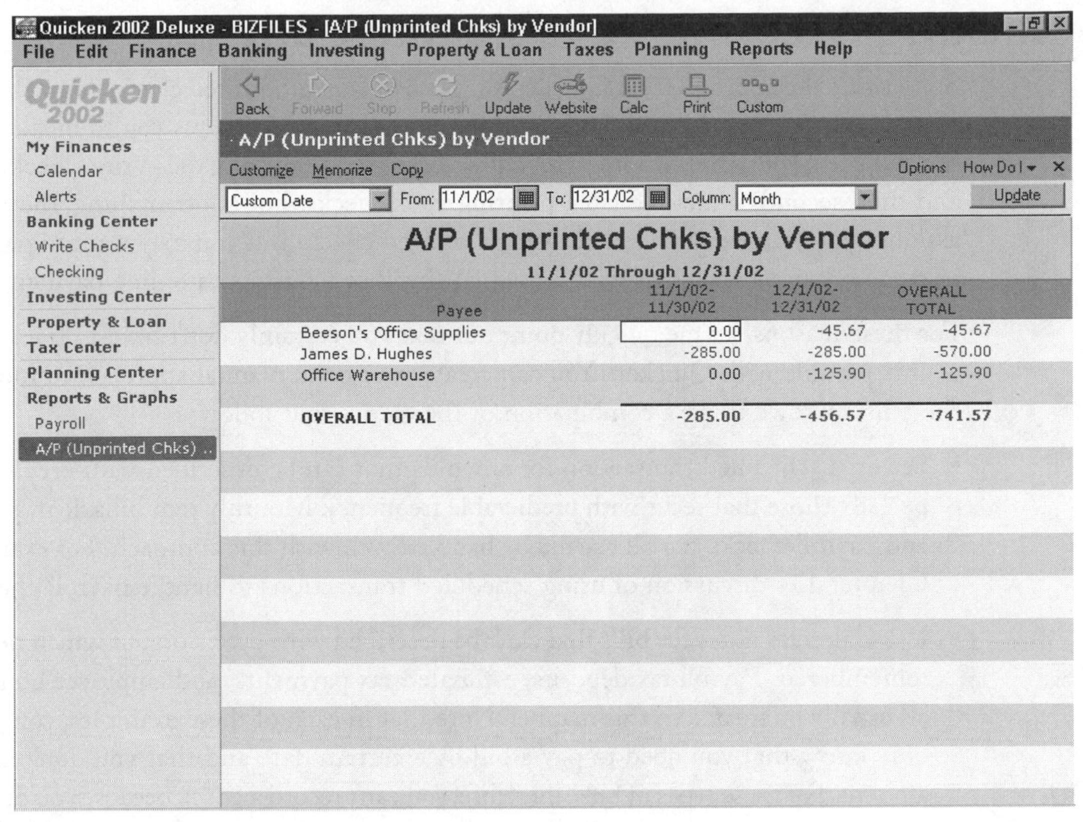

Figure 16.2: An A/P by Vendor report summarizing the unprinted check information from Figure 16.1.

If you use unprinted checks for tracking accounts payable, be sure to enter the same name for every transaction with a particular vendor. When you produce the A/P (Unprinted Checks) by Vendor report, it summarizes your unprinted check transactions by payee names. You can easily keep payee names consistent by using the QuickFill feature, which automatically completes the entry of a payee name it recognizes. (See Chapter 2 for a description of how QuickFill works.) Another good approach is to select the payee name from the Payee drop-down list box.

TIP *To display information about the unprinted checks that need to be paid, display the account register and choose the File ➢ Print Checks command.*

Tracking Accounts Payable Manually

Sometimes the approach that Quicken suggests—using unprinted checks to track accounts payable—isn't very practical. For one thing, the approach requires you to break the work of paying your bills into two steps: first describing your bills using the Write Checks window and then second, sometime later, printing your checks. For another thing, the approach assumes you want to pay the bills using a printed check. But you may want to pay the bill in some other way (such as with a manual check or by using an online payment).

For these reasons, let me quickly point out that you certainly don't have to track your accounts payable with Quicken. You can create your own, manual approach to monitoring the bills you owe using a combination of the tactics that follow:

- Set up a scheduled transaction for any bills that can be described with precision—especially those that recur with predictable frequency. Monthly rent bills, loan payments, and payroll checks can all usually be handled well with this approach. For example, see Chapter 15's discussion of using scheduled transactions to handle payroll checks.
- Use Calendar notes for bills that can't be described with precision but which need to be remembered. Payroll tax deposits, estimated tax payments, and employee bonuses can all usually be treated in this manner. Note that in each of these examples, you probably only know that you need to pay a bill by a certain date and that you don't know the amount. For these types of bills, therefore, you can't record a check because you don't know the amount.
- Set up an "unpaid bills" file folder and use it to hold the bills you need to pay in the next week or next month. Then, on a regular basis, review the bills in the file folder and pay those that are due—such as by printing a check with Quicken, by writing a manual check (which you'll of course later record into the Quicken register), or by making an online payment.

The whole point of tracking your unpaid bills is to make paying and monitoring your bills easy. You should not feel as if you must automate the process in order to be doing it right. The "right way" is just the method that gives you the control you need with the least amount of effort.

Understanding Early Payment Discounts

One related topic, early payment discounts, deserves brief mention here because it relates to successfully managing accounts payment. In a nutshell, some vendors offer to discount, or reduce, the amount you pay if you make the payment early.

The really important point to understand is that usually early payment discounts are too good to pass up. Suppose that a vendor bills you $100 but offers you a 2 percent discount if you'll pay within 10 days instead of the usual 30 days—usually referred to as "2/10 Net 30." So, you can pay $98 on, say, March 10, or $100 if you wait until March 30. In effect, the 2 percent (or $2) early payment discount is interest. And while this may not sound like much, charging a 2 percent interest rate for 20 days works out to an annual rate of more than 36 percent (because there are roughly eighteen 20-day periods in a year). Since there are usually cheaper ways to borrow money, it almost never makes sense to borrow money from your vendors by foregoing early payment discounts.

Table 16.1 shows the precise equivalent annual interest rates for early payment discounts allowed by paying a vendor 20 days early.

Table 16.1: Early Payment Discounts

EARLY PAYMENT DISCOUNT	EQUIVALENT ANNUAL INTEREST RATE
1%	18.43%
2%	37.24%
3%	56.44%
4%	76.04%
5%	96.05%

You can roughly calculate the equivalent interest rate a vendor offers in the form of an early discount by dividing the number of days in a year (365) by the number of days early the vendor wants you to pay. Then, take this number and multiply it by the early payment discount percentage.

TIP *If you must forego some early payment discounts because your business's cash flow requires stretching out your payments, look at the option of taking the discounts that work out to the highest equivalent interest rate. For example, skip the discounts that work out to an 18% or 37% annual interest rate and instead take the discounts that work out to a 76% or 96% annual interest rate.*

Tracking Accounts Payable Using Quicken Home & Business

If you're using Quicken Home & Business, you don't have to use the simple approach to tracking accounts payable described in the preceding paragraphs of this chapter. You can instead set up a more sophisticated and powerful accounts payable system. The big benefit of such a system is that you'll be able to track expenses for which you want to be reimbursed from customers.

NOTE *The accounts payable tools provided by Quicken Home & Business closely resemble the accounts receivable tools provided by Quicken Home & Business. If you learn how to use one set of tools, therefore, you know most of what you need to know in order to use the other set. Chapter 17 discusses and describes the Quicken Home & Business accounts receivable tools.*

Setting Up Your Vendors List

As a first step in setting up the Quicken Home & Business accounts payable system, you want to describe your vendors using Quicken's Address Book. To start the address book, choose Business ➢ Bills And Vendors ➢ Create Vendor. Quicken displays the Edit Address Book Record dialog box, as shown in Figure 16.3.

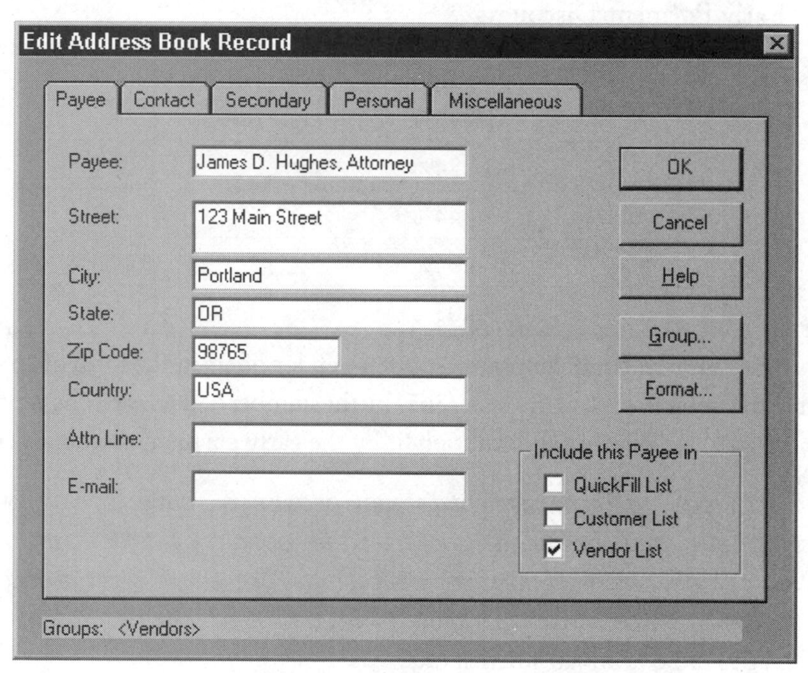

Figure 16.3: The Payee tab of the Edit Address Book Record dialog box.

To identify and describe a vendor, enter the vendor's name and address information into the Payee tab's text boxes. If necessary, mark the Vendor List checkbox. Optionally, you can use the other tabs of the Edit Address Book Record dialog box—Contact, Secondary, Personal, and Miscellaneous—to collect and store other information about the vendor. After you describe a vendor in the desired detail and click OK, Quicken displays the Address Book window, as shown in Figure 16.4.

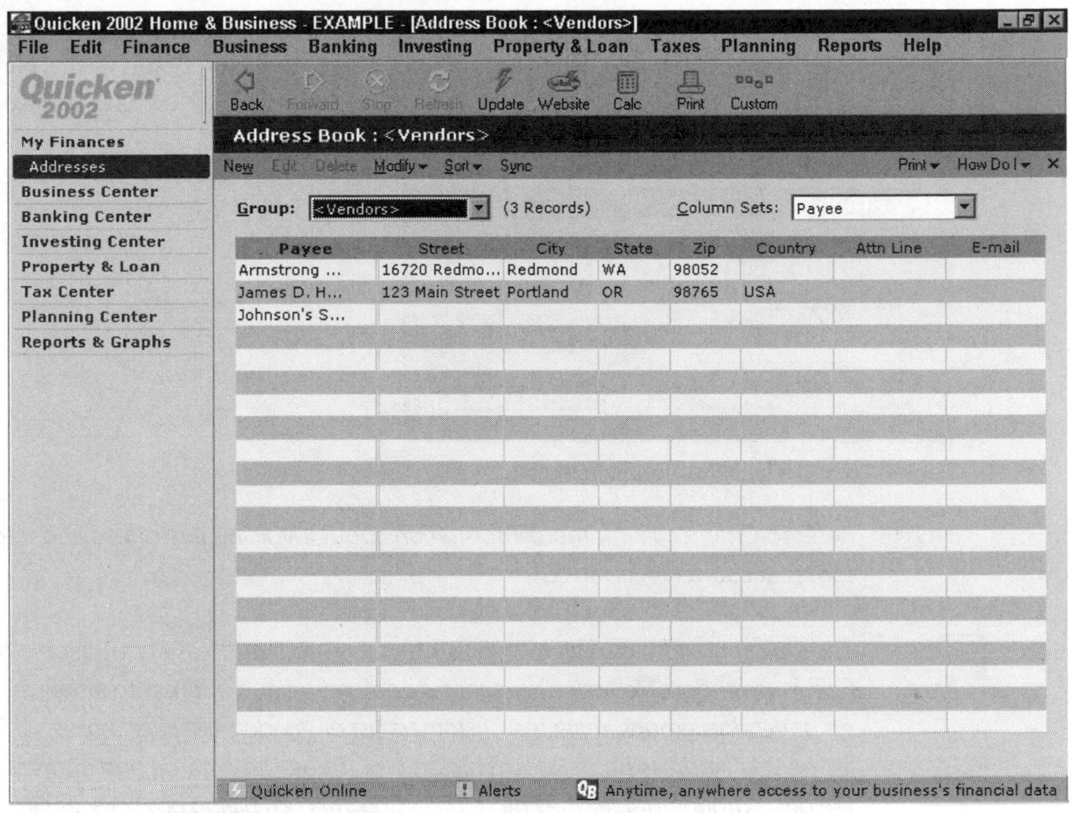

Figure 16.4: The Address Book window after adding information.

To see the name and address information you've collected on a vendor, just double-click his or her name in the Address Book list. If you've collected many names and addresses, you may need to scroll through the list to get to a person's or business's record.

TIP *You can use the Sort menu's commands to arrange and rearrange the names and addresses. For example, choose Sort ➢ By Organization to arrange your address book alphabetically by the entries in that field.*

You can edit an existing name and address by selecting the business or person in the list box, clicking Edit, and then using the Edit Address Book dialog box to make your changes. After you've made your changes, click OK. You can delete someone from the Address Book window by selecting the person's name and clicking Delete.

One important point to make is that Quicken assumes you will organize your address book information using groups. Vendors, for example, are a group. Customers, as you'll read more about in Chapter 17, are another group. But you can use the Address Book window to see other groups as well: friends, family, and so forth. To see the address book entries in a particular group, select the group from the Group drop-down text box. To create a group, choose the <New> entry from the Group box. When Quicken displays the New Group dialog box, shown in Figure 16.5, enter a group name into the New Group box and click OK.

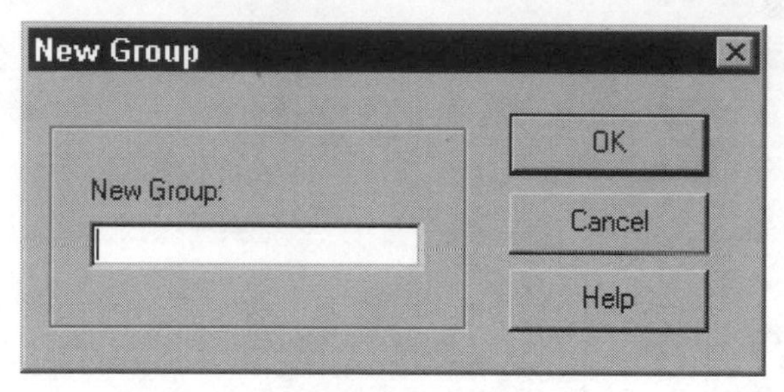

Figure 16.5: The New Group dialog box.

NOTE *Refer to Chapter 17 for more information about invoicing customers and tracking customer accounts receivable.*

TIP *The Quicken address book lets you store names and address about people other than just your vendors. To assign an address book name and address to either the Customers or Vendors groups, mark the Customers List or Vendors List checkboxes, which appear in the Edit Address Book Record dialog box. To assign a name and address to one of the other groups, display the Edit Address Book Record dialog box, click its Group button, and select the group from the dialog box that Quicken displays.*

Setting Up a Vendor Bills Account

To use Quicken to keep accounts payable records, you also need to set up a separate vendor bills account. You then use this account to keep a list of the amounts you owe vendors.

To create a vendor bills account, follow these steps:

1. Choose Business ➤ Business Accounts ➤ Account List.
2. Click New so that Quicken displays the Create New Account dialog box, as shown in Figure 16.6.

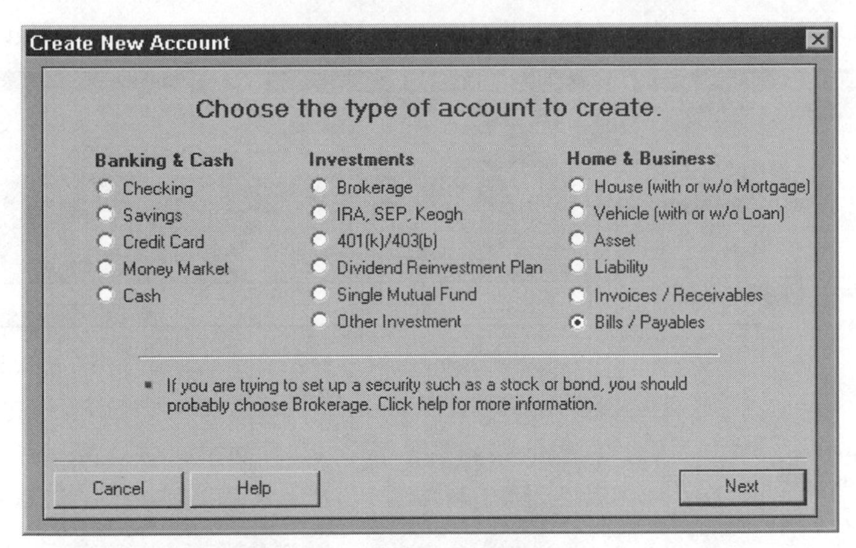

Figure 16.6: The Create New Account dialog box.

3. Mark the Bills / Payables option button, and then click Next. Quicken displays the Bill Account Setup dialog box, as shown in Figure 16.7

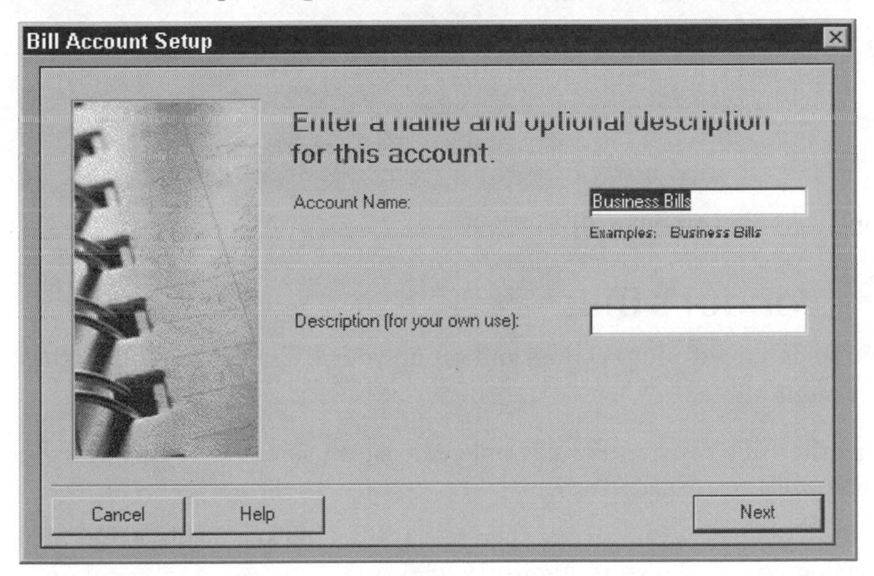

Figure 16.7: The Bill Account Setup dialog box.

4. Optionally, edit the default account name. Quicken suggests the name Business Bills, but you can change this to something that better fits your business or your requirements.
5. Enter a brief description of the new account in the Description text box.
6. Click Next. Quicken displays a message that says you've added the new bills/payables account.

7. Click Done. Quicken shows the Bills: Business Bills register, as shown in Figure 16.8.

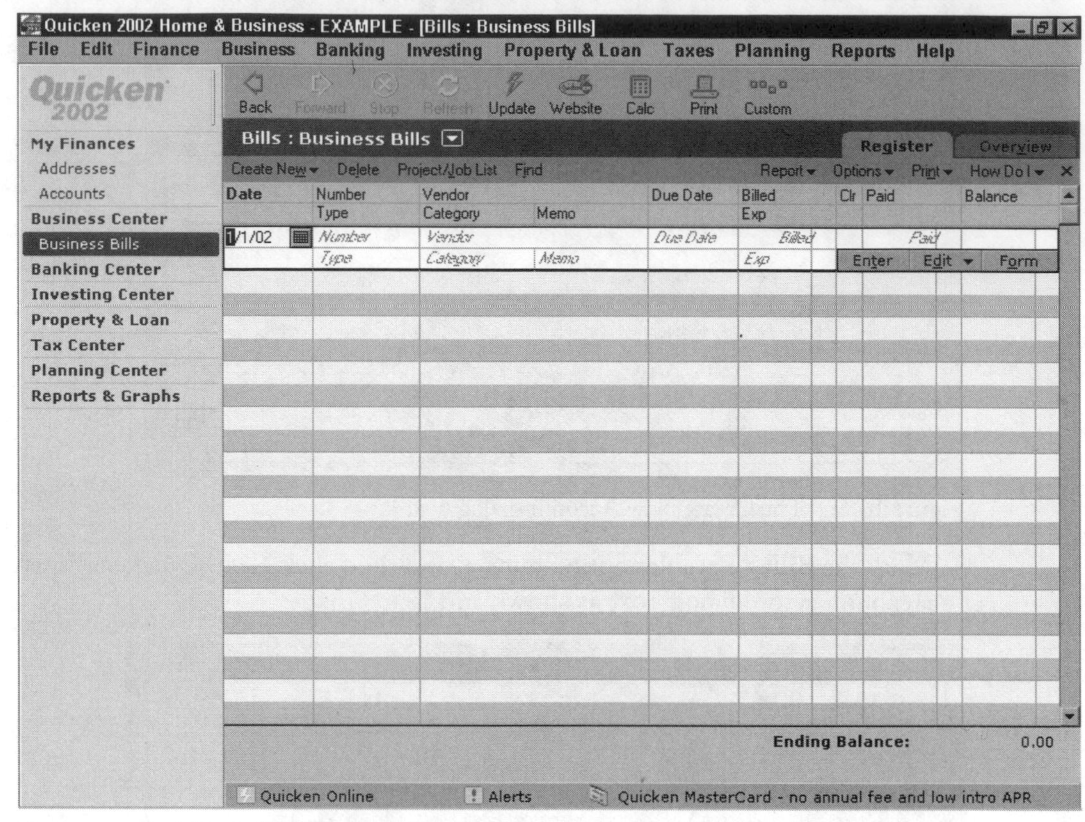

Figure 16.8: The Bills: Business Bills register.

Recording a Vendor's Bills

After you've described your vendors and set up your Bills register, follow these steps to record a vendor bill:

1. Display the Bills register. For example, choose Business ➢ Business Accounts ➢ Business Bills.
2. Click the Create New button and then select Bill. Quicken displays the Bill – Business Bills dialog box, as shown in Figure 16.9.

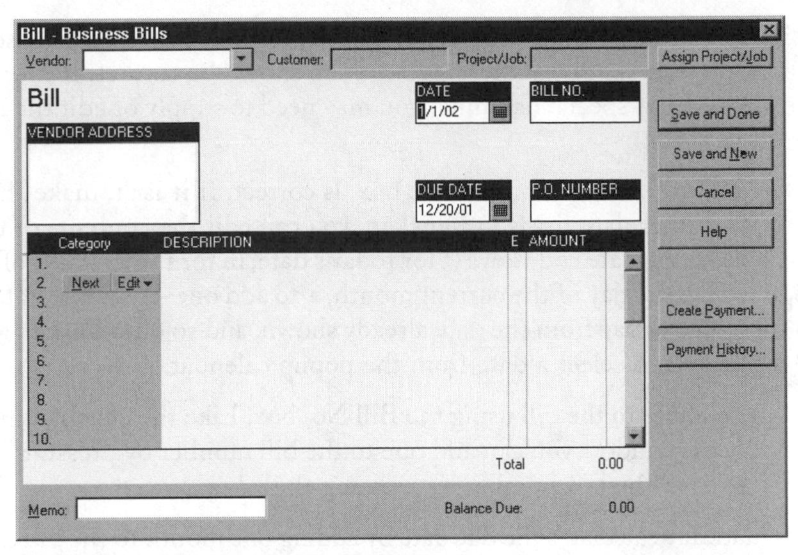

Figure 16.9: The Bill – Business Bills dialog box.

3. Select the vendor from the Vendor drop-down list box. If you don't see the vendor listed—perhaps because it's a new vendor—you can also enter the vendor's name into the Vendor box. Quicken automatically adds the vendor to your address book when you do this, but the information will be incomplete.

4. Optionally, click the Assign Project/Job button. When Quicken displays the Select Project/Job dialog box, as shown in Figure 16.10, select the project or job to which the bill should be assigned. Or, to set up a new project or job, click the New button and use the New Project/Job dialog box to name and describe the job.

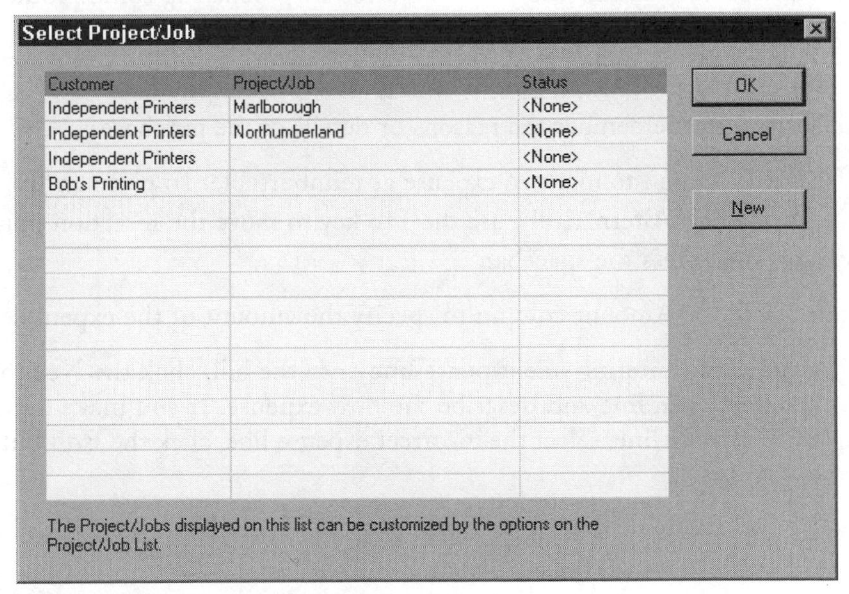

Figure 16.10: The Select Project/Job dialog box.

5. Verify and, if necessary, correct the address. If you've previously and correctly set up the vendor in the address book, this address information should be correct. If the vendor is new or the order requires special handling, you may need to supply or edit the information in the Address box.
6. Verify that the bill date, shown in the Date box, is correct. If it isn't, make the necessary changes. Like other date fields in Quicken, you can edit the contents of the Date box directly by using the date code keys (t for today's date, m for the first day of the current month, h for the last day of the current month, + to add one day to the date already shown, - to subtract one day from the date already shown, and so on). You can also click the Calendar button and select a date from the popup calendar.
7. Assign a unique number to the bill using the Bill No. box. Like the check number field on the Write Checks window you can add one to the bill number by pressing the + key and subtract one from the bill number by pressing the - key.
8. Quicken automatically calculates the due date by adding one month to the bill date. This due date may be incorrect, however, if you've agreed to some other payment terms with the vendor. Accordingly, verify and, if necessary, edit the due date shown in the Due Date box.
9. If you issued a purchase order for the item or service, enter this number into the P.O. Number box.
10. Record each expense category for which you're being billed by entering the following pieces of information:
    - **Category** Use the Category column to identify which expense category you want to use for tracking the expense you've incurred by purchasing some product or service from the vendor.
    - **Description** Use the Description column to describe the product or service in more detail so you later remember the reasons or details of the purchase.
    - **E** Use the E column to mark an expense as reimbursable. To place an "E" in the E box, click the box. Alternatively, use the Tab key to move the insertion point to the E box and then press the spacebar.
    - **Amount** Use the Amount column to specify the amount of the expense.

    When you finishing entering one expense line onto the bill, click the Next button to move to the next open line and describe the next expense. If you make a mistake in entering a bill expense line, select the incorrect expense line, click the Edit button, and make your changes.
11. Optionally, enter some further description into the Memo box.

12. To record paying a bill you're entering, click the Create Payment button. Quicken records the bill and then displays the Payment dialog box, as shown in Figure 16.11. To pay the bill, use the Withdraw From box to select the bank account on which you want to write the check, the Amount box to specify how much you want to pay on the bill, and the Check Number box to specify the number of the check you're using to pay the bill. Note that these are all the same fields you would fill out if you used the Register window or the Write Checks window to record a check or prepare to print a check.

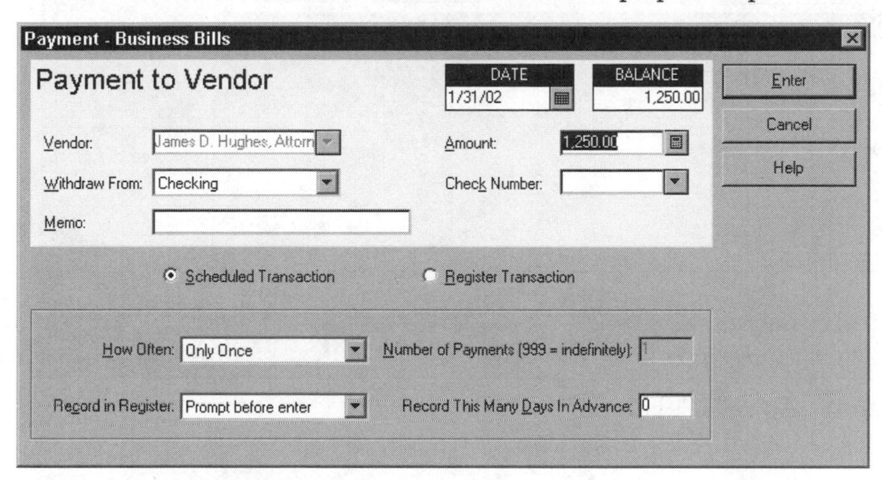

Figure 16.11: The Payment dialog box.

NOTE *The buttons and boxes at the bottom of the Payment dialog box let you set up a scheduled transaction for the bill. To set up a scheduled transaction, mark the Scheduled Transaction option button. Use the How Often box to indicate how frequently you want to schedule paying this bill and the Number Of Payments box to indicate the number of times you'll pay the bill. Use the Record In Register box to specify whether Quicken should automatically record the payment or just prompt you to record the payment. Use the Record This Many Days In Advance box to specify how far in advance the bill should be recorded.*

TIP *You can click the Payment History button, which appears on the Bill – Business Bills dialog box, to see a list of the payments you've made on a bill.*

13. If you didn't record payment of the bill as you were entering the bill in step 12, you must save your bill. If you're recording only one bill, click the Save And Done button to save the bill and close the Bill – Business Bills dialog box. If you're recording several bills, click the Save And New button to save the bill but leave the Bill – Business Bills dialog box open. Figure 16.12 shows an example bill.

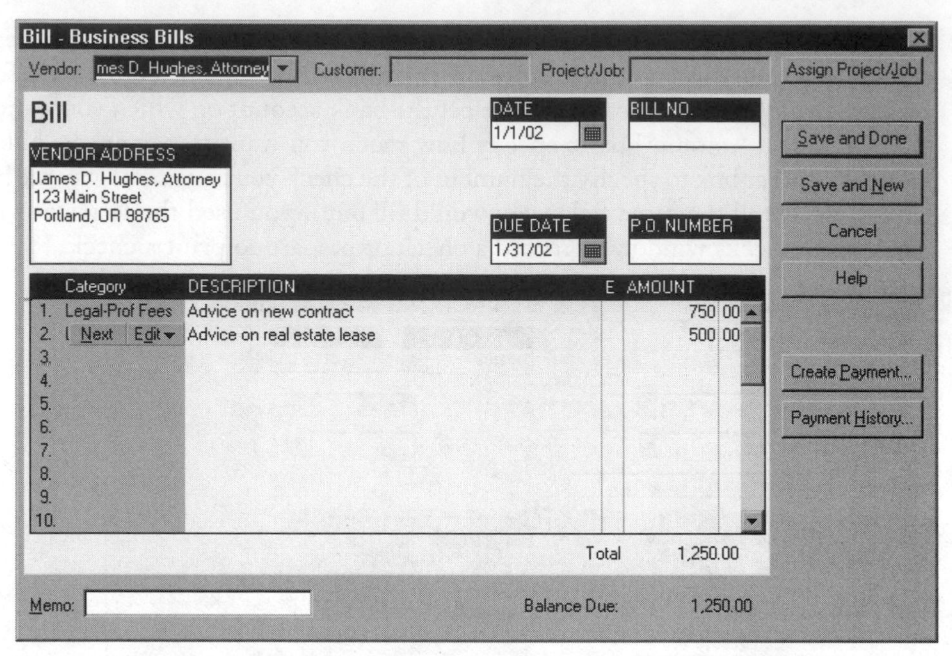

Figure 16.12: An example bill.

Recording Payments to Vendors

As noted in the preceding discussion of recording a vendor's bills, you can record a payment at the time you record the payment. More typically, however, you'll record the bill from a vendor at one time and then make and record the payment at some other time.

When you want to make and record a payment for a vendor bill you've already recorded, follow these steps:

1. Display the bills register. For example, choose Business ➢ Business Accounts ➢ Business Bills.
2. Click the Create New button and then select Payment To Vendor. Quicken displays the Payment – Business Bills dialog box, as shown in Figure 16.13.

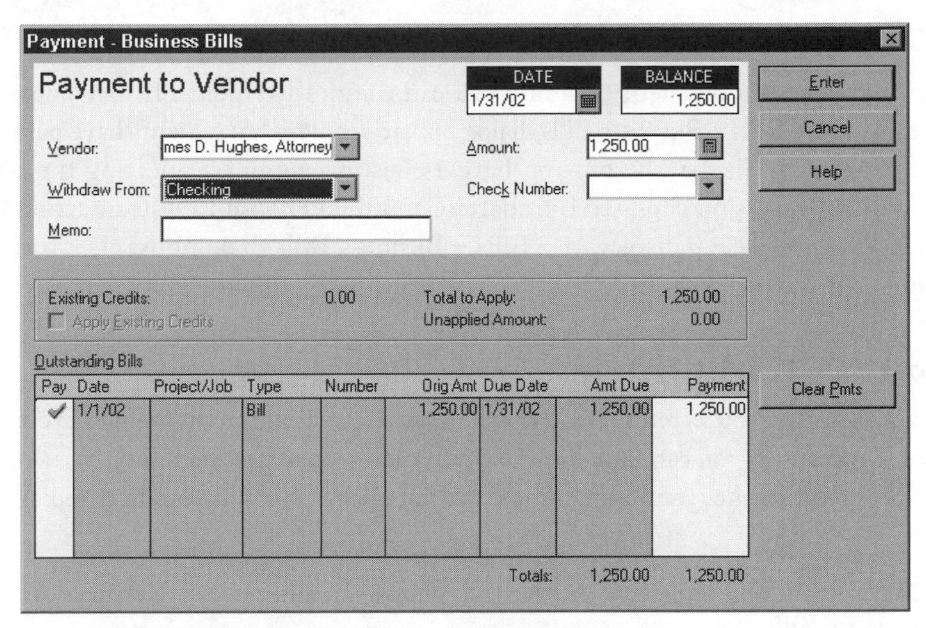

Figure 16.13: The Payment – Business Bills dialog box.

TIP *You can also display the Payment – Business Bills dialog box from the Bills – Business Bills dialog box. Simply click the Create Payment button.*

3. Enter the payment date into the Date box.
4. Select the vendor from the Vendor drop-down list box.
5. Enter the payment amount into the Amount box.
6. Identify the bank account from which you'll make the payment using the Withdraw From box.
7. Record your check number into the Check Number box.
8. Optionally, use the Memo box to collect some bit of information you want to record but which isn't stored in some other box.
9. If, as part of recording the payment, you want to apply a credit memo, mark the Apply Existing Credits checkbox. Quicken applies the outstanding credit memos to the oldest bills. For more information on credit memos, refer to the next chapter section, "Issuing a Credit Memo."
10. Select the vendor bills that you want to pay by clicking. If the payment pays the entire bill, selecting the bill is all you need to do. Quicken assumes that the entire bill amount is paid. If the payment pays only a portion of the bill, however, change the amount shown in the Payment column of the Outstanding Bills list to that portion of the payment that should be applied to the bill.

11. Click Enter to record the payment.

After you record a payment on a bill, you can use the Payment History button, which appears on the Bills – Business Bills dialog box, to see which payments have paid the bills. To do this, first display the bill you have a question about by selecting the bill in the Business Bills register, click the Edit button, and then choose Edit Transaction from the menu. When Quicken displays the Bills – Business Bills dialog box, click the Payment History button.

Issuing a Credit Memo

If a vendor issues you a credit memo, you'll need to record the credit memo in your accounts payable records so you can later use the credit memo to offset the bill or bills you owe. To record a credit memo, you follow almost the same set of steps as you do to record a vendor bill:

1. Display the bills register. For example, choose Business ➤ Business Accounts ➤ Business Bills.
2. Click the Create New button and then select Credit. Quicken displays the Credit – Business Bills dialog box, as shown in Figure 16.14.

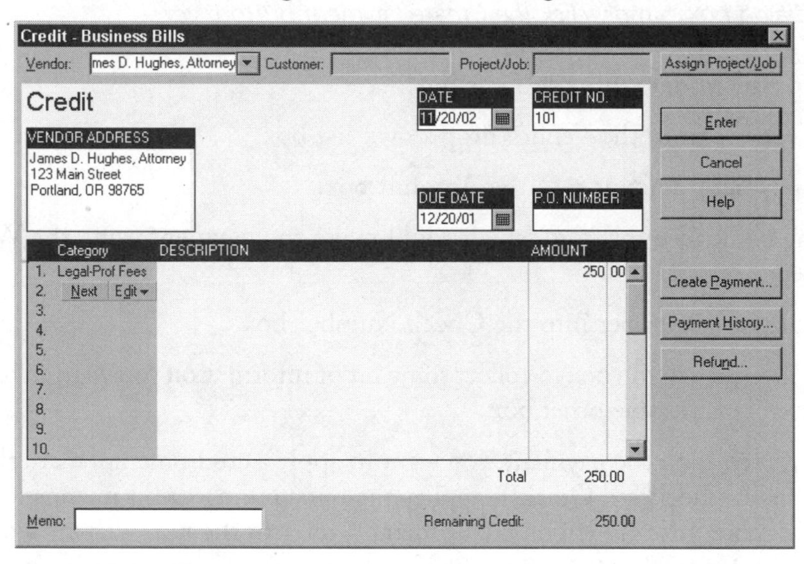

Figure 16.14: The Credit – Business Bills dialog box.

3. Select the vendor from the Vendor drop-down list box.
4. Optionally, click the Assign Project/Job button. When Quicken displays the Select Project/Job dialog box, select the project or job to which the bill should be assigned.
5. Verify and, if necessary, correct the information shown in the Vendor Address box.

6. Verify that the credit memo date, shown in the Date box, is correct. If it isn't, make the necessary changes.
7. Assign a unique number to the credit memo using the Credit No. box.
8. If you issued the vendor a purchase order for the bill related to this credit memo, enter this number into the P.O. Number box.
9. Record each expense line you want to include on the credit memo by entering the following pieces of information:

   - **Category** Use the Category column to identify which expense category you used on the original bill.
   - **Description** Use the Description column to describe the product or service in more detail if necessary.
   - **Amount** Use the Amount column to specify the original amount of the expense.

   When you finish entering one expense line onto the credit memo, click the Next button to move to the next open line and describe the next expense category. If you make a mistake in entering a bill expense line, select the incorrect line, click the Edit button, and make your changes.
10. Optionally, enter any additional information you want to collect about the credit memo into the Memo box.
11. Save your credit memo by clicking either the Save And Done button or the Save And New button.

Issuing Vendor Refunds

Vendors may pay you a refund as part of issuing a credit memo. To record a refund, display the Business Bills register, click the Create New button, and choose Refund. When Quicken displays the Refund – Business Bills dialog box, as shown in Figure 16.15, describe the refund using the text boxes. You need to identify the bank account into which the refund check is deposited, the vendor, check date, project/job (if applicable), amount, and the check number. After you enter this information, click Enter.

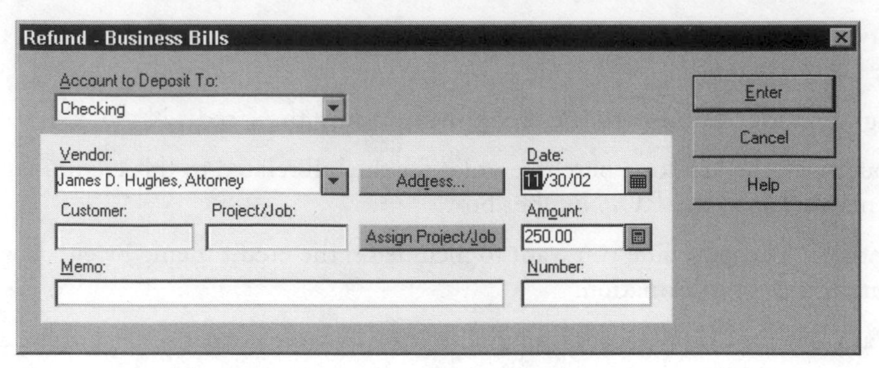

Figure 16.15: The Refund – Business Bills dialog box.

TIP *You can also get to the Refund – Business Bills dialog box directly from the Credit – Business Bills dialog box, which is the dialog box you use to record a credit memo. Just click the Refund button.*

Reviewing Your Accounts Receivable

Quicken Home & Business supplies two useful ways to review your accounts payable information. To see a list of the unpaid vendor bills, credit memos, and any payments, view the Bills register. You can do this by choosing Business ➢ Business Accounts ➢ Business Bills. Figure 16.8, which appears earlier in the chapter, shows an example Business Bills register.

As with other versions of Quicken and as discussed earlier in the chapter, you can also prepare a Quicken report that summarizes accounts payable information. To see such a report, choose Reports ➢ Business ➢ Accounts Payable. Figure 16.2, shown earlier in the chapter, shows an example A/P by Vendor report.

Chapter 17

INVOICING CUSTOMERS AND ACCOUNTS RECEIVABLE

In This Chapter

- Identifying your customers
- Setting up an invoices account and your invoice items
- Invoicing a customer
- Preparing customer estimates
- Preparing and printing customer statements
- Recording customer payments
- Issuing credit memos and refunds
- Delivering invoices and credit memos
- Assessing finance charges
- Reviewing your accounts receivable

One of the most basic business accounting tasks is billing your customers and accepting their payments. You can use Quicken to automate this work as long as you have the Home & Business version of Quicken.

NOTE *If you don't have the Home & Business version, you need to prepare your invoices manually using, for example, your word processor or a spreadsheet. For very low volumes of invoices, such an approach is fine. Review the examples of Quicken invoices in this chapter, however, to see how your invoices should look. If you do use a manual approach, you'll record customer payment directly into the bank account register when you receive them. You'll also need to manually monitor your customer's unpaid invoices—such as by using a file folder.*

Identifying Your Customers

Both Quicken Deluxe and Quicken Home & Business come with an address book you can use to maintain a database of names, addresses, and telephone numbers. While the using the address book is optional for Quicken Deluxe users, Quicken Home & Business users need to use the address book because that's where Quicken stores customer information.

Describing Customers in the Address Book

As a first step in invoicing customers and tracking receivables, accordingly, you want to describe your customers using Quicken's address book. To start the address book, choose Business ➢ Customers ➢ Create Customer. Quicken displays the Edit Address Book Record dialog box, as shown in Figure 17.1.

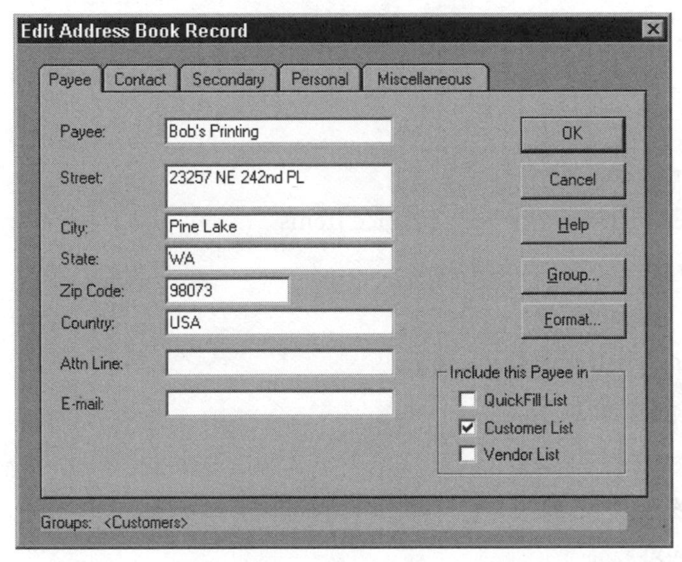

Figure 17.1: The Payee tab of the Edit Address Book Record dialog box.

To identify and describe a customer, enter the customer's name and address information into the Payee tab's text boxes. Then, mark the Customer List check box. Optionally, you can use the other tabs of the Edit Address Book Record dialog box—Contact, Secondary, Personal, and Miscellaneous—to collect and store other information about the customer. After you describe a customer in the desired detail and click OK, Quicken displays the Address Book window, as shown in Figure 17.2.

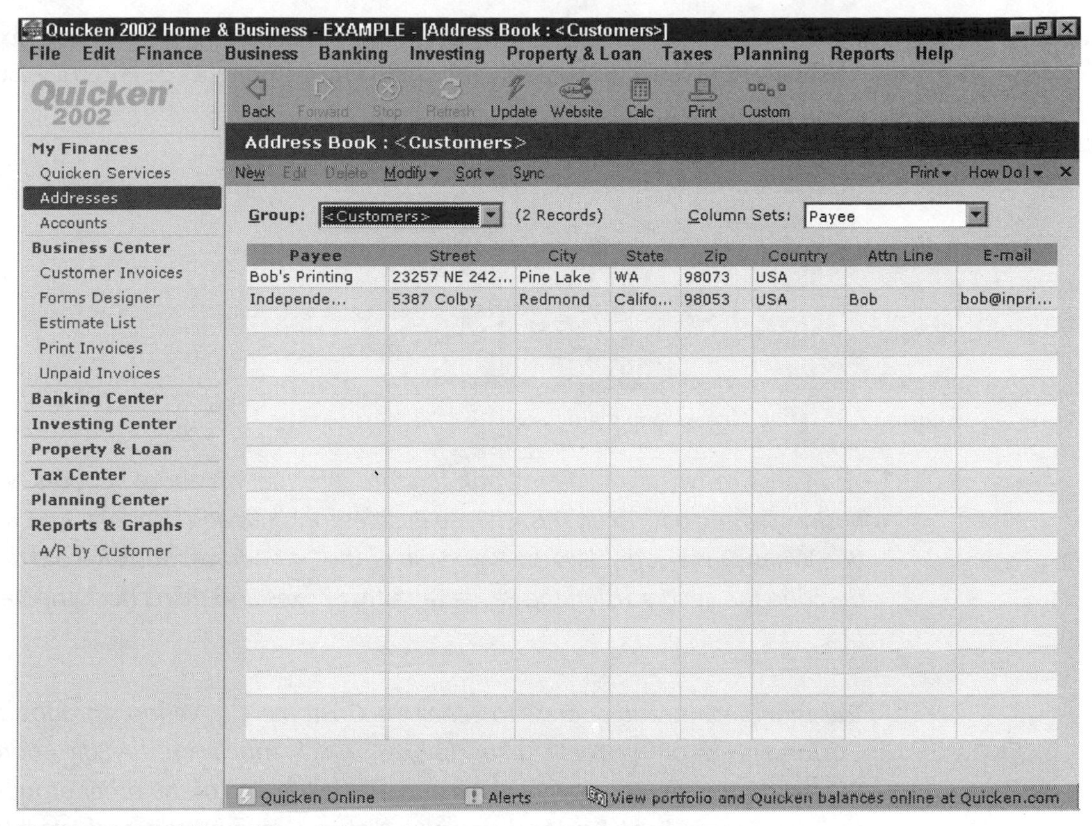

Figure 17.2: The Address Book window after adding information.

To see the name and address information you've collected on a customer, just double-click his or her name in the list. If you've collected many names and addresses, you may need to scroll through the list to get to a person's record.

TIP *You can use the Sort menu's commands to arrange and rearrange the names and addresses. For example, choose Sort ➢ By Organization to arrange your address book alphabetically by the entries in that field.*

You can edit an existing name and address by selecting the person in the list box, clicking Edit, and then using the Edit Address Book Record's dialog box's text boxes to make your changes. After you've made your changes, click Record. You can delete someone from the Address Book window by selecting the person's name and clicking Delete.

One important point to make is that Quicken assumes you will organize your address book information using groups. Customers, for example, are a group. But you can use the Address Book window to see other groups as well: friends, family, vendors, and so forth. To see the address book entries in a particular group, select the group from the Group box. To create a group, choose the <New> entry from the Group drop-down text box. When Quicken displays the New Group dialog box, shown in Figure 17.3, enter a group name into the New Group box and click OK.

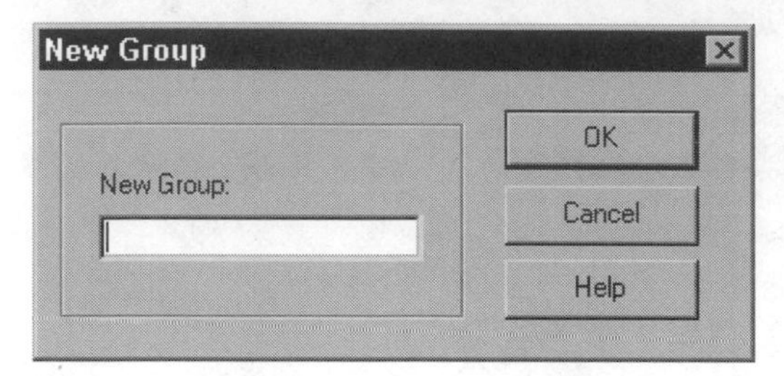

Figure 17.3: The New Group dialog box.

NOTE *You can also use the address book to store information about vendors, which are businesses you pay. To do this, choose Business ➤ Bills and Vendors ➤ Create Vendor. When Quicken displays the Payee tab of the Edit Address Book Record dialog box, describe the vendor using the Payee tab's text boxes and then check the Vendor List box.*

TIP *To assign a name and address to either the Customers or Vendors groups, mark the Customers List or Vendors List checkboxes, which appear on the Edit Address Book Record dialog box. To assign a name and address to one of the other groups, display the Edit Address Book Record dialog box, click its Group button, and select the group from the dialog box that Quicken displays.*

Printing Address Book Information

You can print the names and addresses in your list after you've sorted them or grouped them. To print names and addresses, follow these steps:

1. Select the address book entries that you want to print. You can do this by choosing the group you want from the Group box and then choosing Modify ➤ Select All. If you want to print only a subset of the address book entries in a group, you can individually select those entries by clicking them.
2. Click the Print button and choose one of the commands that Quicken displays: List (to print a list of the address book entries), Labels (to print mailing labels for the address book entries), and Envelopes (to print envelopes for the selected address book entries).
3. When Quicken displays the Print dialog box, use it to describe how you want the address book entries printed. If you're printing on labels or envelopes, you need to tell Quicken what type of label or envelope you're using. Figure 17.4 shows the Print Labels dialog box.

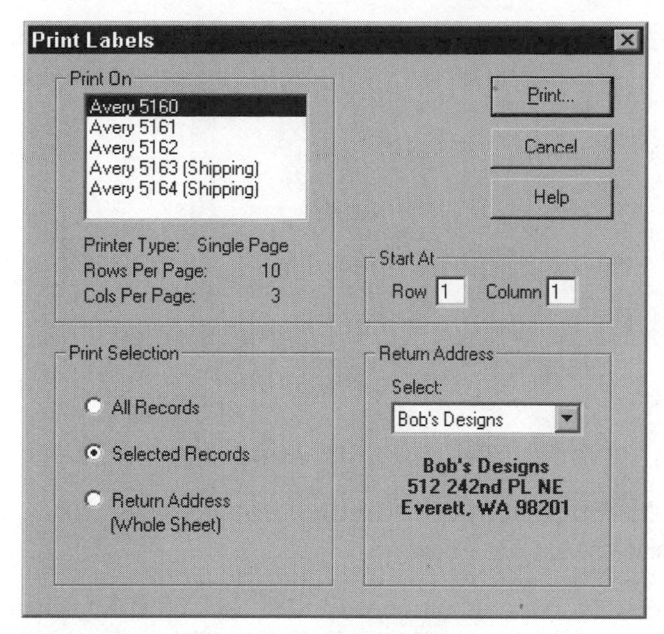

Figure 17.4: The Print Labels dialog box.

4. If needed, feed the labels or envelopes into your printer and then click Print.

Setting Up an Invoices Account

To use Quicken to keep accounts receivable records, you first need to set up a separate invoices account. You then use this account to keep a list of the amounts customers or clients owe and pay.

To create an invoices account, follow these steps:

1. Choose Business ➢ Business Accounts ➢ Account List.
2. Click New so that Quicken displays the Create New Account dialog box, as shown in Figure 17.5.

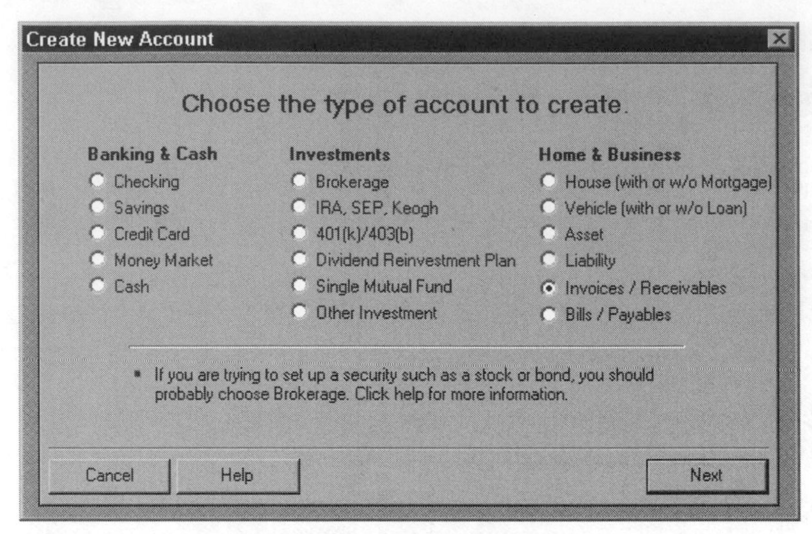

Figure 17.5: The Create New Account dialog box.

3. Mark the Invoices / Receivables option button, and then click Next. Quicken displays the Invoice Account Setup dialog box, as shown in Figure 17.6

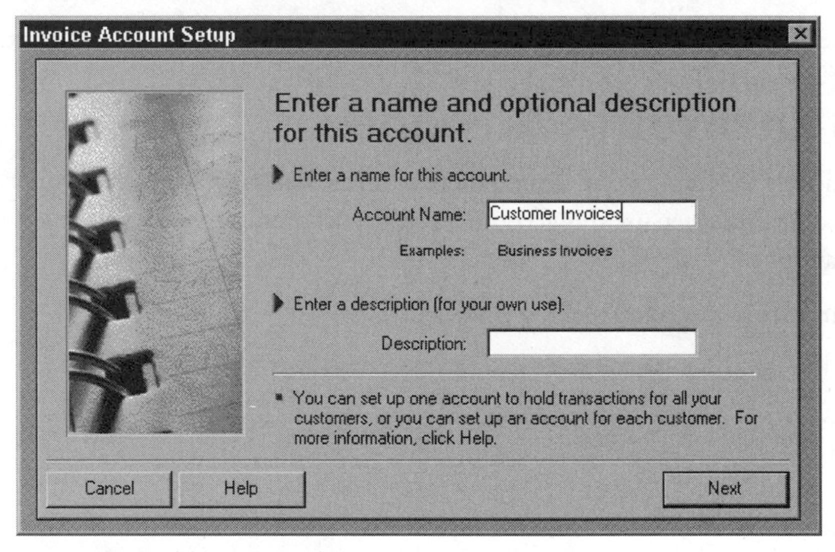

Figure 17.6: The Invoice Account Setup dialog box.

4. Optionally, edit the default invoices accounts name. Quicken suggests the name Customer Invoices, but you can change this to something that better fits your business or your requirements.
5. Enter a brief description of the new account in the Description text box.
6. Click Next. Quicken displays a message that says you've added the new invoices setup dialog box.

7. Click Done. Quicken displays the Introduction To Invoices dialog box, which describes how Quicken's invoicing works. You can read this message if you like, but I'll provide all of the same information (and more) in the paragraphs that follow.
8. When you finish with the Introduction To Invoices dialog box, click Done. Quicken shows the Invoices register, as shown in Figure 17.7.

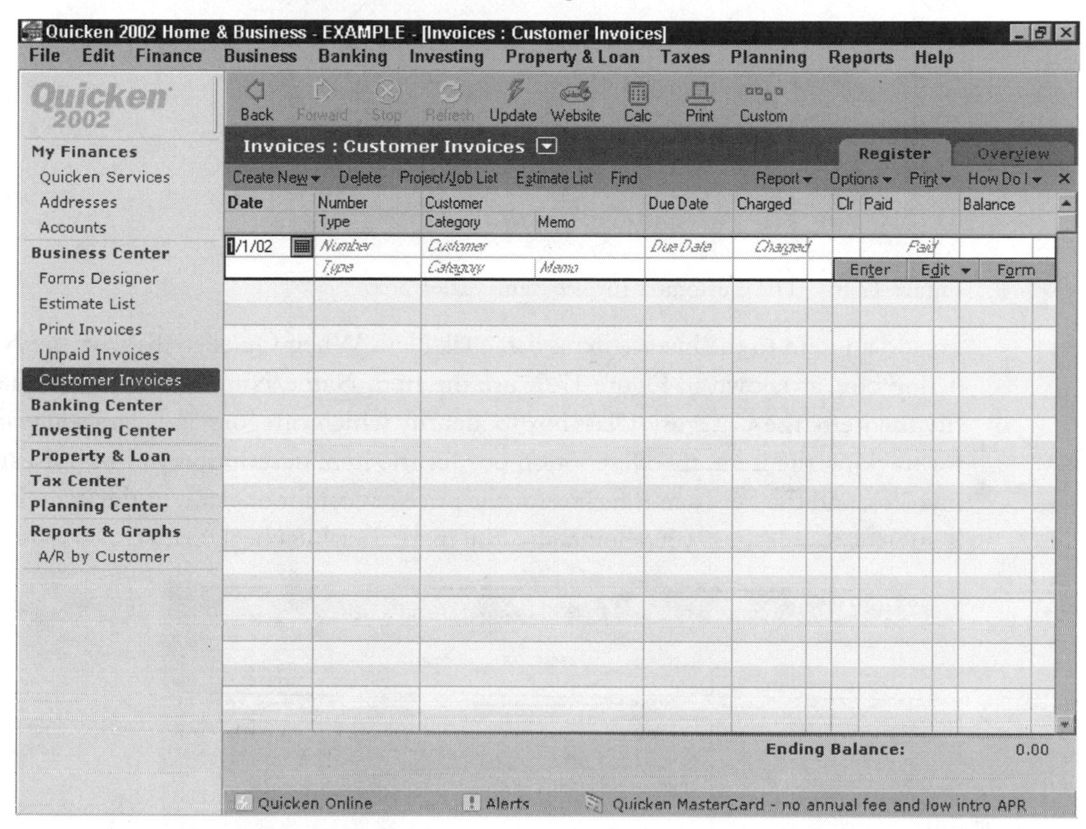

Figure 17.7: The Invoices register.

Setting Up Your Invoices Items List

You need to describe each of the items you'll list on your invoices and credit memos. To build this list of the items you sell, choose Business ➢ Invoices And Estimates ➢ Invoice Items so that Quicken displays the Customize Invoice Items dialog box, as shown in Figure 17.8.

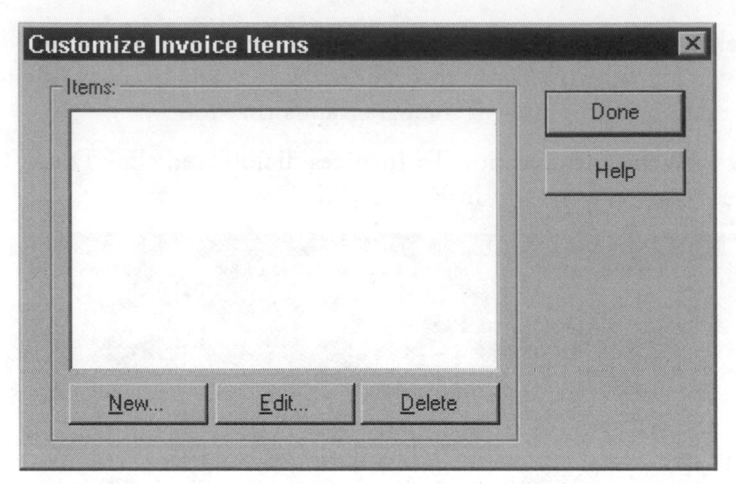

Figure 17.8: The Customize Invoice Items dialog box.

To add an item to the invoice items list, click New. When Quicken displays the New Item dialog box, as shown in Figure 17.9, use the Item Name/Number box to uniquely identify the item, the Category/Class box to identify which category and class you want to use for tracking the item, the Description box for the item description you want to appear on invoices, and the Per Item Rate box for the price or cost for one unit or the item. If the item is subject to sales tax, you should also the mark Taxable checkbox.

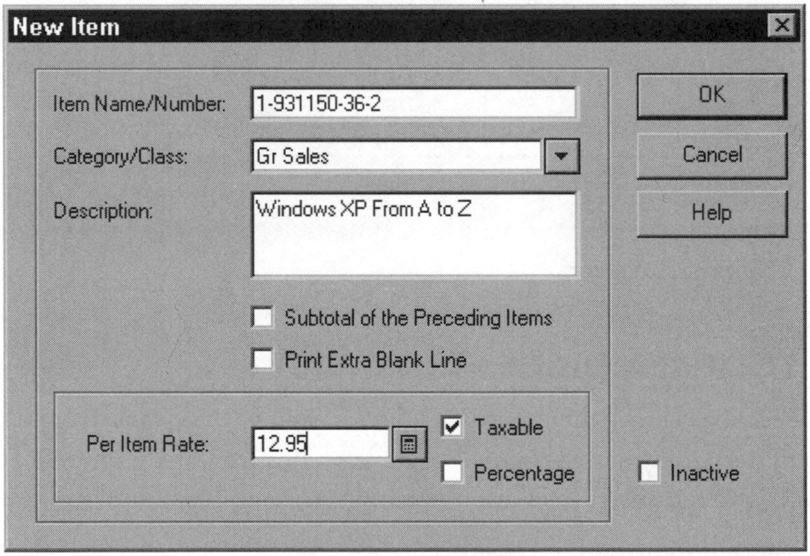

Figure 17.9: The New Item dialog box filled in to define an example item.

Most of the items that you'll list on your invoices will be products you sell or services you provide. You can, however, create subtotal items which simply total all of the preceding items and items which add or subtract a specified percentage to the invoice. To create a subtotal item, create the item in the usual way but mark the Subtotal Of The Preceding Items checkbox. Figure 17.10 shows the New Item dialog box filled in to define an example subtotal item. To create a percentage item which adds or subtracts a specified percent from the previous item on the invoice, create the item in the usual way but mark the Percentage checkbox and enter the percentage to be added as a positive number or the percentage to be subtracted as a negative number into the Per Item Rate box.

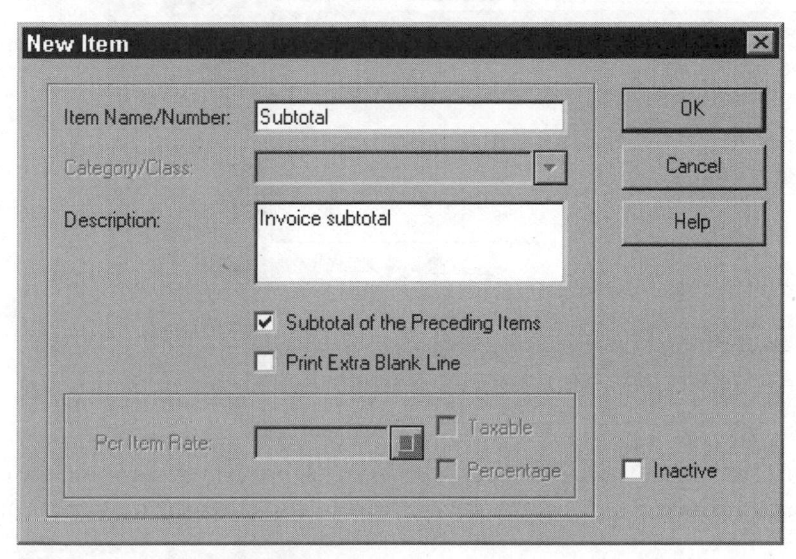

Figure 17.10: The New Item dialog box filled in to define an example subtotal item.

Invoicing a Customer

After you've described your customers, set up your invoices register, and listed your items, you'll find it very quick to invoice customers. Simply follow these steps:

1. Display the invoices register. For example, choose Business ➢ Business Accounts ➢ Customer Invoices.
2. Click the Create New button and then select Invoice. Quicken displays the Invoice – Customer Invoices dialog box, as shown in Figure 17.11.

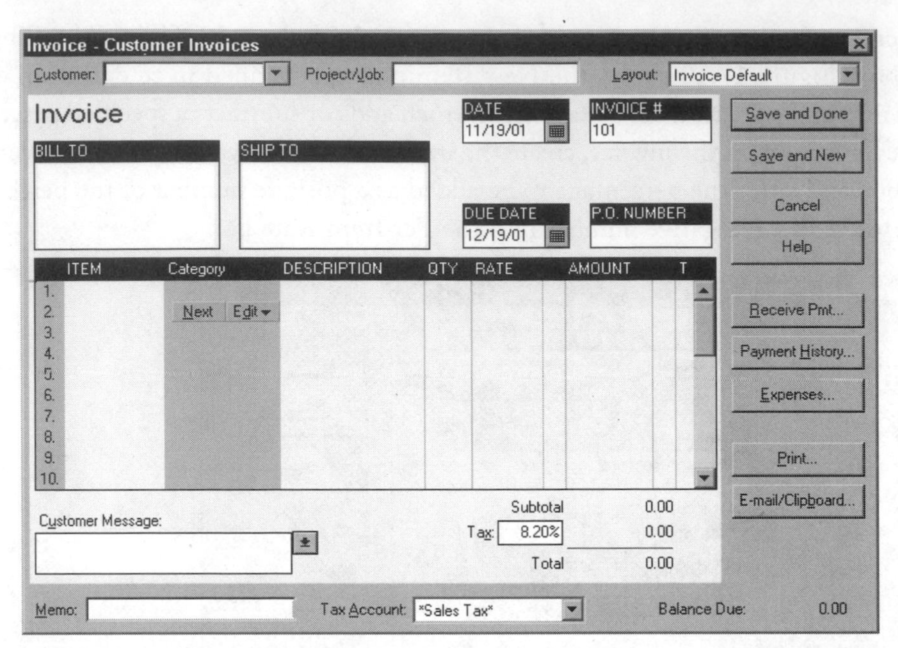

Figure 17.11: The Invoice – Customer Invoices dialog box.

3. Select the customer from the Customer drop-down list box. If you don't see the customer listed—perhaps because it's a new customer—you can also enter the customer's name into the Customer box.

4. Enter the project or job name into the Project/Job box. If you enter a project or job name that Quicken doesn't recognize, Quicken asks if you want to create a new project or job.

NOTE *You can also set up projects and jobs by choosing Business ➢ Customers ➢ Create Project/ Job and using the New Project/Job list, which Quicken displays, to describe the job. You can see a list of the projects or jobs you've set up by choosing Business ➢ Business Lists ➢ Project/Job List. You create projects and jobs, by the way, to further segregate a customer's invoices and vendor bills. This gives you the ability to assess your profits by projects or jobs. For more information about using projects and jobs, refer to Chapter 18.*

5. Optionally, if you've created a custom invoice form or more than one custom invoice form, choose the invoice layout from the Layout box.

NOTE *Quicken doesn't force you to use its invoice form. If you display the Invoices – Customer Invoices dialog box and select <Customize> from the Layout box, Quicken displays the Forms Designer window. This window walks you through the steps of designing an invoice form. In essence, what you do is select which bits of information you want to appear on the invoice. You can also change the labels used on the form to refer to the bits of information. The Forms Designer window is also available by choosing Business ➢ Invoices And Estimates ➢ Design Forms.*

TIP *Quicken's default invoice form doesn't include your company name or address. This means that either you need to print your invoices on letterhead—a fine solution—or you need to use the Forms Designer window to add your company name and address. To add this information, display the Forms Designer window, check the Company Address box, click the Company Address Properties button, and then enter the company name and address into the box provided.*

6. Verify and, if necessary, correct the Bill To and Ship To addresses. If you've previously and correctly set up the customer in the address book, this address information should be correct. If the customer is new or the order requires special handling, you may need to supply or edit the information in the Bill To and Ship To boxes.
7. Verify that the invoice date, shown in the Date box, is correct. If it isn't, make the necessary changes. Like other date fields in Quicken, you can edit the contents of the Date box directly by using the date code keys (t for today's date, m for the first day of the current month, h for the last day of the current month, + to add one day to the date already shown, - to subtract one day from the date already shown, and so on). You can also click the Calendar button and select a date from the popup calendar.
8. Assign a unique invoice number to the invoice using the Invoice # box. Like the check number field on the Write Checks window you can add one to the invoice number by pressing the + key and subtract one from the invoice number by pressing the - key.
9. Quicken automatically calculates the due date by adding one month to the invoice date. This due date may be incorrect, however, if you've agreed to some other payment terms with the customer. Accordingly, verify and, if necessary, edit the due date shown in the Due Date box. Common payment terms, by the way, are to pay in 10 days, 20 days, 30 days, 60 days, and even 90 days. Remember, too, that most businesses don't pay bills everyday. Therefore, even if a customer agrees to pay you upon receipt of the invoice, you won't receive the payment for several days.
10. If the customer issued you a purchase order for the item or service, enter this number into the P.O. Number box. Large companies almost always use purchase orders to control their spending, so in many cases, you need a purchase order on the invoice in order for the invoice to be paid. When you haven't been supplied with a purchase order number, you can try entering ***verbal*** or even the name of the person ordering the item or service.

NOTE *A purchase order is a firm contract to buy some item or service.*

11. Record each item you want to bill using the invoice by entering the following pieces of information:

- **Item** Use the Item column to enter the item number or code. Some businesses don't use these item numbers or codes. But many do. Book publishers, for example, use ISBN numbers to uniquely identify their books. The first time you enter an item number into the Item box, Quicken asks if you want to set up a new item. If you indicate you do, Quicken displays the New Item dialog box, as shown in Figures 17.9 and 17.10, which lets you set up a new item.
- **Category** Use the Category column to identify which income category you want to use for tracking income you earn from selling the item.
- **Description** Use the Description column to describe the item in terms that the customer will understand.
- **Qty** Use the Quantity column to describe the number of items purchased.
- **Rate** Use the Rate column to provide the per item price to the customer.
- **Amount** Quicken should calculate the value shown in the Amount column, but you want to verify the value. Note that if you change the Amount value, Quicken adjusts the price-per-unit shown in the Rate box.

When you finish entering one item onto the invoice, click the Next button to move to the next open line and describe the next item. If you make a mistake in entering an invoice line item, select the incorrect line item, click the Edit button, and make your changes.

12. Enter the sales tax rate into the Tax box.
13. Optionally, enter a new note or select an existing note using the Customer Message box. What you enter in this box appears at the bottom of the invoice.

TIP *You can add messages to the Customer Messages list by choosing Business ➢ Invoices And Estimates ➢ Customer Messages. Just choose the command, enter your new message into the Message To Add/Replace box, and click Add. To edit an existing message, choose the command, select the message from the Customer Messages list, edit the message shown in the Message To Add/Replace box, and click Replace.*

14. Print your invoice by clicking the Print button. When Quicken displays the Print Invoice box, use it to select the printer and the page orientation. Then, click OK and Quicken prints the invoice.
15. Save your invoice. If you're creating only one invoice, click the Save And Done button to save the invoice and close the Invoice – Customer Invoices dialog box. If you're creating several invoices, click the Save And New button to save the invoice but leave the Invoice – Customer Invoices dialog box open. Figure 17.12 shows an example invoice. Note, though, that the printed invoices provide all the same information and look essentially the same way.

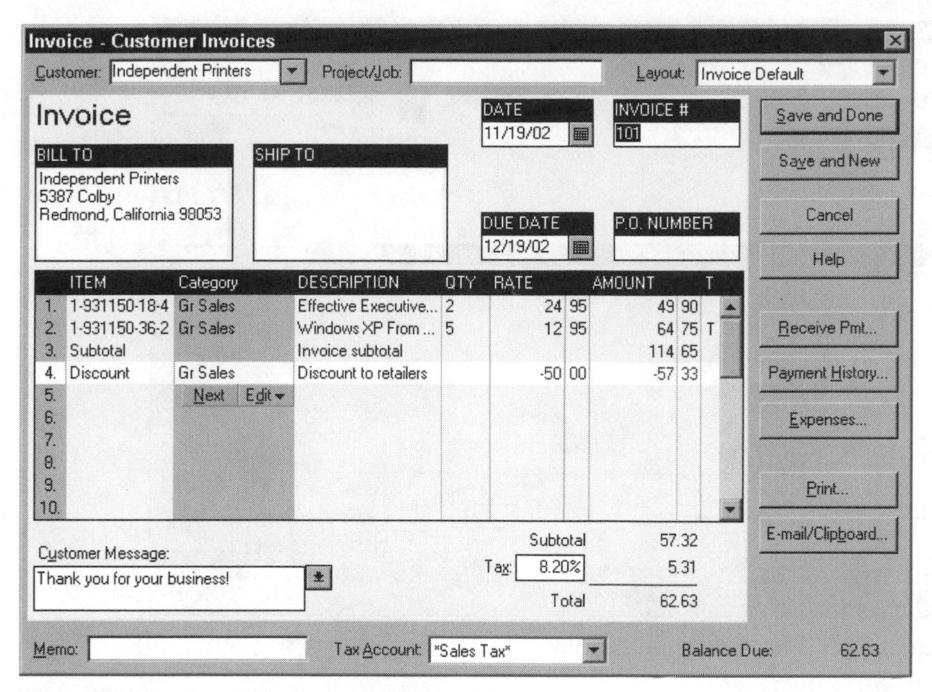

Figure 17.12: An example on-screen invoice.

Preparing Customer Estimates

Quicken lets you prepare estimates, which are, essentially example invoices. With an estimate, you basically say to a customer, "Here's what my invoice will look like if I sell you these items or perform these services." Predictably, the steps for preparing an estimate mirror the steps for preparing an invoice. You choose the Business ➢ Invoices And Estimates ➢ Create Estimate command and fill in the text boxes provided in the Estimate dialog box. Figure 17.13 shows the Estimate dialog box.

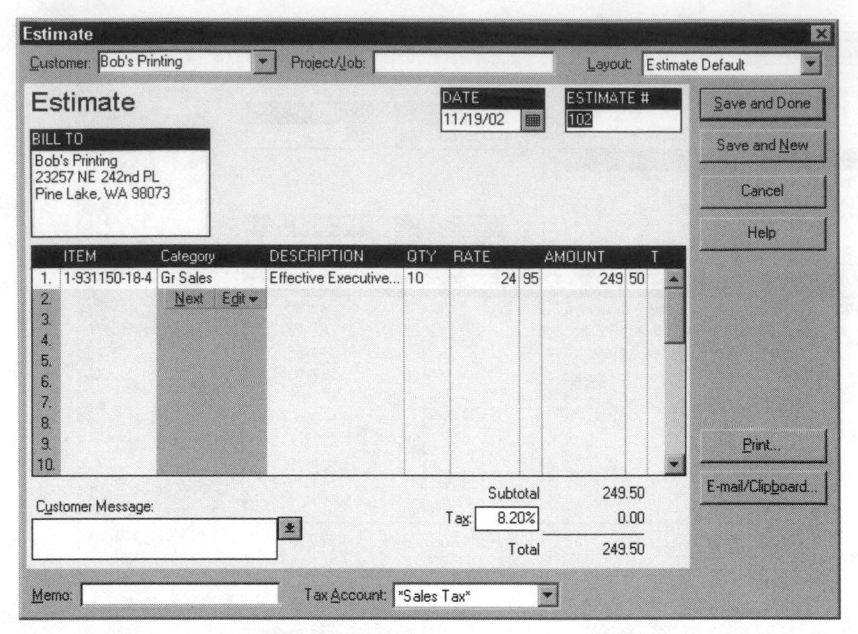

Figure 17.13: The Estimate dialog box.

You can use an estimate to prepare an invoice. Display the Estimate List by choosing the Business ➢ Business Lists ➢ Estimate List command so that Quicken displays the Estimate List window, as shown in Figure 17.14.

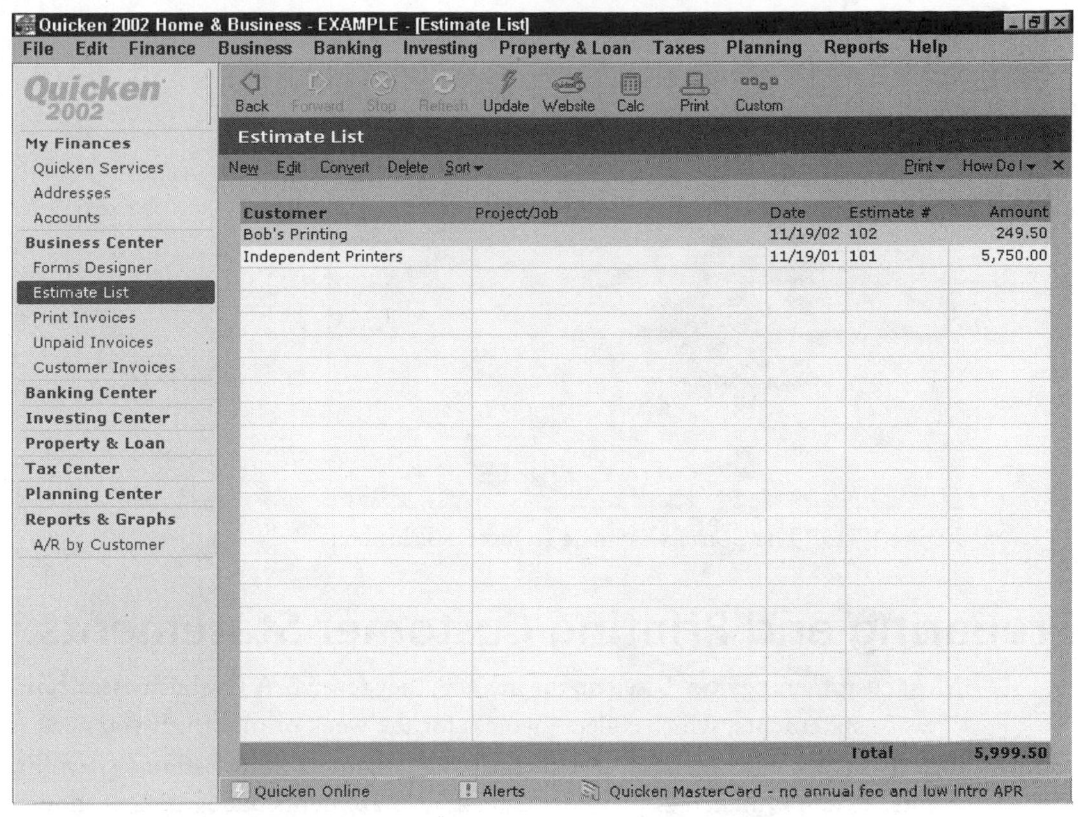

Figure 17.14: The Estimate List window.

Select the estimate you want to turn into an invoice and click the Convert button. Quicken displays the Convert Estimate To Invoice dialog box, as shown in Figure 17.15. If you've set up more than one invoices register, tell Quicken into which invoices register to place the invoice using the Convert It To The Following Account drop-down list box. Use the After Conversion option buttons to tell Quicken what to do with the estimate after you use it to create an invoice. Then click OK. Quicken creates an invoice based on the estimate and displays the Invoice – Customer Invoices window. Make whatever other changes you need and click Save And Done.

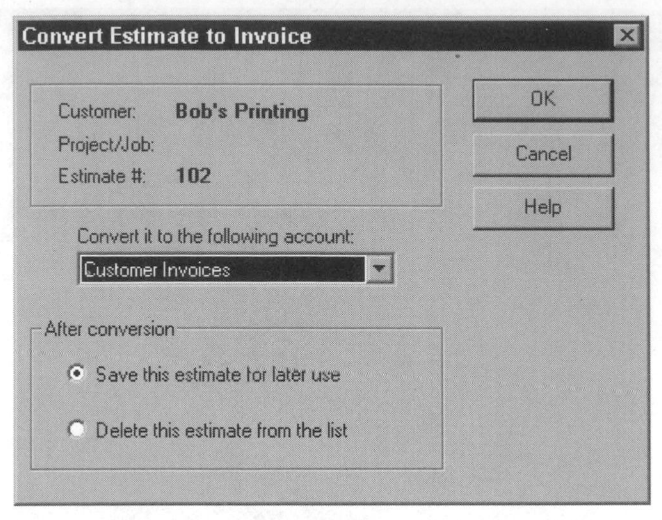

Figure 17.15: The Convert Estimate To Invoice dialog box.

Preparing and Printing Customer Statements

Most customers pay you based on the invoices they receive. A few businesses, however, need or want statements, which collect invoices for the week or month. If you need to produce statements for customers, choose Business ➢ Invoices And Estimates ➢ Print Statements. When Quicken displays the Customer Statements dialog box, as shown in Figure 17.16, use the Dates From and To boxes to select the date range for which a statement should be prepared and the Statement Date box to choose the date of the statement.

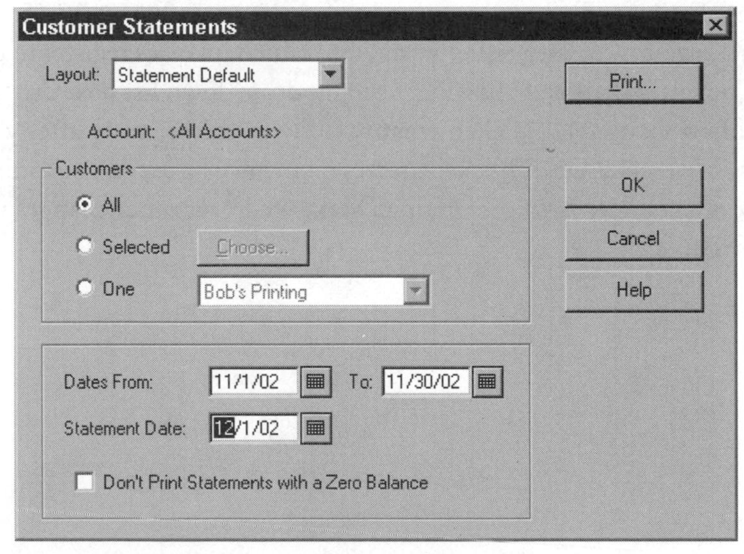

Figure 17.16: The Customer Statements dialog box.

If you want to prepare statements for all your customers, mark the All option button. Otherwise, use the Selected button and Choose box to select a subset of customers or the One button and box to select a specific customer.

After you describe for what time period the statement or statements should be prepared and for whom, click the Print button.

Recording Customer Payments

When a customer makes a payment, follow these steps to record the payment:

1. Display the invoices register. For example, choose Business ➢ Business Accounts ➢ Customer Invoices.
2. Click the Create New button and then select Customer Payment. Quicken displays the Payment – Customer Invoices dialog box, as shown in Figure 17.17.

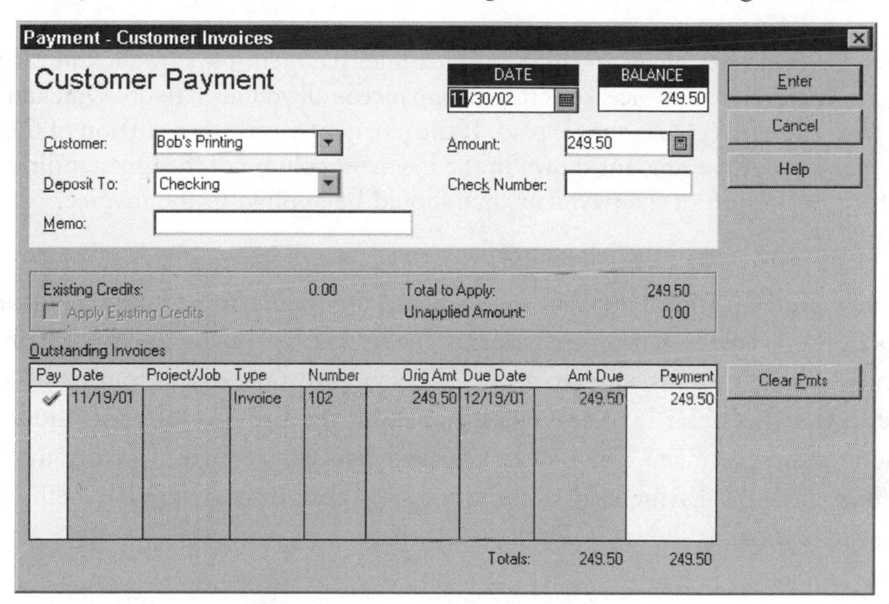

Figure 17.17: The Payment – Customer Invoices dialog box.

TIP *You can also display the Payment – Customer Invoices dialog box from the Invoices – Customer Invoices dialog box. Simply click the Receive Pmt button.*

3. Enter the payment date into the Date box.
4. Select the customer from the Customer drop-down list box.
5. Enter the payment amount into the Amount box.

6. Identify the bank account into which you'll deposit the customer payment using the Deposit To box.
7. Record the customer's check number into the Check Number box.
8. Optionally, use the Memo box to collect some bit of information you want to record but which isn't stored in some other box.
9. If, as part of recording the payment, you want to apply a credit memo, mark the Apply Existing Credits check box. Quicken applies the outstanding credit memos to the oldest invoices. For more information on credit memos, refer to the next chapter section, "Issuing a Credit Memo."

TIP *You don't have a choice about which invoices Quicken applies a credit memo to. Quicken applies credit memos to the oldest invoices. As a practical matter, what this means is that you often don't want to record a credit memo until the invoice to which the credit memo can be applied is the oldest invoice.*

10. Select the customer invoices which the customer payment pays by clicking. If the payment pays the entire invoice, selecting the invoice is all you need to do. Quicken assumes that the entire invoice amount is paid. If the payment pays only a portion of the invoice, however, change the amount shown in the Payment column of the Outstanding Invoices list to that portion of the payment that should be applied to the invoice.
11. Click Enter to record the payment.

After you record a payment on an invoice, you can use the Payment History button, which appears in the Invoice – Customer Invoices dialog box, to see which payments have paid the invoice. To do this, first display the invoice you have a question about by selecting the invoice in the Customer Invoices register, clicking the Edit button, and choosing Edit Transaction from the menu. Then, when Quicken displays the Invoice – Customer Invoices dialog box, click the Payment History button. Quicken displays the Payment History – Invoice dialog box, as shown in Figure 17.18.

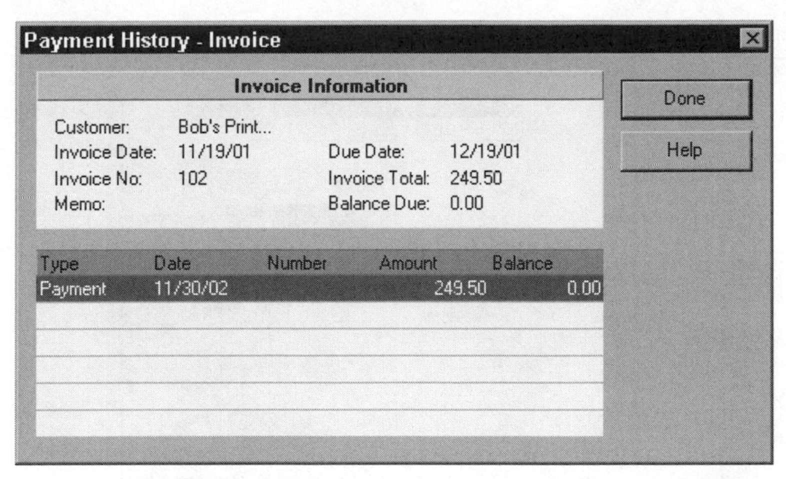

Figure 17.18: The Payment History – Invoice dialog box shows which payments you've applied to an invoice.

Issuing a Credit Memo

If you incorrectly invoice a customer or need to adjust a previously invoiced amount, you do so by issuing a credit memo. In essence, a credit memo is a backwards invoice. It tells a customer that he or she doesn't owe amounts (and why) that you've previously billed.

To issue a credit memo, you follow almost the same set of steps as you do to invoice a customer. Here are the steps:

1. Display the invoices register. For example, choose Business ➢ Business Accounts ➢ Customer Invoices.
2. Click the Create New button and then select Credit. Quicken displays the Credit – Customer Invoices dialog box, as shown in Figure 17.19.

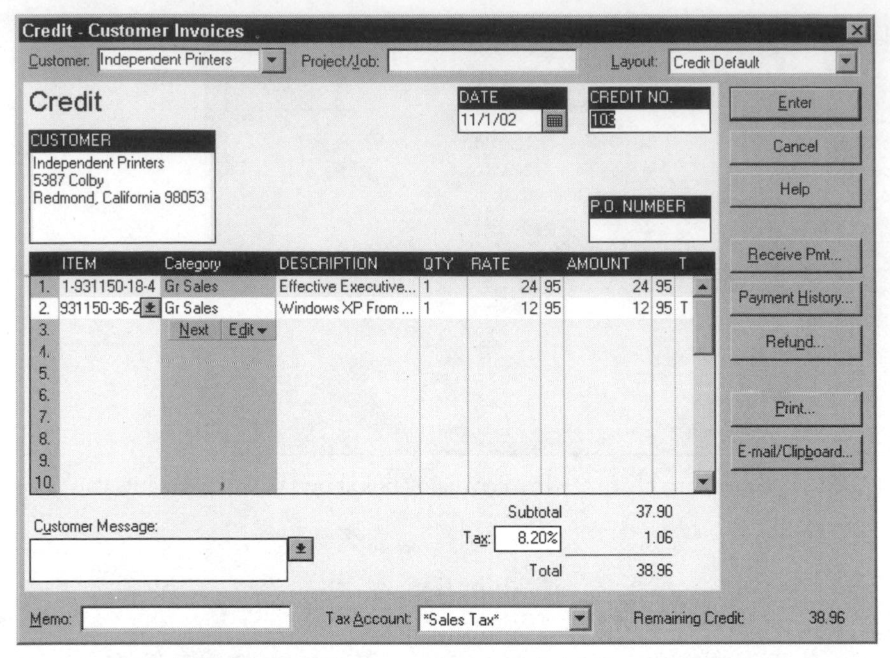

Figure 17.19: The Credit – Customer Invoices dialog box.

3. Select the customer from the Customer drop-down list box.
4. Enter the project or job name into the Project/Job box.
5. Optionally, if you've created a custom credit memo form, choose the credit memo layout from the Layout box.

NOTE *Just as for invoices, Quicken doesn't force you to use its credit memo form. If you display the Credit – Customer Invoices dialog box and select <Customize> from the Layout box, Quicken displays the Forms Designer window. This window walks you through the steps of designing a customized credit memo form.*

6. Verify and, if necessary, correct the address.
7. Verify that the credit memo date, shown in the Date box, is correct. If it isn't, make the necessary changes.
8. Assign a unique number to the credit memo using the Credit No. box.
9. If the customer issued you a purchase order for the invoice related to this credit memo, enter this number into the P.O. Number box.
10. Record each item you want to include on the credit memo by entering the following pieces of information:
    - **Item** Use the Item column to enter the item number or code.

- **Category** Use the Category column to identify which income category you want to reduce for the effect of the credit memo.
- **Description** Use the Description column to describe the credit memo item in terms that the customer will understand.
- **Qty** Use the Quantity column to describe the number of items being credited.
- **Rate** Use the Rate column to provide the per item price by credited to the customer.
- **Amount** Quicken should calculate the value shown in the Amount column, but you want to verify the value. Note that if you change the Amount value, Quicken adjusts the price-per-unit shown in the Rate box.

When you finish entering one item into the credit memo, click the Next button to move to the next open line and describe the next item. If you make a mistake in entering an invoice line item, select the incorrect line item, click the Edit button, and make your changes.

11. Add any reimbursable expenses to the invoice by clicking the Expenses button and then identifying which expenses you want to add to the invoice. Note that the only expenses that appear on Quicken's list of reimbursable expenses are those that you've entered using the Business ➢ Bills And Vendors ➢ Create Bill command and marked as reimbursable.
12. Enter the sales tax rate into the Tax box.
13. Optionally, enter a new note or select an existing note using the Customer Message box. What you enter in this box appears at the bottom of the invoice.
14. Print your credit memo by clicking the Print button.
15. Save your credit memo by clicking either the Save And Done button or the Save And New button.

Issuing Customer Refunds

In addition to credit memos, which are the preferred way of repaying customers or adjusting past overpayments, you can refund a customer's money. To do this, display the Customer Invoices register, click the New button, and choose Refund. When Quicken displays the Refund – Customer Invoices dialog box, as shown in Figure 17.20, describe the refund using the text boxes. You need to identify the bank account on which you write the refund check, the customer, check date, project/job (if applicable), amount, and the check number. After you enter this information, click Enter.

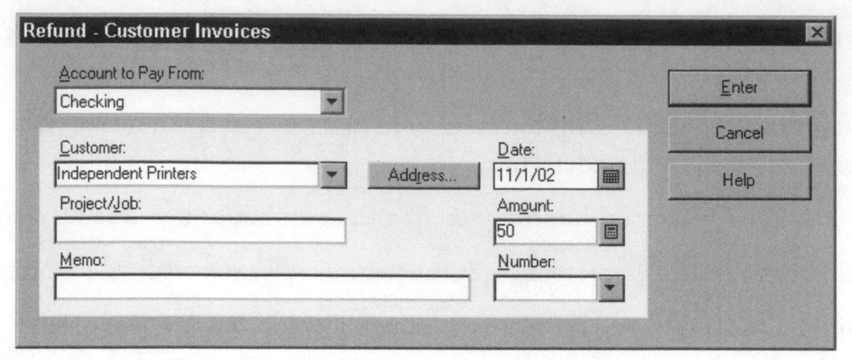

Figure 17.20: The Refund – Customer Invoices dialog box.

Delivering Invoices and Credit Memos

You can deliver invoices and credit memos to your customers in both the standard ways you would expect and using electronic mail.

Printing Invoices and Credit Memos

To deliver an invoice or credit memo in the standard way, print the invoices and any credit memos. Then, batch up the invoices and credit memos by customer, place these forms into envelopes, and then either mail or hand-deliver the envelopes.

You can print invoices individually as you create them by clicking the Print button in the Invoice – Customer Invoices window or the Credit – Customer Invoices window. You can also print invoices in a batch by choosing the Business ➢ Business List ➢ Print Invoices/Invoices List command. When you choose this command, Quicken displays the Print Invoices window, as shown in Figure 17.21. To print all of the invoices listed, click the Print button and choose List. To print only the selected invoices, click the Print button and choose Selected Invoices.

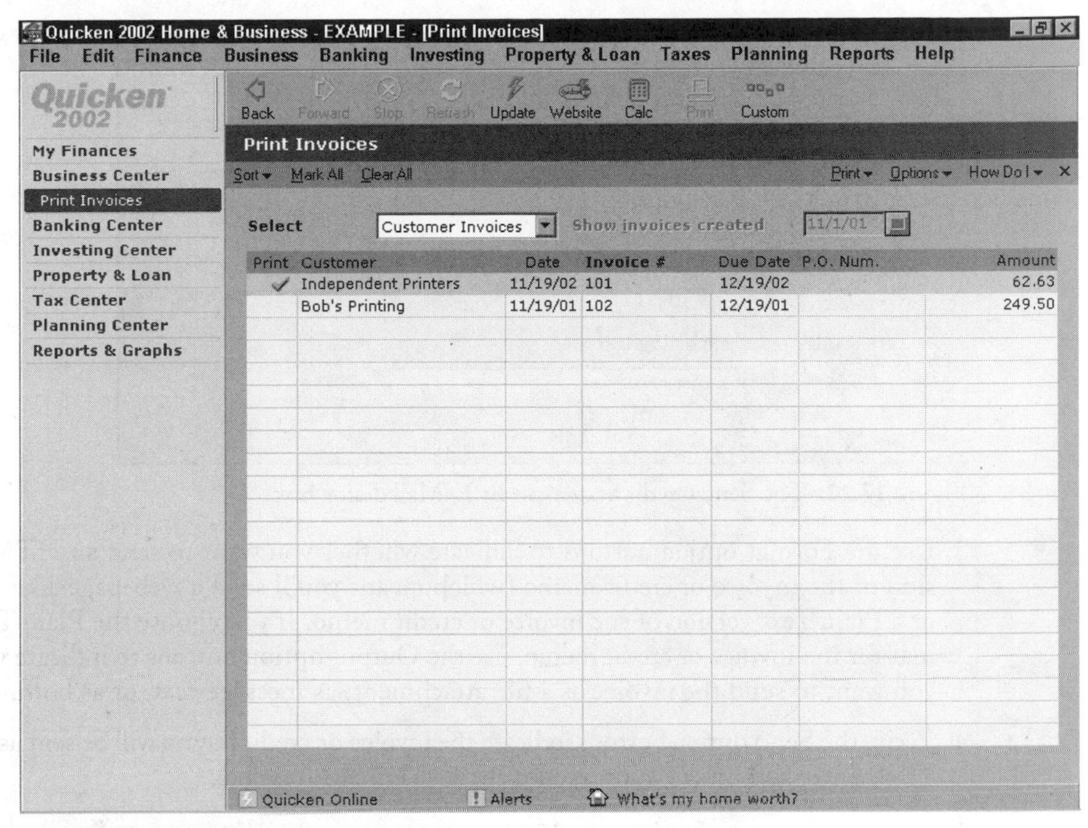

Figure 17.21: The Print Invoices window.

E-Mailing Invoices and Credit Memos

To deliver an invoice or credit memo using electronic mail, follow these steps:

1. Display the specific invoice or credit memo. Select a specific invoice using the Invoice – Customer Invoices window or using the Credit – Customer Invoices window. Click Edit ➢ Edit Transaction to open the Invoice – Customer Invoices or Credit – Customer Invoices dialog box.
2. Click the E-Mail/Clipboard button. Quicken displays the Send Invoice By E-Mail dialog box or the Send Credit Statement By E-Mail dialog box, as shown in Figure 17.22.

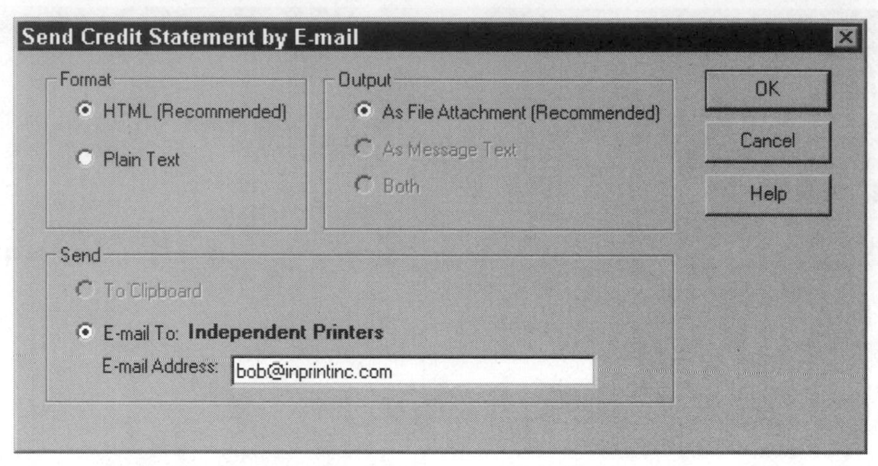

Figure 17.22: The Send Credit Statement By E-Mail dialog box.

3. Use the Format option buttons to indicate whether you want to send an HTML version of the invoice or credit memo (which means you'll send a web-page-like invoice) or a Plain Text version of the invoice or credit memo. If you choose the Plain Text format for the invoice or credit memo, use the Output option buttons to indicate whether you want to send the invoice as a file attachment, as message text, or as both.
4. Verify the Send option buttons indicate the invoice or credit memo will be sent as e-mail. Then enter the e-mail address into the E-Mail Address box.

TIP *You can use a service called PayPal to automatically collect payments on invoices you sent to customers. For more information about this service, click the Tell Me More button. The unusual thing about PayPal is that it lets your customers pay you using their credit cards. For this service, PayPal deducts a small fee from your invoice.*

5. Click OK. Quicken opens your default e-mail program and creates a message for the invoice or credit memo. You send the e-mail invoice or credit memo in the usual way. In Microsoft Outlook and Outlook Express, for example, you click Send.

Assessing Finance Charges

I suspect that most small businesses don't charge their customers finance charges unless absolutely necessary. The goodwill you lose by dinging customers with late payment fees often isn't something you want to do until you decide that a particular customer is no longer worth your time or your trouble.

You should know, however, that Quicken does include a finance charge calculation command which makes it easy to add finance charges to a customer's balance. To charge a customer finance changes, display the Invoices register, click the Create New button, and choose Finance Charge. When Quicken displays the Finance Charge – Customer Invoices dialog box, as shown in Figure 17.23, select the customer you want to calculate finance charges for.

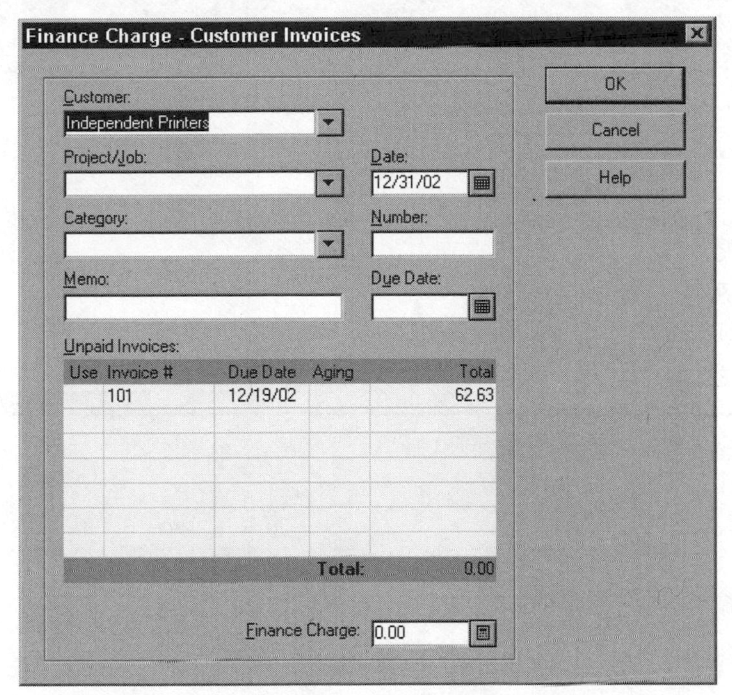

Figure 17.23: The Finance Charge – Customer Invoices dialog box.

After Quicken lists unpaid invoices for the customer, identify the project/job (if applicable), the finance charge calculation date, the category to which finance charges should be assigned (probably Finance Charge if you're using the standard category list), the invoice number to use for the finance charge invoice, and the finance charge invoice's due date. Next, select the unpaid invoices you want to include as the reason or explanation for the finance charge, enter the dollar amount of the finance charge into the Finance Charge box, and then click OK.

Reviewing Your Accounts Receivable

Quicken supplies several useful ways to review your accounts receivable, unpaid invoices, and customer payments.

To review all the details of customer invoices, payments, credit memos, refunds, and finances, choose Business ➢ Business Accounts ➢ Customer Invoices. Quicken then displays the Customer Invoices account register, which lists each of the accounts receivable transactions, as shown in Figure 17.24.

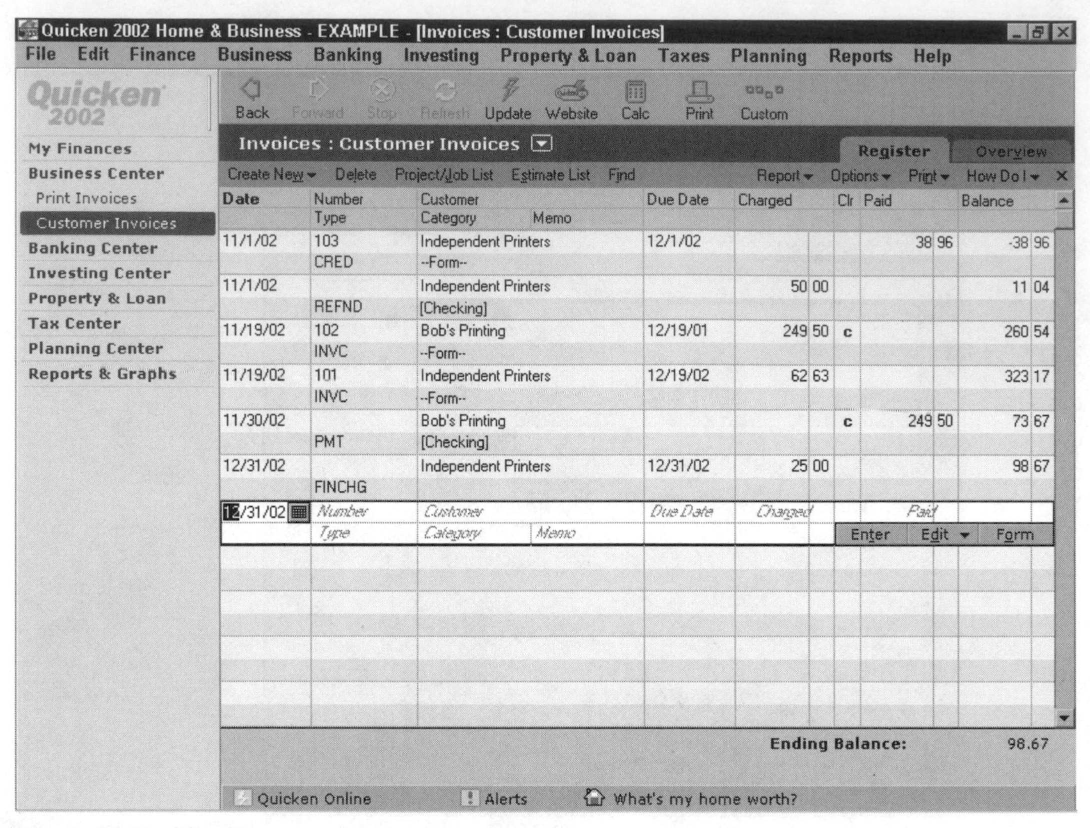

Date	Number / Type	Customer / Category	Memo	Due Date	Charged	Clr	Paid	Balance
11/1/02	103 / CRED	Independent Printers / --Form--		12/1/02			38 96	-38 96
11/1/02	REFND	Independent Printers / [Checking]			50 00			11 04
11/19/02	102 / INVC	Bob's Printing / --Form--		12/19/01	249 50	c		260 54
11/19/02	101 / INVC	Independent Printers / --Form--		12/19/02	62 63			323 17
11/30/02	PMT	Bob's Printing / [Checking]				c	249 50	73 67
12/31/02	FINCHG	Independent Printers		12/31/02	25 00			98 67

Figure 17.24: The Customer Invoices account register.

To see a list of the unpaid customer invoices, choose Business ➢ Business Lists ➢ Unpaid Invoices List. Quicken then displays a list of just those invoices that remain unpaid, as shown in Figure 17.25.

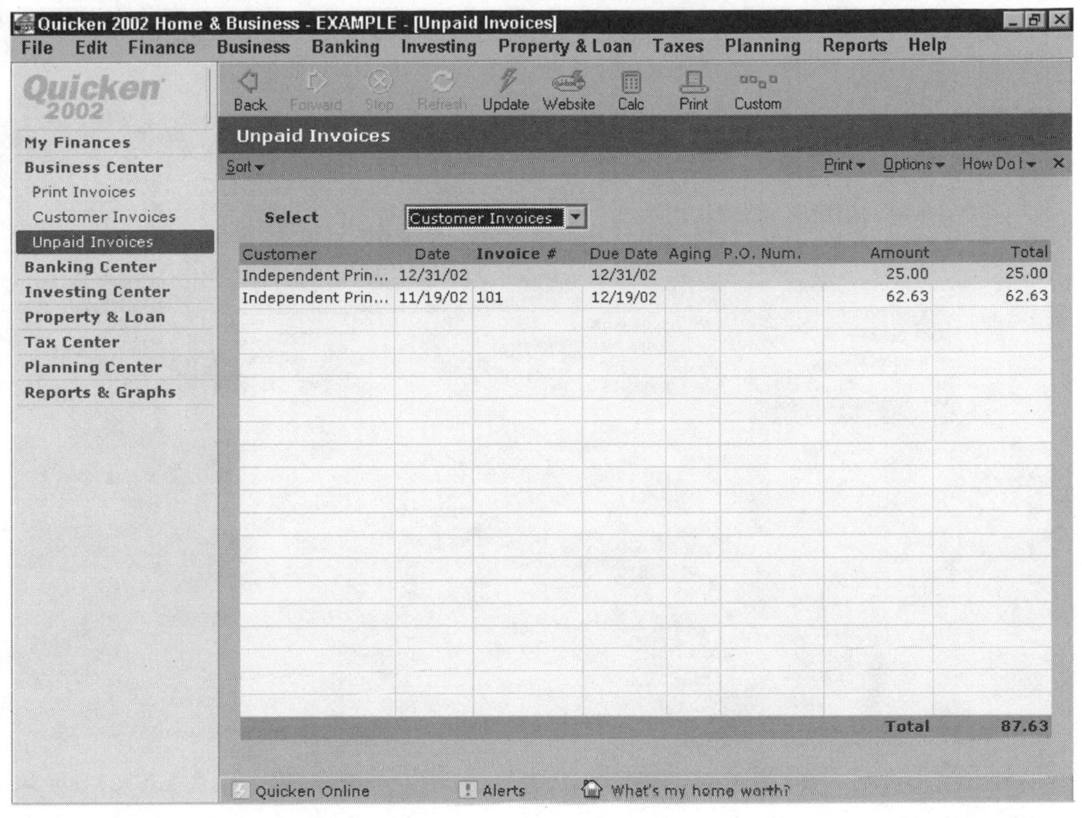

Figure 17.25: The Unpaid Invoices list.

To see a report that summarizes accounts receivable by customer and ages accounts receivable by invoice date, choose Reports ➢ Business ➢ Accounts Receivable to display the A/R By Customer window, shown in Figure 17.26. You may need to use the date boxes to fine-tune the reporting period. You can further customize the report by using the options in the Customize A/R By Customer dialog box. See Chapter 4 for a discussion of report customization options.

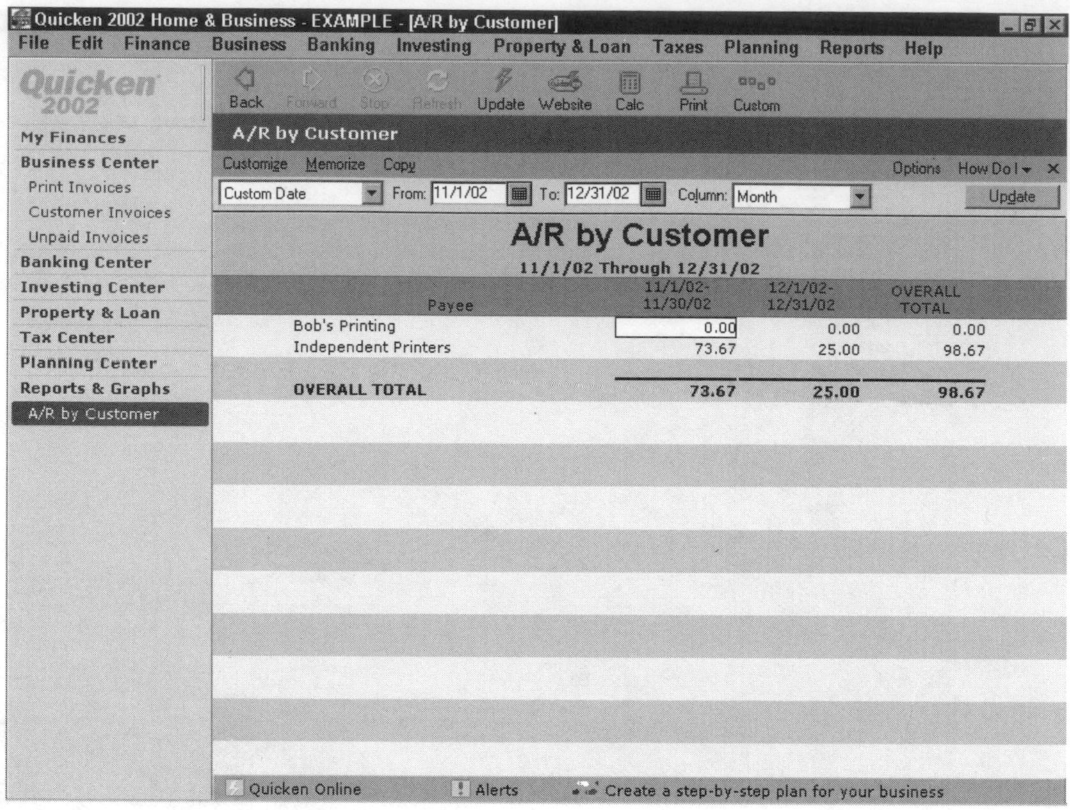

Figure 17.26: The A/R By Customer window.

TIP *You can—and probably should—use the A/R by Customer report as a guide to your collection activities. When a customer owes amounts from a previous month, for example, you might want to verify that the customer received the invoice and that payment is forthcoming. When a customer owes amounts that are from the months before the previous month (meaning at least one invoice is one or more months past due), you might want to consider more aggressive collection measures, such as a letter from you, your attorney, or even a collection agency.*

Chapter 18

FIXED ASSETS ACCOUNTING

In This Chapter

- Setting up your depreciation expense category
- Setting up fixed asset accounts
- Recording periodic depreciation expense
- Retiring assets
- Tracking vehicle mileage

Quicken is not set up to let you easily perform fixed assets accounting, which is the record keeping that's required to track your major equipment, furniture, and business real-estate assets. However, if you want to include depreciation expense in your profit calculations—something I talk more about in Chapter 19—or if you want to prepare business balance sheets that report on your business's assets, liabilities, and owner's equity, you need to perform some simple fixed assets record-keeping with Quicken.

This short chapter explains the basic process, which is to set up Quicken asset accounts for your major fixed assets and then use those accounts for recording depreciation expenses.

Before You Begin

To use Quicken for fixed assets accounting, you need only know how to use the Quicken register and Quicken's income and expense categories to summarize payments and deposits (see Chapters 1 and 2).

Setting Up Your Depreciation Expense Category

You need an expense category for tracking your depreciation. To set this category up, follow these steps:

1. Choose Finance ➤ Category & Transfer List.
2. Click New. Quicken displays the Set Up Category dialog box, as shown in Figure 18.1.

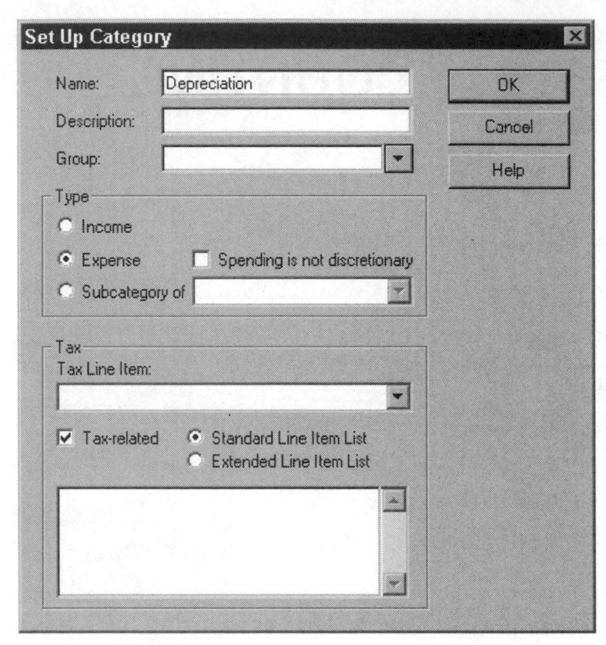

Figure 18.1: The Set Up Category dialog box.

3. Enter a name for the depreciation expense category—such as ***Depreciation***—into the Name text box.
4. If you want, enter a description of the category in the Description text box.
5. Verify that the Expense option button is marked so Quicken knows this is a category used to track spending.
6. Mark the Tax-Related checkbox because this expense category is tax deductible. Don't worry about or attempt to describe the Tax Line Item on which depreciation amounts are reported. Quicken won't let you export depreciation expense amounts to the tax form on which this information is reported.

NOTE *As you may recall from discussions in earlier chapters, the Subcategory Of drop-down list box allows you to create more detailed categorization. If you want to track depreciation both in total and then by type of fixed asset, you could set up an expense category for Depreciation and then separate subcategories for each of the types of depreciation that you want to track.*

Setting Up Fixed Asset Accounts

In order to create a balance sheet and more accurately estimate your business profits, you need to set up an asset account for each major fixed asset: equipment, furniture, real estate, and so on. As a practical matter, however, this is more difficult than you might at first think. You need to be careful that you don't create a greater record-keeping burden than is necessary or worthwhile.

Your overall purpose in setting up these accounts is to more accurately describe your financial condition and to more accurately estimate your profits by including depreciation in your calculations. For these reasons, you should probably not set up fixed asset accounts for anything that has modest value. In many cases, for example, your business furniture (unless you have a lot of furniture) and your computer peripherals don't need to be tracked. Why? Omitting these items from your balance sheet doesn't materially misstate your financial condition, assets, or owner's equity. The items aren't worth that much anyway as compared to assets like your bank account, the larger fixed assets, and your accounts receivable. What's more, because these items are often frequently replaced, you may not give up too much precision in your profit calculations if you just write off the item's purchase price to depreciation when you pay for the item.

TIP *U.S. taxpayers can use a special depreciation rule called a Section 179 election. A Section 179 election allows a business taxpayer to immediately depreciate, or write off, all of the price of a fixed asset. In 2001, a business can usually write off $24,000 of assets that would otherwise have to be depreciated. In 2002, a business can usually write off $25,000 of assets that would otherwise have to be depreciated. To record such a write-off, you simply categorize the check that pays for the asset as falling into the Depreciation category—or, if you want to be more precise, as falling into the Section 179 Depreciation expense category. Consult your tax advisor if you have questions.*

For those fixed assets that have substantial value—and these items would include vehicles, real estate, and in some cases computers—you need to set up an asset account by following these steps:

1. Choose Finance ➢ Account List to display the Account List. This window is just a big list box of the accounts you are using Quicken to track.
2. Click the New button at the top of the Account List window to display the Create New Account dialog box, as shown in Figure 18.2.

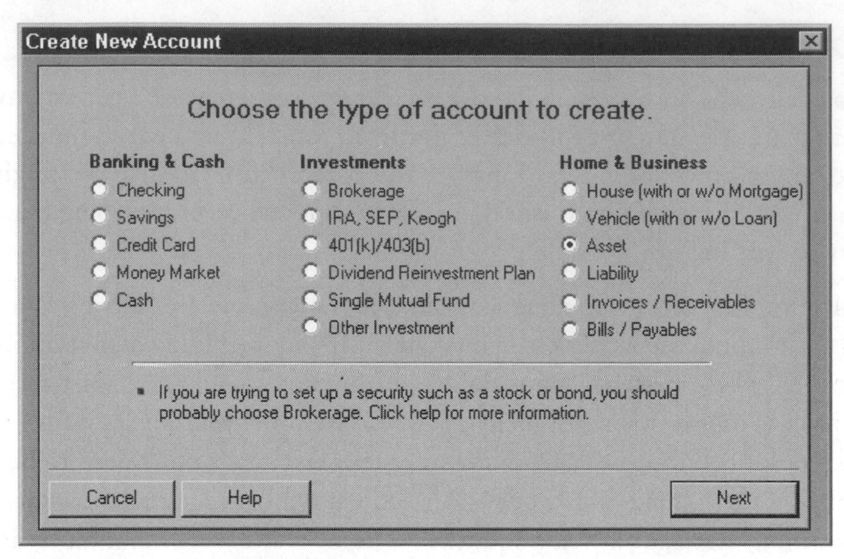

Figure 18.2: The Create New Account dialog box.

3. Mark the Asset option button to tell Quicken that you want to set up an asset account, and then click Next. Quicken next displays the first Asset Account Setup dialog box, as shown in Figure 18.3.

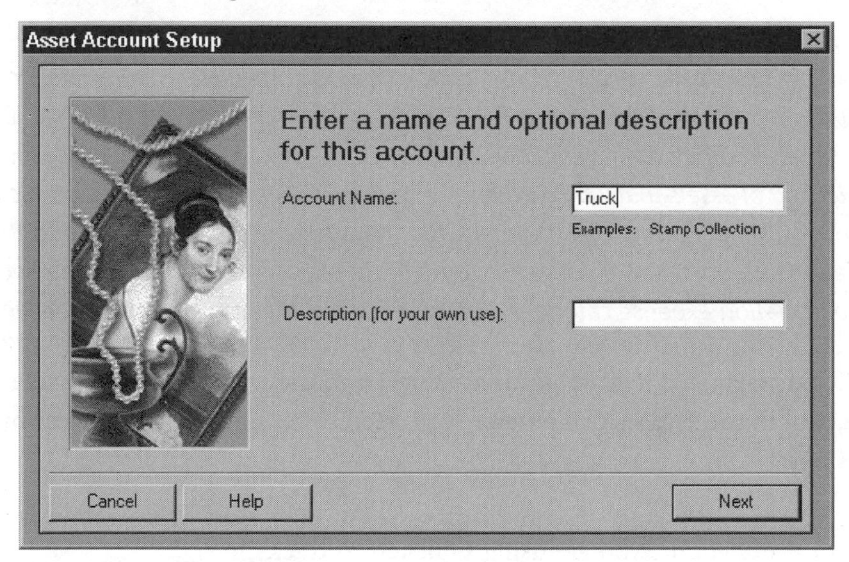

Figure 18.3: The first Asset Account Setup dialog box.

4. In the Account Name text box, enter the asset name.
5. In the Description text box, you have the option of describing the account in more detail.
6. Click Next to move to the next Asset Account Setup dialog box, as shown in Figure 18.4.

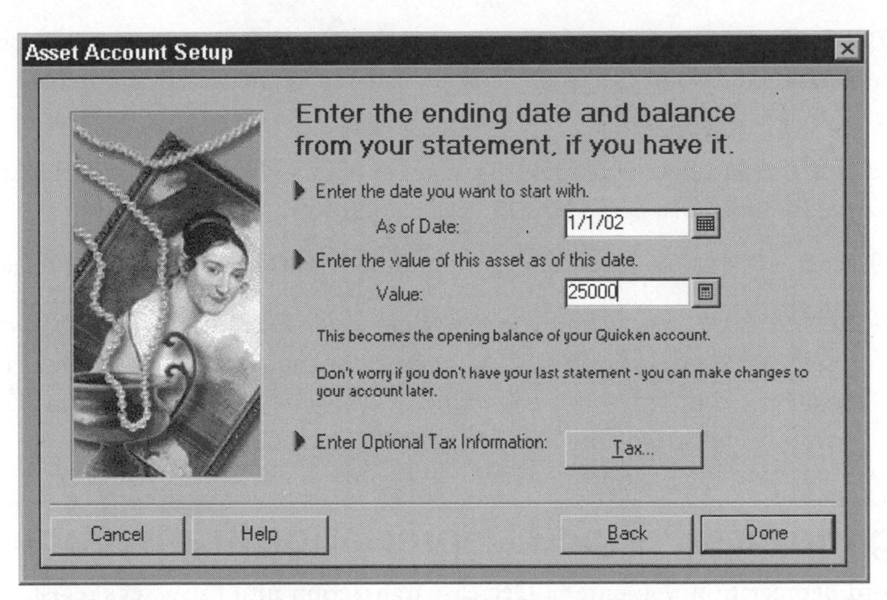

Figure 18.4: The second Asset Account Setup dialog box.

7. Enter the asset purchase date into the As Of Date box and the asset purchase price into the Value box.
8. Click Done. Quicken adds the new account and displays its register.

You can add any other asset accounts you need by repeating steps 1 through 8.

Recording Periodic Depreciation Expense

After you've set up the asset accounts you need to accurately prepare a balance sheet, you record the periodic depreciation expense transactions into those registers. Quicken makes it easy to record these depreciation expense transactions, but you need to first determine whether you want to enter monthly depreciation amounts, quarterly amounts, or annual amounts. To make this determination, you decide how often you want to prepare profit and loss statements that include depreciation. If you want to prepare monthly profit and loss statements, you should record monthly depreciation. (This will be the usual case.) If you only need to prepare quarterly or annual profit and loss statements, however, you can record quarterly or annual depreciation.)

Calculating Periodic Depreciation

Because depreciation seems like an abstract concept until applied in practice, let me describe an example situation and then show you how the accounting works. For the sake of illustration, suppose that you've purchased a $25,000 delivery truck for your business. Further suppose that you can use this vehicle for five years and will then be able to sell the truck for a $7,000 salvage value. These facts mean that over the next five years, or 60 months, you will depreciate $18,000 of the truck's cost (calculated at the $25,000 purchase cost minus the $7,000 salvage value).

If you divide the $18,000 by 60 months, you get $300, which is the monthly depreciation charge. In a formula, here's how the calculation works:

($25,000 cost - $7,000 salvage value) / 60 months = $300 a month in depreciation

NOTE *Tax laws usually specify how you should depreciation an asset for tax accounting purposes. For this reason, you probably want to use the same depreciation calculation as the tax law specifies. For help with this, you may be able to consult the IRS web site at* www.irs.gov *or you may need to get help from your tax advisor.*

Recording the First Period's Depreciation Transaction

To record depreciation, you enter a Decrease transaction into the asset's register for each month. The transaction amount equals $300 and the expense category is Depreciation. To enter the first monthly depreciation transaction, for example, take the following steps:

1. Enter the month-end date for the month you're recording depreciation for into the Date box.
2. Move to the Payee field by clicking it or pressing Tab until you reach it. Then enter ***Monthly Depreciation Charge*** as the payee.
3. Move to the Decrease field and enter the amount of the monthly depreciation charge.
4. Categorize the transaction by moving the cursor to the Category combo box and then entering your Depreciation category.
5. If you want to add a memo description of the depreciation transaction, highlight the Memo text box by clicking it or by pressing Tab. Then enter a brief description. You might want to name the specific asset, for example.
6. Click the Enter button to enter the transaction data into the register. Figure 18.5 shows the asset account register after entering the first monthly depreciation transaction.

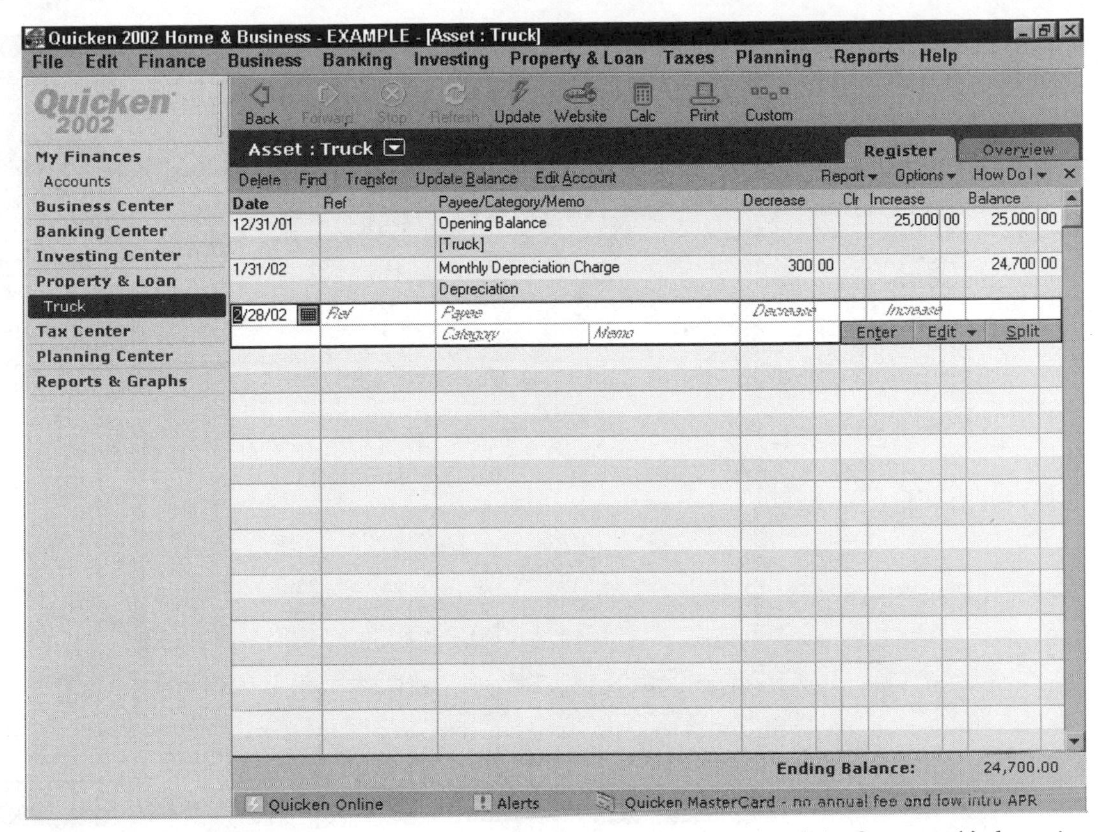

Figure 18.5: The Truck register after the opening balance transaction and the first month's depreciation have been recorded.

Scheduling Subsequent Period Depreciation Transactions for Automatic Entry

The real trick to entering depreciation transactions is to make sure that for the second and subsequent months the transaction is scheduled so that Quicken does the work of entering the transaction for you. You don't want to have to enter the same transaction sixty times.

To set up a scheduled transaction for the second and subsequent month's depreciation, take the following steps:

1. Choose Finance ➢ Calendar to display the Financial Calendar, as shown in Figure 18.6.

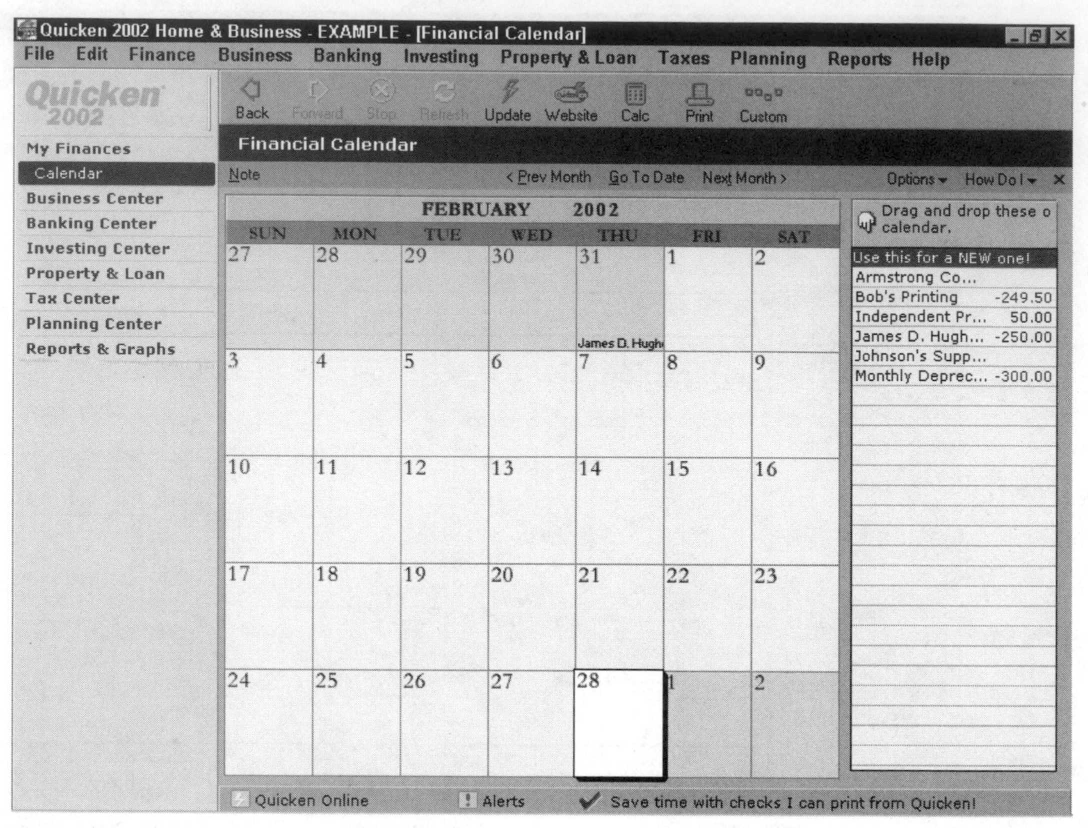

Figure 18.6: The Financial Calendar.

2. Display the next month for which you want to schedule the transaction by using the Prev Month or Next Month buttons.

3. Select the Monthly Depreciation Expense transaction by clicking it. Then drag the transaction to the day it should be scheduled—probably the last date of the second month the asset is used. Quicken displays the New Transaction dialog box, as shown in Figure 18.7. The information displayed in the dialog box describes the transaction you've just dragged.

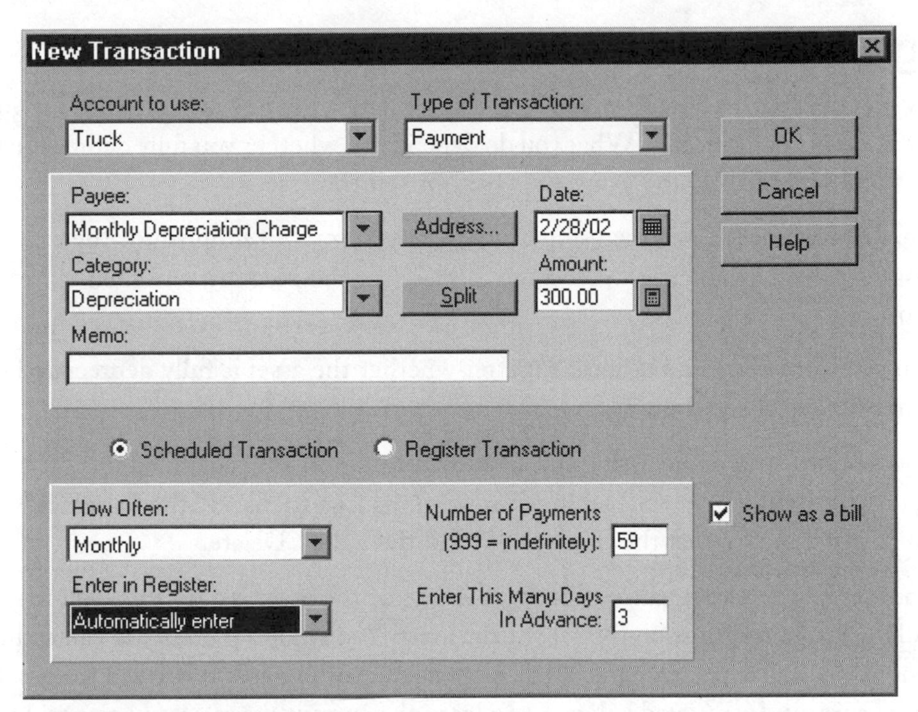

Figure 18.7: The New Transaction dialog box.

4. Activate the Account To Use drop-down list box and choose the asset account into which the transaction should be recorded.
5. Activate the Type Of Transaction drop-down list box to indicate whether you want Quicken to record a payment transaction.
6. Mark the Scheduled Transaction option button.
7. Use the How Often drop-down list box to indicate the frequency of the transaction as Monthly.
8. Use the Number Of Payments text box to enter the number of monthly depreciations you want Quicken to enter. If you want to record 59 months of monthly depreciation transactions, for example, enter *59*.
9. Select Automatically Enter from the Enter In Register drop-down list box to specify whether you want Quicken to automatically enter the transaction at the end of each month.
10. Click OK. Quicken schedules the transaction. To show the scheduled transaction, it puts the payee name on the calendar for each day the transaction will be recorded. Quicken also reminds you of the scheduled transactions in the Alerts window. You can view the Alerts window by choosing Finance ➢ Alerts.

Retiring Assets

How you deal with assets after you stop using them is the one other important and tricky fixed assets accounting task. What you do depends on whether you fully depreciate the asset (and then presumably stop using the asset) or sell the asset.

If you fully depreciate and then stop using the asset, you can simply hide the asset. To hide an asset, choose Finance ➤ Account List, select the account, and then click the Hide button.

If you sell the asset—and it doesn't matter whether the asset is fully depreciated or not—you need to do three things:

1. You need to stop depreciating the asset by turning off the scheduled transaction. To do this, choose Banking ➤ Scheduled Transactions List to display the Scheduled Transactions List window, select the transaction, and then click Delete.

2. You need to record a gain or loss on the sale of the asset. To do this, you first need to calculate the gain or loss on the sale of the asset. You enjoy a gain if you can sell the asset for more than its current, depreciated balance. You suffer a loss if you sell the asset for less than its current depreciated balance. (To learn the current depreciated balance, look at the asset's balance in the register.) After you know the gain or loss, you can record the asset sale transaction into one of your bank accounts. The transaction appears as a deposit for the amount of the sale. You need to use the Split Transaction Window, however, to zero out the asset account balance (through an account transfer transaction) and to record the gain or loss on the sale.

Figure 18.8 shows how the Split Transaction Window looks if after five years of $300-a-month depreciation you sell the truck for $7,500, which means you've enjoyed a $500 gain. Figure 18.9 shows how the Split Transaction Window looks if after five years of $300-a-month depreciation you sell the truck for $6,500, which means you've suffered a $500 loss. Remember that after five years of $300-a-month depreciation, the truck, which you originally purchased for $25,000 (in our example) carries an account balance of $7,000. After either of the transactions shown in Figures 18.8 or 18.9, the truck's ending account balance is zero.

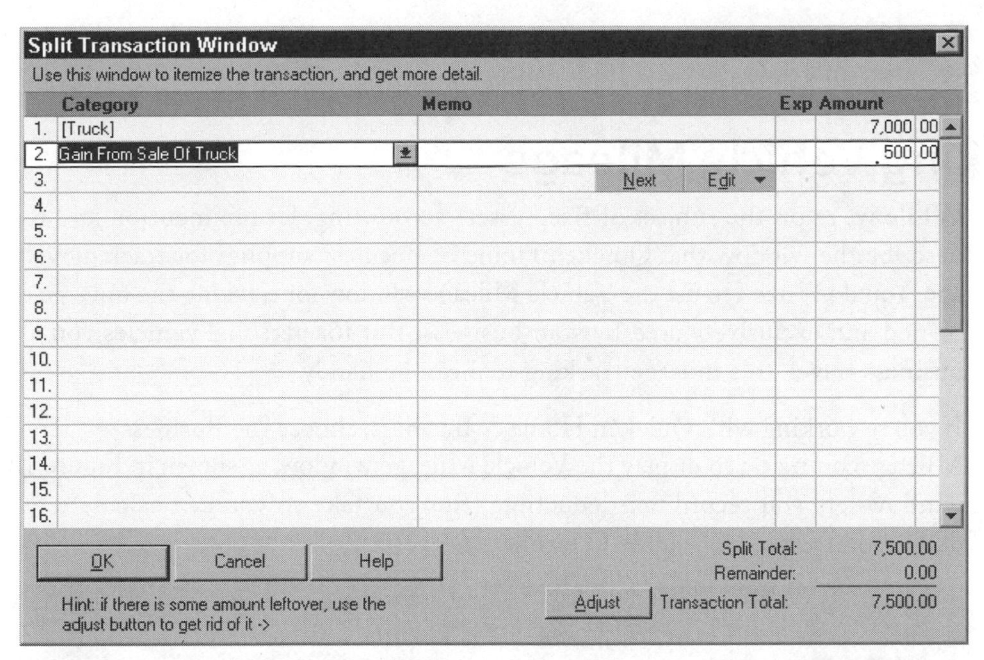

Figure 18.8: The Split Transaction Window recording the sale of the $25,000 delivery after five years and for a $500 gain.

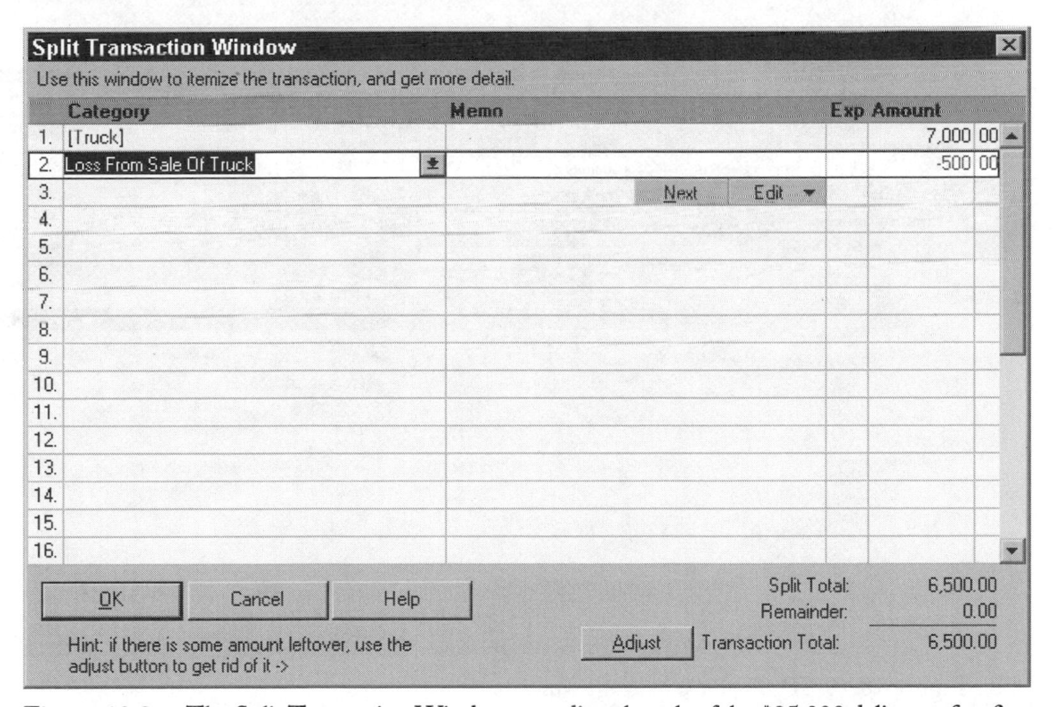

Figure 18.9: The Split Transaction Window recording the sale of the $25,000 delivery after five years and for a $500 loss.

3. You need to hide the asset. Again, to do this, choose Finance ➢ Account List, select the account, and then click the Hide button.

Tracking Vehicle Mileage

While we're on the subject of fixed assets accounting, let me mention and then briefly describe the window that Quicken Home & Business supplies for tracking vehicle mileage. You don't need to use the Vehicle Mileage window for tracking the mileage on vehicles owned and exclusively used by your business. But for personal vehicles you also use for business travel, this mileage tracking tool can be handy.

If you're working with Quicken Home & Business, choose the Business ➢ Track Vehicle Mileage command to display the Vehicle Mileage window, as shown in Figure 18.10. This window lets you record tax-deductible trips you take so you can calculate the mileage deduction for your Schedule C business tax return.

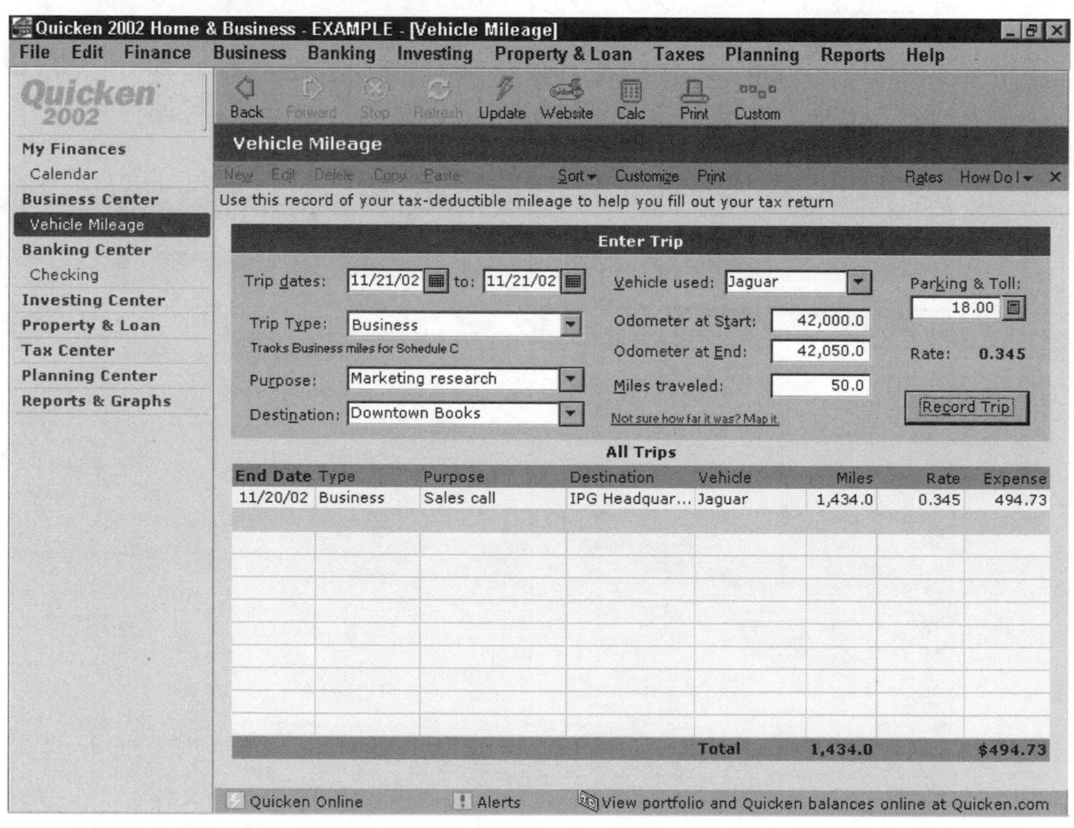

Figure 18.10: The Vehicle Mileage window.

NOTE *Business mileage traveled by the owner is deductible only on a Schedule C. Note, however, that you don't need to track business miles for vehicles that are used exclusively and owned by the business. This is true for sole proprietorships, partnerships, corporations, and other business forms, too.*

To record a business trip using the Vehicle Mileage window, follow these steps:

1. Use the Trip Dates boxes to specify when the trip started and ended.
2. Use the Trip Type box to identify the trip as one for business. You can use the Vehicle Mileage window to also track charity, medical, rental property, unreimbursed business travel, and other mileage, too. If you were recording a trip that falls into one of these other categories, of course, you select the other category from the Trip Type box.
3. Use the Purpose box to identify the trip's purpose.
4. Use the Destination box to identify where you went.
5. Use the Vehicle Used box to identify which vehicle you drove.
6. Use the Odometer At Start box to record the starting mileage on your vehicle's odometer.
7. Use the Odometer At End box to record the ending mileage on your vehicle's odometer. After you enter the starting and ending mileage numbers, Quicken calculates the length of the trip and enters this value into the Miles Traveled box.
8. Record any parking or toll charges you paid using the Parking & Toll box.
9. Click Record Trip to record your trip's mileage and out-of-pocket expenses. Quicken enters the trip on the All Trips list shown at the bottom of the Vehicle Mileage window.

NOTE *The Vehicle Mileage window provides a row of buttons you can use to add new trips, edit existing trips, delete a trip, copy a trip, sort the list of trips, and print the trip information. For the most part, these buttons are self-explanatory. The one button, however, that is unique to the Vehicle Mileage window is the Rates button. The Rates button displays a dialog box that shows the mileage rates the IRS allows for business miles, charitable miles, medical miles, and so on. You can't manually update these rates. However, the Quicken One Step Update, an online update of the Quicken program, will update these rates for you. To perform a one-step update, click the My Finances tab, scroll down the My Finances page, and click the One Step Update hyperlink.*

Chapter 19

MEASURING CASH FLOWS AND PROFITS

In This Chapter

- Measuring cash flows
- Measuring profits
- Forecasting profits and cash flows
- Using project and job costing
- Calculating a business's break-even point
- How to be a better business owner

By collecting income and expense information with Quicken's registers, you can easily track the cash flows and profits of your business. All of your business cash flows, income, and expenses move into and out of these accounts. Nevertheless, there are some tricks to accurately and efficiently producing this cash flow and profit information. This chapter discusses these tricks.

Before You Begin

To measure cash flows, you need to set up Quicken bank accounts for each of the actual bank accounts you have. You should also know how to use income and expense categories to summarize payments and deposits (see Chapters 1 and 2).

To most accurately measure profits, you also need to set up loan and liability accounts (as discussed in Chapter 12), and also be using Quicken Home & Business to track accounts payable (as described in Chapter 16) and track accounts receivables (as described in Chapter 17). If you have major fixed assets, such as expensive furniture and equipment or real estate, you also need to perform fixed assets accounting (as described in Chapter 18).

Measuring Cash Flows

To monitor a business's actual cash flows in Quicken, choose the Reports ➤ Business ➤ Cash Flow command. Quicken produces a Cash Flow report like the one shown in Figure 19.1. (See Chapter 4 for more information about producing Quicken reports.)

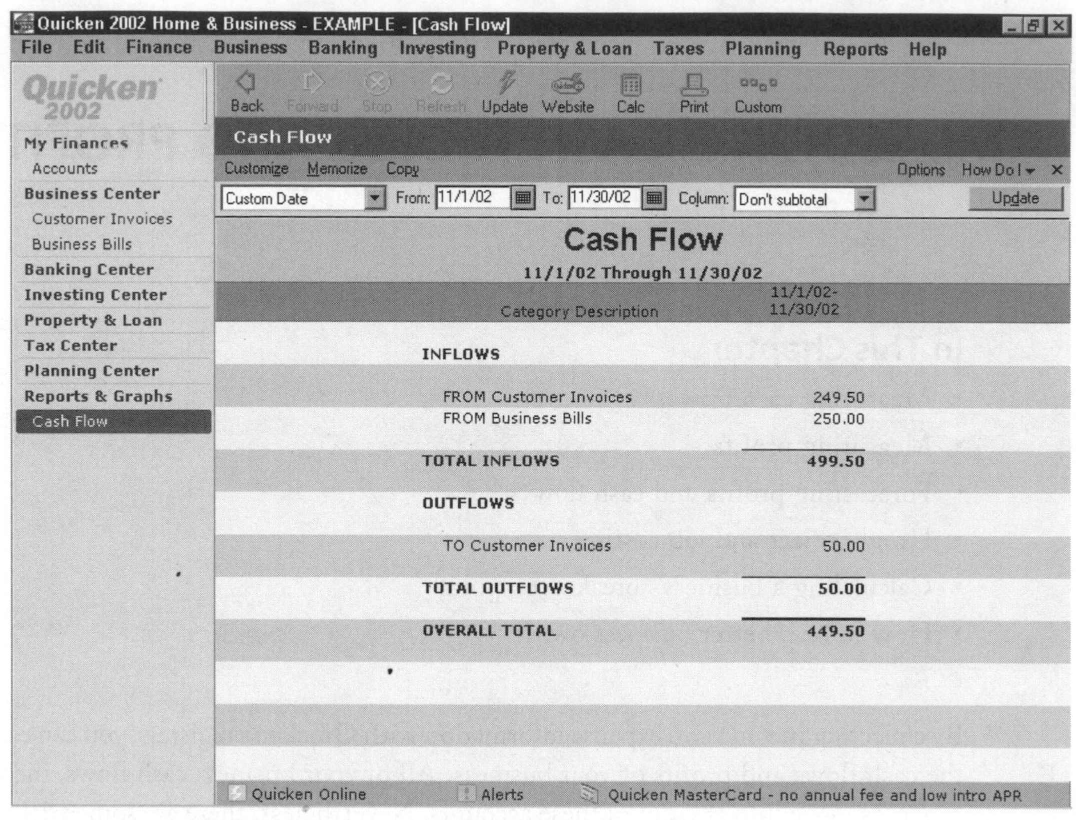

Figure 19.1: A Cash Flow report.

As Figure 19.1 shows, a Cash Flow report summarizes by income and expense category the money flowing into and out of bank accounts and cash accounts. A checkbook program like Quicken does a better job of describing and summarizing cash flows than any of the full-featured, double-entry bookkeeping systems because it uses the cash-basis method of accounting.

TIP *Because Quicken summarizes income and expense cash flows, you budget by cash flows too. This means that the Budget window really amounts to a cash-flow budgeting spreadsheet. Chapter 14 discusses Quicken's budgeting tools.*

Measuring Profits

Cash flow is important, but it doesn't indicate whether a business is profitable. Cash flows into a business, for example, when a bank loans you money, a customer makes a deposit, or an investor contributes cash—yet none of these actions has anything to do with profit.

Similarly, a business earns revenue when it does work for or sells items to a customer. And a business incurs expenses when it receives goods or services. Yet, unless cash is immediately collected or immediately disbursed, these items don't "appear" in the business's accounting records until later.

Figure 19.2 shows a Profit & Loss Statement based on the same set of financial data as the cash flow statement in Figure 19.1. The differences between the two statements stem from customer invoices and vendor bills which were recorded into the Quicken registers but for which cash has been neither collected nor disbursed.

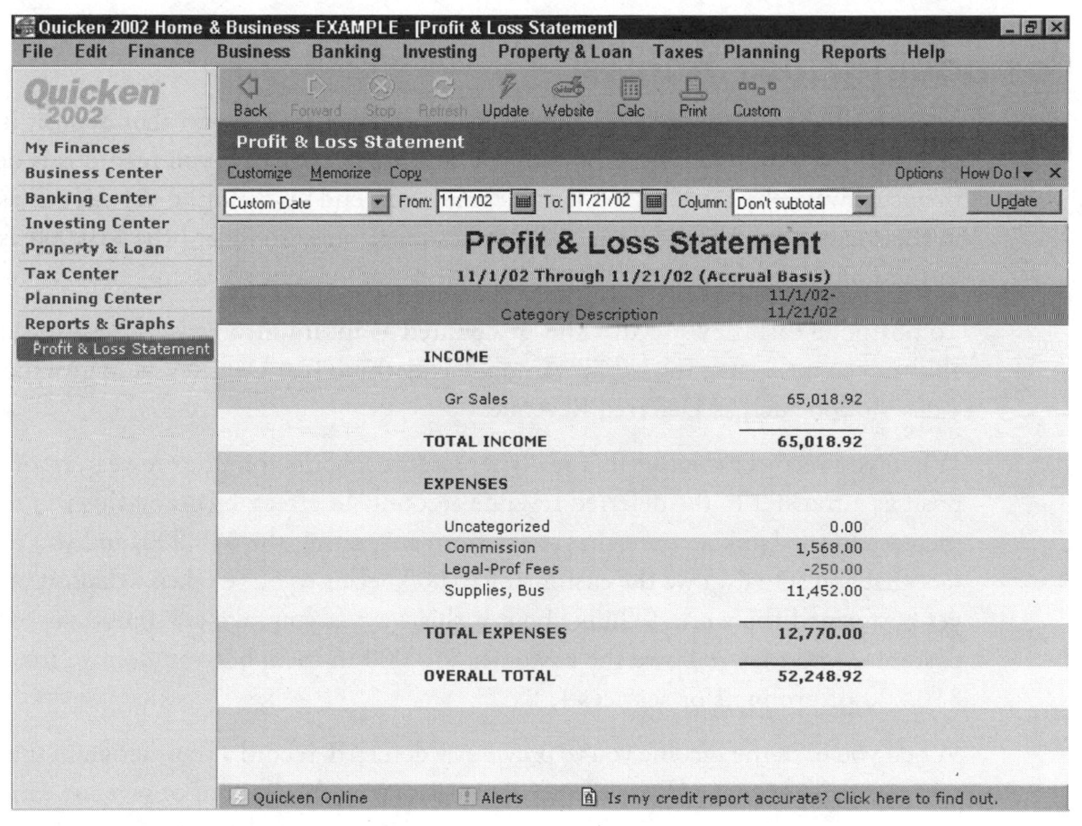

Figure 19.2: A Profit & Loss Statement.

NOTE *Quicken Home & Business produces profit and loss statements on either a cash flow basis or a simplified accrual basis. To specify how you want your profit and loss statement prepared, click the Customize button. When Quicken displays the Customize Profit & Loss Statement dialog box, click its Advanced tab and then mark either the Accrual or Cash option buttons.*

To measure your profits precisely, you need to employ four techniques:

- Postpone cash inflows so that they are counted as future income.
- Postpone cash outflows so that they count as future expense.
- Count future cash inflows as current income.
- Count future cash outflows as current expense.

Each of these techniques is discussed in the following paragraphs.

Postponing Cash Inflows

Suppose that you receive a $10,000 deposit from a customer and that deposit is a down payment for work the customer wants performed next year. If you record this deposit in the usual way—by categorizing it as income—you end up counting the deposit as income in the current year. However, it really makes more sense to record the $10,000 as income in the following year.

To postpone cash flows so that they're counted as future income, you need to set up a liability account. Name the liability account something like Def. Rev., and give the account a description such as Deferred Revenue.

When you record a deposit that really represents income for a future year, record the deposit as a transfer to the deferred revenue account. In effect, by doing this you record the increase in the bank account that stems from depositing the $10,000, and you record the fact that you actually owe the customer $10,000 because you've taken a deposit but haven't yet performed the work. (Think about it this way: If you take a $10,000 deposit from a customer, you may not owe the customer $10,000 in cash, but you do owe the customer $10,000 of products or services.)

When you earn the income you've previously deferred, record a transaction in the deferred revenue account that reduces the account balance by the amount of revenue earned. Categorize this transaction using the appropriate income category.

Figure 19.3 shows a liability account with two transactions: a $10,000 increase in the liability account, such as would occur if you deferred $10,000 of revenue, and a $10,000 decrease in the liability account, with the decrease categorized as income.

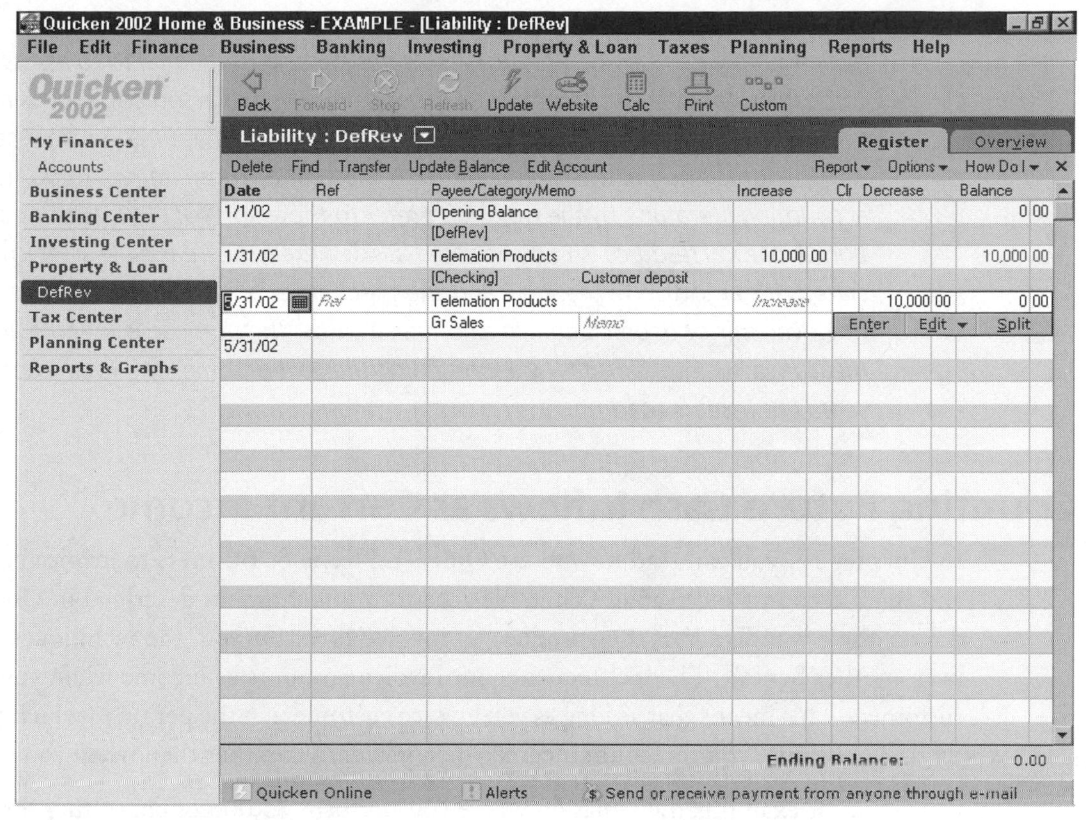

Figure 19.3: How a deferred revenue liability account might look.

Postponing Cash Outflows

In some cases, you may want to postpone counting all or part of a cash outflow as an expense. Suppose you purchase a $50,000 truck. If you will use the truck for five years, it probably makes sense to allocate, or depreciate, the truck's cost over those five years. (In this case, you might want to record $10,000 of truck expense in each of the five years.)

To postpone cash outflows so that they're counted as future expenses, you need to set up an asset account. In the case of a truck, for example, you would set up an account for the truck.

When you record the payment that really represents expenses for a future year or for future years, record the payment as a transfer to the new asset account. (Think about it this way: The amounts you pay for future years' expenses add up to prepaid expenses.)

For more information about how to work with depreciation, refer to Chapter 18. It describes how to set up asset accounts and record depreciation.

TIP *The mechanics of depreciation—a systematic allocation of an asset's cost over a period of time—can also be used for assets besides the traditional fixed assets. Mining companies, for example, can depreciate the value of natural resources (such as the gravel in a quarry or the oil in a field). And businesses that purchase intangible assets (such as copyrights and patents) can depreciate the cost of these items. Accountants and accounting literature, by the way, don't refer to these sorts of allocations as depreciation. A natural resource isn't depreciated, it's* depleted. *An intangible asset isn't depreciated, it's* amortized. *The logic and the mechanics of depletion and amortization, however, mirror depreciation. In all of these cases, the purpose is to more accurately measure a business's profits by apportioning the cost of some long-lived asset over the years the asset is used up.*

Counting Future Cash Inflows as Current Income

In Chapter 17, you can read how to use Quicken Home & Business to invoice customers and track accounts receivable. While the accounting techniques described in Chapter 17 deliver the advantage that they produce an invoice form for you, the techniques also deliver another benefit: The techniques count invoice amounts as income when you invoice customers. This means that as long as you invoice customers in the period in which you earn the sales revenue, you can count income when you earn it rather than when you collect it.

Consider, for example, the situation where you perform $5,000 of consulting for a client in one year but don't collect the cash until the following year. You probably want to correctly count the $5,000 as income in the year you perform the consulting services rather than wait until you collect the cash—because that more accurately measures your profits.

NOTE *Accrual-based accounting, which is what we're talking about here, sometimes seems confusing to non-accountants. You typically need to understand just two points, however, in order to appreciate the concept. First, recognize that you're not giving up cash flow information by using accrual-based accounting. You can and should monitor cash flow for a business—but you do that with a cash flow statement, not an income statement. Second, accrual-based accounting tries to more closely estimate your business profit or loss by counting invoices as income when you sold the item or did the work and by counting bills as expenses when you received the service or used the purchased item.*

Essentially, what Quicken Home & Business does is set up an accounts receivable asset account for each customer. When you want to create an invoice, Quicken records income, entering an increase transaction in the accounts receivable account—probably an account called Customer Invoices—and categorizes the increase by using an income category. When you ultimately collect the income, Quicken records a deposit in the appropriate bank account and categorizes the deposit as a transfer from the accounts receivable account.

TIP *You can do manually what Quicken Home & Business does automatically—in fact, in the years before Quicken Home & Business was available I used to describe how to do this. With Quicken Home & Business, however, you should either let it do the tedious bookkeeping or forgo the extra precision of counting income when you earn the income rather than when you collect income.*

Counting Future Cash Outflows as Current Expense

In Chapter 16, you can read how to use Quicken Home & Business to record vendor bills and track accounts payable. In Chapter 16, I suggested that the principal reason for setting up a vendor bills and accounts payable tracking system was to track expenses that you can later bill to customers and be reimbursed for. That's true, but there's also a subtle benefit to using Quicken Home & Business's vendor bills and accounts payable tracking. When you use those features, Quicken counts bill amounts as expense when you record the bill. This means that as long as you record vendor bills in the period in which you truly incur the expense, you can count expenses when you incur them rather than when you disburse the money to pay the bill.

If Quicken Doesn't Work for Your Accrual-Based Accounting...

All this said, Quicken isn't really set up to handle accrual-based accounting, which is what you're doing when you try to record income when you earn it and expenses when you incur them.

If your business needs the increased precision of accrual accounting and you can't practically or successfully employ the techniques described here, it may be time to consider one of the other, more powerful—but more complicated—accounting programs, such as Intuit's QuickBooks (which is relatively easy to use) or Peachtree Accounting for Windows (which is slightly more challenging to use but also much more powerful).

Forecasting Profits and Cash Flows

Quicken comes with a Forecasting tool that lets you estimate your future cash flows and profits by extrapolating past information. In essence, what Quicken does is look at your register and scheduled transactions, assume that these transactions will occur in the future, and then create *pro forma* registers for producing cash flow and income statement reports.

NOTE *This forecasting tool can also be used for personal financial management for someone whose personal finances are very complex. Using the forecasting tool in this way is probably overkill, however, for most individuals.*

Creating a Forecast

The steps for creating a forecast are relatively simple:

1. Choose Planning ➢ Cash Flow Forecast. Quicken displays the Cash Flow Forecast – Base Scenario window and the Automatically Create Forecast dialog box. If necessary, click Options ➢ Update Forcast to display the Automatically Create Forecast dialog box, shown in Figure 19.4.

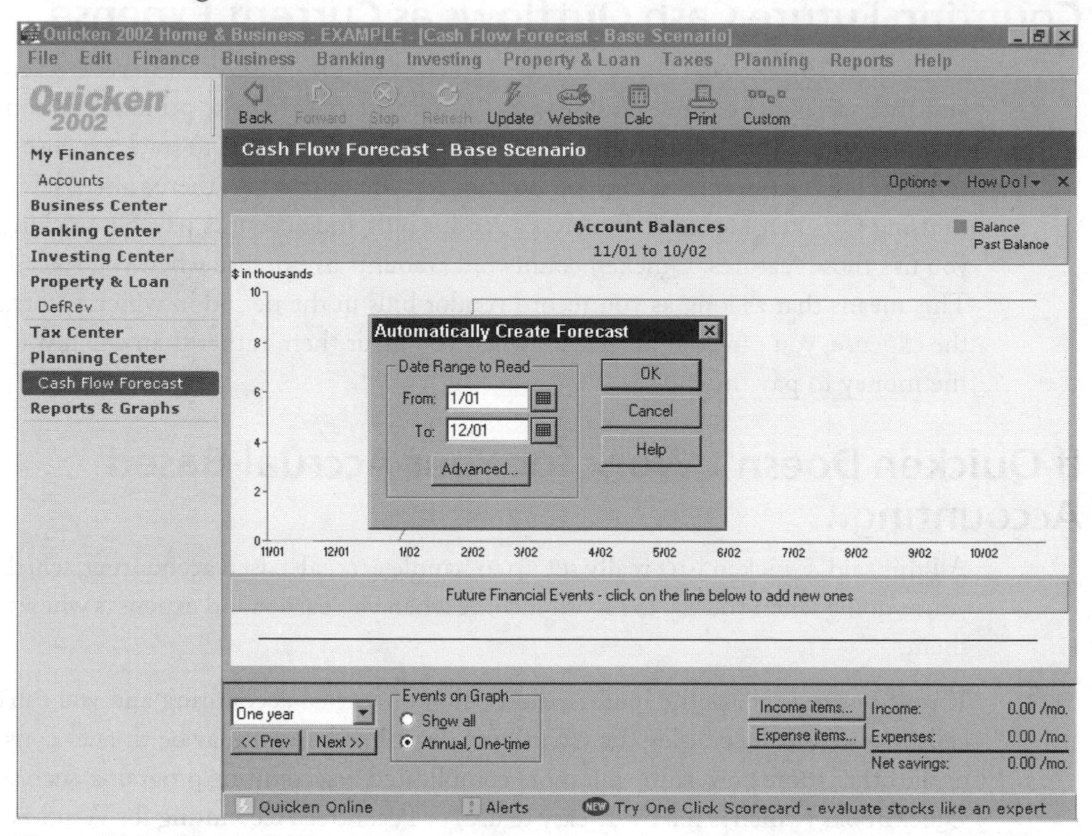

Figure 19.4: The Cash Flow Forecast window with the Automatically Create Forecast dialog box showing.

2. Use the Date Range To Read text boxes, From and To, to describe the period of time that should be used to create the forecast.
3. Click the Advanced button to access the Forecast Items To Create option buttons, and then use these buttons to indicate the type of transactions Quicken should use as the basis for the forecast:
   - **Known Items** (from Scheduled Txns) Tells Quicken to use scheduled transactions to create the forecast.
   - **Estimated Items** Tells Quicken to forecast future income and expense amounts by using average income and expense amounts from either your register or your budget.

- **Create Both** Tells Quicken to use scheduled transactions and average income and expense amounts.

4. Use the From Register Data or From Budget Data option buttons to indicate whether Quicken should create estimates using the register transactions or your budget.
5. If you want Quicken to forecast only certain income and expense categories, click the Categories command button. Quicken displays the Select Categories To Include dialog box. Indicate which categories you want to forecast by marking them, and then click OK.
6. If you want Quicken to forecast only certain account balances, click the Accounts command button. Quicken displays the Select Accounts To Include dialog box. Indicate which accounts you want to forecast by marking them, and then click OK.
7. Click Done to save your advanced options.
8. Click OK in the Automatically Create Forecast dialog box. Quicken displays the Cash Flow Forecast – Base Scenario window, as shown in Figure 19.5.

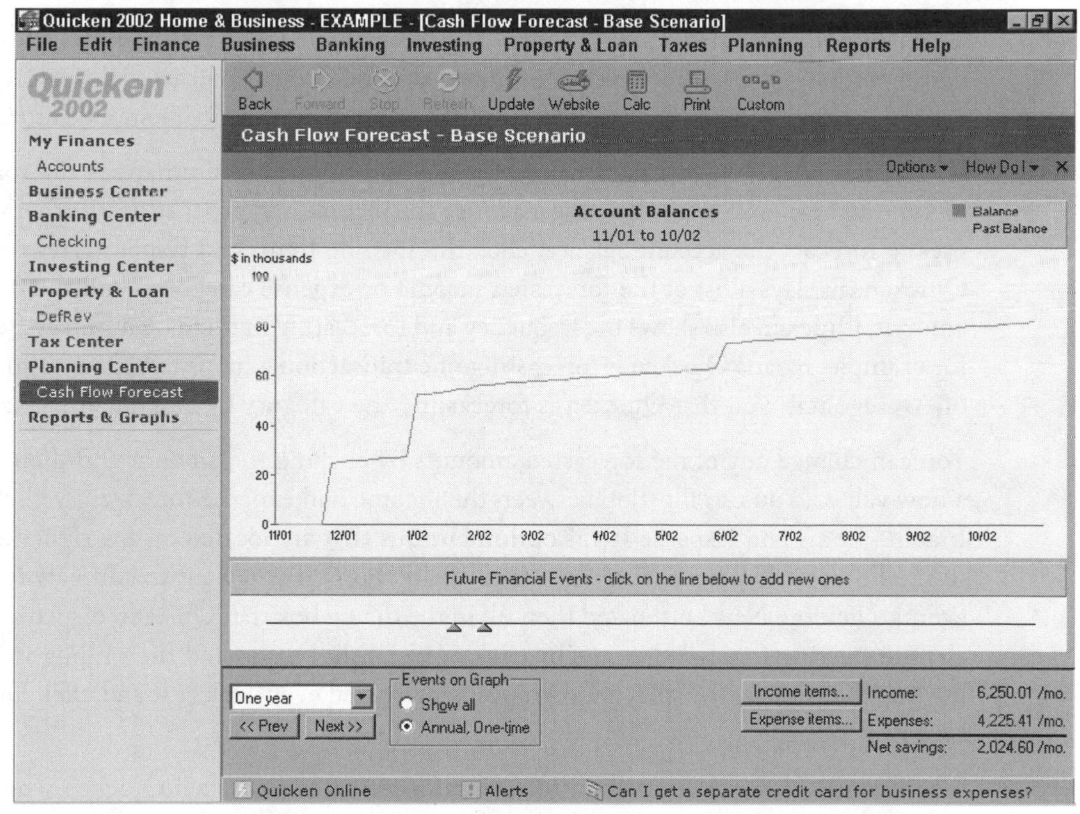

Figure 19.5: The Cash Flow Forecast – Base Scenario window.

Working with a Cash Flow Forecast

The line chart shows the forecasted account balance in either all or a selected group of accounts. You can select which accounts to include in the account balances line by clicking Options and choosing Select Accounts. When Quicken displays the Select Accounts To Include dialog box, mark the accounts you want to include.

You can change the forecasting interval—to month, half-year, full-year, and so on—by activating the drop-down list box in the lower-left corner of the window. You can change the forecasting period, such as from April to May if you've selected months as the period, by clicking the Prev and Next arrow buttons. Clicking the Prev (left arrow) button displays the account balances line chart for the previous period. Clicking the Next (right arrow) button displays the account balances line chart for the next period.

If you click Options and choose Update Budget, you can build a budget based on your forecast. (You may need to provide additional data to Quicken in order for it to build a budget in this manner.)

To change the parameters used to create the forecast, click Options and then choose Update Forecast. Quicken redisplays the Automatically Create Forecast dialog box (see Figure 19.4). From here you can change any of the parameters you initially supplied to Quicken.

In the lower-right corner of the Forecast window, Quicken summarizes the forecasted income and expense totals. If you want to see the income and expense details that Quicken uses to forecast the account balance, click the Income Items and Expense Items buttons. Quicken displays a list of the forecasted income or expense categories and the forecasted amount. Quicken also shows the frequency and forecasting method. A monthly frequency, for example, means Quicken is forecasting one transaction a month. A Date column entry of Average tells you that Quicken is forecasting the category by looking at past averages.

You can change any of the forecasted amounts by clicking the amount and then entering a new value. (You can flip-flop between the income and expense forecasts by clicking the Income Items and Expense Items option buttons that are located on the right-hand side of the Forecast Income or Expense Items dialog box.) If you want to add new forecasted events, click the New button and then fill in the dialog box that Quicken displays. You can change existing forecasted events by clicking the Edit button and then filling in the dialog box that Quicken displays. To remove a forecasted event, select it and click Delete. To save your changes to these forecast items, click Done.

The Events On Graph option buttons in the Forecast window tell Quicken whether you want to see all the financial events for a forecasting interval or just those that occur on a one-time or annual basis.

Creating Multiple Forecast Scenarios

You can work with multiple forecasts, or scenarios, by clicking Options ➢ Manage Scenarios In The Cash Flow Forecast – Base Scenario window. Quicken displays the Manage Forecast Scenarios dialog box, as shown in Figure 19.6. To name and save the current forecast, click the New button and enter a name for the scenario when Quicken displays the Create New Scenario dialog box. (By default, when you create a new scenario, the Copy Current Scenario button is marked and Quicken actually makes a copy of the current scenario.) When you click OK to save this scenario name, you go back to the Manage Forecast Scenarios dialog box. To later display a forecast, click the Scenario button and simply select it from the Scenario Data drop-down list. You can also edit and delete scenarios by using the Edit and Delete command buttons.

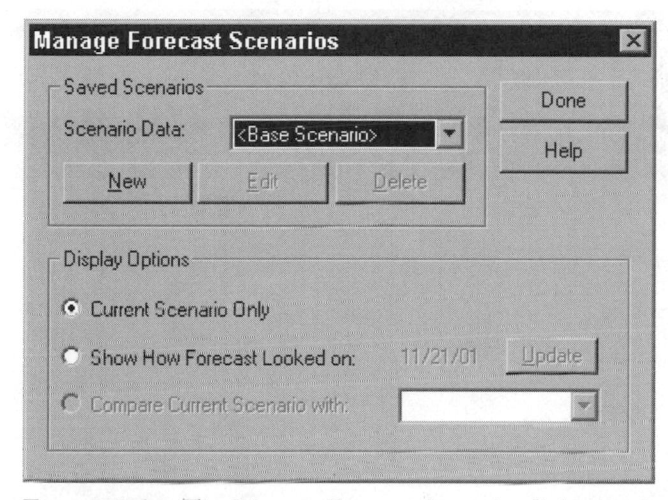

Figure 19.6: The Manage Forecast Scenarios dialog box lets you work with multiple forecasts.

If you create a baseline scenario that you always want to show, create a comparison line. To do this, first make sure the scenario you want is the one currently shown. (You may need to use the Scenario Data drop-down list box to activate the scenario.) Then click New and enter a name in the dialog box that Quicken displays.

Using Project and Job Costing

When people talk about measuring cash flows and profits, they usually mean measuring the cash flows and profits of a business. And, certainly, that's essential. But many businesses, including many small businesses, should also measure profits and cash flows by project or job. A consultant, for example, should look at profits and cash flows by consulting engagement to determine which projects and which sorts of projects are most profitable. And a general contractor should look at profits and cash flows by job to determine which jobs and which sorts of jobs are most profitable.

Fortunately, Quicken makes it easy to track profits and cash flows by project or job. How you account for projects depends on whether you're using Quicken Deluxe or Quicken Home & Business, however.

Project and Job Costing with Quicken Deluxe

If you have Quicken Deluxe, you can perform project or job costing by setting up a class for each project or job, by recording a class when you enter income and expense transactions, and by then preparing project/job reports.

To set up a class, follow these steps:

1. Choose Finance ➢ Class List to display the Class List window, as shown in Figure 19.7.

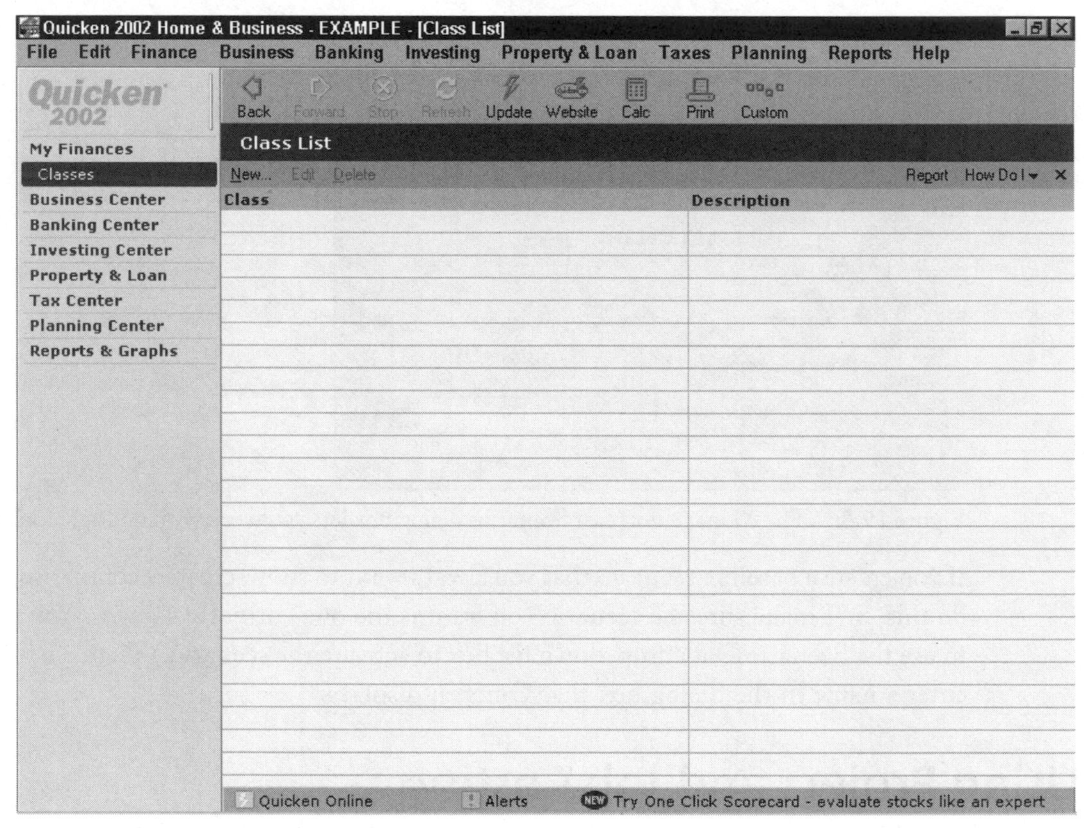

Figure 19.7: The Class List window.

2. Click New to display the Set Up Class dialog box, as shown in Figure 19.8.

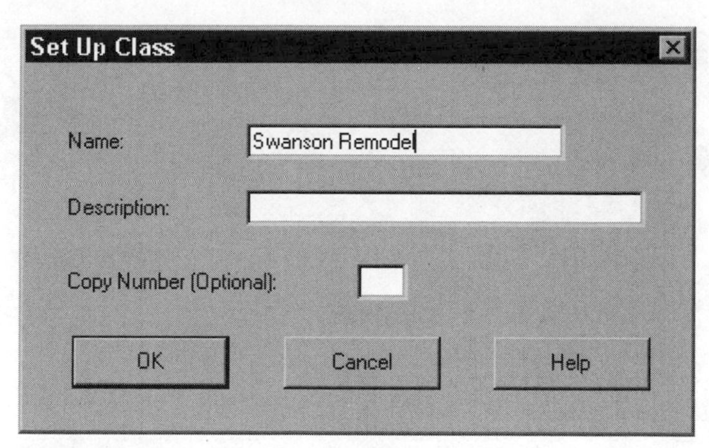

Figure 19.8: The Set Up Class dialog box.

3. Name and describe the project or job using the Name and Description boxes.

4. Click OK to save the new class.

To use project or job classes, you simply append the class name to the income or expense category when you enter income and expense transactions in a register. Figure 19.9 shows a bank account register with several transactions. Note that the Category box shows both a category name and then, following the backslash symbol, a portion of the class name, Swanson Remodel, set up in Figure 19.8. You can't see all of the class name because the Category box isn't long enough.

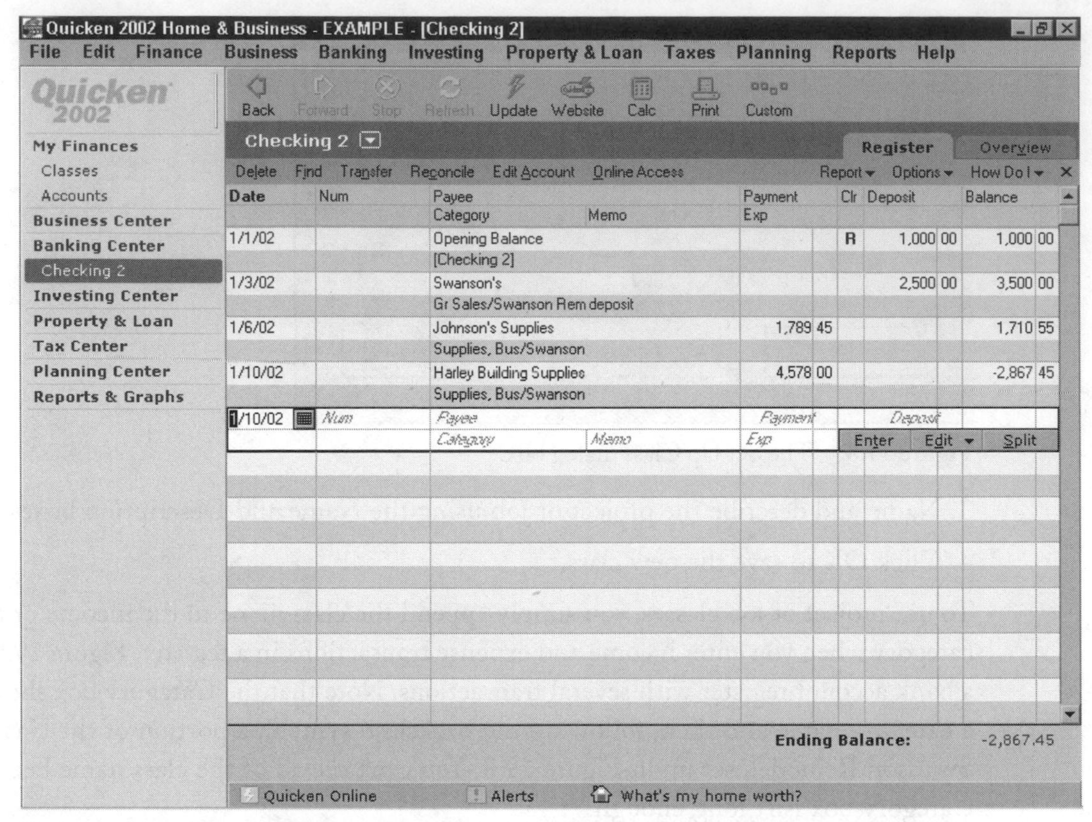

Figure 19.9: A bank account register with the transactions that use project classes.

If you use classes to further describe your income and spending, you can prepare a report that summarizes your income and expense not just using categories but also by using classes. To prepare such a report, choose Reports ➢ Business ➢ Project/Job or Reports ➢ Business ➢ Project/Job By Project. Figure 19.10 shows a Project/Job report that uses the transactions shown in Figure 19.9.

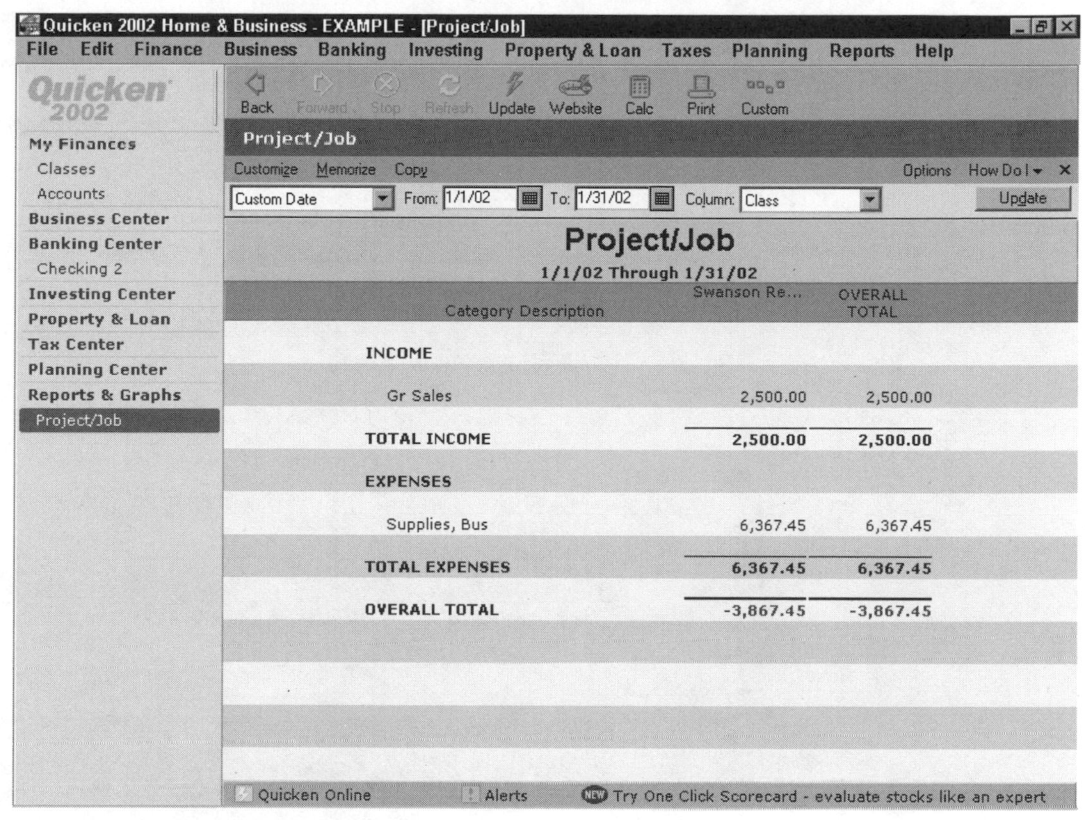

Figure 19.10: A Project/Job report.

Project and Job Costing with Quicken Home & Business

If you have Quicken Home & Business, you can perform project or job costing by setting up a project or job using the Project/Job List, by recording a project or job when you enter income and expense transactions, and by then preparing project/job reports.

To set up a project or job, follow these steps:

1. Choose Business ➤ Business Lists ➤ Project/Job List to display the Project/Job List window, as shown in Figure 19.11. The Project/Job List window shows customers, outstanding invoices and estimates, and any jobs or projects you've already set up.

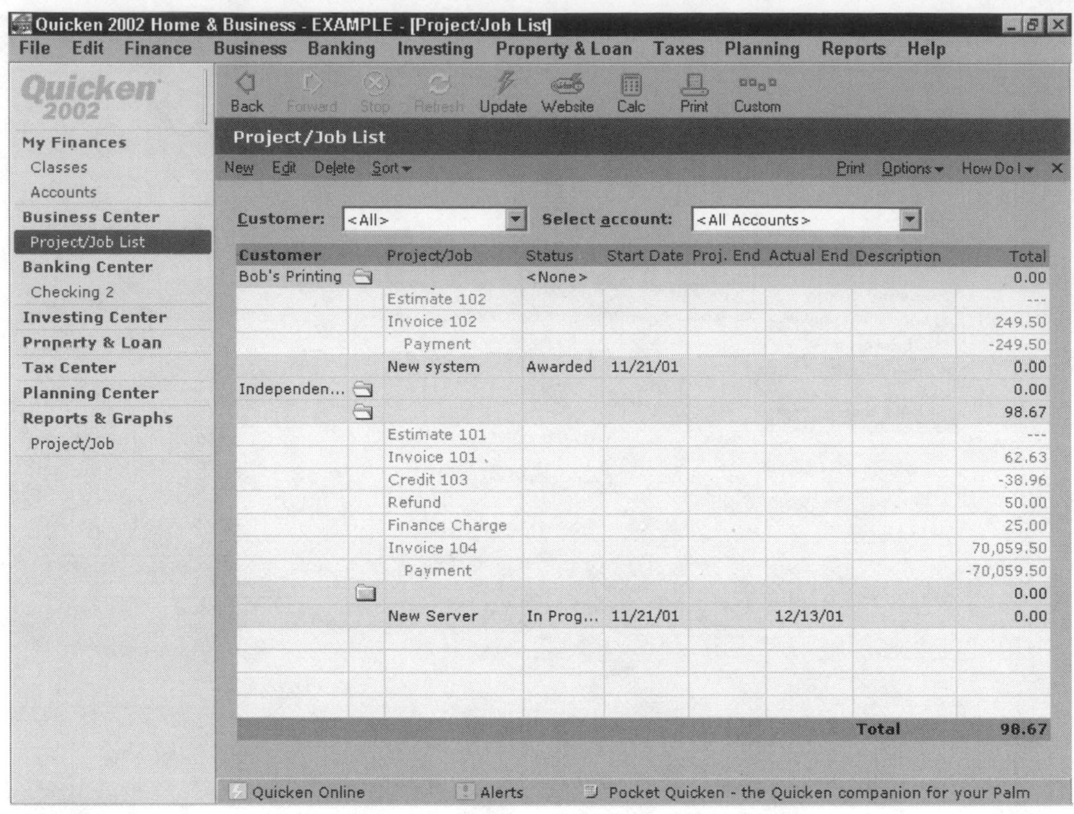

Figure 19.11: The Project/Job List window.

2. Click New to display the New Project/Job dialog box, as shown in Figure 19.12.

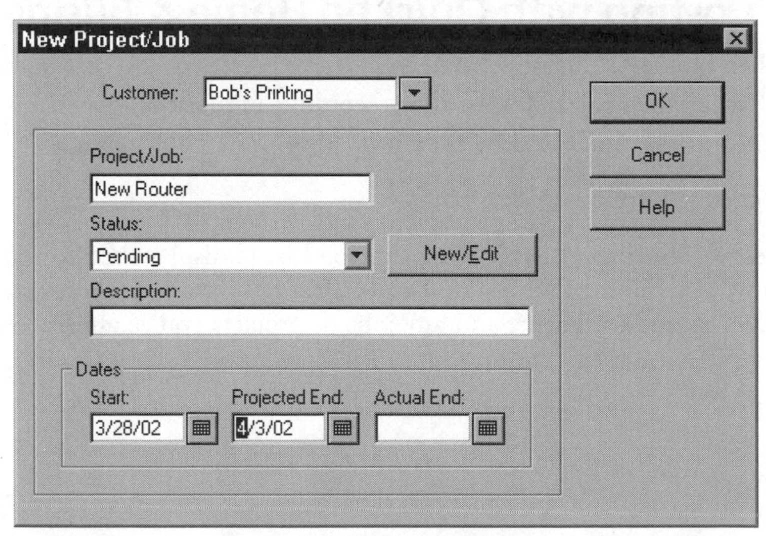

Figure 19.12: The New Project/Job dialog box.

3. Identify the customer for whom you're performing the project or job using the Customer drop-down list box.
4. Name the project or job using the Project/Job box.
5. Select a project or job status from the Status drop-down list box. The Status box lists several typical project or job statuses: Awarded, Closed, In Progress, Not Awarded, and Pending. You can sort the projects and jobs listed in the Project/Job List by status, so if you have large numbers of jobs, this bit of information can be useful to collect.
6. Optionally, use the Description box to further describe or document the project or job.
7. Use the Dates boxes to describe the timing of the project or job. Enter the project start date in the Start box, the anticipated end date in the Projected End box, and the actual finish date in the Actual End box. As with other bits of project and job information, you can sort projects and jobs using this information, which means that you probably want to collect this information if the data is useful in itself or useful for sorting through your job list.
8. Click OK to save the new project or job.

To use project or job classes, you simply record the project or class when you enter a customer invoice, vendor bill, or credit memo transaction. The dialog boxes that Quicken Home & Business supplies for recording these sorts of transactions includes a Project/Job drop-down list box, as shown in Figure 19.13. You can use this box to identify the project or job associated with a transaction.

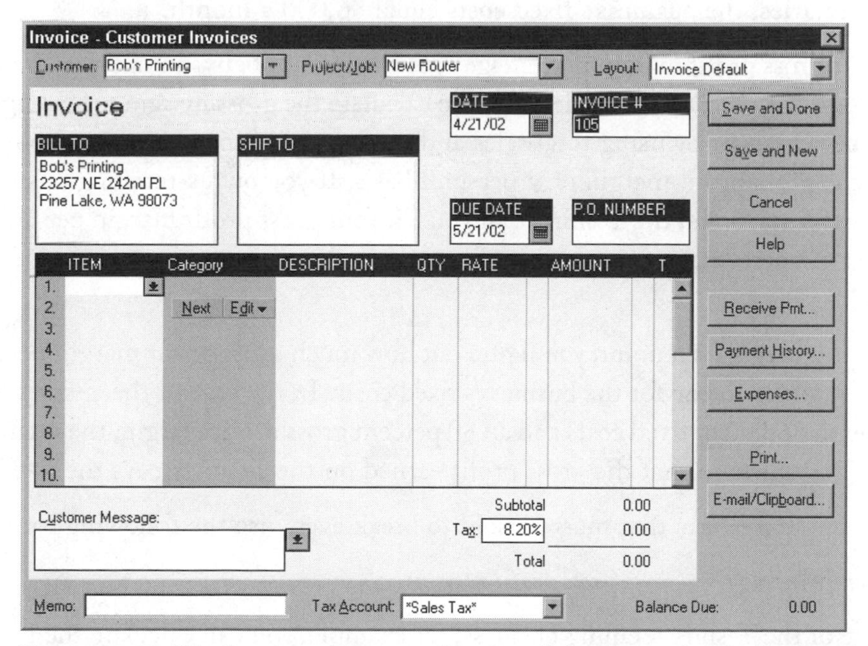

Figure 19.13: The Invoice – Customer Invoices dialog box includes a Project/Job box.

As long as you assign projects or jobs to your customer invoices, vendor bills, and credit memos, you can prepare a report that summarizes your income and expense not just by using categories but also by using classes. To prepare such a report, choose Reports ➢ Business ➢ Project/Job or Reports ➢ Business ➢ Project/Job By Project.

Calculating a Business's Break-Even Point

Break-even analysis allows you to determine the income necessary to pay all your expenses. Break-even analysis is a simple and powerful financial-management technique related to business profits. At the break-even point, a business doesn't make any money, but it also doesn't lose any money. In general, you want to know a business's break-even point because it represents a sales level you must surpass to make money.

The Trick to Calculating a Break-Even Point

To calculate a business's break-even point, you need to determine the total fixed costs of a business and its gross profit margin as a percentage.

A business's fixed costs are those expenses a business must pay regardless of the sales volume. In a retailing business, for example, fixed costs probably include rent, salaries of sales clerks, and other overhead expenses such as utilities and insurance. If a business's fixed costs include $2,000 in monthly rent (which also includes utilities and property insurance) and $4,000 in salaries, the business's fixed costs equal $6,000 a month.

A business's gross profit margin percentage is the difference between sales and its variable costs expressed as percentage of sales. You can calculate the gross margin percentage either on a per-unit basis or by using total sales and total variable costs. Suppose you want to calculate the gross profit margin on a per-unit basis. If you own a retailing business that sells T-shirts for $15 and the T-shirts cost you $3, your gross profit margin per unit is $12 or, restated as a percentage, your gross profit margin is 80 percent, calculated as $12 divided by $15.

To calculate a break-even point, you figure out how much gross profit margin needs to be generated in order to pay for the business's fixed costs. In the case of the T-shirt retailing business with $6,000 of fixed costs and an 80 percent gross profit margin, the retailer must sell enough T-shirts so that the gross profit earned on the T-shirts pays the fixed costs.

To calculate the T-shirts that must be sold to break even, use the following formula:

Break-even point = (fixed costs/gross profit margin)

In the case of the T-shirt retailing business, for example, you can calculate the number of T-shirts that must be sold to break even like this:

Break-even point in units = ($6,000 fixed costs/80 percent)

When you divide the $6,000 by 80 percent, you calculate the sales necessary to break even: $7,500. (At $15 a T-shirt, this works out to 500 T-shirts.) You can test this number by creating a worksheet that describes the income and expenses expected if the retailer sells 500 T-shirts, as shown here:

Income	$7,500	Calculated as 500 T-shirts @ $15 each
T-shirt expenses	$1,500	Calculated as 500 T-shirts @ $3 each
Fixed expenses	$6,000	
Profit (Loss)	0	

Using Quicken to Make Break-Even Calculations Easier

The preceding discussion described how you can determine your business's break-even point if you know your fixed costs and your gross profit margin. As a practical matter, however, you probably don't know these two figures—at least not right off the bat. Does not knowing them mean you can't calculate your break-even point? No, you can easily use Quicken to develop the raw data you need.

To collect the raw data you need for your break-even analysis, you set up a couple of classes: one named Fixed, for tracking your fixed costs, and one named Variable, for tracking your variable costs.

NOTE *You can't, therefore, use classes for break-even analysis if you're also using them for project/job costing.*

Setting Up the Fixed and Variable Cost Classes

To set up classes for segregating your fixed and variable costs, follow these steps:

1. Choose the Finance ➤ Class List command to display the Class List window, as shown in Figure 19.14.

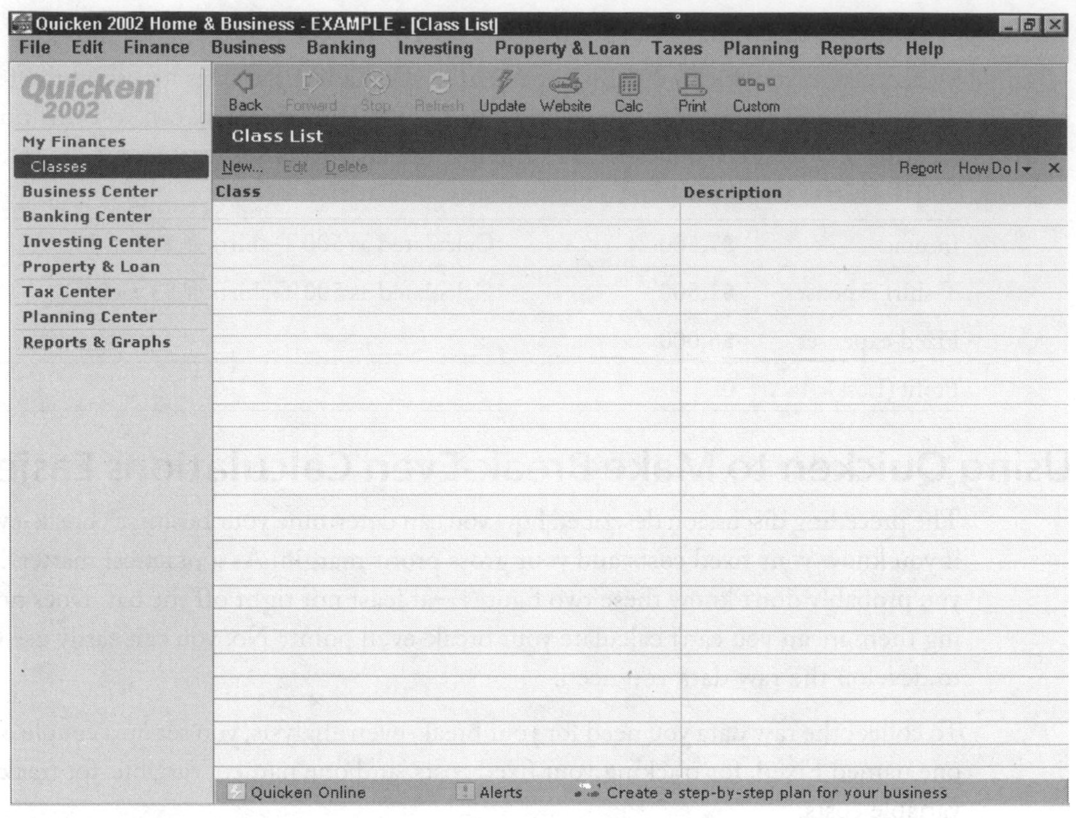

Figure 19.14: The Class List window.

2. Click the New command button to display the Set Up Class dialog box, shown in Figure 19.15.

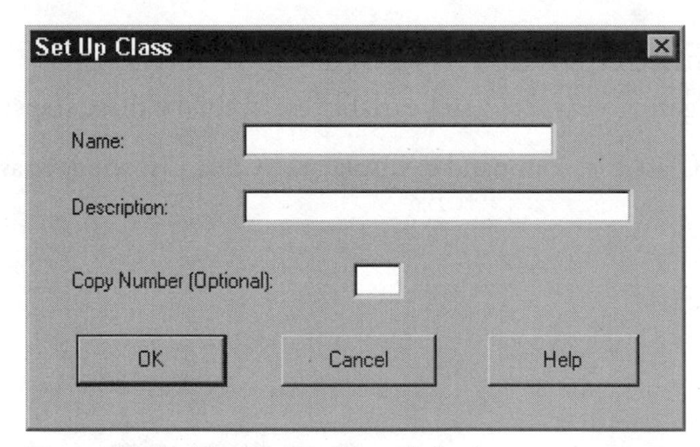

Figure 19.15: The Set Up Class dialog box.

3. Use the Name text box to enter the class name, Fixed.
4. If you want to further describe the cost classification, use the Description text box.

5. Click OK. Quicken adds the new class to the list shown in the Class List window.

Repeat steps 2 through 5 to set up the Variable class. You can set up subclasses in the same way.

Collecting the Break-Even Raw Data

Once you set up the fixed and variable cost classes, classify each cost you incur as either fixed or variable. Things such as rent, utilities, insurance, and salaries are probably fixed; items such as sales commissions, costs of products or services you sell, and delivery or freight charges are probably variable.

To classify an expense as either fixed or variable, follow the expense category with a forward slash and the class name. Figure 19.16 shows a register with transactions classified as Fixed and Variable.

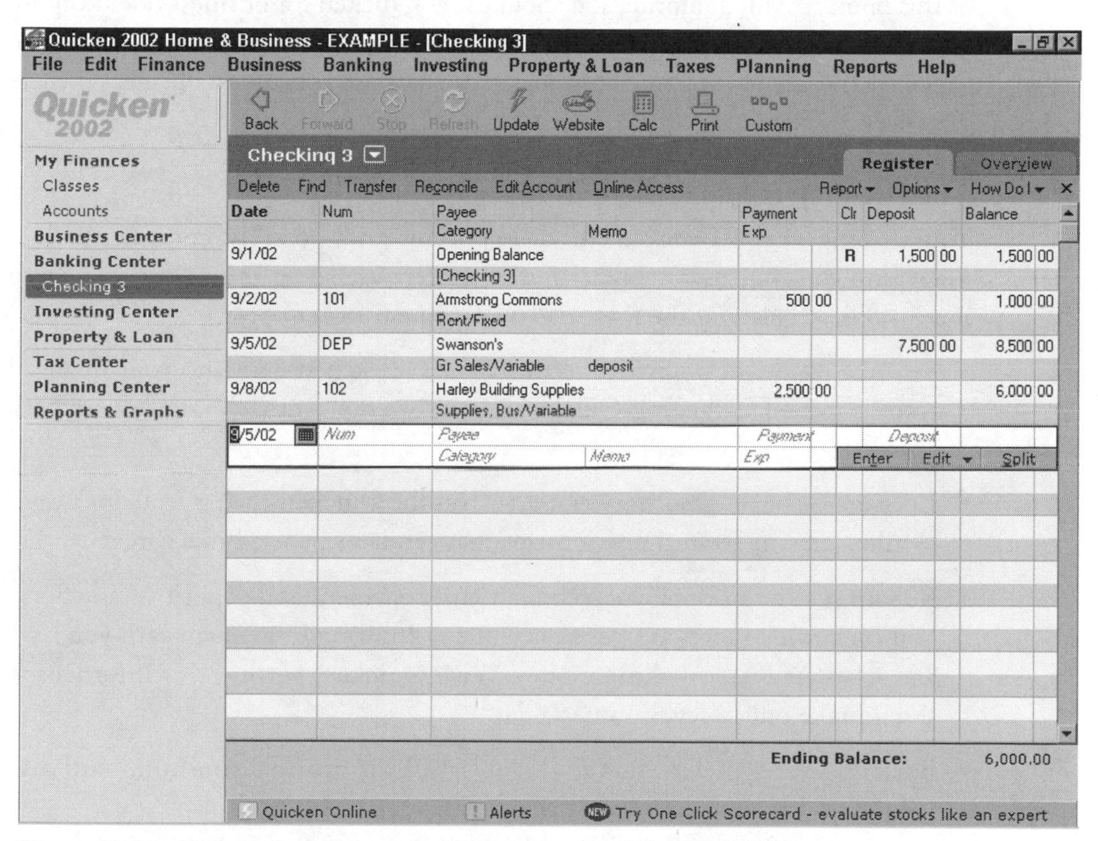

Figure 19.16: Transactions that are both categorized and classified.

To see what fixed and variable costs you've incurred in a year or month, produce a Profit & Loss Statement that summarizes costs by both category and class. This will give you the total fixed costs—one of the pieces of data you need.

To calculate your gross profit margin, you can use the total sales and total variable costs figures and the following formula:

Gross profit margin = (sales–variable costs)/sales

If the data you collect shows sales of $20,000 and variable costs of $16,000, you calculate your gross profit margin percentage as 80 percent ($16,000/$20,000). Then you simply divide the fixed costs by the gross profit margin percentage to calculate the break-even point. If the fixed costs were $6,000, your break-even point would be $7,500 ($6,000 divided by 80 percent equals $7,500).

How to Be a Better Business Owner

If you're a business owner, this part of the chapter is for you. The earlier chapters of this book provided information about using Quicken for business bookkeeping and accounting. This chapter takes a slightly different tack by discussing some financial and accounting management issues that are specific to business owners who use Quicken.

Thinking about Security

You're going to use Quicken for an important and, possibly, confidential job: managing your business's financial affairs. Here are some things you can do to increase the security of the financial-management system:

- Set up a password to restrict access to the Quicken system and your financial records if the PC running Quicken is used by employees who don't work with Quicken (see Chapter 7).
- Lock up the business forms you use, such as the Quicken checks. You don't want to allow anyone to steal check forms that can later be used in a forgery.
- Be sure you (or an employee) regularly enter payment and deposit transactions. You can't run a successful business without knowing how much cash you have and whether you're making money. With Quicken, getting this information should take only a few minutes a day.
- Back up your Quicken data files regularly. This protects you from hard disk failures and human error (see Chapter 7).
- Reconcile your bank accounts on a monthly basis. This will help you catch the errors that people make (see Chapter 5).

The Problem of Embezzlement

Employee theft is extremely common. People steal office supplies in the fall (to use as school supplies for their children), deal with vendors who provide kickbacks (often in the form of expensive gifts and services), and sometimes even find clever ways to steal inventory and pilfer cash.

Most people don't steal, but it does happen; so it makes sense for you to consider what you can do to minimize your employees' opportunities to steal.

Sign Checks Yourself

It's a good idea to sign all checks—even small ones—yourself. This can be a lot of work (as a corporate controller, I used to sign about $100,000 of checks every week), but you can have an employee prepare the checks for your review and signature. The benefit of signing all your checks is that your signature will be a requirement for money to leave the business. No cash will be deducted from the business bank account without your knowing about it.

If you sign all checks, an employee who wants to steal cash from you might try to convince you to write a check that the employee can cash. (You wouldn't write out, say, a $1,000 check to the employee without asking questions.) This means that the employee would need to set up a fictitious vendor and then convince you to pay this vendor some amount. Or the employee might have you pay someone the employee needs to pay anyway. (I saw an employee have the employer write a check that paid the employee's Visa bill.) By carefully reviewing the checks that you sign, you minimize an employee's opportunities for committing these crimes.

If you'll be on vacation for, say, a couple of weeks, the business will probably need to pay some bills while you're away. You can deal with this in a couple of ways. You can decide to trust an employee enough to leave behind a signed check or two; the employee can then use these signed checks to pay for things such as an unexpected C.O.D. shipment. Or you can decide to simply require vendors to wait. If you leave signed checks, be sure to leave specific instructions as to what these checks should be used for, and review the checks when they come back from the bank to be sure that your instructions were followed.

Review Canceled Checks

Be sure to intercept the bank statement when it comes and review the canceled checks. (An easy way to do this is to have the bank send the bank statement to your home.) This way, you can make sure that no one is forging your signature and writing a check or two for nonbusiness reasons. This might seem unlikely, but if your business writes a hundred checks a month totaling tens of thousands of dollars, would you really notice an extra check or two if the amounts were "only" a few hundred dollars?

Separate Mailroom Duty from Bank Deposit Duty

One of the most common ways to embezzle money from an employer is called *lapping*. To lap, an embezzler skims a little bit of the cash that comes in each month and then adjusts the books to hide the skimming. As long as the person skimming the cash also maintains the checkbook, it's easy for the theft to go unnoticed. The embezzler simply ignores or hides the fact that, for example, the $500 Customer A owes you has been paid. You can minimize the opportunities for lapping if you have one employee open the mail and make a list of the incoming cash and another employee enter the bank deposit information into the checkbook. For this approach to work, you simply compare the list of incoming cash maintained by the mailroom person with the bank deposit information shown in the check, and you contact customers about past-due payments. This way, you can discover, for example, that Customer A actually paid the $500 owed and that the check has cleared the bank.

Protect Other Valuable Assets

From an embezzler's perspective, cash is the most convenient item to steal. It's portable, easy to store, and easy to convert to other things an embezzler might want. Because cash is usually watched so closely, however, embezzlers often steal other items of value, such as office equipment, inventory, and supplies.

You can follow a couple of general rules to minimize losses such as these. You can keep a record of the things that your business owns and periodically compare what your records show you have with what you actually hold. If you own a bunch of computer gear, for example, you might want to keep a record or list of the items. You don't need to do this with Quicken unless, as discussed in Chapter 18, you're using Quicken for fixed assets accounting. You just need a simple list. Then, once a month or once a year, compare what your records show with what you have in your warehouse or storeroom or office.

NOTE *If you buy and sell inventory in your business, Quicken will not meet your needs. Consider upgrading from Quicken to a small business accounting system that tracks inventory, such as Intuit's QuickBooks Pro or Peachtree Accounting for Windows.*

You can also restrict access to any valuable assets that the business owns. Warehouses and storerooms should be locked. Access should be limited to people who really need what is being kept behind lock and key. If you have items of high value in a storeroom, for example, and several employees have access, it's also a good idea to make it a rule that people go into the storeroom only in pairs. (A dishonest employee is less likely to steal if someone else is present who may see and report the theft.)

Require Vacations

There's a final embezzlement prevention tool that many big businesses use and that you should probably consider: Require regular vacations of a week or two. (Banks almost always do this.)

Here's the rationale: Some embezzlement schemes are so clever that they're almost impossible to catch. The one typical weakness of these super-clever schemes, however, is that they usually require ongoing maintenance on the part of the embezzling employee. By making the employee take a vacation, you can see what happens when the employee's not around. Here are a couple of examples.

One embezzler who managed a concession stand had a simple but clever technique: He always pocketed a few hundred dollars of cash sales each week. This scheme worked for years. The owner assumed that cash sales were typically about $4,000 a week, even though they were really quite a bit more than that, and that he was losing about $200 a week of ice cream cones, soda pop, and popcorn because of spoilage and, perhaps, a little shoplifting. The concession stand manager never did take a vacation, but he did eventually have a heart attack. And a funny thing happened. Cash sales increased overnight (literally). Even more dramatic, profits jumped because sales increased while expenses stayed level. When the owner looked into the situation in the employee's absence, he figured out that sales and profits had increased because the employee was no longer pilfering cash from the till.

Another embezzler who got tripped up by a vacation requirement was a salesman selling profitable remodeling jobs for a company I'll call *ABC Construction*. His scheme was to have every fourth or fifth job done by a company he had set up, which I'll call *ABC Remodeling*. He regularly used the resources and reputation of ABC Construction to sell a remodeling job for ABC Remodeling and thereby collect the 40 percent profit his employer (ABC Construction) would have made rather than his usual 10 percent sales commission. As long as he stayed in town, his little ploy worked reasonably well. He could answer all his telephone calls—both those from ABC Construction customers and those from ABC Remodeling customers—and handle any problems that surfaced for either set of customers. When he went on vacation, however, the whole thing blew up as soon as an ABC Remodeling customer called ABC Construction to ask about a remodeling project in progress.

Finding Good Bookkeeping Help

In any business, it's a challenge to find and keep good people. It can be even more difficult to find good people to do something such as bookkeeping when you are not particularly knowledgeable about the subject, but there are some guidelines you can follow.

First, if you're hiring someone who simply is going to keep your checkbook, that person needs to know basic arithmetic, of course, but doesn't need to know how to use Quicken. If Quicken works well for you and you have no plans to upgrade to a more powerful program, the person can learn to use Quicken on the job. It will help if the employee already knows a thing or two about computers and has worked with Windows or a program that runs under it, such as Microsoft Word.

One other thing: You'll do well to find someone who knows how to do payroll net wages and payroll tax calculations. Mechanically, preparing payroll is one of the more complicated things you do in Quicken. An employee who understands these procedures will have an easier time using Quicken for payroll.

NOTE *The IRS and many state revenue agencies sponsor free small-business taxpayer education programs (sometimes referred to as STEP workshops) that explain how things such as payroll taxes work. If a bookkeeper needs to learn how to do payroll, find out if there are any such workshops in your area.*

How to Tell if You've Outgrown Quicken

Small-business accounting systems (Quicken is one when you use it in a small-business setting) are supposed to do three things:

- Measure your profits and cash flow so that you can prudently manage your business.
- Track the assets and liabilities of the business so that you know what you own and what you owe.
- Generate the business forms that you use to transact business.

As long you keep these three accounting system tasks in mind, you'll find it easy to tell when you've outgrown Quicken and should move up to a more full-featured small-business accounting system.

Quicken measures income and expenses using either cash-based accounting or very simple accrual-based accounting. If you want to do sophisticated accrual-based accounting rather than cash-based accounting, you can't use Quicken. You'll need a more full-featured accounting system, such as QuickBooks from Intuit or Peachtree Accounting for Windows.

To keep detailed records of assets besides cash and your investments, you also need to use a small-business accounting system. For example, if you buy and sell inventory items and want to track those items, you need an accounting system that includes inventory management features. (Most small-business accounting packages provide these features.) If you own a lot of depreciable assets and want to track them, you need an accounting system that includes a true fixed-assets module that easily handles depreciation. (This is a less common feature, by the way.) If you want point-of-sale accounting, or other special features, you also need to upgrade to a more powerful accounting system.

One other issue is business forms. Quicken produces check forms and Quicken Home & Business produces invoices and customer statements, but you may need to produce other business forms, such as purchase orders. If you want to automate production of these other forms with an accounting system rather than prepare them manually, you need to upgrade to a more powerful system.

Before you purchase a new accounting system to take care of the tasks I've just described, there are a couple of things to keep in mind. First, no accounting system is perfect. I've seen more than one business waste enormous amounts of time, energy, and money pursuing the perfect accounting system. If you have a system that works reasonably well, lets you gauge the performance of your business, and in general does most of the things you need it to do, you may create more problems than you solve by converting to a more complicated new system. (If Quicken works reasonably well and presents you with only a handful of minor problems and irritations, I'd suggest you stick with Quicken.)

Also, the more powerful small-business accounting systems generally require you (or someone who works for you) to know a lot more about accounting than you need to know to operate Quicken. When you get right down to it, all you need to know to operate Quicken is how to use a checkbook and enter payments and deposits into a check register. In comparison, to use a full-featured small-business accounting system, you (or your employee) should know how to perform double-entry bookkeeping, understand the tricks and techniques used in accrual-based accounting (accruals, deferrals, reversing journal entries, and so on), and be able to read and use the financial information contained in a standard set of accrual-based financial statements (income statements, balance sheets, and cash flow statements). Note that the cash flow statement produced by an accrual-based accounting system won't look anything like the Cash Flow report produced by Quicken.

Two Things Business Owners Should Never Do

As a business owner, you know that there are plenty of things that you should do. Here, I'll point out two things that you should never do.

Don't Misrepresent Your Financial Affairs

You should never misrepresent your financial condition and your business's financial performance. You may think that you would never do this, but let me tell you how it always seems to start. You go to the bank for a loan (perhaps a home mortgage). The bank loan officer looks at your Quicken Profit & Loss statement and then tells you that you're not making quite enough money or that your debts seem a bit high.

It appears that a fair number of business owners go home, mull things over, and then think, "What if I made more money?" Asking and answering this question leads quite naturally to a careful review of the Quicken register, and suddenly the business owner has recategorized a series of business transactions as personal expenses. This has the nice effect of increasing the business profits. When the bank loan officer looks at your new Quicken Profit & Loss statement, the loan is approved.

This may seem like a harmless solution, but misrepresenting your finances subjects you to two extremely serious risks. First, by misrepresenting your finances, you've committed a felony because you fraudulently obtained your loan. In a worst-case scenario, the bank can probably force you to repay the loan immediately. Many of the laws that normally protect you if you're a borrower don't protect you if you've fraudulently obtained a loan. (In a bankruptcy proceeding, for example, you probably can't escape repayment of fraudulently obtained loans.)

Another serious risk you run by misrepresenting your finances occurs if the IRS audits your return. If the IRS agent sees that expenses you claimed as business deductions on your tax return are later described as personal expenses on a Profit & Loss statement, the IRS can probably disallow the business deductions. If you assured the bank that $3,000 of travel expenses were for a personal vacation, you'll need to do a lot of backpedaling to convince the IRS that the $3,000 was really for business travel.

Don't Borrow Payroll Tax Deposit Money

Never borrow the money you've deducted from an employee's payroll check for taxes, and never spend the money you've set aside for the payroll taxes that you owe as the employer. If for any reason you can't repay the money, the IRS will pursue you with merciless vigor.

If you get to the point where you can't continue business without dipping into the payroll tax deposit money, don't compound your problems by getting into trouble with the IRS. It doesn't matter what you want to use the money for. If you can't make payroll, can't get a supplier to deliver goods, or can't pay the rent without borrowing a bit of the payroll tax deposit money, you simply can't make payroll, receive the goods, or pay the rent. If you did borrow the payroll tax deposit money, you would be stealing from the IRS. And when the IRS finds out, the IRS may padlock your business some afternoon, thereby putting you out of business; seize any valuable personal assets you own, including your home; and garnish your wages if you get another job. In short, the IRS will do anything it legally can to collect the money you should have paid.

Because of all this, I can't imagine a situation in which it makes sense to borrow the payroll tax deposit money. If things are so bad that you can't go on without taking the payroll tax deposit money, it's time for you to consider drastic action—perhaps closing the business, filing for bankruptcy, laying off employees, or finding an investor.

Part 3

INVESTMENTS AND INSURANCE

In This Part

Chapter 20

MUTUAL FUND INVESTMENTS

In This Chapter

- What to do about IRAs and 401(k) mutual fund investments
- Setting up a mutual fund account
- Describing the mutual fund shares you buy
- Describing mutual fund profit distributions
- Describing the mutual fund shares you sell
- Handling account fees, stock splits, and reminders
- Editing mutual fund transactions
- Success strategies for mutual fund record keeping
- How to be a smart investor

Mutual funds deliver big benefits to investors: tremendous diversification, low costs, and in many cases outstanding professional management and investment advice. Unfortunately, mutual-fund record keeping can be tricky. When the profits you earn from a mutual fund investment are taxable, the profit calculations—in particular, the capital gain or loss calculations—quickly become cumbersome. Fortunately, Quicken can help you with these calculations, as well as your other mutual-fund tracking activities.

TIP *Even if you don't invest using mutual funds but instead invest directly in stocks and bonds, this chapter is a good place to start learning. Quicken's stock and bond record-keeping features represent an extension of its mutual fund record-keeping features. So read through this chapter and then continue onto the next one, which covers stock and bond record keeping.*

Before You Begin

Here are the prerequisites for tracking a mutual fund investment in Quicken:

- You need to keep records that document the mutual fund shares you've purchased and sold. Quicken is, after all, a record-keeping tool. If you don't have the raw data you want to record in Quicken, you can't use Quicken.
- You should know the mechanics of using the Quicken register. To keep records of investments, you use many of the same windows and commands you do to keep records of bank accounts, credit cards, and other assets and liabilities.

What to Do about IRA and 401(k) Mutual Fund Investments

It probably doesn't make sense to track tax-deferred mutual fund investments in Quicken. There's no harm in doing so, but you don't get anything extra for your effort.

If your mutual fund investing is through tax-deferred accounts such as employer-sponsored 401(k) accounts, Individual Retirement Accounts (IRAs), and self-employed pension plans like Simplified Employee Pensions (SEPs), Keogh plans, and SIMPLE-IRAs, your investment profits aren't taxed. Dividends and interest aren't taxed, capital gains aren't taxed, and capital losses aren't tax-deductible.

Instead, money you withdraw from the account is taxed. Restated in terms of Quicken mechanics, when you deposit money that has been withdrawn from, say, your IRA account into a bank account, you just categorize the bank account deposit as income. (The income category could be named something like IRA Distribution.)

Because you don't need to keep records for the purpose of tracking your mutual fund profits, there's little reason to go to the extra work of keeping mutual fund investment records in Quicken. You can easily obtain information about these accounts in several ways:

- If you want to know the current value of your mutual fund investment, you can just look at your last statement from the mutual fund investment management company or give that company a telephone call. The big mutual fund management companies have toll-free numbers that give fund price and account value information. You can also look up the fund on the Web.
- If you want to see what taxable income you have because of the mutual fund, you can look at your bank accounts and summarize the deposits you've made into these accounts.
- You can get the annual return on the investment by looking at the annual report the mutual fund management company sends you at the end of the year.

NOTE *Roth-IRAs, as you might know, work differently from regular IRAs. With a Roth-IRA, you don't get a tax deduction for money you put away into the IRA and when you withdraw money during retirement from a Roth-IRA (assuming you meet certain requirements) you don't count the money as income. Accordingly, Roth-IRAs produce neither tax deductions nor taxable income. While these characteristics mean that Roth-IRAs appear very different from a regular IRA, they mean the same thing for your investment record-keeping: You don't need to set up separate investment accounts for Roth-IRA investments made using mutual funds. You can get all the information you want from the mutual fund manager.*

There are other, similar situations in which it doesn't make sense to track a mutual fund investment with Quicken because you don't get any new information or added value from your record-keeping effort. Suppose you have retirement money in a mutual fund, you don't buy and sell shares, and you don't reinvest your mutual fund profits (because you live on these profits). In this case, it doesn't make sense to track your mutual fund investments in Quicken. You can keep a record of the mutual fund profits by using appropriate income categories when you deposit the dividend, interest, or capital gains distributions check into your bank account. And you can get investment activity and current market value information by looking at a recent statement or by telephoning the mutual fund investment company.

That much said, if you feel compelled to set up an account for an IRA, Roth-IRA or 401(k) mutual account, you can do so. The extra work you go through to set up and then keep records of your retirement account will deliver some modest benefits. By doing so, for example, you can have all your investment information in Quicken, thereby making managing this money easier. You can also prepare more accurate estimates of your net worth if you have Quicken accounts set up for all your assets.

NOTE *You can use the Paycheck Wizard (described in Chapter 2) to describe any 401(k) contributions you deduct directly from your paycheck.*

Setting Up a Mutual Fund Account

To track a mutual fund investment in Quicken, you need to set up an investment account. It will be into this account that the mutual investment transactions are recorded. You'll set up one investment account for each mutual fund in which you own shares.

To set up a mutual fund account, follow these steps:

1. Choose Finance ➢ Account List to display the Account List window.
2. Click the New command button to display the Create New Account dialog box, as shown in Figure 20.1.

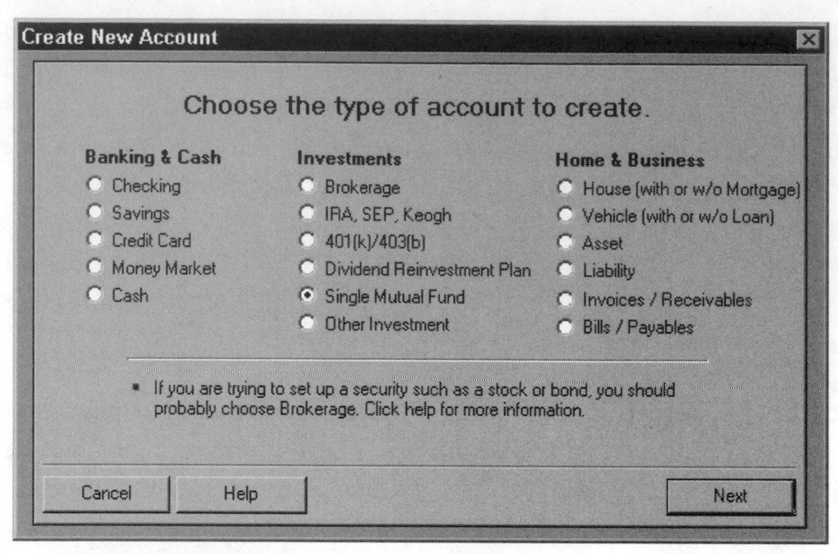

Figure 20.1: The Create New Account dialog box.

3. Mark the appropriate Investment option button:

   - **IRA, SEP, Keogh** Sets up an account to track a mutual fund you're investing in through an IRA, SEP, or Keogh retirement plan.
   - **401(k)/403(b)** Sets up an account to track a mutual fund you're investing in through a 401(k), 403(b), or SIMPLE-IRA retirement plan.
   - **Single Mutual Fund** Sets up an account to track a taxable mutual fund investment.

NOTE *If you're investing in a money market mutual fund, mark the Money Market option button.*

4. Click Next to display the first Investment Account Setup dialog box, as shown in Figure 20.2.

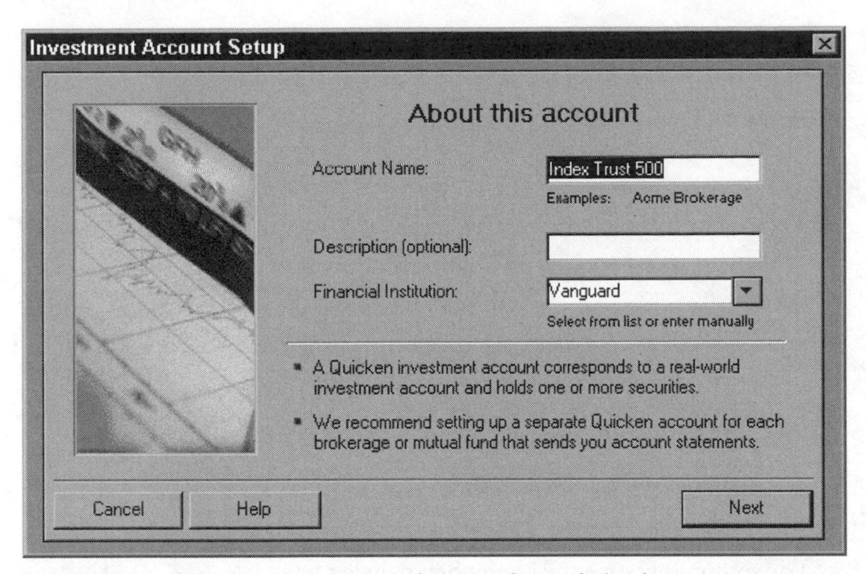

Figure 20.2: The first Investment Account Setup dialog box.

5. Enter an account name in the Account Name text box. You can use the mutual fund's name as your account name. If you have Mutual Fund shares in the Vanguard Index 500 trust fund, for example, you might choose to name the account Vanguard or Index 500.
6. If you want to further describe or collect additional information about an account, use the Description text box. You can enter a maximum of 54 characters.
7. Select the mutual fund management company or financial institution from the Financial Institution list box.
8. Click Next to display the second Investment Account Setup dialog box, as shown in Figure 20.3. Answer the question that Quicken asks about the tax-deferred or tax-exempt status of the mutual fund account by marking the Yes or No option button.

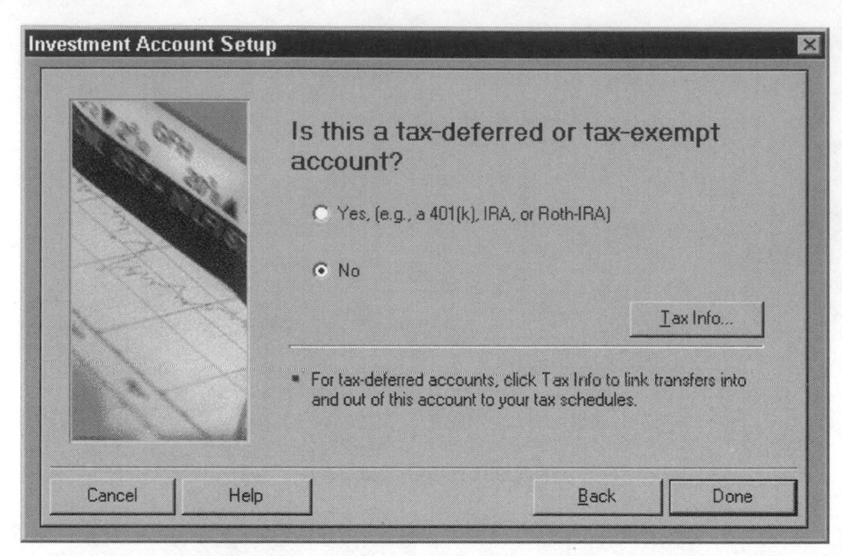

Figure 20.3: The second Investment Account Setup dialog box.

9. Click the Tax Info command button to display the Tax Schedule Information dialog box, as shown in Figure 20.4.

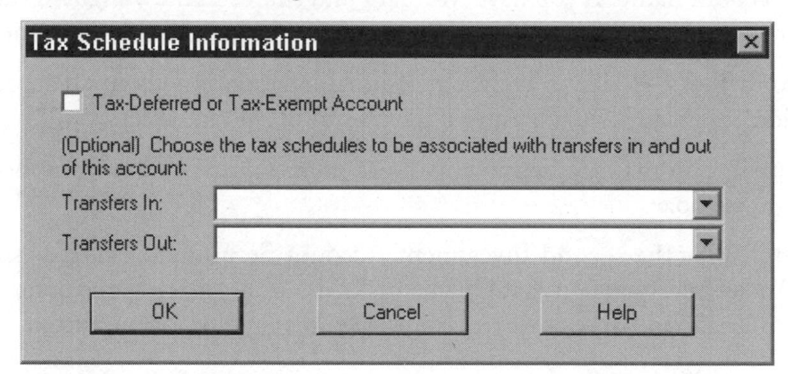

Figure 20.4: The Tax Schedule Information dialog box.

10. If the mutual fund account won't produce taxable income or tax-deductible capital losses, mark the Tax-Deferred Or Tax-Exempt Account checkbox. This tells Quicken that it should not count this account's income and expense amounts as taxable or tax deductible.

11. If the transfers into and out of the investment account should be reported on your income tax return, use the Transfers In and Transfers Out drop-down list boxes to identify on which tax return form or schedule (and on which line on the form or schedule) these transfers should be reported. In the case of a mutual fund investment that's part of your IRA, for example, transfers to the account are reported as IRA contributions.

12. Click OK to close the Tax Schedule Information dialog box.

13. Click Next in the Investment Account Setup dialog box. If the financial institution holding your investment account offers online financial services, Quicken may display another Investment Account Setup dialog box that lets you enroll for online services. Complete this dialog box.

14. Click Next again. Quicken displays the Create Opening Share Balance dialog box, as shown in Figure 20.5. Usually, you don't want to use this dialog box because it doesn't allow you to enter the actual cost data that is useful for tax calculations. Don't enter anything into the Number Of Shares and Price Per Share text boxes here. You will enter the opening shares and price information later.

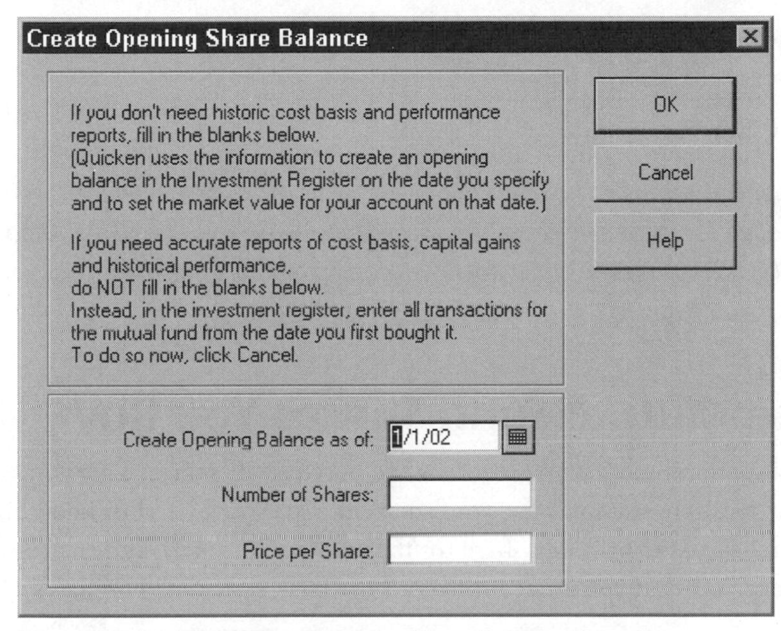

Figure 20.5: The Create Opening Share Balance dialog box.

NOTE *You can enter the date, number-of-shares, and price-per-share information in the Create Opening Share Balance dialog box if you won't use the data for calculating the tax basis and, as a result, for calculating taxable profits or tax-deductible losses. But if you don't need to calculate taxable investment profits or tax-deductible losses, you also don't need to use Quicken for your investment record keeping.*

15. Click Cancel to close the Create Opening Share Balance dialog box. Quicken displays the Welcome To Your Investment dialog box.

16. Click Continue. Quicken displays the Easy Actions Assistant dialog box, as shown in Figure 20.6. This dialog box walks you through the steps of recording the mutual fund share purchases that you've already made. You can use Easy Actions Assistant to record these purchases by following the on-screen instructions. Alternatively, you can just read through and follow the instructions described in the next section of the chapter.

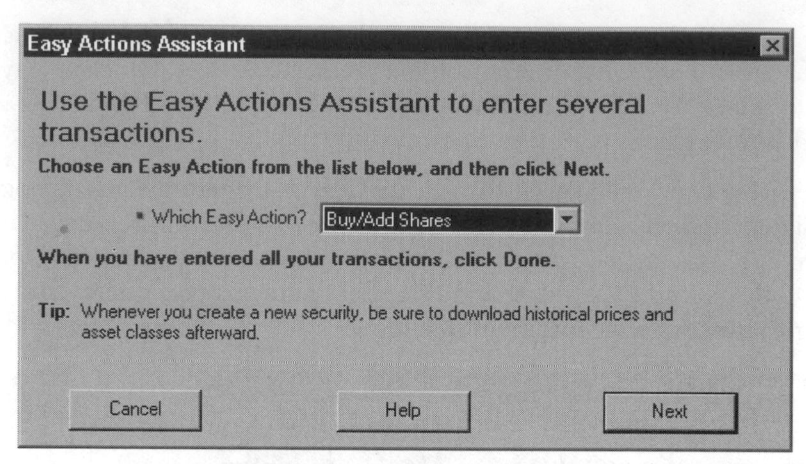

Figure 20.6: The Easy Actions Assistant dialog box.

NOTE *If the financial institution holding your investments offers online financial services and you enrolled for these services when you set up the account, the Easy Actions Assistant dialog box includes an option for downloading mutual fund investment transactions directly. If you're given this option, you want to take it.*

Describing the Mutual Fund Shares You Buy

The first mutual fund transaction you record is the purchase of shares. This is easy as long as you have your monthly statement or confirmation slip. You'll need to know the number of shares purchased, the price per share (or the transaction total), and the commission paid (if any). Note, too, that you'll need to record the past, historical purchases of mutual fund shares.

Quicken provides two methods for recording transactions such as share purchases:

- You can enter a purchase transaction directly into the register.
- You can use an investment form dialog box to collect the share purchase transaction and then have Quicken enter the purchase transaction into the register for you.

Both methods work in the same way. Which one you choose depends on which window you're currently working in.

Entering a Purchase Directly into the Register

To enter the first and any subsequent purchases of mutual fund shares directly into the register, follow these steps:

1. Display the investment register and move to the first empty row of the register. You can display the investment register by choosing Finance ➤ Account List and then double-clicking the investment account.

2. Enter the purchase date in the Date text box. Be sure to enter the actual purchase date and not the date you mailed the check to the mutual fund management company or the broker or the date you recorded the purchase. Quicken categorizes any capital gain or loss as short-term or long-term based on the difference between the purchase and sales dates shown in the register.

3. Enter the action, as follows:

   - *If you made this purchase sometime in the past,* enter the action as ShrsIn. Place the cursor in the Action combo box and type ***ShrsIn*** or select the ShrsIn entry from the Action list box.

   - *If this is a purchase you're currently making,* enter the action as BuyX. Type ***BuyX*** in the Action combo box or select that entry from the Action list box.

4. Enter the name of the mutual fund into the Security text box. If this is the first time you've recorded a purchase of the mutual fund, Quicken displays the Set Up Security dialog box, as shown in Figure 20.7. Enter the security symbol for the mutual fund in the Symbol text box. (If you don't know the security symbol, click the Look Up button.) Activate the Type drop-down list box and select the Mutual Fund entry. To monitor your mutual fund investments by the type of investments made, activate the Asset Class drop-down list box and select the asset class that most closely matches the mutual fund's principal investments. To segregate your investments by investment goal, activate the Goal drop-down list box and select one of the goals listed. Then click OK to close the Set Up Security dialog box and return to the investment register.

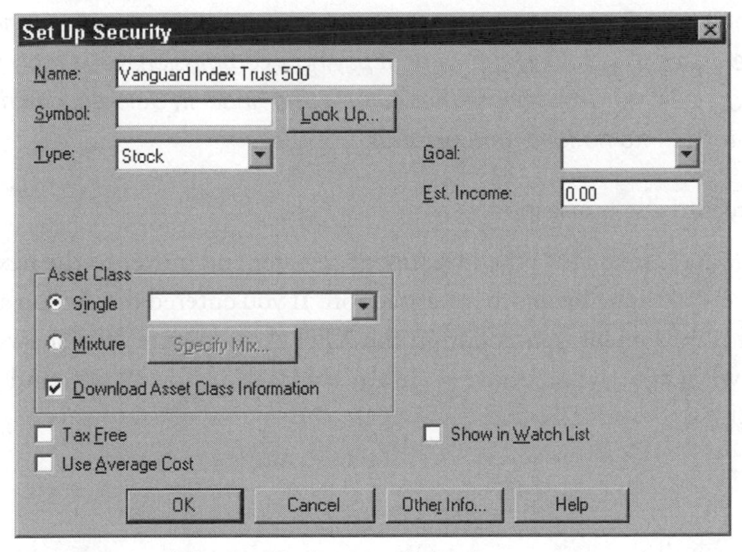

Figure 20.7: The Set Up Security dialog box.

5. Enter the price per share you paid in the Avg. Cost or Price text box. (Quicken changes the name of the box that holds the share price data from Avg. Cost to Price if you record a BuyX transaction.) You can enter the share price in dollars and cents, such as 10.25, or in dollars and eighths, such as 10 1/8.
6. Enter the number of shares you purchased in the Shares text box or the total amount you paid in the Basis or Amount text box. (Quicken changes the name of the box that holds the total price from Basis to Amount if you record a BuyX transaction.)

Quicken calculates whatever piece of data you didn't enter. For example, if you enter the price as $10.00 and the number of shares as 100, Quicken calculates the total as $1,000.00.

7. If you want to record some additional piece of information, such as the order number, use the Memo box.
8. If you're recording a BuyX action, use the XFer Acct combo box to show which account you used to pay for the purchase.

NOTE *If you enter an account name in the XFer Account field, Quicken records a payment transaction in the account equal to the value you enter in the XFer Amt text box.*

9. If you're recording a BuyX action, either enter the amount you paid for the mutual fund shares and any commission in the XFer Amt text box or enter the commission you paid in the Comm Fee text box. (If you purchased shares of a no-load mutual fund, the commission equals zero.)

Quicken calculates whatever piece of data you didn't enter. For example, if you enter the total paid for the mutual fund shares as $1,000.00 and the commission as $50.00, Quicken calculates the XFer Amt as $1,050.00.

TIP *You don't need to pay commissions, or loads, when you purchase mutual fund shares. To purchase shares of a mutual fund without paying a commission, you simply purchase shares of a no-load mutual fund. Use the Mutual Fund Finder in Quicken, described later in the chapter, to find no-load mutual funds.*

10. Click Enter to record the transaction.

Quicken records the transaction into the investment register and moves to the next empty row of the register so you can enter another transaction. If you entered the Action as BuyX, Quicken also records a payment transaction in the XFer Acct. Figure 20.8 shows the investment register with two transactions: a ShrsIn transaction for $2,000 and a BuyX purchase for $5,000.

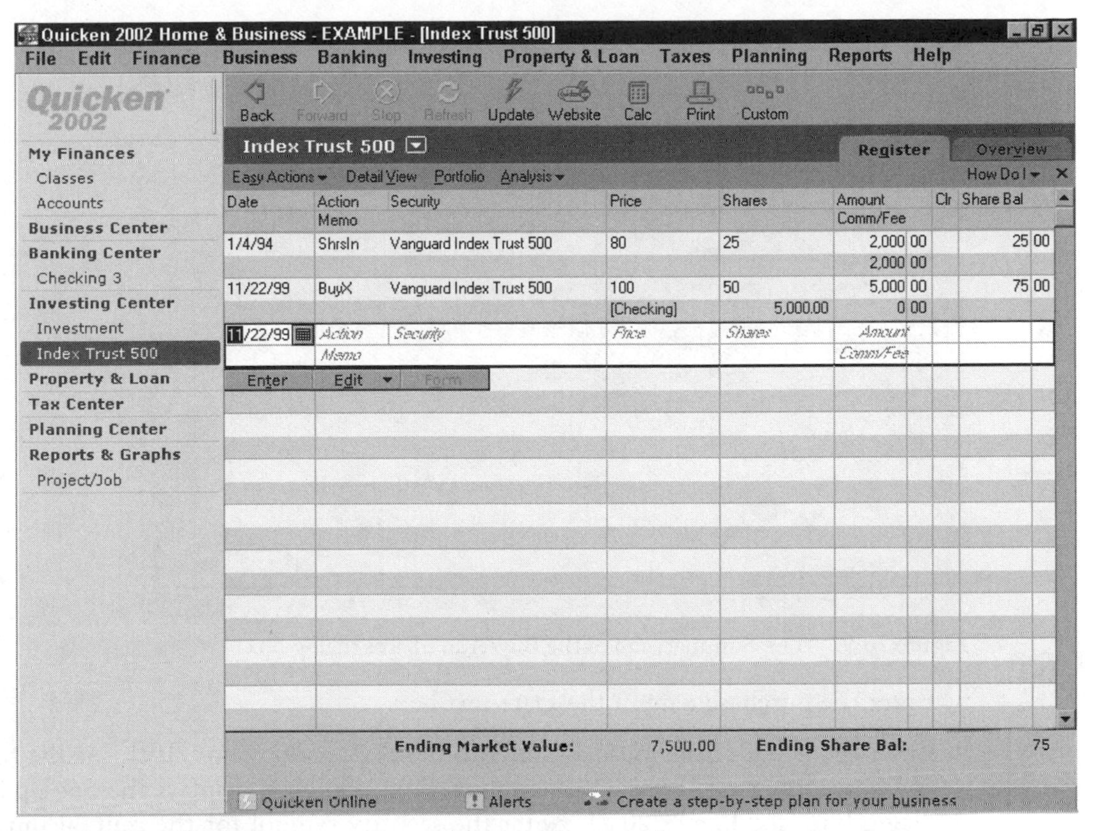

Figure 20.8: An investment register with some share purchases.

Using a Form to Record a Purchase

Instead of recording information directly into the investment register, you can use the Buy/Add Shares dialog box to record a current purchase or an earlier purchase of mutual fund shares. A current purchase is one for which you not only want to record the purchase of the mutual fund shares but also need to record the corresponding payment transaction (probably the check you wrote to purchase the shares). An earlier purchase is one for which you want to record only the purchase of the mutual fund shares but not the corresponding payment transaction. Here's how both transactions work:

1. Display the investment account in a register, move the cursor to the next empty row of the investment register, and click the Easy Actions button to display the Easy Actions menu. Choose the Buy/Add Shares command to display the Buy/Add Shares dialog box.
2. Click the Summary tab of the Buy/Add Shares dialog box. This tab is shown in Figure 20.9.

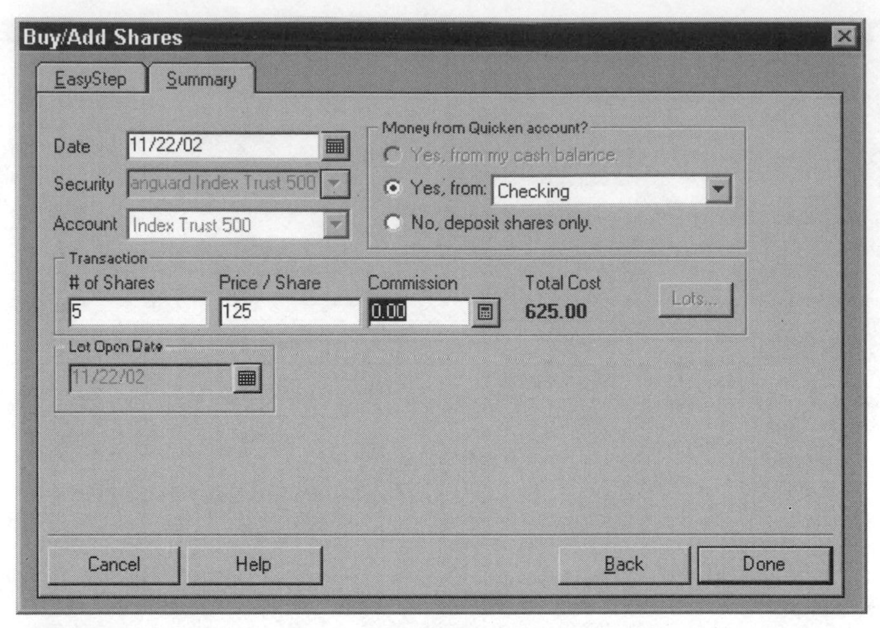

Figure 20.9: The Summary tab of the Buy/Add Shares dialog box.

3. Enter the purchase date in the Date text box.

4. Enter the name of the mutual fund into the Security text box. If this is the first time you've recorded a purchase of the mutual fund, Quicken displays the Set Up Security dialog box (see Figure 20.7). Enter the security symbol for the mutual fund in the Symbol text box. (If you don't know the security symbol, click the Look Up button.) Activate the Type drop-down list box and select the Mutual Fund entry. To monitor your mutual fund investments by the type of investments made, activate the Asset Class drop-down list box and select the asset class that most closely matches the mutual fund's principal investments. To segregate your investments by investment goal, activate the Goal drop-down list box and select one of the goals listed. Then click OK to close the Set Up Security dialog box and return to the investment register.

5. Press Tab to move past the Account text box. Quicken fills in the Account text box with whatever you named the mutual fund account.

6. Enter the shares you purchased in the # Of Shares text box, the price per share you paid in the Price/Share text box (in dollars and cents or dollars and eighths), and the commission you paid, if any, in the Commission text box.

7. If you're recording a current purchase, mark the Yes From option button in the Money From Quicken Account? section of the dialog box, and then use the Yes From drop-down list box to identify the account from which the payment was made.

8. If you're recording an earlier purchase, mark the No option button in the Money From Quicken Account? section of the dialog box.

9. Click Done.

Quicken uses the information you've entered in the Buy/Add Shares dialog box to record a current purchase or an earlier purchase in the investment account register.

Describing Mutual Fund Profit Distributions

Periodically, a mutual fund distributes profits to the shareholders. On a monthly basis, for example, a money market or bond mutual fund may distribute interest income. On a quarterly basis, a stock mutual fund probably distributes dividend income. And on an annual basis, most mutual funds make distributions of capital gains or losses.

NOTE *A capital gain occurs when the fund sells a stock, bond, or other security held by the fund for more than the security originally cost. A capital loss occurs when the fund sells a security held by the fund for less than the security originally cost.*

What to Do When You Receive a Check from the Mutual Fund Manager

With Quicken, you can record mutual fund distributions you receive either directly into the register or by using an investment form. The advantage to using the investment form is that it lets you describe the distribution just once. When you record the amount directly into the register, you must sequentially describe each type of distribution separately: the dividend distribution, the short-term capital gain distribution, the long-term capital distribution, and so on.

To record a mutual fund distribution you receive by check using an income form, follow these steps:

1. Display the investment account's register, move the cursor to the next empty row of the register, click the Easy Actions button, and then choose the Income command. You see the Record Income dialog box, as shown in Figure 20.10.

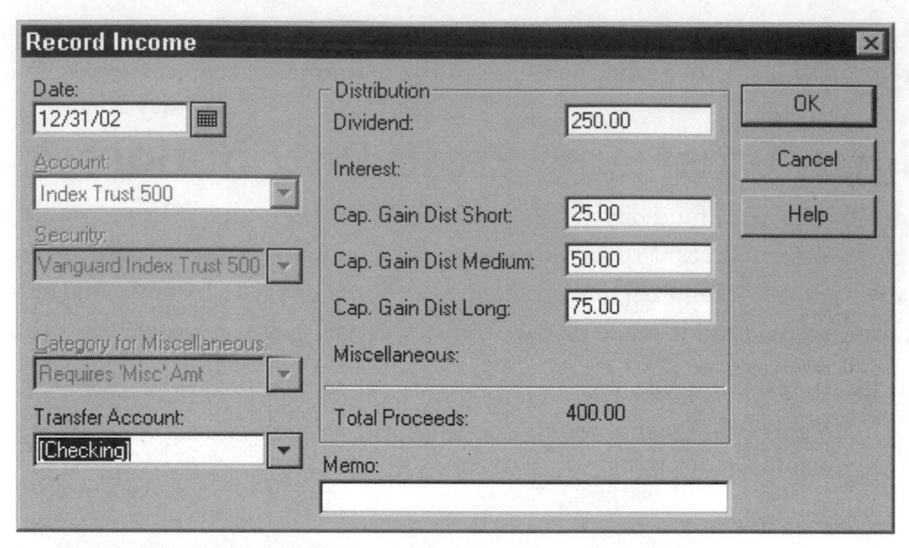

Figure 20.10: The Record Income dialog box.

2. Enter the distribution date in the Date text box. Be sure to enter the actual distribution date, not the date you received the distribution or the date you recorded the distribution. The date you enter determines in which year's income the distribution is counted. For example, if you receive a distribution of 2002 capital gains in 2003, you need to enter the distribution date as 2002 so that the capital gains are counted in 2002's taxable income and not in 2003's taxable income.
3. Press Tab to move past the Account and Security boxes to accept the mutual fund security name.
4. Enter the dividend income amount in the Dividend text box. (The mutual fund statement will give the amount of each type of distribution.)
5. Enter the short-term capital gain amount in the Cap. Gain Dist Short text box, the medium-term capital gain amount into the Cap. Gain Dist Medium text box, and the long-term capital gain amount in the Cap. Gain Dist Long box.
6. Enter the name of the account into which you'll deposit the distribution check in the Transfer Account combo box.
7. If you need to collect any additional information, use the Memo text box.
8. Click OK.

Quicken takes the information entered in the Record Income dialog box and records transactions into the investment register. Quicken records one transaction for each type of distribution. Figure 20.11 shows the investment register with a $250 dividend distribution (the third transaction). The figure also shows a $25 short-term capital gain distribution, a $50 medium-term capital gain distribution, and a $75 long-term capital gain distribution.

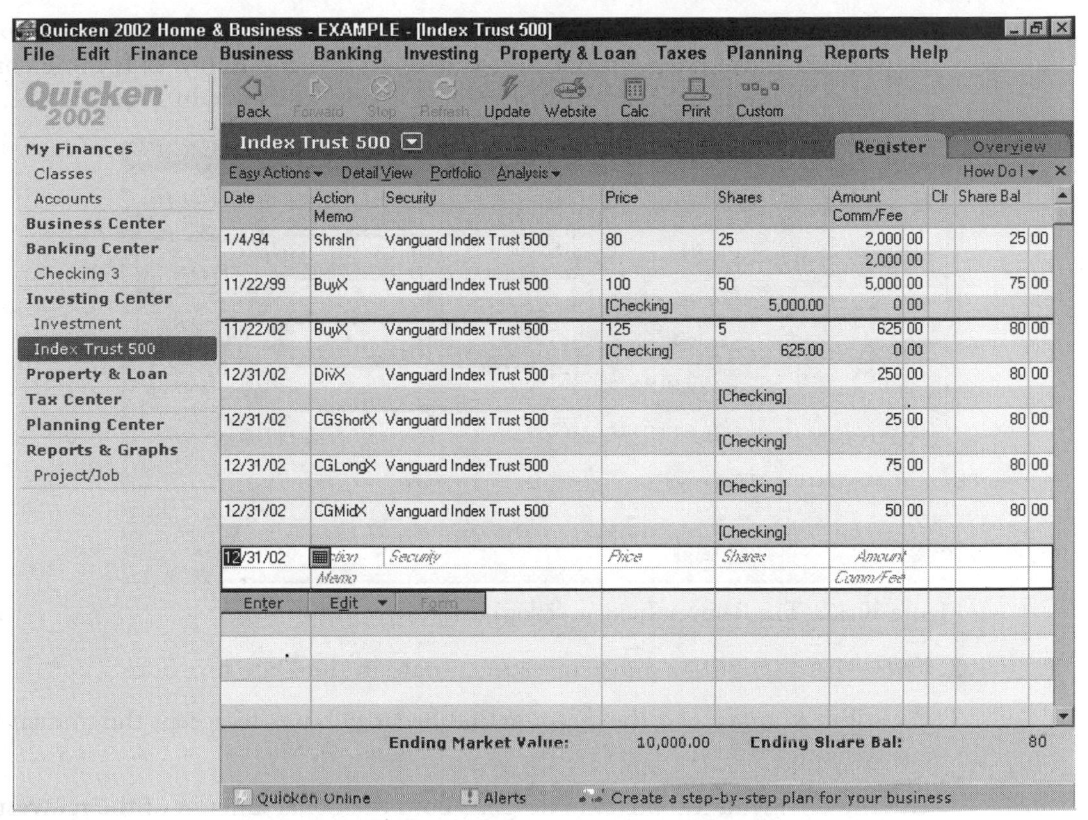

Figure 20.11: How Quicken records an income distribution into the register.

As noted earlier, you don't need to use the Record Income dialog box to enter income distribution transactions into an investment register, but it makes things easier. To record them directly into the register, enter each distribution individually, as in Figure 20.11.

What to Do When You Reinvest a Mutual Fund Distribution

When you reinvest a mutual fund distribution by buying additional shares, you essentially combine two of the transactions already described in this chapter: receiving a distribution and buying shares. You can record this sort of transaction directly into the register, but as with income distributions you don't reinvest, the easiest approach is to use an investment form.

To record a reinvested mutual fund distribution using the investment form, follow these steps:

1. Display the investment account's register, move the cursor to the next empty row of the register, click the Easy Actions button, and choose the Reinvest Income command. Quicken displays the Reinvest Income dialog box, as shown in Figure 20.12.

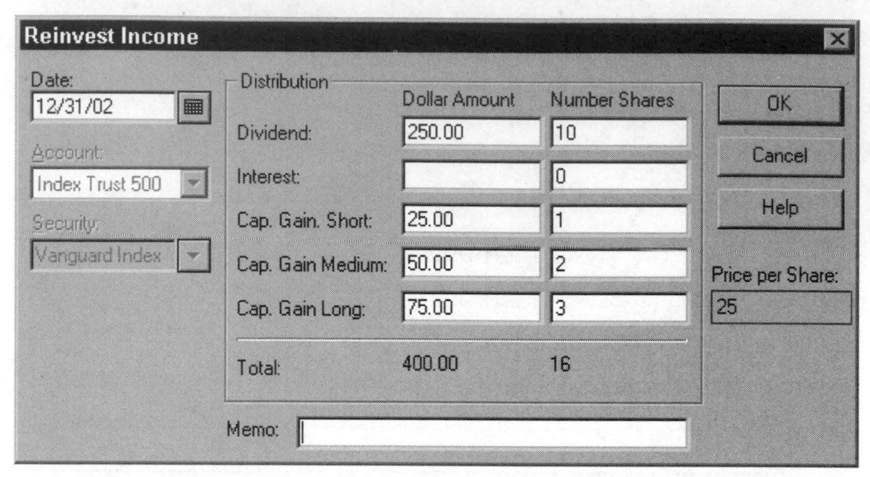

Figure 20.12: The Reinvest Income dialog box.

2. Enter the distribution and reinvestment date in the Date text box.
3. Press Tab to move past the Account and Security boxes to accept the mutual fund security name.
4. Use the Dividend text boxes to describe both the dollar amount of the reinvested dividends and the number of shares acquired through reinvestment.
5. Use the Interest text boxes to describe the reinvested interest income.
6. Use the Cap. Gain. sets of text boxes to describe any capital gains you reinvest. As with descriptions of reinvested dividends and interest, you record both the dollar amount of the reinvestment and the number of shares purchased. Your mutual fund statement will identify the character of the capital gains as short-term, medium-term, or long-term.

Quicken calculates the total dollar amount of the reinvested distribution, the total number of shares purchased, and the average price per share based on the information you entered in steps 4 through 7. These totals and the average price values will agree with what your mutual fund statement shows if you've correctly completed these steps.

7. If you need to collect any additional information, use the Memo text box.
8. Click OK.

Quicken takes the information you entered in the Reinvest Income dialog box and records transactions into the investment register. As with an income distribution that isn't reinvested, Quicken records one transaction for each type of distribution. Figure 20.13 shows an investment register with a $250 reinvested dividend distribution, as well as a $25 reinvested short-term capital gain distribution, a $50 reinvested medium-term capital gain, and a $75 reinvested long-term capital gain distribution.

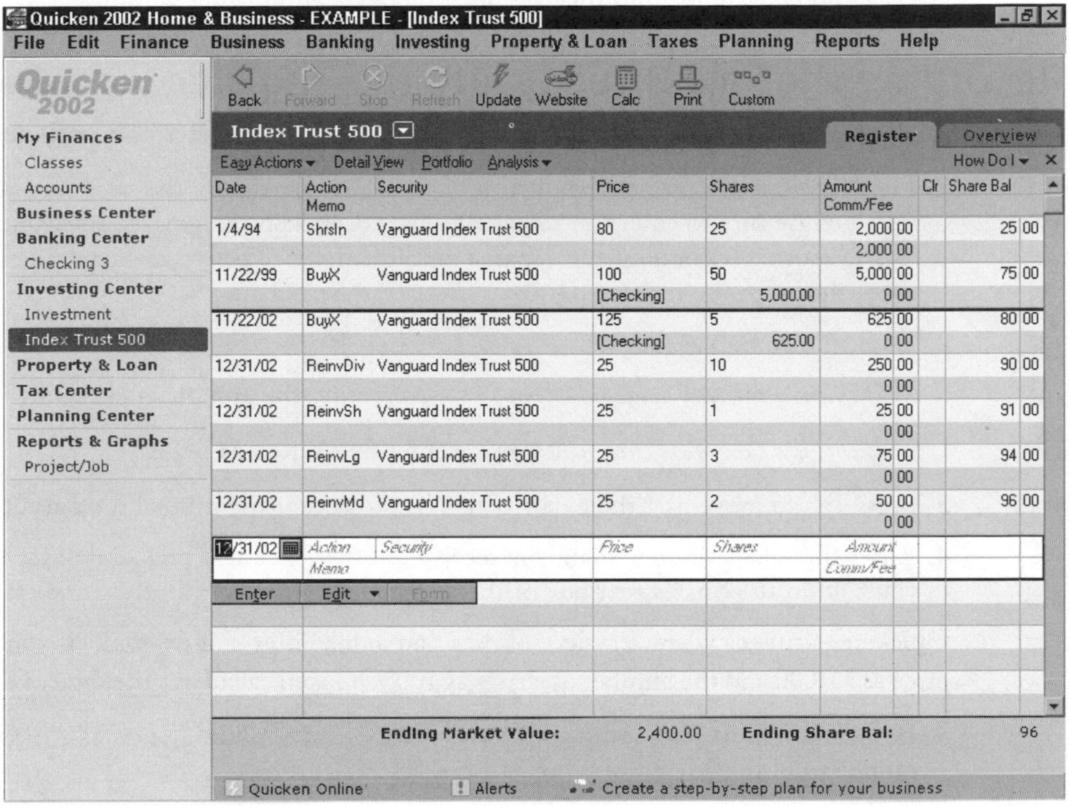

Quicken 2002 Home & Business - EXAMPLE - [Index Trust 500]
File Edit Finance Business Banking Investing Property & Loan Taxes Planning Reports Help
Back Forward Stop Refresh Update Website Calc Print Custom
Index Trust 500
Register Overview
Easy Actions Detail View Portfolio Analysis How Do I
My Finances
Classes
Accounts
Business Center
Banking Center
Checking 3
Investing Center
Investment
Index Trust 500
Property & Loan
Tax Center
Planning Center
Reports & Graphs
Project/Job
Date Action Memo Security Price Shares Amount Comm/Fee Clr Share Bal
1/4/94 ShrsIn Vanguard Index Trust 500 80 25 2,000 00 2,000 00 25 00
11/22/99 BuyX Vanguard Index Trust 500 100 [Checking] 50 5,000.00 5,000 00 0 00 75 00
11/22/02 BuyX Vanguard Index Trust 500 125 [Checking] 5 625.00 625 00 0 00 80 00
12/31/02 ReinvDiv Vanguard Index Trust 500 25 10 250 00 0 00 90 00
12/31/02 ReinvSh Vanguard Index Trust 500 25 1 25 00 0 00 91 00
12/31/02 ReinvLg Vanguard Index Trust 500 25 3 75 00 0 00 94 00
12/31/02 ReinvMd Vanguard Index Trust 500 25 2 50 00 0 00 96 00
12/31/02 Action Memo Security Price Shares Amount Comm/Fee
Enter Edit Form
Ending Market Value: 2,400.00 Ending Share Bal: 96
Quicken Online Alerts Create a step-by-step plan for your business

Figure 20.13: How Quicken records an income distribution into the register when the money is reinvested.

Again, you are not required to use an investment form—in this case, the Reinvest Income command and dialog box—to enter the reinvested distribution transactions. You can enter the transactions shown in Figure 20.13 directly into the register, one transaction at a time; just be sure to specify the correct action for each transaction.

Describing the Mutual Fund Shares You Sell

At some point, you'll probably sell the mutual fund shares you originally purchased with a check or that you acquired by reinvesting the dividends or capital gains. As with the other types of mutual fund transactions you record, this is easy as long as you have the necessary information: the number of shares sold, price per share (or transaction total), and commission paid (if any).

Again, you have two ways to record the sale of mutual fund shares: directly into the register or through an investment form. However, for this task, both record-keeping approaches are fast and convenient, and they are described in the following sections.

Recording the Sale Directly into the Register

To record the sale of mutual fund shares directly into the register, follow these steps:

1. Place the cursor in the next empty row of the register and enter the sales date in the Date text box. Be sure to enter the actual sales date. Quicken categorizes any capital gain or loss as short-term or long-term, based on the difference between the purchase and sale dates shown in the register.
2. Enter the Action as follows:
   - *If this is a sale you made sometime in the past*, enter the Action as ShrsOut.
   - *If this is a sale you're currently making*, enter the Action as SellX.
3. Press Tab to move past the Security text box to accept the mutual fund security name.
4. Enter the sales price per share you received in the Price text box, and enter the shares you sold in the Shares text box or the total amount you sold in the Amount text box.

Quicken calculates whatever piece of data you didn't enter. For example, if you enter the price as $10.00 and the number of shares as 100, Quicken calculates the total as $1,000.00.

5. If you want to record some additional piece of information, such as the sales order number, use the Memo text box.
6. If you're recording a SellX action, use the XFer Acct combo box to show the account into which you will deposit the check you receive from the sale of the shares.

If you enter an account name in the XFer Account text box, Quicken records a deposit transaction in the account equal to the value you enter in the XFer Amt text box.

7. If you're recording a SellX action, either enter the amount you received for the sale of the mutual fund shares less any commission you paid in the XFer Amt text box or enter the commission you paid in the Comm Fee text box. Again, Quicken calculates whatever piece of data you didn't enter.
8. Select Enter to display a message box that asks if you want to specifically identify the shares you're selling.

Specific identification of the shares you sell gives you control over the capital gain or loss stemming from the sale. People often use this control to minimize or postpone capital gains taxes and accelerate or maximize deductible capital losses. For example, by selling the most expensive shares first, you minimize the capital gain or maximize the capital loss on the sale of these shares. If you don't use specific identification, Quicken assumes that the first shares you purchased are the first shares you sell. You may have heard this costing assumption referred to by its initials, FIFO (first in, first out).

9. If you don't want to specifically identify the shares, click Cancel, and you're finished.

10. If you want to use specific identification, click Specify Lots. Quicken displays a dialog box similar to the one in Figure 20.14.

Specify Lots for Vanguard Index Trust 500

Date	Holding Period	Price	Available	Selected
1/4/94	**SLT**	**80**	**25**	**0**
11/22/99	LT to 11/23/04	100	50	0
11/22/02	ST to 11/23/03	125	5	0
12/31/02	ST to 1/1/04	25	10	0
12/31/02	ST to 1/1/04	25	1	0
12/31/02	ST to 1/1/04	25	3	0
12/31/02	ST to 1/1/04	25	2	0
Totals:			96	0

Shares to Sell: 60
Total Selected: 0

Auto Select
First Shares In
Minimum Gain
Last Shares In
Maximum Gain

OK
Cancel
Reset
Help

Figure 20.14: This dialog box lets you tell Quicken which shares you're selling.

You can indicate which lots or parts of lots you're selling (a *lot* is just a set of shares you purchased at the same time). As you make your selections, Quicken shows you how many shares you've said you'll sell and how many you've identified. If you make a mistake in your specific identification and want to start over, choose Clear. When you've specifically identified as many as you've said you'll sell, click OK.

- To specify a lot, click it or highlight it and click OK.
- To select a portion of a lot, highlight it and enter the number of shares in the Total Selected box. Quicken displays a message box that asks for the number of shares from the lot you want to sell. You can enter some number of shares or accept Quicken's suggestion. (Quicken suggests you sell as many shares as you need to complete the specific identification.)
- To tell Quicken to sell the oldest lots first, click the First Shares In command button.

- To tell Quicken to sell the newest lots first, click the Last Shares In command button.
- To tell Quicken to pick lots that minimize your capital gain (and therefore your capital gains taxes), click the Minimum Gain command button.
- To tell Quicken to pick lots that maximize your capital gain (and therefore your capital gains taxes), click the Maximum Gain command button.

Quicken records the transaction into the investment register and selects the next empty row so you can enter another transaction. If you entered the action as SellX, Quicken also records a deposit transaction in the XFer Acct. Figure 20.15 shows 60 shares of the Vanguard Index 500 Trust being sold on December 31, 2003, for $40 a share.

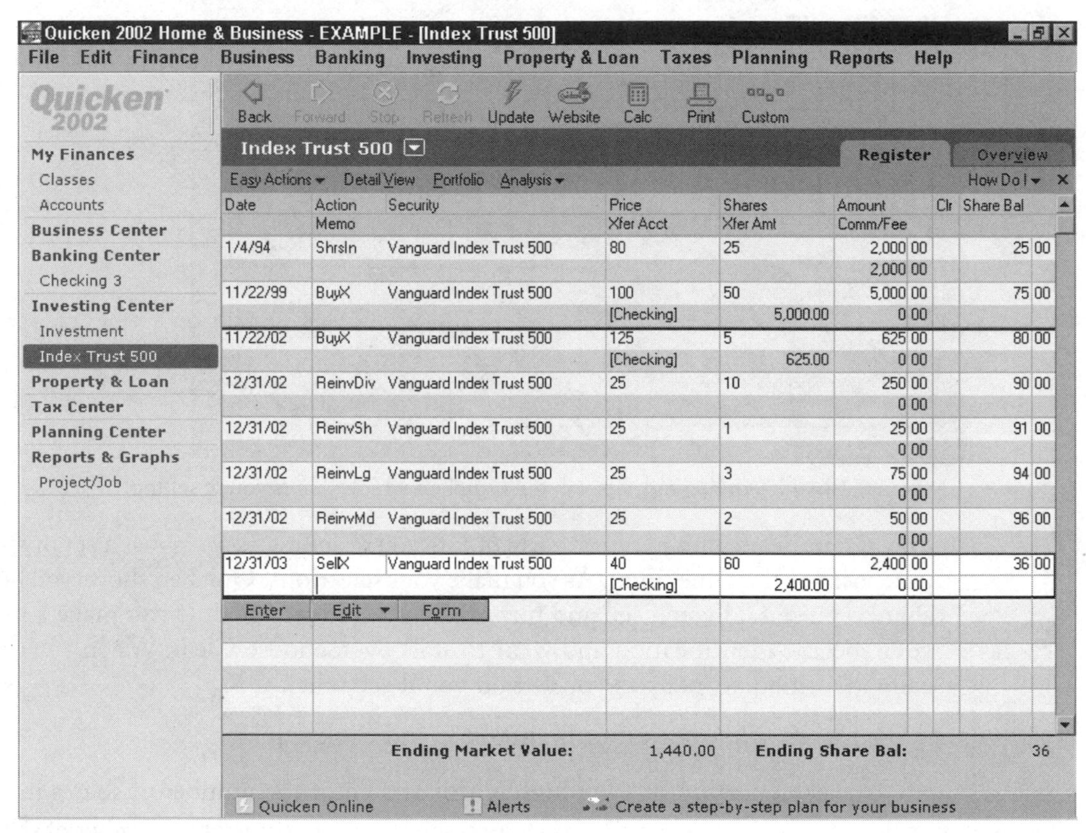

Figure 20.15: An investment register with a sale transaction.

Using a Form to Record a Sale

To record the sale of shares using an investment form, follow these steps:

1. Display the investment account's register and place the cursor in the next empty row of the register.

2. Click the Easy Actions button and choose the Sell/Remove Shares command to display the Sell/Remove Shares dialog box. Then click the Summary tab, which is shown in Figure 20.16.
3. Enter the sale date in the Date text box.
4. Press Tab to move past the Security and Account boxes to accept the mutual fund security name.
5. Use the # Of Shares text box to indicate how many shares you are selling.

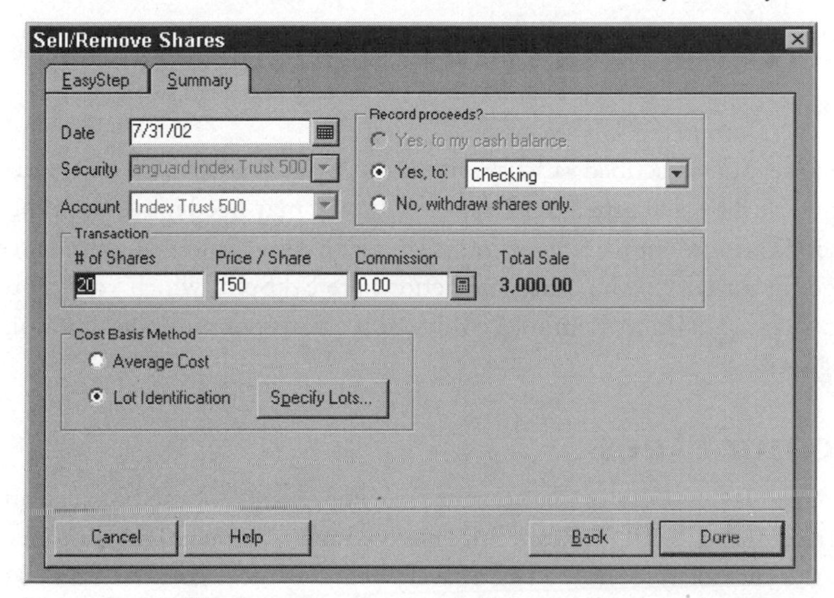

Figure 20.16: The Summary tab of the Sell/Remove Shares dialog box.

6. If you want to specifically identify the shares, click the Specify Lots command button. Quicken displays the Specify Lots For dialog box (see Figure 20.14). You can make your selections as described in step 10 in the previous section. When you've specifically identified as many shares as you've said you'll sell, click OK to close the dialog box and return to the Sell/Remove Shares dialog box.

If you don't use the Specify Lots command button to specifically identify the shares you're selling, Quicken uses a first-in, first-out costing assumption to calculate the capital gain or loss on the sale. In other words, it assumes the shares you sell are always those you've held the longest.

7. Enter the share sales price in the Price/Share text box and the sale commission you are paying, if any, in the Commission text box. Quicken calculates the total amount of the sale.

You need to enter only three of the following four inputs: number of shares, price, commission, and total. Quicken can use any three of these inputs to calculate the fourth input.

8. If you're recording a current sale, indicate the account into which you'll deposit the sales proceeds by marking the Yes To option button in the Record Proceeds? section of the dialog box. Then select the account from the Yes To drop-down list box.
9. If you're recording an earlier sale and don't want to adjust a bank account balance for the sale, mark the No option button in the Record Proceeds? section of the dialog box.
10. Click Done. Quicken records the sale and enters a transaction describing the sale into the register.

Handling Account Fees, Stock Splits, and Reminders

The preceding sections described various record-keeping actions for a mutual fund account. There are three additional mutual fund transactions you may need to record. Probably the most common is an account fee transaction (such as a mutual fund management company might charge for an IRA). The other two actions are StkSplit, which you use to record mutual fund share splits, and Reminder, which you use to put reminder notes in the investment register.

Recording Account Fees

Some mutual funds periodically levy account fees. For example, I used to have an IRA in a T. Rowe Price mutual fund. T. Rowe Price charged me an annual IRA custodian fee of $10. To pay the custodian fee at the end of every year, I could either write a $10 check to T. Rowe Price Company or let T. Rowe Price sell $10 worth of the mutual fund shares.

When You Write a Check to Pay the Account Fee

If you write a check to pay an account fee, you don't need to do anything special in the investment register. You just write the check in the usual way.

Categorize the check that pays an account fee as investment expense or a similar expense category. Items such as IRA account and custodial fees are miscellaneous deductions. At the time I'm writing this, a miscellaneous deduction in excess of 2 percent of your adjusted gross income may be used as an itemized deduction.

When You Sell Shares to Pay an Account Fee

If you sell shares (or, more likely, the mutual fund manager sells shares) to pay an account fee, you need to do a little more work to record the account fee. You need to record a SellX transaction in the investment register, as described in the section "Describing the Mutual Fund Shares You Sell" earlier in this chapter.

There's a slight trick to recording this type of SellX transaction. The entry for the commission or fee equals the total sales amount. For example, if you record the sale of $10 of mutual fund shares to pay for, say, a $10 account fee, both the Total Amount and Comm/Fee text boxes show 10. The XFer Amt text box, as a result, shows as 0. (When you record this transaction, Quicken sets the Price text box value back to 0, so both the Price and XFer Amt text boxes show 0.)

If you use the Sell/Remove Shares dialog box (displayed when you choose the Sell/ Remove Shares command from the Easy Actions menu) to record an account fee transaction, you enter the number of shares you need to sell to pay the account fee, the sales price per share, and the commission. If you've correctly entered these inputs, the total sale shows as 0 because the commission—really the account fee—consumes the entire sales proceeds.

WARNING *Check with your tax advisor concerning investment expenses such as account maintenance fees paid for by selling shares. While the approach described here is the only one you can easily do in Quicken, it causes your account maintenance fees to show up as capital losses equal to whatever you originally paid for the shares. Unfortunately, this overstates your capital loss by the amount of the account fee and understates your investment expenses by the amount of the account fee. On your tax return, therefore, you need to adjust your capital losses or gains and your investment expenses (a possible miscellaneous deduction) for this discrepancy.*

Recording a Mutual Fund Share Split

A share split occurs when the mutual fund company gives each current shareholder new shares. In a two-for-one split, for example, a shareholder receives one new share for each share already held. Someone who holds 100 shares prior to the split, for example, holds 200 shares after the split. You can record share splits directly into the register or with an investment form.

Recording the Share Split Directly into the Register

To record a mutual fund share split directly into the register, follow these steps:

1. Place the cursor in the next empty row of the register and enter the split date in the Date text box.
2. In the Action combo box, enter ***StkSplit*** as the action.
3. Press Tab to move past the Security text box to accept the suggested security, the mutual fund name.
4. If you want to update your mutual fund price per share data, enter what the price per share will be after the split in the Price text box.

5. Enter the number of new shares you'll receive for a specified number of old shares in the New Shares text box. (When you indicate the action as StkSplit, Quicken replaces the Number Of Shares text box with the New Shares text box.)
6. If you want to record some additional piece of information about the split— perhaps to cross-reference the mutual fund statement that explains or reports the split—use the Memo text box.
7. Enter the number of old shares you'll give up to receive a specified number of new shares using the Old Shares text box. (When you indicate the action as StkSplit, Quicken replaces the XFer Account combo box with the Old Shares text box.)
8. Click Enter.

Quicken records the transaction into the investment register and adjusts the number of mutual fund shares you're holding according to the new-shares-to-old-shares ratio. Then it selects the next empty row of the investment register so that you can enter another transaction. Figure 20.17 shows the investment register with a stock split transaction (the last transaction shown in the figure).

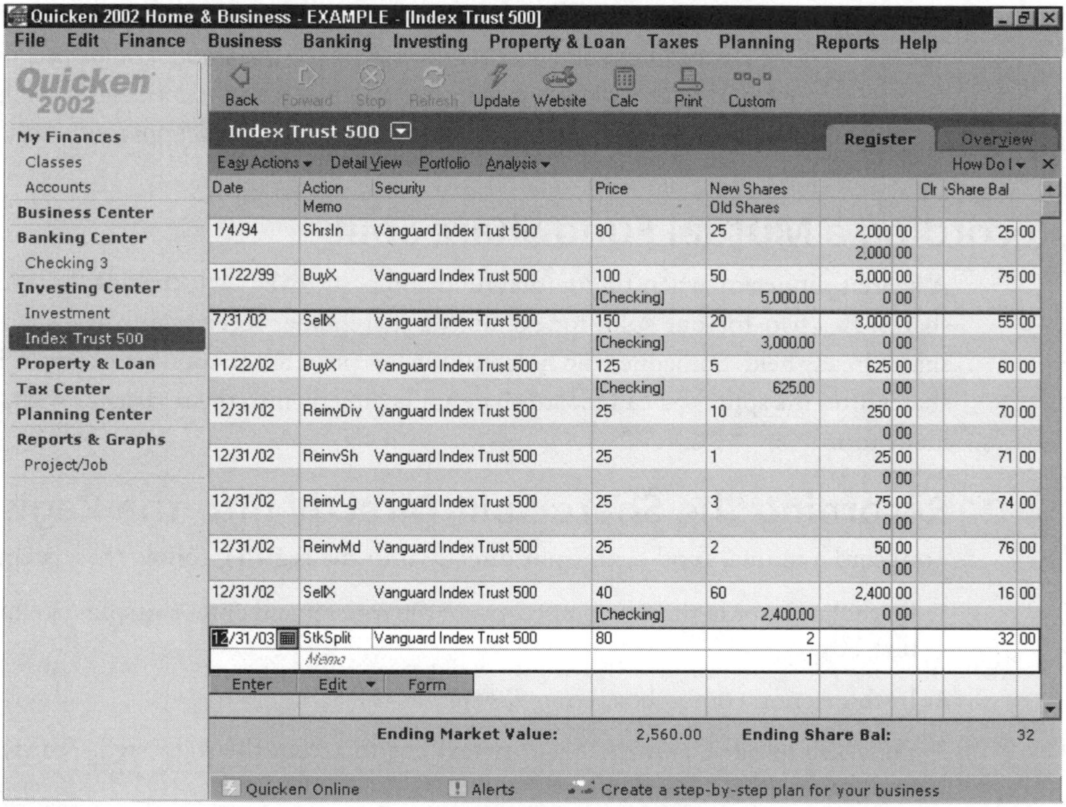

Figure 20.17: An investment register with a stock split transaction.

Using a Form to Record a Share Split

To record a share split transaction using an investment form, follow these steps:

1. Display the investment account in a register and move the cursor to the next empty row of the investment register.
2. Click the Easy Actions button and choose the Stock Split command to display the Stock Split dialog box, as shown in Figure 20.18.

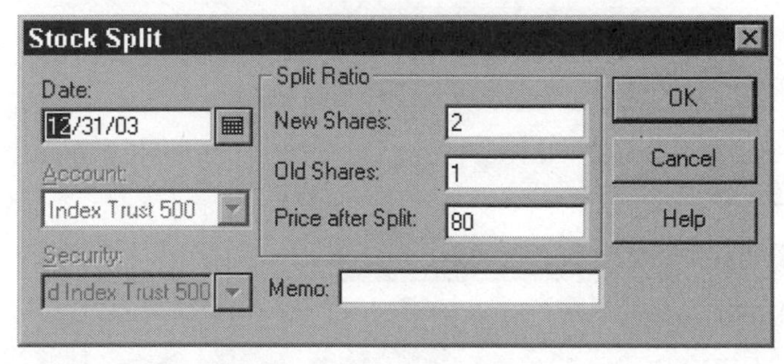

Figure 20.18: The Stock Split dialog box.

3. Enter the split date in the Date text box.
4. Press Tab to move past the Account and Security boxes to accept the mutual fund security name.
5. Enter the number of new shares equal to one old sharc in the New Shares text box.
6. Enter the number of old shares equal to one new share in the Old Shares text box.
7. If you want to update the share price information, enter the price per share after the split in the Price After Split text box.
8. If you want to describe some additional piece of information about the stock split, use the Memo text box.
9. Click OK. Quicken uses the information you've entered to record a stock split transaction for the investment account.

Storing Reminders in the Investment Register

Your investment activities may require you to do things by certain dates—cash a certificate of deposit by June 3, for example. You can use the investment register to store reminder messages, which alert you about these types of events.

To enter a reminder message directly into an investment register, just enter the date by which you want to be reminded in the Date text box, enter the action as Reminder, and then type your message in the Description text box. If you wanted to remind yourself about a certificate of deposit (CD) that needs to be either cashed or rolled over by June 3, 2003, for example, set the date as 6/3/2003 and the action as Reminder. You might enter the text ***Cash Big National CD*** in the Description text box and any other notes to yourself about this transaction in the Memo text box.

To enter a reminder message with an investment form, click the Easy Actions button and then select Advanced ➢ Reminder Transaction. Quicken displays the Reminder dialog box shown in Figure 20.19, which collects the date and the reminder message.

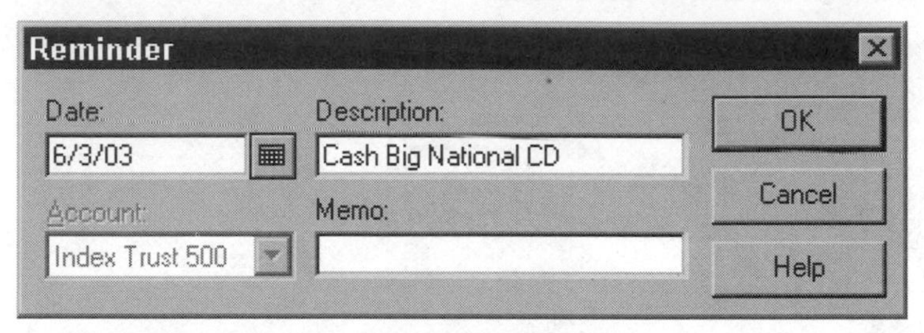

Figure 20.19: The Reminder dialog box.

To stop Quicken from reminding you, you can delete the reminder message transaction or enter a *c* in the Clr text box to mark the reminder message as cleared.

Editing Mutual Fund Transactions

Just as with the transactions that appear in any other account, you can edit investment account transactions. There are two ways to do this:

- Highlight the incorrect transaction in the register, and then fix the incorrect pieces of the entry. Be sure to click the Enter button after you've made your changes.
- Use an investment form to make your corrections. First, select the transaction that needs to be edited, and then choose the Form button. Quicken displays an investment form like the one you might have used originally to record the transaction, but the dialog box is already filled out with the transaction's information. Make your changes and click OK.

Success Strategies for Mutual Fund Record Keeping

Once you're familiar with the mechanics, you'll find it very easy to use Quicken to keep records of your mutual fund investments. When you use Quicken for your mutual fund record keeping, there are some strategies to consider, as described in the following sections.

ShrsIn and ShrsOut versus BuyX and SellX

It can be confusing to choose between the ShrsIn and BuyX actions and between the ShrsOut and SellX actions. Follow this basic rule: Use the ShrsIn and ShrsOut transactions when the cash effect of an investment purchase or sale has already been recorded, and use the BuyX and SellX transactions when the cash effect of an investment purchase or sale hasn't yet been recorded.

In general, you should use the ShrsOut and ShrsIn actions when you're entering old investment transactions so that you have a historical record. And this raises an important question: Is it worth it to go back and enter historical records? I think it is if you're dealing with a taxable mutual fund, which is a mutual fund that's not being used as an IRA or a 401(k) plan account.

One of the biggest benefits of using Quicken for your mutual fund record keeping is that it lets you more easily track the tax basis, or cost, of the mutual fund shares you've acquired through the years. When you sell the mutual fund shares, you need to report the capital gain or loss stemming from the sale on a Schedule D tax form. And to do this, you'll need to know not only the sales proceeds, but also the cost of the shares you sell.

TIP *Quicken's reports and graphs provide a handy means of summarizing and organizing the investment information stored in the investment account registers. See Chapter 4 for details on producing Quicken's investment reports and Chapter 8 for more information about Quicken's graphing capabilities.*

Tracking Market Values

You can store current share price information about investments. By doing so, you'll be able to track the market value of your mutual fund investments over time. You'll also be able to calculate the performance of your mutual fund investment over any time period. Your mutual fund probably provides the quarterly and annual returns of the fund in its quarterly and annual reports. If you invested some time other than at the start of the year or the start of the quarter, however, these performance figures don't actually give the performance of your shares.

WARNING *When Quicken produces a Net Worth or Balance Sheet report, it uses the most recent market price per share to calculate the value of an account balance. This approach is probably fine for personal net worth reports as long as the valuation method is clearly disclosed, but reporting securities at their fair market value on a business's balance sheet isn't the accepted convention unless the fair market value is less than the original cost.*

Entering Market Price Information

To provide the current price-per-share information to Quicken, follow these steps:

1. In the investment account register, display the Portfolio View window of the investment account by clicking the Portfolio button at the top of the register or by choosing Investing ➤ Portfolio View. Figure 20.20 shows this view.

The Portfolio View window lists each of the securities you hold. (In the case of a mutual fund account with only one security, the list contains a single entry.) An *est* shows next to the prices of those security prices that are only estimates. (In the Investment Portfolio Value report, this *est* changes to an asterisk.)

2. If the As Of date shown beneath the Portfolio View's button bar isn't the current date, use the Calendar button located just to the right of the date display to select the current date.

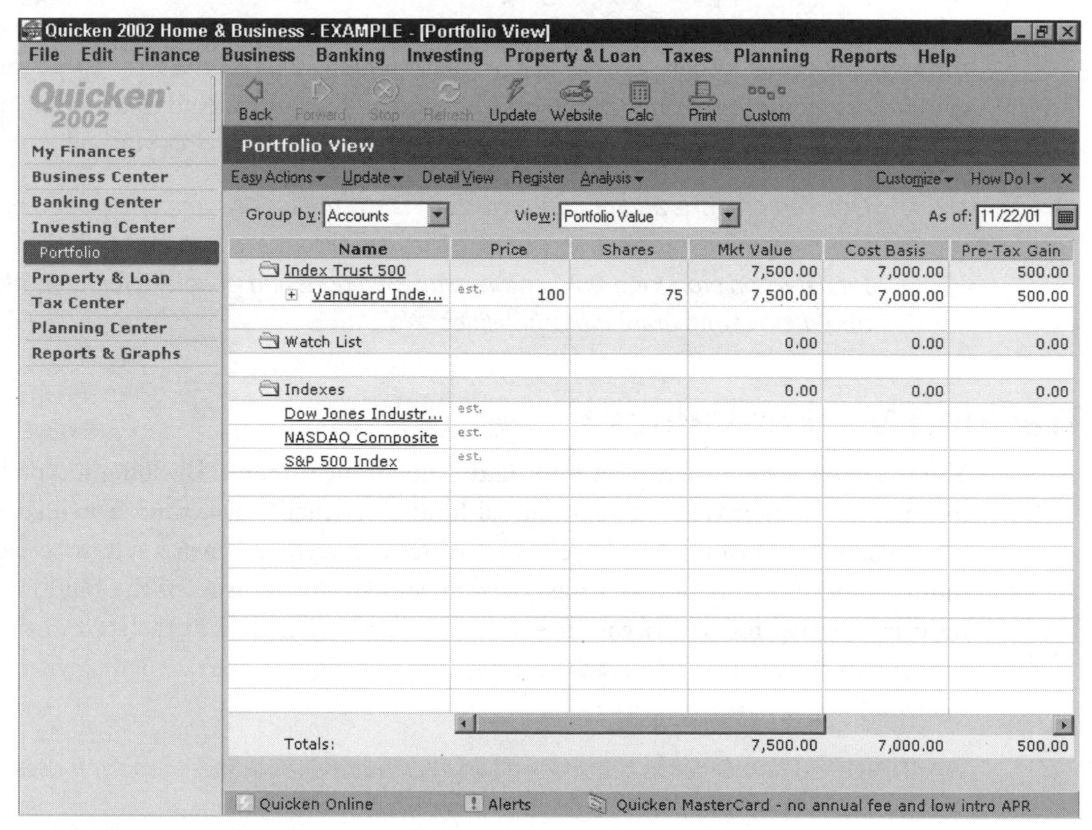

Figure 20.20: The Portfolio View window displays investment information by security.

3. If you want to reorder the list, use the Group By list box to specify how you want Quicken to arrange your investment portfolio information: by account, industry, security, security type, investment goal, asset class, or sector.

4. Select the security for which you want to record the current market price.
5. Enter the current market price in the Mkt Value column. Typically, you can enter mutual fund prices in dollars and cents, such as 13.87, but you can also use fractional prices, such as 8 7/8. (Use the + and – keys to incrementally adjust the price by one-eighth.) If the estimated price is correct, you can just press the asterisk key.
6. Repeat steps 4 and 5 to enter the current market price for each of the other mutual funds shown in the Portfolio View window. You will see the results of each adjustment as you move your cursor to the next security.
7. If you want to return to the Register window, click the Register button.

NOTE *In general, a mutual fund will have only one security. You can, however, put more than one mutual fund security in an account—for example, if you invest in a mutual fund family.*

Creating Custom Portfolio Views

You can create customized portfolio views that show the information and calculations that you specify. To customize the view, click the Customize button in the Portfolio View window and choose Customize Current View. Quicken opens the dialog box shown in Figure 20.21. This dialog box provides a set of list boxes for specifying which investment information a custom view should display. You can also use the Accounts To Include and Securities To Include list boxes to tell Quicken you want to see only a subset of the investment accounts and securities.

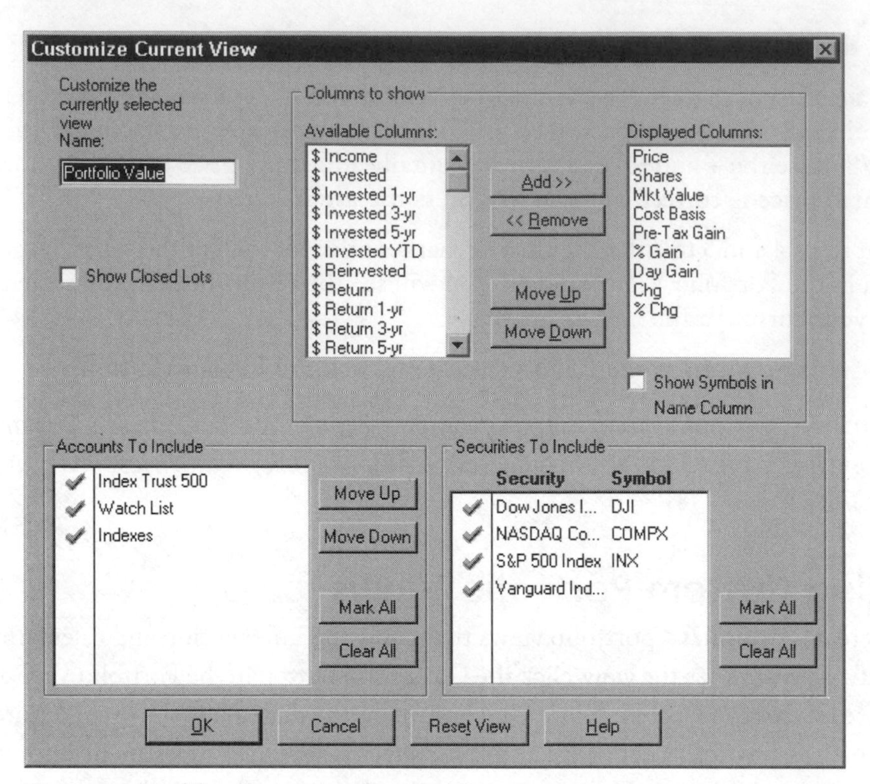

Figure 20.21: The Customize Current View dialog box.

To change the date used for investment return calculations and the tax bracket used for capital gain calculations, click the Customize button in the Portfolio View window and choose Options. Quicken opens the Portfolio View Options dialog box, as shown in Figure 20.22. You can mark the From button and then enter a date into the From box to specify that return calculations should be made from a certain date forward. You can use the Tax Bracket drop-down list box to select the marginal tax rates you want Quicken to use for its capital gains calculations.

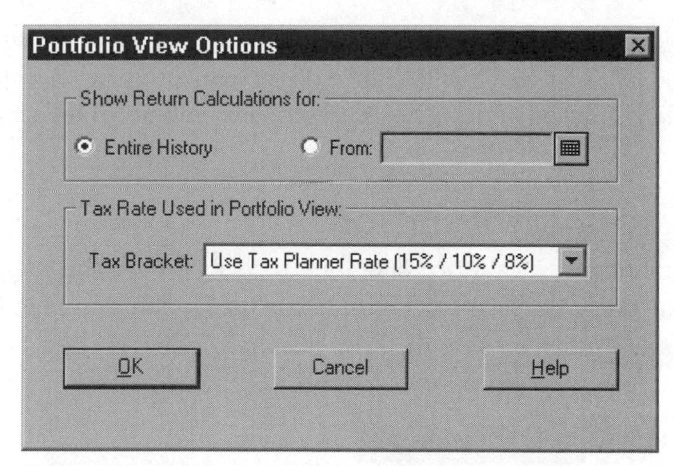

Figure 20.22: The Portfolio View Options dialog box.

Updating Prices Online

You can quickly and easily retrieve security price information using Quicken's Online Quotes feature. If you have an Internet connection, and have entered ticker symbols for all of the securities you want to track, Quicken can update the price and adjust the market value automatically. Simply click the Update button in the Portfolio View window and choose the Get Online Quotes command. You will see a series of messages as Quicken connects, transmits, and receives information over the Internet.

NOTE *In order to use Quicken's Online Quotes, you need to have entered ticker symbols for each of the securities you want to track. If you want to go back and do this, select the investment in the Detail View window and click the Properties button. Then enter the ticker in the Symbol text box and click OK.*

You can also update quotes online by choosing the Finance ➢ One Step Update command. Just select the information you want to update from the dialog box Quicken displays and click Update Now.

Updating Prices Manually

If you don't have an Internet connection, you can enter price updates manually. Updating prices manually usually doesn't take much more time than downloading price information, so you may want to update prices by hand even if you do have an Internet connection (especially if you infrequently track a small number of mutual funds).

To update prices, display the Portfolio View window and click the Mkt Value column. Then enter the current price, and press Enter. (You can get daily prices from your local paper or from the *Wall Street Journal.*) Quicken updates the Market Value amount to reflect the new price.

Editing Price History Information

You may want to enter or edit historical price data for a security. To do this, display the Portfolio View window and select the security. Then choose the Update command button and select Edit Price History. Quicken displays the Price History window, as shown in Figure 20.23.

Price History for: Vanguard Index Trust 500

New Edit Delete Print Close

Date	Price	High	Low	Volume
12/31/03	80			
12/31/02	40			
11/22/02	125			
7/31/02	150			
11/22/99	100			
1/4/94	80			

Figure 20.23: The Price History window.

To enter a new price, click the New command button. Quicken displays the New Price For dialog box, as shown in Figure 20.24.

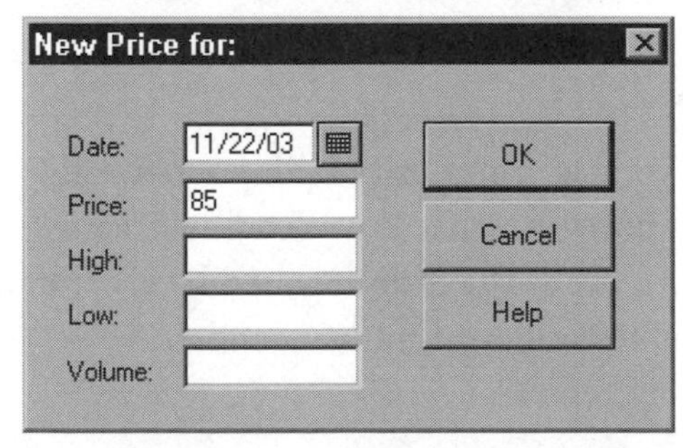

Figure 20.24: The New Price For dialog box.

This dialog box provides five text boxes: Date, Price, High (Price), Low (Price), and Volume. To add a new price to the history, enter the date and price and click OK. Optionally, enter the daily high price, daily low price, and trading volume for that day. When you click OK, Quicken adds the price to the price history.

To correct a price that already shows in the Price History window, select the price and then click the Edit command button. Quicken displays the Edit Price dialog box, which asks what the correct share prices and volume should be for the selected date. To correct the prices or volume shown, enter this data and click OK. Quicken updates the price history.

You can also delete a price from the Price History window. To do this, select the price and then select Delete.

If you want to print the data in the Price History window—perhaps to compare a hard copy list of the prices to an annual or quarterly mutual fund report—click the Print command button, complete the Print dialog box, and click OK.

Charting Market Price and Value Information

You can plot the total value of the selected security in the Portfolio View window as well as the price per share. Just click the Detail View button. Quicken displays a window like the one shown in Figure 20.25. The Security Detail View window shows the price-per-share values and share volumes in a chart. The window also lists all transactions for a security using a scrollable list box and summarizes your holdings of a particular security and provides other useful financial data.

NOTE *If a security has been split, you can mark the Adjust For Split checkbox (above the chart) to tell Quicken to plot shares as if they were split from the very beginning.*

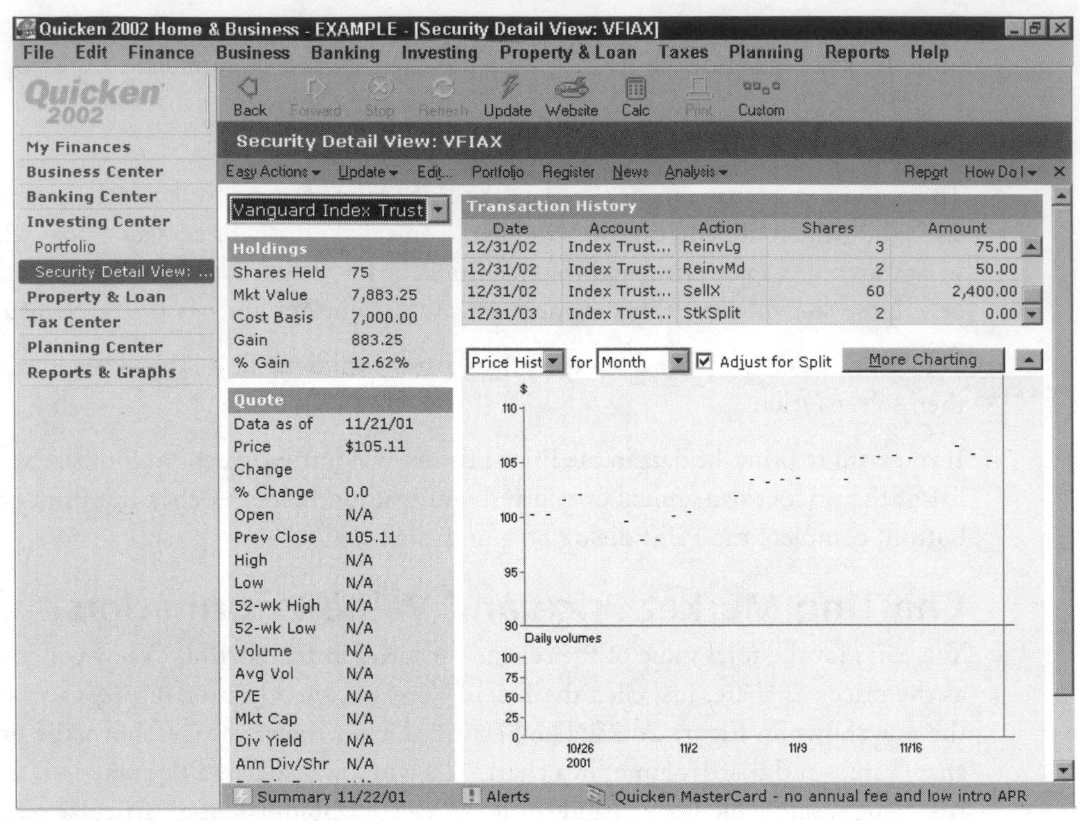

Figure 20.25: The Security Detail View window plots share prices and volumes in graphs and provides other security-specific information.

You can record investment activity when the Security Detail View window is displayed. This approach doesn't make as much sense for mutual funds as it does for brokerage investment accounts, but you should know that the capability exists. To record investment transactions when the Security Detail View window is displayed, click the Easy Actions button to display the Easy Actions menu and use its menu commands to display the appropriate investment form dialog box. Then fill in the dialog box's text and combo boxes. For example, to record the purchase of mutual fund shares, click the Easy Actions button, choose the Buy command, and use the Buy/Add Shares dialog box to describe the purchase.

You can expand the size of the share price and share volume graphs by clicking the up arrow that appears above the top-right corner of the graph. Figure 20.26 shows the expanded graph.

You can print the price history graphs by clicking the Print button that appears in the upper-right corner of the window, or by choosing the File ➢ Print Graph command.

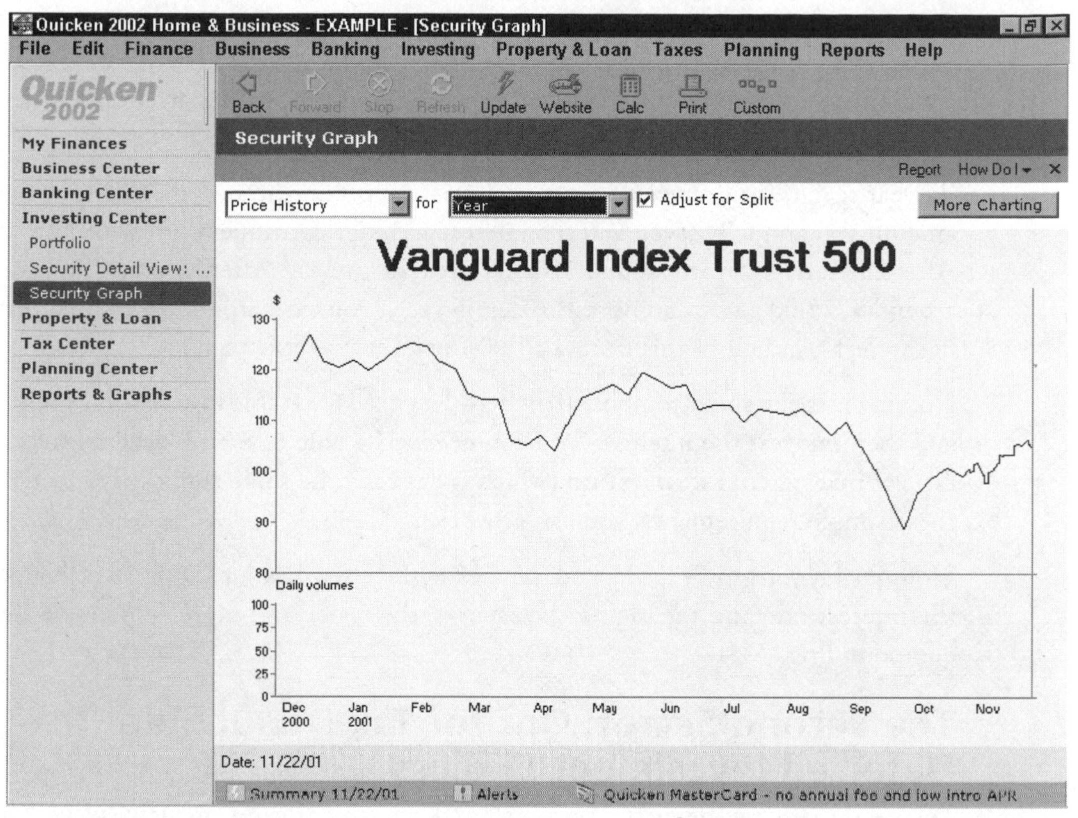

Figure 20.26: The Price History Graph window shows an expanded version of the same graphs shown by the Security Detail View window.

How to Be a Smart Investor

A lot of people think smart investing means complicated investing. That's not true. Smart investing is usually simple investing. In fact, the most important things you can do relate to the way you go about investing, not the specific investments you pick. Here, I offer five secrets that can help you become a smart investor.

The First Secret: Compound Interest

Compound interest represents the first secret. Does that seem strange? Compound interest doesn't seem very powerful at first blush. You put, say, $1,000 into an investment that returns a 10 percent profit. The first year, the $1,000 earns $100. Let's say you leave the $100 in the savings account and add another $1,000. The second year, you earn $210. If you continue saving this way (every year putting $1,000 into the account), you earn $330 in the third year.

Compound interest produces a very interesting result. Your interest earnings grow because you continue to add to your investment. Some of the addition comes from additional savings. But more and more of the interest earnings come from the interest you're earning on the interest—what's called compound interest.

By year seven, for example, you typically earn more in interest than the regular amount you annually save. And the interest earnings continue to grow and grow. After 25 years, you earn around $10,000 a year in interest. After 35 years, you earn around $27,000 a year in interest. After 45 years, you earn around $72,000 a year in interest. And all of this from a $1,000-per-year savings plan.

Nothing is tricky about compound interest. You need to be able to save some money and then reinvest the interest. And you need to be able to earn a decent interest rate, or investment rate of return (which is basically the same thing). By meeting these simple requirements, you can grow rich.

How quickly you grow rich depends on the interest rate and your savings. The higher the interest rate and the bigger the savings, the faster and more impressive the compounding.

The Second Secret: Opt for Tax-Deductible, Tax-Deferred Investment Choices

You need to use tax-deductible, tax-deferred investment vehicles such as IRAs or, even better, an employer's 401(k) or 403(b) plan. Let me show you how powerful these two tools are.

To provide a backdrop against which to discuss your future investing, let's suppose that your personal wealth target requires you to save $6,000 a year. And just to make things fun, let's also pretend that $6,000 is an absolute impossibility. Let's say that you're currently spending every dollar you make and you couldn't come up with an extra $500 a month unless your life depended on it.

Here's the secret of meeting the $6,000-per-year goal: Tax-deductible investments let you borrow a huge chunk of the money from the federal and state government. Suppose, for example, that you're working with an employer who provides a 401(k) plan but doesn't contribute any matching money. You want to save $6,000 a year because that amount will ultimately allow you to become financially independent. By using a tax-deductible investment such as a 401(k), you would, in effect, be able to borrow roughly $2,000 a year. Here's why: If you stick $6,000 in your 401(k) plan, you will save about $2,000 in income taxes. Of the $6,000 in annual savings, then, $4,000 would come from your pocket and $2,000 would come from the federal and state government.

Notice what you've already accomplished by using the powerful concept of tax-deductible investing: You've cut your out-of-pocket cash by around a third.

Things get even better if you happen to work for an employer who matches a portion of your 401(k) contribution. Let's say, for example, that your employer matches your contributions by contributing $.50 to your savings for every $1.00 you contribute. The math gets a little tricky in this case. If you contribute $4,000, you get another $2,000 from your employer. You also get roughly $1,500 in government contributions in the form of tax savings. The bottom line is that you need to come up with only about $2,500 of your own money to reach your $6,000-per-year savings goal.

If you or your spouse work for an employer who generously matches a portion of your 401(k) contributions, most of the money you need to achieve financial independence will come from your employer and the government. That's right—*most of the money comes from your employer and the government.*

In a tax-deferred investment vehicle like a 401(k) or an IRA, income taxes on your interest or investment profits are deferred. For this reason, you effectively earn a much higher rate of interest inside a tax-deferred account. The reason is that the federal and state income taxes you pay on interest and investment income wipe out anywhere from 15 to 40 percent of your profit, with most people paying about a 30 percent tax on their profits. But inside a tax-deferred investment vehicle like a 401(k) or an IRA, you might earn compound interest at the annual rate of 10 percent. Outside a tax-deferred investment vehicle, on the other hand, you might earn around 7 percent.

Those differences may not seem very big, but over time they have a cumulative impact on compound interest calculations. For example, suppose that you are a 20-year-old adult just entering the work force and you're trying to decide how to invest $2,000 a year for retirement at age 65. If you compound interest using a 7 percent annual rate, you end up with around $570,000 by the time you retire. If you instead compound interest using a 10 percent annual rate, you end up with around $1,400,000—roughly $800,000 more.

To sum things up, tax-deductible, tax-deferred investment vehicles are the best and most effective method of accumulating wealth. There is no better method for moving toward financial independence—none. You can save up to roughly $10,000 a year by using a 401(k) or 403(b) plan.

What If You're Unlucky?

The financial power of tax-deductible, tax-deferred investment choices such as 401(k)s begs an important but awkward question. Let's say your employer doesn't offer a 401(k) plan, 403(b) plan, or an equivalent tax-deductible, tax-deferred savings program. Is this whole tax-deductible, tax-deferred investing business such a big deal that you should consider switching employers?

I doubt that's necessary. First of all if I were you, I would start by talking to other employees and gauging their interest. Then, assuming you're not alone in your feelings, I would approach management. As you know now, such a plan delivers enormous benefits. If it were me, I would rather have a 401(k) plan than a fancy holiday party or a summer picnic. If the truth be told, I would even forgo part of my next raise.

Note, too, that you may be eligible to contribute up to $2,000 a year in a tax-deductible IRA. (IRA earnings on allowable contributions are always tax-deferred.) If you're married and your spouse works, you both may be able to contribute $2,000 a year. Even if your employer doesn't provide a 401(k) plan, it may be worthwhile to save several thousand dollars a year by using tax-deductible investment choices. They may be all you need to progress toward your wealth target.

Finally, if you or your spouse own and operate a small business, you can set up a pension plan for that business. Something like a SIMPLE-IRA, which is essentially a small company 401(k) plan is very easy to set up and administer. All you do is sign a few documents and distribute some literature to your employees (if you have any). With a SIMPLE-IRA, you can contribute up to $6,500 of your earnings to a tax-deductible, tax-deferred investment account. If you're married and your spouse also works in the business, he or she can contribute another $6,500 of his or her earnings. To learn more about setting up a SIMPLE-IRA, visit one of the large mutual fund management companies' web sites. The *www.vanguard.com* web site, for example, provides very useful information about retirement planning options for self-employed people.

The Third Secret: Work Your Money Hard

Most people don't make their money work very hard. Not surprisingly, their profits reflect this. They earn returns of 3 or 5 percent. By working their money harder, they could double or triple their returns and earn 9 percent, 10 percent, or more.

You make your money work harder by investing in riskier investments. If the idea of investing in, say, the stock market, scares the living daylights out of you, you've made way too big a deal out of stock market risks.

Let's start by discussing the concept of risk. What you mean by risk, I'll venture, is really two things: volatility and the fear of losing your investment.

As for the volatility of the stock market, some days the market is up, and some days the market is down. Up and down, up and down. It's enough to make some people sick. However, people make way too big a deal over day-to-day fluctuations in the weather. Stock prices are like the weather. Some days it's warmer, and some days it's colder. Some days the market is up, and some days the market is down. This up-and-down business gives the nightly news anchor something to talk about, but it's only so much blather. It's pseudo-news.

You don't let day-to-day temperature fluctuations bother you. The fact that it was two degrees colder last Thursday doesn't matter. Neither should you let day-to-day stock market fluctuations bother you. It's just plain silly. The only thing that really matters is the change in price between the time you buy a stock and the time you sell it.

The other feeling about risk, based on the fear of volatility, is that what you buy today for, say, $1,000, won't be worth $1,000 when you sell it. You have only to look at day-to-day fluctuations in the market to realize that. However, if you take the long view, you will see that the general trend in the stock market is always up. You can't buy a handful of stocks today and be certain that they will increase in value over the coming weeks, but you can be certain that they will grow in value over a decade or, even better, over two or three decades.

"Well, even so," you're thinking, "I'll still stick with something a little safer. All that bouncing about makes me nauseous." Unfortunately, there is a simple problem with so-called safe investments: They appear to be safe because their values don't jump around, but they aren't profitable. Your money doesn't earn anything or much of anything.

Here are a few simple facts: Since 1926, common stocks have delivered an average 10.5 percent return. Since 1926, long-term corporate bonds have delivered an average 5.7 percent return. U.S. Treasury Bills over the same time period have delivered an average 3.7 percent return.

If you adjust the historical long-term bond return for inflation and income taxes, you just break even. If you adjust the historical U.S. Treasury Bill return for inflation and income taxes, you lose about a percent a year. These two options, remember, are so-called safer investments.

History teaches investors two lessons. One is that you profit by sticking your money in riskier investments such as stocks and real-estate-ownership investments. The other is that you don't make any real profit by loaning your savings to the government, a corporation, or a local bank. To profit from your investments, you need to be an owner, not a loaner.

"Now, wait a minute," you're thinking. "That may be true over recent history. But the world is a far more dangerous place today. We can't be sure things will run so smoothly in the future."

Actually, I agree with you. But I would say that the last 70 or so years haven't been smooth. The stock market collapsed. The world suffered a global recession. A demonic madman named Adolf Hitler almost succeeded in turning the entire world into a place of darkness. We saw the first use of nuclear weapons. We had a 50-year cold war that, for peace, relied upon the threat of thermonuclear exchange.

The world *is* a dangerous place, but it's been a dangerous place for a long time. And yet, despite all the terrible things that have happened, ownership investments have been profitable. For that reason, I firmly believe that the only way to achieve financial independence—the only way to accumulate any significant amount of wealth—is by investing money in ownership investments such as stocks or real estate.

The Fourth Secret: Broadly Diversify

There is one other point of which you need to be aware, and it's crucially important: You need to be well-diversified. Ideally, in fact, you should have a couple dozen, equal-sized investments in different areas.

You should also make sure that you're not heavily dependent on a single industry or tied to a particular geographical location. You don't, for example, want to own twenty rental houses in the same town. And you wouldn't want to own twenty bank stocks.

This business about broadly diversifying is a statistical truth. Unfortunately, the statistics are too daunting—and darn unpleasant—to explain here. Suffice it to say, the only way you can hope to achieve the average returns I've talked about in the preceding secret is by having enough individual investments so that they "average out" to the historical average.

Diversification has a really interesting ramification, by the way. Even with several thousand dollars of savings a year, you need, as a practical matter, to invest in mutual funds. To own a portfolio of, say, 20 or 25 common stocks and to keep your commission costs reasonable, you would probably need to be able to invest $40,000 or $50,000 at a time. That way, you can purchase round, 100-share lots of stocks, thereby lowering your expenses. To own a portfolio of 20 or 25 rental houses, you probably need to invest several times that much. You also have the challenge of geographically diversifying yourself. It is much harder, obviously, to own houses in many different parts of the country than it is to own stocks in many different places. So picking a mutual fund is the way to go.

Picking a stock mutual fund isn't tough. But rather than try to give you a bird's-eye view of this subject, I encourage you to read a good book on the subject by Richard D. Irwin, called *Bogle on Mutual Funds* (Richard D. Irwin, Inc., 1994). John C. Bogle was chairman of The Vanguard Group of Investment Companies. This easy-to-read book provides hundreds of pages of worthwhile and honest advice on picking mutual funds.

The Fifth Secret: You Don't Have to Be a Rocket Scientist

None of this investment business requires anywhere near as much know-how as is needed to be a rocket scientist. All you need to know is the following, which is a summary of what I've explained in the preceding pages:

- Compound interest is a mathematical truth that says you should regularly save and reinvest your profits.
- Use tax-deductible and tax-deferred investment choices such as 401(k)s and IRAs. These investment vehicles boost your savings and the interest rate you earn on your investments.
- The case for investing in ownership investments is simple: It's the only real way to make money over time.
- Diversification is important because it increases the probability that investment profits closely match the stock market's historical returns. However, for diversification to work, you must invest for long enough periods of time.

Chapter 21

STOCKS, BONDS, AND OTHER INVESTMENTS

In This Chapter

- Setting up a brokerage account
- Keeping records of your stock purchases, sales, and profits
- Handling tricky stock investment transactions
- Bonds and other debt securities
- Tips for tracking other debt securities
- Understanding Quicken's annual return calculations
- How to avoid investment mistakes

If you invest in common stocks through a brokerage account, you can set up a special investment account that tracks all the securities you hold in the brokerage account. In addition, this special investment account keeps a record of the brokerage account's cash balance if the account includes an associated cash or money market account.

Tracking stocks and other equity securities with Quicken works very much like tracking mutual funds, as described in Chapter 20. The main difference is that Quicken provides a lengthier list of investment actions for stocks and other equity securities, since these transactions can affect the cash account associated with a brokerage account or your regular bank account.

NOTE *You can track shares of mutual funds that invest in stocks and shares of publicly traded real estate investment trusts in the same way that you track stocks. You may want to set up securities for these other equity investments, too.*

Before You Begin

Here are the prerequisites for tracking stock investments in Quicken:

- You need to have records that document the securities you've purchased and sold (the raw data you want to record in Quicken).
- You need to know the mechanics of using the Quicken investment register. To keep records of stock investments, you use many of the same windows, dialog boxes, and commands you do to keep records of mutual funds (see Chapter 20).

Setting Up a Brokerage Account

You'll need to set up a separate investment account for each brokerage account you have. If you have one brokerage account with a full-service broker and another with a discount broker, you need two investment accounts. If you also hold stocks (and other securities) outside a brokerage account, you can set up another investment account for these.

TIP *A good rule of thumb is to set up an investment account for each brokerage statement you receive.*

Setting Up the Quicken Investment Account

To set up an investment account for tracking stocks and other securities, follow these steps:

1. Choose Finance ➢ Account List to display the Account List window.
2. Click the New command button in the Account List to display the Create New Account dialog box.
3. Click the Brokerage button and then click Next to display the first Investment Account Setup dialog box, which is shown in Figure 21.1.

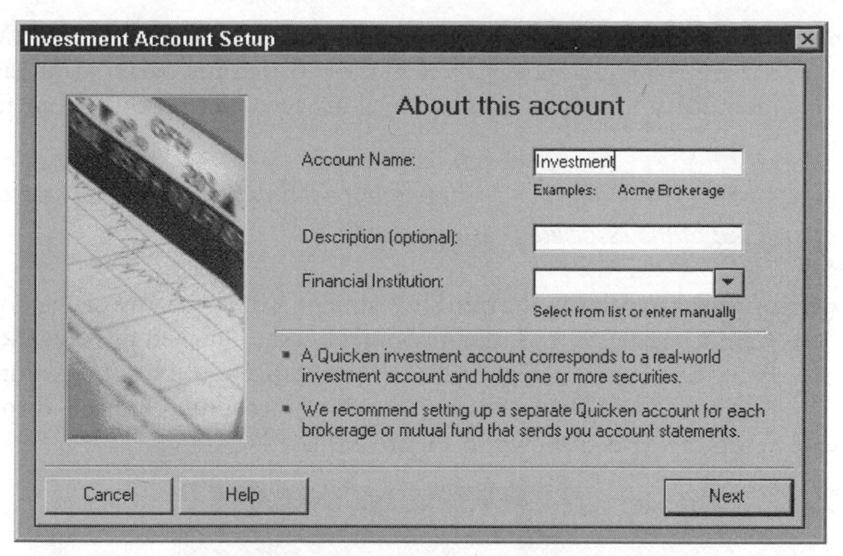

Figure 21.1: The first Investment Account Setup dialog box.

4. Enter an account name in the Account Name text box.
5. If you want to enter a description of the brokerage account or additional account information, such as the account number, use the Description text box.
6. Name the brokerage company or financial institution that holds the securities in your account using the Financial Institution box. You can select the firm from the box if the firm is listed. Or you can type the firm name into the box.
7. Click Next and Quicken displays the second Investment Account Setup dialog box, as shown in Figure 21.2

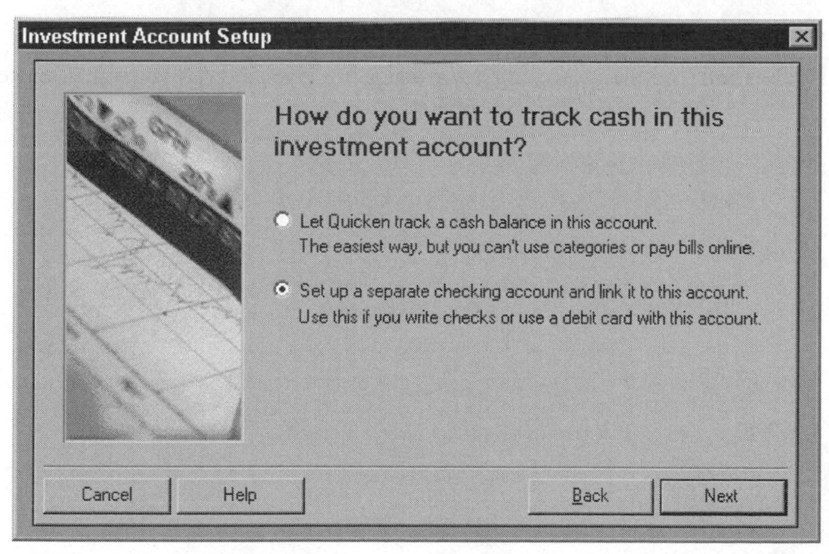

Figure 21.2: The second Investment Account Setup dialog box.

8. Tell Quicken how you want to track the cash associated with brokerage account. You have two choices: either to let Quicken keep track of the cash account balance (the easiest but least flexible method) or to set up a separate checking account (more work but also more flexible).

NOTE *Quicken assumes that any time an investment action affects cash, the cash goes into or comes out of the associated cash account.*

9. Click Next and Quicken displays the third Investment Account Setup dialog box. If you indicate you want Quicken to track the investment cash, Quicken displays the Investment Setup dialog box shown in Figure 21.3. If you indicate you want to set up a separate checking account or use an existing checking account, Quicken displays the Investment Setup dialog box shown in Figure 21.4.

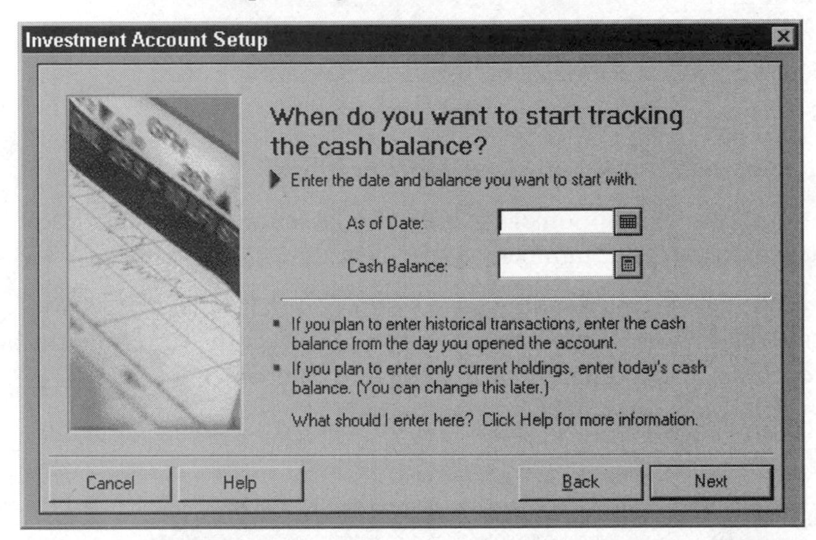

Figure 21.3: The third Investment Account Setup dialog box if you indicate you want Quicken to track your cash.

Figure 21.4: The third Investment Account Setup dialog box if you indicate you want to set up a new or use an existing checking account to track your investment cash.

10. If in step 8 you told Quicken that you want Quicken to track your investment cash, Quicken uses the Investment Account Setup dialog box shown in Figure 21.3 to collect the starting balance and starting date for the cash account. To provide these pieces of information, you enter the requested information into the As Of Date and Cash Balance boxes.

    If in step 8 you told Quicken that you want to set up a separate checking account to track the cash associated with this brokerage account, Quicken uses the Investment Setup dialog box shown in Figure 21.4 to collect the information about this other account. To create a new account, mark the New Quicken Account option button and then provide the starting account balance and starting date using the Balance and As Of boxes. To use a Quicken checking account you've already created, mark the Existing Quicken Account option button and then select the account you want from the drop-down list box. Click Next to continue.

11. Click Next. When Quicken displays the fourth Investment Account Setup dialog box, shown in Figure 21.5, use the Yes and No option buttons to indicate whether the investment account is tax-deferred or tax-exempt.

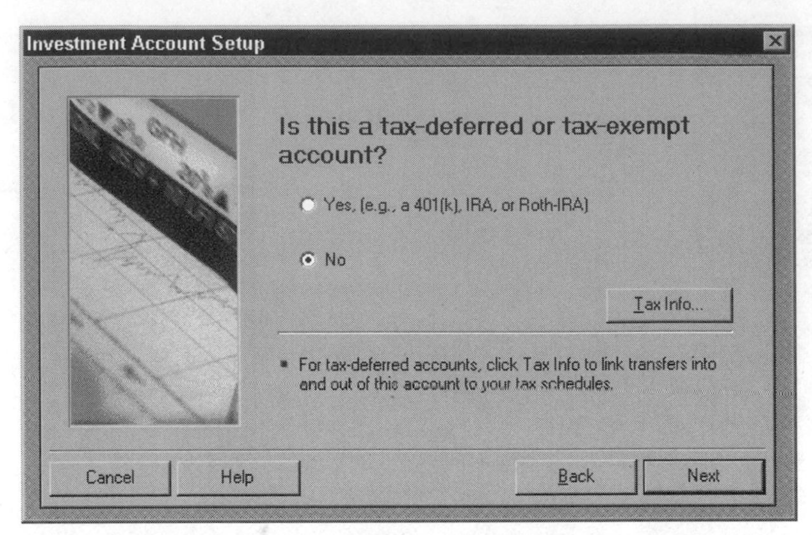

Figure 21.5: The fourth Investment Account Setup dialog box.

12. Optionally, click Tax Info. Quicken displays the Tax Schedule Information dialog box, as shown in Figure 21.6. If the transfers into and out of the investment account should be reported on your income tax return, use the Transfers In and Transfers Out drop-down list boxes to identify on which tax return form or schedule (and on which line on the form or schedule) these transfers should be reported. Then click OK.

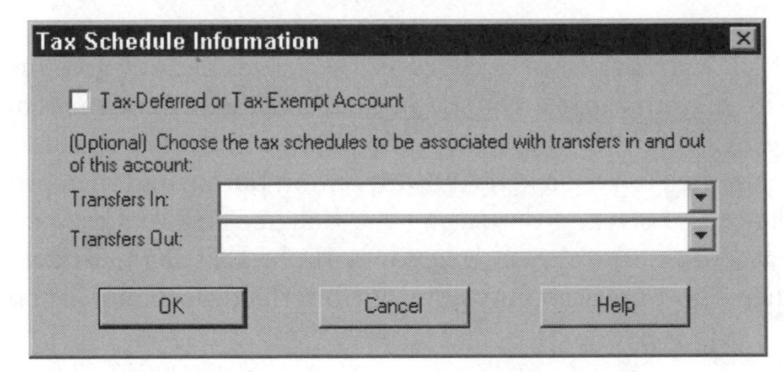

Figure 21.6: The Tax Schedule Information dialog box.

TIP *If your broker supports online investing with Quicken, Quicken prompts you to set up the investment account so that you can automatically retrieve investment transactions from the broker's computer. You want to do this. What this means is that you don't have to record the transactions you affect with an online investment account. Instead, you can tell Quicken to retrieve these transactions directly from the online investment broker.*

13. Click Done in the Investment Account Setup Information dialog box. Quicken displays a welcome message that asks how much historical data you want to include in your accounting records. If you're going to use Quicken for record keeping, you want to track complete historical data so that you can calculate accurate capital gains. And you want to set up your account so Quicken automatically retrieves information about your investment transactions from your broker. The welcome message also provides a Continue button that, if clicked, starts the Easy Actions Assistant, which steps you through the process of recording historical transactions. You can use the Easy Actions Assistant (by following its on-screen instructions). Or you can just follow the steps provided in the next section, "Describing the Securities You Already Hold."

Describing the Securities You Already Hold

Once you've set up the brokerage account, you're ready to describe the securities you hold in the account. To do this, you record the individual stocks or securities and provide the number of shares and original purchase price information.

Naming the Stocks or Securities You Hold

To name the stocks or securities you hold once you've provided the starting cash balance, display the brokerage account's register. Then follow these steps:

1. Choose Investing ➢ Security List to display the Security List window, as shown in Figure 21.7.

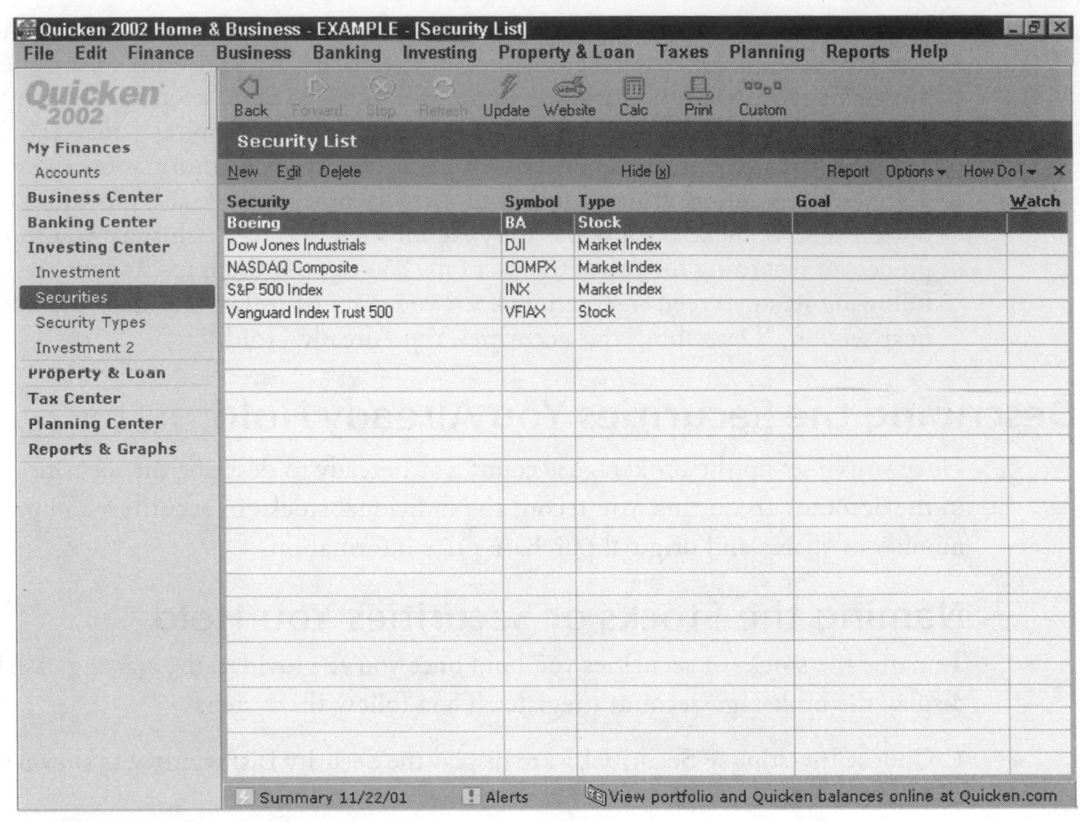

Figure 21.7: The Security List window.

2. Click the New command button in the Security List window to display the first Set Up A New Security dialog box, as shown in Figure 21.8.

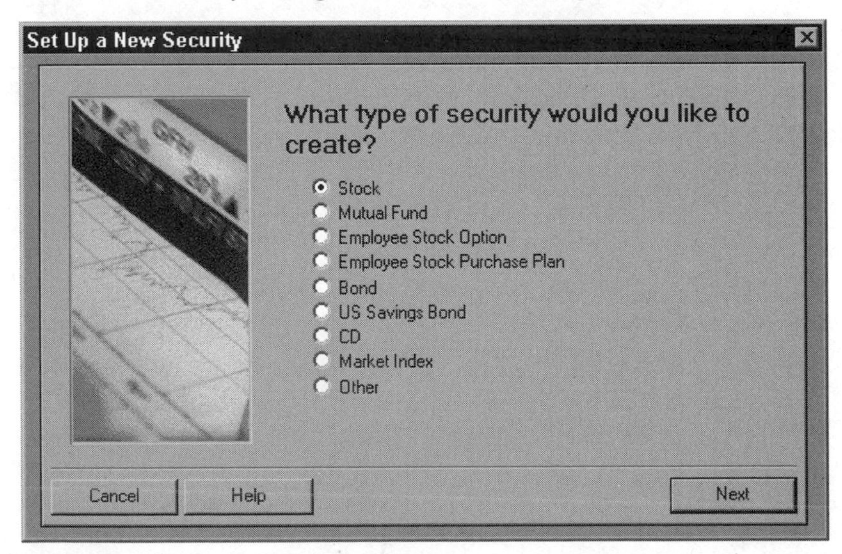

Figure 21.8: The first Set Up A New Security dialog box.

3. Mark the option button that corresponds to the type of security you are describing and then click Next. Quicken displays the second Set Up A New Security dialog box, as shown in Figure 21.9.

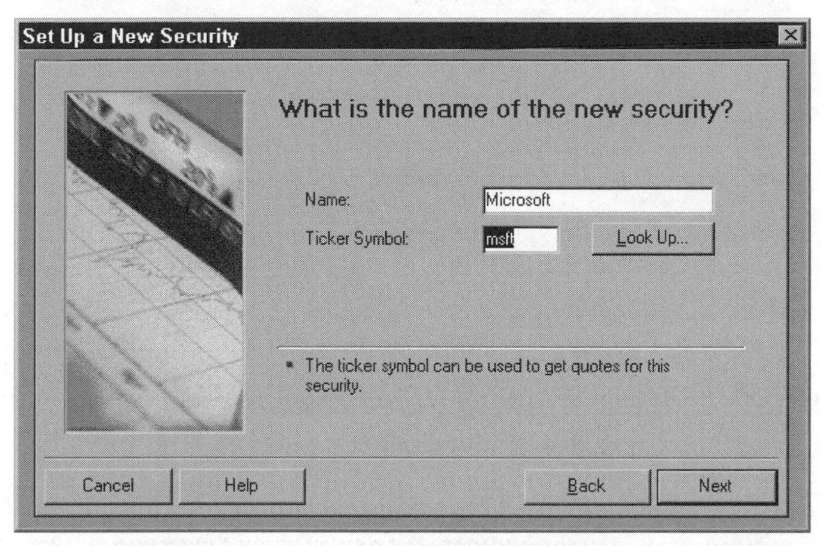

Figure 21.9: The second Set Up A New Security dialog box.

NOTE *The following steps here describe setting up a stock security. The steps for setting up other securities closely resemble these steps. However, setting up other securities may require you to collect other bits of information. For example, if you set up a bond security, Quicken prompts you to collect information about the bond's interest rate, maturity date, and accrued interest. As long as you understand the characteristics of security you're adding—and you should if you've chosen to invest in it—you should have no trouble setting up the security.*

4. Enter the name of the security in the Name text box.

5. If you want to use Quicken's Online Quotes feature to download security prices over the Internet, enter the symbol used to identify the stock in the Ticker Symbol box. Then click Next. Quicken displays the third Set Up A New Security dialog box, as shown in Figure 21.10.

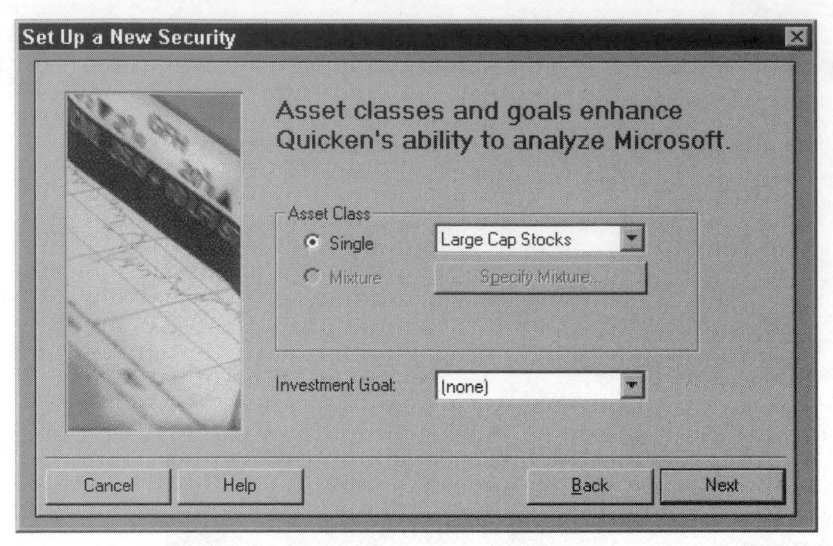

Figure 21.10: The third Set Up A New Security dialog box.

NOTE *If you provided symbols for each of your securities as you describe the securities, you can download prices over the Internet. Just display choose Investing ➢ Portfolio View, click the Update button, and choose Get Online Quotes. (This is the same information you get from the stock page of your local newspaper or from the* Wall Street Journal.*)*

6. Optionally, mark the Single option button and then select the asset class description from the list box. Or, alternatively, in the case of a mutual fund, mark the Mixture option button, click Specify Mixture, and then use the dialog box that Quicken displays to describe the mixture of asset classes that a mutual fund represents.
7. If you've earmarked this investment as funds for a specific purpose, select the appropriate investment goal from the Goal drop-down list box.

NOTE *You can create your own goal by choosing Investing ➢ Investment Goal List. Quicken displays the Investment Goal List window. Select New to display the Set Up Investment Goal dialog box. Then enter a goal in the Goal box. Optionally, select an investment goal from the Investment Goal drop-down list box.*

8. Click Next to display the fourth Set Up A New Security dialog box, as shown in Figure 21.11. Mark the Lot Identification option button to indicate that you want to individually track each lot, or purchase, of a security. You do want to use lot identification because it provides the most control over realization of any capital gains.

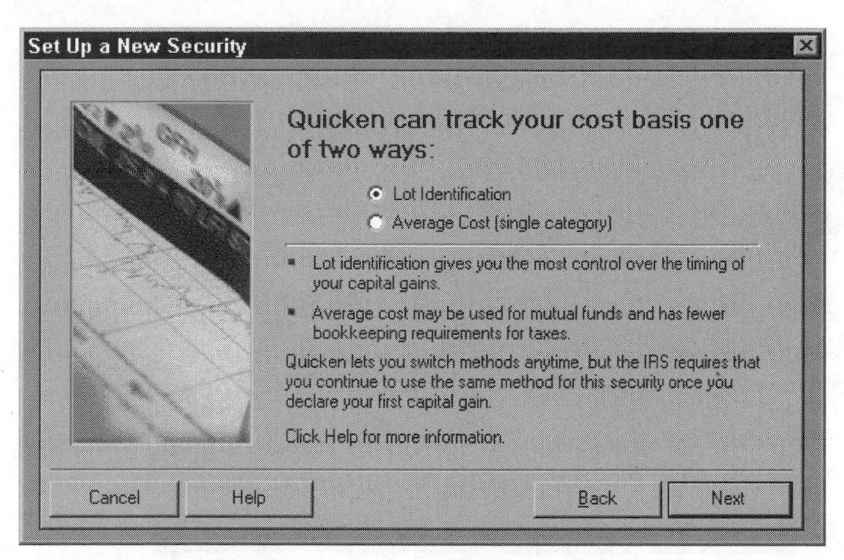

Figure 21.11: The fourth Set Up A New Security dialog box.

9. Click Next to display the fifth Set Up A New Security dialog box (not shown). The fifth Set Up A New Security dialog box asks whether you want to really track holdings of a security or merely put the security on your watch list. Assuming you really do want to track your investment in a security, mark the Track My Holdings option button. Then use the Starting From buttons to select from what point you want to keep your records. Almost always, you want to keep records from the time of purchase, and in this case, you can mark The Date You Purchased This Security button and enter the original purchase date.

10. Click Next to display the sixth Set Up A New Security dialog box (not shown). The sixth Set Up A New Security dialog box asks which investment account you want to use. Select the investment account from the Account Name drop-down list box.

11. Click Next to display the seventh Set Up A New Security dialog box, as shown in Figure 21.12. Describe the original purchase of the security by entering the shares held into the Number Of Shares box, the amount paid per share into the Cost Per Share box, and any transaction costs into the Commission/Fee box.

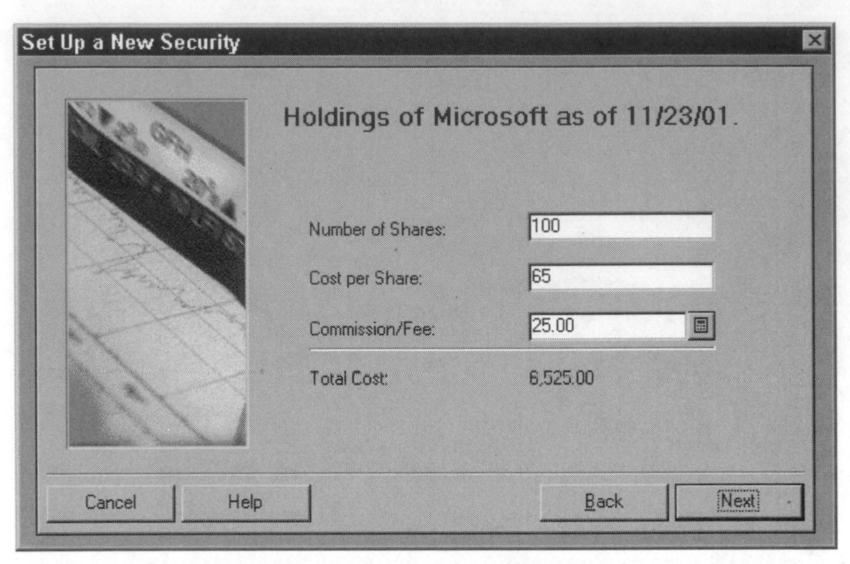

Figure 21.12: The seventh Set Up A New Security dialog box.

NOTE *In step 11, you only describe your first lot, or purchase, of a security if you're using Lot Identification. Subsequent lots need to be described using purchase transactions, as described in the section "Describing Subsequent Lots and Purchases."*

12. Click Next to display the eighth Set Up A New Security dialog box, as shown in Figure 21.13. Review the security information. If some bit of information isn't correct, click the Back button to return to the dialog box where you supplied some piece of information and make the correction.

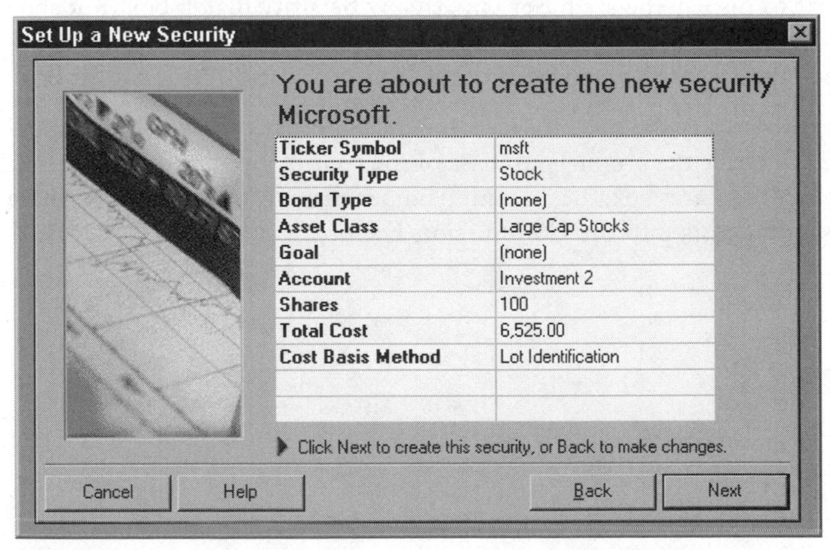

Figure 21.13: The eighth Set Up A New Security dialog box.

13. Click Next to display the ninth Set Up A New Security dialog box (not shown). The ninth Set Up A New Security dialog box asks if you want to set up another security. To answer this question, you use the Yes and No option buttons. If you click Yes, Quicken walks you through the steps 3 to 13.
14. Click Next to display the tenth Set Up A New Security dialog box (not shown). Quicken asks if you want to download historical price information for any of the securities for which you supplied a ticker symbol. Answer this question by using the Yes and No option buttons, then click Done.

Describing Subsequent Lots and Purchases

You describe the first lot, or purchase, of a security when you set up the security. To describe subsequent lots and subsequent purchases, you need to record additional investment transactions, giving the number of shares of each stock or lot, the price per share (or the stock or lot total), and the commission paid (if any).

You can describe the shares you hold either by entering them directly in the investment account register or by using an investment form. I described the "directly into the register" approach in Chapter 20. Because the investment form approach makes the most sense for brokerage accounts, I'll describe that method here.

To describe each of the subsequent lots and purchases using an investment form, display the Security Detail View window (by choosing Investing ➤ Security Detail View). Then follow these steps:

1. Choose the security from the drop-down list box in the upper-left corner of the Security Detail View window.
2. Click the Easy Actions command button and then choose the Buy/Add Shares command to display the Buy/Add Shares dialog box. Click the Summary tab to display the buttons and boxes you'll use to describe your holding. This tab is shown in Figure 21.14.

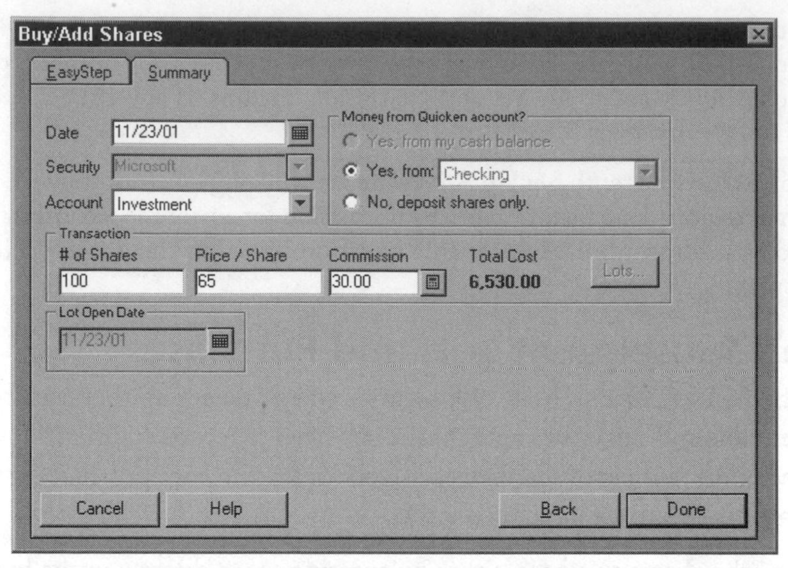

Figure 21.14: The Summary tab of the Buy/Add Shares dialog box.

TIP *Quicken automatically enters your investment transaction into the next empty row of an investment register. To display an investment account's register, choose Finance ➢ Account List to display the Account List window and then double-click the investment account.*

3. Enter the lot purchase date in the Date text box. Be sure to enter the actual purchase date. Quicken categorizes any capital gain or loss as short-term or long-term based on the difference between the purchase and sales dates shown in the register.
4. Select the investment account using the Account drop-down list box.
5. Enter the shares you purchased in the # Of Shares text box.
6. Enter the price per share you paid using the Price/Share text box. You can enter stock prices either as dollars and cents (7.50) or as fractional amounts (7 1/8.) If the Price text box is highlighted, you can incrementally adjust the price by eighths using the + and – keys.
7. Enter the brokerage commission you paid in the Commission text box.
8. Verify the Money From Quicken Account? option buttons to identify the source of the funds used for the purchase. If you're recording a new purchase, for example, mark the Yes From option button and verify the Yes From box identifies the account you used. If you're describing an old purchase—perhaps a subsequent lot—mark the No, Deposit Shares Only option button so that Quicken doesn't adjust the balance in one of your bank accounts for the purchase.
9. Click Done. Quicken records the transaction into the investment register.

NOTE *If you hold mutual funds in a brokerage account, you can treat them as stocks for purposes of your investment record keeping.*

Keeping Records of Your Stock Purchases, Sales and Profits

Once you've set up the brokerage account records, you're ready to begin recording subsequent stock purchases, sales, and any profits. If you've used Quicken for mutual-fund record keeping (as described in Chapter 20), you'll notice many similarities in the way stock-investment record keeping works.

Describing the Shares You Buy

Whenever you buy additional shares of a stock, you'll need to record the purchase. To do this, you follow the same sequence of steps as just described in the section "Describing Subsequent Lots and Purchases."

Describing Dividend Interest and Capital Gains Distributions

Many companies disburse a quarterly dividend to their shareholders, and sometimes they even disburse special dividends—as the result of a particularly good year, perhaps. And mutual funds, which you can also track in a brokerage account, may pay interest or capital gains.

You can record these sorts of investment profits either directly into the register (as described in Chapter 20) or by using an investment form. The investment form approach is easier, and it is the one described here.

TIP *You don't need to worry about which kind of distribution is which. The 1099 statement, and probably your brokerage statement, will tell you what kind of distribution you've received.*

To record a dividend, interest, or capital gains distribution using an investment form, display the Security Detail View window (by choosing Investing ➢ Security Detail View). Then follow these steps:

1. Choose the security from the drop-down list box in the upper-left corner of the Security Detail View window.

2. Click the Easy Actions button and then choose the Income (Dividend, Interest) command to display the Record Income dialog box, as shown in Figure 21.15.

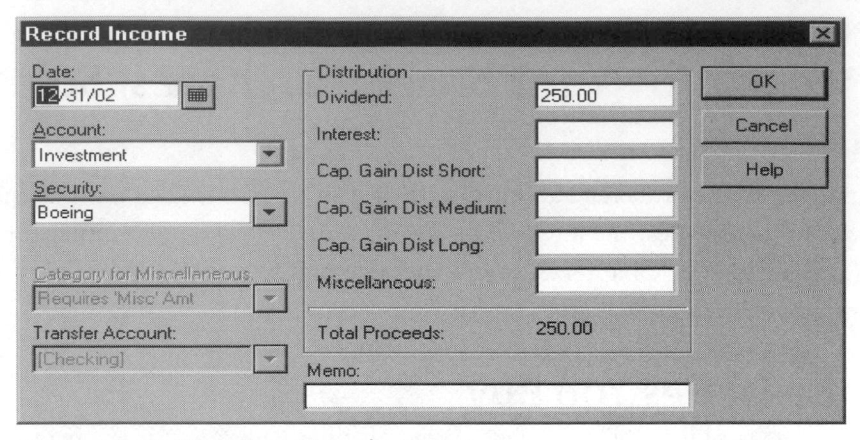

Figure 21.15: The Record Income dialog box.

3. Enter the distribution date, stock name, amount of the dividend, interest payment, short-term capital gain payment, and long-term capital gain payment in the appropriate text boxes.
4. Enter the amount of any other payment in the Miscellaneous text box. Use the Category For Miscellaneous combo box to show how the miscellaneous payment should be categorized. (Quicken doesn't show this combo box until you enter an amount in the Miscellaneous text box.)
5. If you will deposit the distribution in another account (in other words, not the brokerage account), use the Transfer Account combo box to identify the other account. (This combo box isn't available unless you're using an account that doesn't have a linked cash account.)
6. If you need to record some additional piece of information—for example, to cross-reference the source that documents the distribution—use the Memo text box.
7. Click OK.

Recording Reinvestment Transactions

You may reinvest investment profits by purchasing additional shares of a stock or mutual fund. Some companies even have formal reinvestment programs called Dividend Reinvestment Programs (DRIPs). With a DRIP, you can buy additional shares of a company using your dividends, often without needing to pay any commissions or transaction fees.

To record reinvested investment profits, using an investment form, display the Security Detail View window (by choosing Investing ➤ Security Detail View). Then follow these steps:

1. Choose the security from the drop-down list box in the upper-left corner of the Security Detail View window.
2. Choose Easy Actions ➤ Reinvest Income to open the Reinvest Income dialog box, as shown in Figure 21.16.

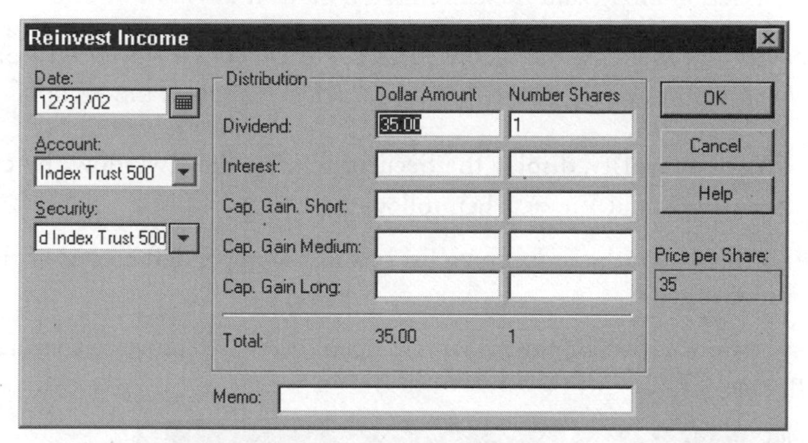

Figure 21.16: The Reinvest Income dialog box.

3. Enter the reinvestment date and stock name in the appropriate text boxes.
4. Use the Dividend Dollar Amount and Number Shares text boxes to describe the dividends you reinvested and the number of shares acquired with the dividends.
5. Use the Interest Dollar Amount and Number Shares text boxes to describe the number of shares acquired with the interest.
6. Use the Cap. Gain Short Dollar Amount and Number Shares text boxes to describe the short-term capital gains you reinvested and the number of shares acquired with the capital gains money.
7. Use the Cap. Gain Long Dollar Amount and Number Shares text boxes to describe the long-term capital gains you reinvested and the number of shares acquired with the capital gains money.

Using the values you enter in the Dollar Amount and Number Shares text boxes, Quicken calculates the total dollar amount reinvested, the total number of shares purchased by reinvesting, as well as the average price per share you're paying.

8. If you need to record additional information about the reinvestment, use the Memo text box.
9. Click OK. Quicken records the distribution and the purchase of new shares.

Describing the Shares You Sell

As with the other types of stock transactions you record, describing the shares you sell is easy as long as you have the necessary information: the number of shares sold, the price per share (or the transaction total), and the commission paid (if any).

NOTE *You can record a short-sale transaction. Choose Easy Actions ➢ Advanced ➢ Short Sale and fill in the boxes similar to what you would do for a sale in this section.*

To record the sale of a security, display the Security Detail View window (by choosing Investing ➢ Security Detail View). Then follow these steps:

1. Choose the security from the drop-down list box in the upper-left corner of the Security Detail View window.
2. Choose Easy Actions ➢ Sell/Remove Shares to open the Sell/Remove Shares dialog box, as shown in Figure 21.17. Click the Summary tab.

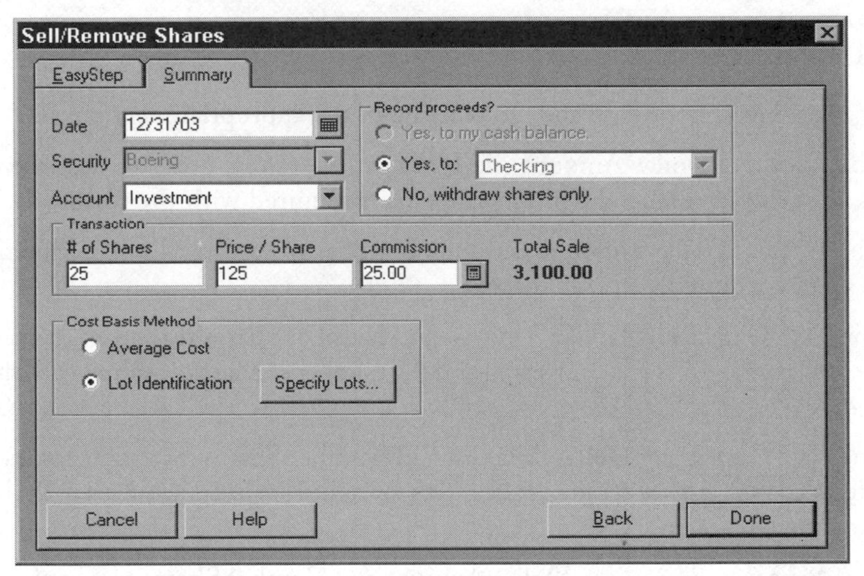

Figure 21.17: The Sell/Remove Shares dialog box.

3. Enter the sale date in the Date text box. Be sure to enter the actual sale date. Quicken categorizes any capital gain or loss as short-term or long-term based on the difference between the purchase and sale dates shown in the register.
4. Name the stock you're selling using the Security combo box.
5. Enter the number of shares you sold in the # Of Shares text box.
6. Enter the sales price per share you received in the Price/Share text box.
7. Enter the sales commission or transaction fee in the Commission text box.

8. If you will deposit the sales proceeds in some account other than the brokerage one, mark the Yes, To option button and use the combo box to show the account. Alternatively, mark the No option button if you don't want to record the proceeds. (By default, Quicken assumes that you will deposit proceeds into a cash, or linked, account.)
9. If you want to use specific identification, mark the Lot Identification option button in the Cost Basis Method section, and then click Specify Lots. In the Specify Lots dialog box, identify the lots you want to sell. (For more information about specific identification of shares, see the section "Describing the Mutual Fund Shares You Sell" in Chapter 20.)
10. Click Done. Quicken records the transaction.

Stock Splits, Dividends, and Reminders

Chapter 20 explained how you record stock split transactions and investment reminder transactions in mutual fund accounts. These two transactions work the same way for brokerage accounts.

Stock dividends are really just stock splits. With a stock dividend, a company increases the number of shares held by each shareholder by a set percentage. A company, for example, might give current shareholders a 20 percent stock dividend. In this case, the company increases the number of shares held by each shareholder by 20 percent.

To record dividends, enter the ratio of old shares to new shares. If a company issued a 10 percent dividend, for example, the ratio is 1 to 1.1. In other words, for every old share, a stockholder receives 1.1 new shares.

TIP *Quicken also provides a special advanced action for stock dividends. To use this action, click the Easy Actions command button, and then choose Stock Dividend (non-cash). Quicken displays a dialog box that collects the information it needs to record a stock split transaction that shows the effect of the stock dividend.*

Recording Brokerage Account Fees

Many brokerage accounts levy annual fees. Some also charge exit fees when you close the account. Recording these account fees isn't difficult, but how you record them depends on the type of investment account you've set up.

If you've set up an investment account that has a linked cash account, you record these fees directly into the linked cash account's register as an account withdrawal. When you record the withdrawal, you categorize the expense as falling into an investment expense category.

This process works in the same way as recording bank service charges for a regular bank account.

If you've set up an investment account that doesn't have a linked cash account, you can record the fees either directly in the investment register or by using an investment form. Using an investment form is easier. To record one of these fees using an investment form, follow these steps:

1. Choose Easy Actions ➤ Miscellaneous Expense to open the Miscellaneous Expense dialog box.
2. Enter the date the fee is charged in the Date text box.
3. If the fee is tied to a specific stock or you have only one stock in the account, enter the stock's name in the Security text box.
4. Enter the amount of the fee in the Amount text box.
5. In the Category drop-down list, select the expense category you use to track and tally investment expenses. (Investment expenses may be deductible as miscellaneous deductions.)
6. If you want to further describe the fee—for example, to note that a fee is charged annually for account maintenance—use the Memo text box.
7. Click OK. Quicken records the account fee and adjusts the brokerage account's cash balance accordingly.

NOTE *If you write a check to pay an account fee, you don't need to do anything special in the investment register. You just write the check in the usual way—probably by using the Write Checks window or the Register window. Be sure, however, to categorize the check that pays an account fee as investment expense since it may qualify as a miscellaneous deduction.*

Recording Cash Balance Interest and Miscellaneous Brokerage Account Income

It's likely that you'll earn interest or other income on the cash balances you hold in your brokerage account. To record this interest or income, choose Easy Actions ➤ Income (Dividend, Interest), and then fill out the Record Income dialog box as described earlier in the chapter. The only difference in recording cash balance interest and miscellaneous brokerage account income rather than stock income is that you don't identify a specific security.

NOTE *The 1099 or brokerage account statement will indicate what kind of distribution the check is for.*

Reconciling Investment Accounts

You can reconcile mutual fund investment accounts and brokerage investment accounts. In a mutual fund, you reconcile just the shares. In a brokerage account, you reconcile shares and the cash balance.

Mechanically, reconciling an investment account works like reconciling a bank account. After you've read Chapter 5 of this book and performed a few bank account reconciliations, you'll have no trouble reconciling investment accounts.

Handling Tricky Stock Investment Transactions

The earlier portions of this chapter describe the most common investment transactions you need to record for common stocks you hold in a brokerage account. There are, however, several additional transactions you may need to record, particularly if you're an aggressive investor (one who's willing to bear increased risk in the pursuit of greater returns). These transactions involve short sales, margin loans and interest, call and put activities, employee stock options, and corporate reorganizations. The following sections briefly describe how you record these other types of transactions.

Short Sales

A *short sale* occurs when you sell stock you don't actually hold. The logic of a short sale is that rather than buying low and later selling high, you first buy high and then sell low. (To make the transaction, you actually borrow the stock from your broker.)

To record a short sale transaction in Quicken, you just sell a stock you don't own. Select Easy Actions ➢ Advanced ➢ Short Sale and fill in the appropriate categories in the Short Sale dialog box. To show that these are shares you actually owe your broker, Quicken displays the number of shares and the current market value as negative amounts in the Portfolio View window.

To record the transaction in which you close out your short position by buying the stock you've previously sold, you record a stock purchase in the usual way.

Margin Loans and Margin Interest

If you purchase a security and the total purchase cost exceeds the cash balance in a brokerage account, Quicken assumes that you've borrowed the needed cash on margin from your broker. To show the margin loan, it displays the cash balance as a negative value.

To record margin loan interest in cases where you have a linked cash account, you record the margin loan interest as an expense when you record the withdrawal from the linked cash account that pays the margin interest.

To record margin loan interest in cases where you don't have a linked cash account, choose Easy Actions ➤ Margin Interest Expense. When Quicken displays the Margin Interest Expense dialog box, use it to describe the margin interest.

Calls and Puts

A *call* is an option to buy a share of stock. A *put* is an option to sell a share of stock. You may write, buy, or exercise calls and puts.

Writing Calls and Puts

When you write a call or put, what you really do is collect money from someone in return for promising the person the option, or chance, to buy or sell a share of stock at a specified, or *strike*, price by some future date.

When a call or put expires without being exercised—and this is the usual case—recording the transaction is simple. If you're the one writing the call or put, just record the transaction as miscellaneous income.

Buying Calls and Puts

If you're the one buying the call or put, you just record the option purchase the way you do any other stock purchase. If the call or put expires and becomes worthless, just record the sale as a stock purchase with the amount set to zero. (This is the most common case.)

If, on the other hand, you sell the call or put before the expiration date because the call or put can be profitably exercised, you record the sale as a stock sale with the amount set to whatever you sell the option for.

Exercising Calls and Puts

You probably won't actually exercise a call or put. You'll probably sell it, as described above. If you do exercise a call or buy option, however, you need to record two transactions.

To record the exercise of a call option, first record a transaction that sells the call option for zero. Then record a transaction that purchases the optioned number of shares at the option price.

To record the exercise of a put option, first record a transaction that sells the put option for zero. Then record a transaction that sells the optioned number of shares at the option price.

TIP *For income tax purposes, what you pay for a call needs to be counted as part of the purchase price if you exercise the call option and purchase shares. What you receive for a put needs to be counted as part of the sales price if you exercise the put and sell shares. This can get complicated, so you may want to consult your tax advisor.*

Employee Stock Options

You can track the value of employee stock options in the same way that you track shares of stock. (The purchase price in this case is zero if you don't pay anything for the option.) The value of the option, of course, is the difference between the exercise price and the fair market value of the vested shares.

The income tax accounting for stock options can get a little tricky, depending on whether the options are part of a qualified incentive stock-option plan or a nonqualified stock-option plan. You may have a taxable gain when you are granted or when you exercise the option, or you may have a taxable gain only later when you sell the shares. If you have questions about the income tax treatment, consult your tax advisor. You'll need to show him or her the stock option plan document, so be sure to bring that with you.

Dealing with Corporate Reorganizations, Mergers, and Spin-Offs

Several of the commands on the Advanced submenu of the Easy Actions menu are useful for investment actions that stem from corporate reorganizations, mergers, or spin-offs:

Short Sale Lets you record the sale of stock you don't own so that you can record short salc transactions.

Cover Short Sale Lets you record the purchase of shares you've previously sold short.

Corporate Name Change Lets you change the name of a security without losing any of your financial records for the security.

Corporate Securities Spin-Off Lets you describe new securities you're adding to an account as coming from existing securities you already own. In this way, your rate of return calculations don't ignore "spun-off" securities in their calculations of investment profits.

Corporate Acquisition (Stock for Stock) Lets you record stock-for-stock corporate mergers.

Transfer Cash Into Account Lets you move cash into a brokerage account's associated cash account.

Transfer Cash Out Of Account Lets you move cash out of a brokerage accounts' associated accounts.

Transfer Shares Between Accounts Lets you move securities between investment accounts.

Bonds and Other Debt Securities

To keep records for bonds and other debt securities, you use the same brokerage account described earlier in the chapter. Tracking these securities works very much like tracking stocks.

Getting Ready for Bond Record Keeping

You'll need to set up a separate investment account for each brokerage account you have. If you have one brokerage account with a full-service broker and another with a discount broker, you need to set up two investment accounts. If you also hold stocks and bonds outside a brokerage account, you can set up another investment account for these.

Once you've set up the brokerage account, you're ready to describe the bonds and any other debt securities you hold in the account. This process works the same way for bonds and debt securities as it does for stocks and mutual funds.

NOTE *Bond prices are quoted as a percentage of their face, or par, value. A $1,000 par value bond that sells for $950, for example, has a price of $95. Because Quicken calculates the total security amount as the price times the quantity, however, you can't enter the bond price as a percentage. Instead, you need to enter the actual dollar price. To describe a bond you've purchased for $950, for example, you enter the price as $950.*

Keeping Records of Your Bond Purchases, Sales, and Profits

Once you've set up the brokerage account records, you're ready to begin recording bond purchases, sales, and any profits. If you've used Quicken for stock-investment record keeping, you'll find that bond record keeping works pretty much the same way.

Describing the Bonds You Buy

Whenever you buy additional bonds, you need to record the purchase and any accrued interest, so you actually record two transactions. As with stocks and mutual funds, you can record bond purchases directly into the register or by using an investment form. Because the investment form approach is easier, it's the one I'll describe here. To learn how to record transactions directly into the register, see Chapter 20. It describes how you record mutual fund transactions directly into the register, but the same basic approach works for stocks and bonds.

Recording a Bond Purchase

To record a bond purchase, follow these steps:

1. Go to the Portfolio View window and choose Easy Actions ➤ Buy/Add Shares to open the Buy/Add Shares dialog box, and then click the Summary tab.
2. Enter the purchase date in the Date text box, the bond name in the Security combo box, and the quantity of bonds you purchased in the # Of Shares text box.
3. Enter the dollar price per bond you paid in the Price/Share text box. Remember that Quicken expects you to enter the actual dollar price you paid, not the price as a percentage of the bond's face, or par, value.

NOTE *You don't include the accrued interest in the bond price in step 3. You record that bit of information later.*

4. Enter the brokerage commission you paid in the Commission text box.

You can enter any three of the following four inputs: number of shares, price, commission/fee, or total of sale. Using the three values you do enter, Quicken calculates the fourth value.

5. If you will use cash from some other account for the purchase instead of cash from the brokerage account, mark the Yes, From option button and use the combo box to add the account. Do this only if you're not using a linked cash account.
6. Click Done. Quicken records the transaction.

Recording Accrued Interest

After you record the bond purchase, you usually need to record accrued interest paid to the previous holder. In effect, what you're really doing by paying accrued interest is giving the previous bond holder his or her share of the next interest payment. To record this accrued interest, follow these steps:

1. Choose Easy Actions ➤ Return Of Capital to open the Return Of Capital dialog box, as shown in Figure 21.18.

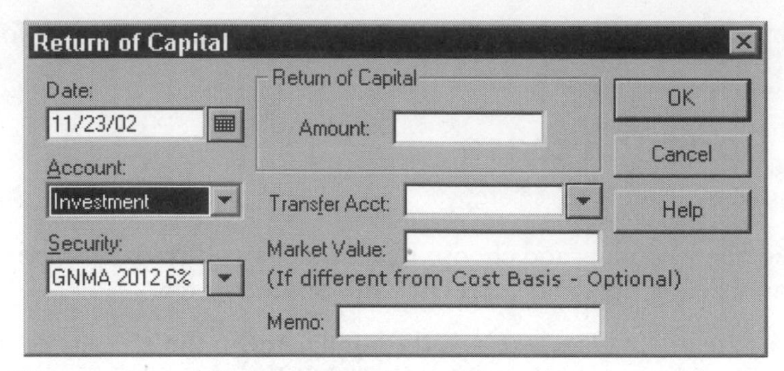

Figure 21.18: The Return Of Capital dialog box.

2. Enter the purchase date in the Date text box and the bond or lot name in the Security text box.
3. In the Amount text box, enter the accrued interest you paid as a negative number.
4. If you want to identify the transaction as an accrued interest adjustment, use the Memo text box.
5. Click OK. Quicken records the accrued interest transaction.

NOTE *You can also record accrued interest when you set up a bond as a new security. If you do that, you don't need to use the Return Of Capital dialog box.*

Describing Bond Interest and Return of Capital Distributions

Most bonds pay monthly or semi-annual interest. In addition, some bonds—for example, mortgage-backed securities such as GNMA bonds—return a portion of the bond principal with each interest payment.

TIP *Don't worry about which kind of distribution is which. The 1099 statement, and probably also your brokerage statement, tells you what kind of distribution you've received.*

As with other investment transactions, you have a choice as to how you record bond interest and return of capital transactions. You can enter these transactions directly into the register, as discussed in Chapter 20, or you can use an investment form.

To record an interest payment, choose Easy Actions ➢ Income (Dividend, Interest). In the Record Income dialog box, identify the interest payment date, the security paying the interest, and the amount. Fill in the Record Income dialog box's text and combo boxes as described in Chapter 20 and earlier in this chapter. The steps for recording bond income are similar to those for recording stock or mutual fund income.

To record a return of capital distribution, including the payment of interest you previously accrued, choose Easy Actions ➢ Return Of Capital. In the Return Of Capital dialog box, give the interest payment date, name the security paying the interest, and indicate the amount of previously accrued interest you're now receiving.

Recording Accrued Interest Shown on a 1099-OID

You aren't always paid the interest that you've earned. If you purchase a negotiable certificate of deposit (CD), for example, the bank issuing the CD may accrue the interest you've earned through the end of the year and then add this amount to the CD's value. If you purchase a zero-coupon bond, you don't receive periodic interest payments at all. Rather, the bond issuer accrues interest each year and then repays the bond and the total accrued interest at maturity. Even though you aren't paid interest, however, you need to record the interest you've earned because you need to report the accrued interest as taxable income. Fortunately, in most cases the bond issuer sends a 1099-OID form that reports the amount of accrued but not paid interest.

NOTE *Bond issuers also report the amortization of original-issue discounts on 1099-OID forms. In fact, OID stands for Original Issue Discount. Because original-issue discounts effectively increase the annual interest earnings, you also need to record these.*

To record accrued interest, you actually record two transactions, as described in Chapter 20 and earlier in this chapter:

- Choose Easy Actions ➢ Income (Dividend, Interest), and then complete the Record Income dialog box.
- Choose Easy Actions ➢ Return of Capital, and fill in the Return Of Capital dialog box. Describe the accrued but unpaid interest as a negative return of capital. (This is the same technique used earlier in the chapter to deal with accrued interest paid with the bond purchase.)

TIP *By entering the return of capital as a negative number, Quicken increases the bond cost, or carrying value, by the accrued interest amount.*

Accrued Interest and the 1099-OID Form

Accrued interest income can get messy when, for income tax purposes, you need to record accrued interest that isn't reported on a 1099-OID form. The reason is that you're required to report the accrued interest—even though you won't get a 1099-OID amount. Later on, when you ultimately do get a 1099-INT or 1099-OID that includes the previously recorded accrued interest, you need to adjust this figure so it doesn't double-count the accrued interest.

Many people don't report accrued interest income until it's reported on a 1099-OID form or actually paid and reported on a 1099-INT form. With this simplified approach, you don't evade income taxes on the interest income, but you do delay paying the income taxes. Once the interest is accrued, the IRS does insist that you pay income taxes. If this applies to your situation, talk to your tax advisor.

Describing the Bonds You Sell

Describing the bonds you sell is easy as long as you have the necessary information: the number of bonds sold, the price per share (or the transaction total), and the commission paid (if any). You also need to know the amount of accrued interest you will be paid.

As with other investment transactions, you can record bond sales either directly into the register or by using an investment form; using an investment form is easier. To record a bond sale, choose Easy Actions ➢ Sell/Remove Shares. In the Sell/Remove Shares dialog box, click the Summary tab. Enter the sales date, name the bond being sold, give the sales amount and sales commission, and indicate where you'll deposit the money. (Chapter 20 and earlier sections in this chapter describe how investment sale transactions work.)

After you record the bond sale, you need to record the amount of accrued interest you're being paid. In effect, the bond purchaser pays you your share of the next interest payment. To do this, choose Easy Actions ➢ Income (Dividend, Interest), and fill out the Record Income dialog box so that it describes the accrued interest being paid. From your perspective, it's irrelevant that the bond purchaser rather than the bond issuer pays the interest, so recording this accrued interest payment works just like recording a regular interest coupon payment, as described earlier in this chapter.

Recording Early Withdrawal Penalty Transactions

Early withdrawal penalties on certificates of deposit are a special type of tax-deductible expense. Like IRA contributions, alimony, and a few other items, these penalties are deductions from your total income and are used to calculate your adjusted gross income. Because of this, be sure to record any early withdrawal penalties you pay with a separate transaction. If you're using an investment account with a linked cash account, record the early withdrawal penalty as if it were paid from the cash account. If you're not using an investment with a linked cash account, use the Easy Actions menu's Miscellaneous Expense command. In either case, when you do record the early withdrawal penalty, categorize the early withdrawal penalty expense in a way that lets you easily report this penalty on your income tax return. (You might want to set up a new expense category called Early Withdrawal Penalty.)

Tips for Tracking Other Debt Securities

You can use Quicken to keep records of most other debt securities. Here's a list of some of the other common debt securities, along with suggestions for how you can treat them in Quicken:

DEBT SECURITY	HOW TO HANDLE IT
Certificates of deposit	Treat negotiable certificates of deposit like bonds. (Mechanically, jumbo negotiable CDs are almost identical to corporate and government bonds.) Consider treating non-negotiable certificates like bank accounts.
U.S. Savings Bonds	Treat these as you do a regular bond. You won't record interest payments, but you will need to accrue interest.
Zero-coupon bonds	Treat these the same way as U.S. Savings Bonds. You won't need to record interest payments (the bond won't pay these), but you will need to accrue interest.

Understanding Quicken's Annual Return Calculations

Quicken's Investment Performance report calculates an internal rate of return for each security, as described in Chapter 4. Here I'll describe why you use the internal rate of return (IRR) tool and how it compares with the other standard performance measurement tools.

What Is an IRR?

The IRR tool calculates the annual profit an investment delivers as a percentage of the investment's value at the start of the year. For example, in a simple case, if you buy an investment for $100 and the investment pays $10 in dividends at the end of the year and then is sold for $95, your IRR is 5 percent.

There are actually two steps to making this calculation:

- You need to calculate the annual profit. You can do this by combining the $10 of dividends with the $5 capital loss (calculated as $95–$100) for a result of $5 of annual profit.
- You divide the $5 of annual profit by the $100 investment value at the start of the year. $5/$100 equals 5 percent, and that's the IRR.

By calculating an IRR, you can quantify the performance of a stock that you've purchased and of your investment portfolio as a whole. This is particularly true with individual stocks and brokerage accounts because you often don't really know how your stock picks, your broker's picks, and your portfolio have done and are doing relative to the market as a whole and relative to other investments.

NOTE *In comparison, you usually have a pretty good idea as to how well a mutual fund does on a quarterly or at least an annual basis. The fund manager will report to you on the quarterly and annual returns.*

Some Mechanical Problems with the IRR

Now that you understand the basic logic of the IRR tool, you should know that the IRR, for all of its usefulness, isn't flawless. Quicken (and every other investment record-keeper's computer program) calculates a daily IRR and then multiplies this percentage by the number of days in a year to get an equivalent annual IRR.

This sounds right, but it presents problems in the case of publicly traded securities because a short-term percentage change in a security's market value—even if modest—can annualize to a very large positive or negative number. If you buy a stock for $10.125 and the next day the stock drops to $10, the annual return using these two pieces of information is a whopping –98.9 percent! If you buy a stock for $10.125 and the next day the stock rises to $10.25, the annual return using these two pieces of information is an astronomical 8,711 percent.

To minimize the problems of annualizing short-term percentage changes, you probably want to refrain from measuring IRRs for only short periods of time. An annualized daily return can be very misleading.

One other thing to note is that the IRR calculation becomes more difficult when you try to calculate the average annual profit percentage, or IRR, for a series of years when the starting value is changing from year to year. The basic problem is that the IRR formula is what's called an *n*th root polynomial (*n* is the number of days in the IRR calculation). A one-year IRR calculation is a 365th root polynomial. (Remember that Quicken calculates daily IRRs and then annualizes these daily percentages.)

The problem with an *n*th root polynomial is that, by definition, it can have up to *n* real and imaginary solutions. An annual IRR calculation could theoretically have 365 correct IRRs. You would not normally have this many solutions, but you could still have several correct solutions. So you can see that by using IRR-based return calculations, there's an opportunity for real confusion. Quicken, recognizing these problems, does not attempt to calculate IRRs for investments that look like they may have more than one IRR. You'll know for which investments you can't calculate an IRR, but you won't know how those investments did.

How to Avoid Investment Mistakes

Smart people sometimes make dumb mistakes when it comes to investing. Part of the reason for this, I guess, is that most people don't have the time to learn what they need to know to make good decisions. Another reason is that oftentimes when you make a dumb mistake, somebody else—an investment salesperson, for example—makes money. Fortunately, you can save yourself lots of money and a bunch of headaches by not making bad investment decisions.

Don't Forget to Diversify

At the end of Chapter 20, I mentioned that the average stock market return is 10 percent or so, but to earn 10 percent you need to own a broad range of stocks. In other words, you need to diversify.

Everybody who thinks about this for more than a few minutes realizes that it is true, but it's amazing how many people don't diversify. For example, some people hold huge chunks of their employer's stock or some important customer's or vendor's stock but little else. Or they own a handful of stocks in the same industry.

To reduce your risks to a prudent level and earn returns roughly similar with the stock market's average returns, experts used to say that you needed around 15 to 20 stocks in a variety of industries. More recently, the finance professors who study such topics say you probably need more like 50 stocks. And in my very rough experiments, I've found that one needs closer to 200 stocks in order for a portfolio's returns to approximate the market's "average." The point is you need more than just a few stocks; otherwise, your portfolio's returns will very likely be something greater or less than the stock market average. Of course, you don't care if your portfolio's return is *greater* than the stock market average, but you do care if your portfolio's return is *less* than the stock market average.

By the way, to be fair I should tell you that some very bright people disagree with me on this business of holding a large number of stocks. For example, Peter Lynch, the tremendously successful manager of the Fidelity Magellan mutual fund, suggests that individual investors hold four to six stocks that they understand well. His feeling, which he shares in his books, is that by following this strategy, an individual investor can beat the stock market average. Mr. Lynch knows more about picking stocks than I ever will, but I nonetheless respectfully disagree with him for two reasons. First, I think that Peter Lynch is one of those modest geniuses who underestimate their intellectual prowess. I wonder if he underestimates the powerful analytical skills he brings to his stock picking. Second, I think that most individual investors lack the accounting knowledge to accurately make use of the quarterly and annual financial statements that publicly held companies provide in the ways that Mr. Lynch suggests.

Another important point for business owners is that spending the time required to be a successful, active investor often doesn't really make economic sense. Usually, you'll enjoy far greater profits by investing that time and energy in your business. Spending a couple of hours every Saturday to earn an extra $2,000 or even $5,000 over the year in investment income might actually work out to a pretty modest hourly rate—especially when compared to what you would earn by investing that time in your business.

Have Patience

The stock market and other securities markets bounce around on a daily, weekly, and even yearly basis, but the general trend over extended periods of time has always been up. Since World War II, the worst one-year return has been −26.5 percent. The worst 10-year return in recent history was 1.2 percent. Those numbers are pretty scary, but things look much better if you look longer term. The worst 25-year return was 7.9 percent annually.

It's important for investors to have patience. There will be many bad years. Recently, the stock market returns have, for most investors, been terrible. But over time, the good years outnumber the bad. They compensate for the bad years, too. Patient investors who stay in the market in both the good and bad years almost always do better than people who try to follow every fad or buy last year's hot stock.

Invest Regularly

You may already know about *dollar-average investing.* Instead of purchasing a set number of shares at regular intervals, you purchase a regular dollar amount, such as $100. If the share price is $10, you purchase 10 shares. If the share price is $20, you purchase five shares. If the share price is $5, you purchase 20 shares.

Dollar-average investing offers two advantages. The biggest is that you regularly invest—in both good markets and bad markets. If you buy $100 of stock at the beginning of every month, for example, you don't stop buying stock when the market is way down and every financial journalist in the world is working to fan the fires of fear.

The other advantage of dollar-average investing is that you buy more shares when the price is low and fewer shares when the price is high. As a result, you don't get carried away on a tide of optimism and end up buying most of the stock when the market or the stock is up. In the same way, you also don't get scared away and stop buying a stock when the market or the stock is down.

One of the easiest ways to implement a dollar-average investing program is by participating in something like an employer-sponsored 401(k) plan or deferred compensation plan or by setting up your pension plan for you and any of your employees. With these plans, you effectively invest each time money is withheld from your paycheck.

To make dollar-average investing work with individual stocks, you need to dollar-average each stock. In other words, if you're buying stock in IBM, you need to buy a set dollar amount of IBM stock each month, each quarter, or whatever.

Don't Ignore Investment Expenses

Investment expenses can add up quickly. Small differences in expense ratios, costly investment newsletter subscriptions, online financial services, and income taxes can easily subtract hundreds of thousands of dollars from your net worth over a lifetime of investing.

To show you what I mean, here are a couple of quick examples. Let's say that you're saving $7,000 per year of 401(k) money in a couple of mutual funds that track the Standard & Poor's 500 index. One fund charges a 0.25 percent annual expense ratio, and the other fund charges a 1 percent annual expense ratio. In 35 years, you'll have about $900,000 in the fund with the 0.25 percent expense ratio and about $750,000 in the fund with the 1 percent ratio.

Here's another example: Let's say that you don't spend $500 a year on a special investment newsletter, but you instead stick the money in a tax-deductible investment such as an IRA. Let's say you also stick your tax savings in the tax-deductible investment. After 35 years, you'll accumulate roughly $200,000.

Investment expenses can add up to really big numbers when you realize that you could have invested the money and earned interest and dividends for years.

Don't Get Greedy

I wish there was some risk-free way to earn 15 or 20 percent annually. I really, really do. But, alas, there isn't. The stock market's average return is somewhere between 9 and 10 percent, depending on how many decades you go back. The significantly more risky small company stocks have done slightly better. On average, they return annual profits of 12 to 13 percent. Fortunately, you can get rich earning 9 percent returns. You just need to take your time. But no risk-free investments consistently return annual profits significantly above the stock market's long-run averages.

I mention this for a simple reason: People make all sorts of foolish investment decisions when they get greedy and pursue returns that are out of line with the average annual returns of the stock market. If someone tells you that he has a sure-thing investment or investment strategy that pays, say, 15 percent, don't believe it. And, for Pete's sake, don't buy investments or investment advice from that person.

If someone really did have a sure-thing method of producing annual returns of, say, 18 percent, that person would soon be the richest person in the world. With solid year-in, year-out returns like that, the person could run a $20 billion investment fund and earn $500 million a year. The moral is: There is no such thing as a sure thing in investing.

Don't Get Fancy

For years now, I've made the better part of my living by analyzing complex investments. Nevertheless, I think that it makes most sense for investors to stick with simple investments: mutual funds, individual stocks, government and corporate bonds, and so on.

As a practical matter, it's very difficult for people who haven't been trained in financial analysis to analyze complex investments such as real estate partnership units, derivatives, and cash-value life insurance. You need to understand how to construct accurate cash-flow forecasts. You need to know how to calculate things like internal rates of return and net present values with the data from cash-flow forecasts. Financial analysis is nowhere near as complex as rocket science. Still, it's not something you can do without a degree in accounting or finance, a computer, and a spreadsheet program (like Microsoft Excel or Lotus 1-2-3).

What's more, and here we get back to a point I made earlier in this discussion, you've probably got a small business you're running (inasmuch as you're reading this book). Your time and energy is almost certainly far more profitably invested in that business than it is in getting fancy in your investing.

Chapter 22

TRACKING REAL ESTATE INVESTMENTS

In This Chapter

- Tracking your home as an investment
- Tracking rental property
- How to choose a home and a mortgage

Quicken isn't really set up specifically for tracking real estate investments. Yet because it's probably the place where you'll keep all your other personal and business financial records, and because real estate often amounts to one of your most valuable assets, you may want to use it for real estate record keeping. In this chapter, I describe how you can use Quicken to keep tax records for your home and income property investments.

Tracking Your Home as an Investment

Tracking the value and cost of a home delivers one of two benefits:

- You can track your home in a way that lets you include your home's value in your net worth report.
- You can track your home in a way that lets you minimize the capital gains tax you may ultimately pay when you sell your home.

This chapter will help you decide whether it's worth more to you to focus on and track your home's market value or worth more to save capital gains taxes at some point in the future.

Focusing on Your Home's Market Value

To track your home's market value and, as a result, the home equity you've accumulated, you need to set up an asset account for your house and a liability account for your mortgage. Chapter 12 explains how to set up liability accounts for mortgages. Here, I'll explain how to set up an asset account for your house.

Setting Up the House Account

To set up an asset account for tracking your home's value, follow these steps:

1. Display the Account List window (Finance ➢ Account List) and click the New command button.
2. Select the Asset button to indicate that you want to set up an asset account, and then click Next to display the first Asset Account Setup dialog box.
3. Enter a name for the new account (such as House) in the Account Name text box, as shown in Figure 22.1.

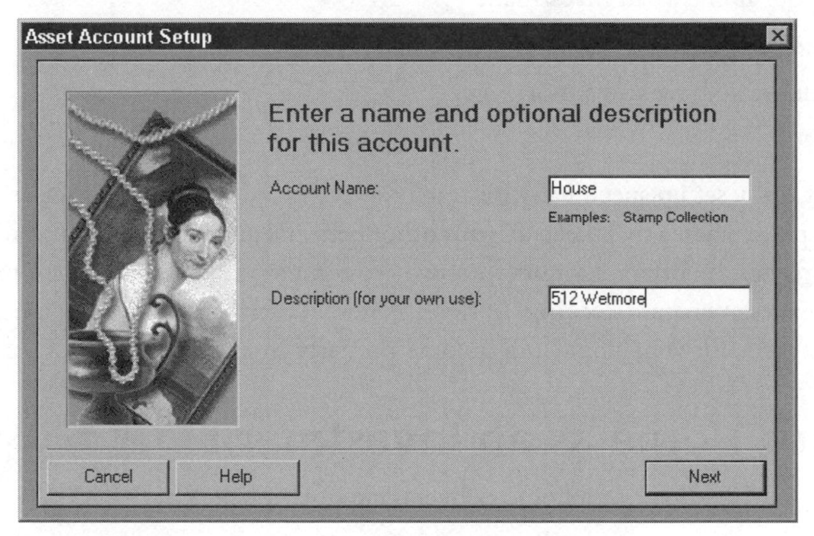

Figure 22.1: The first Asset Account Setup dialog box.

4. If you want to provide an additional description, such as the street address, use the Description text box.
5. Click Next to display the second Asset Account Setup dialog box, as shown in Figure 22.2.

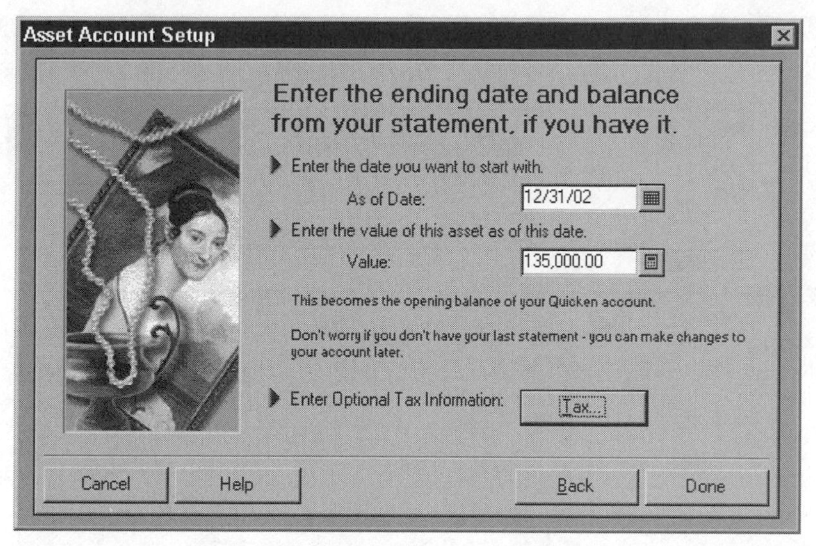

Figure 22.2: The second Asset Account Setup dialog box.

6. Enter the date as of which the current market value is correct in the As Of Date text box and the current market value of the house in the Value text box.
7. Click Done. Quicken adds the new account and then redisplays the Account List window.

Updating Your Records for Changes in the Market Value

To update your records for changes in your home's market value, follow these steps:

1. In the Account List window, select the House account and click Open to display the House account information in its own Register document window, as shown in Figure 22.3.

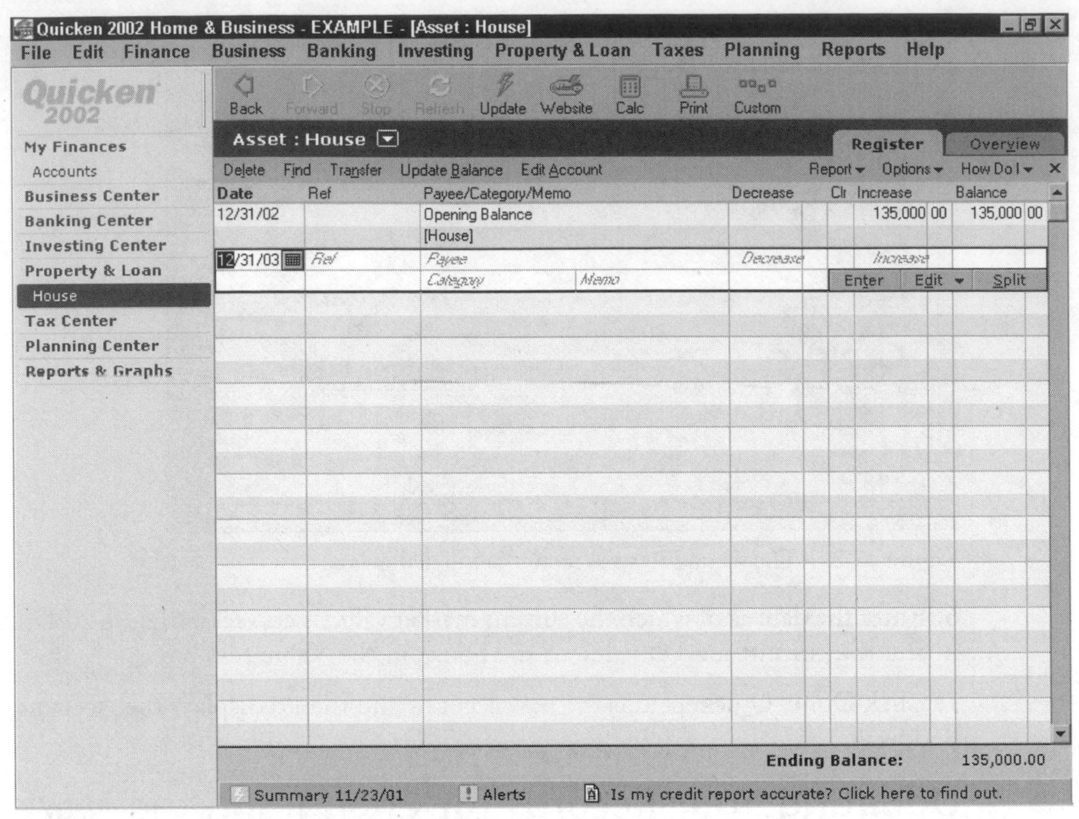

Figure 22.3: The House account in its own register.

2. Click the Update Balance button to display the Update Account Balance dialog box, as shown in Figure 22.4.

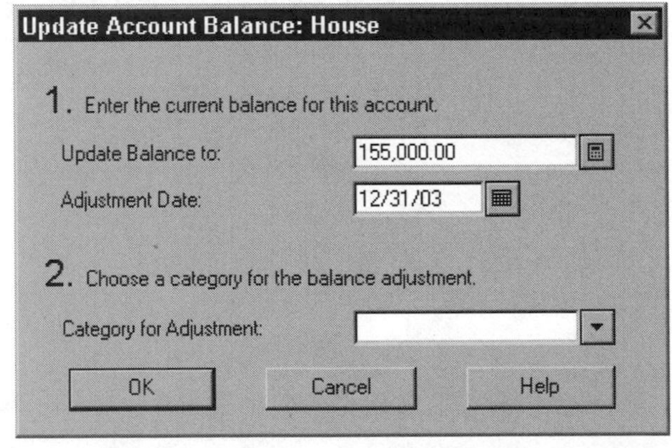

Figure 22.4: The Update Account Balance dialog box.

3. Enter the current market value in the Update Balance To text box, enter the date as of which the current market value is correct in the Adjustment Date text box, and click OK.

4. Clear the Category For Adjustment text box, and click OK. (By convention, you don't include changes in a home's market value in your income and expense summaries.)

Quicken adds an adjustment transaction to the register that changes the House account balance to whatever you specified in step 3. Figure 22.5 shows a House asset account register with a single adjustment transaction.

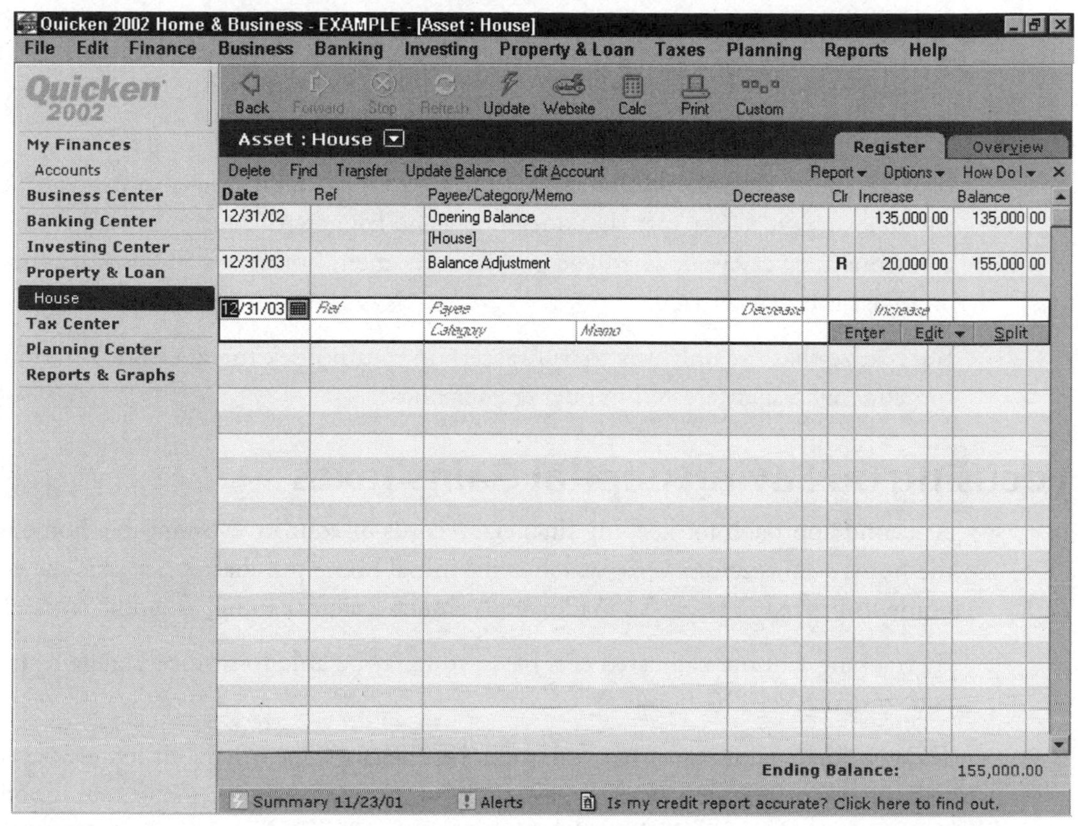

Figure 22.5: The House asset account register with an adjustment transaction that increases a home's value to $155,000.

What's Wrong with the Current Market Value Approach

The current market value approach presents a problem: It's difficult to pick the correct current market value. You could periodically have your home appraised, of course, but appraisals are expensive and imprecise. You might be able to get reasonable estimates of your home's value from your annual property tax assessment if it's based on the estimated market value, but again, this number is only an estimate.

If you do use the assessed value as your current market value, one advantage is that you'll have a piece of paper that documents and triggers the current market value adjustment. Every year, when you get the assessment notice, you'll know it's time to adjust the market value.

But realize that the only way to truly ascertain your home's market value is to find someone who is interested in buying your house.

Focusing on Saving Capital Gains Taxes

A second approach for keeping financial records of your investment in a home is to track the home's *adjusted cost basis,* which is the initial home purchase price plus the cost of any home improvements you've made: new cabinetry, landscaping, an addition, and so on.

By tracking a home's adjusted cost basis, you may be able to save capital gains taxes when you someday sell the home.

To keep financial records that will minimize the capital gain you ultimately pay when you sell a home, you set up an asset account as described in the previous section, but you set the starting balance to the home's initial purchase price. Be sure to include any of the related costs you incurred to purchase the home, such as escrow and closing fees, appraisals, and so on.

Then, whenever you make an improvement to the home, record the improvement as an increase in the House account's balance.

TIP *Usually it's easiest to just categorize the check you write to pay for the improvement as a transfer to the House account.*

As long as the home improvements are considered capital improvements, they increase the home's tax basis. Since the capital gain on which you'll ultimately be taxed when you sell the home is based on the difference between the home's sale price and the home's tax basis, the larger the home's tax basis, the smaller the capital gains tax.

If you sell your home, be sure to show a copy of your House account register to your tax advisor, who can review each of your increase transactions and make sure they can be counted as capital improvements. If you have specific questions about deferring or avoiding capital gains on the sale of a home, confer with a tax advisor. Your advisor will be aware of nuances in the law that apply to your specific situation. In addition, it's always possible that Congress will once again change the income tax laws relating to calculation of capital gains on sales of a principal residence.

What's Wrong with the Saving Capital Gains Taxes Approach

I used to recommend that everybody use the "saving capital gains taxes" approach, and I still think it's a pretty good idea, but the approach isn't perfect. Here's the problem: The approach doesn't necessarily save you any capital gains taxes. Why? Because you may be able to avoid capital gains taxes on the sale of your home by taking advantage of a loophole or two.

Here's the first loophole. You may never need to pay income taxes on a home sale—even if you've made a lot of money—because the federal income tax laws include an interesting provision related to the capital gains taxes owed on the sale of your principal residence (the place you live most of the time): You can take an exemption of up to $250,000 ($500,000 for married couples filing joint returns) for any gain on the sale of your principal residence. This probably means that most homeowners in many parts of the country stand a good chance of never having to pay income taxes on gains from home ownership. Of course, in other parts of the country where real estate is very expensive to start with, it's very possible that over a few decades, a homeowner might enjoy capital gains in excess of $250,000 or even $500,000.

Here's the second loophole. For purposes of calculating the capital gain on an asset held in your future estate, including your home, the estate's trustee will probably subtract the asset's value at the date of your death from the sales price. This means that if you never sell your home and just leave it in your estate for your heirs, your estate won't need to pay capital gains taxes (although the estate may be required to pay federal and state estate taxes).

Because of these factors, it's possible that you won't get anything for tracking the cost of your home plus any improvements. For the "saving capital gains taxes" approach to actually save you money, you'll need to be someone who can't avoid a capital gain on the sale of a home (perhaps because the home isn't a principal residence) and who can't avoid capital gains tax by using the exemption (perhaps because a home is very expensive to start with).

Tracking Rental Property

Quicken's account registers and categories provide a handy format for tracking real estate investments such as income property. By using Quicken for this record keeping, you can prepare summaries of income and expenses by property for monitoring your individual real estate investments. You can also easily complete the Schedule E income tax form you use.

Moreover, if you set up asset accounts for each of the individual real estate properties you hold and then use these to record both capital improvements and any depreciation, you can easily calculate any capital gains or capital losses stemming from the sale of a piece of real estate.

Describing Your Real Estate Holdings

To track income and expense by individual real estate property, you need to do two things:

- Set up the income and expense categories needed to describe this income and expense. As noted in Chapter 13, make sure that whatever income and expense categories you set up support completion of the Schedule E tax form.
- Set up a class for each individual real estate property, and then, whenever you categorize an income or expense item for a particular property, identify the property by providing the class.

NOTE *If you have only a single real estate investment and you know for certain that you'll never add another real estate investment to your portfolio, you don't need to set up classes.*

Setting Up Classes for Real Estate Investments

To set up classes for your real estate investments, follow these steps:

1. Choose the Finance ➢ Class List command to display the Class List window, as shown in Figure 22.6.

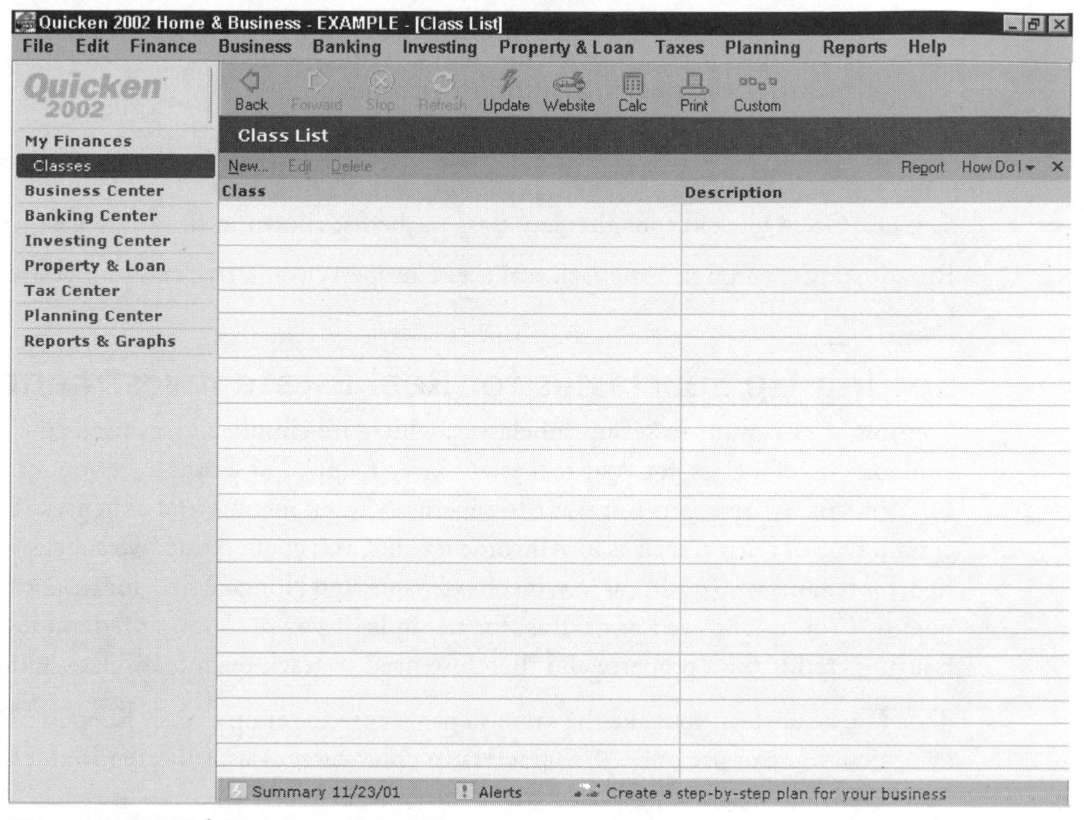

Figure 22.6: The Class List window.

2. Click the New command button to display the Set Up Class dialog box, as shown in Figure 22.7.

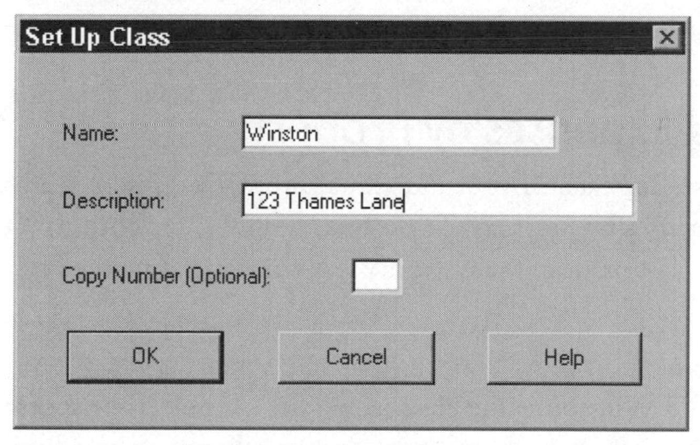

Figure 22.7: The Set Up Class dialog box.

3. Use the Name text box to provide a brief name for the real estate property. For example, if you're setting up a class for a rental property and the property has the name Winston Apartments, you might shorten this to Winston.
4. If you need to describe the property in more detail, such as noting the street address, use the Description text box.
5. Click OK. Quicken adds the new class to the list shown in the Class List window.

Repeat steps 2 through 5 for each real estate property you'll track as an investment using Quicken.

Setting Up Subclasses for Real Estate Investments

You might also want to set up subclasses, which are simply classes used to classify the components of a class, for your real estate investments. For example, if you set up a class for Winston Apartments but want to separately track income and expenses related to a certain type of tenant, such as low-income tenants, you could create two subclasses: Qualified, for tenants who qualify as low-income tenants, and Nonqualified, for tenants who don't qualify. (You might need to do this, for example, if you're claiming federal low-income housing credits for a property and therefore need to track tenants by class, too.)

To set up a subclass, you take the same steps you use to set up a class. Keep in mind, however, that you can use only 31 characters to enter categories, subcategories, classes, and subclasses. All this information goes into the Category combo box, so use short names. For example, you might use Qual and Nonq for Qualified and Nonqualified.

NOTE *Quicken lets you use subclasses and classes interchangeably: You can use a class as a subclass and a subclass as a class. Therefore, if you do choose to use subclasses, you need to be more careful in your data entry.*

Tracking Income and Expenses by Property

Once you've set up classes for each of your individual properties, you're ready to begin tracking income and expenses by property. To do this, simply enter both the income or expense category and the class name in the Category text box, separating the category from the class with a slash.

To record a rent check from one of your Winston Apartments tenants when Rental Income is the income category and Winston is the class name, for example, type ***Rental Income/Winston*** in the Category combo box.

If you've used subclasses, such as Qual and Nonq for Qualified and Nonqualified to identify tenants as qualified and nonqualified (low-income) tenants, follow the class name with a colon and then the subclass name. To record a rent check from one of your Winston Apartment "qualified" tenants when Rental Income is the income category and Winston is the class name, for example, type ***Rental Income/Winston:Qual*** in the Category combo box.

NOTE *Classes can be a little tricky for a couple of reasons. As mentioned earlier, you can flip-flop the classes and subclasses because Quicken doesn't track your classes and subclasses separately. From its perspective, they're both the same. And you can't tell Quicken to always remind you to enter a class, which you can do for categories. So be careful to always use classes and subclasses, and if you find that a report shows unclassified amounts, use QuickZoom to locate the unclassified transactions you need to fix.*

When you want to print an income and expense report by property, produce the Job/Project report by choosing Reports ➢ Business ➢ Project/Job. (For more information about how to produce and print reports, refer to Chapter 4.)

Setting Up Real Estate Investment Accounts

You can use Quicken accounts to track the adjusted cost basis of individual real estate investments. You calculate the gain or loss upon sale by subtracting the adjusted cost basis of a property from the net sales price. To do this, set up an asset account for individual real estate properties the same way you do for your home if you're keeping records to minimize any future capital gains taxes, as described earlier in this chapter.

As with a home, whenever you make an improvement to the property, record the improvement as an increase in the property's balance. Usually, the easiest way to do this is to just categorize the check you write to pay for the improvement as a transfer to the house account.

NOTE *As with a home capital gain calculation, be sure to show a copy of your property account register to your tax advisor, who can review each of your increase transactions and make sure that they can be counted as capital improvements.*

You can also record the periodic depreciation you'll use for calculations of the taxable profit or loss on the real estate investment. To do this, first set up a depreciation expense category, such as Depreciation. Then record an annual depreciation expense transaction that decreases the property's account balance. To record a depreciation on Winston Apartments when Depreciation is the expense category and Winston is the class name, for example, type ***Depreciation/Winston*** in the Category text box.

NOTE *Chapter 18 describes how depreciation works with business fixed assets, but you would use the same basic approach for depreciating investment real estate.*

Figure 22.8 shows an asset account register for the fictitious real estate investment, Winston Apartments. Note that I've recorded more than a single year's depreciation and used both a category and a class. For income tax purposes, the adjusted cost basis is the account balance at the date of sale.

Quicken 2002 Home & Business - EXAMPLE - [Asset : Winston Apartments]

Asset : Winston Apartments

Date	Ref	Payee/Category/Memo	Decrease	Clr	Increase	Balance
1/1/02		Opening Balance [Winston Apartments]			250,000 00	250,000 00
12/31/02		Depreciation Depreciation/Winston	10,000 00			240,000 00
12/31/03		Depreciation Depreciation/Winston	10,000 00			230,000 00
12/31/04		Depreciation Depreciation/Winston	10,000 00			220,000 00
12/31/05		Depreciation Depreciation/Winston	10,000 00			210,000 00

Ending Balance: 210,000.00

Figure 22.8: The asset account register for Winston Apartments.

TIP *You can learn what depreciation expense is allowable on a property for tax purposes by consulting your tax advisor or telephoning the IRS.*

How to Choose a Home and a Mortgage

Home ownership is usually considered the most important part of the so-called American Dream. Many consider home ownership the national birthright. It's often called the average American's best investment. And, usually, it results in the single largest debt a person takes on, in the form of a 30-year mortgage. Given these major financial characteristics, it makes sense to talk about home ownership. Here, I'll discuss some important aspects of home ownership: the decision to purchase a home, home affordability, and how to choose a mortgage.

Deciding Whether to Buy or Rent

The first decision you need to make, of course, is whether to buy a home or rent one. This decision isn't an easy one to make, at least if you look at the impact of a home in purely economic terms.

Since World War II, a single-family home has been, on the average, a very reasonable investment. Calculating the profits of home ownership is quite complicated, but I can sum things up quite nicely by stating that home ownership produces two benefits: rent savings and appreciation. Home ownership has been profitable for people because these benefits have more than paid the average homeowner's property ownership expenses and mortgage interest. When you boil down home ownership to its financial essence, it's really that simple.

A few years ago, an economist at the Mortgage Banking Association did a national survey of the investment returns of home ownership. He found that, on average, home ownership produced returns of around 10 to 12 percent. This figure is very respectable in light of the stock market's 50 year average of 10 percent and the 12 to 13 percent average of small-company stocks.

Before you trot off and use this bit of real estate trivia in your decision-making, however, it's important to understand the fundamental reason why home ownership has been a good investment. Suppose a person is considering two options: renting a three-bedroom house for, say, $600 a month or purchasing the same house for $135,000 with a $120,000 (7 percent) mortgage. Initially, the renter pays just $600 a month, while the homeowner pays a mortgage payment equal to $798 plus another $220 in property taxes and maintenance. So, renting costs $600 a month and owning costs $1,024 a month. With gradual inflation, however, things change over time. Assume that there's a 3 percent inflation rate, for example (3 percent is the historical average of this century).

After 10 years of 3 percent inflation, the renter pays around $760 a month in rent; after 20 years, the renter pays around $1,020 in rent; after 30 years, when the homeowner's mortgage is presumably paid off, the renter pays around $1,413 a month in rent. Even when the home owner has paid off the mortgage in 30 years, he or she would still pay about $549 a month in property taxes and maintenance, but this figure is still roughly $900 a month less than what the renter pays.

The following graph shows this financial reality by comparing monthly housing costs when you purchase versus monthly housing costs when you rent. At first, purchasing is more expensive. Gradually, over time, however, the costs of renting and purchasing converge and then flip-flop. The big change, however, comes when the homeowner finally pays off his or her mortgage. In the graph, this is when the homeowner line drops. At that point, the homeowner pays only property taxes and maintenance costs. The renter, meanwhile, is still writing a monthly check to a landlord.

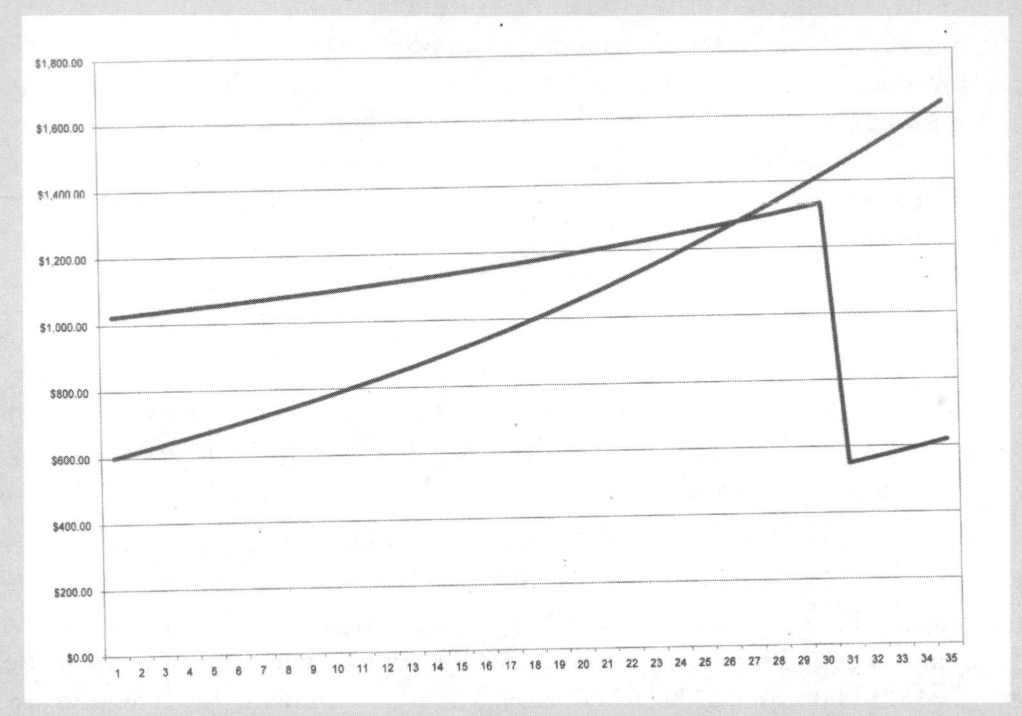

If you understand this graph, you understand why home ownership can be a good investment. In recent history, rents and real estate values have inflated at annual rates in excess of the 3 percent average. People who purchased their own homes locked in, or froze, the major portion of their housing expenses. With higher inflation, of course, the two lines cross much earlier. In the 1970s, when the nation suffered double-digit inflation, it didn't take long at all for buying to be cheaper than renting.

However, as you might know, one of the very best ways to boost your investment profits is to take advantage of investment vehicles that either increase your investment (such as the matching that employers sometimes provide to their employees with 401(k) plans) or that produce immediate tax savings (such as tax-deductible individual or self-employed retirement accounts). Home ownership produces neither of these benefits. Employers don't pay more to homeowners. And you can't claim your down payment as a tax deduction. A home ownership investment is probably a respectable investment, but it doesn't hold a candle to a 401(k) plan, a SIMPLE-IRA, or a regular deductible IRA.

About the Tax Benefits of Home Ownership

Many people claim that mortgage interest deductions are a tax benefit, but this isn't always true. For most people, the interest on a mortgage is an itemized deduction that reduces taxable income and therefore income taxes. But the same thing is usually true of interest on a loan used to purchase an investment. Deductible mortgage interest really isn't a tax benefit when you're talking about the investment qualities of buying a home versus, say, the investment qualities of putting money into a mutual fund.

One loophole that may benefit homeowners, however, concerns the gain on the sale of a principal residence (the place where you live most of the time). As mentioned earlier in the chapter, you might be able to postpone indefinitely paying income taxes on any appreciation in the value of your house. If you sell your home, you can take an exemption of up to $250,000 ($500,000 for married couples filing joint returns) for any gain on the sale of your principal residence.

The Problems of Home Ownership as an Investment

As an investment, however, home ownership isn't flawless. Financially, you must consider several things if you're trying to decide whether to buy or to rent. Perhaps the first thing to consider is this: Home ownership is very illiquid. In other words, it's very difficult to turn an investment in a home into cash. The value of liquidity is debatable. Suppose that you need money for an unexpected expense, perhaps because you've lost your job. An investment in a publicly traded stock or a stock mutual fund takes only minutes to convert to cash. Equity in a home takes weeks or months or even years to reach. (This illiquidity business, by the way, is the reason it's not really a good financial idea to repay debts such as mortgages, despite what some of the popular financial writers say.) Another problem with real estate as an investment is that the transaction costs are extremely high. To buy a home, for example, you must pay for things like loan fees and appraisal expenses. To sell a home, you usually need to pay a real estate broker a commission that can be as much as 7 percent of the home's value. Due to high transaction costs, home ownership loses its investment shine if you frequently buy and sell homes. In fact, if a home appreciates, say, 3 percent a year and your transaction costs amount to 9 percent, as they easily can, it takes three years of steady 3 percent inflation just to pay for the 9 percent transaction costs of trading homes.

One final problem that's more important than most people realize is the financial principle of diversification. When you store a large chunk of your financial wealth in one place—your home—it's much easier for a single event to damage or destroy your financial situation. It's easy to think of these sorts of "single events" as hurricanes, tornadoes, or fires. But when you're thinking about a home as an investment, the real danger (if you want to call it that) is that your home won't appreciate in value or, even worse, that its value will depreciate. Take another quick look at the housing costs graph shown earlier. If you look closely at the data, you'll see that it takes more than 20 years of steady 3 percent inflation before home ownership becomes less expensive on a monthly basis than renting. If home values fall or they just don't rise in value for a few years, home ownership isn't a good investment. In fact, it becomes a very poor investment.

One final problem of home ownership as an investment is that it's a leveraged purchase. *Leverage* simply means you borrow much of the money you use to make the purchase. Financial leverage can dramatically impact the goodness or badness of an investment, including a home.

The problem of financial leverage is a simple one. You owe the mortgage company the money you borrowed plus any accrued interest regardless of whether the home you purchased with the borrowed money increases in value or decreases in value. Suppose that you borrow $95,000 to purchase a $100,000 home. If the home increases in value a mere 10 percent to $110,000, you still owe only $95,000, so your $5,000 investment grows to $15,000—a 200 percent return. On the other hand, if the home decreases in value a mere 10 percent to $90,000, you still owe $95,000, and you've actually lost your entire investment—the down payment. You need to come up with an additional $5,000 if you sell the home.

What's the Bottom Line?

Focusing entirely on the financial issues, you can draw several conclusions. First, be sure to take advantage of superior investment options such as employer-sponsored 401(k) plans, small business retirement programs you set up for your own business, and deductible IRAs before you invest in a home. You probably need a certain amount of money for things like retirement. A home isn't the best way to accumulate the financial wealth you need when you no longer work.

If you have exhausted the superior investment opportunities available (like 401(k) plans, SIMPLE-IRAs, and deductible IRAs, home ownership is usually a very prudent investment. It is prudent if you will be able to live in the home for at least five years and preferably 10 to 20 years. As a diversification measure, a real estate investment in home ownership nicely balances retirement savings invested in the stock market. Real estate often represents a reasonable hedge against inflation. What's more, most of the problems of real estate, such as illiquidity and leverage, aren't serious if you're willing to live someplace for a long time and you have other savings.

Don't, however, make the mistake of believing that the bigger a house is, the better the investment is. People often and erroneously justify a larger, more expensive home because "it's a good investment." Admittedly, I haven't seen a lot of good data that conclusively disproves this particular theory. There is evidence, however, that suggests modest and middle-class housing is the better investment. What's more, luxury housing is often much more illiquid.

Maybe the most important thing to say, after all of this, is that if you can't afford a home, don't worry about it. There are better investments. Not owning a home means being far more mobile than you would be if you owned one. Remember, too, that it takes renters years and years before they spend more for housing than their home-owning friends. Finally, even when your home-owning friends have repaid their mortgages, you'll be in very good shape if you've been salting money away in investments like 401(k)s or IRAs.

Can You Afford It?

A home costs more than you probably have in your checking account, so to buy one you need to borrow money from either the seller or a lender. It's impossible to generalize about what an individual seller might do. In fact, most of the creative financing schemes available today, including most of the "nothing down" schemes, rely on a seller doing what a regular lender won't do: take a down payment in a form other than cash, trade properties, loan money at below-market interest rates, and so on.

Regular lenders, such as banks and mortgage companies, usually follow three rules to determine how much money to lend and how much house you can afford: the housing expenses rule, the long-term debt payments rule, and the down payment rule.

The Housing Expenses Rule

Typically, a lender suggests that your total monthly housing expenses should not exceed 25 to 28 percent of your gross monthly income. Monthly housing expenses include mortgage payments and insurance, property taxes, maintenance, and utilities. Your gross monthly income might include your wages (before taxes), investment income, and miscellaneous income items such as pension benefits or alimony. (In some areas of the country, higher standards apply because housing expenses in general are very high.)

Because the loan calculations are complicated without a financial calculator, I created a table that rates how many "dollars" of 30-year mortgage a "dollar" of income supports at various interest rates. The figures all suppose that you can spend 25 percent of your monthly gross income on a mortgage payment. This really means that a lender will be applying the 28 percent rule and that the extra 3 percent will go for the non-mortgage payment part of your housing expenses.

MORTGAGE INTEREST RATES (%)	MORTGAGE DOLLAR PER INCOME DOLLAR
5.00%	$3.88
5.25%	$3.77
5.50%	$3.67
5.75%	$3.57
6.00%	$3.47
6.25%	$3.38
6.50%	$3.30
6.75%	$3.21
7.00%	$3.13
7.25%	$3.05
7.50%	$2.98
7.75%	$2.91
8.00%	$2.84
8.25%	$2.77
8.50%	$2.71
8.75%	$2.65
9.00%	$2.59

Using the numbers in this table, if interest rates are 7 percent, for example, someone making $40,000 a year would be able to qualify for a mortgage of $3.13 times $40,000, or $125,200.

Long-Term Debt Payments Rule

This loan qualification rule sets a limit on the amount of long-term debt you can have. The general rule is that long-term debt payments shouldn't exceed 33 to 36 percent of your monthly gross income. Lenders want to be sure that you can comfortably bear the total debt burden you'll have after you get the mortgage. Long-term debt includes mortgage payments and any other debt borrowers still have in 10 to 12 months.

As long as your long-term debts don't exceed about 10 percent of your income, the long-term debt rule usually isn't the limiting factor that determines how large a mortgage you can afford. If you have a lot of long-term debt—car payments, student loans, and so on—you may have a problem finding a mortgage you can afford.

The Down Payment Rule

In addition to the rules that have to do with the size of the mortgage, there's another rule for determining affordability. Lenders typically do not lend the full purchase price of homes. Most lenders want the borrower to pay 10 to 20 percent of the purchase price, although some might require as little as 5 percent down. Federal Housing Administration and Veterans Administration loans allow even smaller down payments, from 0 to 5 percent. However, if you put down less than 20 percent, you need to pay private mortgage insurance. This type of insurance protects the lender against loss if you default on your mortgage payments.

Another way to look at the down payment business is by expressing the mortgage you can have as a percentage of the price of the house. With a 20 percent down payment, for example, a lender puts up 80 percent of the purchase price in the form of a mortgage; with a 10 percent down payment, a lender puts up 90 percent; and with a 5 percent down payment, a lender puts up 95 percent.

To take our earlier example, if interest rates are 7 percent and your family gross income is $40,000, you can't go out and buy a house for $125,200, because the lender doesn't want to put up 100 percent of the purchase price. You need to pay part of the purchase price—at least 5 percent in most cases—in the form of a down payment.

By the way, lenders aren't concerned only with the percentage of the purchase price that you can supply. Usually, the lender is also interested in how you come up with the down payment. From a lender's perspective, some sources are acceptable and some are not. Acceptable sources include savings, investments, and gifts from parents and relatives. Unacceptable sources include draws on credit cards and loans (not gifts) from parents and relatives.

A Final Word about Affordability

The rise in home values in many parts of the country has made it very difficult for many people to afford a home. If you've spent time working through the numbers and found yourself thinking that owning a home is more like the impossible dream than the American dream, don't give up for a couple of reasons.

- Don't depend too much on what I've said here. Lender guidelines often vary, so you should place a telephone call to your local bank.
- Interest rates have a dramatic impact on home affordability. They bounce up and down. Although you can't afford a home today, a lower interest rate next month or next year might mean you can afford a home then.

Choosing a Mortgage

Choosing a mortgage is easier than you might think, thanks to federal truth-in-lending laws. You basically have two choices: a fixed-interest rate loan or an adjustable-interest rate (ARM) loan. The first question to ask yourself is whether you should go with a fixed-interest rate or an adjustable-interest rate mortgage. I explained how adjustable-rate mortgages and fixed-rate mortgages work at the end of Chapter 12. Here, I'll briefly review the pros and cons of each type of mortgage.

Fixed-Rate versus Adjustable-Rate Mortgages

Some financial writers and perhaps most of your neighbors think ARMs are worse than bad. To be quite blunt, their advice is influenced more by fear and emotion than by the hard facts. Several studies have shown that, for the most part, ARMs cost homeowners with mortgages less money. This cost-savings feature is particularly true of ARMs with capped, or increase-limited, interest rates in which the rate of interest cannot rise above a certain rate.

The cost-savings can add up quickly. As you may know, in the early years of a mortgage, very little of the mortgage payments are actually applied to reducing the principal. This fact suggests an interesting money-saving and risk-reduction technique when there's a substantial difference between fixed rate mortgages and adjustable rate mortgages. Suppose a homeowner chooses an ARM and then uses the interest rate savings (as compared to a fixed-rate mortgage) to reduce the cost of the mortgage. In other words, the borrower gets an ARM but makes the larger fixed-interest rate payment. If interest rates don't jump up for at least a few years, the homeowner is very unlikely to lose money because the mortgage balance ends up getting reduced so quickly.

As part of writing this chapter, in fact, I constructed a little computer-based model that did just this. My model calculates what happens if a person looking for a $90,000 mortgage chooses an adjustable-rate 7 percent mortgage with a $598-per-month payment but then makes the $724.16-per-month payment that would be required on the alternative 9 percent fixed-rate mortgage. In this case, the extra payment amount—roughly $125—is applied directly to principal.

Here's the interesting thing about all this: It turns out that even if interest rates rise by a full percent each year, you would pay less with an ARM than you would with a fixed-rate mortgage until the fourth straight year of rising interest rates. At this point, the ARM borrower ends up paying about an extra $50 a month.

However, if interest rates don't immediately rise but stay level for even a few years, the person with the ARM saves a bundle of money. And even if interest rates skyrocket later on, this person will never pay more than the person with the fixed-rate mortgage because the extra monthly principal payments made early on so quickly reduce the mortgage balance.

Another thing to consider about all this is that if interest rates are rising rapidly, as you would assume if you're seeing back-to-back interest rate increases, it probably means that inflation has kicked up again. With strong inflation, it's very possible that your wages or salary or business profits will be adjusted annually for inflation and that your house will be inflating in value as well.

Given these characteristics, many people really should consider an ARM rather than a fixed-rate mortgage when ARM interest rates are significantly below fixed-rate mortgage interest rates. Sure, there's a little more risk, as there always is in any financial investment. But with a limit on the year-to-year increases a lender can make (such as 1 percent) and on the total increases a lender can make (such as 5 percent), you are more likely to save money by going with an ARM.

If fixed-interest mortgage rates are low—the case as I'm writing this late in 2001—fixed-interest mortgages certainly are worth considering. What's more, to truly reduce the financial risk of an ARM, you need to be the sort of person (or the sort of family) who has the discipline to always add that extra amount to the payment.

It's not a good idea to use an ARM if it's the only mortgage you can afford. The reason for this—and, admittedly, I'm pretty conservative—is that if this is the case, it likely means that you can't afford an increase in your mortgage payments, and that is what will happen the next time interest rates jump up. By picking an ARM when that is the only kind of mortgage you can afford, you're almost certain to have the unpleasant task of someday trying to figure out how to pay for something you can't really afford.

Note, too, that many ARM lenders use what are called *teaser rates*. Teaser rates amount to a marketing ploy where a lender offers a special, temporary, lower-than-normal interest rate. The problem with a teaser rate is that even if the underlying interest rate index doesn't change, your payment still increases the next time it's recalculated because the lender used a special rate to entice you. Teasers aren't bad, by the way. They do save you money. It's just that you need to be ready for the payment bump that occurs when the teaser interest rate is adjusted.

Comparing Mortgages

Once you make the fixed-rate versus adjustable-rate decision, the rest is easy. To compare fixed-interest rate mortgages, all you need to do is compare the annual percentage rates, or APRs. Then pick the one that's lowest. That's it.

APRs measure the total cost of a mortgage, including the periodic mortgage interest you need to pay and all other costs of obtaining credit, such as the loan origination fee and processing costs. By comparing APRs, you don't need to get bogged down wondering whether, for example, an 8.5 percent mortgage with a 2 percent fee is a better deal than a 9 percent mortgage with no fee. The APR combines all the costs into one easy-to-understand number that, in effect, expresses all the loan costs as an effective interest rate.

ARMs also can be compared by using APRs. Unfortunately, it's often more difficult to get the lender to provide an APR because the calculation is more complicated. Nevertheless, you should still be able to get an APR if you press the lender for it.

Chapter 23

MAKING BETTER INSURANCE DECISIONS

In This Chapter

- Determining how much life insurance you need
- Constructing a property insurance list
- Using the Emergency Records List
- How to get the right insurance policy

Quicken supplies two useful tools for insurance purposes. One is the Savings Calculator, which lets you make a sophisticated estimate of how much life insurance you should have in place. The other tool is an asset-account type of register, which helps you to build useful lists of the items you've insured.

NOTE *There are no prerequisites for using Quicken to make better insurance decisions.*

Determining How Much Life Insurance You Need

When considering life insurance, you're planning and preparing for an event most of us would rather not think about. But life insurance represents a critical step in managing your personal finances and ensuring your family's well-being.

The Two Approaches to Life Insurance

You can use one of two approaches to estimate how much life insurance you should buy: the needs approach or the replacement-income approach. Using the needs approach, you calculate the amount of life insurance necessary to cover your family's financial needs if you die. Using the replacement-income approach, you calculate the amount of life insurance you need to equal the income your family will lose. Let's look briefly at each approach.

NOTE *At the end of this chapter, you'll find a sidebar with tips on making decisions about obtaining life insurance.*

The Needs Approach

Using the needs approach, you add up the amounts that represent all the needs your family will have after your death, including funeral and burial costs, uninsured medical expenses, and estate taxes. However, your family depends on you to pay for other needs, such as your child's college tuition, business or personal debts, and food and housing expenses over time.

The needs approach is somewhat limiting. The task of identifying and tallying family needs is difficult, and separating the true needs of your family from what you want for them is often impossible.

The Replacement-Income Approach

Using the replacement-income approach for estimating life insurance requirements, you calculate the life insurance proceeds that would replace your earnings over a specified number of years after your death. Life insurance companies sometimes approximate your replacement income at four or five times your annual income. A more precise estimation considers the actual amount your family members need annually, the number of years for which they will need this amount, and the interest rate your family will earn on the life insurance proceeds, as well as inflation over the years during which your family draws on the life insurance proceeds.

Using the Savings Calculator to Estimate Life Insurance Needs

Using the Quicken Savings Calculator, you can calculate what life insurance you need to replace earnings over a specified number of years. You can then add to this figure any additional needs-based insurance. The total insurance would be the amount calculated by Quicken as necessary to replace earnings plus the amount calculated by you as necessary to pay for any additional needs.

NOTE *The Quicken Savings Calculator is available in Quicken Deluxe and in Quicken Home & Business.*

Be careful not to count items twice. For example, if you consider paying off your mortgage on the family home to be a final expense, your estimate of the annual living expenses should reflect this. Similarly, if you include the costs of a spouse's returning to and finishing college as a prerequisite for supporting the family, reduce the number of years your family will need replacement income.

To use the Quicken Savings Calculator to estimate the life insurance necessary to replace earnings over a specified number of years, follow these steps:

1. Choose Planning ➤ Financial Calculators ➤ Savings to display the Investment Savings Calculator dialog box, as shown in Figure 23.1.

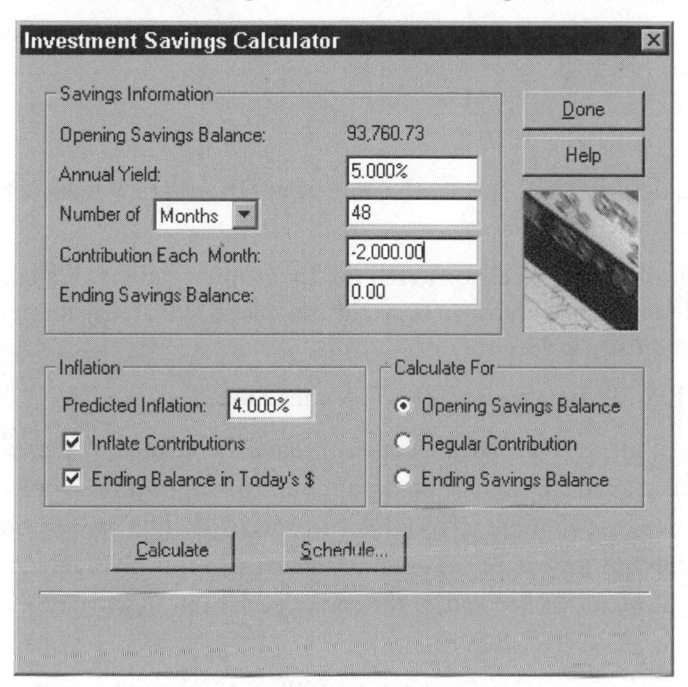

Figure 23.1: You can use the Investment Savings Calculator dialog box to estimate insurance needs.

2. Mark the Opening Savings Balance option button in the Calculate For section.
3. In the Annual Yield text box in the Savings Information section, enter your estimate of the annual interest rate you expect your savings, investments, and life insurance proceeds to earn when they are invested. Because this money might need to provide basic living expenses for your family, you might want to assume that this money is invested in conservative, lower-risk investments, which means you should expect lower interest rates.
4. In the Number Of drop-down list box, select Months.
5. In the Number Of text box, enter the number of months you will use the life insurance proceeds and the interest earned on those proceeds to replace earnings of the insured. You might need replacement income only until a child completes an education or until your spouse returns to work.

6. In the Contribution Each Month text box, enter the monthly amount your family members will withdraw from the life insurance savings money at the end of each month to supplement their living expenses. For example, if you want your family to be able to withdraw $2,000 at the end of each month, enter *–2000*. (You enter the amount as a negative number because your family will be withdrawing this amount from your savings, not adding it.)

TIP *If you have children and pay Social Security taxes, there's a good chance that Social Security survivors' benefits will provide several hundred dollars a month. Call your local Social Security office for more information.*

7. Enter the Ending Savings Balance as *0*.
8. In the Predicted Inflation text box, specify the annual inflation rate you expect over the years your income needs to be replaced.
9. Mark the Inflate Contributions checkbox to tell the Investment Savings Calculator that you want the monthly amounts withdrawn from the life insurance savings money to grow each month by the monthly inflation rate.
10. Make sure that the Ending Balance In Today's $ checkbox is marked.

As you enter the values, Quicken calculates an opening savings balance, which equals the amount of life insurance needed to produce enough money to support or supplement the support of your family over the number of months you specified. The assumption is that your family will place the life insurance in a savings account or an investment that will produce the annual return you forecasted and, at the end of each month, withdraw a monthly amount to replace your income.

To see a schedule that shows the monthly withdrawals and the end-of-month life insurance proceeds balance, click the Schedule command button. Quicken displays the Deposit Schedule dialog box, as shown in Figure 23.2. The Number column identifies the months. The Deposit column actually shows the withdrawals. (This is confusing, but remember you're using the Investment Savings Calculator to do something the folks at Intuit never intended.) The Total column shows the balance after the monthly withdrawal.

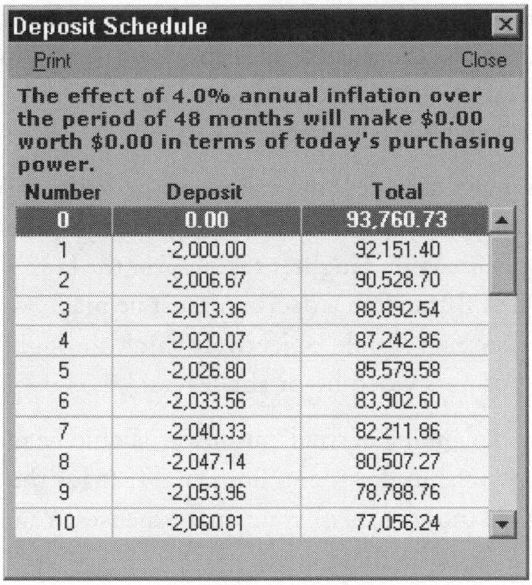

Deposit Schedule

Print Close

The effect of 4.0% annual inflation over the period of 48 months will make $0.00 worth $0.00 in terms of today's purchasing power.

Number	Deposit	Total
0	0.00	93,760.73
1	-2,000.00	92,151.40
2	-2,006.67	90,528.70
3	-2,013.36	88,892.54
4	-2,020.07	87,242.86
5	-2,026.80	85,579.58
6	-2,033.56	83,902.60
7	-2,040.33	82,211.86
8	-2,047.14	80,507.27
9	-2,053.96	78,788.76
10	-2,060.81	77,056.24

Figure 23.2: The Deposit Schedule dialog box shows potential monthly withdrawals.

NOTE *The monthly withdrawal amounts increase every month by the monthly inflation rate. Allowing for increasing withdrawal amounts is important if you want to replace earnings over a long period of time.*

If you use the approach described here to plan life insurance needs, remember that you must add any additional special needs (such as final expenses or extraordinary debts) to the opening savings balance amount in order to come up with a life insurance amount that both replaces earnings and provides for special needs.

Two Other Important Estate-Planning Issues

Because we've just talked about estimating appropriate levels of life insurance, let me mention that you want to consider two other related issues as part of this analysis: succession planning and Social Society survivors' benefits.

Succession Planning for a Small Business

Succession planning refers to your plans for your business if you're no longer able to operate the business. Succession planning plans for the day you step away from your business—perhaps because you retire or pass away or become disabled.

For many of the business owners reading this book, the implicit succession plan is simple. The business will be shut down when the owner-operator leaves. And that often makes sense in the case of very small businesses. It's frequently the case that such businesses can't be easily acquired and then operated by someone else. A consulting practice, for example, that relies on your network of contacts and business experiences probably can't be sold to and then operated by some other consultant. A part-time crafts business that relies on your artistic skills can't just be taken over by your neighbor or daughter.

Nevertheless, you ought to reflect for at least a few moments on the issue of succession planning. You probably want to communicate your ideas and thoughts to your heirs. I don't think you should count on, for example, a son or daughter taking over the family business. That's not fair to them or their families. But before a decision must be made, you and the other people involved in any succession plan should objectively think through the question, "What should we do with the business when he or she leaves?"

Two other points concerning succession planning of small businesses should be made: First, many small businesses will cost money to shut down and liquidate. If that's the case with your small business, you should include those costs in your final expenses. You may want to bump up any life insurance a bit to include these costs.

A second important point is that many small businesses aren't worth that much more than their liquidation value—the cash that the accounts receivable and any other assets can be sold for—after you adjust the profits for a fair salary to the owner. For example, if a business makes $60,000 a year and a fair salary for someone with your skills doing what you do for the business is $50,000, the business profits equal $10,000. In other words, the "business" doesn't make $60,000: an employee (you) makes $50,000 and the business makes $10,000. The business profits determine the business's value. Small companies that can be sold are often worth two to five times their profits. That means the business that made you $60,000 but really produces "adjusted for a salary" profits of $10,000 is perhaps worth as little as $20,000 (2 x $10,000) and probably only as much as $50,000 (5 x $10,000). These amounts are probably not all that much more than the liquidation value.

Given these succession planning factors, you typically don't want to assume that your business is a major asset that your heirs can liquidate for cash or can operate to produce income. Instead, you want to assume your heirs will need to shut down the business—and you need to include the costs of shutting down in your estimates of final expenses.

Survivors' Benefits

If an employee who paid Social Security taxes or a business owner who paid self-employment taxes dies, that person's dependent children may be eligible for monthly survivors' benefits. To determine whether your family is eligible for survivors' benefits and for how much, you need to refer to the Personal Earnings and Benefits Statement (or PEBS) which the Social Security Administration may have recently sent you and will send you again upon request.

I mention survivors' benefits here because they can amount to a rather substantial sum relative to the income you may want to replace with life insurance. It's very possible, for example, that your family will receive as much as $2,000 a month. This amount depends on your earnings, by the way. You must refer to your PEBS to see what your family might receive. The point is that survivors' benefits should be included in your estimations of life insurance requirements.

TIP *For more information about survivors' benefits, including information about how to sign up, you can visit the Social Security Administration's web site at* http://www.ssa.gov/pubs/10084.html.

Constructing a Property Insurance List

There's one other important insurance-related task you can do with Quicken: You can build a list of the items that you have insured or will insure with property insurance. You simply use an asset account to build a list of items and values. This list is not only useful for your records, but your insurance agent or property insurer may also want to see a copy.

One benefit of this kind of list is that you'll get an idea of how much property insurance you should really have. You can compare the total value of the items on such a list with the personal property limit on your homeowner's or renter's policy. Another benefit is that, should something destroy your personal property, you'll have a record of what you've lost.

If you have the Deluxe version or Home & Business version of Quicken, you can use the Quicken Home Inventory program to create a list of your personal property, insurance policies, and pending claims. If you don't have Quicken Deluxe or Quicken Home & Business, you can just use a separate file and account. Both approaches are detailed in the paragraphs that follow.

Using the Home Inventory Program

The Quicken Home Inventory program provides tools for making a complete personal inventory of all of your property. Such an inventory might come in handy in any situation where you may need to have a record of what you own. For instance, if you were robbed and needed to tell the police what had been taken, a home inventory would be useful in making sure that you did not forget anything. You begin Quicken Home Inventory by choosing Property & Loan ➤ Quicken Home Inventory. Quicken displays a welcome message and you click Continue. Quicken then opens a window, that after you add a few items, looks similar to Figure 23.3.

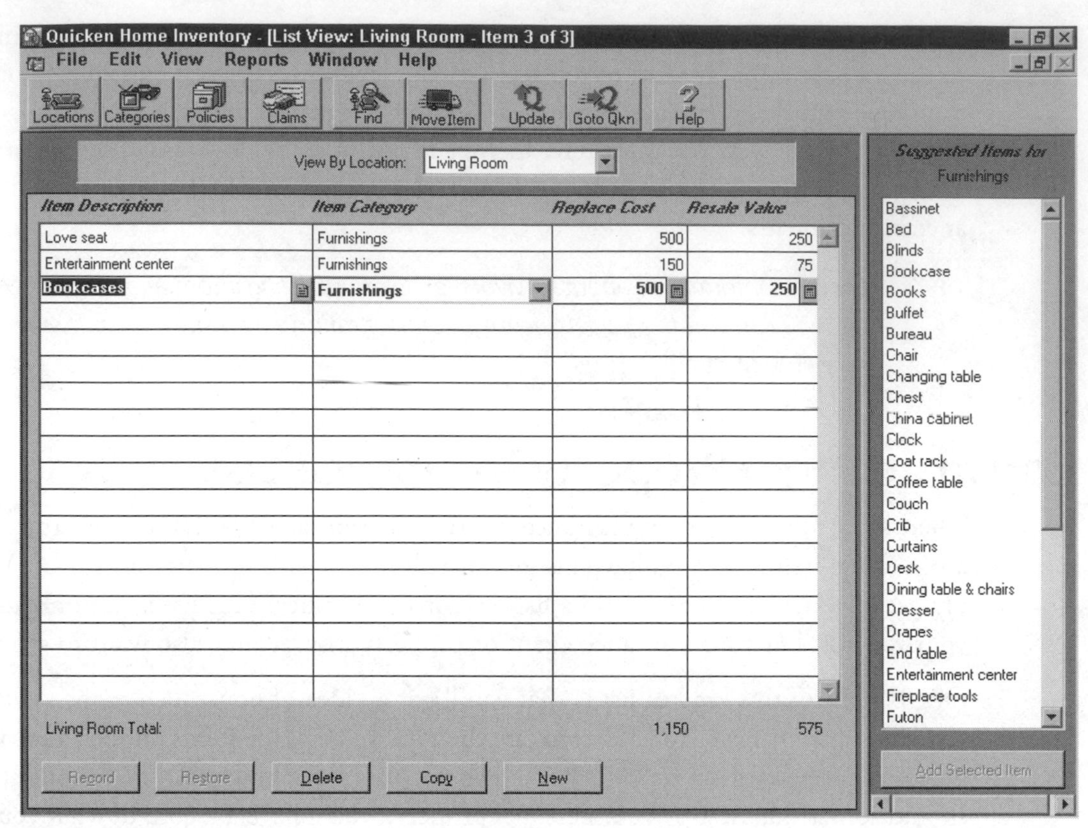

Figure 23.3: The Quicken Home Inventory helps you keep track of your belongings in case of an emergency.

Here's how to complete your home inventory list:

1. Choose a room in the View By Location drop-down list box.
2. Click the first blank Item Description box and type the name of the item.

TIP *If the Suggested Items For scroll box lists an item you own, you can double-click it and Quicken will add the item to your current list, along with its best guess as to the Replace Cost and Resale Value. If Quicken's guess is inaccurate, highlight the incorrect amount by double-clicking it, and then type the correct amount.*

3. Use the Item Category drop-down list box to categorize the item.
4. Click the Replace Cost box and type in the amount that it would cost to buy an exact replacement of the same item.
5. The Resale Value is the amount you would get if you sold the item today. Quicken assumes that it would half the Replace Cost. If it isn't, select the incorrect Resale Value amount and then type the correct value

6. Click Record.

Repeat steps 1 through 6 to record each item of value.

Note that along the top edge of the Quicken Home Inventory window, a row of buttons appears. Three of these buttons are worth briefly mentioning:

- **Locations** Displays a dialog box that you can use to add or change the Home Inventory window's list of locations. If you have an attic loft, for example, where you also store items, you would use the Locations dialog box to add this storage place.
- **Categories** Displays a dialog box that you can use to add or change the categories that the Home Inventory window uses to organize your items.
- **Claims** Displays a dialog box that you can use to document and monitor outstanding claims you've filed.

TIP *You should also keep a list of any unique identifying marks with this information. For example, note the make and serial and model numbers of the item, whether you have an etched ID number somewhere on the item, whether you once scratched the item when you dropped it and similar information. If the item is stolen and recovered, this information may be the difference in getting the item back or not.*

The Quicken Home Inventory program also allows you to track your insurance policies, including special riders, using its Policies list. To see this list, click the Policies button. Figure 23.4 shows an example of the Policies window.

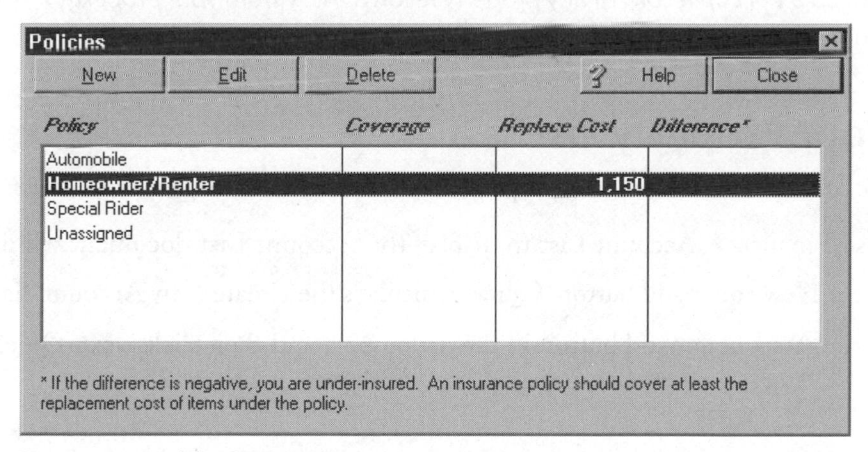

Figure 23.4: The Policies list helps you keep your insurance policies straight.

To describe a new insurance policy after you've displayed the Policies window, click the New button and then use the New Policy dialog box, which Quicken displays, to describe the policy. To edit an existing policy's description after you've displayed the Policies window, click the Policy and then click the Edit button. When Quicken displays the Edit Policy dialog box, fill in or edit the text boxes so they contain the correct information.

Creating a New File for Your Property List

If you have Quicken Basic and so don't have access to the Quicken Home Inventory tool, consider putting the asset account that lists the property in a separate file, especially if you've listed items such as clothing that have a substantial replacement value or cost (which is why you've insured them) but don't have much market value. This way, the value of things you've insured won't get included in your net worth.

To create a separate file, choose the File ➤ New command to display the Creating New File: Are You Sure? dialog box. Mark the New Quicken File option button, and then click OK. When Quicken displays the Create Quicken File dialog box, use the File Name text box to give the file a name such as homeinv.qdf and then click OK. Quicken creates the new file in the Quicken directory. It is to this file that you'll add the asset list account.

To switch between your two Quicken files, choose the File ➤ Open command. When Quicken displays the Open Quicken File dialog box, select the file you want to work with from the File Name list box.

NOTE *Keep a backup record of any property records away from your property. If something happens, you don't want whatever destroys your property to also destroy your records.*

Creating Your Property List

To create an asset list account for property insurance records, follow these steps:

1. Choose Finance ➤ Account List to display the Account List document window.
2. Click the New command button. Quicken displays the Create New Account dialog box.
3. Click the Asset command button in the dialog box, and then click Next. Quicken displays the Asset Account Setup dialog box, as shown in Figure 23.5.

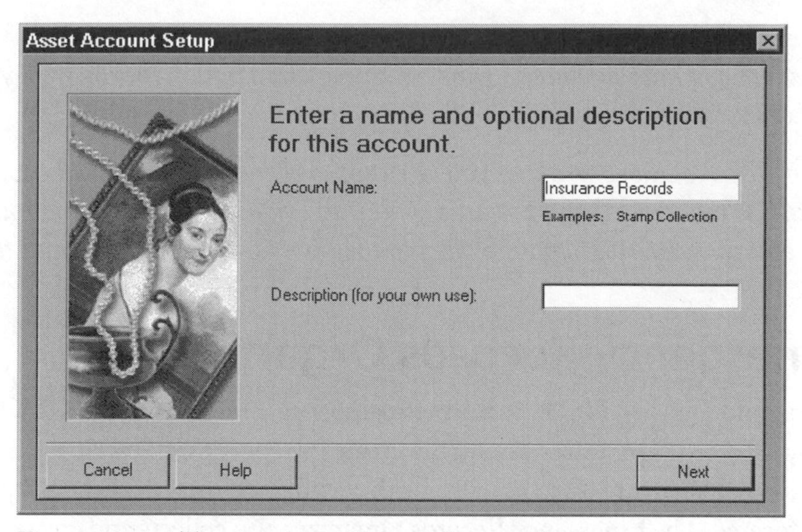

Figure 23.5: The first Asset Account Setup dialog box.

4. Use the Account Name text box to identify this register as a list of your insured items. In Figure 23.5, for example, I named the account Insurance Records.
5. In the Description text box, you have the option of describing the account in more detail.
6. Click Next to move to the next Asset Account Setup dialog box, as shown in Figure 23.6.

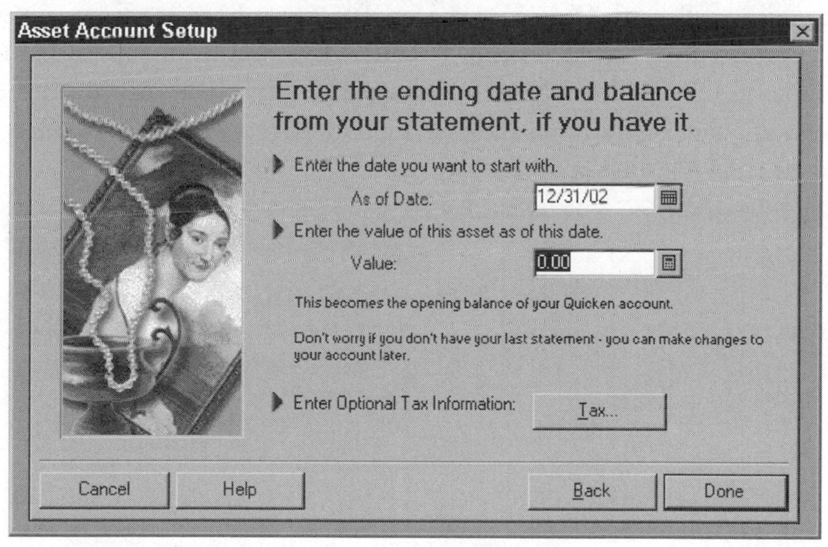

Figure 23.6: The second Asset Account Setup dialog box.

7. Because you'll use this account to build a list of insured items, the account shouldn't have a starting account balance value. Therefore, enter ***0*** into the Value box. The As Of Date box, because there's no starting balance doesn't matter. You can set it to the current date.
8. Click Done. Quicken adds the new account and displays its register.

From the account list, locate and open the new asset account that you just created. Quicken displays the asset register in a document window. Enter a transaction for the item you want included on the list.

NOTE *If you can, make a video of things you've stored in all the rooms of your house, including closets, the garage, and the attic. And if the video camera records sound, add comments about the items you're filming, their prices, and where you got them.*

Using the Emergency Records Organizer

Quicken Deluxe and Quicken Home & Business supply an Emergency Records Organize. The Emergency Records Organizer essentially creates a report that describes where your important personal documents (such as wills, birth certificates, trust documents, passports and so on) are located. The Emergency Records Organizer also collects and creates a report that summarizes personal and financial information, such as family member physicians, bank accounts, safe deposit box locations, and dozens of other important pieces of financial information. In short, the Emergency Records Organizer produces a document that would be absolutely invaluable in an emergency situation (such as if you're injured or if a family member dies).

To use the Emergency Records Organizer, choose Property & Loan ➢ Emergency Records Organizer. The first tab of the Emergency Records Organizer displays information about why and how to use this tool, as shown in Figure 23.7. After you read this information, click the Create/Update Records tab and then fill in the boxes provided to collect personal information, as shown in Figure 23.8.

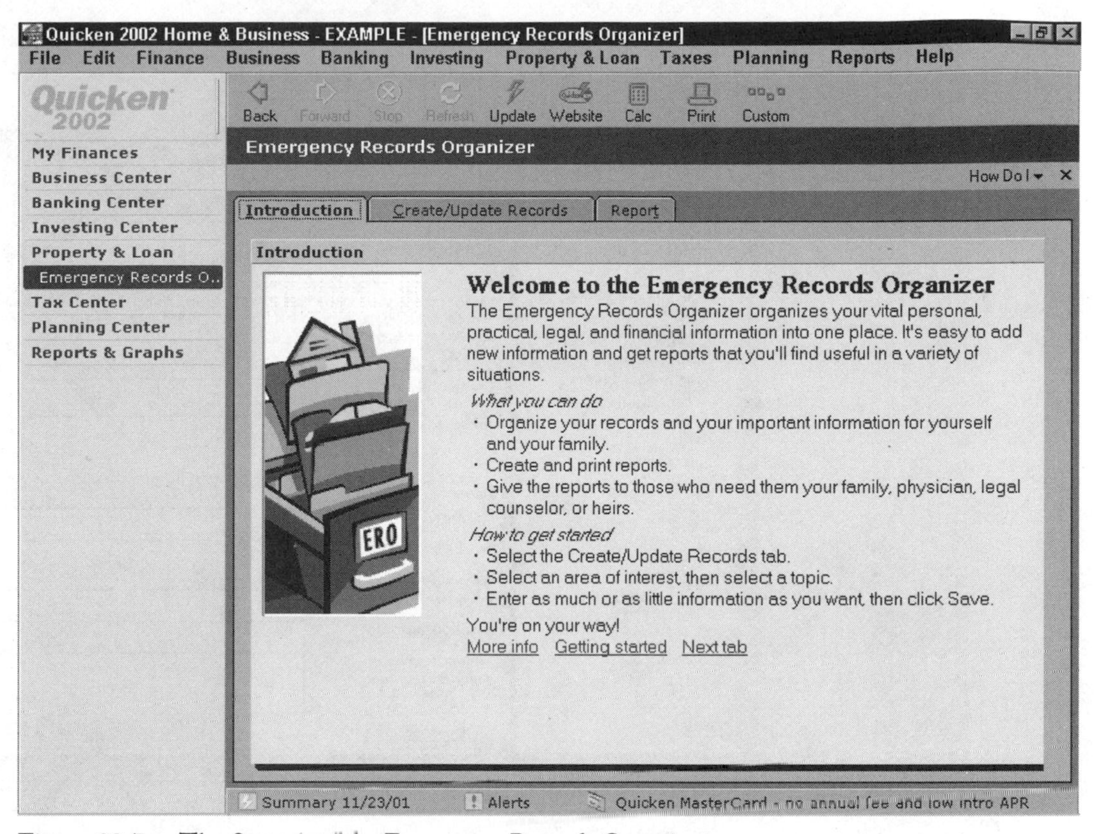

Figure 23.7: The first tab of the Emergency Records Organizer.

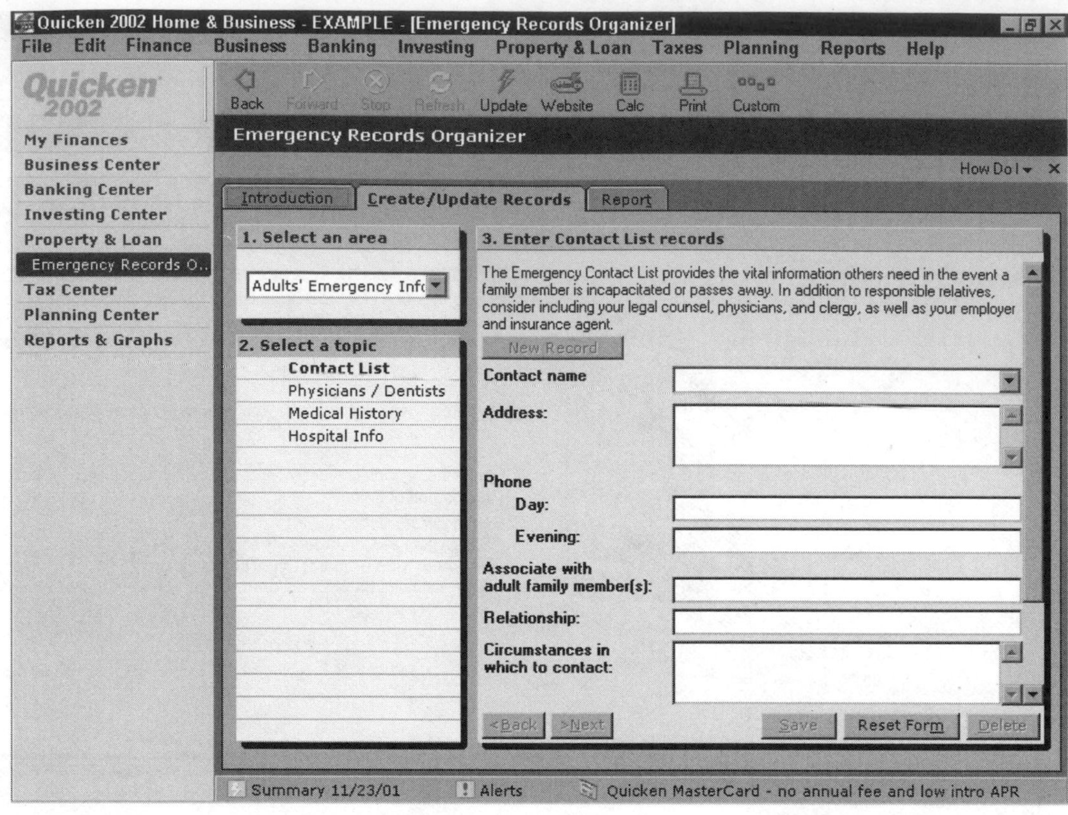

Figure 23.8: The Create/Update Records tab of the Emergency Records Organizer.

The Emergency Records Organizer can also provide reports that summarize your personal and financial affairs. Click the Report tab and use the drop-down list box to select the report you want. Then click Print.

How to Get the Right Insurance Policy

A lot can be said about making smart decisions when it comes to getting insurance. Rather than write a lengthy and encyclopedic description of how insurance policies work, I want to focus on eight general rules for buying insurance of any kind. Then I'll explain how to buy the two kinds of insurance that most everyone needs: life insurance and health insurance.

Eight Rules for Buying Insurance of Any Kind

By following the eight rules explained here, you can save money, and just as important, you can save yourself from making serious mistakes when you shop for and acquire insurance policies.

Rule 1: Buy Insurance Only for Financial Risks You Can't Afford to Bear on Your Own

The purpose of insurance is to cover catastrophes that would devastate you, your business, or your family. Don't treat insurance as a chance to cover all your losses no matter how small or insignificant, because if you do you'll fritter away money on insurance you really don't need. For example, if your house caught fire and burned down, you would be glad you had homeowner's insurance. Homeowner's insurance is worth having, because you likely can't—and you certainly don't want to—cover the cost of rebuilding a house. On the other hand, collision insurance on an old clunker is a waste of money if the car is only worth $800. You would be throwing away money for something you could cover yourself if you had to.

Rule 2: Buy from Insurers Rated A or Better

Insurance companies go bust, they are bought and sold, and they suffer the same economic travails that all companies do. Between 1989 and 1993, 143 insurance companies declared bankruptcy. You want to pick a reliable company with a good track record.

A.M. Best is an insurance company monitoring service that rates insurance companies on reliability. Look for insurers rated A or better by A.M. Best, and periodically check to see whether your insurer is maintaining its high rating. If your insurer goes down a notch, consider finding a new insurance company. You can probably get A.M. Best's directory of insurance companies at your local public library, and you can find A.M. Best on the Web at *www.ambest.com*.

Rule 3: Shop Around

There are many, many, many kinds of insurance policies, and insurers don't advertise by price. You need to do some legwork to match your needs with the cheapest possible policy. Talk to at least two brokers to start with. Look for no-load insurance companies—companies that sell policies directly to the public without a broker taking a commission—since they usually offer cheaper prices.

Rule 4: Never Lie on a Policy Application

If you fib and get caught, the company can cancel your policy. If you lie on an application for life insurance and die during the first three years you hold the policy, the company will cancel your policy, and your beneficiaries will receive nothing. Health, life, and disability insurers run background checks on applicants through the Medical Information Bureau, so you can get caught lying. The medical examination you take for life insurance can also turn up a lie. For example, if you smoked tobacco in the previous year, it will come up in the test.

Rule 5: Don't Buy Specific-Risk Policies—Buy General Policies Instead

When it comes to insurance, you want the broadest coverage you can get. Buying insurance against cancer or an uninsured motorist defeats the purpose of having an insurance policy. If you have ulcers, your cancer insurance will not help you. Get comprehensive medical coverage instead.

Uninsured motorist insurance is supposed to protect you if you get hit by someone who doesn't have car insurance or doesn't have adequate car insurance. But, in my opinion, you don't need it if you have adequate car insurance yourself, as well as health, disability, and life insurance. I should point out that some attorneys advise you to carry uninsured motorist insurance because, by doing so, you may be able to recover damages for "pain and suffering."

Rule 6: Never Cancel One Policy until You Have a Replacement Policy in Place

If you cancel a policy without getting a replacement, you will be uninsured for however long it takes to get a new policy. And if disaster strikes during this period, you could be financially devastated. This rule goes for everyone, but especially for people getting on in years, since older folks sometimes have trouble getting health and life insurance.

Rule 7: Get a High Deductible

You save money by having insurance policies with high deductibles. The premium for high-deductible policies is always lower. Not only that, but you save yourself all the trouble of filing a claim and needing to haggle with insurance company representatives if you have a high deductible and you don't need to make as many claims.

People who buy low-deductible policies usually do so because they want to be covered under all circumstances. But the cost, for example, of a $400 fender-bender is usually worth paying out of your own pocket when compared to the overall cost of being insured for $400 accidents. Statistics show that most people have a fender-bender once every 10 years. The $400 hurts to pay, but the cost of insuring yourself for such accidents over a 10-year period comes to far more than $400.

One other thing: If you have a low deductible, you will make more claims. That means you become an expensive headache for the insurance company. That means your rates will go up, and you don't want that to happen.

Rule 8: Use the Money You Save on Insurance Payments to Beef Up Your Rainy Day Account

While you can save money on your insurance premiums by following the rules mentioned earlier, it's probably a big mistake to use that money for, say, a trip to Hawaii. Instead, use any savings to build a nice-sized rainy day fund that you can draw on to pay deductibles. A big enough rainy day fund can cover both periods of unemployment and your insurance deductibles.

Buying Life Insurance

Not everyone needs life insurance. The first thing to do is make sure you need it. Life insurance is really meant for your family members or other dependents who rely on your earnings. You buy life insurance so that, if you die, your dependents can live the same kind of life they live now. Strictly speaking, then, life insurance is only a means of replacing your earnings in your absence. If you don't have dependents (say, because you're single) or you don't have earnings (say, because you're retired), you don't need life insurance. Note that children rarely need life insurance because they almost never have dependents and other people don't rely on their earnings.

If you do need life insurance, you should know that it comes in two basic flavors: *term insurance* and *cash-value insurance* (also called "whole life" insurance). Ninety-nine times out of 100, what you want is term insurance.

Term life insurance is simple, straightforward life insurance. You pay an annual premium, and if you die, a lump sum is paid to your beneficiaries. Term life insurance gets its name because you buy the insurance for a specific term, such as 5, 10, or 15 years (and sometimes longer). At the end of the term, you can renew your policy or get a different one. The big benefits of term insurance are that it's cheap and it's simple.

The other flavor of life insurance is cash-value insurance. Many people are attracted to cash-value insurance because it supposedly lets them keep some of the premiums they pay over the years. After all, the reasoning goes, you pay for life insurance for 20, 30, or 40 years, so you might as well get some of the money back. With cash-value insurance, some of the premium money is kept in an account that is yours to keep or borrow against. This sounds great. The only problem is that cash-value insurance usually isn't a very good investment, even if you hold the policy for years and years. And it's a terrible investment if you keep the policy for only a year or two. What's more, to really analyze a cash-value insurance policy, you need to perform a very sophisticated financial analysis. And this is, in fact, the major problem with cash-value life insurance.

While perhaps a handful of good cash-value insurance policies are available, many—perhaps most—are terrible investments. And to tell the good from the bad, you need a computer and the financial skills to perform something called discounted cash-flow analysis. If you do think you need cash-value insurance, it probably makes sense to have a financial planner perform this analysis for you. Obviously, this financial planner should be a different person from the insurance agent selling you the policy.

What's the bottom line? Cash-value insurance is much too complex a financial product for most people to deal with. Note, too, that any investment option that's tax-deductible—such as a 401(k), a 401(b), a deductible IRA, a SEP/IRA, a SIMPLE-IRA, or a Keogh plan—is always a better investment than the investment portion of a cash-value policy. For these two reasons, I strongly encourage you to simplify your financial affairs and increase your net worth by sticking with tax-deductible investments.

NOTE *Remember, too, that if you're a business owner, you have even more flexibility about the sorts of tax-deductible investments you can make because you can set up your own pension plan.*

If you do decide to follow my advice and choose a term life insurance policy, be sure that your policy is noncancelable and renewable. You want a policy that cannot be canceled under any circumstances, including poor health. (You have no way of knowing what your health will be like 10 years from now.) And you want to be able to renew the policy even if your health deteriorates. (You don't want to go through a medical review each time a term is up and you need to renew.)

Buying Health Insurance

Everybody needs health insurance. With medical costs skyrocketing, you simply can't pay for this stuff on your own. Too many families get wiped out by a stroke, a car accident, or some other major medical emergency because they didn't have medical coverage and were forced to pay for the surgeries and hospital visits themselves. Even worse, if you don't have health insurance, you may not be able to get the treatment that you need to save your life.

The problem, however, is that heath insurance is very expensive. Fortunately, there are some good ways to save money on health insurance.

Buy Major Medical Coverage and Self-Insure the Minor Stuff

The amounts of your deductible and co-payments are the biggest determining factors in how much you pay in premiums. If you have a large deductible, your premiums will fall accordingly. If you co-pay the first $2,000 to $5,000 in medical bills—that is, if you pay a certain percentage of these bills, usually 20 to 50 percent—your premiums drop dramatically.

The surest way to save money on health insurance is to get a high deductible and a large co-payment. Under this plan, you pay for checkups and minor cuts and scrapes. The insurance company starts paying only when your bills soar due to a major medical emergency. Follow this plan only if you're healthy and you have enough tucked away in a rainy day account to pay the deductible and make the co-payments. You don't want to be stuck in a hospital bed wondering how you can make co-payments or pay a deductible.

Investigate Preferred Provider Plans

Several major health insurance companies offer discounted insurance plans if you agree to see your family doctor first for all of your medical care. You select a primary care physician from a list of participating doctors in your area, and then you agree to see only this physician, except in the case of an emergency. If this physician cannot provide you with the help you need, he or she can refer you to a specialist. Usually, the insurance company pays for specialist services only if you have a referral from your family doctor.

Don't Get One-Disease Insurance

Some insurers prey on people's fears by offering them cancer or other types of one-disease insurance. The problem with cancer insurance is that it won't do you any good if you get ulcers, the gout, athlete's foot, or any other disease except cancer. Buy broad health insurance that covers all the illnesses you might get. One-disease insurance is too expensive, and it can too easily leave holes in your coverage.

Make a Living Will

A *living will* tells the doctor and your family that, if you're dying, you don't want your life extended by aggressive life-support measures. Although a living will seems like a strange topic for anyone who's healthy, drawing up a living will is a really smart thing for you to take care of now. For a set of blank living-will documents, visit the *www.partnershipforcaring.org* Web site, which has downloadable living wills and healthcare power of attorney forms for each state.

Skip Maternity Coverage—As Long As Your Policy Covers Complications from Pregnancy and Newborn Care

Having a baby is expensive. But even so, maternity coverage usually isn't a good deal. If you work out the numbers, you need to have a baby about every year or every other year just to break even on the extra cost (the premiums, in other words) of having this benefit.

You do need to be very careful about skipping maternity coverage if there's even the slightest chance that you or your spouse will have a baby in the near future. If there are any complications from the pregnancy or if your newborn needs special care, the costs of having the baby can increase astronomically. Ideally, you want a policy that either includes all maternity benefits or one that doesn't cover delivery, but does cover pregnancy complications and newborn care. If you choose the latter policy, you may save some money in the long run, but make sure you have enough money in your rainy day fund to pay the delivery costs out of pocket.

Compare Doctor and Hospital Prices

It would be great if doctors wore prices on their foreheads the way that used cars have prices on their windshields. Comparing doctor and hospital prices is not easy, but it can be done simply by asking.

Look for a Doctor Who Accepts Assignment If You're on Medicare

Accepting assignment means that the doctor charges no more than what Medicare deems appropriate. You still pay the deductible and the co-payment, but you can rest assured that the bill will not go above that.

Ask for Generic Drugs

Once you take the tiny little words off the capsules or pills, brand name drugs are exactly the same as their generic counterparts. Did you know that generic drugs and name brand drugs are often made in the same laboratories? Always opt for generic drugs, and use the money you save to see a good movie.

Use 24-Hour Emergency Clinics instead of Hospital Emergency Rooms

Clinics are much cheaper than hospital emergency rooms. Cheaper still is seeing your own doctor. Most doctors' offices have an after-hours telephone number that puts you in contact with the physician or nurse on call. If you get sick or injured at a time during which your doctor's office is closed, and you are not sure if you need to go to an emergency clinic, call the after-hours telephone number to find out if your condition can wait until you can see your doctor.

Get a Guaranteed Renewable Policy

You should be able to renew your policy without needing to pass a medical exam. A nonrenewable policy defeats the purpose of having health insurance. You buy health insurance in case you get sick. You don't buy it for when you're healthy.

Part 4

APPENDIXES

In This Part

Appendix A

INSTALLING QUICKEN AND SETTING UP YOUR FIRST ACCOUNT

This appendix describes how to install Quicken 2002 and set up your first bank account in Quicken. After you've completed these two tasks, you can turn to Chapter 1 to begin learning how to use Quicken.

Automatically Starting the Quicken Installation

You should be able to automatically install the Quicken program. By inserting the Quicken CD into your CD drive, you implicitly tell Windows to look at the Quicken CD. The Quicken CD includes an autorun file that tells Windows it should automatically start the Quicken installation program.

If the Quicken installation program doesn't start automatically after you insert the Quicken CD—and you may need to wait a minute or two—you can manually start the installation program, as described in the next sections of this appendix.

Manually Starting the Quicken Installation under Windows 2000

To install Quicken under Windows 2000, follow these steps:

1. Close any running applications. Remove any floppy disks from your floppy drives.
2. Choose Start ➢ Settings ➢ Control Panel.
3. In Control Panel, double-click Add/Remove Programs to display the Add/Remove Programs Properties dialog box.
4. In the Add/Remove Programs dialog box, double-click Add New Programs and then the CD or Floppy button. Quicken displays the Install From CD or Floppy dialog box.

5. Click Next. Windows looks at the Quicken CD—it will still be in the CD drive if you first attempted to automatically start the Quicken installation program—and finds the install.exe program. This is the Quicken installation program.
6. Click Finish. Quicken starts the installation program.

Manually Starting the Quicken Installation under Windows 95, Windows 98, or Windows NT

To install Quicken under Windows 95, Windows 98, or Windows NT, follow these steps:

1. Close any running applications.
2. Choose Start ➢ Settings ➢ Control Panel.
3. In Control Panel, double-click Add/Remove Programs to display the Add/Remove Programs Properties dialog box.
4. Click Install to display the Install Program from Floppy Disk or CD-ROM dialog box.
5. Insert the Quicken CD-ROM into your CD-ROM drive.
6. Click Next to display the Run Installation Program dialog box. Windows will locate the installation program on your disk or CD-ROM, and the program command line will appear in the text box.
7. Click Finish. Windows starts the Quicken installation program.

Running the Quicken Installation Program

The Quicken installation program, once it has started, is not difficult to run. You can, in fact, choose to accept all of the suggested installation settings. The two or three questions that the installation program asks can be answered by clicking yes and no buttons. Nevertheless, let me provide step-by-step instructions here just in case you have questions. Here are the specific steps you take to run the Quicken program.

1. When the Quicken installation program displays the Welcome message, as shown in Figure A.1, click Next.

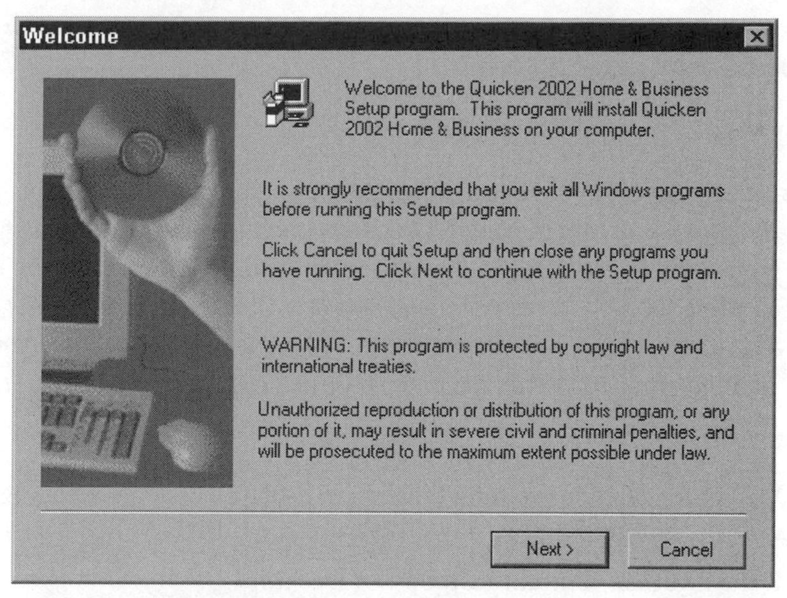

Figure A.1: The Welcome message box.

2. Quicken next displays a message box which displays the Quicken licensing agreement—the terms under which Intuit expects you to use Quicken. Read the agreement and, assuming you agree, click Yes.
3. The installation program asks questions about the type of installation you want, as shown in Figure A.2. Click the Express button. You can also choose between the U.S. or Canadian version of Quicken. Mark your choice, and then click Next.

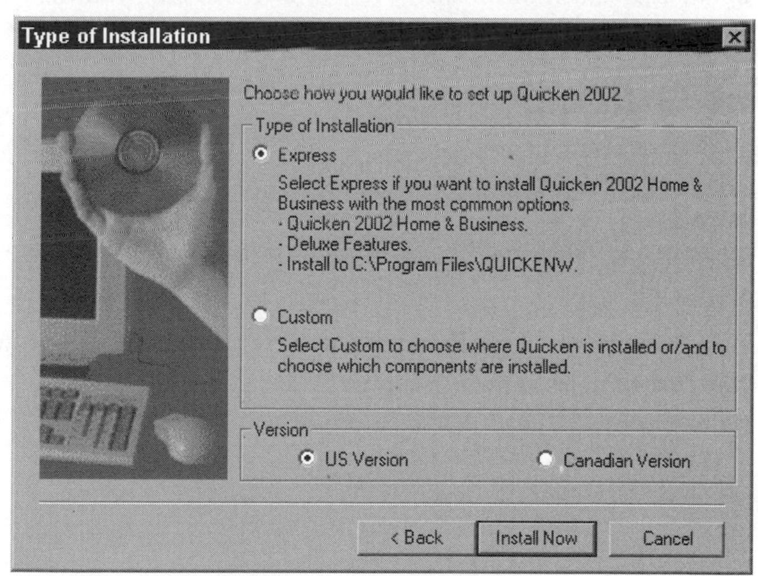

Figure A.2: The Type Of Installation dialog box.

NOTE *If you choose to install the Canadian version of Quicken, see Appendix B for information about using Quicken in Canada.*

4. Click Install Now to begin the installation.

TIP *If you selected the Custom installation, you can choose which components you want to install, as well as accept the default folder location for Quicken or specify another folder. (You should use the default location unless you have a good reason for designating a different one, such as if you are installing Quicken on an external drive.) To define a new path, click Browse, select or type the name of the path you want Quicken to use, and then click OK. When the path is correct, click Next. Then click Start Copying.*

5. When the Quicken installation program finishes, it displays a dialog box telling you that the installation is complete. Remove any disks from their drives. Click Finish.
6. Double-click the Quicken shortcut icon on the Desktop.
7. Quicken asks if you want to register Quicken, which you probably want to do. To register, click OK. Then fill in the text boxes in the dialog boxes that the installation program displays to ask about your name, address, and use of Quicken.

TIP *Intuit wants your name for its mailing list, of course. But even though you probably have an aversion to junk mail, it's a good idea to register. By registering, you're notified of product updates and add-on products. (Sometimes existing users get special, discount prices on upgrades!) And in the unlikely event of a serious bug, you will be notified.*

Setting Up Your Quicken File

Installing a record-keeping system like Quicken isn't just a matter of copying program files to your computer's hard disk. You also need to set up your first accounts.

If you've been using an earlier version of Quicken, Quicken upgrades your data when you first start up Quicken 2002.

If you haven't used Quicken before, Quicken runs the New User Setup wizard when you start Quicken for the first time, as shown in Figure A.3.

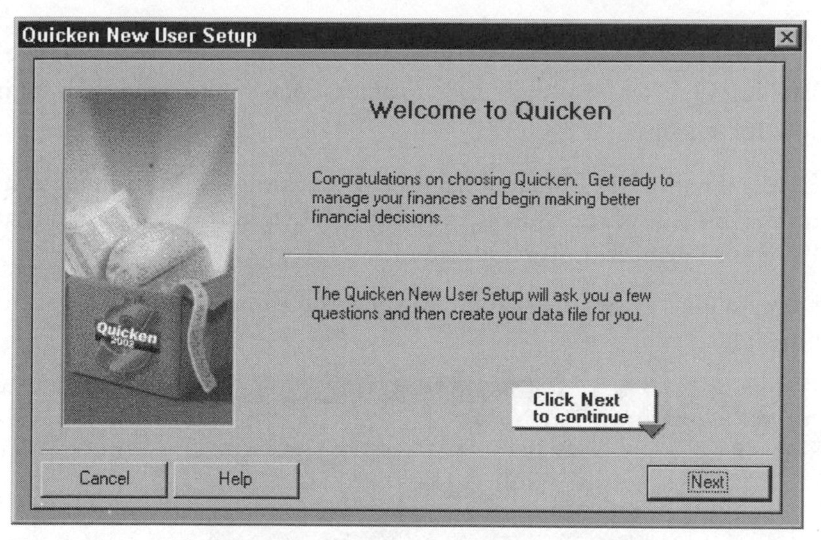

Figure A.3: The first New User Setup dialog box.

To run the New User Setup, follow these steps:

1. Click Next to start the setup process. Quicken displays the second New User Setup dialog box, as shown in Figure A.4.

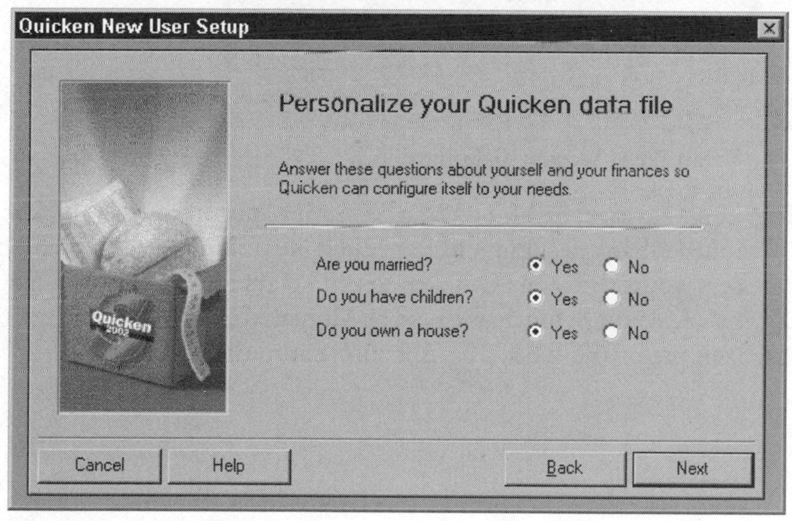

Figure A.4: The second New User Setup dialog box.

2. Answer the setup dialog box's questions by clicking the Yes and No buttons.
3. Click Next. Quicken displays the third and final New User Setup dialog box. If you want to see a video that describes how Quicken works, click Show Video. Otherwise, click Done.

Setting Up Your First Bank Accounts

As part of installing Quicken, you should set up at least one bank account. To set up a bank account, follow these steps:

1. If necessary display the My Finances window by clicking the My Finances hyperlink, which is on the left side of the Quicken window. Note that this window may already be displayed if you've just set up the Quicken file.
2. Click the Create New Account button to display the Create New Account dialog box, as shown in Figure A.5.

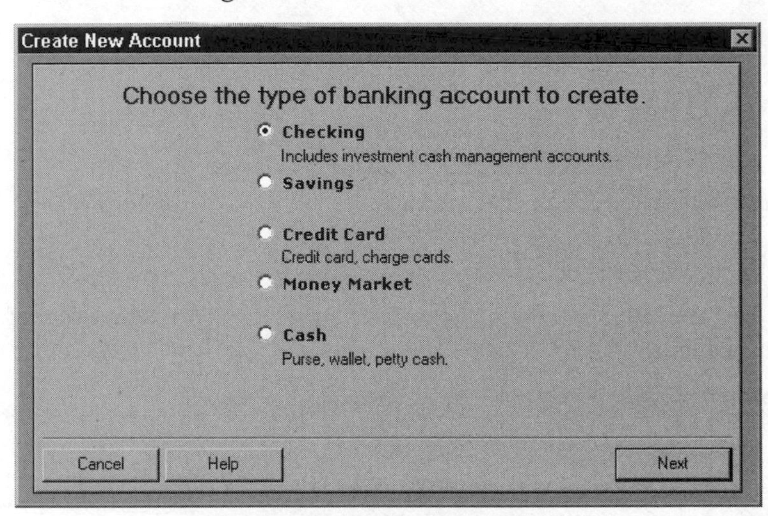

Figure A.5: The Create New Account dialog box.

3. Click the Checking, Savings, or Money Market option button to tell Quicken that you want to set up another bank account and then click Next. No matter which button you choose, the process works the same: Quicken next displays the Checking Account Setup dialog box, Savings Account Setup dialog box, or Money Market Setup dialog box. Figure A.6 shows an example of the Checking Account Setup dialog box.

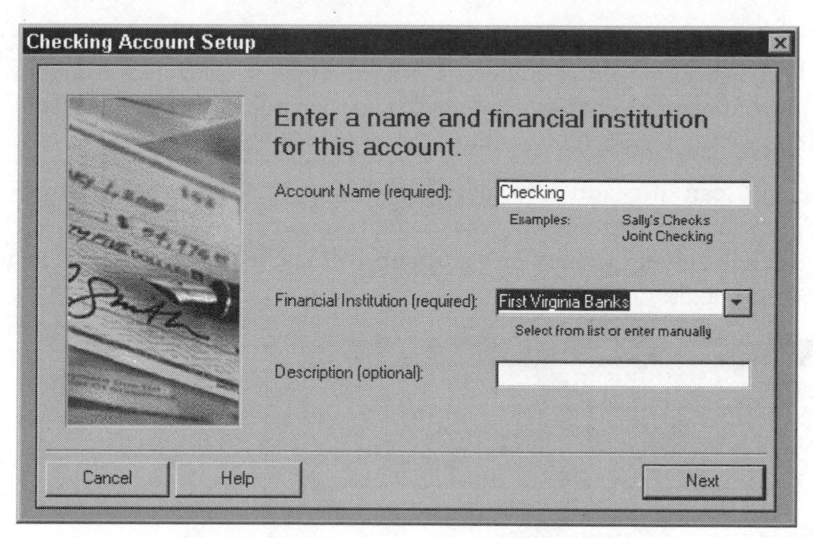

Figure A.6: The first Checking Account Setup dialog box.

4. In the Account Name text box, enter a bank account name.
5. Select the name of your bank from the Financial Institution list box. Or, if your bank isn't listed, type its name into the Financial Institution list box.
6. In the Description text box, you have the option of describing the account in more detail, such as by providing the bank name or account number.
7. Click Next to move to the next Account Setup dialog box, as shown in Figure A.7.

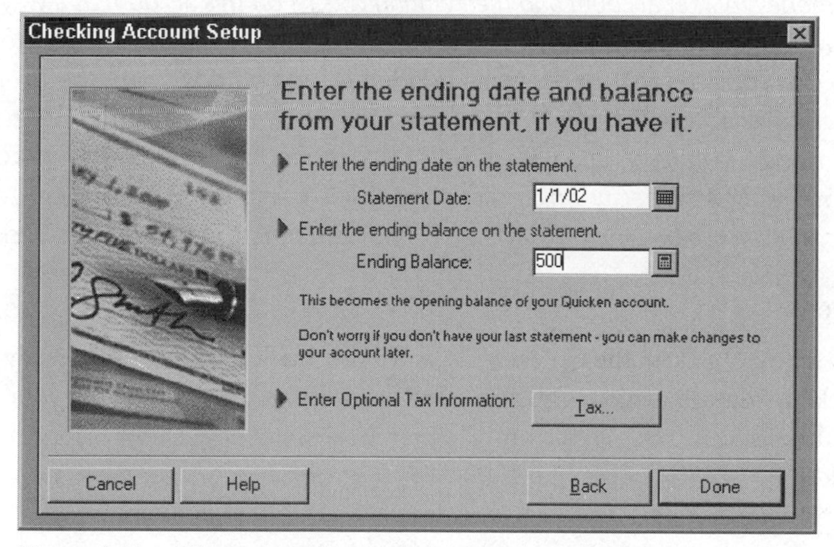

Figure A.7: The second Checking Account Setup dialog box.

8. Enter the bank account balance and bank statement date information in the text boxes provided. Unless you have meticulous records, the best approach is usually to use the balance from your most recent bank statement and then adjust this balance (so it's correct) by recording any uncleared transactions.
9. If you like, you can also add information about taxes. Click the Tax button in the Account Setup dialog box to display the dialog box shown in Figure A.8. This lets you tell Quicken that moving money into and out of this checking account has an impact on your income taxes.

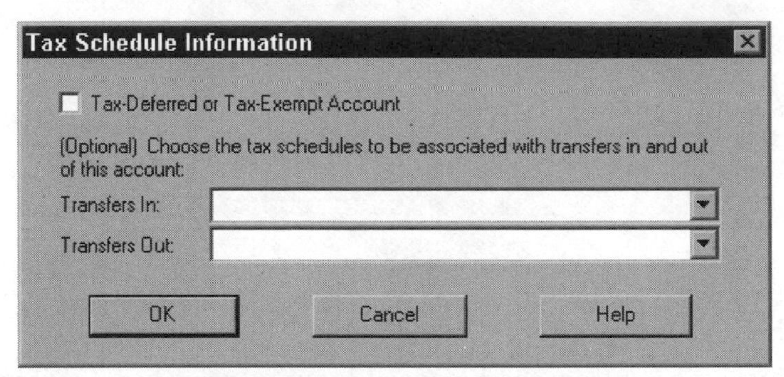

Figure A.8: The Tax Schedule Information dialog box.

NOTE *Most people and most businesses won't need to worry about the Tax button. However, if your transactions into and out of the account affect your taxes, you should keep track of that information. For example, if you're keeping IRA money in a checking account or money market account and then writing checks on this account as a way to withdraw money from the IRA account, you probably want to click the Tax button. When Quicken displays the Tax Schedule Information dialog box, mark the Tax Deferred Account checkbox. Then use the Transfers In drop-down list box to specify which tax form and line transfers into this account should be reported. Use the Transfers Out drop-down list box to specify which tax form and line transfers (or withdrawals) from this account should be reported. When you finish entering this information, click OK.*

10. Click Done.

You've now set up Quicken, the Quicken file, and a first bank account. You're ready to begin using Quicken. You can explore Quicken on your own if you want to begin your learning that way. Alternatively, you can turn to Chapter 1 and read about how to begin working with Quicken.

Appendix B

USING THE CANADIAN VERSION OF QUICKEN

If you live in Canada and want to use Quicken to track your finances, you can take advantage of several features included in the Canadian version of Quicken. This appendix describes how you set up Windows and Quicken for use in Canada and outlines special features included in the Canadian version of Quicken.

Reconfiguring Windows and Quicken

If your system is not already set up for Canadian use, your first task is to reconfigure Windows with settings for Canada. This is quite easy to do:

1. Click the Start button and choose Settings.
2. Choose Control Panel.
3. When the Control Panel window opens, double-click the Regional Options icon. The Regional Options Properties dialog box appears.
4. On the Regional Options General tab, use the drop-down list box to choose English (Canada). Now Canadian English is the default for your system, as is the Canadian date style of *DD/MM/YY.*
5. Click OK.

After configuring Windows for Canadian use, you must also configure Quicken with the settings for Canada. If you've already installed Quicken on your computer, you will need to reinstall it. If you have not yet installed Quicken, you need to choose the Canadian configuration during the installation process. In either case, install Quicken according to the instructions in Appendix A of this book. When you get to the Type Of Installation window, mark the Canadian Version option button. (This option is selected by default if you have configured Windows for Canadian use.) Then complete the installation, as described in Appendix A.

TIP *To see whether you've installed the Canadian version of Quicken, choose Help ➢ About Quicken. The words Canadian Edition should appear atop the About Quicken 2002 dialog box.*

Using Canadian Categories

Before you start processing transactions, you need to be aware of the ways in which the Canadian version differs from the U.S. version. One of the major differences has to do with the categories you use for your record keeping.

As explained in Chapter 2 of this book, when you create a new file for keeping financial records, you are given the opportunity to choose which kinds of categories you want: various home categories, business categories, or both. When you tell Quicken to configure the program for use in Canada, in addition to including almost all the categories for Quicken users in the United States, Quicken adds the following income and expense categories unique to Canada:

- **CPP-QPP** Describes Canada or Quebec Pension Plan benefits
- **Old Age Sec.** Describes Old Age Security income
- **RRIF Income** Describes registered retirement income fund payments
- **RRSP Income** Describes registered retirement savings plan payments and similar products such as annuities and deferred profit sharing.

Quicken also adds several categories for describing expenses:

- **Private and Prov H-care** Describes out-of pocket health care expenses
- **RPP Contrib** Describes Registered Pension Plan contributions through an employer

Quicken also adds tax subcategories for tracking employment insurance premiums and Canada Pension Plan contributions. These categories become essential when you begin describing transactions.

If you specify in the installation that you want to include business categories in your category list, Quicken also adds categories for tracking the federal goods and services tax (GST) and provincial retail sales taxes (PST). All provinces except Alberta collect retail sales taxes. The Yukon, Nunavut, and Northwest Territories do not collect retail sales taxes either. New Brunswick, Nova Scotia, and Newfoundland collect a harmonized sales tax (HST). If the default category list does not include the categories you need for tracking business income or expenses in your province or territory in Canada, you can easily add and delete categories, as described in Chapter 14.

Tracking Business Finances

Tracking GST and PST becomes a necessity when you use Quicken to track business finances. Accurate records are extremely important when you're dealing with taxes, and this is where Quicken can save you a lot of time.

Rather than using the GST and PST categories in your banking transactions, create separate liability accounts for them. This way, you can get up-to-the-minute reports on the status of those accounts and separate any GST you collect from the amounts that are reported as your net worth in reports.

First, create a GST (and, if necessary, a PST) liability account as described in Chapter 12. Be sure to name the account or accounts appropriately. After you click Done, answer No when Quicken asks whether you want to set up an amortized loan to go with the account.

After you've set up the necessary liability accounts, you can use them for your split transactions. For example, suppose that you sold 1,000 widgets to Bob's Widget Warehouse. To record this sale, you put the information in your business account as you would normally. The amount you charge for the widgets, in this case, is $600, which you can write in the Amount box of the register. You then split the categories and include lines that transfer the tax amounts to the appropriate liability accounts (*not* the categories).

When you are recording a business *purchase* you have made, however, the PST you pay should *not* be credited to you, although the GST should be credited to you. Because the amount of the PST should not appear as a credit in your liability account, when you record a business purchase, process the transaction by using the PST *category* and not as a transfer to the PST *liability account* in the Split Transaction Window.

To pay the GST and PST to the tax authorities, find out how much you owe for each tax by looking at the ending balances of the tax liability accounts. Then write a check to the tax authority from a bank account, entering a transfer to the tax payable account in the Category field. This reduces the balance of the liability account.

Describing Canadian Mortgages

Installing the Canadian version of Quicken also allows you to set up loan accounts with semiannual compounding. Most Canadian mortgages are compounded semiannually. This means that interest is added to the principal every six months instead of monthly, as is predominant in the United States.

For example, if you were to take out a $10,000 loan, with a 10 percent annual interest rate compounded annually, the interest payment is $1,000 per year. With a 10 percent interest rate compounded semiannually, the interest payments total $1,025 per year, meaning that the effective annual interest rate is 10.25 percent. With a 10 percent interest rate compounded monthly, the interest payments total $1,047.13 per year, meaning that the effective annual interest rate is 10.47 percent.

Investing in Canada

The Canadian version of Quicken includes a couple of special features for investors as well. If you report capital gains, Quicken uses the average cost basis of your investment to calculate your capital gains, as is required for Canadian taxpayers.

NOTE *Do not use Quicken's lot handling features (described in Chapter 21) to specify lots. Doing so makes the Capital Gains report amounts incorrect.*

Quicken allows you to download security prices from Canadian exchanges. To specify Canadian exchanges, you need to precede the stock ticker symbol with T: for Toronto, V: for Vancouver, or M: for Montreal in the Symbol text box when you set up your investments.

Index

C

D

E

F

N

O

P

Q

R

S

T

U

W

Z

The manuscript for this book was prepared and submitted to Redmond Technology Press in electronic form. Text files were prepared using Microsoft Word 2000. Pages were composed using PageMaker 6.5 for Windows, with text in Frutiger and Caslon. Composed files were delivered to the printer as electronic prepress files.

Project Editor
Paula Thurman

Layout

Minh-Tam S. Le

Indexer

Joann Woy

Technical Editor

Michael Yang